CHASING
GOLD

CHASING GOLD

The Incredible Story of
How the Nazis Stole Europe's Bullion

GEORGE M. TABER

PEGASUS BOOKS

NEW YORK LONDON

CHASING GOLD

Pegasus Books LLC
80 Broad Street, 5th Floor
New York, NY 10004

Copyright © 2014 by George M. Taber

First Pegasus Books cloth edition December 2014

Interior design by Maria Fernandez

Library of Congress Cataloging-in-Publication Data is available.

ISBN: 978-1-60598-655-5

10 9 8 7 6 5 4 3 2 1

Printed in the United States of America
Distributed by W. W. Norton & Company

To Curt Prendergast, my first boss at *Time* magazine. In the summer of 1966, he asked me to investigate what happened to Belgium's central bank gold during World War II. That started my long interest in this dramatic saga.

A NOTE ON THE MAPS

Maps are not to scale, and intended only for reference to show the movement of gold throughout Europe during the specified time periods.

CONTENTS

MAJOR CHARACTERS

Hubert Ansiaux, Belgian Central Bank official who in May 1940 rescued millions of dollars of his country's currency and attempted to do the same for its gold.

Vincenzo Azzolini, president of the Bank of Italy 1931-1944.

Bernard Bernstein, staff member of Treasury Secretary Morgenthau and then financial aide for General Dwight Eisenhower. He directed the gold recovery operation late in the war.

Johan Willem Beyen, president of the Bank for International Settlements (1935-1937).

Robert E. Brett, Captain of the *SS Eocene*, which rescued the Polish gold in September 1939.

William C. Bullitt, Jr., the U.S. ambassador in Paris in 1940, who helped get a large share of the French gold to the U.S.

Basil Catterns, the deputy governor of the Bank of England, who directed British gold shipments.

Neville Chamberlain, British Prime Minister from 1937 to 1940.

Winston Churchill, British Prime Minister from 1940 to 1945.

Count Galeazzo Ciano, Benito Mussolini foreign minister and son-in-law.

Henryk Floyar-Rajchman, one of the leaders of the Polish gold evacuation program.

Pierre Fournier, president of the Bank of France in May 1940 and directed the rescue of the French gold.

Walther Funk, president of the Reichsbank from 1939 to 1945.

Joseph Goebbels, Minister of Propaganda for Nazi Germany from 1933 to 1945.

Hermann Göring, second most powerful man in the Third Reich after Hitler. He was head of the Luftwaffe and the Four Year Plan that prepared the country's economy for war.

Camille Gutt, Finance Minister of Belgium in 1940, who directed the country's gold rescue.

George L. Harrison, President of the New York Federal Reserve Bank, 1928-1941.

Fredrik Haslund, Directed the Norwegian gold rescue, carrying the first shipload all the way to the U.S.

Adolf Hitler, dictator of Germany from 1933 to 1945.

Harry Hopkins, trouble-shooter for President Roosevelt, who went to Moscow in July 1941 to meet with Stalin about sending the Soviet Union military aid.

Georges Janssen, president of the Central Bank of Belgium from 1938 to 1941.

Princess Juliana, heir to the throne of the Netherlands in 1940.

L. Werner Knoke, New York Federal Reserve vice president, who handled gold operations.

Hans Lammers, the head of Hitler's Reich Chancellery.

Charles Moreton, a regional French National Bank official who played a major role in rescuing French gold.

Ignacy Matuszewski, one of two men who directed the evacuation of Polish gold from Warsaw to France.

Thomas H. McKittrick, president of the Bank for International Settlements during World War II.

Stefan Michalski, Polish Central Bank board member who traveled with his country's gold to Dakar in 1940 and also helped rescue it there in 1944.

Henry Morgenthau, Jr., Secretary of the Treasury and close confidant of President Roosevelt from 1933 from 1945.

Benito Mussolini, fascist ruler of Italy from 1922 to 1943.

Juan Negrín, finance minister of Spain who arranged the Spanish gold shipment to the Soviet Union during the Spanish Civil War.

Montagu Norman, Governor of the Bank of England and the most influential central banker of the era.

Alexander Orlov, Soviet agent in Spain who handled the Spanish gold shipment to Moscow.

Domenico Pellegrini Giampietro, Italian Finance Minister who gave the order to turn over Italian gold to the Nazis.

Sir Frederick Phillips, undersecretary of the British Treasury, who directed Britain's gold evacuation.

Pope Pius XII, Roman Catholic pontiff from 1939 to 1958.

Emil Puhl, vice president of the Reichsbank during the war. He ran the day-to-day operations of the central bank.

Rudolf Rahn, German Plenipotentiary to the Italian Social Republic after the fall of Mussolini in 1943.

Friedrich Josef Rauch, the *SS Obersturmbannführer* who directed the evacuation of the last Nazi gold in Bavaria in May 1945.

Paul Reynaud, French Premier, 1940.

Joachim von Ribbentrop, Minister of Foreign Affairs from 1938 to 1945.

Franklin D. Roosevelt, president of the United States 1933-1945.

Nicolai Rygg, president of the Norwegian Central Bank in 1940.

Hjalmar Schacht, Hitler's leading economic advisor from 1933 to January 1939, when the Führer fired him as president of the Reichsbank.

Kurt Schuschnigg, Chancellor of Austria in 1938 when Germany took over the country.

Albert Speer, private architect of Hitler and then Minister of Armaments and War Production from 1942 to 1945.

Joseph Stalin, dictator of the Soviet Union from 1922 to 1953.

Albert Thoms, the head of the Reichsbank Precious Metals Department. He directed the movement of Nazi gold from Berlin to Merkers in the spring of 1945.

L.J.A. Trip, president of the Dutch Central Bank in 1940.

Harry Dexter White, top aide to Treasury Secretary Henry Morgenthau, Jr. 1934-1945. White was also architect, along with John Maynard Keynes, of the Bretton Woods Conference, which set up the postwar international monetary system. White was an undercover communist agent during that whole time.

Sir Kingsley Wood, the Chancellor of the Exchequer, who had overall responsibility for the British gold evacuation.

Queen Wilhelmina, queen of the Netherlands in 1940.

King Zog of the Albanians, ruled his country from 1928 to 1939.

PROLOGUE

In early spring 1945, the Third Army of General George Patton, Jr. was rolling across Germany, crushing the dispirited Wehrmacht in its path. His G.I.s had already scored victories on the Normandy beaches, bailed out the Battle of the Bulge, and crossed the Rhine River into the Third Reich's Vaterland late in the evening of March 22. In a special message to his men, Patton bragged that between late January and late March, "You have taken over 6,400 square miles of territory, seized over 3,000 cities, towns, and villages including Trier, Koblenz, Bingen, Worms, Mainz, Kaiserslautern, and Ludwigshafen. You have captured over 140,000 soldiers, killed or wounded an additional 100,000, while eliminating the German 1st and 7th Armies. Using speed and audacity on the ground with support from peerless fighter-bombers in the air, you kept up a relentless round-the-clock attack on the enemy. Your assault over the Rhine at 2200 last night assures you of even greater glory to come."[1]

Along the way, the general wrote doggerel verse about warfare such as:

> For in war just as in loving,
> You must always keep on shoving,
> Or you will never get your just reward.[2]

On April 4, Patton's 358th infantry regiment captured Merkers, a village in central Germany about 80 miles northeast of Frankfurt and 180 miles southwest of Berlin. The whole area around there was known for its salt mines. Some of them had thirty miles of tunnels. The area's dense forests gave it the nickname "the green heart of Germany." The 358th was in the process of cleaning up pockets of enemy resistance and arresting retreating German soldiers trying to disappear into the sea of refugees. When the G.I.s went through Merkers, they heard rumors that the German Reichsbank had been moving gold there in recent days, but nothing was confirmed, so they moved on and set up a command post in Kieselbach a mile and a half down the road.[3]

At 8:45 on the morning of April 6, American military policemen Clyde Harmon and Anthony Klein, two privates first class, were guarding a road, when they stopped a pair of French women entering Kieselbach on foot. They were violating the U.S. army curfew that prohibited civilians from being on the streets. One of the women was obviously well along in her pregnancy. The two explained that they were displaced persons from Thionville in northeastern France and were on their way to a midwife in Kieselbach to deliver the baby. The women were taken to the Provost Marshal's Office and questioned. Their story seemed honest, and they were offered a ride back to Merkers.[4]

PFC Richard Mootz, who spoke German, drove them. When the three entered the town, the soldier asked the women about the huge Kaiseroda mine facility that they were passing. Sitting in the middle of a green valley of rolling hills, it looked more like a steel mill than a mine. There were large brick buildings plus bridges and cobblestone streets. It resembled a small village. Smokestacks and a giant elevator dominated the skyline, but they were no longer operating. The women explained that the Germans had recently stored gold and paintings underground there, adding that it took local citizens and displaced people three days to unload the first train. PFC Mootz passed the information up the chain of command to Colonel Whitcomb, the chief of staff, and Lt. Col. Russell, the military government officer.

Armed with that information, Russell immediately went to the mine with a few G.I.s where he talked with other displaced people and local Germans, who corroborated the French women's story. Mine officials told him that the assistant director of the National Galleries in Berlin was also there to care for confiscated artworks. A British POW, who had been captured in 1940 and was working at the mine as a mechanic's assistant, told Russell that he had helped unload the gold. The soldiers learned that there were five more entrances to the labyrinthine mine, with one of them still behind enemy lines. Russell immediately ordered a tank battalion to guard the entrances and arrested all the mine executives.[5]

On April 7 at 10:00 A.M., Lt. Colonel Russell, accompanied by mine officials, soldiers, and Signal Corps photographers, entered the mine. The group immediately noticed at the entrance several hundred bags. When they opened them, they found them full of Reichsmark currency, which the Germans had apparently left behind in their rush to escape. Soldiers later found over a hundred more in another location. They determined that each sack contained one million Reichsmark. They also found a locked steel door and speculated that they would find more valuables behind it. Germans told the G.I.s that it was called simply "room number eight." At 2:00 P.M., soldiers attempted unsuccessfully to open the vault's door and then left.

With all that evidence in hand, Russell interrogated Werner Veick, who worked for the Reichsbank, Germany's central bank, and said that he had been part of a group that recently brought gold, along with both German and foreign currencies, to the mine from Berlin. He said most of it was stored in the room behind the steel door. Russell quickly sent word to his superiors that there was a vault that reportedly contained gold and other valuables. Eventually the news reached General Patton, who ordered the soldiers to blow off the door the next day and find out what was inside. In the meantime, reinforcements were sent to guard the mine.

The next morning, a group led by Lt. Colonel Russell was back at the mine to blast their way into the vault. They gathered up both Kaiseroda officials and Paul Ortwin Rave, the curator of the

German State Museum, to investigate what was underground. Newspaper photographers and reporters traveling with Patton's army accompanied them. The soldiers tried at first to get into the room by digging around the door; but when that didn't work they blew a five-foot hole in a masonry wall.

Inside, the soldiers found riches to rival King Solomon's mines. The room was approximately 75 feet wide, 150 feet long, and had a 12-foot ceiling. Bags of gold bars and gold coins were neatly arranged in rows only a few feet apart. The G.I.s broke the seals of a few bags to confirm the contents and then resealed them. At the back of the room were 207 battered suitcases, boxes, and packages in addition to 18 bags containing gold or silver jewelry, gold watches, and other valuables. Much of it appeared to have been flattened with a hammer to fit as much as possible into the containers. The soldiers speculated it was war loot collected by Nazi soldiers. The boxes actually contained valuables that Gestapo guards had taken from concentration camp inmates on their way to the gas chambers. Bales of currency were stacked along another side of the room. There were also several balances, seemingly to weigh precious metals. Later that day, the group found elsewhere in the mine 550 bags of Reichsmark plus paintings and other museum treasures. They were haphazardly packed in cardboard or wooden containers.[6]

General Manton S. Eddy, the commander of the XII Corps, arrived at the mine three hours later and quickly telephoned Patton to report that they had found a huge treasure of gold and artworks. In a rare reaction for a general famous for his oversized ego, Patton decided that the discovery was a political rather than a military matter, and asked General Dwight D. Eisenhower, the commanding general of the Allied European Theater of Operations, to take over responsibility. The Berlin museum paintings and art pieces, which included the famous bust of Empress Nefertiti, were priceless. The gold alone in room number eight was worth $238.5 million. At today's gold price, that would be about $9 billion. The Merkers mother lode was the largest recovery of stolen property in world history, but the story behind this incredible cache and the plight of Europe's wartime gold was still to be discovered.[7]

Chapter One

THE GLITTER OF GOLD

Throughout history the glitter of gold has mesmerized mankind. Gerald M. Loeb, the founding partner of the Wall Street brokerage firm E. F. Hutton, once observed, "The desire for gold is the most universal and deeply rooted commercial instinct of the human race."[1] For as long as records have been kept, people have had an obsession with gold that is second only to their preoccupation with sex. Wrote historian Peter L. Bernstein in his book *The Power of Gold*: "Over the centuries, gold has stirred the passions for power and glory, for beauty, for security, and even for immortality. Gold has been an icon for greed, a vehicle for vanity, and a potent constraint as a monetary standard. No other object has commanded so much veneration over so long a period of time."[2]

Of course, the metal has also had its enemies. The Roman poet Virgil wrote in the *Aeneid*, "To what extremes won't you compel our hearts, you accursed lust for gold?" Shakespeare wrote in Romeo and Juliet, "There is thy gold, worse poison to men's souls, doing more murder in this loathsome world, than these poor compounds that thou mayst not sell." In December 1921, Thomas Edison called it "an invention of Satan." The British economist John Maynard Keynes dismissed it as "a barbaric relic."[3]

Gold is beautiful, malleable, and rare. It is also indestructible, which probably accounts for its connection to eternal life. Treasure hunters still today find shiny coins from Spanish galleons that sank in the early 1700s off the coast of Central Florida. Gold does not rust. Even if buried in the ground for thousands of years it still sparkles. The metal is extremely heavy: a cubic foot of it weighs a half-ton. It can be easily turned into products ranging from wedding rings to teeth. It is used in computers and has even gone to the moon. An ounce of gold can be stretched to a string fifty miles in length or made into a sheet measuring one hundred square feet. It can be pounded down into gold leaf one-tenth of the diameter of a human hair. The world's total gold holdings amount to only about 165,000 tons. A metric ton in the form of a cube is only fifteen inches on each side. All the gold mined in world history would fit into three-and-a half Olympic-sized swimming pools.[4]

The ancient Chinese and Egyptians practiced alchemy, a quack science that attempted to turn base metals into gold. King Croesus of Lydia, who ruled the area of modern Turkey, introduced large-scale gold coinage. French historian Fernand Braudel called the metal the "lifeblood of Mediterranean trade in the Second Millennium B.C."[5] Thucydides in the fifth century B.C. wrote admiringly of the Carthaginians, "If willing to help, of all existing states they are the best able; for they have abundance of gold and silver, and these make war, like other things, go smoothly."[6]

Explorers during the Age of Discovery set off in sailing ships to look for gold. The objectives of Columbus were gold, god, and glory. On October 12, 1492, the day after he landed on the island of Guanahani in the Bahamas, he set out on a quest for the metal. He wrote of his first experience: "Seeing some of them with little bits of this metal hanging at their noses, I gathered from them by signs that by going southward or steering round the island in that direction, there would be found a king who possessed large vessels of gold, and in great quantities."[7]

Two years after that first voyage to the new world, the proud Columbus proposed to his Spanish patrons, King Ferdinand and

Queen Isabella, the rules for gathering gold from the new territories. Colonists, for example, should be obliged to get a license from the Spanish governor, and all gold found should be smelted immediately. He wrote them, "Without doubt there is in these lands a very great amount of gold." In the century after Columbus, the world's stock of gold increased five-fold setting off one of the world's most productive eras of gold discovery.[8]

Under the mercantile system, which dominated the world economy from the sixteenth to the eighteenth century, countries imported as few goods as necessary, exported as much as feasible, and sold as little of their gold as possible. This was followed by the international gold standard, which was the bedrock of global finance for the next century, leading up to World War I.

The British in the early eighteenth century established the value of a country's currency on the basis of gold. Sir Isaac Newton, the master of London's Mint, in 1717 tied the value of the pound sterling at 113.0016 grains of pure gold. Britain was such a dominant economic power that other countries had no choice but to follow its lead. That gold system became the foundation of world trade and fostered economic prosperity. The U.S. dollar in that era was worth 23.22 grams of gold. From the 1830s to the 1930s, the international price of gold was about $20 an ounce.[9] During that time, Britain was the international lender of last resort and helped countries out of financial troubles. The system had credibility and fostered close cooperation among the leading nations as well as widespread prosperity. If a country followed irresponsible economic policies, it had to devalue its currency by decreasing its gold value. It was a humiliating and painful process that nations fought hard to avoid.

Governments often ignored the gold standard in times of war, but they returned to it in peacetime. Britain and other nations suspended it during World War I. In April 1925, though, Chancellor of the Exchequer Winston Churchill put his country back on the gold standard at the pre-war level.[10] It was an unrealistic price that fostered the world depression. Nonetheless, Joseph Schumpeter, the great Austrian-American economist of the mid-twentieth century, praised gold as an automatic system that reacted quickly to changing conditions, writing, "Gold imposes restrictions upon governments or bureaucracies that are much more powerful than is parliamentary criticism. It is both the badge and guarantee of bourgeois freedom— of freedom not simply of the bourgeois interest, but of freedom in the bourgeois sense."[11] Robert Mundell, the winner of the Nobel Prize for Economics, has said, "Gold will be part of the international monetary system in the twenty-first century."[12] George Bernard Shaw, the playwright, in *The Intelligent Woman's Guide to Socialism and Capitalism*, wrote, "You have to choose between trusting the natural stability of gold and the honesty and intelligence of members of the government. And, with due respect for those gentlemen, I advise you, as long as the capitalist system lasts, to vote for gold"[13]

On January 24, 1848, James W. Marshall discovered a few flakes of gold at the sawmill he owned with John Sutter in Northern California. Ambitious miners from around the world rushed to California by land and sea to seek their fortune, and in the process helped settle the nation from sea to shining sea. When the Union Pacific and Central Pacific railroads met on May 10, 1869 at Promontory Summit in the Utah Territory, a golden spike completed the job. The United States had become a global power.

Gold has always been the last refuge of people in times of crisis. In July 1864, Confederate military units invaded the District of Columbia and were within sight of the nation's capital. Union Secretary of War William Stanton took $5,000 in government bonds and $400 in gold belonging to his wife Ellen out of his safe at the War Department next door to the White House, gave them to his secretary, and told her to go to his home and hide the valuables in his mattress.[14]

In *Lords of Finance*, which recounts the history of central banking between the two world wars, Liaquat Ahamed wrote that Montagu Norman, the governor of the Bank of England, the predominant banker in that period, considered gold to be "one of the pillars of a free society like property rights or habeas corpus, which had evolved in the Western liberal world to limit the power of government."[15]

At the beginning of World War II, when nations fell in a matter of days and millions of refugees flooded the roads to escape the conflict, people turned to gold as their last hope for survival. In June 1940, twelve-year-old Felix Rohatyn, who would later become the chairman of the international financial giant Lazard Frères and rescue New York City from bankruptcy in 1975, was one of millions of European Jews trying to escape from the Nazis in France. His mother instructed him to empty tubes of Kolynos toothpaste and refill them with gold coins from his grandfather's collection. Two years later, when Rohatyn finally arrived in New York City to end his long escape odyssey, the gold was still in the toothpaste tubes.[16]

In a similar but less successful tale, Prime Minister Paul Reynaud, who had led his country's battle against Hitler, fled France after the armistice and was trying to get into Spain in June 1940. Spanish customs officers at the border inspected the luggage of his mistress Helène de Portes and found $2 million worth of gold.[17]

The world's central banks are the traditional home for most gold. That is where the vast majority of it is stored, and the biggest trades in the metal have traditionally been made among national financial institutions. Governments looked to central bankers to run their economies, and for most of history nations settled their foreign trade exchanges with gold. Countries buying more than they were selling usually made up their trade gap with bullion. Sweden established the first central bank in 1664 following the failure of a prominent private financial institution. The Bank of England was established thirty years later and was the preeminent one for nearly three centuries. During that time, it was the custodian of gold. The New York Federal Reserve, the American central bank, took over that international role during World War II.

Adolf Hitler knew nothing about economics and cared little for gold. He wrote in his opus *Mein Kampf*, "It may be that today gold has become the exclusive ruler of life, but the time will come when man will again bow down before a higher god."[18] The people working for Hitler, such as Hjalmar Schacht and Hermann Göring, however, believed strongly in bullion. Schacht wrote in his book *Gold for Europe*, "With all peoples and at all times gold has always been a welcome means of exchange, and it was possible to acquire all other goods in current commercial use with gold long before rulers and governments took control of the monetary system by legal measures." They used the precious metal as an important way to finance Nazi wars and achieve their goal of dominating Europe. The Nazis systematically attempted to steal gold from each of the nearly two-dozen countries they invaded. Sometimes they succeeded; other times they failed. Nations made heroic efforts to safeguard the national treasury. The most despicable gold thefts were the tons of dental gold that elite *SS (Schutzstaffel)* guards ripped from the mouths of people who had died in the gas chambers. That, however, represented only a small portion of total Nazi theft. Willy Sutton, the Depression era crook, apocryphally said that he robbed banks because that's where the money was. The Nazis robbed central banks because that's where the gold was. Between 1938 and 1944, the government in Berlin stole some 600 tons from Europe's national depositories.[19]

Gold was the centerpiece of the Nazi economic policy and war strategy during World War II. They stole it, and then used the booty to finance their war machine. They could have been taking their marching orders from King Ferdinand of Spain, who in the sixteenth century told his conquistadores: "Get gold humanly if possible, but at all hazards get gold."[20]

Chapter Two

SPANISH PRELUDE

Spain
October–November 1936
Tons of gold: 510

Four ships departed Cartagena on
October 25, 1936

Gold Route
- - - - - ▸

The Spanish Civil War of 1936 to 1939 set the stage for World War II and left a half million people dead.[1] Germany, Italy, and the Soviet Union used Spain as a real live testing ground for their soldiers, weapons, and tactics. The first urban carpet-bombing, which would be used extensively in the battles of Britain and Berlin, was the German attack of April 26, 1937 on the Basque town of Guernica, a tragedy that Picasso immortalized in a painting. Tank combat, while first seen in World War I, was vastly improved in Spain. The first airlift of war materiel took place when Germany landed caches of weapons and men to help anti-government forces.

The Spanish Republic also used its stockpile of gold, built up by the conquistadors, as a weapon of war. At the outbreak of the conflict, the Spanish government had 635 tons of it in its vaults.[2] That was the world's fourth largest national holding after the U.S., France, and Britain. By the end of the conflict, Stalin would have much of it.

The Spanish Civil War was the culmination of a half-century of chaos and violence in a country struggling to move from the medieval to the modern. A social revolution spun out of control, and politicians from extreme right to extreme left who had little experience in democracy believed every disagreement was a fight in which no prisoners would be taken. At one point twenty-six political parties were represented in the Cortes, the national parliament.[3] The spectrum went from royalists to anarchists. In addition, Basque and Catalan separatists fought to win freedom for their regions from the central government in Madrid.

On one side was a democratically elected leftist government; on the other a rightist military. Government supporters called themselves Republicans, while those backing the armed forces were Nationalists. To their opponents, Republicans were communists, while Nationalists were fascists. The rallying cry of the right was *Viva España*, and that of the left was *Viva la Republica*.

The war brought about the bloodshed and cruelty so often seen in wars of religion and ideology. The Roman Catholic Church struggled to preserve long-held privileges, while its opponents considered the church the epitome of everything wrong in Spain. In the opening weeks of the war, thirteen bishops, 4,184 diocesan priests, 2,365 religious brothers and 283 religious sisters were killed.[4] At the same time, Pope Pius XI in the encyclical *Dilectissima Nobis* (On Oppression of the Church of Spain) called on Catholics to join "a holy crusade for the integral restoration of the Church's right." The Pontiff condemned the Spanish government as an "offense not only to religion and the church."[5]

There was no limit to vicious rhetoric. Dolores Ibárruri, the left's *Pasionaria*, bellowed, "It is better to kill one hundred innocents than to let one guilty person go," while Franco wailed that communists "should be crushed like worms." Assassination became the continuation of politics by other means, and tit-for-tat murders of two politicians set off the war.

Passionate volunteers from around the world rushed to join one side or the other. An estimated 32,000 foreigners from fifty-two nations joined the International Brigades that fought alongside the Republicans. Others supported the Nationalists. Portugal, where António de Oliveira Salazar in 1932 set up a fascist state, sent some 10,000 soldiers to help Franco, and 75,000 Spanish Moroccan troops joined the Nationalists. Germany dispatched 10,000 men to Franco, while Italy sent between 40,000 and 50,000. Seven hundred Irish Catholics formed the Blue Shirts to fight for the Nationalists and Catholicism.[6]

After fascists came to power in Italy, Germany, and Portugal, the Comintern, the coordinating organization of national communist parties that did Moscow's bidding, urged leftist parties to form Popular Front coalitions to oppose right-wing groups. The Spanish national election on February 16, 1936, pitted the leftist Popular Front against the rightist National Front. The Popular Front won 4,451,300 votes or 47.03 percent, while the National Front garnered 4,375,800 or 46.48 percent. Despite the lack of a clear mandate, the Popular Front moved to implement its program. Manuel Azaña, a long-time leftist leader, became first prime minister and then president. At the same time, Spanish generals plotted a *coup d'etat*.[7]

Spain soon slipped into chaos. In a speech to the Cortes on June 16, José María Gil Robles, a leader on the right, counted off the toll in the four months since the national election: 160 churches burned, 269 political murders, 1,287 political assaults, 69 party offices destroyed, 113 general strikes, 228 partial strikes, 10 newspaper offices sacked. He pleaded, "A country can live under a monarchy or a republic, with a parliamentary or a presidential system, under Communism or Fascism. But it cannot live in anarchy. And we are today at the funeral of democracy!"[8]

Only a month later during the night of July 16-17, military units in Spanish Morocco staged a *coup d'etat*. The code broadcast over the radio to signal the revolt: "The skies are cloudless all over Spain." At the time, General Francisco Franco was stationed eight hundred miles away on the Canary Islands and had only a few troops under his command, but a Spaniard in London hired a plane to fly him to Spanish Morocco, where he took over leadership of Spain's Army of Africa, the country's premier fighting unit. While rebel units quickly captured a few key towns in the north and south, the big population centers remained in government hands. After some uncertainty, the navy remained mostly loyal to the Republic and blocked the Nationalists from moving Moroccan troops to the mainland.

The Republican government of Socialist José Giral quickly armed its supporters by distributing weapons, including machine guns, to anyone with a union card. The resulting bloodbath left an estimated 50,000 people from both sides dead. The night of July 19-20, some fifty more Catholic churches were set ablaze just in Republican-controlled Madrid.[9]

With no way to get his troops out of Africa, Franco appealed to the fascist governments of Italy and Germany for logistical support in the form of an air convoy. On July 19, a journalist close to Franco flew to Italy to ask Mussolini for twelve bombers, three fighter aircraft, and a supply of bombs. Three days later, Franco through an intermediary asked Berlin if he could buy "ten transport aircraft with maximum seating capacity." A Nationalist delegation also arrived in Berlin on July 25 with a letter from Franco to Hitler making a similar request.

German Foreign Minister Konstantin von Neurath met with them, but opposed the sale, fearing it might lead to a general European war. Hitler also talked with the Spaniards in Bayreuth, where he was attending a presentation of the Wagner opera *Siegfried*. Intense talks lasted until 2:00 A.M., when Hitler finally overruled his foreign minister and agreed to send Franco more equipment than he had even requested. Luftwaffe pilots quickly flew an initial twenty Junker-52 transport planes to Franco.[10]

At exactly the same time, the Republic was trying to get military hardware, especially aircraft, from the European democracies. On the evening of July 19, Prime Minister Giral sent a cable to French Prime Minister Léon Blum, who had taken office only two weeks before in another Popular Front election victory. The Spaniard stressed their common crusade against fascism, writing: "Beg of you to help us immediately with arms and airplanes. Fraternally yours, Giral." The Spanish ambassador in Paris followed up with specific requests for bombers, fighters, machine guns, and more. Blum agreed. The Spanish Republic used its gold to pay for the weapons. On July 24, Giral authorized the first shipment to France to pay for the materiel Blum promised. Gold worth $720,000 arrived a day later aboard a Douglas DC-2 airplane at Le Bourget airport outside Paris. Further payments were delivered to France on July 26 and July 30 and then sporadically until March 1937.[11]

On July 25, Prime Minister Giral also sent a message to Joseph Stalin asking for "supplies of armaments and ammunition of all categories, and in very great quantities, from your country."[12] The Soviet leader was uncertain about whether to get involved in Spain. He had several reasons to stay out of the conflict. The Spanish Communist Party had just three thousand members and none in the government, although it had been part of the Popular Front during the election. Stalin was also preoccupied with internal problems. The Great Terror, his purge of old Bolsheviks from the government, party, and secret service, was just beginning. The first trial started on August 19. The country's economy was weak after his collectivization of agriculture, rapid industrialization, and state-created famine that left millions dead. Stalin was also waging an international battle with Leon Trotsky, his old revolutionary comrade-in-arms, for leadership of the international communist movement. Because of all those troubles, Stalin at first watched developments in Spain from the sidelines.

Britain and France were meanwhile trying to find a way to stop the Iberian conflict. After a quick trip to London to explain his strategy to a skeptical Foreign Minister Anthony Eden, Blum arrived back in Paris on July 24 to face a cabinet rebellion. Part of his coalition strongly opposed selling arms to Spain. French President Albert Lebrun told the prime minister that it would drag France into a war, and the speaker of the Chamber of Deputies and the president of the Senate also both voiced opposition. Following a blustery meeting, the cabinet on July 25 announced that France would not sell arms to Spain. That, however, did not entirely stop them, and leftist cabinet members, particularly Air Minister Pierre Cot, succeeded in getting French planes to the Republicans. The famed author André Malraux helped deliver French aircraft to the Spanish Republic.[13]

With massive military support rolling in from Italy and Germany, the Nationalists began doing better on the battlefield. From July 29 to August 5, German transport planes shuttled 1,500 soldiers from Morocco to Seville. Italy also airlifted troops from North Africa.

On August 6, Franco took command of the Army of Africa, and his force of some 8,000 men, mostly Moors, began moving north, advancing three hundred miles in the following month. The Republicans repeatedly condemned Franco for using Moors, a sensitive issue in Spain because Arabs had occupied parts of the country from 711 to 1492. The Moors were perhaps the best fighters in the war, and by August the Nationalists controlled half the country.

The French were anxious to halt the supply of materiel to both sides in the civil war out of fear that they would be dragged into a major war on its border, and the government on August 2, sent out to other countries a proposal for "An International Agreement of Non-Intervention in the Present Spanish Crisis." The British liked the idea and agreed to be a co-sponsor. Paris was particularly anxious that Germany, Italy, and the Soviet Union support the plan. On August 6, Italy announced it would accept the non-intervention accord. The Germans signed it on August 24, and four days later Stalin forbid weapons exports to Spain. In the end, twenty-seven European countries signed the agreement, but the flow of weapons continued nonetheless.

Throughout the month of August, the Madrid government used the Bank of Spain's gold to purchase armaments from France. After the acceptance of its own non-intervention policy, the Paris government could no longer make direct shipments of weapons to Spain. Nonetheless, the Spanish banks still sold a significant amount of its bullion to France in exchange for weaponry.[14]

By early August, Stalin was becoming concerned about a quick Franco victory. Intelligence reports coming to him through the Comintern showed that government forces were desperately short of weapons. An intelligence estimate made in late August was that Republican units had just one rifle for every three soldiers and one machine gun for 150 to 200 men. Stalin's first move was to get better on-the-ground information. On August 6, he sent Mikhail Koltsov, the country's most famous journalist, to be a war correspondent for *Pravda* and also a secret agent. In Hemingway's novel *For Whom the Bell Tolls*, Koltsov's name was changed to Karkov, and is described as a savvy *Pravda* journalist with a fine taste in women. A week later, a two–person film crew followed. Ilya Ehrenburg, a writer and journalist, went as the *Izvestia* correspondent. They all were soon sending Stalin pessimistic reports.[15]

The Soviet Politburo on August 21 asked state planners to draw up a large-scale program of military assistance to the Republican government. The program was dubbed Operation X. The plan recommended shipping fighter aircraft, bombers, light tanks, heavy tanks, armored cars, and torpedo boats. In addition to the hardware, the communist leadership proposed sending military advisors and combatants such as pilots, mechanics, radio operators, and code-breakers.[16]

The Soviet government at the time did not have diplomatic relations with the Republican government, but it quickly appointed Marcel Rosenberg, formerly the Soviet representative at the League of Nations in Geneva, to be ambassador. He arrived in Madrid on August 27. A phalanx of Soviet attachés and advisors quickly joined Rosenberg in the capital. Vladimir Antonov-Ovseyenko, the commander of the Red Guard unit that captured the Winter Palace during the Russian Revolution, went to Barcelona as consul general. A few days later on September 2, Soviet agents in Western Europe received instructions to set up a clandestine network to "purchase and transport arms to Spain." Stalin, though, instructed anyone going to Spain to "stay out of range of the artillery fire."[17]

Among the new Soviet officials was Alexander Orlov, a top operative in the secret police, who had the title of political attaché. Orlov, a man of many names, was born on August 21, 1895, as Leiba Lazarevich Feldbin in Bobruysk, Belarus. He later took the name Leon Feldbin. He came from a line of Ashkenazy Jews, who had migrated from Austria. He studied law briefly before World War I, before being drafted into the Czar's army. In 1918, Feldbin went over to the Red Army and directed guerilla operations during the Russo-Polish war, which won him the attention of Feliks Dzerzhinsky, the founder of the *Cheka*, the first Soviet secret police. After the conflict, Feldbin went to work for that organization, and by 1920 his name was Lev Nikolayevsky or Lev Nikolsky. His obvious gift for foreign languages landed him in overseas operations for the secret service. He went to Paris as an undercover agent posing as trade delegate Léon Nikolayev. In January 1928, he was transferred to Berlin with the same title and the name Lev Lazarevice Feldel. In April 1931, Moscow called him back home to head the agency's economic department.[18]

After only a short stay, he went to Berlin, where he got to know a General Motors employee and used that contact in September 1932 to make a trip to the U.S., which still did not have diplomatic relations with the Soviet Union. General Motors thought he was interested in buying a fleet of cars for Moscow, but he was actually trying to obtain a U.S. passport in the name of William Goldin. While in New York City, he also checked out dead-drop sites that might someday be useful for smuggling or making clandestine deals. He returned to the Soviet Union on November 30.

In July 1934, the star spy was off to London. Using the "William Goldin" passport and professing to be a European-born American working for a U.S. refrigerator company, he recruited university students with leanings toward Marxism. His plan was to nurture them until they reached high government positions. In February 1935, William Goldin took over responsibility for Kim Philby (code-named *Söhnchen*) and taught him the basic tricks of the trade. Philby went on to become a top Soviet spy. By early 1935, Goldin was back in Moscow.

In the spring of 1936, the peripatetic spy was one of the six men giving intelligence briefings to the Soviet Politburo and foreign ministry. In that position, he had frequent contacts with Stalin. On August 26, Security Boss Genrikh Yagoda told Lev Nikolsky, as he was still known in Moscow, to go to Spain and organize a counter-intelligence service that would make guerrilla attacks. Before departing, he met with Foreign Secretary Maxim Litvinov, who told him that he would need a new undercover name. Litvinov threw out several suggestions, including Alexander Orlov, the name of an obscure Russian writer. On September 5, Litvinov signed the passports of the new Alexander Orlov, his wife Maria, and daughter Veronika, who would be accompanying him to Spain. He arrived in Madrid on September 16.[19]

A photo of Orlov taken in Spain shows someone who looks more like a bank senior vice president than a spy. He was about 5 ft. 7 in. and wore a dark suit and white shirt, with just a touch of cuff showing. His dark hair was slightly receding and parted on the left. A white handkerchief peaked out of his vest pocket. With his feet well planted, he was the image of someone accustomed to being in charge. His most striking feature was a neatly trimmed mustache. Hollywood in the 1930s would have cast Adolphe Menjou to play Orlov.

A Republican cabinet shuffle on September 4, ushered in several new cabinet ministers as the government shifted sharply to the left. Socialist Francisco Largo Caballero, 67, a labor leader who had once worked as a plasterer, became prime minister, and for the first time communists were in the cabinet. With the military situation deteriorating and the Italians and Germans continuing to ship materiel and men to the Nationalists despite the non-intervention agreement, the Republicans were desperate to get more weapons. France and Britain clearly were not going to help them, and in fact might block their efforts to sell gold for armaments. The Spanish Republic's only option was the Soviet Union. The Politburo discussed a deal called Operation X on October 17 and gave it the go-ahead two days later. It involved the delivery of fifty T-26 tanks plus fuel and ammunition and also bombers and small arms. The Soviet aid to the Spanish government eventually more than balanced out the amount of munitions the Germans and Italians gave to Franco.[20]

The driving force of the new government was Juan Negrín, the 43-year-old finance minister. He was a medical doctor and polyglot who had studied in Germany and spoke English, French, and German. Negrín and Arthur Stashevsky, who had arrived in mid-October to be the Soviet trade envoy in the new Madrid embassy, were soon fast friends. Stashevsky had once served in the Red Army, but left following the Bolshevik victory to reorganize the country's fur industry, a key sector that supplied the state with badly needed foreign currency. He married a French woman and enjoyed the good life.[21] Negrín and Stashevsky shared long lunches, where they discussed Spain's need for weapons. In a locked drawer of his desk, the finance minister kept a card with a list of all the financial resources the government had available to fight the war, broken down into gold, silver, and pesetas. He told American journalist Louis Fischer in September 1936 that the Republic had "approximately 600 million gold dollars."[22] Some of it was in the form of coins, often dating back to the Spanish conquistadores, which probably had greater numismatic value than the gold price.

While the Soviets quickly established a strong presence in Madrid, the Republican government was much slower off the ground diplomatically. On September 21, Prime Minister Largo Caballero named Marcelino Pascua ambassador to Moscow, but he didn't arrive in the Soviet capital until October 7. Pascua was a medical doctor by training and had no previous diplomatic experience. His main qualification for the job was that he had once traveled to the Soviet Union to study its health system. Shortly before the ambassador left for Moscow, he met with Largo Caballero and asked for specific instructions. The Prime Minister replied, "Well now, you know the political and military situation. You've got to convince them to help us immediately with military equipment—above all with aviation."[23]

Franco's armies were now only twenty miles from the capital, and the government had received reports that Catalan anarchists, radical supporters of the government, were planning to grab the gold in Madrid and take it to Barcelona. Only nine days after taking office, Largo Caballero and Negrín got President Azaña to sign a secret decree that authorized the finance minister to move some 10,000 cases of gold and silver from Madrid to a "place which in his opinion offers the best security."[24]

On September 13, Prime Minister Largo Caballero authorized Negrín to ship the bullion from the Madrid vaults to a naval installation overlooking the port of Cartagena on the country's Mediterranean southeastern coast. At 11:30 P.M. on September 15, the first convoy of 800 cases of gold coins in bags left the Madrid central bank for the city's Atocha railroad station. The next day it was loaded onto train wagons and arrived at its final destination at 2:30 A.M. on September 17. Eventually all 10,000 cases of gold and silver in Madrid were sent there. About one-fifth of the shipment was immediately sent to Marseilles to be turned into hard currency for the government.[25] The remaining cases, which contained 510 tons of gold, would be sent to Moscow. Only Negrín, Azaña, Largo Caballero, and Francisco Méndez Aspe, the director general of the Treasury, knew that it had been moved.

The location was as far away from Franco's armies as possible while still being in Spain. The gold was stored in a naval ammunition dump inside a large cave hewn out of rock. At the front were two heavy wooden doors. Guards were told that the boxes contained munitions. The national treasure was now better protected in Cartagena, but the government still needed weapons to fight Franco's well-armed rebels.

No one knows for certain whether it was a Spaniard or a Soviet who first proposed sending the Spanish gold to Moscow. The reality was that with the arms embargo put in place by leading European nations, Spain had no other choice for getting military hardware. Walter Krivitsky, a Soviet spy working at the time in The Hague but also involved in Spanish affairs, later wrote, "Stashevsky offered to take the Spanish gold to Soviet Russia, and to supply Madrid with arms and munitions in exchange. Through Negrín, he made the deal with Largo Caballero's government." According to Krivitsky, Soviet agents began calling Stashevsky the "richest man in the world" because he controlled the Spanish gold.[26] Alexander Orlov maintained in his autobiography that Finance Minister Negrín first sounded out Soviet Trade Attaché Winzer "about storing the gold in Soviet Russia."[27]

On October 15, Largo Caballero sent a letter to Stalin asking if he would "agree to the deposit of approximately 500 tons of gold, the exact weight to be determined at the time of delivery."[28] Stalin sent back his acceptance two days later.

Orlov was in his Soviet embassy office on October 20, when the code clerk brought him an encrypted telegram. The aide had read only the first line: "Decode immediately. Absolutely secret. This telegram must be decoded by Schwed personally."[29] Schwed was Orlov's code name. The cable read: "Arrange with the head of the Spanish Government Caballero for shipment of the gold reserves in Spain to the Soviet Union. Use a Soviet steamer. Maintain utmost secrecy. If the Spaniards demand from you a receipt, refuse. I repeat refuse to sign anything. Say that the State Bank will issue a formal receipt in Moscow. I hold you personally responsible for this operation." The name at the end of the message was Ivan Vasilevich, the moniker Stalin used for his most secret communications. It is also the Russian name for the person known in the west as Ivan the Terrible, the brutal medieval czar whom the Soviet leader greatly admired.

Ambassador Rosenberg was officially in charge of the whole operation, but Orlov handled the details. Both were flabbergasted that the Spaniards would entrust their gold to Stalin. Orlov later wrote of Negrín: "The finance minister seemed the very prototype of the intellectual—opposed to communism in theory, yet vaguely sympathetic to the 'great experiment' in Russia. This political naïveté helps to explain his impulse to export the gold to that country."[30]

Two days later, the two Soviet officials met Negrín to go over transportation details. That was Orlov's job, so he and Negrín conducted business in a mixture of English, French, and German. The finance minister repeated that his government wanted to send its gold to the Soviet Union to buy weapons, adding that the shipment involved about 700 tons. The actual figure turned out to be closer to 500 tons. The Soviet Secret Service already knew independently that it had been shipped to Cartagena, but Orlov asked him where it was just to test him. Negrín replied that it was there and was safely "in one of the old caves north of the town used by the navy to store munitions."[31]

That location made things easier for Orlov because the Soviets were already unloading arms and munitions there. *Campeche*, a Spanish tanker and the first ship bringing Soviet arms to Spain, arrived in Cartagena from the Crimea on October 4. A Soviet tank brigade had also docked a few days later and was still housed nearby. Negrín offered to get a team of Spanish soldiers to transfer the gold to the boats, but Orlov begged off, saying that was too risky. He wanted to use his own soldiers.

Orlov asked the finance minister to provide him with false documents that would show he was a British or American official. If the Spanish police stopped him, he could claim that the Republican government had decided to send the gold to that country for safekeeping. The two men quickly agreed that Orlov would be a representative of the Bank of America, not realizing that it was a private financial institution that had its headquarters in California and not the U.S. Central Bank. He should have been representing the Federal Reserve Bank. Negrín proposed that Orlov take the name Blackstone for the operation, and had his office draw up an official-looking document bearing Negrín's signature that asked Spanish authorities to give whatever assistance was needed to

"Mr. Blackstone, plenipotentiary representative of the Bank of America."[32]

The following day, Orlov had just left for Cartagena on a Spanish air force plane when two German bombers and several fighters spotted his aircraft. One of them strafed his plane, which had to make an emergency landing. The next day he continued by car to Cartagena, where he met with Soviet Naval Attaché Nikolai Kuznetzov. Orlov explained that he was arranging shipment of "a highly strategic material" and asked to send it home on any arriving Soviet vessel.[33] The Soviet ship *Volgoles* was already in port and was the first to be loaded. Orlov decided it was safer to split the precious cargo among several ships, eventually using four.

He then returned to Madrid to work out the final details with Largo Caballero and Negrín. Everyone agreed that the most dangerous part of the ocean journey was going to be around Italy, in particular in the narrow area between Tunisia and Sicily. Defense Minister Indalecio Prieto was brought into the plan, and provided escort ships to follow the Soviet convoy at the beginning of the trip until it reached Odessa on the Black Sea. The Spanish captains of the escort ships would each be given a sealed letter with instructions to open it only if one of the Soviet vessels were attacked at sea. The captains were then to go to the vessel's aid and bring it to a safe port. Orlov also sent a message to Moscow suggesting that the Soviet navy station warships in the eastern Mediterranean to protect the convoy. He never got a reply, but later learned that Stalin had ordered that to be done.

Orlov received plenty of local help for the job. The Spanish commander at Cartagena provided sixty sailors to move boxes of gold from the cave to the trucks. The Soviet tank brigade officer supplied twenty five-ton trucks and tank men to drive the cargo the five miles from the cave to the docks. Two secret service men were assigned to provide security. Kuznetzov also provided sixty Soviet sailors to move the cargo onto the ships once it reached the harbor.

Orlov worked out the plan to the last detail. The 7,800 cases of gold would be split between four Soviet ships. The most, 2,697 boxes, would be on the *Neva*, and the least, 963 containers, would be on the *Volgoles*. He ordered that each truck carry exactly fifty boxes from the cave so that it would be easier to keep count of the boxes. The containers each weighed 145 pounds and were all the same size: nineteen inches long, twelve inches wide, and seven inches high. Since the Spanish workers were generally short and lightly built, two men were assigned to carry a box.[34] Working from 7:00 P.M. to dawn, the crew loaded the gold over a three-day period.

It was still on October 22, when Orlov's car led the first convoy of ten trucks toward the harbor. Sitting next to him was Francisco Méndez Aspe, the director general of the Treasury. Each round trip, including the unloading, took two hours. When those vehicles returned to the cave, another ten left for the docks. The transport took place on three moonless nights. Cartagena was also under a blackout because of the danger of German attacks, so neither Orlov's car nor the trucks could use their lights. Orlov grabbed an hour of sleep when he could.[35]

Sixty Spanish sailors during the day remained in the caves with the gold, passing their time listening to dance records and playing cards. They still thought they were guarding munitions. Negrín came one afternoon to check things out, and Orlov showed him some newly arrived Soviet tanks at a nearby camp. None of them had yet been in battle in Spain, and Negrín became emotional as he ran his hand across a tank like a man petting a dog. With his eyes tearing up, he said, "Now we'll lick them! Now they will do the running! Send our thanks to Stalin, tell him this war will soon be over!"[36]

At about 3:30 A.M. on the third night of the gold transports, German aircraft attacked the Cartagena harbor. Orlov was at the cave when it took place, but he could hear explosions hitting the piers. Drivers told him later that bombs had damaged a Spanish ship near the Soviet ones. He decided to speed up the process in order to get his cargo out of the harbor and on its way to Odessa as soon as possible. The last box was loaded on the *Volgoles* just after 10:00 A.M. on October 25. Méndez Aspe and Orlov kept separate records as the boxes were loaded. At the end, the Spaniard counted

7,900, but Orlov had one hundred less. He recognized the discrepancy, but decided not to tell him and to let officials in Moscow settle the problem.[37]

Just before the ships were ready to leave, Méndez Aspe asked Orlov for a receipt for the gold, and the Soviet remembered the order he had received in the cable. He casually replied, "A receipt? But, *compañero*, I am not authorized to give one. Don't worry, my friend, it will be issued by the State Bank of the Soviet Union, when everything is checked and weighed."[38]

Méndez Aspe was visibly upset and impatiently said he wouldn't be able to explain this to his bosses in Madrid. So a Spanish official was assigned to travel on each of the four vessels as "official chaperones" for the gold. Two Bank of Spain officials who were already at the harbor were told to make the trip. Méndez Aspe then went into Cartagena and dragooned another two Spaniards to go along. The four ended up getting a longer voyage than they expected, since once they arrived they were not allowed to leave the country. With the gold and escorts now on board, the four Soviet ships carrying the Spanish state treasury left the Cartagena docks. The destination was the port of Odessa on the Black Sea. The *Volgoles* sailed out first. The ships in the convoy were as protected as they could be given the war conditions.

Once the convoy of gold ships had departed, Foreign Minister Litvinov sent Vyacheslav Molotov, the Chairman of the Council of People's Commissars, asking him to get the Spanish ambassador in Moscow to "write a letter to us with a request to receive the gold, but, since he is unable to indicate the weight nor the value of the gold, such letter would be legally meaningless."[39]

Orlov spent the week after the shipment departed on tenterhooks, worrying about whether the vessels and their cargo would safely get through the Mediterranean. As soon as he figured the ships had arrived at their destination, he sent a message to Moscow explaining the difference in totals between him and Méndez Aspe. Nikolai Yezhov, the head of the secret police, replied and asked whether he was sure of his figure.[40] Orlov responded that he was "almost certain," and then received another cable, saying, "Do not worry about figures. Everything will be counted anew in Moscow." A last message several hours later told him: "Do not mention your figure to anybody."[41]

The first Soviet ship carrying the gold landed in Odessa on November 2. Local officials were fearful that someone would see the material being offloaded, so they cleared the port and surrounded it with security troops. A team of Soviet secret service officers from Moscow and Kiev carried boxes of gold on their backs to a waiting freight train guarded by one hundred armed men. A Soviet official who participated in the transfer later told Soviet spy Walter Krivitsky that there were enough boxes to cover Red Square from end to end.[42] The first shipment arrived at the Soviet Depository of Precious Metals in Moscow at 3:00 A.M. on November 6, and deliveries continued until 1:00 A.M. on November 7.[43] The street where the agency was located had been closed to traffic and troops guarded the operation.

On November 7, the Spaniards finally received their official receipt for the gold in the form of a four-page protocol that was written in both Russian and French, then the international language of diplomacy. Ambassador Pascua and three of the Spaniards who had accompanied the gold signed for Madrid, while eight Soviet officials signed for their country. It noted that 5,619 standard cases plus 126 partly damaged ones had been delivered to the Precious Metal Depository of the People's Commissariat for Finance. It also said that the quantities of gold in the boxes did not always agree with the figures on the manifesto.

It was not until February 5, 1937 that Soviet officials finally finished counting the Spanish gold. They calculated that the shipments totaled 453 tons. The cargo contained only thirteen cases of bars. The rest were 60 million gold coins, most of them Portuguese.[44]

At a dinner in the Kremlin to celebrate the arrival of the Spanish gold, Stalin said, "They will never see their gold again, just as they do not see their own ears."[45]

Chapter Three

ADOLF HITLER'S ARGONAUT

In the aftermath of its defeat in World War I, Germany was an angry and economically decimated nation that spent years on the brink of revolution. Street battles pitting the far left against the far right took place daily around the country, especially in the capital Berlin. Germans agreed on little except their desire to annihilate their opponents and the current government. The victorious Allies, led by France, had inflicted on Germany a Carthaginian peace with the Versailles treaty of 1919 that crushed the country in hopes that it would never again rise to be a military power. That left Germans determined for revenge. The result was nearly two decades of political, social, and economic upheaval that ended in a Nazi dictatorship that brought Adolf Hitler to power in January 1933.

During the period of runaway chaos, Germany had few national heroes. There was one, though, with the unusual name Hjalmar Horace Greeley Schacht. In 1923 he became famous for rescuing the country that stood on the brink of collapse due to one of history's greatest inflations. Schacht was almost born an American. His father, Wilhelm Schacht, was from Schleswig-Holstein, a border region that in the nineteenth century went back and forth between Germany and Denmark. After the Prussians took it over following the Austro-Prussian War of 1866, Wilhelm left his native land with hopes of starting a new life in America. He became a U.S. citizen on December 11, 1872. Wilhelm Schacht's hero in his new country was Horace Greeley, the founder of the *New York Tribune*, an ardent foe of slavery and champion of the country's westward expansion, who wrote in a famous editorial on July 13, 1865, "Go west, young man, and grow up with the country."

After immigrating to the U.S., Wilhelm Schacht got a job at a brewery in Brooklyn and wrote to his girlfriend back home asking her to join him so that they could get married, which they did on January 14, 1872, at the Episcopal Church in Manhattan. The couple stayed in the U.S. for another five years, as Wilhelm bounced from one mediocre job to another and a first son named Eddy was born. In the fall of 1876, Wilhelm packed up his pregnant wife and son and returned to Germany. Shortly after they arrived, a second son was born on January 22, 1877. His father wanted to name the child Horace Greeley Schacht, but his maternal grandmother, who was from Danish nobility, was outraged and insisted that he have the proper Scandinavian first name Hjalmar. The baby's birth certificate gave his name as Horace Greeley Hjalmar Schacht, but he was always called Hjalmar.[1]

Young Schacht performed well in school and earned a doctorate in economics, while dabbling in journalism. In a country where academic degrees carry great prestige, and someone with two PhDs is called "Doktor Doktor," he was Dr. Schacht for the rest of his life. He moved into banking at an early age and excelled. Tall, thin, and standing ramrod straight, he could have been a stand-in for Washington Irving's Ichabod Crane. Schacht had a long neck and generally wore tall starched collars that made him look as if his head were on a platter. He plastered down his hair and parted it in the middle. Pince-nez glasses rested just above a neatly trimmed military mustache.

But unlike the charmingly awkward fictional schoolteacher, Schacht's dour demeanor made him look like a heartless banker who was about to foreclose on farmer Schmidt's home. He was also an unrepentant showman with an immense ego. He told jokes in four languages and liked to write humorous poems that belied his stiff formality.[2] In January 1938, George Ogilvie–Forbes, the *chargé d'affaires* at the British embassy in Berlin, sent Foreign Minister Anthony Eden a word portrait of the man: "Schacht is composed of the most diverse qualities. Vanity, arrogance, overweaning ambition, simplicity, good nature, wit, repartee, malice, technical ability, inconsistency alternate with kaleidoscopic effect in his complex character."[3]

Schacht was a strict classical economist and follower of Adam Smith, David Ricardo, and John Stuart Mill. They all advocated limited government in a free economy and thought that the market would regulate itself. He, and they, also believed firmly in the importance of gold. In his book *Gold for Europe*, Schacht wrote, "Money, to be internationally stable, must be based upon a commodity which, independent of governmental and economic influence, is in demand and accepted everywhere and at any time. Of such commodities, gold is the one that has best stood the test of time." Schacht could have been listening to the nineteenth century British economist David Ricardo, who once wrote, "Gold, though of little use compared with air or water, will exchange for a great quantity of other goods."[4]

The German was also a fierce advocate of national self-sufficiency that economists still called the Schachtian system. Similar to the mercantilism that reigned from the sixteenth to eighteenth centuries, this called for a country to produce at home as much as possible of the goods and services it needed and import only those that it could not make locally. Following that strategy, Germany would shepherd its gold, the internationally accepted form of payment, and also build up stashes of world currencies such as the British pound and American dollar. Then it would have sufficient funds to buy the products it couldn't make.

Hjalmar Schacht rose to national esteem during the national trauma that followed World War I. Inflation began picking up in April 1918 shortly after the conflict ended, and blasted off to hyper levels in May 1922, when prices increased more than fifty percent in just that one month. Government expenditures in 1923 totaled six quintillion Reichsmark (the number six followed by eighteen zeros). Central bank printing presses turned out bank notes in ever-higher denominations that quickly became almost worthless. In November the government introduced the 100-trillion Reichsmark note. The government printed money on only one side of the paper in order to turn it out more quickly. The inflation wildfire sucked air out of civilized society. Food fights broke out between farmers, who hoarded their products, and city dwellers. Consumers resorted to barter. People paid their dental bills with condensed milk, and the Ministry of Finance gave its staff potatoes in lieu of cash. On November 1, 1923, a loaf of bread cost 3 billion marks, a pound of meat 36 billion marks, and a glass of beer 4 billion marks. Germans looking for a scapegoat turned on each other, and anti-Semitism ran rampant. The middle class was ruined, while currency specula-tors enriched themselves and flaunted their wealth. Gold became the only means of payment in which people believed, and prices in stores were often listed in both Reichsmark and gold. Schacht, the managing director of the Danat Bank, became so fearful for the safety of his wife and two young children that he sent them to live in Switzerland.

On November 8, 1923, Schacht had a late dinner at the Hotel Continental in Berlin with the new German Chancellor Gustav Stresemann to discuss the country's inflation crisis. The two men were old friends, and Stresemann was looking for someone to take an unenviable new job as the country's currency commissioner. The government was anxious to replace Karl Helfferich, the longtime head of the central bank, who was one of the fathers of these cata-strophic runaway prices. Bank rules, though, did not allow him to be fired. So Stresemann wanted to put someone above him who would have the mandate to save the country's currency. Shortly before midnight as the two men were about to leave dinner, they learned that Nazi party leader Adolf Hitler had staged a *putsch* by marching on Munich's Bürgerbräukeller, a beer hall. The coup failed, but sixteen Nazis and four police officers were killed. Schacht later wrote in his autobiography that the country at the time was "living on the edge of a volcano."[5]

Four days later, Hans Luther, the Minister of Finance, officially offered Schacht the job of trying to end Germany's inflation. Two eminent bankers had already turned it down. Luther explained that he would have unlimited power and could even overrule decisions from the Reichsbank president. Schacht asked for a few days to consider the offer, but Luther said he needed an immediate decision. Schacht accepted and went to work the following day.

The new currency czar had only one employee, a secretary with whom he shared a converted janitor's closet. Schacht's secretary later described her boss's working habits during the crisis: "He sat on his chair and smoked in his little dark room at the Ministry of Finance, which still smelled of old floor cloths. He read no letters. He wrote no letters. He telephoned a great deal to German or foreign bankers to gauge the mood of international markets. He usually went home late, often by the last suburban train, travelling third class."[6]

At first, the value of the Reichsmark continued falling. Less than a week after Schacht took office, the government stopped printing the old currency, and introduced a new one called the Rentenmark. It had the distinction of being backed by the country's land, but was also linked to gold at the mark parity rate prior to World War I, even though there was a new rule that no one could exchange it for the precious metal in order to preserve government gold reserves. Schacht saw the Rentenmark as a way to get back to the gold standard as quickly as possible. On November 20, Schacht fixed the exchange rate at 1 trillion Reichsmark to one Rentenmark. Now 4.2 Rentenmark were worth one U.S. dollar, the exact exchange rate as before the war. That same night, Helfferich died unexpectedly, and a month later Schacht was named president of the Reichsbank, a job with a lifetime tenure.[7]

Schacht considered the Rentenmark to be only "a bridge between chaos and hope."[8] Although many countries were already off the gold standard because of the global economic slump, he still wanted to have a strong, gold-backed currency and advocated the establishment of a separate Gold Discount Bank. Before World War I, Germany had $1 billion in gold holdings and even in the immediate aftermath it still had $577 million. But because of war reparations and rampant inflation, the Reichsbank on December 31, 1923 was down to only $111.2 million worth of gold.

Once the inflation had been stabilized, the veteran banker and economic internationalist realized that his country could not solve its currency problem alone and reached out for help. The preeminent custodian of world financial power in the years between the world wars was a man named Montagu Norman, the governor of the Bank of England. When he suggested that the new German central banker come to see him, Schacht jumped at the opportunity, arriving at the Liverpool Railroad Station in London at eight o'clock on New Year's Eve. He was surprised to see Norman standing on the platform to greet him. The two agreed to start work the next morning at eleven, despite the holiday. The central bankers quickly struck up a warm friendship, and at the end of the visit Norman agreed to give him a three-year loan to start a new Gold Discount Bank that would help finance German recovery.[9]

In the first months of the New Year, runaway German inflation ended like a patient's fever breaking. Germany's economy stabilized for the first time in nearly a decade. Schacht was immediately hailed at home and abroad as the savior of his country's economy.

With the crisis over, Schacht began enjoying the trappings of being a central banker. He traveled extensively to hobnob with his fellow mavens of money. One of his trips took him to New York City to meet Federal Reserve Chairman Benjamin Strong. Schacht had earlier sent him a case of the best wine from Germany's Palatinate region, even though the U.S. was still under Prohibition. Strong nonetheless served the wine at a lunch at the Federal Reserve building in lower Manhattan. He also wanted to show his German counterpart the gold Berlin had stored in the Fed vaults below the streets of Lower Manhattan after the end of World War I. Unfortunately, Fed staffers couldn't quickly find the specific German bullion amidst all the various national deposits. Finally an employee admitted: "Mr. Strong, we can't find the Reichsbank gold." Schacht comforted his host by saying, "Never mind; I believe you when you say the gold is there. Even if it weren't, you are good for its replacement."[10]

Although Germany's runaway inflation was over, the country still faced the problem of the unrealistic reparations that the World War I victor nations had demanded. The payments seemed only natural to the victors. In 1870 at the end of the Franco-Prussian conflict, the victorious Germans demanded that Paris pay 5 billion gold francs in war reparations. In the Treaty of Versailles in 1919 ending World War I, the victorious Allies demanded even higher war payments. The three big powers had vastly different demands against the Germans. The French sought revenge and to crush the German economy so Berlin could never again wage war on them. The British were not as angry since they had not been invaded. The U.S. was the least demanding. The French wanted Germany to pay $220 billion; the British $24 billion, and the Americans $22 billion. The final settlement was 132 billion gold marks or $34 billion. That was later negotiated down to 112 billion gold marks, with annual payments of two billion per year.[11] The final German payment for World War I reparations was made on October 3, 2010.

The Versailles Treaty was naturally unpopular with the German public, and Britain's John Maynard Keynes warned in his book *The Economic Consequences of the Peace* that it would ruin the country's economy. Schacht refused to publicly recognize the war debt, but participated in negotiations with the Allies for better treaty conditions that became known as the Young Plan. He got somewhat better terms that reduced the amount and spread it out over a longer period, but the German public nonetheless turned against him. The national hero suddenly turned into a fall guy. When Schacht returned from a trip to Paris in June 1929, after signing the latest plan, his wife met him at the Berlin railroad station with the stinging rebuke: "You ought never to have signed!"[12]

On October 3, 1929, Schacht's friend and mentor Chancellor Gustav Stresemann died of a stroke. Having lost public support within the increasingly dangerous German political scene where radicals of the right and left polarized politics, Schacht on March 7, 1930, resigned from his lifetime job. When asked at a farewell press conference what he was going to do, the banker replied that he was going to become "a country squire and raise pigs."

The new retiree enjoyed traveling, and that summer visited Romania, Switzerland, Denmark, and Sweden. In the fall, he went to the U.S. for a two-month speaking tour. While on his ocean crossing in September 1930, he read a copy of Mein Kampf by Adolf Hitler, the country's rising politician.

By the time Schacht returned home, he had forgotten about being a country squire and ventured into German politics. Although he had been one of the founders of the German Democratic Party, a center-left group founded largely by intellectuals in 1918, he left it eight years later on the grounds that it no longer supported private property. The Nazis were now coming on strong. In the May 1928 parliamentary elections, they had won only twelve seats, but in the September 1930 balloting they captured 107, making them the second largest party in the Reichstag.

In December 1930, Emil Georg von Stauss, the CEO of the Deutsche Bank and the man who loaned Hitler the Remington typewriter on which Mein Kampf was written, invited Schacht to a dinner with Hermann Göring, a top Nazi leader who had asked to meet him. Table talk among the three men quickly turned to politics and economics. In a sign of his compulsive arrogance, Schacht later speculated that Göring probably hadn't yet paid for the tuxedo he was wearing that night.[13]

A month later on January 5, 1931, Göring invited Schacht to a dinner party that he and his wife were holding at their apartment in the Wilmersdorf section of Berlin. In another condescending observation, Schacht noted that the Nazi leader lived in a modest rented dwelling. A message accompanying the invitation said that Hitler would be present. The Führer, wearing his Nazi uniform of dark trousers and brown jacket, arrived only after everyone had eaten and proceeded to speak for two hours. Schacht described him as "neither pretentious nor affected—on the contrary he was natural and unassuming." He also noted that Hitler spoke ninety-five percent of the time. Hitler showed Schacht respect, which he appreciated, but treated his fellow Nazis with disdain. The banker was impressed and later wrote that Hitler's "skill in exposition was most striking. Everything he said he demonstrated as incontrovertible truth; nevertheless his ideas were not unreasonable and were entirely free from any propagandist pathos." Schacht's bottom line: "The thing that impressed me most about this man was his absolute conviction of the rightness of his outlook and his determination to translate this outlook into practical action."[14]

During his post-war trial at Nuremberg, Schacht said that his own political view at the time was that he "wanted a big and strong Germany; and to achieve that, I would ally myself with the devil." The banker who the British economic journalist Paul Einzig once called "the most Machiavellian statesman in Europe" was about to make a dangerous power play.[15]

Unlike almost everyone else surrounding Hitler, Schacht was not a Nazi party man and found it hard to hide his contempt for people he considered only slightly better than street brawlers. He alone among the Führer's inner circle never wore either the Nazi or military uniform. He was always the quintessential central banker. And while he might have fought the temptation, he treated most Nazis as inferiors. He had few contacts with leading party members outside of Hitler, who repeatedly invited his banker to attend his intimate daily lunches at the Reich Chancellery, where he held court and gossiped. Schacht attended only twice. Despite his initial favorable impression, he later came to regard Hitler as "half educated," adding that although he had read a lot, it was all from a distorted point of view. When Wilhelm Vocke, who had served with Schacht on the Reichsbank board, warned him about the Nazis, Schacht replied, "One must give these people a chance. If they do no good, they will disappear. They will be cleared out in the same way as their predecessors."[16]

In the spring of 1931, the American journalist Dorothy Thompson interviewed Schacht and voiced skepticism about the ability of the

Nazis to handle the country's economy, asking, "Who will run it?" Schacht replied, "I will. The Nazis cannot rule, but I can rule through them."[17]

The world economic crisis accelerated on May 11, 1931, when Austria's largest bank, the Rothschild's Kreditanstalt, collapsed. That set off an international financial crisis that hit neighboring Germany particularly hard. On July 11, Chancellor Heinrich Brüning called Schacht and asked him to come immediately to Berlin. When the banker arrived the next day, he learned that the Reichsbank's gold and foreign currency reserves were quickly evaporating. In the first three weeks of June, the country had lost more than half its gold to speculators. On July 13, the Danat Bank, one of the country's major financial institutions and Schacht's old bank, did not open. A new full-scale national economic crisis had begun.

Schacht was regularly in contact with Hitler during those tense times, often expressing his support in sycophantic letters. On August 29, 1932, the banker offered him a strategic suggestion: "Do not put forward any detailed economic program." He also pledged his loyalty: "Wherever my work may take me in the near future, even if you should see me one day within a fortress, you can always count on me as your reliable helper." Schacht signed the letter, "With a forceful Heil."[18]

Schacht urged Brüning's successor Franz von Papen to resign in favor of Hitler, saying, "Give him your position. Give it to Hitler. He is the only man who can save Germany."[19] Schacht's name was prominently at the top of a list of the country's leading economists who publicly urged President Paul von Hindenburg to name Hitler chancellor.

In a surprising development in the November 6, 1932 election, the Nazi vote declined for the first time, giving hope to German democrats that the party's power had peaked. That tempted some politicians to propose bringing the Nazis into a new government in hopes that they would begin acting responsibly once they were in power. That was naïve.

Schacht was showing his loyalty to the Nazis at a crucial moment. Joseph Goebbels, the party's chief propagandist and a member of

Hitler's inner circle, wrote in his diary on November 21, 1932, "In a conversation with Dr. Schacht, I assured myself that he absolutely represents our point of view. He is one of the few who accepts the Führer's position entirely."[20]

On a snowy January 30, 1933, and after years of increasing social chaos, violence in the streets, weak governments, and inconclusive elections, President Paul von Hindenburg reluctantly asked Adolf Hitler to form a government. The following day, the new chancellor convinced the president to dissolve the Reichstag and call new elections to be held on March 5. Goebbels wrote in his diary: "The struggle is light now, since we are able to employ all the means of the state."[21]

In order to ensure the party's electoral victory, the Nazis wanted to raise as much money as possible to finance the campaign, and turned to Schacht to help deliver large donations from the country's wealthy industrial leaders. Göring asked him to invite a group of businessmen to a meeting with Hitler on February 20 at the Reichstag's Presidential Palace. Some twenty-five attended, including Gustav Krupp von Bohlen und Halbach, the armaments magnate; Carl Bosch, the head of I.G. Farben, the chemical giant; and Albert Vögler, the founder of Vereinigte Stahlwerke, a steel giant.

Schacht and Göring were joint hosts and spoke first while waiting for Hitler, who as usual arrived late. Once there, the Führer explained his political agenda for after his expected election success. He promised to "eliminate" Marxists, rearm the Wehrmacht, and bluntly said, "We must not forget that all the benefits of culture must be introduced more or less with an iron fist."[22] He also made a menacing prediction: "We stand before the last election." It was time to "crush the other side completely."

When Hitler finished speaking, Krupp jumped up and thanked him "for having given us such a clear picture."[23]

After Hitler left the room, Schacht asked the business executives to make major contributions to the election campaign. He said the overall goal was three million Reichsmark. Göring said it was time for them to make "financial sacrifices," adding that it would "surely be easier for industry to bear, if it realized that the election of March fifth will surely be the last one of the next ten years, probably even for the next hundred years." Schacht requested that each man write down the amount his company would contribute to the Nazi campaign fund. Hitler had already asked Schacht to undertake the job of administering the contributions. When he totaled them up, the businessmen of Germany had pledged the requested three million marks.

Two nights later on February 27, a mysterious fire largely destroyed the Reichstag building. The Nazis blamed Marinus van der Lubbe, a Dutch communist, for the crime. The next day, Hitler convinced President von Hindenburg to sign emergency measures suspending part of the constitution as a "defense measure against Communist acts." Göring later bragged that he had set the fire, but then later denied it.[24]

Despite their ruthless election tactics, the Nazis did not get the two-thirds majority that Hitler sought, which would have allowed him to push through his radical agenda and grab total control of the country. His party increased its vote only to 43.9%, but he was able to put together a small majority government with the help of Franz von Papen's Center Party.

Shortly after the election, Hitler called in Reichsbank President Hans Luther and asked him how much money the central bank could advance for a job-creation program, which is how the new chancellor planned to masquerade German rearmament. The new regime did not want to finance this through unpopular new taxes. The banker said he could only provide 100 million Reichsmark or about $23 million, which was a pittance compared to what Hitler wanted.

So the new chancellor called in Schacht and put the same question to him. After saying it was necessary to "do away with unemployment," Hitler asked if there was a way to raise "a very large sum of money" through the Reichsbank. Schacht replied that the central bank "should provide the money needed." Hitler pressed him for a number, but he would not commit, saying only, "I am honestly not in a position, Chancellor, to mention any particular sum. My opinion is this: whatever happens we must put an end to unemployment, and therefore the Reichsbank must furnish whatever will be necessary to take the last unemployed off the street."[25]

Hitler paused briefly and then asked, "Would you be prepared to take command of the Reichsbank again?" Schacht replied that he didn't want to force Luther out of office, but Hitler quickly said that he had other plans for him. Schacht said that in that case he would take the job. In a second meeting with Luther, Hitler offered him the post of German ambassador to Washington, which he readily accepted.

On March 17, almost exactly three years after he had left the job, Schacht was once again president of the Reichsbank. Every central banker should be born under a lucky star, and fortune smiled on him. Experts now agree that the German economy hit bottom in late 1932 and started expanding in early 1933, although no one knew that at the time. The following month, the central banker was also named a member of the secret Reich Defense Council, which was charged with preparing the country for war. Hitler's first demand of his banker was money for a Nazi priority program to repair and reconstruct houses, and Schacht readily complied. Another of his preliminary actions was to sanction an initial credit of 600 million Reichsmark to pay for the construction of the new highway system called the *Autobahn*, which was a pet Hitler project. The Führer considered the limited-access roads as a way to move army troops and weapons rapidly around the country in time of war. The government also spent heavily on building new housing. Schacht was accommodating on the Reichsbank's gold policy. When the Nazis took power, Germany's currency had to be backed 40% by gold or foreign exchange, but in October that requirement was quietly dropped. That made it easier to increase spending.

On March 23, 1933, the Reichstag by a vote of 441 to 94 passed the Enabling Act, which allowed Hitler to pass laws without legislative approval. The heavy hand of Nazi dictatorship was quickly descending on Germany.[26]

The German people left World War I with a national consensus that they could not count on any other nation for their safety or prosperity. They believed that their country faced the world alone and had to provide for its own defense, economy, and wellbeing. Britain, the country's main adversary during the earlier conflict, had cut off vital supplies with a naval blockade that left the country's people starving. During the infamous "turnip winter" of 1917, Germans on the home front had little to eat except turnips, which had previously been used for cattle fodder. In that tragic period, 763,000 people died of starvation.

Germans were now united with the angry attitude of "never again." The country, in the future, had to be master of its own domain. The widespread German name for this policy was *autarky*. The word goes back to the Greeks, and the more common English expression is "self-sufficiency." The foundation of this national policy was gold, the historic last refuge of people in trouble. If all else failed, the country needed enough gold to buy food. Germans of all political stripes and classes supported the policy. The public universally believed that British, French, and American armies had not defeated them on the battlefield, but rather had cut off Berlin's trade ties to the world and starved them into submission. The food blockade continued even after the armistice was signed on November 11, 1918, burning the humiliation even deeper into the national psyche. Autarky was not a national policy dictated by Berlin politicians on the general public, but was based on the country's painful experience and unity in the belief that it should never happen again.[27]

Members of the growing Nazi party, the street thugs who brought Hitler to power, were among the strongest believers in autarky. For them, the words in the country's national anthem said it all: *Deutschland über alles in der Welt* (Germany above all in the world).

Hitler himself had an expansionist view of Germany's place in Europe and believed that the nation could achieve not just self-sufficiency, but growth. Although he didn't often spell it out in detail to the world's public or political leaders, he envisaged a much larger country that would stretch from the Atlantic Ocean to the Ural Mountains. That was his concept of *Großraumwirtschaft*, a Nazi plan for the reorganization of Europe with a new continental economic system under Berlin's control and for its benefit. Germany could not achieve its historic role within the restrictive borders that the Allies had dictated at the end of World War I, where 66 million people lived when Hitler came to power in 1933. Hitler envisaged a German super nation that, in the west, would include parts or all of Belgium, Holland, and even France. In the east, Germany would take over the breadbaskets of Poland and Ukraine. Those countries had the rich soils that could produce both the food and natural resources that the enlarged Germany would need, as well as a population that Hitler planned to subjugate to perform the menial labor necessary to support this new, expanded state. This Great Germany would have a population of 140 million and have vassal states on its borders that would pose no military threat.

Big business such as I.G. Farben backed the autarky program that foresaw the production of man-made substitutes for goods such as rubber and oil that were not indigenous to Germany. Göring's Four Year Plan in 1934 forced all the major brown coal producers to form a joint venture to produce synthetic fuel. It invested heavily in synthetic fuel during the 1920s, when it looked as if the world's known sources of oil were running out. New discoveries in countries such as Saudi Arabia, though, set back their plans because the artificial product became uneconomic. Farben was a major financial backer of Hitler during his rise to power, and the Führer supported spending on synthetics when he became chancellor in 1933. Now the company was going to get its payoff.[28]

On August 9, 1942, when Hitler was still optimistic about the success of his invasion of the Soviet Union, he gleefully told his dinner companions, "There is here a million tons of wheat in reserve from last year's harvest. Just think what it will be like when we get things properly organized, and the oil wells are in our possession! The Ukraine produces thirteen or fourteen million tons a year. Even if we show ourselves to be half as successful as organizers as the Russians—that's six million for us!" There would be plenty of everything. He added, "We shall become the most self-supporting state, in every respect, including cotton in the world. The only thing we shall not have will be a coffee plantation—but we'll find a coffee-growing colony somewhere or other! Timber we shall have in abundance, iron in limitless quantity, the greatest manganese-ore mines in the world, oil—we shall swim in it."[29]

Hitler revealed his lack of knowledge of the economics of modern warfare in his *Second Book*, the sequel to *Mein Kampf* that he wrote in 1928, but which was not published in his lifetime. In it he said flatly, "The sword has to stand before the plough and an army before economics."[30]

That nirvana, however, would arrive only once Germany ruled the European mainland. In the meantime, Hitler's wars of conquest would have to be waged with the mineral resources that nature had given the country. Nazi Germany could not produce certain key raw materials. The Führer's entourage accepted without question his unrealistic orders to produce everything needed for his wars no matter what the cost or where it could be bought.

As an international banker with frequent and friendly contacts abroad, Schacht was not a natural advocate of autarky. But he knew his country; he knew its needs; and he knew its political leaders. Germany was dependent on world markets for a few essential raw materials and some food imports. Perhaps the most important one for Hitler's wars was the weapons-grade iron ore needed to make steel for tanks, cannons, and rifles. The country had plenty of low-quality ore, but not the higher level. At the time the Nazis took power, Germany imported eighty percent of its iron ore, with half of it coming from Sweden. The process of improving the country's low-grade ore to make better products was well known. It required adding tungsten, a mineral also known as wolfram. While Germany had virtually none, Portugal and Spain had plenty. Germany also lacked other raw materials including petroleum, aluminum, nickel, rubber, and chromium that would be necessary to turn it into a military superpower. But these supplies and more could be bought on the world market with gold. Chromium was abundant in Turkey. Romania had plenty of oil. And no nation ever turned away gold.

In a November 10, 1943 memo to Hitler, Albert Speer, his one-time architect who by then was the minister for armaments and munitions, wrote, "Chromium is indispensable to a highly developed armaments industry. Should supplies from Turkey be cut off, the stockpile is sufficient only for 5-6 months. The manufacture of plants, tanks, motor vehicles, tank shells, U-boats, and almost the entire gamut of artillery would have to cease from one to three months after this deadline." He noted that chromium was in shortest supply of the elements the Nazis needed.[31]

Schacht had to establish an economy that made the most of Germany's own natural resources, while also husbanding major foreign currencies such as the American dollar and the British pound, but gold reigned above all. He knew that once a new war started, the U.S. and Britain would take measures to make it difficult to get either of those currencies, making gold more important than ever: it was the one thing that the neutral countries would take in payment. When all else failed, Germany could buy whatever products it needed with gold.[32]

Gold was even useful in achieving Germany's strategic goals. When the Nazis were recruiting the minor Norwegian politician Vidkun Quisling in December 1939, to run a pro-Nazi party in that country, they gave him some gold to get the operations started. Foreign Minister Joachim von Ribbentrop soon demanded his own independent source of gold to finance his clandestine operations abroad.[33]

Schacht quickly put autarky into practice. In his early months in office, he worked closely with Nazi officials to set out a multifaceted strategy to solve the country's economic problems and get it on the road to self-sufficiency. Everyone knew that during wartime Germany had to expect that its military opponents would again attempt to starve the country into submission. The Nazis wanted to make sure that didn't happen again, and Schacht was ready to help them.

Only two months after returning to the Reichsbank, Schacht traveled to the U.S. to meet the leaders of the new Franklin D. Roosevelt administration. The new president greeted him on the White House terrace and had four separate sessions with him. The president and his top aides, though, did not look favorably on the new Nazi government. Nonetheless, Roosevelt, who once called Schacht a "bastard," and had been suspicious of the Nazis almost from day one, still hosted him at a White House lunch, and Hull honored him with a dinner. The German basked in the glow of all the attention.[34]

Back in Germany, the central banker soon took on more titles that reflected his growing power within the Hitler regime. On July 26, 1934, the Führer was in southern Germany at the Bayreuth Wagner festival when he asked him to come down from Berlin to meet with him. He offered his banker the additional post of Minister of Economic Affairs. Two loyal Nazis who occupied the position previously had been complete flops.[35]

When he learned of the proposal, Schacht asked, "Before I take office, I should like to know how you wish me to deal with the Jewish question." Hitler replied, "In economic matters the Jews can carry on exactly as they have done up to now." Schacht then accepted the new position. Less than a year later on May 21, 1935, a secret law also named Schacht the General Plenipotentiary of War Economy. That gave him authority over the entire German economy in time of conflict. He would be the co-equal to the commander of the country's armed forces. He was charged with placing "all the economic resources in the service of warfare."[36]

The first step in the autarky program was to reorient as much as possible of Germany's trade away from the country's traditional economic partners. Berlin would simultaneously reduce its commerce with Britain, France, and the U.S., while increasing it with peripheral and less developed nations with whom Germany had historically done little trade. Those countries would be much less likely to demand payment in gold or major currencies and be willing to accept barter trades. Berlin could sell its surplus production of non-vital products in exchange for important ones that it needed to buy abroad. That would keep the country's sparse financial resources for only the most important imports. The two areas with the greatest potential were the Balkans and Latin America. Both were rich in natural resources.

As far as can be determined from historic records, Schacht never wrote out his autarky policy or presented it in any public speech, although he explained it clearly to top Nazi officials. He repeatedly insisted on the need to husband precious foreign currency so that the country could buy vitally needed imports, especially war materiel. The use of foreign currencies and gold turned into a major subject of conflict between the General Plenipotentiary of War Economy and other top Nazis. It was a classic case of the historic choice between guns and butter. Nazi leaders such as Hitler and Göring believed they could have both, and the central banker never succeeded in changing their view.

Schacht's immediate challenge in the early months of the Third Reich was to find a way to finance Hitler's huge military buildup. The Führer's goal was to make Germany the mightiest military power in Europe, if not the world, in just five years. Moreover, this had to be accomplished without setting off a new 1920s-style inflation, which still terrified Germans. Initially, at least, it also had to be done without attracting attention from other countries. Schacht not only had to pull a financial rabbit out of his hat, he had to do it without anyone noticing.

The centerpiece of Schacht's plan was a new corporation called the Metallurgische Forschungsgesellschaft (Metal Research Company), which soon became known as Mefo for short. In financial terms, it would issue promissory notes permitting the government to get around the law that limited central bank lending to 100 million Reichsmark. All the money went to rearmament. At the behest of the Berlin government, four major German companies, Siemens, Krupp, Rheinstahl, and Gutehoffnungshütte, started a dummy company that had no employees, but capital of one million Reichsmark. German businesses doing rearmament work would present their bills and be paid in Mefo currency, which they could either sell at a discount to a German bank or hold. In addition, the companies would get four percent interest on the Mefo bills. They were to have a total longevity of four years, after which repayment would begin. The Metallurgische Forschungsgesellschaft would raise 12 billion Reichsmark in capital over four years, and the Reichsbank would buy back the Mefo bills. In effect, the companies doing rearmament work were giving Berlin a loan that the government promised to start paying back in four years. The repayment date continued to lengthen, and at one point was pushed out to seventeen years. One of the best-kept secrets of the Mefo bills was that foreigners bought a majority of them from the Reichsbank without knowing how the money was being spent. In a memo to Hitler in May 1935, Schacht gleefully wrote, "Our armaments are, therefore, being financed partially with the assets of our political opponents."[37]

Schacht came up with the target of 12 billion Reichsmark because he thought that was the most he could spend without setting off new inflation. He called it "an ingenious and well-adapted method of providing funds." During his interrogation at the Nuremberg trials, Schacht proudly said, "The 12 billion Mefo bills were exclusively appropriated for armament, so I knew that money was not spent on dinners."[38]

Another attraction of the Mefo bills was that they were hidden from the world. No reference to them appeared in the published statements of the Reichsbank or the German national budget. Even within the government, few officials knew about them. Hans Lammers, Hitler's chief of staff, told interrogators after the war that he had seen the term in documents but had no idea what it meant. German defense spending between April 1935 and March 1940 totaled 20.5 billion Reichsmark, of which 12 billion came from the Reichsbank via Mefo financing.[39]

In early 1934, Schacht ran into unexpected balance of payments difficulties because rearmament spending almost wiped out the country's holdings of gold and foreign currency. Secret reserves and official bullion reserves fell to just $55.5 million on June 30,

1934. Schacht's reaction to that crisis was to put through his New Plan on September 24, which introduced state control over foreign trade. The name was in homage to Franklin Roosevelt's New Deal. The German objective, though, was very different. According to Schacht's plan, Germany should buy nothing that could not be paid for with exports. The program promoted bilateral trade and limited imports to essential products, in particular raw materials and agricultural products. This was to be done by reorienting Germany's trade to just twenty-five states, with most of them in the Balkans and South America, where countries were still suffering from the lingering effects of the global depression and would accept almost any deal. Berlin thus began importing large quantities of goods from countries such as Romania, Spain, Argentina, and Turkey, which became the main supplier of chromium, the still coveted key resource in the making of certain products essential to the war effort.

The policy achieved its goals. Germany's balance of trade had a deficit of 284 million Reichsmark in 1934, but a 111 million surplus the following year. The benefits kept increasing. In a letter to Göring in August 1937, Schacht bragged that Germany had a trade surplus of a half billion Reichsmark.[40]

Thanks to Schacht's economic policies, the German economy was soon flourishing. The Gross National Product, which in 1932, the year before he took over the economy, had been 58 million Reichsmark, rose to 83 billion by 1936. From 1934 to 1937, imports of non-essential finished products such as consumer goods fell by 63%, while imports of raw materials increased sharply: iron ore by 132%, petroleum 116%, grain 102%, and rubber 71%.

Hitler came to power in 1933 largely because the country had six million people unemployed, but by the end of 1934 that number was down to 2.6 million and falling. In fact, Germany would soon face a shortage of skilled workers. In early 1934, Germany bought $1 million worth of high-quality air force hardware from American manufacturers and paid for it with bullion. In 1936, Hitler, Schacht, and War Minister General von Blomberg argued about the importance of gold in the military buildup. Schacht thought that the purchase of military equipment from the Americans in the early days of the Reich was proof that it could now buy needed goods. Hitler, though, continued to believe that he could fight wars without gold. Blomberg listened to both sides in several discussions without taking a position, but Georg Thomas, his top economist, shared Schacht's views, telling a group of young military leaders in November 1937, "In wartime, Germany will need a considerable reserve of gold and foreign exchange for propaganda, espionage, and other purposes."[41]

Schacht hid German gold by spreading it into five different places in the country's books. He also kept the world in the dark about what he was doing by creating a whole variety of accounts on the Reichsbank's books, some hidden and some public. He and only a handful of associates understood what was going on. Officials referred to these as the country's "war reserve accounts" and nick-named them the "new Julius Tower," a reference to the location where gold had been hidden during World War I. Reserves at the end of 1933 were $174.5 million, with $156.1 million in official records and $18.4 million hidden off the books. After the 1934 run on the currency, the numbers were $28.4 million in public documents, but $40.4 million hidden. By the end of 1935, gold holdings started heading back up, with $33.3 million acknowledged and $81.6 million not made public. Because of heavy spending on the military, though, both published and hidden reserves remained in overall bad shape.

Most of the credit for the economic prosperity in the early Hitler years went to Schacht, and he thoroughly enjoyed the adulation. When the central banker celebrated his sixtieth birthday in January 1937, General Blomberg told him, "Without your help, my dear Schacht, none of this rearmament could have taken place."[42]

Only three years after he had joined the Hitler government, Hjalmar Schacht's economic policies had been a major success. Perhaps because of that success, Schacht could not help treating the Nazi leaders, even Hitler, as his intellectual inferiors. A British intelligence report from its Berlin embassy to London said Schacht was "one of few if not the only man who dares to speak out to Hitler." U.S. Ambassador William Dodd wrote in his diary on June 21, 1935, "No man in Germany, perhaps none in Europe, is quite so clever as this 'economic dictator.' His position is always delicate and even dangerous."[43]

Confident that he had become indispensable to the Nazi regime and therefore untouchable, Schacht on August 18, 1935, at the Ostmesse, a major business fair held annually in the Baltic city of Königsberg, voiced opposition to major party policies, including the treatment of Jews. Top Nazis attended his speech, which was also broadcast nationally on the radio. An SS general walked out in protest, and when Schacht sat down Erich Koch, the party boss of East Prussia, whispered to him, "Little monk, little monk, you are on a difficult road." Martin Luther had received that same warning, which any educated German would recognize, at his trial at the Diet of Worms after launching the Protestant Reformation.[44]

Hitler reluctantly recognized the importance of a strong economy in building his Nazi state. At the same time, he was instinctively and frequently at odds with Schacht, who never paid him the homage others did. He arrogantly told Hitler early in the Third Reich, "You need me. And you'll continue to need me for several years. After that, you can shoot me if you want to. But you can't shoot me yet." Ironically, the better the economy, the less Hitler needed Schacht. The Führer also had an underlying contempt for economic advisors, once saying, "The nation does not live for the economy or for the leaders of the economy . . . The leaders of the economy and all theories have to serve exclusively this struggle for the maintenance of the nation." In his post-war memoirs Schacht wrote candidly, "From the middle of 1936 onwards my relations with Hitler had slowly but steadily deteriorated."[45]

Chapter Four

FRANKLIN D. ROOSEVELT'S ARGONAUT

enry Morgenthau, Jr. was the brother that President Franklin D. Roosevelt never had. The two men shared much in common, and both even wore pince-nez glasses. Each was born into great wealth and to families who believed that privileged people had a duty to help those less fortunate. Morgenthau's father, Henry Sr., made a fortune in New York City real estate; Roosevelt was from old money. Henry and Franklin were both gentlemen farmers in upstate New York. In some ways, however, they were polar opposites. Roosevelt was the happy-go-lucky politician who charmed voters, while Morgenthau was reserved and reflective. His main mission in life now was to serve his friend.

Morgenthau's parents knew early on that their eldest son suffered from some kind of learning disability that may have been dyslexia, which at the time was not easily diagnosed or treated. He entered the prestigious Exeter Academy, but didn't do well in class and left. He eventually graduated from high school and went to Cornell University with plans of becoming an architect, but again failed academically despite the help of a tutor, and soon dropped out.[1]

In 1911, Morgenthau traveled to Texas to recover from typhoid fever, and while there became attracted to agriculture and ranching. The following year, he told his father he had decided to become a farmer, and in the fall of 1913 at age 22, Henry Jr. bought 1,000 acres of land for $55,000 up the Hudson River in Dutchess County, New York. He named it Fishkill Farms, and the property became the centerpiece of his life. He loved working outdoors and had finally found a calling where he excelled. Christmas trees were one of his early crops. He returned to Cornell to study agriculture, but left again without a degree.[2]

Franklin Roosevelt, who was nine years older, lived 25 miles away in Hyde Park, where he ran his family's Springwood estate. The first known communication between the two men took place on December 11, 1914, when Morgenthau sent a letter to Roosevelt, who was by that time assistant secretary of the navy, seeking his support for a blacksmith who was a candidate for postmaster. Roosevelt responded in detail, and that seemingly innocuous beginning started a long and deep friendship.[3]

When the U.S. entered World War I in 1917, the recently married Morgenthau tried to enlist in the army, but failed the eye exam. Still anxious to help the war effort, he came up with the idea of shipping tractors to France so that the country could increase its food production and thus help the Allied troops. Few French farmers at that time had tractors. Morgenthau's father was then serving as President Woodrow Wilson's ambassador to the Ottoman Empire, and the father lined up a meeting with Herbert Hoover, the head of the Food Administration, who was enthusiastic about the plan. Working with both Hoover's agency and the International Red Cross, Morgenthau arranged to get 1,500 Ford tractors sent to France and traveled along with them. When he returned to the U.S., he tried again to join the military, and this time was accepted into the Naval Quartermaster Corps. He received the news in a letter signed by Franklin D. Roosevelt. Morgenthau served his military time in New York City for the last two months of the war as a lieutenant (junior grade).

After the war ended, Morgenthau returned to his farm in Dutchess County, where he concentrated on dairy farming and growing apples. He frequently called on Cornell professors in upstate New York to help him improve production. Through local Democratic Party politics, he stayed in touch with Roosevelt, who was planning to run for statewide office. Morgenthau, Roosevelt, and their wives, Elinor and Eleanor, soon became friends. Roosevelt was on the political fast track and was the vice presidential candidate on the 1920 Democratic ticket; Morgenthau organized a rally in the county that attracted national figures and a large crowd. The Democratic ticket lost the election, and the following year Roosevelt came down with polio. Many thought his political career was over.

In addition to having a farm, Morgenthau wanted to establish himself as a farm expert. In a letter to his father he explained, "There is nothing I would rather do than own an agricultural paper." In 1922 he bought the *American Agriculturist*, a New York State weekly.[4] His goal was to educate farmers on new and better ways to work the land. Both Henry and his wife were activists in local Democratic politics and frequently saw Franklin and Eleanor Roosevelt both in Hyde Park and in the Florida Keys. The newspaper regularly lost money, and his father reprimanded him, once pointing out that he had revenues of $185,000 a year, but expenses of $200,000.

When Roosevelt ran for governor of New York in 1928, Morgenthau served as an advance man, preparing voter rallies and rustling up crowds at campaign stops. After winning in a squeaker, Roosevelt moved to Albany, with Morgenthau in tow. The new governor appointed him to head the Agricultural Advisory Commission. Morgenthau received neither a salary nor an office, and had to work from a desk located outside the governor's office. Roosevelt liked to give people nicknames, and since Morgenthau was always so deadly serious he called him "Henry the Morgue." He wrote studies for the governor, and reached out to professors at Cornell's College of Agriculture. Roosevelt was reelected in 1930 with a huge majority and quickly set his sights on the White House. Morgenthau, who by then was his Conservation Commissioner, was soon traveling the country learning about the situation down on the farm, one of the nation's most serious economic problems. He also wrote memos on the subject to increase Roosevelt's knowledge of farm issues in anticipation of the expected campaign against incumbent Herbert Hoover.[5]

Roosevelt won a landslide victory in 1932, and the president-elect and his best friend both headed to Washington. Agriculture was one of the most pressing of the many challenges facing the new administration. Farm prices had collapsed. Wheat in 1932 sold for sixty-three percent below the 1929 level, and cotton was down sixty-seven percent. "The smell of revolution was in the air," Morgenthau wrote. To the surprise of many, the new president did not name him to be Secretary of Agriculture. That job went instead to Henry Wallace, whose father had held the same position in the 1920s. The younger Wallace was an agriculture graduate from the University of Iowa and a farmer, and had switched from the Republican party to support FDR.

Some people, especially those in the Jewish community, saw this as a sign of America's persistent anti-Semitism. Up to that point, there had been only one Jewish cabinet member in American history, Oscar Straus, who was Secretary of Commerce and Labor in the Theodore Roosevelt administration. Morgenthau's father had expected to be named as a cabinet member in the second Wilson administration after being one of his biggest contributors during the campaign, but he had been shuttled off to be an ambassador.

The younger Morgenthau was disappointed when he lost the job he coveted, but he remained loyal to Roosevelt and would take whatever job was offered. FDR named him to head the Federal Farm Board. Herbert Hoover had started the agency in early 1929, and it was his main weapon against the farm depression. It tried to stabilize agriculture prices by buying up and storing surplus grain and cotton, but the new administration had other plans for farm relief. Roosevelt thought that the major problem farmers faced was the heavy debts they were carrying. Thousands of them were losing their property to foreclosure, and he wanted to consolidate a host of federal agriculture agencies into a new one that would concentrate on reducing farm debt. In its place, Roosevelt started by executive order the Farm Credit Administration. Morgenthau was its first governor. He had a war chest of $2 billion to slow down foreclosures, and was soon financing twenty percent of the country's farm loans. Morgenthau worked closely with Jesse Jones, the new chairman of the Reconstruction Finance Corporation, another Hoover-era agency that made loans to banks, railroads, and other businesses.[6]

Although normally a staunch supporter of all Roosevelt programs, Morgenthau broke with the president for ethical reasons on one important aspect of farm policy. He opposed the section of the 1933 Agriculture Adjustment Act that paid farmers to plow crops into the ground in order to take fields out of production. The strategy was to decrease production in order to increase prices and the money that went to farmers. Morgenthau simply could not accept reducing food output at a time when people were starving. "Something within me revolted at the destruction of existing crops," he wrote. He argued that instead of paying farmers $100 million to grow less wheat, the government should buy it and make flour that could be given to the needy. Eventually, and with the support of Eleanor Roosevelt herself, Morgenthau introduced a policy of giving surplus food at reduced prices to people on relief.

Whenever Henry Morgenthau, Jr. faced an important economic issue, he turned for help to George F. Warren, who had taught him agricultural economics twenty years earlier at Cornell. Morgenthau regularly consulted the professor while working in Albany, and appointed him to the State Agricultural Commission. Warren had grown up in Nebraska herding sheep on his family's farm and had his own 500-acre spread near the Cornell campus. The professor joined Roosevelt and Morgenthau in Washington after the election and was soon writing them private memos about his new idea for solving the farm problem. Warren worked out of a bare office on the ground floor of the huge new Commerce Building. If anyone knocked on the door, he would shout back, "No one's here."[7]

The professor argued that low farm prices had seriously distorted the American economy's general price structure. He and fellow professor Frank Pearson had just published a book entitled simply *Prices*, which maintained that an increase in the price of gold would lead to higher prices for cotton, wheat, and other agricultural goods. In a memo to Roosevelt, Warren said that "the simplest way to proceed" was to devalue the dollar "at once." The professor argued that such a step would raise agricultural prices and farm incomes. In order to devalue its own currency, the U.S. government should buy gold at above world-market prices. It was a radical idea and diametrically opposed to conventional economic thinking. Warren believed the price should be increased to at least $35 an ounce. The official U.S. price since 1837 had been $20.67, and it had still been selling at about that before Roosevelt's election.[8]

Roosevelt was no fan of the precious metal. Between his election victory in November 1932 and his inauguration the following March, outgoing president Herbert Hoover tried to solicit his support for a global economic conference to stabilize the international financial system. Hoover wrote Roosevelt, "Confidence cannot be reestablished by abandonment of gold as a standard for the world."[9] The appeal fell on deaf ears. Americans worried about the country's economic future were sending their money abroad or buying gold, always the last refuge of the truly frightened. During the month of February 1933, $160 million left the country. In just the four days before Roosevelt took office on March 4, the public turned in $200 million in paper currency for gold coins. Soon after his inauguration, the new president had Congress pass the Emergency Banking Act, which prohibited the exporting or hoarding of bullion, and a month later issued an executive order that people had to turn in their gold for paper currency.[10] At a White House meeting with his top economic staffers on April 18, the president jauntily told them, "Congratulate me. We are off the gold standard."[11]

FDR's disdain for gold and international financial cooperation was blatantly on display two months later during the World

Economic Conference outside London, which lasted from June 12 to July 27. The meeting had been called to save the world economy by stabilizing currency values, slowing the march toward trade restrictions, and reducing European war-debt payments to the U.S. All other countries sent their top economic and central bank officials to London, but the American delegation at the conference was stunningly second rate. None of the members knew much about international economics. World moneymen were outraged by the American blunt show of power and Washington's unwillingness to join in the effort to prop up world currencies.[12]

While the meeting in London was in process, the White House effectively killed it before it even had a chance to really hit its stride. The president and Morgenthau were cruising off the Maine coast on the USS *Indianapolis* and decided to give Professor Warren's ideas a chance from across the sea. They sent a presidential radio message from the ship saying that the U.S. would no longer stabilize the dollar at the existing official level of $20.67 an ounce (to the gold standard). Adding insult to injury, the Roosevelt and Morgenthau statement said that ideas about going back to old gold prices were "old fetishes of so-called international bankers."[13] That was heresy to the London crowd, and leading governments put out a statement affirming their commitment to gold. The meeting dragged on for another week, but it had been essentially torpedoed.

Although Roosevelt was falling under Warren's spell, several other members of the president's staff vehemently opposed the professor's theories. Dean Acheson, who was running the Treasury Department for the ailing secretary William Woodin, thought such action was unconstitutional. Oliver Sprague, a Harvard economist who had taught FDR at Harvard and was now a Treasury Department consultant, also objected to his former student's gold policy. Lewis W. Douglas, the budget director, lamented, "This is the end of western civilization."[14] They all warned that if the U.S. dropped the value of the dollar by raising the price of gold, the world would face competitive devaluations and uncontrollable inflation similar to that of 1920s Germany. FDR responded that arguing with his advisors was like "punching your fist into a pillow."[15]

Despite Roosevelt's hundred-day program of emergency measures to rescue the U.S. economy by moving off the gold standard, farm prices that summer and fall continued to drop. Never one to sit idly by, Roosevelt was anxious to take further action. The evening of October 16, he called Morgenthau at home to tell him that they had to stop the price of wheat from sinking further. The next morning Morgenthau began buying wheat on commodity markets in an attempt to push up the price. The initial purchase was one million bushels, but by the end of the day the price had increased only slightly. Clearly something more had to be done.

In his fourth radio fireside chat on Sunday night October 22, Roosevelt announced to the world a new American gold policy. He spoke in the plain-talk style that made his radio talks so successful. He began by painting a glum picture of the American economy, and he was near the end of the talk when he finally got around to gold. He blamed the country's troubles on it by saying, "Our dollar is now altogether too greatly influenced by the accidents of international trade, by the internal policies of other nations, and by political disturbance in other continents. Therefore the United States must take firmly in its own hands the control of the gold value of our dollar." He announced that he was authorizing the Reconstruction Finance Corporation to buy all the gold mined in the U.S. at prices to be determined by the president and the secretary of the treasury. He also said that the American government would buy and sell gold on the world market.[16]

Three days later, the president began meeting daily at 9:00 A.M. in his White House bedroom with top aides to fix the U.S. price for gold. Henry Morgenthau, Jr., Jesse Jones, and Professor Warren usually attended. During the sessions, Roosevelt wore pajamas and sat up in an antique mahogany bed. As they talked, the president ate soft-boiled eggs and sipped coffee. His wife Eleanor wasn't there because she had refused to sleep in the same room with him after she learned, in 1918, about his affair with her social secretary, Lucy Mercer. On the left side of the presidential bed was a table with stacks of government papers, detective novels, and a telephone. On the right side on a matching table were his watch, pads and pencils, cigarettes, and a plate of fruit. The walls were covered with seascape prints from the president's days as assistant secretary of the navy.[17]

During the first meeting and at Morgenthau's suggestion, Roosevelt decided that the U.S. should buy gold at $31.36 an ounce, a sharp increase over the official U.S. price of $20.67 and even more than the daily London price of $31.02, which had been increasing in anticipation of U.S. action. The next day the bedroom group pushed it up another 18 cents, and then 6 cents more the third day. The price moved generally higher a few cents at a time. Sometimes the group dropped it slightly in hopes of burning speculators, but usually the next day it continued a relentlessly consistant climb. Over afternoon tea at the White House on October 28, Roosevelt and Morgenthau came up with a medium-range plan to raise the price to $33.02. On Friday, November 3, a dour-looking Morgenthau recommended increasing it between 19 cents and 22 cents. The jovial president looked at Henry the Morgue and suggested 21 cents, adding with a laugh, "It's a lucky number because it's three times seven." That night Morgenthau noted in his diary, "If anybody ever knew how we really set the gold price through a combination of lucky numbers, etc., I think they would be really frightened."

Originally, Roosevelt and Morgenthau bought only U.S. gold, but when the price went above the world market level they also began purchasing it in foreign markets. When George Harrison, the president of the New York Federal Reserve, told Montagu Norman, the head of the Bank of England, about the new policy, Norman replied in horror, "This is the most terrible thing that has happened. The whole world will be put into bankruptcy."[18] When Roosevelt and Morgenthau heard that reaction, they burst into wild laughter. Roosevelt, who had a nickname for everyone, called spade-bearded Norman "old pink whiskers."[19]

Many politicians and statesmen around the world condemned the policy. Former Democrat presidential candidate Al Smith spoke for many Americans when he said, "I am for gold dollars as against baloney dollars." John Maynard Keynes, the most famous economist in the world and no fan of gold, dismissed Roosevelt's maneuvers as "the gold standard on the booze."[20]

At the end of the breakfast meeting on November 13, Roosevelt asked Morgenthau to stay behind and told him he wanted him to take over as Secretary of the Treasury. The president explained that Secretary Wooden, Under Secretary Acheson, and Special Assistant Sprague were all being swept out of office largely because their opposition to the gold program had found its way into the press. Roosevelt said he wanted his best friend to have his hand on the tiller of the American economy, which remained the administration's toughest challenge. The president complimented Morgenthau by saying he was "one of the two or three people who have made an outstanding success here in Washington." With the jaunty optimism that the nation had witnessed often in those dark economic times, the president concluded by saying, "So let's you and I go on to bigger things. We will have lots of fun doing it together."[21]

As a gesture of conciliation toward Britain and France, the U.S. at the end of November agreed to let the international price of gold stabilize at between $32 and $35 an ounce. The White House, though, still wanted a little more time to maneuver before once again fixing the official U.S. dollar value.

Warren's theory on farm goods seemed to be working, as prices were finally going up at an annual rate of about 10%. Farmers, consumers, and industrialists all began to feel more confident, and an economic recovery finally took hold. The Great Depression would not really conclude until after the U.S. entered World War II at the end of 1941, but both in corporate boardrooms and down on the farm the country's economy appeared to be on the mend at last.

When Morgenthau was sworn in at the White House, the president was naturally in attendance for the event as were Professor Warren and members of the extended Morgenthau family, who were particularly happy because they thought he was getting the job that President Wilson should have given his father. The appointment, though, was not universally praised. Gladys Straus, a major Republican donor and herself Jewish, quipped that Roosevelt had found the "only Jew in the world who doesn't know anything about money." The new secretary, though, had the president's confidence, and that was what really mattered.

After settling into his new job, Morgenthau dealt with a couple of personal matters. He sold *American Agriculturist* to the Gannett newspaper chain to avoid charges that he was using it to push his agenda. It was still losing money, but had served its purpose of providing him with a national platform. He also installed in his office a voice recording system that he could activate at his desk. That may have been official Washington's first taping device. Most people attending meetings did not know they were being taped. It later provided the raw material for the voluminous Morgenthau Diaries, a collection of typed notes of meetings or conversations that is now housed at the Franklin D. Roosevelt Presidential Library in Hyde Park, New York.

The president on January 15, 1934, sent Congress a message stating that "the time has come for a more certain determination of the gold value of the American dollar." This, he wrote, would "bring some greater degree of stability to foreign exchange rates."[22] That was a U-turn for the Roosevelt Administration, which less than year before had fought stabilized exchange rates at the London Economic Conference. Politicians, though, have never been known as paragons of consistency. An additional reason for the administration's change in position was that it wanted to lock in the lower dollar value, which was helping American exports. Officials were also fearful that the country's trading partners would start pushing the price of gold around to get their own competitive trade advantage. Morgenthau asked New York Fed Chairman George Harrison to check with Montagu Norman to see if he were interested in fixing the price of gold. The British were not interested in a long-term set price, but agreed to a temporary one.

Two weeks later, Congress passed, by a huge majority, the Gold Reserve Act, and the following day the president officially fixed the price from $20.67 to $35 an ounce, an increase of 69%. That became the standard world price. It also automatically increased the fixed value of U.S. gold reserves by $2 billion, as it did for other institutions holding bullion. With the U.S. once again on the gold standard, the Federal Reserve also bought and sold the metal at $35 an ounce to other central banks around the world. One result was a massive inflow of gold into the U.S., which was also stimulated by growing war threats in Europe. In the next four years, the value of the gold in the vaults of the New York Federal Reserve tripled, reaching $12 billion.[23] As anyone could have predicted, the production of gold around the world also soared, especially in the Soviet Union, where output went up nearly ten-fold between 1923 and 1934.[24]

Jacob Viner, a conservative economist from the University of Chicago and a strong believer in a balanced budget, was Morgenthau's first economic advisor at the Treasury. The professor, though, didn't enjoy working in Washington and suggested in June 1934 that Harry Dexter White, a Harvard graduate then teaching at Lawrence College in Wisconsin, join him in Washington to work on monetary and banking legislation. Morgenthau grew to depend greatly on White and trusted his judgments on economic questions, an area where Morgenthau was weak.

White was born in Boston of parents who had emigrated from Lithuania, which, at the time, was part of the Russian empire. After army service in World War I, he studied economics at Stanford before going to Harvard. He joined the Treasury Department staff in June 1934 and in November was named head of the department of research and statistics. The following year he went to Britain, where he met with John Maynard Keynes, who was impressed by him. The time in Europe expanded White's expertise and established his credentials as Morgenthau's closest advisor. White rose in rank to become director of monetary research and eventually assistant secretary. Morgenthau's son, in a family biography, described him as "short-termed and arrogant" as well as "meticulously civil to anyone in a position to afford him access to the powerful."[25]

The legality of raising the price of gold was challenged in court in a case that eventually reached the Supreme Court. The New Deal at the time had lost several cases in the court, so the decision was not a sure thing. Finally on February 18, 1935, the Supreme Court sided with the administration largely on legal, rather than economic, grounds, with a 5 to 4 ruling. Top government officials received the news in the White House cabinet room and celebrated for an hour. Morgenthau reported in his diary that Roosevelt was "very natural, laughing and smiling practically all the time."[26]

Just as Professor Warren had predicted, the American economy was soon on the mend, although it was a slow recovery. The U.S. gross national product grew from $58.7 billion in 1932, Herbert Hoover's last year in office, to $83.8 billion in 1936, the last year of Roosevelt's first term. That's better than 6% annual growth. During that same period unemployment fell from about 24% to 17%. It was a good start, but more still needed to be done.

Morgenthau bought gold on the international market to keep the price from falling below $35, picking up $385 million in 1933, $1.9 billion in 1935, and $1.1 billion in 1936. Professor Warren wanted him to push the price even higher, but the Treasury Secretary refused largely because it would be too costly to maintain a higher price in world markets. Warren returned to teaching at Cornell, but he had made his mark. As economic historian Liaquat Ahamed has written, "Breaking with the dead hand of the gold standard was the key to economic revival."[27]

Chapter Five

HERMANN GÖRING
GRABS CONTROL

At the Nazi's annual September rally in Nuremberg, Hitler liked to announce with great fanfare a big and bold new national goal to mobilize the country for the following year. He wanted to set out a new economic target at the 1936 meeting. In a break from what he had done since taking power three years earlier, Hitler did not look to Hjalmar Schacht to manage the new plan this time. The Führer had grown tired of his top economist's haranguing lectures and reluctance to follow orders. Hitler instead turned to Hermann Göring, a trusted *Alter Kämpfer* (Old Fighter), who had been at his side since 1922. Hitler's move marked the beginning of the end for Hjalmar Horace Greeley Schacht.[1]

The son of a military officer who also served as governor of Germany's colony in Southwest Africa, Göring grew up in a small, rundown castle near Nuremberg before attending a military school at age twelve and going on to a military college. An ace pilot in World War I, he shot down twenty-two enemy planes and earned the German air force's highest honor, the *Pour le Mérite* award, also known as the *Blauer Max* (Blue Max). He was the last commander of the Red Baron's famous squadron. Following the war, Göring bounced around aimlessly in a variety of jobs that drew on his air force experience. He barnstormed as a stunt pilot, worked for the Dutch aircraft company Fokker, flew for a Swedish airline, and sold parachutes. Along the way, he married the Swedish baroness Carin von Kantzow.[2]

The flying ace eventually wandered into politics, joining the Nazi party only two years after it was founded. For a while he was Hitler's bodyguard and also headed the *Sturmabteilung* or *SA*, the party's private army. During the aborted Munich putsch in November 1923, Göring was shot in the groin. Two Jewish women gave him emergency first aid, and then his wife, doctor, and a Nazi Storm Trooper hustled him out of Germany before he could be arrested. He recuperated in Innsbruck, Austria, but his wound had become badly infected, and as part of the treatment he received daily morphine shots. That led to a drug addiction that plagued him on and off for the rest of his life. In Sweden in 1925, Göring was hospitalized in a drug withdrawal clinic and later in an asylum for the criminally insane, but he recovered, and two years later returned to Germany during a political amnesty. He went back to selling parachutes, and later spent more time in a Swedish drug clinic.[3]

Göring eventually returned to Munich, where he elbowed his way into a high position on the list of Nazi candidates for the Reichstag. That gave him one of only twelve Nazi seats. He then moved to Berlin and after years of living in poverty finally had some money in his pocket thanks to his legislative salary and sideline jobs for Lufthansa and Fritz Thyssen, the steel magnate. The smooth-talking and flamboyant Göring was more debonair than the normal Nazi goons and became known as the "salon Nazi." His aristocratic wife, Carin, was a good hostess. Göring was a dynamic speaker, perhaps the second best in the party after Hitler. His obviously excessive hail-fellow-well-met style was very popular in the early years with the German public.

With Hitler and Göring working in tandem, the Nazi party grew quickly. Göring was leader of the party group in the legislature and was elected Reichstag President in 1932 after a Nazi surge in popularity. When Hitler came to power the following year, Göring received three top posts in the Führer's first cabinet: Minister Without Portfolio, Prussian Minister of the Interior, and Reich's Commissioner for Aviation. He remained a pilot at heart, and he spent lavishly to expand the German air force. During the Night of the Long Knives in June 1934 that purged the party of Ernst Röhm and his followers, Göring and Heinrich Himmler, the head of the SS, directed the operation with brutal efficiency.[4]

As a young high-flying pilot, he had been slim and athletic, but now his weight ballooned until he was obscenely obese. The U.S. ambassador's daughter in Berlin in the early 1930s described him as "three times the size of an ordinary man." Göring collected art, jewelry, rare stones, and precious metals, not because he recognized their beauty or history, but because they symbolized his success. He built an elaborate estate northeast of Berlin called Carinhall after his first wife, who died in October 1931. He stocked it with exotic animals, the bigger the better. He also hunted. Göring personally enriched himself more than any other Third Reich leader. Schacht described Hitler as "immoral," but called Göring "amoral."[5]

Göring's overriding ambition was to bring Hitler to power, and his long-term objective was to eventually succeed him as Führer. In 1933 when he had his first real taste of power as Prussian Minister of the Interior, he told the police, "Shoot first and inquire afterwards. If you make mistakes, I will protect you.[6]

He knew nothing of economics or banking, but had an innate sense of power and recognized the importance of Germany's financial success in achieving the party's political and military goals. Starting in the spring of 1935, he began challenging Schacht for control of the economy. Unlike the stiff Reichsbank president, Göring played to the crowds. In May of that year, he gave a speech in Hamburg promoting the rearmament program and arguing that the country should sacrifice butter for guns. Said the rotund minister to an adoring crowd, "What does butter do but make us fat?" Those in the hall roared.[7]

Hitler soon began giving Göring special economic assignments. The first was to settle a dispute between Schacht and the minister of agriculture over the amount of scarce foreign currency or gold that could be spent buying food in the international markets. In March 1936, Göring began calling himself the Inspector-General of the Petroleum Industry, and Hitler named him Fuel Commissar. Schacht complained to Hitler that Nazi leaders were shipping money abroad to finance their own private and party activities despite his strict monetary controls, which forced the central bank to buy currency abroad. Propaganda Minister Joseph Goebbels, for example, was spending wildly. Schacht first learned of this when foreign central banks such as that of the Netherlands started shipping Reichsmark back to Germany and demanding that they be exchanged for convertible currencies or gold. In a rash move that showed the central banker's political naiveté, Schacht told Hitler that someone else should handle foreign currency issues and suggested Göring. In April 1936, the air minister was named commissioner for foreign exchange, but that later included all raw materials, including gold, although the Reichbank still controlled how the gold was valued. Göring was now steadily expanding his authority into fields that Schacht had previously controlled.

After publishing *Mein Kampf* in 1925 and dictating the secret second book in 1928, Adolf Hitler rarely put this thoughts or plans down in writing, preferring to give oral orders that left no footprints. On August 26, 1936, however, the Führer called Hermann Göring to his Berghof retreat near Berchtesgaden in the Bavarian Alps and presented him with a thirteen-page memorandum that he had written during the summer. The Nazi leader had by then consolidated his power and was ready to launch a new diplomatic and military offensive. Only the year before, the German Ministry of Defense had been renamed the Ministry of War, a change in nomenclature that foreign diplomats noted with concern. Hitler instructed his secretary to make only three copies of his report: one for himself, one for War Minister General Blomberg, and one for Hermann Göring. The memo outlined the Führer's plan to go to war no later than 1940 and established a four-year agenda to get Germany ready to fight major conflicts.[8]

The preface was entitled "The Political Situation." In it, Hitler dismissed the western democracies because they were "ideologically split," adding that the real danger to Germany now was Marxism, which "through its victory in Russia has established one of the greatest empires as a base for its future operations." Hitler acknowledged the importance of gold in his war plans, but then dismissed it: "There is no guarantee during war of realizing the transformation of even gold into raw materials." The clear implication was that Germany quickly had to become self-sufficient in the production of war goods.

Following that political preface, Hitler's set out five conclusions. The first four: Germany must achieve economic self-sufficiency; foreign currency must be saved for necessities that can be fulfilled only by imports; Germany must be self-sufficient in fuel within 18 months; and mass production of synthetic rubber had to be achieved in the same time frame. Hitler's final and most categorical conclusion: "The question of production costs of those raw materials is also of no importance."

The Führer then ordered that within four years Germany had to reach annual production targets for three vital products that would be needed to wage war: 80,000 tons of rubber, three million tons of petroleum, and thirty million tons of iron ore.

The Führer concluded the report with two direct orders:

- The German military must be ready for war within four years.
- The German economy must be mobilized for war within four years on the same deadline.[9]

The overall objective of the Four Year Plan was the same as that of the Schachtian system of autarky. The only significant differences were the scope of Hitler's objectives and the speed with which the goals were to be achieved. The targets were unrealistic and showed his lack of experience in economics and business. That was not unusual since he was regularly unrealistic in dealing with such topics, considering them as matters that could be accomplished purely by German willpower. Hitler knew that Schacht would have insisted that the goals were impossible to reach, which is why the new job was going to Göring. Stolen gold became more important than ever, since bullion could be a stopgap way to finance the ambitious goals and deadlines, and the price of gold was now quite high, thanks to the American price increases.

After meeting with Hitler in Bavaria, Göring returned to Berlin, where he told a few people about his meeting at Berchtesgaden, saying, "Never have I been so impressed by the strength of the Führer, by his logic, and by the boldness of his ideas, which he placed before me at that interview. There will be consternation abroad, but the Führer's instructions will be steadfastly carried out."[10]

Two days later, Göring called a meeting of the cabinet's executive committee known as the Kleine Ministerrat, which was made up of eleven top officials, including Schacht and Blomberg. Göring read parts of the secret memorandum, but did not hand out copies. He said that war with the Soviet Union was now "unavoidable" and added glowingly that "through the genius of the Führer in a short time seemingly unbelievable things are going to take place."

On September 2, Hitler called in Schacht and told him that he would be giving a major speech on economics at the upcoming party meeting. He didn't provide any details, but said he wanted to make sure that Germany would not be dependent on any country for imports.[11]

Schacht was terrified by the developments, knowing that they would have a major, negative, impact on the economy. Worse still, he had not even been consulted. His immediate reaction was to call General Georg Thomas, the top economist at the War Ministry, and ask him to inform his boss General Blomberg. Schacht also requested that the general warn Hitler about the dangers the plan raised. He figured that the military commander was now the only person who could stop Hitler, adding in a letter to the general, "If we now shout out abroad our decision to make ourselves economically independent, then we cut our own throats."

Blomberg simply brushed Schacht off, writing, "I realize fully that you are right, Herr Schacht, but you know I am quite convinced that the Führer will find a way out of all our troubles." The dispirited banker answered, "God grant that your faith is justified."[12]

At the Nuremberg Party Festival on September 9, Hitler announced the Four Year Plan. He said bluntly that the goal was to make Germany "wholly independent of other countries in all those materials which German capacity, our chemistry, our machine industry, and our mining industry can produce at home."[13] There was widespread popular and press support for Hitler's goals. Germans of his generation would never forget the hardships caused by the Allied blockade in the Great War, and the general public was happy to hear that it was not going to be dependent on outsiders. German industrial leaders strongly favored autarky. I.G. Farben had for years wanted to make synthetic fuel in large quantities from the country's plentiful brown coal. Now it had the chance.[14]

Hitler commissioned Göring to direct the ambitious project to make Germany ready for war in four years. Schacht was still the president of the Reichsbank, Minister of Economics, and Plenipotentiary for War Economy, but he no longer directed the Nazi economy. That power was now in Göring's hands, and he was going to take the Schachtian system to its logical conclusion. The central banker who had initially championed the policy suddenly did not agree with it and went public with his criticism even to an American publication. In an article in *Foreign Affairs* magazine in January 1937, Schacht wrote, "I should like to make perfectly clear that autarky, whether natural or produced artificially, cannot possibly be an idea. It is opposed to the general principles of civilization. Autarky means isolation from the rest of the world."[15]

Göring quickly grabbed the steering wheel of the nation's economy, and was not going to let go. Either directly or indirectly he now set the nation's economic policy. One of his first steps was to issue an order outlawing price increases. Germany was rapidly moving toward a wartime economy. Schacht still had all his titles, but Göring now really ran the Nazi economy. The banker claimed that after he left the Ministry of Economics, he rarely saw the Führer.[16]

Making synthetic products was the top priority of the Four Year Plan. Lieutenant Colonel Wilhelm Löb, a staff member of the Luftwaffe General Staff, prepared a report on how Germany could produce synthetic products in some twenty branches of industry to replace imports of those goods. It became known as Löb's Bible. Some of the proposals were totally unrealistic and immediately came under attack by Carl Krauch, a top executive at I.G. Farben. Krauch cut the program back to more realistic levels and concentrated on the production of synthetic oil, synthetic rubber, explosives, and light metals. Göring approved it in July 1938.[17]

The most important of these products was oil. Napoleon once famously said, "An army marches on its stomach." The new Nazi army, though, would be moving in tanks fueled by gasoline. Germany has little indigenous oil, but the country's scientists had discovered early in the twentieth century two different chemical processes to produce synthetic fuels from the country's abundant, but low-quality, coal. Friedrich Bergius and Carl Bosch in 1931 shared the Nobel Prize for their contributions to the invention and development of high-pressure methods to make synthetic petroleum. Later two other German scientists, Franz Fischer and Hans Tropsch, discovered a similar process. At the time, though, both methods were uneconomical because major new oil discoveries had been made in South America and the Middle East, and driven down the price of oil to less than $5 a barrel. That made synthetic fuel uncompetitive, but Göring was willing to subsidize I.G. Farben in order to achieve energy independence, no matter how expensive. A first plant using the Fischer-Tropsch or FT method needed higher quality coking coal and could not produce aircraft fuel, but it was nevertheless still built in 1934. Another synthetic method used brown coal, which was more abundant and could also make airplane fuel. The Four Year Plan turned into a boon for I.G. Farben.

By 1939, annual production was upwards of one million tons of synthetic oil and reached a peak of more than four million by 1944, when the Allies began systematically bombing the factories.[18]

The Reichswerke Hermann Göring, a huge iron ore and steel company established in July 1937, was another temple to self-sufficiency. The corporation's name also reflected the egomania of its founder. The industrial complex was located in the town of Salzgitter in Saxony, where poor quality iron ore had been mined for decades. Göring began spending unlimited government money to support it under Hitler's edict that costs were "of no importance."

The industrial complex started with a series of mergers of several small steel companies and produced its first pig iron in October 1939 and its first steel in August 1940. As Germany began invading its neighbors, Reichswerke Hermann Göring took over iron and steel facilities in conquered Austria, Czechoslovakia, and other countries. The German army even dismantled Soviet iron and steel facilities and shipped them back to the Reich. The company also moved into manufacturing armaments, and by the end of 1941 was the largest corporation in Europe. The massive complex, though, was too large and diffuse to be managed efficiently. Moreover, decisions were often made on the basis of politics rather than economics. The Reichswerke's coal, iron, and steel operations lost money throughout the war.[19]

The Four Year Plan developed into a large bureaucracy that had carte blanche to move into any part of German economic life. Göring found talented bureaucrats to run a shadow government that answered to him. He recruited Reinhard Heydrich, an SS officer, to set up a new group to investigate foreign currency accounts, and Erich Neumann, a Prussian civil servant, to handle foreign exchange and gold issues. That gave Göring personal control over valuables confiscated in occupied countries. Foreign gold was still shipped to the Reichsbank's vaults for safekeeping, but officials of the Four Year Plan controlled how it would be used. Göring also had his own account there and could personally request as much money as he wanted. Reichsbank bureaucrats were savvy enough not to disagree with the second-ranking person in the Third Reich.

Despite Germany's famous reputation for organization and efficiency, the Nazis did not have an overall organization for capturing gold in the central banks of the countries they conquered or from private citizens. It was done in a haphazard fashion and by several different agencies. The Germans were very successful in getting that booty in the early years in countries such as Austria and Czechoslovakia before other nations learned what they were doing. Later, central banks of various countries took care to protect their treasure, and if possible sent it out of Europe to Canada or the United States so that it would be an ocean away from Hitler. Gathering up private gold from citizens, whether Jews or non-Jews, was more difficult because people were dispersed, and valuable property could be easily hidden, except in ghettos.

The centralized place for holding all gold, whether public or private, was the Reichsbank. It had the vaults where it could be safely stored, and also the bank to handle it. Nazi organizations sent their valuable goods there. As the war dragged on, however, some of the more powerful agencies, such as the Foreign Ministry and the *Schutzstaffel (SS)*, the Nazi security unit, had their own stashes, which by the end of the war were substantial, thanks to the countries and the people they conquered, including gold seized from Jews.

The paramilitary *Devisenschutzkommando* (Foreign Exchange Protection Commando), which was controlled by Göring and was under the Four Year Plan, was in charge of collecting valuables such as gold, jewelry, currency, and diamonds from individuals in conquered countries. It was generally known by its initials DSK and reported directly to Göring. The Reichsbank held the property, but he was given anything he wanted. DSK commandos went to banks in newly invaded countries and, accompanied by an employee and a notary, opened and inspected safety deposit boxes. They confiscated such items as gold coins or bars, foreign currency, diamonds, and stock certificates that were later mostly sold on the open market.

The DSK units also did some house searches for valuables. Although it was a paramilitary unit, soldiers often wore civilian clothing. They often gave a nominal payment in Reichsmark to people whose valuables they had taken.

The DSK operations started with Austria, the first victim of German aggression, and were also carried out in Czechoslovakia and Poland. It reached its peak of efficiency under the direction of the SS officer Herbert Staffeldt during the May 1940 invasions of the Low Countries and northern France. Between May 1940 and September 1943, the DSK confiscated $144 million in the Netherlands, $876 million in Belgium, and $21 million in northern France.[20]

Göring retained personal control over stolen art and took his favorite pieces to his hunting retreat Carinhall. While the gold went to the Reichsbank, he could get as much of it as he wished. He reorganized the operation just before the German invasion of the Soviet Union. Nazis units there did similar work, but the people were not as wealthy as in Western Europe, so there was less to steal. The DSK played only a minor role after 1942.

With the Four Year Plan taking over more and more control of the German economy, attacks on Jewish citizens increased. On April 26, 1938, the government required them to declare their property and the estimated value of their private goods. In February of the following year, another decree required that they turn in their jewelry, silverware, and gold to the Municipal Pawn Shop in Berlin. The securities went to so-called currency banks. Jews were paid a pittance of the value. In the first quarter of 1939, the Nazis began melting down confiscated jewelry, so that the gold could it made into bars and be passed along as Reichsbank property.

Göring thought his appointment meant Schacht's role as Plenipotentiary for War Economy would be eliminated, but it wasn't, and bureaucratic turf wars ensued. The first squabble between the two was over mining. Göring issued government ordinances without asking Schacht's opinion or even sending him a copy of the new legislation.

The proud Schacht was outraged, and for a while he fought a rearguard action by simply staying away from the Ministry of

Economics and working only out of his beloved Reichsbank. His staff quipped that he was on a sit-down strike. General Wilhelm Keitel, a Göring supporter, complained in a memo that Schacht was "not exercising his office as the Plenipotentiary General [and] decisions on essential problems of mobilization and conduct of war remain unacted upon." Göring soon gave direct orders to Schacht's Economics Ministry staff, but Schacht responded on December 11, 1936 with a letter under his title as the Plenipotentiary for War Economy telling the staff to take orders only from him.[21]

On December 24, 1936, Schacht sent General Blomberg a long letter explaining the increasing difficulties he was having getting foreign exchange. Many countries were now refusing to trade with Germany because of Nazi racial policies. The Reichsbank president wrote: "The economic and illegal treatment of the press, the anti-church activities of certain party organizations, and the lawlessness that centers in the Gestapo harm our rearmament task." At the same time, Schacht stated that he was not abandoning the country's national goals "in the least."[22]

General Thomas told investigators after the war that "from 1936 on, Schacht used every opportunity" to encourage von Blomberg to reduce the tempo and size of rearmament. Schacht condemned what he called "the excessive rearming of Germany." In both 1937 and 1938, the bank president told Blomberg he was going to resign from the government. The general sent Thomas to Schacht to persuade him to stay in office. In a speech to senior officers at the War College, Schacht outlined all the economic reasons not to go to war.[23]

General Blomberg remained a staunch ally of Schacht even while he was staging his boycott. On February 22, 1937, the general wrote Hitler, "If you, my Führer, agree with my view regarding these jurisdictional questions, it may be possible to induce Reichsbank President Dr. Schacht, whose cooperation as Plenipotentiary for the War Economy is a great significance, to resume his former activity."[24]

Schacht and Göring signed a reconciliation accord on July 7, 1937, and the next day, Schacht sent a letter to General Blomberg saying he would cooperate. Göring, though, still thought that he had authority over Schacht. In any case, the accord changed little when it came to the workings of the Nazi government.[25]

Schacht still valued highly his position at the Reichsbank, where he remained firmly in control. That was the post he really wanted to keep, in part because Göring was uninterested in its obscure technical issues. Schacht also enjoyed the international hobnobbing and travel that the job entailed. After nearly a year of internecine warfare, Schacht on October 5 wrote a long letter to Göring pointing out that "fundamental differences exist in our economic policies, which I hope will induce the Führer to place the further direction of economic policies solely in your hands." He sent a copy to Hitler. By that time, Schacht knew that Göring was lobbying Hitler to get rid of him, including from his position as head of the Reichsbank. Göring responded on August 22 with an equally long, point-by-point rebuttal.

Schacht's four-year term as president of the Reichsbank was coming to a close in March 1937, just as he was becoming increasingly worried that the economy might overheat and cause a new burst of inflation. The man who had stopped runaway prices in 1923 did not want to go into history books as the one who brought them back fifteen years later. He first decided to stop the last three billion Reichsmark installment of Mefo bills that were to finance the next stage of rearmament. As far as he was concerned, the government should now pay for additional rearmament through new taxes or loans, although he didn't think that Hitler would ever take those steps. Schacht even argued that the government should begin paying back the first Mefo loans, which were soon coming due. War Minister Blomberg agreed with him, saying that the initial objectives of the arms build up had been fulfilled by 1937, so there was no need for further Mefo spending.[26]

Twice in early 1937, Hitler sent Hans Heinrich Lammers, the head of the Reich's Chancellery, to Schacht to ask him to sign on for a new term as president of the Reichsbank. Twice the banker told him he did not want to be reappointed. Schacht explained that he could no longer condone the country's loose credit policy, saying that it would eventually lead to inflation. When Hitler heard that, he was furious because it was unthinkable for anyone to turn him down for anything. Schacht's reputation as an economic wizard was still strong, and the Führer worried that the German public would be shocked if he fired him. When Hitler learned that Schacht was telling people, "I must have the right of action in my hands," he responded angrily, "I must have the right of action in my own hands." Schacht finally agreed to extend his term at the bank for just one more year and to issue, in early 1938, the last three billion Reichsmark of Mefo bills.[27]

The deteriorating relations between Hitler and the economic czar who had helped bring him to power exploded in August 1937, in front of top government officials at the Berghof retreat. Hitler and Schacht were meeting in the salon. It was a warm afternoon, so the windows were wide open. Several top aides, including Albert Speer, were outside on the terrace and could hear what was transpiring. Hitler began shouting at Schacht, who replied in an equally loud voice. Schacht maintained that he had to resign because of the conflicts with Göring, and the Führer attempted to get him to stay, saying, "But Schacht—I'm fond of you."[28] The confrontation shocked the outsiders because no one ever shouted at Hitler. Schacht continued to insist that he wanted to resign. Hitler finally urged him to make one more attempt to work with Göring.

After the heated exchange ended and Schacht left, the Führer joined the group outside. He bellowed to them that Schacht was "holding up my rearmament program." At one point Hitler said the entire military project would probably cost 30 billion Reichsmark, but quickly added, "Don't tell Schacht because he'll faint."[29]

In early November 1937, Göring and Schacht had a final showdown. The Reichsbank president was now determined to get out of his job as Minister of Economics. Schacht refused to take instructions because he considered Göring "a fool in economics." Göring told him bluntly, "I must have the right to give you orders." Pulling together all his famed arrogance, Schacht replied, "Not to me, but to my successor."[30]

Schacht at about this time put out feelers to American officials about defecting to the U.S. He contacted Donald Heath, the first secretary of the American embassy in Berlin. He also reached out to Merle Cochran, an old friend who was on the staff of the American embassy in Paris. Cochran passed that information along to Treasury Secretary Morgenthau. The Roosevelt administration, though, didn't act on it.[31]

Schacht wrote Hitler on November 16, asking to be relieved of his job at the Economics Ministry "in the interest of uniform government management." Ten days later, the Führer accepted the resignation. Schacht also lost his post as Plenipotentiary for War Economy, but he remained president of the Reichsbank. Hitler also gave him the title Minister Without Portfolio. Schacht's reputation as the man who stopped Germany's runaway inflation in 1923 was too strong for him to be simply thrown out into the cold. In a letter to Schacht that was made public, Hitler wrote, "If I accede to your wish, it is with the expression of deepest gratitude for your so excellent achievement and in the happy consciousness that, as president of the Reichsbank board, you will make available for the German people and me for many years more your outstanding knowledge and ability and your untiring working strength."[32]

When Göring took over Schacht's office at the Economics Ministry, he was stunned by how modest it was and bellowed, "How can a man have big ideas in such a small room." Then he sat down at the desk, telephoned his predecessor, and announced triumphantly, "I am now sitting in your chair!"[33]

Schacht remained a favorite guest at the home of William Dodd, the American ambassador in Berlin, and enjoyed the prestige of dining at the embassy. The Reichsbank president continued to be reckless in his comments about the Nazis and called Hitler "crazy." Dodd in December 1937 told Schacht that the Gestapo was planning an attempt on his life, but he dismissed the threat.[34]

Schacht's successor at the Economics Ministry was the trusted Nazi Walther Funk. The manner in which he learned the news was indicative of the diminished role the job would have. One night he ran into Hitler at the opera during intermission, and the Führer simply told him he was going to succeed Schacht and told Funk to see Göring to get the details.

A former economic journalist, Funk had been an editor at the *Berliner Börsenzeitung*, a center-right business newspaper. He joined the Nazi party in 1931 and rose quickly to become a major link between the business world and Hitler. Funk had attended the Führer's meeting with business leaders in 1933, when Schacht and Göring hit them up for contributions to finance the party's election campaign. After the Nazis took power in January 1933, Funk became the new government's press spokesman and was then named state secretary, the number two job, in Joseph Goebbels's Ministry of Public Enlightenment and Propaganda.[35]

A fat man with a pudgy face and nearly bald, Funk, according to Albert Speer, had a reputation for a "dissolute love life." Schacht said Funk had been dismissed at the business paper because he was homosexual. Speer also claimed that the SS had a detailed dossier on Funk and had blackmailed him. During the Nuremberg trials following the war, Funk kept his fellow prisoners amused by telling them stories about his erotic excursions to Casablanca, where he said he went "to experience new variants of passion." The Nazis were vehemently anti-gay, but he survived within their ranks.[36] Schacht had contempt for the new economics minister and claimed he had "not the slightest conversation with Funk when he followed me, not before and not after." Göring treated him as an errand boy.

On March 9, 1938, Schacht accepted reappointment as head of the Reichsbank first for just one year and then for a normal four-year term. By then he had no illusions about Hitler's goals or his aggressive military program, but at the same time the central banker enjoyed the trappings of being president of the Reichsbank, where he also had great autonomy. Later that month he agreed to issue the last Mefo bills. At about that same time, Germany had $183.2 million in gold in its vaults, with all but $28.6 million hidden off the official records. Although Schacht had lost a ministry and his plenipotentiary title, he still had what he really wanted: the

Reichsbank. With its gilded armchairs, plush carpeting, and Gobelin tapestries, the new central headquarters in the heart of Berlin, which Hitler helped dedicate in 1934, was a showpiece of the Third Reich. Schacht relished the bank's international prestige and the monthly meetings with other central bankers in Basel. The economic power in Hitler's Reich, though, was now clearly in the hands of Hermann Göring.[37]

Chapter Six

THE CLUB FOR
CENTRAL BANKERS

A handful of central bankers governed the world's financial system in the years immediately following World War I, handling such crucial issues as war reparations, growth, inflation, as well as the handling of central bank gold. These men, who were responsible in many ways to no one but themselves, ruled the economic world from behind a curtain of silence via their control over credit and the money supply in their countries. The most important of them were Montagu Norman of the Bank of England, Benjamin Strong at the Federal Reserve Bank of New York, and the German Reichsbank's Hjalmar Schacht.[1]

There was no convenient place where the central bankers could get together to discuss their common issues and work out shared problems. If the press learned that two of them were meeting somewhere, financial markets immediately assumed that one country or the other was in serious trouble, and a run on some nation's currency would soon develop. At least as far back as the 1880s, central bankers had talked about establishing a venue where they could routinely exchange information, and the idea gathered strength in the 1920s as the world economy bounced from one crisis to the next. Finally in 1930, the leading economic powers established the Bank for International Settlements in Basel, Switzerland.

Basel is at the crossroads of the Germanic and Latin cultures of Europe. Germany, France, and Switzerland come together there on the banks of the Rhine River, Europe's most important transportation artery. Since the nineteenth century, Basel had been a major hub of European travel. It even had three train stations, one for each of the French, German, and Swiss national rail networks. The moneymen decided to locate their new organization in Basel because the city of nearly 150,000 inhabitants was international, intimate, and easy to reach. The American financial writer Adam Smith once noted that while the world spoke darkly about the powerful "gnomes of Zurich" who controlled world finance, the gnomes were actually in Basel.

As with many good ideas, the new bank had many parents. One of them was Hjalmar Schacht. As he remembered it happening, the time was the late spring of 1929, and key players of the world economy were meeting in Paris to work out a plan to reschedule the impossible war reparations that Germany faced after World War I.[2] Owen Young, a leading American businessman who founded the Radio Corporation of America and was president of General Electric, chaired the conference. One day, Schacht and Young were having a private talk at the swank new Hotel George V, where the meetings were being held. Young stretched out in a stuffed chair smoking a pipe, with his legs sticking out far in front of him. Schacht was pacing the floor at what he called his "quarter-deck speed," and as so often happened his mind was in overdrive.

Suddenly Schacht tossed out an idea: why not set up an international bank to handle post-war reparation payments and other global financial issues such as the development of colonial countries, which were rich in precious raw materials. The bank could also play a role in managing the world's gold, the foundation of the world's financial system. It would be something like an economic League of Nations, except that the national representatives would be the central bankers of a variety of countries. When Schacht finished speaking, Young mulled over the idea without initially responding, but then jumped out of his chair and excitedly said, "You gave me a wonderful idea, and I am going to sell it to the world!" The conference ended on June 7, 1929, following an agreement on the Young Plan to settle German war reparations. The meeting's expert report also recommended establishing a group of countries to look into a new institution along the lines that Schacht and Young had first discussed in the hotel room.[3]

The Bank for International Settlements (BIS) was fundamentally an institution to facilitate German war reparations by creating a way to sell Berlin's post-war bonds. Germany would pay off the huge debt by offering long-term securities, which private banks and financial houses would then buy and earn the profit. Governments demanded upfront lump payments, but financial institutions were willing to let Berlin pay off the debt over time with interest. Everyone would get what they wanted. In addition, the BIS would become the place where central bankers could meet on a regular basis and discuss their common problems, swap their economic outlooks, and if possible coordinate national policies.[4]

Schacht took a leading role in talks laying out plans for the new organization, suggesting that it be called the International Settlements Bank. On January 20, 1930, the founding members met in The Hague and signed documents establishing the new institution with a slightly altered name: the Bank for International Settlements. By the time the BIS was up and running, however, Schacht had resigned from his post at the Reichsbank because of a conflict with the Berlin government over the Young Plan. He wanted to accept the deal he had struck on war reparations, but the Berlin government rejected it.

While the Europeans were getting closer together, the United States in the wake of the war had become strongly isolationist and did not join international organizations, including the League of Nations (which was ironic, as one of its key founders was President Woodrow Wilson) or this new bank. American financiers, though, clearly saw that they could make money on war reparations and wanted to get in on the game. So while the U.S. Federal Reserve did not become a member, three U.S. banks, J. P. Morgan, First National Bank of New York, and First National Bank of Chicago, invested in the BIS and played a major role in its birth.

Switzerland offered to provide a home for the new organization in Basel as well as an attractive array of tax and legal perks for its future staff. The first official meeting of the bank's board of directors took place in Basel on May 12, 1930. The bank started with capital of 500 million Swiss gold francs, and its headquarters was to be located in the city's old Grand Hôtel et Savoy Hôtel Univers. It was an ideal location: far from the prying press in Paris or London, but just a few steps from Basel's main train station, which provided good access to European capitals. The BIS signed a two-year lease on the hotel, but ended up staying there for forty-seven years. It also quickly grew to a staff of 100 made up largely of economists.[5]

The central bankers easily slipped into a routine of holding monthly, weekend meetings ten times a year. They enjoyed the informal sessions and camaraderie so much that they were soon stretching their visits from Thursday to Monday. Since the U.S. was not in the club, no Federal Reserve representatives were present. American bankers, though, were on the board, and diplomats from the U.S. embassy in Paris traveled to Basel each month to roam the corridors and sent cables back to Washington reporting on the talk of the international financial and political world.

The epicenter of world finance in those days was still London, which was colloquially known as The City. The personification of that money power was Montagu Norman, the governor of the Bank of England, whom one biographer described as "a strange and lonely man." In addition to being a giant of global finance, he was also a hero of the Boer War and a lover of classical music. He hired string quartets to perform at his home for him alone. With his spade beard and flowing cape, Norman ruled the world of money with panache and cultivated aloofness. A 1929 cover story in *Time* magazine called him the "Paladin of Gold," and in Basel he was always referred to respectfully as Mr. Governor. In the early years, the BIS was essentially Norman's club, and he rarely missed a meeting. He called the bank his "spiritual home away from home," and developed many close friendships. On Monday afternoons after the official weekend events were over, Norman regularly had tea with BIS economist Per Jacobsson's British-born wife Violet. The banker always arrived dramatically via a back road with his cape flowing behind him.[6]

When Hjalmar Schacht returned to his old job as president of the Reichsbank in early 1933, he was delighted to rejoin the Basel meetings. Given Hitler's aggressive foreign policy, the German was a big draw at the weekend sessions. Some governors even checked to make sure he was coming before they committed to attending. Other central bankers and visiting American diplomats pumped him for both the latest Berlin rumors and what Hitler was thinking. Schacht loved being the center of attention and dished out just enough gossip to retain everyone's attention, but held back the last bit of information, to keep them wanting more. When he got back home, he told the Führer about the discussions. Hitler bragged at one of his staff lunches, "I must say that the tricks Schacht succeeded in playing on them proves that even in the field of sharp finance a really intelligent Aryan is more than a match for his Jewish counterpart."[7]

The BIS attracted top executives from the world of finance. American Gates W. McGarrah resigned as chairman of the New York Federal Reserve Bank to become the first head of the organization, even though the U.S. government was not an official member. Other early presidents included the American Leon Fraser, a legal expert on reparations, as well as Dutch bankers Leonardus Trip and J. Willem Beyen. None of them, however, stayed in the job for long.

The bank quickly earned a reputation for having a multinational stable of the world's top economists. The most famous was the Swede Per Jacobsson, who at the age of thirty-seven became the organization's first head of the Monetary and Economic Department. He had earlier worked at the League of Nations. Karl Blessing, another rising star in economics also worked in Basel during the early days. Later Jacobsson served as managing director of the International Monetary Fund, and Blessing became a member of Schacht's Reichsbank board and was president of the West German Bundesbank in the 1950s and 1960s.

While journalists were not initially welcome at the Basel meetings, they nonetheless started showing up soon after the BIS was founded. For a while there was a ban on conversations between bankers and the press. As a result, reporters resorted to writing stories with lots of atmospherics about how Germany's Dr. Schacht, for example, had an expression of disappointment—or joy—on his face after he left a meeting in the suite of Britain's Governor Norman. So much misinformation was being published that the BIS finally gave up and began holding an off-the-record press conference after each meeting. Information was still heavily guarded, though, so these press conferences usually produced little news.

The BIS came into existence at an ominous time in world economics. The already weak world financial system had collapsed completely following the Wall Street crash of October 1929. Britain, Germany, and the U.S. now had combined unemployment of 10 million. No one seemed to have any good ideas about how to get out of the collective mess. In December 1930, John Maynard Keynes wrote in an article that appeared simultaneously in both Britain and the U.S., "We have involved ourselves in a colossal muddle, having blundered in the control of a delicate machine, the working of which we do not understand."[8]

The leaders of the world central banks, though, never wavered in their support for the continuing role of gold. It was their anchor in troubled times. BIS President Beyen later wrote that the BIS was designed to be "the guardian of the gold standard." In fact, both before and during the war, it was the largest channel for gold transactions in Europe. Bullion was the top-of-the-mind concern of central bankers, who nervously saw their national holdings swinging wildly as countries and investors looked around for economic shelter. It was a time of great turmoil in the global economy. All the major countries were in chaos because of the worldwide depression. Nations spent heavily in hopes of ending the downturn, which led to deficit spending and raised questions about the stabilities of their currencies. The result was global instability. The U.S. in 1930 enjoyed an influx of some $300 million in gold, but between the end of September and the end of October 1931 it lost $755 million. Paris saw its gold increase by $500 million in 1930 and another $1 billion in early 1931. Britain, on the other hand, suffered sharp drops in its reserves, and Germany's bullion almost disappeared. Germany's Karl Blessing, who was then on the BIS staff, wrote in a memo on April 8, 1930, that the BIS should "manipulate the gold value in such a way that international price levels remain as stable as possible."[9]

As the worldwide depression grew worse, countries began leaving the gold standard. Germany was the first major nation to depart from it in July 1931, followed in September by Britain and a host of small countries. Eventually some twenty-five British Commonwealth countries from Canada to India joined Britain in dropping the link to gold. The U.S. left in March 1933, and Italy in May 1934. Soon only France, Switzerland, Belgium, and Holland were still on the bullion standard, and none of them allowed their citizens to exchange their paper currency for gold.

Despite all that, the central bankers meeting each month in Basel never lost their attachment to the traditional money system. The troubles were considered only a passing phenomenon, and they were certain that the world would eventually get back on the right track. Their unspoken motto: "In Gold We Trust." The BIS historian Gianni Toniolo later wrote, "The gold standard was still embedded in the very DNA of the BIS."[10]

In April 1935, and with the international money system in tatters, the BIS published its fifth annual report. It was both an autopsy on the economic crisis and an overview of the world's financial future. The author was chief economist Per Jacobsson. While national governments might be temporarily off gold, the central banker's club was convinced more than ever that it should be the centerpiece of the world economy in order to foster growth and global financial stability. He wrote, "It is slowly beginning to be realized in ever-wider circles than an enduring economic progress presupposes more possibilities for international trade and for sound financial relationships, which, in turn, require stability of exchange rates. In the sphere of practical politics, this means stabilization on the basis of gold."[11]

The Bank for International Settlements quickly got into the business of holding gold reserves for its member countries. While the general public might have thought that the metal was being physically moved around the world from country to country to settle trade balances, that rarely happened in these dealings because bullion is extremely heavy and transportation was risky. Transportation might sometimes occur, but more often ownership labels in the vaults of the Federal Reserve of New York or the Bank of England were simply changed. Within the general BIS account in London, the organization's members had their own sub-accounts that were identified only by numbers. Acting on orders from a particular national central bank, BIS officials in Basel would wire instructions to London to transfer bullion from one account to another, and the transaction immediately took place. The Bank of England considered the transfers only bookkeeping operations. Small countries, in particular, liked the gold-earmarking service, which saved them from having to pay for a physical exchange or the expense of the requisite security. Bank of England officials claimed that they did not even know who owned the sub-accounts, although that was not true.

Just nine years after it was first founded, the outbreak of World War II in 1939 put the Bank for International Settlements right in the middle of the Nazi battle for gold, and the Reichsbank sold bullion to BIS up until a few weeks before the end of the war in 1945. American investigators after the conflict concluded that the bank eventually acquired 13.5 tons of stolen gold in the war years. Germany's Schacht had been one of the founders of the organization, and officials at the Reichsbank knew exactly how it operated and how to manipulate BIS rules and policies to achieve their objectives. The top German staffer at the organization was Paul Hechler, who arrived in 1935 and became the general director and head of the banking department. He was a card-carrying Nazi and signed his letters *"Heil Hitler!"*[12]

Chapter Seven

AUSTRIA BECOMES THE FIRST EASY PIECE

Austria
March 1938
Tons of gold: 91

Gold Route
- - - - - ▸

On November 10, 1937, Hitler met with top military and diplomatic officials in his study at Berlin's Reich Chancellery at 77 Wilhelmstraße. The rococo building had been the traditional office of the German Chancellor since the time of Otto von Bismarck in the late nineteenth century. He had unified a number of independent and often-quarrelsome Teutonic states under the leadership of Prussia. Hitler, the wannabe architect, considered the majestic building "fit for a soap company" and had his architect Albert Speer redesign and expand it. Attending the meeting were Hermann Göring, the head of the Four Year Plan and the new Luftwaffe; General Werner von Blomberg, the war minister; General Werner von Fritsch, commander-in-chief of the army; Admiral Erich Raeder, commander-in-chief of the navy; Freiherr Konstantin von Neurath, the foreign minister; and Colonel Friedrich Hossbach, Hitler's military adjutant and official note taker.[1]

When Hitler spoke before a large crowd, he became an actor strutting on the world stage. He pounded the podium; he screamed; he threatened. When he spoke before a small group such as this, he totally dominated discussions, rarely, if ever, letting anyone voice an opinion or challenge him. The wife of Joseph Goebbels once complained to the wife of Italian foreign minister Ciano about this, saying, "It is always Hitler who talks! He may be Führer, but he repeats himself and bores his guests."[2]

The gathering on that November day took place against a troubling economic background. The country was again having balance-of-payments problems, and there was talk about the need to reduce private consumption and cut back on rearmament. The Nazis had made major increases in military spending in the past few years, but internal squabbling continued over where to spend the country's resources. Admiral Raeder argued that the navy was not getting enough steel and munitions allocations. Schacht and Göring were still fighting over control of the economy, although Göring had essentially won. There was also public rumbling about the severe shortage of vital imports, especially food.

Hitler, though, had other things on his mind. He wanted to talk about his next political and military moves. The meeting lasted from 4:15 P.M. to 8:30 P.M. The colonel's notes, which historians have labeled the Hossbach Memorandum, were typed up five days later. They provide the best outline of Hitler's thinking and strategy during the first period of Nazi aggression.[3]

Hitler began by explaining that the topic for discussion was too important to be discussed with the full cabinet. He quickly explained that his overall political goal was "to make secure and preserve the [country's] racial community and to enlarge it." That meant expanding Germany's population beyond the current eighty-five million and enlarging the country's borders by bringing into the Reich territories where ethnic Germans lived, such as Austria and Czechoslovakia.

The chancellor explained that Germany had to become economically self-sufficient, especially in war materiel. It was possible to achieve that immediately in coal, but it would be more difficult with petroleum, iron, copper, and tin. Agricultural self-sufficiency was impossible in the short run, which was why it would be necessary to expand Germany's territory to the east and gain sufficient farmland. Hitler also said that the country had to regain the colonies lost after World War I, notably the area known as German East Africa and German Southwest Africa, which could become a new source of raw materials and foodstuffs.

Hitler spelled out three different political scenarios or what he called cases. The first covered the period from 1943 to 1945, after which he said the German military situation would deteriorate because Britain, France, and the Soviet Union would have rearmed with new weaponry. Therefore action had to be taken before 1943. "Nobody knows today what the situation would be in the years 1943-45," he said. "It was while the rest of the world is still preparing its defense that we are obliged to take the offensive . . . Only one thing is certain: we can not wait longer."

Hitler's second premise was that France would continue to be weak because of the country's ongoing economic and political problems. Hitler believed that would preoccupy its political and military leaders, and as a result France would not react to German military moves despite Prague's mutual defense treaty with France.

The Führer's conclusion was that Germany should take over Austria and Czechoslovakia as soon as possible in order to protect its southern flank. Hitler believed that Britain and France had already written off Czechoslovakia, and Italy would not offer any objections as long as Mussolini was in power; he still considered Austria part of his sphere of influence. Hitler confidently proclaimed that neither Poland nor the Soviet Union would go to war to protect either Austria or Czechoslovakia.

Hitler concluded the presentation by saying that Germany should undertake a diplomatic and military offensive against the two countries early in the following year. The German military move against Czechoslovakia, he said, should be conducted with "lightning speed" to forestall Britain or France from mounting a counterattack. The Führer's overriding strategy was to avoid the protracted conflicts that led to his country's defeat in World War I. His objective was to win a series of small wars with *Blitzkrieg* attacks. His immediate goal: "For the improvement of our military political position, it must be our first aim . . . to conquer Czechoslovakia and Austria simultaneously." The annexation of the two small countries would improve Germany's strategic position in eventual, and expected, conflicts with Britain and France. Securing his southern border would also increase the country's military might during the ultimate, and inevitable, attacks on Western Europe.

Hitler, as always, dominated the meeting by the force of his personality. Not everyone in the room, however, agreed with him, and Hossbach devoted two long paragraphs to objections from Blomberg, Fritsch, and Neurath. They argued that France and Britain "must not appear in the role of our enemies." War Minister Blomberg said that the Czech defenses were now stronger because the country had built a kind of Eastern Maginot Line that would make a German attack both difficult and dangerous. Foreign Minister Neurath argued that conflict with France, Britain, and Italy was more likely than Hitler assumed. Hitler replied that he wasn't thinking of an immediate conflict with the small countries, but perhaps one in the summer of 1938. He also repeated his belief that neither Britain nor France would mobilize its forces to defend Austria or Czechoslovakia.

Göring offered his strong support for the plan and added that in view of Hitler's presentation, Germany should immediately halt its military involvement in the Spanish Civil War. The support for General Francisco Franco's rebels consisted of supplying military equipment as well as providing air cover and undertaking selected aerial bombings. Hitler agreed, but added that he wanted to wait for the appropriate time to make that move. Displaying behaviour he was to exhibit repeatedly throughout the war, he wanted to do everything at the same time and refused to sacrifice one objective in order to achieve another. Militarily, Hitler always desired to push his armies to do more and rebuffed anyone who tried to set limits.

Hossbach's notes ended with a terse one-sentence statement that the second part of the meeting dealt with a detailed discussion of armaments.[4]

Four days later, General Fritsch met with Hitler and objected even more strongly to the plan put forth at the meeting. Foreign Minister Neurath tried to get an appointment with the Führer to voice his opposition, but Hitler slipped out of Berlin and went to his Berghof retreat in order to avoid another confrontation. Three months after the Reich Chancellery meeting, Blomberg, Fritsch, and Neurath had all been relieved of duty. The two military leaders were removed because of sexual charges. Blomberg was accused of having recently married a prostitute, and Fritsch was labeled a homosexual, which was untrue. Joachim von Ribbentrop, a wine salesman before becoming Hitler's diplomatic trouble-shooter, replaced Neurath as foreign minister. General Walther von Brauchitsch, another Prussian nobleman, but one who followed Hitler's orders, replaced Fritsch.

By early in 1938, Hitler had effectively silenced all diplomatic and military opposition. On February 4, he held a cabinet meeting to explain the government shuffle. It was to be the last cabinet meeting Hitler ever held. The same night he went on German radio and declared, "From now on, I personally take over the command of the armed forces."[5]

No one should have been surprised that Hitler had his eyes on Austria. In the second paragraph of his opus *Mein Kampf* he wrote, "German-Austria must return to the great German motherland . . . One blood demands one Reich."[6]

The Führer had already sent agents into Austria to stir up unrest and prepare for military action, and now he sped up his plans to incorporate the country of his birth into his Reich. Immediately after World War I, a majority of Austrians probably wanted to unify their country with Germany, but by the mid-1930s only a minority still desired to take that step. The move in German was called *Anschluss* or annexation. Austria was economically and politically unstable, and thus an easy target. Paramilitary units operated on both the right and the left, and high-level political assassinations had taken place, including the murder of Austrian Chancellor Engelbert Dollfuss in February 1934 during a failed Nazi-led coup attempt. Hitler sent Franz von Papen, the centrist politician who had helped bring him to power, to Vienna as ambassador. The same day that Hitler met with his cabinet in Berlin, he recalled Papen and fired him. Hitler didn't need good relations with the country he was planning to annex.

On February 12, 1938, Hitler demanded that Kurt Schuschnigg, the Austrian chancellor and a strong opponent of *Anschluss*, meet him at Berchtesgaden. Dressed in the Nazi brown-shirt of a Storm Trooper and flanked by three generals, Hitler immediately launched into a two-hour tirade against Austria. Schuschnigg offered no response and did not ask what Austria should do about the complaints. Hitler and Schuschnigg then adjourned for a convivial lunch that totally belied the earlier diatribe. After eating, though, Schuschnigg had to wait for hours before Hitler presented the Austrian leader with a detailed ultimatum that included putting Nazis in key Austrian cabinet posts, integrating the country's economy into that of Germany, and releasing all Nazi political prisoners.

Hitler said there could be no discussion about his demands. "You will either sign as it is and fulfill my demands within three days, or I will order the march into Austria."[7]

Schuschnigg played for time by explaining that under the Austrian constitution only the president had the power to accept the agreement and carry it out. Hitler exploded and ran to the door, shouting to General Wilhelm Keitel, the Supreme Commander of the Armed Forces and a Führer favorite, to join him. Turning to Schuschnigg, Hitler bellowed, "I shall have you called later." Once outside the room, Hitler smiled and told the general that he had no orders to give him. Keitel was simply a bit player in a *pièce de théâtre* to scare the Austrian chancellor.

After letting his guest stew for half an hour, Hitler sent Schuschnigg a message saying that he wanted to see him. When the Austrian arrived, the Führer said, "I have decided to change my mind—for the first time in my life. But I warn you. This is the very last chance. I have given you three additional days to carry out the agreement."

Schuschnigg returned to Vienna, and Austrian political leaders wrestled with how to avoid the inevitable. On February 15, the deadline, the government finally gave in. The next day Vienna granted an amnesty to all Nazis and reorganized the cabinet to include Nazi representatives. Five days later, Hitler made a speech to the Reichstag, thanking Austrians for the concessions and for agreeing to new and closer relations between the two countries. At the same time, he issued an ominous warning: "Over 10 million Germans live in two of the states adjoining our frontiers . . . It is unbearable for a world power to know there are racial comrades at its side who are constantly being afflicted with the severest suffering for their sympathy or unity with the whole nation." That was a none-too-subtle reference to the seven million Austrians and three million Sudeten Germans residing in Czechoslovakia.[8]

Hitler named Wilhelm Keppler his commissioner for Austrian affairs. He was already *Statßecretär*, the number-two position, at the foreign ministry. Keppler was a veteran Nazi and member of the much-feared *Schutzstaffel*. He had joined the party in 1927 and by

1931 was an economic advisor to Hitler. While working at the Reich Chancellery, Keppler formed a group made up largely of business leaders called the *Freundeskreis der Wirtschaft* (Friends Economic Circle). Göring considered him weak, but Hitler liked him. In early March he made a first visit to Vienna in his new role. While there, he met with leading Nazis and with Schuschnigg. Upon his return to Berlin, Keppler briefed Hitler, who was pleased with how things were going.

On the morning of March 8, however, a top Austrian Nazi called Keppler with the rumor that Schuschnigg was going to hold a plebiscite on the question of union with Germany. The information was immediately passed along to Hitler, who doubted it but nonetheless told Keppler to take a government plane back to Vienna and check things out on the ground.

The scuttlebutt was correct. On the evening of March 9, Schuschnigg announced at a rally in Innsbruck that a national plebiscite would be held the following Sunday, only four days later. The Austrian people would be asked to respond either *Ja* or *Nein* to one question: "Are you for a free, German, independent and social, Christian and united Austria, for peace and work, for the equality of all those who affirm themselves for the people and Fatherland?"[9]

When Hitler learned of the referendum, he blew up and ordered that plans for an invasion of Austria be drawn up immediately. The vote had to be stopped! The Führer immediately called Göring, who was relaxing at his Carinhall retreat. As they discussed next moves over the phone, it quickly became clear that Germany would respond militarily. Keppler returned from Vienna to get a lay of the land, while Göring left for Berlin.

The following day was hectic in both Berlin and Vienna. Göring's worries about Keppler had been born out, and the report he presented to Hitler at 10:00 A.M. was a masterpiece of indecision. The Austrian Nazis could not agree on a clear strategy, and he sided with moderates who wanted to let events play themselves out. That was not good enough for Hitler, who had built up a great army and now wanted to use it.

Hitler's only real concern was whether a military action against Austria would push Italy's *Duce* Benito Mussolini to action. The Italian considered Austria to be his protectorate and a symbol that Rome was once again a world power. Hitler feared that if the Italians mobilized their army, France and Britain might take similar steps. In 1934, when Nazis killed the Austrian Chancellor Dollfuss, Mussolini had mobilized five divisions to forestall any German action. After the confrontation at Berchtesgaden, Schuschnigg instructed his military attaché in Rome to meet with the Duce and explain what had happened. Mussolini doubted the Germans would act, saying confidently, "This is something they will never do. We have Göring's word of honor." Il Duce also told the Austrian that the plebiscite was a mistake.[10]

Meanwhile in Berlin, Hitler told General Wilhelm Keitel, the new Supreme Commander of the Armed Forces, that if the Austrians went ahead with the vote, he would invade. Keitel had Colonel Alfred Jodl bring him the Special Case "Otto" plans for an invasion of Austria. The report was skimpy and had been drawn up in case the Austrians tried to restore the monarchy headed by Otto Von Habsburg. "We have prepared nothing at all," reported General Ludwig Beck, the head of the general staff.

When Beck met with Hitler, he told him bluntly, "I cannot take any responsibility for an invasion of Austria." The Führer responded that his own *SS* troops could then carry it out. "They will march in with bands playing. Is that what the army wants?" Later Jodl sent a message to the armed forces telling them that if they encounter Czech troops during the invasion they should treat them as enemies, but any Italian ones should be "treated as friends."[11]

The German generals didn't need to worry about London or Paris. The new government of Neville Chamberlain was anxious to get along with Hitler, and once again a French government was falling. The French thought little of the new British prime minister, joking that his name as a pronunciation pun was *"J'aime Berlin"* or *"I love Berlin."* During a rambunctious session of Parliament, Chamberlain said little more than, "I have no statement to make."

Ribbentrop traveled to London and met with both him and his new foreign secretary Lord Halifax. After the talks, the German sent a cable to Hitler saying, "England will do nothing in regard to Austria."[12]

In the early afternoon, Keppler was handed a message significantly addressed to him as SS *Gruppenführer*. It provided a list of the Austrian Nazis or party sympathizers who were now supposed to run the country. At the top was the name Dr. Arthur Seyss-Inquart. He was a trained lawyer who had grown up in the mixed ethnic area of the Austro-Hungarian Empire. He had been associated with the Austrian Nazi Party since 1931, but did not actually join it until the day after the *Anschluss*. In the Schuschnigg government he had held the crucial post of Minister of Security and Interior.

The Austrian government continued to organize the referendum that was now only three days away. Schuschnigg had a long talk that evening with Seyss-Inquart, who complained that he had not been informed in advance about the plebiscite. Since he didn't have instructions yet from Berlin, he only argued about a few technical issues. At the end of the conversation, he said that his followers would vote for the referendum. Demonstrators both for and against the referendum filled the streets of Austria that night, and a whiff of civil war was in the air.

At 2:00 A.M. on March 11, the Berlin government issued Directive Number One for Operation Otto. It instructed the German army and air force to be ready to invade Austria at noon the following day "at the latest." Hitler wanted to take action before the scheduled referendum.[13]

At 5:30 that morning, the phone rang in Chancellor Schuschnigg's bedroom. The Austrian chief of police informed him that German troops had closed the border at Salzburg, stopping rail traffic between the two countries. Military forces were also building up just over the border. An hour later, Schuschnigg headed for his office, but stopped at St. Stephen's Cathedral to attend mass and pray for his country. As he sat in the last pew, the chancellor could only think of the phone call warning. By the time he got to his office, a telegram from the Austrian Consul General in Munich had arrived with the cryptic message, "Leo ready to travel." The chancellor knew that meant the German army was preparing to invade.

At 11:30 A.M., Arthur Seyss-Inquart arrived at the Vienna chancellery with Edmund Glaise-Morstenau, the vice chancellor in Schuschnigg's cabinet, who had just flown back from Berlin with a letter demanding that the plebiscite be put off for several weeks. In the early afternoon there ensued a series of threatening phone calls that involved Göring in Berlin, who was working out of a phone booth at the chancellery. He was now the puppet master, pulling strings from afar. Seyss-Inquart first presented Schuschnigg with Hitler's order that the plebiscite be called off "within the hour." The Austrian leader refused to comply, but went to see President Wilhelm Miklas, the head of state. The two finally agreed at 2:00 P.M. to comply with the German demand and cancel the referendum. Seyss-Inquart informed Göring by phone at 2:45.[14]

Twenty minutes later, Göring was back on the phone orchestrating a *coup d'état* in Vienna. He told Seyss-Inquart that he and all the Nazi cabinet ministers should resign. In another call less than an hour later, Seyss-Inquart told Göring that Schuschnigg was on his way to the office of the Austrian president to hand in his resignation. Göring responded that a new government had to be in place by 7:30. He added that the referendum also had to be cancelled and that Keppler would be returning to Vienna with the list of new cabinet members. Göring also said that military units would be arriving soon and would be at Seyss-Inquart's disposal. He was also instructed to send Berlin a message asking for German troops to reestablish law and order in the country.

In the middle of a phone call, however, Göring learned that the Austrian president was refusing to appoint Seyss-Inquart. A furious Göring bellowed into the receiver that German forces in that case would march that night and, "Austria will cease to exist . . . There is no time now for jokes."

While frantic phone calls between Berlin and Vienna continued, Prince Philip of Hesse at 10:25 P.M. telephoned Hitler from Rome. The prince said he had just left Mussolini's office in the Palazzo

Venezia with the news that the Duce "accepts the whole thing in a very friendly manner" and "sends his best regards." Hitler was elated and asked the prince to "please let Mussolini know I will never forget him for this. . . . never, never, never, whatever happens." The Führer also sent Mussolini an effusive cable repeating that message. The Nazis could now move in for the kill without facing military opposition.

Schuschnigg that evening went on Austrian radio and told his countrymen what had transpired, saying in conclusion, "President Miklas has asked me to tell the people of Austria that we have yielded to force since we are not prepared even in this terrible hour to shed blood. We have decided to order the troops to offer no resistance." It was after midnight, when Seyss-Inquart drove his predecessor home through streets where Austrian Nazis were celebrating their victory.

While all the cabinet shuffling and threats were taking place over the phone, Reichsbank president Hjalmar Schacht was in Berlin participating in pre-invasion planning with the Wehrmacht's economic staff. He had long been an advocate of a union between the two countries, arguing that Austria was too small to be economically viable, and merging its financial coffers with the Reichsbank would certainly be advantageous. Lt. Colonel Hans Wiedemann from Hitler's office asked Schacht how currency policy for the united country should be handled. The central banker said the exchange rate should be fixed at one Reichsmark to two Austrian schillings, even though that country's currency was trading at the time for about one mark to 1.1 schillings. The under-valuation of the Austrian currency made anything the Germans bought in Austria about half price, and that became the Nazi policy in all countries it later invaded. This manipulation of exchange rates became one of the most successful tools the Nazis had to exploit occupied countries throughout World War II. Occupying German soldiers lived like kings and shipped back home huge amounts of local products at bargain prices. That gave Germans both at home and in occupied nations a much higher standard of living, making the Nazi government even more popular.[15]

At 8:45 that same evening, Hitler signed Directive No. 2 instructing German troops to begin entering Austria at daybreak the next morning. Only three minutes later, Göring dictated a telegram to Keppler that was to be given to Seyss-Inquart. It stated that he should send Hitler a message asking him "in order to prevent bloodshed . . . to send German troops as soon as possible."[16]

At daybreak on March 12, German units marched into Austria at six border crossings. They faced no opposition. By then Nazi paramilitary units were already on the streets of the Vienna, and Austrian Nazis were helping execute the country's quick takeover. Wehrmacht planes flew over the capital dropping leaflets that read: "National Socialist Germany greets its possession National Socialist Austria and its new government in true indivisible union."

That same day, Reichsbank director Karl Friedrich Wilhelm flew on a government plane to Vienna with instructions to oversee the financial takeover of Austria. He was under strict orders to insist on the Reichsmark-Austrian schilling exchange rate Schacht had set. When Wilhelm got to his hotel in a truck requisitioned from the national post office, he telephoned the Reichsbank in Berlin, and officials again repeated the order that the exchange rate should be one Reichsmark for two Austrian schillings. He was also told to be at the Vienna central bank the following morning at 11:00 to meet with the president and director general.

Shortly after lunch, Hitler crossed the German border by car and made a triumphant return to his native land. Teeming, cheering crowds greeted him as he passed through villages. He laid a wreath at the grave of his parents in the town of Leonding and afterward traveled to Linz, where he had once studied. In a self-congratulatory speech, he said, "If providence once called me forth from this town to be the leader of the Reich, it must in so doing have charged me with a mission, and that mission could only be to restore my dear homeland to the German Reich."[17] He then told an Austrian official to draft the legal document for the *Anschluss* of Austria into

Germany. The document stated simply: "Austria is a province of the German Reich." When Hitler saw it, tears rolled down his cheeks.

In anticipation of a possible invasion, the Austrians had already packed some of the country's gold be shipped to Brno, Czechoslovakia. It was anticipated that it would then be sent to the Bank of England for safekeeping. The plans, however, were for naught.

Thanks to his close contacts among European central bankers, Schacht knew that Austria held about $100 million in gold, while Germany in 1938 was down to $28.6 million officially with another $120.5 million in hidden bullion. Hitler and Göring had already met in late February to plan the capture of the bullion. On Saturday morning March 12, Wilhelm Keppler led two Nazi commandoes, who had arrived in Vienna earlier that day, to the Austrian Central Bank and took possession of the country's gold that had been packed and which was ready to be moved. The Germans also arrested several top Austrian bank officials and told the bank's president not to return to the building.[18]

One of the first acts by officials in Berlin was a government order to transfer the assets of the Austrian National Bank to Germany. Hitler, Schacht, Finance Minister Johann Schwerin von Krosigk, and Interior Minister Wilhelm Frick signed it. The four-point statement published in German papers on March 17 was straightforward and clear. The first two decrees:

1. The administration of the Austrian National Bank shall be taken over by the Reichsbank.
2. The Austrian National Bank shall go into liquidation and be liquidated by the Reichsbank for account of the Reich.[19]

World central bankers were attending the regular monthly meeting of the Bank for International Settlements on Sunday, March 13, just as the Nazi mopping up was taking place in Vienna. Before the gathering started, Schacht told the chairman he did not want the developments in Austria to be discussed. Nonetheless, that was still the main topic of conversation in the corridors. The central bankers were already nervously looking toward Czechoslovakia, fearing that would be Hitler's next target. The Italian representatives in Basel voiced their unhappiness that Mussolini had not received any advance notice from his Berlin partner. He had been told, but the official was unaware of it. Several central bankers discussed the increasing importance of gold in a world that seemed to be headed for war. The metal's price soared in London when markets opened the following day. The Bank of England sold $1 million worth in an attempt to keep the price from going even higher.

On March 17, the Nazis put into law the economic measures involved in uniting the two countries. The Reichsmark was made legal tender in the country at a rate of 1:1.5. Austrian protests against Schacht's 1:2 rate were so strong that the Germans made a strategic retreat, but it was still significantly higher than the pre-invasion value of 1:1.[20]

The following day, the commercial attaché at the U.S. embassy in Vienna sent Washington a curt cable with the news, "Reichsbank absorbed Austrian National Bank." He estimated that the Germans had seized $46 million in gold and $34 million in foreign exchange. The actual amount was more than double that. The cryptic end of the message: "Complete absorption Austria proceeding at a rapid rate."[21]

Three days later and before 99.73 percent of Austrians voted in a plebiscite to join the Reich, Schacht arrived in Vienna and officially seized the Austrian Central Bank and its property. He also made a speech to the assembled local staff. The central banker was suffering from a bad cold, but that didn't chill his spirits. He called the event a "celebration" that was part of "one of the greatest moments ever recorded in German history." He added, "I consider it completely impossible that even a single person will find his future with us who is not wholeheartedly for Adolf Hitler." Schacht also introduced Reichsbank director Karl Blessing to the assembled crowd. He would be taking over daily responsibility for the Vienna bank.[22]

After more effusive praise for Hitler, Schacht asked the employees to raise their hands and join him in a pledge of allegiance: "I swear that I will be faithful and obedient to the Führer of the German

Reich, Adolf Hitler, and will perform my duties conscientiously and selflessly."

Schacht then chided his audience, "You have taken this pledge. Anyone who breaks it will be a scoundrel." He ended his presentation by asking the staff to give "a triple *Sieg Heil* to our Führer."

Collecting and sending all the Austrian gold to Berlin turned into a complicated task and involved not only the bars and coins in Vienna but also the gold stored in London. Reich officials were also anxious to get the gold owned by Austrian citizens since it was believed that Jews, who lived primarily in Vienna, had large holdings. All of it was placed in the Reichsbank's Precious Metal Department alongside German gold. The largest part was bullion that had been located in Vienna, but there was also 5.7 tons of gold resting in the London vaults of the Bank of England and 16.6 tons from the Bank for International Settlements. After the war, the Austrian government put in a claim to the Tripartite Commission for the Restitution of Monetary Gold for a whopping 91.3 tons of gold that the Nazis had stolen.[23]

On March 22, the day after Schacht led the *Sieg Heils* at the Austrian National Bank in Vienna, Victor Brauneis, the Vienna bank's general director, sent a cable instructing the BIS to put its gold bars into Germany's account at the Bank of England and to confirm that his telephone instruction earlier that day to move gold bars between the two accounts had already been made. On April 1, Berlin received a cable confirming that the gold was now in the Reichsbank's BIS account in London. Between the amount seized in Vienna and what had been transferred in London, the Reichsbank now controlled the entirety of the gold that the Austrian Central Bank held. Robbing a bank had never been easier. Schacht's intimate knowledge of how the BIS operated and which countries had gold in London made the takeover simple.[24]

There was, however, still more gold to come. Reichsbank board member Emil Puhl sent Keppler a note predicting that they should be able to collect between three and four billion Reichsmark of gold from Austrian Jews.[25] A German law of March 23, 1938, ruled that before April 25 all Austrian citizens had to declare and sell their gold, foreign currency holdings, and foreign stocks to the "National Bank of Austria in liquidation." The prices offered for jewelry, coins, and bars were low, but people knew that later they would be even worse, and the penalty for withholding their valuables would be worse still. Under that program, Austrian citizens sold 14.3 tons of gold to the Reichsbank. The main victims were Viennese Jews, who kept bullion at home because of their tragic history of having to escape from persecution, and history was repeating itself once again.[26]

The Austrian gold played a major role in financing the Nazi war machine at a crucial moment in its development. Germany had been rapidly using up its own holdings of gold and foreign currency to pay for its rearmament program. The Berlin gold reserves, both reported and hidden, dropped from 443.8 million Reichsmark in March 1937 to 138.9 million Reichsmark by the end of June, but the Hitler government now suddenly had more than $100 million in gold that could be used for armaments. Germany was like a driver crossing a desert in a car that had been slowly running out of gas, who all at once comes upon an oasis with a gas station where he refills his tank. Thanks to the Austrian gold, Hitler could now continue, and even expand, his aggressive plan for invading his neighbors. The gold and foreign exchange captured at the Austrian Central Bank totaled 345 million Reichsmark.[27]

On October 3, 1938, Emil Puhl wrote in a secret memo: "The rapid implementation of rearmament was only possible because of the use of available gold, foreign exchange from the former Reich, and the immediate recovery of Austrian gold, foreign exchange, and valuable securities reserves. Without the use of these, it would not have been possible to obtain enough foreign raw materials for ongoing military requirements nor for Field Marshal Göring's modest program to build up stocks of raw materials for warfare."

The memo further itemized what the Germans had obtained in Austria. That consisted of 65 million Reichsmark in privately owned gold coins, 299 million from privately-owned foreign bonds and stocks, 150 million by confiscating foreign shares in companies,

345 million in gold and currency from the Austrian National Bank, and 325 million from accelerated payment of export bills and specialty business contracts. The total haul was 1.2 billion Reichsmark or $470 million. That was only the first of the robberies the Nazis would execute in countries they invaded.[28]

The timing of the Austrian robbery was crucial because the Reich was then running out of money because of its heavy military spending. Economic historian Adam Tooze in *The Wages of Destruction* wrote, "Thanks to the Austrian booty, Germany in 1938 was able to run a trade deficit of almost 450 million Reichsmark, larger than at any time since 1929. For a brief moment, at least, the *Anschluss* freed Hitler's regime from the balance of payments constraint."[29]

Eleven days after the scam plebiscite in which Austrians overwhelmingly approved the German takeover of their country, Hitler met with General Wilhelm Keitel to review plans for his next target, codenamed Case Green. The target: Czechoslovakia.

Chapter Eight

AN INSIDE JOB AGAINST CZECHOSLOVAKIA

Czechoslovakia
February–March 1939
Tons of gold: 45

The victors of World War I forged the country of Czechoslovakia out of the multilingual and multicultural Austro-Hungarian Empire, the major loser in that conflict. The nation was an offspring of Woodrow Wilson's commitment to the national self-determination of ethnic groups. The tenth of his famous Fourteen Points proclaimed that "the peoples of Austria-Hungary" should have "the freest opportunity to autonomous development." The Czechs and Slovaks spoke somewhat similar languages, but their sense of national unity was weak. The country was an ethnic ratatouille that also included Germans, Hungarians, Poles, Ruthenians, Romanians, Gypsies, and Croats. More than three million Sudeten Germans lived in the economically developed and prosperous border area near Germany. They made up one-fourth of the country's total population of nearly 14 million. Hitler, a racial purist, had nothing but contempt for what he considered to be a mongrel country. His goal was to pull German Czechs into the Reich and turn the rest of the nation into his protectorate.

For a young and small nation, Czechoslovakia had surprisingly large gold reserves. Even more astounding was the fact that they came largely from private donations. Dr. Alois Rašín, the country's first finance minister, in 1919 launched a campaign to establish what he called the "Gold Treasure of the Czechoslovak Republic." He asked the new country's citizens to donate their family jewelry and bullion to provide the backing for the new nation's currency. Czechs enthusiastically responded, and by the end of 1924 the central bank had $27.1 million in gold reserves, more than such countries such as Egypt, Greece, and Iran. In the fall of 1938, when the Nazi dismantling of the country started, Czechoslovakia had ninety-five tons of gold.[1]

The new Czech government had already in 1921 established a military alliance with France, which was anxious to have an ally on Germany's southern border. Both countries hoped that accord would keep the German military in check. Czechoslovakia became an industrial power that included the important Škoda industrial complex, one of Europe's leading arms producers. In 1925, France and Czechoslovakia signed a mutual defense treaty promising that if either country were attacked, the other would provide "immediate aid and assistance." The Soviet Union had a similar agreement with Czechoslovakia, although that was contingent on France going to war first. The Czechs invested heavily in their own defense from 1936 to 1938, building a fortification along its border with Germany that became known as the Czech Maginot Line because it matched the formidable defense wall that France had constructed on its eastern border.

Hitler, though, had his own plans for the new nation. He looked to Czechoslovakia's German-speaking minority to help him stir up trouble and provide him with an excuse for military intervention. On March 28, 1938, just two weeks after the annexation of Austria, Hitler, Foreign Minister Ribbentrop, and Rudolf Hess, the Führer's deputy, met with Konrad Heinlein, a schoolteacher and leader of the Sudeten German Party, which Berlin bankrolled. They laid out a strategy for bringing the German-speaking part of Czechoslovakia into the Reich. The basic plan was for Berlin to make ever-greater demands on the Prague government, which it could not fulfill without giving up its own authority over the country. Its supposed non-compliance would then provide the *casus belli* for military action. Just as with Austria, Hitler thought he could accomplish this without provoking a military reaction from Britain or France.

He was right. Initially, London and Paris blamed the Czechs for the political unrest and leaned on the Prague government to find a peaceful settlement with the Nazis. In May, French and British diplomats pressed the Czechs "to go to the utmost limit" to accommodate German demands.

On May 20, General Keitel sent Hitler the Case Green plan for the military takeover of Czechoslovakia that he had ordered up a month earlier. It presented three options. The first was for an attack without warning that would catch the west by surprise. The second was an invasion after months of diplomatic talks. The third was a "lightning action" following an incident such as an anti-German demonstration in Prague that Berlin would instigate. The Führer favored the third option. Propaganda and economic warfare against the smaller country would also play important roles. At a meeting of his top military and diplomatic leaders Hitler bellowed, "It is my unshakable will that Czechoslovakia shall be wiped off the map." He ordered his army to be prepared to launch military action against the country no later than October 2. The opening line of the Case Green document that Hitler signed on May 30 read: "It is my unalterable decision to smash Czechoslovakia by military action in the near future." The new document set the deadline one day earlier, October 1.[2]

Some of Hitler's leading generals had doubts about the Czech operation because of their fear that Britain, France, and even the Soviet Union might move militarily to support Prague. The leader of these dissidents in uniform, just as it had been in the case of Austria, was General Ludwig Beck, the army chief of staff. He told General Walther von Brauchitsch, the army's commander-in-chief, to demand that the Führer stop his reckless military adventures.

Hitler, though, was confident that the western democracies and the Soviet Union would not take up arms to defend Czechoslovakia. On May 14 in London, Prime Minister Neville Chamberlain hosted an "off the record" luncheon for American reporters. He implied clearly that none of the three countries was ready to defend Prague. Although not attributed to Chamberlain, the news soon appeared in New York City papers, and German diplomats forwarded the reports to Berlin. In addition, Sir Nevile Henderson, the British ambassador to Berlin, in early August told a private party in the German capital, "Great Britain would not think of risking even one sailor or airman for Czechoslovakia." That also quickly made its way to German authorities.[3]

With war drumbeats starting to sound, General von Brauchitsch summoned the courage to show Hitler the Beck memo outlining the arguments against military action in Czechoslovakia. The Führer's response was to call a meeting of younger military leaders on August 10 at his Berghof retreat, where he lectured them for nearly three hours on the wisdom of his strategy. Alfred Jodl, the chief of the operations staff of the armed forces high command, wrote in his diary: "Führer becomes furious and flames up."[4] Eight days later, Beck resigned. He was the last general to challenge Hitler until the attempt on the Führer's life on July 20, 1944, in which Beck also played a major role.

The September 1938 Nazi party rally in Nuremberg offered the opportunity to raise German public opinion to a frenzy over the alleged poor treatment of their fellow countrymen living in Czechoslovakia. Göring called the Czechs a "pygmy race" that was oppressing "cultured people." Behind them, he said, was "Moscow and the eternal mask of the Jew devil." Hitler was more cautious, saying that the Czech government had to give "justice" to the Sudeten Germans.[5]

Paris and London then panicked. The day after Hitler's speech, Chamberlain sent a message to Hitler proposing that he come to Germany for consultations about finding "a peaceful solution" to the Czech situation. The Prime Minister, who had never before flown, was now ready to rush to see him. A shocked Hitler said, "I have fallen from heaven."[6]

The British Prime Minister and the Führer met on September 15 at the chancellor's retreat in Berchtesgaden. Hitler, as always, did nearly all the talking, demanding that German-speaking Sudetenland become part of the Reich. He said he "would face war, even a world war, for this." Chamberlain was left speechless and soon proposed splitting Sudetenland off from Czechoslovakia. Chamberlain thought Hitler and he had a confirmed agreement and returned to London to sell the plan to his cabinet and parliament.[7]

On September 22, Chamberlain returned to Germany for a follow-up meeting with Hitler in Bad Godesberg, a small town on the Rhine near Cologne. He expected it would be just a brief encounter to seal the deal on the basis of their previous talk. Hitler, though, had new demands. He wanted to take over the Sudetenland by October 1 at the latest. The Prime Minister left the session shattered, but returned the next evening for a meeting that began at 10:30. Hitler always bullied best late at night, and an exasperated

Chamberlain finally at 1:30 in the morning said he was leaving for London since clearly no agreement was possible. Then in an almost word-for-word repetition of his humiliation of Austrian Chancellor Kurt Schuschnigg only a few months before, Hitler quickly replied, "You are one of the few men for whom I have ever done such a thing. I am prepared to set one single date for the Czech evacuation—October first—if that will facilitate your task." That, of course, had been Hitler's deadline all along. It was no concession. Nonetheless, a relieved Chamberlain left after telling Hitler that they had established a "relationship of confidence."[8]

Meanwhile, a revolt of German generals was gathering force to stop Hitler from invading Czechoslovakia. Top military brass had little respect for the Nazi leader since he was not from their ranks and had only served as a corporal in World War I. They also feared that Britain and France would launch a military offensive for which they thought they were not yet prepared. Officers led by General Franz Halder, Beck's successor as army chief of staff, agreed on a plan to arrest Hitler in order to stop a war over Czechoslovakia. The coup was scheduled to take place two days later on September 29.[9]

Chamberlain spoke to the British people via the BBC at 8:30 P.M. on September 27 and lamented that Europe was preparing for war "because of a quarrel in a faraway country between people of whom we know nothing."[10] He also offered to fly back to Germany for a third time. Two-and-a-half hours later, a conciliatory letter from Hitler arrived. Chamberlain grasped at it like a drowning man reaching for a lifejacket and proposed a four-power meeting in Germany that would include the leaders of Britain, France, Germany, and Italy. Hitler agreed and later sent a message to Chamberlain that no Czech representatives could participate in the conference. The prime minister agreed.

It was during a meeting to coordinate the putsch that Halder received news that Chamberlain, Hitler, and the others had agreed to the summit meeting. The coup of the generals was cancelled, in hopes that a resolution might yet be achieved, and they lost their best chance ever to stop the dictator.

At the Munich meeting Chamberlain and French Premier Édouard Daladier basically caved in to Hitler and Mussolini. Just after 1:00 A.M. on September 30, the four leaders signed an agreement that permitted the German army to march into the Sudetenland the next day, which was exactly Hitler's target date. On his return to London, Chamberlain proudly proclaimed, "I believe it is peace in our time."[11] Winston Churchill was more perceptive when he told the House of Commons, "We have sustained a total, unmitigated defeat." The British public, though, cheered Chamberlain and grasped at peace. Following the Munich meeting, Hitler contemptuously considered Chamberlain and Daladier to be pushovers who would never stand up to him.

When the Führer returned to Berlin, he was met with wild ovation. He was not totally happy, however, because he had been itching to show off his military strength and told his SS entourage, "That fellow [Chamberlain] spoiled my entry into Prague." When Hitler later toured the Czech's Maginot Line, he was stunned by how strong the defenses were and said, "I now understand why my generals urged restraint."[12]

Only a few days after Munich, Hitler sent General Keitel a message asking him how soon Germany could take over the rest of Czechoslovakia. The officer replied he could do it by October 11. Hitler didn't plan to move that fast, but ten days later he received a more detailed plan for "the liquidation of the remainder of Czechoslovakia." In what was now becoming a pattern, German thugs created unrest in the remaining part of the country in late 1938 and early 1939, and on March 15, Hitler browbeat Czech leaders during another middle-of-the-night confrontation in Berlin. Their president fainted in the middle of the harangue. That same day, German troops marched into Slovakia, and a week later, Ribbentrop and Dr. Vojtech Tuka, the new leader of the puppet Czech state, signed the Treaty of Protection that put the country under German control. A secret protocol gave Germany the rights to exploit the Slovak economy.[13]

Despite having picked up the Austrian gold, the Nazis were again short of money to finance Hitler's military adventures. In February

1939, he demanded that the Czech National Bank immediately turn over part of its gold reserve to the Reichsbank. On February 18, Göring sent the urgent message to the German Foreign Ministry: "In view of the increasingly difficult currency position, I must insist most strongly that the 30 to 40 million Reichsmark in gold [from the Czech bank] which are involved come into our possession very shortly; they are urgently required for the execution of important orders of the Führer."[14]

Following the German takeover of the rest of Czechoslovakia, Chamberlain realized that his country, which was virtually unarmed, faced a mortal danger. On March 17, he told his country: "We must all review [our national security] position with that sense of responsibility which it greatly demands. Nothing must be excluded from that review which bears upon the national safety. Every aspect of our national life must be looked at again from that angle."[15]

At the time of the Munich crisis in September 1938, Czechoslovakia's gold reserves totaled ninety-five tons, but the Czech government had moved most of it abroad because of the danger Germany posed. Only a little over six tons were in the country's bank vaults when Nazis troops finally arrived in Prague in March 1939. The rest had been shipped to other European central banks and to the Bank for International Settlements in Basel. An American diplomat in London reported back to Washington that the Germans found that "the cupboard was bare."

As part of the dismemberment of Czechoslovakia, the Germans came up with the creative, but outrageous, argument that the Czechs should pay them in gold for the part of the country Berlin took over under the Munich accord. The rationale was that since the Sudetenland was now part of Germany, the Czechs should give them the gold to back the paper currency that would be circulating in that region. Prague authorities stalled for time, but Berlin kept pressuring to get their hands on the bullion. Berlin sent the Czech government an ultimatum on February 23, 1939, with the threat that the Wehrmacht would invade the country if the bullion were not quickly sent. The Czechs, on March 7, finally caved in. Prague instructed the BIS to send two tons of gold to Berlin and the Swiss National Bank to deliver 12.5 tons of Czech gold.[16]

After all the transactions, the Czech government still had 74 tons left.[17] More than one-third of it was stored in the Bank of England, the traditional location for European bullion storage. Another one-third of its holdings were at the Bank for International Settlements.

The French embassy in Berlin on March 14 tipped off the Czech ambassador in the German capital, that the Nazis were getting ready to take over the Slovak rump state. The French diplomat specifically added that the Germans were anxious to get their hands on all the remaining Czech gold in addition to annexing yet another region of the country. At dawn the next day, German troops crossed the Czechoslovakian border. Accompanying the conquering armies were Dr. Friedrich Müller, a special Reichsbank commissioner, and members of the special commando unit known as *Herresgruppenkommando 3*. When it arrived in Prague, Müller went directly to the headquarters of the Bank of Bohemia and Moravia, the successor of the Czech Central Bank. The soldiers immediately took two bank directors, Peroutka and Malík, into custody. With soldiers pointing pistols at them, Müller demanded that they sign two orders that effectively put the country's remaining gold under German control.[18]

Both the Czech and German central banks had accounts at the Bank for International Settlements that were held at the Bank of England. The first directive ordered the BIS to transfer 23.1 tons of Czech gold to the Reichsbank account. The second one instructed the Bank of England to transfer 26.8 tons of bullion that the Czech Central Bank had in London to the BIS account there. Those two accounts comprised all the remaining Czech gold.[19]

Johan Willem Beyen, the Dutch president of the BIS and manager of day-to-day operations, on March 18 received a telegram with the instructions. According to the bank's normal procedures, such changes in ownership would have been handled on the same day a transfer order arrived, and the bank's rules did not allow officials to refuse a member's instructions. Beyen knew that the Germans had invaded the remaining part of Czechoslovakia, although he was not aware that the gold-transfer orders had been made at gunpoint. He consulted with the institution's legal advisor about the Bank of Bohemia and Moravia order, who told him the bank had to execute the transactions spelled out in the telegram.[20]

Shortly after the message arrived in Basel, Beyen received a phone call from Roger Auboin, the BIS general manager. The Frenchman happened to be in Paris on a routine visit to the Bank of France and told Beyen that Pierre Fournier, the head of the bank, had heard about the telegram instructions and wanted to know how Beyen was going to handle it. The Dutchman replied that he would not execute the transfer if he received, before the end of the day, a message from Fournier requesting that the issue be brought before the BIS board.

Beyen thought he was off the hook, but at 6:00 P.M. he received another call from Auboin, saying that the French and British central banks governors had discussed the matter and did not want to interfere with the order. Montagu Norman felt strongly that it should not be stopped since it was a bank transaction, and the French were not anxious to act unilaterally to block it.[21]

At 6:00 P.M. on March 20, the BIS sent a cable to the Bank of England instructing officials to execute the transfers. The British government would later claim that the Bank of England did not know the ownership of accounts or that they even had the right to know. That was false; they knew. The two transfers changed the ownership of 1,845 bars from the Czechs to the Germans.[22]

The Reichsbank then quickly emptied their account in London. They swapped most of their gold in London with the Dutch and Belgian central banks for bullion stored in those countries. The whole charade was a clever deal. Berlin had outmaneuvered the well-planned Czech strategy to protect the country's gold. By early April it was in Berlin. Wrote BIS historian Gianni Toniolo: "The timing and details of these operations are essential for the understanding of this carefully planned and skillfully executed action by Germany in anticipation of war."[23]

At their next monthly meeting the BIS board members discussed whether Beyen had properly handled the politically delicate Czech gold affair. France's Fournier insisted the transfer should not have taken place, even though he could have stopped it. The Bank of England's Otto Ernst Niemeyer, who was chairman of the BIS board of directors, said that the organization should not "concern [itself] with political questions." Montagu Norman considered it a purely financial transaction that bankers, rather than politicians, should handle.

The Chamberlain government, however, soon faced outrage in Parliament over how it had handled the case. Critics charged that the Bank of England had facilitated the Nazi robbery of Czech gold. Treasury Minister Sir John Simon lamely told Parliament that he had asked the Bank of England not to make any such moves in the future without contacting the government. On March 27, the government passed legislation to impound Czech assets in the country, including gold. By then, though, it was too late.

The story of the Czech gold burst into the minds of the international public on May 19, when the British *Financial News* broke the story about the handling of the Czech gold. The author of the story was Paul Einzig, an editor of the paper. His source of the information was the Czech central bank's Josef Malík, who had escaped from occupied Czechoslovakia and was now a refugee in London. The rest of the press quickly picked up the story, and it became a national scandal. Prime Minister Chamberlain soon faced a whirlwind of rage in Parliament. In an attempt to minimize the issue, he called the whole matter a "mare's nest," insisting incorrectly that the government had not agreed to release Czech gold earmarked in the Bank of England. Government officials also claimed that the Bank of England didn't even know the countries involved in gold transfers. That was a lie.[24]

Churchill used the scandal to attack the government, saying that it was "so butter-fingered that £6 million worth of gold can be transferred to the Nazi government." He added that Hitler "only wishes to use it, and is only using it, as it does all its foreign exchange, for the purpose of increasing its armaments." Montagu Norman came under particularly sharp criticism and was accused of being the dullard who turned Czechoslovakia's national treasure over to the Nazis. The Chamberlain government tried to maintain that, under the Hague Protocol of 1930 and the Brussels Protocol of 1936, the Bank of England had to execute the order from the Prague officials. Norman won few friends with either the public or politicians when he argued that it was "even more important to keep the Bank for International Settlements as a non-political body than to keep £6 million out of Hitler's hands."[25]

Beyen also came under attack for his handling of the Czech gold, and the British press pointed out that he had recently resigned from the BIS to take up a top job in London with the Anglo-Dutch company Unilever, which had important financial interests in Germany. Beyen later argued in his memoirs that the whole thing was the fault of feckless politicians: "It is strange that the blame for the transfer of the Czech gold has been put on the B.I.S. as an institution—or even on me as its President—while it clearly belonged at the doorsteps of appeasing governments of those days."[26]

The United States had not paid much attention to Germany's seizure of the Austrian gold, but after the Munich sellout and Hitler's takeover over the remaining part of Czechoslovakia, Washington became more attentive. On March 21, 1939, Treasury Secretary Morgenthau telephoned Roosevelt and explained what had happened. The president was unhappy, but lightheartedly suggested that his Treasury Secretary should find a "friendly judge" in the New York State Supreme Court to agree to issue an injunction to block any money from being sent to the former Czechoslovakia. The president quipped, "I am a bit of a devil," and Morgenthau replied, "I'll say you are."[27]

Morgenthau had already become concerned about developments in Europe. He was also worried about the role the Bank for International Settlements was playing in sending gold to Berlin. The bank had never been particularly popular in official Washington circles, and its reputation slipped to a new low. The Treasury Secretary now read the daily telegraph reports about European financial markets that the Bank of England sent regularly to the New York Federal Reserve Bank. Ambassador Joseph P. Kennedy also sent critical reports to Washington from London, as did his counterpart William C. Bullitt from Paris.

On July 27, 1939, Harry Dexter White, Morgenthau's key staff member, sent him a four-page memo entitled, "What Happened to the Czech Gold in the Bank of England?" It was mainly a day-by-day account of how the bullion ended up in German hands and made no recommendations about what the U.S. might do at that point.[28]

The day after getting the White report, Morgenthau spoke up strongly during that morning's London-New York phone call when global financial markets were discussed. He said that "no matter who's guilty or not guilty," it was unfortunately "water over the dam." He added that the more important thing was that "the Czechs still have a chance." White jumped into the call to add that the U.S. government, a year before, had decided it didn't "want to deal with BIS" because "we anticipated some possibility of this sort." Morgenthau added, "Well. It's a dirty business whichever way you look at it."[29]

In October 1939, the Bank of Bohemia and Moravia asked the Bank for International Settlements to send to them the remaining gold ingots left in London. Beyen this time refused to execute the order. The Germans, on August 22, then changed the directive and ordered that half of the gold be sent to Holland and half to Switzerland.[30] Beyen believed that since they were both neutral countries, he could not deny the transfers, and so the gold was moved. A little over two tons arrived in those locations on August. The bars remained untouched through most of the war, and at the end of the conflict were returned to the reestablished Czech National Bank.

Dr. Friedrich Müller, who became the head of the Bank of Bohemia and Moravia in Prague, diligently rounded up any remaining gold and shipped it to Berlin. On June 14, 1940, the bank sent to Germany the remaining 6.4 tons of gold in the form of coins of largely historic value. In the fall of the same year, the bank also transferred to the Reichsbank just over a ton of gold that it had been holding for the Skoda Works and Brno Munitions. After that point, no central bank gold was left in the former Czechoslovakia.[31]

Chapter Nine

MUTINY AT THE REICHSBANK

I n 1938, Hjalmar Schacht was proud of the contributions he had
made to Germany's economy and rearmament. In a speech on
November 29, he pointed to his achievements during nearly seven
years in office. He had laid down the economic foundation for
the Third Reich and the mightiest army in Europe. He particularly
cited his program to build up trade surpluses, noting that between
1934 and 1937, imports of finished goods were down sixty-three
percent, and imports of mineral ores, petroleum, grain, and
rubber, all needed for war, were up sharply. Schacht flamboyantly
said, "It is possible that no central bank in peacetime carried on
such a daring credit policy as the Reichsbank since the seizure of
power by National Socialism. With the aid of this credit policy,
Germany created an armament second to none, and this armament in turn made possible the results of our policy."[1]

Hitler never worried about economic issues because he never
understood them. He thought that willpower was all that mattered.
His easy successes in conquering Austria and Czechoslovakia, and
getting large amounts of gold out of them to finance future wars,

had shown him that the western powers would not stand up to him and reinforced his belief that economic nuance was not necessary. While Schacht wanted him to slow down and consolidate, Hitler wanted to conquer more countries before Germany's opponents could catch up with him militarily. Just after the Munich agreement, General Thomas wrote in his diary, "By telephone I receive instructions: all preparations now for war against England, target 1942!"[2] Acting on the Führer's orders, Göring revved up even further his already ambitious armaments program. On October 14, 1938, he told a conference of aircraft manufacturers that Hitler had instructed him to put together an armament program that would make earlier ones look insignificant. Overall military spending would be tripled, and the Luftwaffe budget would increase fivefold. The army would soon have a massive increase in tanks and heavy artillery. Göring put the arms manufacturers on notice that they needed to expand their industrial capacity to meet the new demand.[3]

Schacht's hopes that Hitler could be stopped were crushed when he replaced generals Blomberg and Fritsch in January and February 1938. He would later maintain that was when he "started working for my own retirement." The central banker suspected that the Gestapo was bugging his office, and independent inspectors found listening equipment. The Nazis had put a servant on the payroll to spy on him. Nonetheless, he had an uncontrollable habit of speaking up. While attending a private dinner at the home of a wealthy Swedish banker in Berlin in the summer of 1938, Schacht imprudently and impatiently told his host's wife, "Madam, how could I have known that we have fallen into the hands of criminals."[4]

Recklessly or courageously, he reached out to anti-Hitler opposition. He first contacted Hans Bernd Gisevius, a leader of the small and loosely organized movement. Schacht boastfully told Gisevius, "I have got Hitler by the throat."[5] Schacht had been aware of General Ludwig Beck's aborted coup in September 1938, and also met with two other highly placed Hitler opponents: Admiral Wilhelm

Canaris, the head of German military intelligence service, and Ulrich von Hassell, a top foreign ministry official. At a meeting on September 4, 1938, he told Hassell, "Economically we have pumped ourselves more and more dry: the secret funds, foreign exchange reserves of Austria et cetera have already been used in an irresponsible way." Hassel met him again on December 19, when Schacht said he would stay in power "until the impossible is demanded of me."[6]

Schacht also confided in his close friend Montagu Norman at the monthly meetings at the Bank for International Settlements. He tried to get a message to Prime Minister Chamberlain that he should stand firm against Hitler. But when Norman tried to set up a meeting with Chamberlain, the prime minister dismissed him, saying that he had to deal with Hitler.

In November 1938, Schacht attended a political rally, sitting in the second row facing Hitler. While the rest of the audience cheered the Führer wildly, Schacht sat with this arms folded and coldly stared at him. Hitler noticed the insubordination, but did nothing. The central banker later wrote a twenty-page memo that included strong attacks on both the party and the Führer. When he showed it to a military officer, the person responded, "This is dynamite; one doesn't leave something like this lying around the desk!" Schacht answered, "Let the swine read it and then hang me!"[7]

Schacht traveled to London that same fall to promote his project to let Jews and Nazi opponents immigrate to Madagascar. It was a non-starter from the beginning. During his time in London, he met several times with Norman at the German embassy, but no records were ever made of their conversations. The British banker simply wrote in his diary that he had gone alone to the German embassy to see him.

Christmas was the biggest holiday of the year even in Hitler's Germany, and the Reichsbank held an annual party for the office staff where the president would make a speech thanking people for their work. The 1938 party took place shortly after the infamous *Kristallnacht* of November 9th and 10th, when Nazi mobs attacked

Jews, burned more than 1,000 synagogues, and destroyed some 7,000 businesses. Dr. Joseph Goebbels, the minister of propaganda, selected that date because it was the twentieth anniversary of Germany's surrender to the Allies in World War I, which Hitler considered the country's worst humiliation.

At the Reichsbank's holiday party, Schacht called the anti-Semitic violence "a wonton and outrageous undertaking as to make every decent German blush for shame." Then he added, "I hope none among you had any share in these goings-on. If any one of you did take part, I advise you to get out of the Reichsbank as quickly as possible. We have no room in the Reichsbank for people who do not respect the life, the property, and the convictions of others." Several Nazi members on the bank staff were present, and Hitler soon learned of his central banker's attack on *Kristallnacht*.[8]

Schacht was now clearly searching for an exit from the Reichsbank job that he loved so much. His protégé Emil Puhl said later that by the end of 1938, the bank president was looking for a way to get fired. The weakening German economy was not just an excuse, though numbers were indeed bad. Reichsbank debt had gone from 750 million Reichsmark in 1932 to 14 billion at the end of 1938. During that same period the Nazi government had spent 35 billion on armaments. The weakness of Schacht's strategy was that to the person on the street or even to many foreign observers, the Nazi economy outwardly appeared to be doing well.

Finance Minister Lutz von Krosigk, the man who paid the government's bills, had warned Hitler in a memo on September 1, 1938, that the country was "steering towards financial crisis." Starting on April 1, 1939, the state would have to begin repaying the money investors for the Mefo bills that had financed Nazi rearmament. Lutz von Krosigk asked Schacht to tide over his ministry with 100 to 200 million Reichsmark ($40 to $80 million) because he could not pay government salaries in early 1939. Schacht responded to the minister that he considered the request "monstrous," insisting that the state had to pay its bills. The Reichsbank would not bail out the government. He added that the best thing that could happen for Germany would be a bankruptcy so that the country would see that its failed financial system could not continue. He told Lutz von Krosigk that he wanted it made clear to Hitler that the Reich was bankrupt.[9]

When Schacht told the finance minister that he was ready to resign or be fired, Lutz von Krosigk replied that he would follow him. That was fine rhetoric, but the reality was different. At the end of November 1938, the Nazi government could not raise 1.5 billion Reichsmark in the private equity market because one-third of the bonds went unsold. The country was also running out of foreign exchange and was having trouble paying for vital imports, including food. The government even had to borrow money from the state-run post office and railroad to make ends meet. Nazi Germany was on the brink of financial collapse.[10] Economics Minister Walther Funk, the former reporter, heard of Schacht's critical comments and passed the news along to the Führer. At that point it appears that Hitler had had enough of his central banker. An aide contacted Schacht and told him to make an appointment to see Hitler after the holidays.[11]

The German leader celebrated New Year's Eve 1938 at the Berghof in Berchtesgaden with his mistress Eva Braun and friends. The evening was full of levity, and he wore a tuxedo. Hitler, though, was morose most of the time, which worried Braun. He was scheduled to meet Schacht at the Berghof on January 2, but wasn't looking forward to the encounter. Hitler wanted to keep the banker as a showpiece to give the Nazi regime legitimacy, but that looked increasingly unlikely.

The post-New Year's conference was all business. Schacht spelled out in detail Germany's economic situation, painting a bleak picture and warning that the country could go into a new hyperinflation similar to the one it had known in 1923. Germany, the banker said, was simply spending too much money on weapons, and there was no sign that it would end. In fact, military expenditures were slated to double in the new year. Schacht explained that the country had now reached full employment, and new war spending would likely lead to inflation.[12]

The central banker also pointed out that the government had not been able to raise the first installment of the so-called Jewish Atonement Tax, which was supposed to bring in 1 billion Reichsmark in new revenue. This tax had been levied on the country's Hebrew community in retaliation for a Polish Jew's assassination of a German diplomat in Paris. Hitler then jumped in to say that he had a plan for that. The Reichsbank should simply issue banknotes against the unpaid amount of the Jewish Atonement Tax. It would be a variation of the Mefo bills. Schacht later wrote, "A cold shiver went down my spine." He later wrote, "The danger of inflation was now definitely imminent." He realized that the time had come to disassociate both himself and the bank from what he called "Hitler and his methods."[13]

With the confrontational meeting drawing to an end, Schacht said that he and his fellow Reichsbank board members would soon present the Führer with a memorandum outlining in detail the country's financial situation.[14]

Despite his dominating personality and international reputation, Schacht ran the Reichsbank board more as the *primus inter pares* than as a dictator. The board, which was made up of some of the country's leading bankers and economists, was a mixture of veterans as well as younger officials such as Emil Puhl and Karl Blessing. Puhl really ran the central bank for most of the war. If Count Claus Graf von Stauffenberg's assassination attempt in July 1944 had been successful, Blessing would have become Reichsbank president or minister of economics in a post-Hitler government. He headed the German Bundesbank, the successor organization, from 1958 to 1969.

Board members for months had been discussing the danger of inflation, and three months earlier two of them had drafted a memo outlining their opposition to more inflationary defense spending. Schacht agreed in principle, but was waiting for the right moment to present it. When he returned to Berlin from the Berghof, he told the board that the time had come. All they had to do was agree on a few final points and send Hitler the memorandum. The bank board realized that they were sending a political document, although it was based on solid economic facts and reasoning.

After returning to Berlin, Schacht also played host to Montagu Norman, who had come to the German capital to participate in the christening of Schacht's new grandson, Norman Hjalmar. At the previous month's BIS meetings in Basel, Schacht had warned his colleagues that he and some of his fellow Reichsbank board members might be resigning. Schacht would certainly have told his British counterpart that a showdown with Hitler was coming.[15]

Just before the two men left Berlin by train on January 7 to attend the next meeting in Basel, Schacht sent Hitler a seven-page board report outlining the case against more defense spending. The most direct passage stated: "The reckless expenditure of the Reich represents a most serious threat to the currency. The tremendous increase in such expenditure foils every attempt to draw up a regular budget; it is driving the finances of the country to the brink of a run despite a great tightening of the tax screw, and by the same token it undermines the Reichsbank and currency."[16]

The bankers tried to balance that attack with some praise for the country's successful foreign policy and noted that the Reichsbank had "gladly cooperated" with the national rearmament. That was probably a Schacht touch since he knew how to flatter Hitler.

The report stated flatly that the bank simply could not continue on that path because "the gold or foreign exchange reserves of the Reichsbank no longer exist." What had been stolen from Austria and Czechoslovakia was largely already gone, while government printing presses were working overtime. The German money supply grew nearly three-fold between January 1933 and the end of 1938. The country, the board argued, was on the cusp of major inflation.

The memorandum ended with a surprisingly personal attack on Hitler, stating, "The Führer and Reichskanzler himself has considered the inflation danger again and again to be dumb and useless."[17] No one in the Nazi government had ever dared address him in that manner.

As a sign of solidarity, all eight board members signed the document, with Schacht's name leading the list. The board stood as one. After learning of the content of the memo during a phone call from Berlin, Hitler bellowed: "This is mutiny!" Nonetheless, the Führer coolly waited a few days before taking any action. He probably wanted to gain a better understanding of the situation on the ground at the bank, or he may have been trying to decide if he could finally cut ties with the still prestigious Schacht. In either case, it was an unusual delay from someone who usually acted spontaneously when confronted.

For more than a week, the Reichsbank directors heard nothing. Finally on the evening of January 19, Schacht returned home late from the opera to find several telegrams instructing him to be at the Chancellery the following morning at 9:00. That was an unusually early meeting for Hitler, who normally talked into the night and then got up late. That morning, Schacht received a phone call telling him that the meeting had been put off to 9:15.[18]

Schacht was punctual and had just entered a waiting room at the Chancellery, which overlooked a garden. Hitler entered and without any pleasantries immediately said, "I sent for you, Herr Schacht, to hand you the written notice of dismissal from the office of president of the Reichsbank." The Führer handed him the document and said, "You don't fit in the general National Socialist scheme of things." Hitler then berated him for not putting party members into key positions at the bank, adding that the financial institution was not sufficiently Nazi.[19]

Schacht did not immediately respond, and there was a moment of uneasy silence. Then Hitler continued, "You have refused to allow your staff to submit to political scrutiny by the party." Another silence. "You have criticized and condemned the events of November 9 [Kristallnacht] to your employees." This time Schacht answered, saying, "Had I known, Mein Führer, that you approved of those events, I might have kept silent."[20]

The central banker wanted to ask Hitler some questions, but the Führer seemed stunned and cut him off by saying, "I'm much too upset to talk to you any more now."[21]

Schacht responded, "I can always come back when you have grown calmer."

Hitler then shot back, "And what you think will happen, Herr Schacht, won't happen. There will be no inflation!"

Schacht calmly replied, "That would be a very good thing, Mein Führer."[22]

Without another word spoken, Hitler and Schacht strolled through two Chancellery rooms, and the now ex-banker then left the building and exited the Nazi regime.[23]

Later that day, Hitler issued an official statement that seemed to have been written to soothe German public opinion in the wake of the financial wizard's departure. It was in the form of a letter to Schacht and started by thanking him for the "services that you have rendered repeatedly to Germany and to me personally." Hitler poured it on thick, adding, "Your name, above all, will always be connected with the first epoch of the national rearmament. I am happy to be able to avail myself of your services for the solution of new tasks in your position as Reich Minister."[24]

That was the first Schacht knew he would continue to be in the cabinet with the honorific title of Minister Without Portfolio. There was never a job behind that title, and he worked in a home office outside the capital.

Treasury Secretary Morgenthau heard that Schacht was out at 9:30 in the morning on the U.S. east coast. He immediately phoned President Roosevelt and told him, "Mr. Hitler fired Dr. Schacht with orders to Nazify the Bank . . . I just thought you would like to know . . . Very bad!" Morgenthau then sent over to the White House the Dow Jones report on the firing.

That same busy day, Hitler named Walther Funk, who had succeeded Schacht as Economics Minister, to also take on the Reichsbank job. In his hiring letter, the new president was given three main tasks: "First, maintenance of the absolute stability of wages and prices, also the value of the Reichsmark; second, opening up the capital market to a larger extent and making it available to private money requirements; third, bringing to a conclusion compatible with the National Socialist principles the reorganization of the Reichsbank."[25]

Hitler fired five other Reichsbank board members shortly after getting rid of Schacht. The only two survivors were Emil Puhl and Max Kretzschmann, both Nazi party members. Puhl soon became managing vice president, and actually ran the bank for the rest of the war. Funk enjoyed the perks of being president of the Reichsbank, but let Puhl run the shop.

Early on in his tenure, Schacht had arrogantly told the Nazi leader, "You need me. And you'll continue to need me for several years. After that, you can shoot me if you want to. But you can't shoot me yet."[26] Hitler wasn't going to shoot him, but he felt he no longer needed this troublesome moneyman. The day after he was fired, Schacht sent a note addressed to "My Work Comrades," telling them that he had been "relieved" of the presidency. He added that the success of the Austrian and Sudetenland occupations reflected the "success of the armaments policy" and ended the message with *"Heil Hitler."*[27]

A few days later, Schacht told Ulrich von Hassell, a diplomat and Hitler opponent, "You have no idea how exuberantly happy I am to be out of all this."[28]

Hitler soon signed a secret law that required the Reichsbank to print any amount of money that he requested. No one in the future was going to deny the Führer the money he wanted for the Wehrmacht. By the end of the war, Germany had nearly ten times more currency in circulation than when Schacht left office. The bonfire had been lit for another disastrous German inflation, which took place at the end of World War II.

Schacht moved out of his official residence in the Reichsbank headquarters to a house he owned in the Charlottenburg section of Berlin. He met later in Basel with Montagu Norman, who told people in London that Schacht was in great personal danger. Concerned that word might get out about his earlier contacts with the opposition, Schacht decided it might be wise to leave the country and asked Hitler if he could visit East Asia, China, and Japan. The

Führer agreed, but Foreign Minister Ribbentrop only permitted him to go to India, probably out of fear that he might defect to the Allies. The trip lasted from March to August of 1939.

With the Schacht distraction now gone, Hitler's attention quickly turned to his next target. On April 3, 1939, he issued a directive for war preparations to begin on *Fall Weiss* (Case White), the code name for the invasion of Poland. First, however, Hitler wanted to eliminate the danger of fighting a two-front war against Britain and France in the west as well as the Soviet Union in the east.[29]

Chapter Ten

POLAND'S LONG ODYSSEY

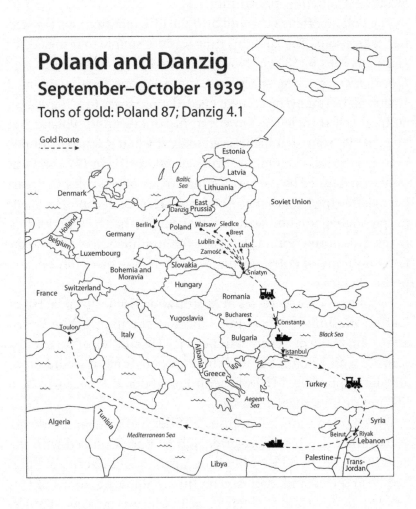

O n May 23, 1939, Hitler met again with top military leaders in his study at the Chancellery in Berlin. It was almost a repetition of the strategy session held in the same room on November 5, 1937, when he laid out plans for the takeover of Austria and Czechoslovakia. His target this time: Poland. Fourteen German military officers listened to his plan to wipe the country literally off the map of Europe. Lieutenant Colonel Rudolf Schmidt, the Führer's adjutant on duty, took notes. Hitler concluded his long diatribe by saying, "We are left with the decision: to attack Poland at the first suitable opportunity.[1]

The Poland offensive would be quite different from his two earlier aggressions. The goal this time was not simply to bring ethnic Germans into his Reich. Now he wanted more blatantly to find *Lebensraum*, or living space, in Eastern Europe for the enlarged *Vaterland*. Germany, he argued, needed more space to achieve agricultural self-sufficiency. Moreover, in Hitler's mind, Poland was an artificial state that had ceased to exist when it was partitioned between the Russian Empire, Prussia, and Austria in 1772 and was only reestablished by the anti-German treaty of Versailles 123 years later. Following Hitler's thesis of the master race, the inferior Slavic people should be eliminated, and their land settled by superior Germans. This meant nothing less than the annihilation of thousands, if not millions, of Poles, starting with their religious, cultural, and political elites.

Despite his easy successes in Austria and Czechoslovakia, Hitler had no illusions. "We cannot expect a repetition of the Czech affair," and added, "There will be war." He still hoped to avoid a conflict with Britain, but told those gathered that it would probably be impossible. "The war with England and France will be a life-and-death struggle," he said.

The German arms buildup since Hitler had come to power six years earlier had been staggering and had been funded with the help of the nearly $150 million in Austrian and Czech gold that had been seized and by the secret financial machinations of Hitler's economic wizard Hjalmar Schacht, who was now out of office.

When the Nazis took power in January 1933, the German army had only six divisions, three infantry, and three cavalry, but now it had fifty-one, including four motorized and four tank units. In 1933, Germany had a skeleton air force. Now it had twenty-one air squadrons and 7,000 first-line planes. Moreover, Göring's Luftwaffe during the Spanish Civil War had developed new techniques of air warfare and gained valuable combat experience. In 1933 the Reich's navy had one heavy cruiser and six light ones. By 1939, it had four battleships, one aircraft carrier, six cruisers, twenty-two destroyers, and fifty-four submarines. It also had 6,000 tanks, and 1.25 million men in arms. Hitler was ready to throw all that military might at Poland.[2]

Before attacking Poland, Hitler first wanted to eliminate the possibility that the Soviet Union would enter the war. Only four days after the Munich agreement, Werner von Tippelskirch, the German counselor in Moscow, sent a cable to Berlin, saying that as a result of the agreement the communist country was likely to "reconsider its foreign policy," becoming less favorable to the western democracies and "more positive" toward Germany. Hitler, who had previously engaged in verbal warfare against the Soviet Union, stopped haranguing Moscow. German diplomats in Moscow were also instructed to make overtures about possible economic agreements.

Joseph Stalin was also looking for a way to avoid war with Berlin, realizing that his country was still weak following the Russian Revolution and the economic chaos resulting from the introduction of communism. After Munich, Stalin doubted that the western countries would ever have the backbone to stop Hitler and was anxious to make his own deal with the German leader. Stalin realized that his Jewish foreign minister, Maxim Litvinov, a revolutionary veteran and colleague of Lenin, would have to go if there were to be a deal. So on May 3, 1939, Stalin replaced him with Vyacheslav Molotov, a faithful, and non-Jewish, party hack. In early May, the French ambassador in Berlin sent a cable warning the French government that the Soviets were seeking an "understanding" with Germany. One of Molotov's first moves was to meet with the German ambassador in Moscow to reinvigorate discussion of a long-delayed economic treaty.[3]

Britain's Neville Chamberlain had resisted pressure from within his own Conservative party to form an anti-German coalition, but finally in late May a British and French delegation left for Moscow to open talks on a military agreement to oppose Hitler. The group, though, was in no mood for quick action and arrived in the Soviet capital after a long sea voyage. Two weeks later, talks were going nowhere fast. The Soviet Union's deceptive diplomacy was to deal simultaneously with the French and British as well as with the Germans, although neither side knew that.

Negotiations for a trade agreement between Berlin and Moscow began in July, the same month that German Foreign Minister Joachim von Ribbentrop instructed one of his top diplomats to take two Soviet diplomats to a ritzy Berlin restaurant and propose a major improvement in relations. During the meal the German official told them that any such deal would be dead if the Soviets made an agreement with London and Paris. Outside of that, the German insisted that there were no outstanding issues between the two countries from the Baltic Sea to the Black Sea.

Following that diplomatic icebreaker, Germany quietly and quickly stepped up its game. On August 3, Ribbentrop dispatched a message to his ambassador in Moscow, who was due to see Molotov the next day. Ribbentrop instructed the ambassador to tell the foreign minister that Germany was interested in "concrete talks" about remolding German-Soviet relations. On the evening of August 14, the German foreign minister sent the ambassador another message with instructions that it should be read to Molotov. The cable stated: "There exist no real conflicts of interests between Germany and Russia . . . I am prepared to make a short visit to Moscow in the name of the Führer to lay the foundation for a final settlement of German-Russian relations." The next day, Molotov played it coy, implying he was not interested in rushing to an agreement.

Nonetheless, he asked casually if the Germans might be interested in a non-aggression treaty. The German ambassador had no instructions about that and gave only a vague reply.

On August 25, Walther Funk sent a memo to the Führer saying, "I have in a wholly inconspicuous manner converted into gold all assets of the Reichsbank and of the German economy abroad on which we could possibly lay our hands."[4]

At the time, Hitler was meeting with his generals at his mountain retreat in Bavaria to work out final details for a Polish invasion. It was now due to start on August 26. The Russians finally replied to Ribbentrop on August 19, saying that he could come to Moscow on August 26 or 27. For the Germans, however, that was too late, so they pressed for an earlier meeting. Hitler sent a personal message to Stalin asking if Ribbentrop could arrive on August 22 or "at the latest on Wednesday, August 23." Stalin replied that that Ribbentrop could come on the latter date.[5]

The German foreign minister arrived on schedule, and that same day the Germans and Soviets signed a non-aggression treaty. The most important part of it was a secret protocol that set out Europe's new borders after the dismantling of Poland. The Soviets got Finland, Estonia, Latvia, part of Romania, and eastern Poland. The Germans took western Poland and Lithuania. The accord was later amended so that the Soviet Union took possession of Lithuania in exchange for giving up more Polish territory to Germany. On the afternoon of August 25 and after learning of the Moscow agreement, Hitler delayed the day of attack on Poland to September 1.[6]

The world was stunned by the news of an accord between the two countries that historically had never had anything good to say about each other. Two days after learning of the non-aggression treaty, the British hurriedly signed a mutual-assistance treaty with Poland. The French already had in place a 1921 agreement to defend Poland, but no one knew how, of even if, they would honor it. Hitler was briefly concerned, and German units were temporarily halted in their war preparations.

On August 31, however, Hitler issued Directive No. 1. The attack was to start September 1 at 4:45 A.M. The time in the typed document was written by hand and with a red pencil.[7]

Propaganda Minister Joseph Goebbels quickly orchestrated a charade of Poland's supposedly outrageous offenses to justify a Nazi invasion. Already on August 11, he had sent an order to newspaper editors that their front page every day had to contain "news and comments on Polish offenses against ethnic Germans and all kinds of incidents showing the Poles' hatred of everything German." Heinrich Himmler, the head of the *Schutzstaffel* Nazi protection squadron, had some of his men dress up in stolen Polish uniforms and attack a radio station in Gleiwitz in Upper Silesia near the Polish border. Nazi concentration camp inmates wearing Polish uniforms were shot and left at the radio tower as proof of the attack. Journalists were taken to the site and shown the alleged victims.[8]

With political tensions mounting, British and French leaders urged the Poles not to make any provocative moves lest they give the Germans an excuse to invade. That only delayed Polish military preparations, and the country was poorly prepared for what hit it on September 1.

Britain and France were obliged by their treaties to wage war immediately upon a German invasion. The two countries again tried to stop a conflict with a flurry of diplomatic cables just as they had during the Austrian and Czech crises. The Italians attempted anew to play the role of mediator, but Hitler was determined this time to have his war and turned back all peace efforts.

The German invasion was a masterpiece of the new type of warfare that combined airplanes, tanks, infantry, and artillery units. Journalists around the world adopted the German term for the strategy, calling it *Blitzkrieg* or lightning warfare. Germany's Luftwaffe quickly controlled the skies, while its ground army launched a major offensive in the north across the Danzig Corridor toward the German enclave of East Prussia as well as a second one toward Warsaw.

The Polish army opposing the new German army was built around the proud cavalry that had waged a victorious war against the Soviet Union in 1919-1920. It had sliced through enemy lines and inflicted heavy damage. Marshal Józef Piłsudski, the Polish commander in that war, was one of the country's greatest strategists. He had died in 1935, and Poland never again had his equal. From 1926 to 1939, a group of military officers known as the Piłsudski Colonels dominated Polish political and military life. When war dangers mounted, Warsaw began spending heavily on the military, but Poles on horses were no match for Germans in tanks in this new era of modern warfare.

After two days of futile diplomacy, the British set a final deadline, demanding that the Germans stop the invasion by 8:00 A.M. Sunday morning, September 3. It was a beautiful day in Berlin. William Shirer, the CBS News reporter in the city, wrote in his diary, "It was the sort of day the Berliner loves to spend in the woods or on the lakes nearby." With no signs of a German pullback, Prime Minister Chamberlain finally went on the BBC at 11:15 A.M. and announced, "The country is at war with Germany."[9] France declared war that afternoon. Neither country, though, backed up its diplomatic moves with military action. Some German generals had been concerned that the French would attack their poorly guarded western border. They need not have worried. Shirer also wrote further, "In 1914, I believe, the excitement in Berlin on the first day of the World War was tremendous. Today no excitement, no hurrahs, no cheering, no throwing of flowers, no war fever, no war hysteria."

While war dangers were growing ever stronger in the late 1930s, Polish officials squabbled about how to handle the country's gold holdings. Some military officials claimed it no longer served its traditional role as the backing for the national currency and that it should be used to buy war materiel. At the end of 1937, military authorities demanded that part of the country's bullion be recognized as a national treasure and remain within the borders of the country. Zygmunt Karpiński, the governor of Narodowy Bank Polski, the Polish national bank, argued that as a precaution, given the country's precarious spot between an increasingly aggressive Germany and the equally ideologically persistent Soviet Union the country's gold should be shipped abroad. In June and July 1939, the Polish Central Bank sent about half of the country's gold from Warsaw to regional bank offices in Brest, Lublin, Siedlce, Zamość, and also to the military fortress in Brest. The minister of finance, though, until mid-August opposed shipping it outside the country. The Poles eventually sent some to the Swedish Central Bank, which exchanged it for Swedish gold in London. So part of the Polish nest egg was at least now in Britain. The Polish Treasury advocated sending more bullion to Britain, Switzerland, and the U.S., but no new or further action was taken.

In August 1939, just before the German invasion, the Polish Central Bank owned 87 tons of gold. Of that just over three-quarters was located in the country. $36.4 million was at the central bank headquarters in Warsaw, and the rest was in regional locations: Siedlce $15.1 million; Brest, $7.6 million; $5.7 million in Zamość; and $3.8 million in Lublin. Abroad it had $4.8 million at the Bank of France, $12.1 million with the Bank of England, $2.2 million at the U.S. Federal Reserve, and a small amount at the Société de Banque Suisse.[10]

The Free City of Danzig on the Baltic, a product of the World War I peace settlement, was a city-state independent of either Poland or Germany, although it was contiguous with both. It consisted of the city of Danzig plus 200 surrounding villages and also had its own central bank. Beginning in 1934, the Bank of Danzig started shipping its gold to the Reichsbank in Berlin. On September 4, 1939, its account was closed, and the four tons of bullion was added to the Reichsbank's holdings.[11]

The declared German gold holdings looked as if they were very low, but in reality were still holding strong enough, thanks to the stolen Austrian and Czech bullion. On September 1, 1939, Germany had declared reserves of 28.6 tons but hidden gold of 82.7 tons. In addition, it had 12.1 tons in regional German banks, 99 tons of Austrian gold, and 43.3 tons of Czech bullion. The total came to a comfortable 265.7 tons.[12]

The first two days after the war broke out, Polish central bank officials were confident that the nation's army would stop, or at least slow, the invading German forces. The distance between Berlin and Warsaw was more than three hundred miles. Nonetheless, the Polish government on September 3, decided to send 13.5 tons of gold east one hundred miles to an ancient military fortress in the city of Brest. At the same time, the bank's staff also began packing up the rest of the Warsaw gold plus other valuables so that they could be moved quickly. Blaring air-raid alarms often interrupted the work, and staff members had to scramble to take refuge in the bank's main vault.

At 11:00 P.M. on September 3, the first five shipments left the central bank's office for Brest in buses that belonged to the State Printing office. With the war deteriorating for Poland by the hour, bank officials ordered that 15.1 tons located in its branch office in Siedlce, the largest concentration outside Warsaw, also be shipped to Brest. That same night, Treasury Minister Stanisław Sadkowski instructed the bankers to prepare to send all the gold in Warsaw to a destination in the east that was still to be determined. Officials quickly finished packing the bullion into wooden crates and then waited for instructions.[13]

On September 5, the Polish government decided to evacuate Warsaw and move to Lublin one hundred miles southeast of the capital. Foreign diplomats followed them out of the capital. The Polish army took control of whatever remained of the country's telegraph and telephones, trains, cars, and gasoline.

That night, the central bank president and four members of the board left Warsaw in automobiles, carrying the last remaining gold. Before departing, bank official Stanisław Orczykowski made a detailed inventory of the gold that had been packed. He ended his memo: "The vault is empty. Not even one bar is left inside."[14]

The treasury ministry that same day, finally ordered the central bank to ship all its valuables in Warsaw to the central bank's branch office in Lublin. Colonel Adam Koc arrived at the Polish bank's headquarters to take over responsibility for the operation. With a bald head and owlish eyes behind rimless glasses, the slender Koc was both a military and a political veteran. Born in 1891 in Suwałki in the Polish part of the Russian Empire, he became politically active while a student at his trade school and a member of a combat-and-rifle club. After graduating from military school in 1912, he joined the fight for Polish independence. His *nom de guerre* was Witold. By 1915, he was a courier in Scandinavia for General Piłsudski. Koc was wounded in September 1916 and taken prisoner, but was released in April 1918 and returned to the Polish military headquarters, where he took on increasingly important military jobs. He served as deputy minister of the Treasury from 1930 to 1936 and was later elected to the Polish Senate in 1938. He was also a board member of Warsaw's Handlowy Bank.[15]

Koc's first stop after receiving his new assignment was to go to Warsaw's Paderewski Park, the capital's large forest area, where ten buses from the Polish National Railway and the Warsaw bus company plus two trucks were waiting. The vehicles, though, badly needed repair, and he immediately ordered Lt. Andrzej Jenicz to take care of the ailing vehicles. Koc next went to the Bank of Poland, where he met with Managing Director Władysław Bryka and director Leon Barański, who showed him that the gold had already been packed and was ready to be shipped.[16]

Koc decided for security reasons to use fifteen buses to transport the gold so that the cargo was less likely to attract attention amid the flood of refugees trying to go south. In addition, it was put in ordinary packing boxes to make it less conspicuous. They were secured with steel bands. A few carefully selected people were chosen to travel in the buses to add to the camouflage. Koc ordered that the buses travel mostly at night without headlights. The destination was Lublin, one hundred miles southeast of the capital.

Warsaw by then was in total chaos, with government officials, diplomats, soldiers, and average citizens all trying to evacuate. Everything moved at a crawl, and Nazi planes frequently strafed the mobs. Ryszard Zolski, a young film director, later wrote: "Most of the people were walking, pushing anything on a wheel or wheels, handcarts or simply prams laden with bundles of clothes, pots and pans, babies and small toddlers."[17]

Although the gold convoy had to travel just one hundred miles, it arrived only the next morning. All the crates were immediately stored in the branch bank's cellar; but the following day the bankers received orders to move again, this time to Lutsk, 130 miles southeast. A few hours after the bankers departed Lublin, German planes bombed the area. Still traveling in buses and cars originally picked up in Warsaw, the convoy again drove through the night. Travel on the treacherous roads was made worse by having to move in darkness. The gold was hidden in forests during the day, and drivers would set off again after dusk. The last stopover was at a village manor. Despite the risk, the convoy of buses and cars arrived safely in Lutsk, and the crates of gold were stored this time in the cellar of the bank office there.[18]

While the central bank treasure was on the road, Koc recruited two other Piłsudski Colonels to help him with his assignment. The first was Henryk Floyar-Rajchman, who was two years younger than Koc but shared the same experience of growing up in the Polish part of the Russian Empire. Born in Warsaw as Henryk Rajchman, he went into the anti-Russian underground while still a youth, where he took the *nom de guerre* Floyar and later added that to his surname. He was a devoted follower of Piłsudski and served during World War I in one of his units. Floyar-Rajchman left the army in 1931 to enter politics and served as Minister of Industry and Trade from 1933 to 1935. While he only attained the rank of major, he was still considered a Piłsudski Colonel.

Koc also asked Ignacy Matuszewski, who was the same age, to join the taskforce. He had studied philosophy at Jagiellonian University in Krakow, the oldest institute of higher education in Poland, as well as studying architecture in Milan. In early World War I, he served in a Russian intelligence unit, but after the Soviet revolution organized a group of Polish fighters in Petrograd who called themselves the Matuszewski Poles. After the Bolsheviks condemned him to death in absentia, he fled to Kiev and eventually joined the new Polish army. While a long-time supporter of Piłsudski, Matuszewski broke with him over economic policy. He left the army in 1927 and from 1929 to 1931 was treasury minister. Matuszewski then edited the daily newspaper *Gazeta Polska* and wrote extensively on political issues, warning of the German threat and advocating increased military spending.

Many central bank officials joined the gold team. Among them were Zygmunt Karpiński, the governor, Stanisław Orczykowski, the chief cashier, and twenty-one other bank employees. The three Piłsudski Colonels, though, directed the operation.

On September 9, Koc arrived in Lutsk from Warsaw to explain his plan for getting the national treasure out of the country. Polish leaders had already decided that the gold's final destination was the French National Bank in Paris, with Romania as an intermediate stop. That was about 150 miles south. The plan was to get the treasure to the Black Sea and then somehow take it to France by ship. Since Koc had just been named minister of treasury, he would have to stay with the government, which was moving frequently around the country as the war situation deteriorated. He appointed Floyar-Rajchman to be responsible for the vehicles, and he discarded useless equipment, stocked up on fuel, and organized the police escorts. Matuszewski was put in charge of protecting the gold after it crossed the border into Romania and getting it safely to France.[19]

Koc instructed bank governor Karpiński to leave the group and travel to Paris as soon as possible to handle matters there. That same day, the Bank of Poland president gave him a document authorizing him "to dispose on his own authority the stocks of gold which are now or will [in the] future be deposited to the account of the Bank of Poland in foreign banks." In his rush to get out of Warsaw, Karpiński hadn't brought along his passport, so he first had to get a new one in Kremenets, fifty miles to the south, where the Polish Foreign Ministry was temporarily housed. By the time he arrived there it was dark, and the town was under a blackout. Nonetheless he and others worked by candlelight in the cellar of the town's castle to send cables to Polish embassies in Bucharest and Paris. The French ambassador Léon Noël, who had also taken temporary refuge in Kremenets, suggested that the gold be sent to

Paris on French warships traveling first through the Black Sea and then to the Mediterranean.

The Polish gold by now was spread out all over the country. The largest amount was in Brest, but there was also some in Lutsk and still more was in Zamość. The new goal was to get all of it to the village of Sniatyn, a Jewish *shtetl* on the border with Romania that was also a rail crossing point between the two countries.

Soldiers and central bank employees poured over maps to determine the best routes to take and set up strict rules for the operation. The buses and trucks would travel only at night since in daylight they would be easy targets for German planes that controlled the skies. Two drivers were assigned to each truck, and they would alternate periods of driving. Vehicles were instructed to travel in a tight formation at the speed of the slowest one. There was plenty of light from the moon that had been full on September 9. The convoy would stop at daybreak and park in a wooded area until it was dark.

The first gold train left Brest. During a stop in Dubno, an ancient town famous for its castle, Polish military officials took seventy crates containing four tons of gold off the train, saying that they needed it for some unknown eventuality such as buying weapons abroad. At about the same time, a train left Zamość also heading to the Polish-Romanian border. The convoy of buses, trucks, and cars left Lutsk under the leadership of Floyar-Rajchman.[20]

On September 11, the fleet of trucks and buses reached a large but very old bridge over the Siret River, the border between Poland and Romania. The load capacity for it was one ton, but the loaded vehicles each weighed about twelve tons. The last thing the leaders wanted to do was to have to pull trucks from the water below. They finally decided to send just three trucks across to test the bridge. It then took them three hours to get all the trucks to the Romanian side.[21] One of the members of the group had a short-wave radio and picked up transmissions among Soviet agents who knew about the gold and were desperately trying to find it. Meanwhile, German planes bombed an area that the Poles had recently passed.[22]

After setting out the overall strategy, Koc on September 11 departed for Romania, arriving there the next day. He went immediately to see the Polish ambassador, who was in talks with Romanian government officials. While the trains, buses, and cars were heading toward the border, the Polish Ministry of Foreign Affairs formally requested that the Romanian government permit the gold to pass travel through its territory and also provide a train to make that happen.

With the Polish high command continuously retreating, the war was worsening by the hour. By September 12, the top military leaders were in Młynów near the Romanian border, and their southern front was on the verge of collapse. In addition, the Poles feared that the Soviet Union would enter the conflict at any moment.

War refugees were overflowing the village of Sniatyn. Fate, though, was for once smiling on the beleaguered Poles. On the evening of September 13, the first gold train arrived in Sniatyn. Two hours later, the one from Zamość pulled into town with more bullion. Later that day, the convoy from Lutsk also arrived. With the exception of the four tons handed over to the military, all of the Polish national treasure was now in the same place ready to move into Romania.

By then, Koc and the Polish ambassador in Bucharest had worked out a deal that allowed the gold to be transported through Romania. A bridge separated the two countries, and the plan was for Polish engineers to drive a train to the other side of the bridge, where Romanians would take it over and transport it to the Romanian-Turkish border. Matuszewski feared that the bridge might have been sabotaged, but finally decided to risk everything and load all 1,208 crates of gold onto the train. The job took four hours, with policemen, railroad workers, soldiers, and bank employees all helping.

At half-past midnight on September 14, the gold train began creeping across the bridge into Romania. There were no glitches, and the cargo immediately departed on an eighteen-hour trip to its next destination: Constanţa, a Romanian port on the Black Sea.

The Germans, however, were still determined to get the gold. The ambassador in Bucharest sent a telegram to Berlin saying that Koc had arrived in the capital and incorrectly reported that he had tried to deposit the gold at its national bank. "The Romanian government gave no permission," the ambassador cabled. The next day, the German Foreign Ministry instructed their ambassador in Bucharest to tell the Romanian government that allowing the Polish gold to pass through the country would be "considered a heavy violation of the neutrality policy." That same day, the Romanian government finally closed its border with Poland. On September 18, the German ambassador sent Berlin a message saying, "The minister of foreign affairs promised me that no further transportations shall be permitted to leave Romanian borders."[23]

When everyone else was settled, Floyar-Rajchman went back to Poland to pick up the four tons of gold that the National Defense Fund had been holding to buy weapons since that looked increasingly unlikely, given the rapid advance of German and Soviet forces. He had to dodge attacks from both German and Soviet troops, who had invaded Poland on September 17 to claim their part of the dismembered country. Just before the Soviets took over Sniatyn, Floyar-Rajchman and his team arrived and picked up the gold. It was impossible to load it onto a train because enemy air attacks had destroyed the local railroad station. So Floyar-Rajchman and his men went to the town of Kuty on the Romanian border, where the Polish army had established its last defensive outpost in the country. He and his team finally slipped fifty-one boxes holding three tons of gold into Romania on two trucks, a bus, and a car, which took it to the Polish embassy in Bucharest. The men and the gold arrived there at 2:00 in the morning of September 24. Romanian troops, though, were waiting for them in the courtyard and seized the gold. The Bucharest government kept it for the rest of the war on the pretext that the proceeds would be spent on the care of the Polish refugees now in the country.

The British had been closely watching the Polish gold saga from a distance in hopes that it could be kept out of German hands. When the Poles asked if Britain could help get their national treasure to France, London sent instructions to its embassy in Bucharest to find a ship large enough to carry the heavy cargo. Few vessels were available, but on the afternoon of September 14, the British vice consul in Constanţa hired the SS *Eocene*, a 4,000-ton tanker that had been transporting oil from Baku on the Caspian Sea to Greece. Socony-Vacuum Oil, the forerunner of Mobil Oil, had chartered it, and the captain was the Englishman Robert E. Brett. Almost immediately, he received two telephone messages. One was from the German ambassador protesting the transportation of the gold through Romania. The second call was a warning about air attacks. At about 10:00 that night, the vice consul instructed Brett to move his ship to a new berth and keep "full steam up," so that he could depart on short notice.[24]

Just after midnight, the train with the Polish gold arrived at the new dock. Since the vessel had no mechanical cranes to move the heavy material, bank employees and local longshoremen started moving the 1,200 cases onto the *Eocene*. The tanker was not designed for carrying such heavy boxes, which had to be stored wherever possible. In addition to the cargo, twenty-seven passengers, including six women and two children, came aboard. Most of them were Poles who had helped bring the gold to Constanţa.

By 7:15 A.M., the cargo was finally loaded; but by then six members of the ship's original Romanian crew had deserted out of fear that the vessel would be attacked.[25] It took several hours to find replacements, and Captain Brett had to pay them hefty bonuses to take on the risky job. Finally just after 4:00 P.M., the *Eocene* pulled up anchor and headed at full speed for Istanbul, Turkey. As he departed, the captain stayed as long as he could in shallow waters so that if a German U-boat attacked, the ship's cargo could still be rescued.

German diplomats in Bucharest were outraged when they learned that the *Eocene* had departed. At 5:30 that afternoon, they sent a cable to Berlin saying, "It has been confirmed from Constanţa that the English tanker *Eocene* sailed in empty on 14 September and then set out towards Istanbul. There were fifty Poles on board and fourteen freight cars, three of which contained the gold."

Without realizing that the Polish gold had already left Romania for Turkey, German Foreign Minister Ribbentrop sent a cable to his ambassador in Bucharest with instructions that it be passed along to the government. The dispatch read: "I draw your attention to the fact that if the Polish gold actually finds itself within Romanian territory, the Romanian government should have it confiscated and secured."[26]

After departing Constanța, Captain Brett sailed south along the coastline toward Istanbul. On September 16 at 3:30 P.M., the *Eocene* dropped anchor in the port of Kabataç in the middle of the Bosphorus, which connects the Black Sea to the Mediterranean Ocean. Directly ahead of the ship was the German embassy, flying a large swastika flag. A German yacht soon began circling the ship, taking pictures from every angle.

No one was sure how the Turkish government would handle the situation. Both sides in the war were leaning on Turkey to join it in the war, so Brett told harbor authorities that the ship was in transit. Fifteen minutes after landing, he contacted the British consul-general in Istanbul and learned that only he would be allowed to leave the ship. The Poles had to remain on board, although local Polish officials could come out to meet them.

With the British now determining the fate of the Polish gold, the first proposal was to transfer the cargo to a British or French warship and take it to either London or Paris. The Turks vetoed that plan. The only other alternative was to send it overland by train across Turkey and the French-controlled Levant, the colonial name for the region of Syria and Lebanon, to Beirut. From there it could be shipped to France.

Two hours after the *Eocene* landed, the Polish consul in Istanbul arrived with the news that the Turkish government had agreed to let the cargo be transported across its territory to Beirut. The consul also suggested that it be deposited temporarily in a local bank. Matuszewski rejected that suggestion. It was staying on board. The consul also passed along a rumor that Germans were attempting to buy a Greek boat so that they could ram into the *Eocene* and sink both the vessel and its cargo.

It took Matuszewski and the others two days to work out all the details. The final issue was payment. The Turks were demanding that the Poles pay the equivalent of $30,000 in Turkish lira before the train could leave the country. They would not accept any other currency or even payment in gold. The Poles were not carrying that kind of money, but the local ambassador's wife suggested asking Archibald V. Walker, the wealthy Middle East representative for Socony-Vacuum, who had that kind of cash on hand. Walker agreed, and the ambassador wrote him out a receipt.[27]

The next afternoon on September 20, the *Eocene* pulled up anchor and moved to Istanbul's majestic Haydarpaşa Terminal, where during the evening the gold was offloaded to a train that consisted of a dining car, two sleeping cars, and nine baggage wagons. Late that evening, the passengers left the ship and boarded the train. Captain Robert Brett then returned to his routine life in Kabataç.

Two days later, the Polish gold train in the evening reached the Syrian border, where a French military unit took over responsibility for it. The trip went smoothly and quickly, until it arrived in Riyak, a no-man's-land between Syria and Lebanon, where the gold had to be unloaded once again to go from a standard to a narrow-gauge train. With that mission accomplished, the new train started up again, traveling through a pine forest that was a pleasant change after the barren Turkish desert. The Poles soon saw the lights of Beirut in the distance. The shipment arrived there on September 23, and went directly to the harbor, where the cruiser *Émile Bertin*, the fastest ship in the French fleet, was waiting to take the gold.[28]

The city and the port were swelteringly hot, which may have been the reason why Matuszewski soon got into an argument with Gabriel Puaux, the French high commissioner for Syria and Lebanon. He wanted all the gold immediately loaded aboard the *Émile Bertin* so that it could depart for France before the German submarines knew what was happening. The vessel, he explained, was the fastest warship in the world and could make a rapid getaway. Its commander, Robert Battet, was ready to leave. Matuszewski disagreed, saying that they should split the cargo into two ship-ments to reduce the risk of losing everything in one sinking.

Rear Admiral M.F.L.F. de Carpentier, the commander of the fleet, agreed with Matuszewski, and it was decided that three-quarters of it would go on the *Émile Bertin*. The rest would follow later. On the evening of September 23, three hundred men loaded 886 crates of Polish gold onto the cruiser. The project took three hours.[29]

French naval regulations did not allow civilians on board a war-ship, but an exception was made so that two Polish central bank employees, Tomasz Kuśnierz and Władysław Bojarski, could accom-pany it on the voyage to France. Bojarski was watching a crane lift crates of gold and lower them into the ship's hold, when a French sailor suddenly shouted to him to get below deck. When he arrived there, he saw that a net carrying several crates had ripped, sending the containers crashing down and breaking open. French sailors stood in stunned silence looking at the gold bars. They had never been told about the ship's new cargo. A French boatswain quickly told the sailors to get to work nailing the boxes back together. Bojarski watched in the miserable heat below deck until the job was completed.

Near midnight on September 23, and with its lights blacked out, the *Émile Bertin* headed out to sea. Its destination: the Toulon naval base on the French Mediterranean coast. The ship left on a zigzag course in order to make it harder for U-boats to attack. With French sailors manning anti-aircraft guns and mid-range artillery, the departure went smoothly. Once the ship was out to sea, the com-manding naval officer in Beirut sent a message to his superior that the Poles had refused to send all the gold on one ship, so eighteen tons still remained there. It would have to come later. West of Malta, the *Émile Bertin* passed two convoys going in the opposite direction.

The two Poles bunked in the cabin normally reserved for Admiral Jean-François Darlan, the commander of the French fleet, and his wife, when they were on board. The guests also ate in the officer's mess and were delighted with the French cuisine and the wines that were served. Commodore Battet, on the other hand, remained on the bridge for the entire voyage, even eating his meals and sleeping there.

The French officers and crew grew nervous when the ship approached the Italian coast near Sicily. Everyone on board worried that German U-boats might be stationed there, but nothing untoward occurred. The *Émile Bertin* reached the French coast at sunrise on September 27. A small scouting plane took off from the deck to make a reconnaissance flight, but immediately went into the sea because the strong morning sun had temporarily blinded the pilot. The ship's crew quickly pulled both the pilot and plane out of the water. In Toulon, Commodore Stanislaw Lasocki, the Polish naval attaché in Paris, welcomed the ship, its passengers, and the gold to France. The ship's cargo was temporarily stored in the base's armory.

On October 2, two French cruisers, *Épervier* and *Vauban*, left Beirut for Toulon under the command of Commodore Chardenot with the remaining 205 crates and 93 bags of Polish gold. A Bank of Poland official was on each ship, which arrived safely in Toulon on October 6.[30]

After all the gold had landed, it was sent by armored train to the Banque de France's regional office in Nevers, three hundred miles northwest of Toulon. On October 18, Zygmunt Karpiński and Stanislaw Orczykowski, two Bank of Poland officials, inspected and counted all the crates and bags of gold at Nevers. The gold was exactly the same amount that had left Sniatyn, Poland on September 13. Only the three tons that Floyar-Rajchman and his men lost to the Romanians at the Polish embassy in Bucharest, were missing.

Pierre-Eugène Fournier, the governor of the Banque de France, offered the Polish bankers two options for storing their gold. It could be handed over as an earmarked account, the popular way central banks held foreign bullion, or he would give vault space at no cost in one of their branches. In the latter case, the Poles would have total responsibility for it. They selected the second option. The Polish government-in-exile sold eight tons of the bullion to the Banque de France in order to obtain money to run this new set of operations.[31]

A total of 70 tons of Polish gold had been shipped out of Warsaw in the early days of September 1939. All but the small amount left in Poland or confiscated in Romania had safely reached France. The long saga of the Polish gold, though, was far from over.

Chapter Eleven

NORTHERN LIGHTS GO OUT

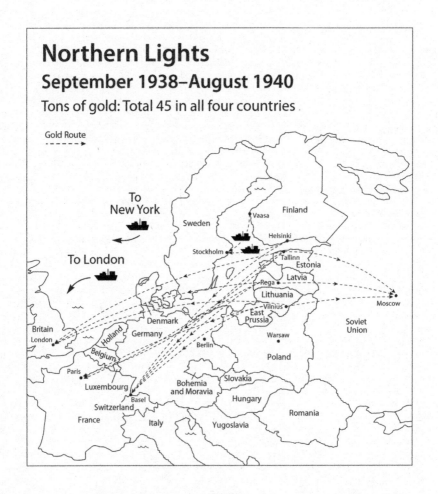

Northern Lights
September 1938–August 1940
Tons of gold: Total 45 in all four countries

A t the end of World War I, several new nations were on the map of northern Europe. Three of them were called the Baltic States, and they were Latvia, Lithuania, and Estonia. The fourth was Finland. None had been independent prior to the war. The Russian Empire had ruled Latvia for nearly two centuries. Lithuania had been incorporated into either Poland or Russia. Estonia had been part of Denmark and Sweden. Finland had been part of the Kingdom of Sweden from the thirteenth century to 1809, and then most of the Finns became citizens of an autonomous part of the Russian Empire. The czar then ruled the area as its Grand Duke.

The small states had received their independence thanks to Woodrow Wilson's policy of promoting ethnic self-determination. As part of establishing their new nationhood, these four set out to establish or strengthen their central banks. The new Soviet government helped the Baltic states get started, and in early 1920 sent them 31.5 tons of the remaining Russian imperial gold. Estonia received just over eleven tons, and Latvia and Lithuania received slightly less. Finland's Central Bank already existed, and dated back to 1812. With the European political situation growing worse in the 1930s, all four countries tried to protect their gold by moving it to France, Britain, Sweden, and the U.S. as well to the Bank for International Settlements.[1]

No sooner had Germany and the Soviet Union crushed Poland in September 1939 than the Germans and the Soviets quickly moved in to redraw the map of northern Europe and grab back land that had once been theirs. Article One of the secret protocol of the Ribbentrop-Molotov Treaty of August 1939 divided the area into Nazi and Soviet spheres of influence and allowed for future "territorial and political rearrangements." Estonia, Latvia, and Finland plus eastern Poland basically went to the Soviet Union, while Germany took western Poland and Lithuania. Stalin and Ribbentrop sealed the deal on the new political boundaries of northern Europe by autographing a map that showed the new borders and their respective spheres of influence.[2]

The dismantling of Poland in September along the lines of the Molotov-Ribbentrop Treaty, though, did not go exactly according to plan. The Nazis had seized area around Lublin, Poland that was supposed to be in the Soviet zone, while the Soviets had captured Vilnius, Lithuania, which was to go to Germany. In late September, Stalin suggested that the two countries have another look at the zones of influence. The second secret accord put Lithuania into the Soviet sphere and gave the Germans more of Poland.[3]

The Soviets now quickly moved to consolidate their gains in the four nations in their sphere. Stalin was not enthusiastic about bringing the small countries into the ethnic hodgepodge that was already straining his country's national unity, but he still wanted to make sure that his militarily weak neighbors were firmly under Moscow's control. He may also already have been thinking about an ultimate conflict between Nazi Germany and the Soviet Union, and saw the small countries as a buffer zone for his young communist nation.

In late September and early October 1939, the Soviets demanded that all the Baltic States agree to mutual assistance pacts that gave Moscow the right to establish military bases in those countries. Estonia complied first on September 28; Latvia came next on October 5, and Lithuania agreed only after heavy pressure on October 10. The Soviet Union by then already had thousands of troops in each country.[4]

That, however, was not enough for Moscow. In June 1940, while the world was fixated on German victories over Holland, Luxembourg, Belgium, and France, Stalin brought the Baltic countries totally under his control. On June 15, Soviet forces invaded Lithuania, and the following day they entered Estonia and Latvia. Only the Estonians put up any defense against the overwhelming Soviet might. In mid-July elections were held for the People's Parliaments in all three nations. Results were announced twenty-four hours before the polls even closed. The new legislative bodies met and voted on only one issue: to request becoming republics within the Soviet Union. They naturally passed the legislation, and the next month the Supreme Soviet accepted their applications.[5] The Council of the People's Commissar of the U.S.S.R. passed a resolution instructing the three central Baltic banks to liquidate on June 15 and to send all their precious metals and stones plus securities to Gosbank, the Soviet state bank.[6]

During three days in the middle of July, the central banks of the three Baltic States sent out to several central banks around the world and also to the Bank for International Settlements instructions to send all the gold that had been deposited in those institutions to Gosbank. The cable to the Federal Reserve Bank in New York from the Latvian Central Bank in Riga was dated Monday, July 14, and read in telegram style: "Close our account transfer balance account state bank U.S.S.R. Moscow with you. Under cable advise Moscow and us. Likewise transfer account State Bank U.S.S.R. Moscow with you any amounts received our account subsequently."[7] The Latvian bank at the time had only 4.4 tons of gold at the New York Fed. The central banks of Lithuania and Estonia sent similar cables with the same wording and instructions.

When the messages arrived, officials at the New York Fed Reserve were reluctant to make the transfers and quickly turned the highly sensitive issue over to the Treasury Department. Bernard Bernstein, the key staff person dealing with monetary and legal issues, took over the issue. He had been watching the situation in Europe closely because it hit him close to home. His parents were both Russian immigrants, and he was one of the many young men who had idealistically gone to work for Roosevelt's New Deal. One admirer described him as looking like a football quarterback. His parents had escaped their native country's virulent anti-Semitism, which he learned about at an early age and which left him with a deep respect for their religion. Accounts of *Kristallnacht* and other Nazi atrocities against Jews in Germany touched Bernstein personally and poignantly. Nevertheless, he was able to write dispassionately about what he called, in one memo, the *Götterdämmerung*, which he was witnessing as Allied armies marched across Europe.

Bernstein took the problem of the Baltic gold to Morgenthau, who bumped it over to the White House. On Monday, July 15,

President Roosevelt used a presidential power dating back to 1917 to block the transfer of Latvian, Estonian, and Lithuanian gold to Moscow.[8] The Federal Reserve two days later informed Moscow of that action.[9]

The amount of gold the Soviets seized in the Baltic States upon annexation was relatively small since by then the countries had sent most of their bullion abroad. They all had some in London and in Sweden. Lithuania had its mainly in France and the U.S, while Latvia had its largely in Britain, and Estonia had it spread out to Britain, Sweden, and the U.S. They all also had small amounts with the Bank for International Settlements. The stock remaining at the Latvian Central Bank, for example, was just 1.6 tons. The amount at the Lithuanian bank was equally small. Some of the countries used the gold stored in the U.S. during the war and even afterward to pay for their diplomatic offices there.

The French Central Bank soon received a message also asking that the gold be sent to the Soviet Central Bank. By that time, however, the gold from the two countries had already gone to Senegal along with the French, Belgian, and Polish bullion.[10]

The Bank for International Settlements also received cables from the three Baltic banks with virtually the same wording asking that their gold be sent to Moscow. President Thomas McKittrick was suspicious when he received the messages and asked a Swiss legal expert to provide him an opinion on whether he was obligated to follow Moscow's instructions. The expert view was that he didn't need to make the payments, and McKittrick informed his board members.[11]

In July 1940, the Bank of England sequestered the Baltic gold reserves deposited in the U.K., but Barclays Bank in Britain confirmed in a cable to the Latvian bank that it had transferred $190,864.38, minus 3.25% for expenses, to the State Bank of the U.S.S.R. The Swedish State Bank also sent Moscow small amounts that it was holding for the Baltic States.[12]

There was no way for the foreigners to know the situation that existed in those countries, but the similar wording indicated that the requests were done under duress. Under the treaties that made them part of the Soviet Union, the countries gave Moscow the right to buy their gold and whatever the three countries held abroad.[13]

The Nazis initially supported the Soviet claims for the Baltic gold, but after their invasion of the Soviet Union, Berlin sent a cable to the New York Federal Reserve requesting cancellation of the earlier order to ship the bullion to Moscow. By then, though, it was too late. The Soviet Union had successfully seized a small chunk of what the Baltic states had once hoped would protect their independence.[14]

Foreign central banks generally continued to keep the gold the Baltic states had put in their charge. Come the early 1990s and the breakup of the Soviet Union, France and Britain sent 5.1 tons of gold back to Lithuania, and the Bank for International Settlements sent bullion to the Bank of Lithuania account at the Bank of England. Latvia received eight tons, and Estonia also got a small amount. Russia, though, did not return any to the newly independent countries, arguing that they had assumed all their debts.[15]

The Soviet cruiser *Kirov* was due to pick up 3.1 tons from the Estonian Bank gold stocks between August 22-28, 1941, but by then the German invasion of the Soviet Union was well underway.[16]

Soviet troops retreated from the Estonian capital Tallinn on the morning of August 27, when the Nazis overran the city. A flotilla of 225 ships steamed out of the harbor. Nazi mines and torpedoes plus Luftwaffe attacks destroyed more than sixty ships. Luckily, the Estonian Soviet government and their gold left on the *Kirov* and reached the port of Kronstadt near Leningrad. The bullion was sent first to Moscow and then further east.

As a newly independent country following World War I, Finland tried to build up its gold stocks. About one-third of its international reserves was in bullion, while the rest was in foreign currencies. In the summer of 1939, the Bank of Finland held eighteen tons of bullion at the Bank of Finland in Helsinki and at one of its regional offices. After the German invasion of Poland, however, it began moving gold abroad, first to Sweden and then to more distant locations. At the start of the Winter War in November 1939, the bank had 4.5 tons at the Bank of England, 18.1 tons at the Swedish National Bank, 1.3 tons at the Federal Reserve in New York, and 0.7 tons at the Bank for International Settlements.[17]

Despite the German-Soviet alliance, Moscow was nervous about Nazi intentions and wanted to enlarge its buffer with Germany even beyond the Baltic states. Stalin first tried to convince Helsinki through negotiation to surrender to it the province of Karelia, which lies between the Gulf of Finland and Lake Ladoga. That was an important piece of territory for the defense of Leningrad, since artillery fire from Finland could hit that city. After talks failed, Stalin decided to invade, expecting that the war would be a walk in the park. Nikita Khrushchev, who then administered Ukraine, was involved in the war planning and shared the optimism. As he wrote in his memoir, "All we had to do was raise our voices a little bit, and the Finns would obey."[18] On November 30, 1939, the Soviet Union invaded Finland.

The war, however, quickly turned into a disaster for Moscow. The Finnish military was well led by Carl Mannerheim, a former czarist general, and his brave soldiers were better at winter warfare than the Soviets. A favorite Finnish tactic was to wear white uniforms that made soldiers all but invisible in the snowy countryside. Then they would shoot passing invaders at point-blank range. The Soviet army was also poorly led because the officer corps had not recovered from Stalin's purges of military leaders only two years before and was lacking in combat experience.

The ragtag Finnish army initially pushed back the mighty invaders, which shocked the world. The Swedes and other Scandinavian countries supported the Finns, and donations to the Finnish cause came rushing in from around the world. Former American president Herbert Hoover and New York City Mayor Fiorello LaGuardia in December 1939 attended a rally in Madison Square Garden in New York City that both showed American public support and raised lots of money.

With everything going wrong, Stalin at one point tongue-lashed Marshal Nikolai Voronov, the People's Commissioner of Defense, for the military's failures. In an unheard of response, the military man blasted back at him screaming, "You have yourself to blame for all this! You're the one who had our best generals killed." He then picked up a platter with a roast suckling pig on it and smashed it on the table.[19] Incredibly, and despite this confrontation, Voronov had a long and successful career in World War II.

In the end and despite international support, the Finns could not hold on. Helsinki sued for peace after 105 days of war and signed a peace accord with Moscow on March 12, 1940. In the settlement, Finland lost eleven percent of its land and one-third of its economic assets. Stalin essentially got everything he had wanted.

Historians believe that the poor Soviet showing in the Winter War strongly encouraged Hitler to invade the Soviet Union in June 1942. The Nazi leader figured that if a small country with limited resources such as Finland could hold the Red Army off for months, then his mighty Wehrmacht would crush it in no time. Military leaders around the world shared that view.

Finland spent almost half of its gold holdings on weapons to fight the war and had only 14 tons left at the end of the conflict. At the beginning of 1940 and with the war still being fought, the Bank of Finland rushed to get its remaining gold out of Europe. In January, it sold some bullion to Sweden and shipped 12.8 tons from Stockholm to the New York Federal Reserve. It already had 4.5 tons at the Bank of England in London, which was moved to the New York Fed. On March 7, only a week before the end of the Winter War, it sold 1.9 tons more.

In the spring of 1941 and after the Winter War, Finland had 11.8 tons of the bank's total holdings of 12.5 tons at the New York Fed, while the rest remained at the Bank for International Settlements in Basel. With Finland still living dangerously between the Soviet Union and Germany, the country's leaders soon sold most of the gold that it had built up in the U.S. Only three tons remained, and that was soon frozen due to Washington's wartime regulations.[20]

Chapter Twelve

THE WORLD'S FORT KNOX

Fort Knox
May–September 1940
Tons of gold: 10,000

Gold Route
- - - - - - ▶

New Hampshire   Maine

Vermont

Massachusetts

Rhode Island

New York

Connecticut

Wisconsin

Michigan   New York City

Pennsylvania   New Jersey

Iowa

Ohio   Delaware

Illinois   Indiana   West Virginia   Maryland

Virginia

Fort Knox

Missouri   Kentucky

North Carolina

Tennessee   South Carolina   Atlantic Ocean

Arkansas

After European central bankers witnessed what had happened to the gold holdings of Austria and Czechoslovakia, the moneymen became anxious to protect their national treasures. Some central banks decided it was probably enough to send their bullion to Britain, the traditional storage place for the world's central bank treasure. Others, though, began looking for ways to get it all the way across the Atlantic Ocean to the United States, to put an ocean between their gold and the Nazis.

Henry Morgenthau was the member of Franklin D. Roosevelt's cabinet most concerned about the threat Hitler posed, even though that was not directly in his area of responsibility. Thankfully, Morgenthau had a direct line to the White House because of his close relationship with the president. The two men lunched together every Monday at 1:00 P.M., and Morgenthau never hesitated to pick up the phone and call the Oval Office when something was on his mind. He worried in particular about the Nazi attacks first on Germany's Jews and then on others when he conquered new countries. Morgenthau was particularly sensitive to the issue because of his own Jewish heritage but also as a result of his father's experience as U.S. ambassador to the Ottoman Empire from 1913 to 1916. The elder Morgenthau witnessed at first hand the Turkish extermination of Armenians that left as many as one-and-a-half million people dead. He tried to bring their plight to the attention of both President Woodrow Wilson and the world, but with little success. That case of ethnic genocide showed to both father and son the horrors that a modern state-run terror could produce. The Treasury Secretary also realized that the Nazis could use modern methods to do even more harm.[1]

American political leaders and the general public believed that U.S. bankers and munitions manufacturers, who were tagged with the moniker "merchants of death," had dragged the country into World War I. They wanted to make sure that would not happen again, which made it difficult for Morgenthau to raise public concerns about a new European war. The Neutrality Act of 1935, which was followed by similar legislation in 1936 and 1937, forbade the sale of weapons to belligerents. Roosevelt lobbied Congress to permit some arms purchases, but Congress refused.[2]

The Roosevelt Administration, and the American public, did not pay much attention to Germany's seizure of the Austrian gold in 1938. But after the Munich sellout to Hitler later that same year, the White House became more concerned about developments on the continent. Morgenthau's department was particularly critical about the role the Bank for International Settlements had played in turning over the Czech gold over to Berlin. William C. Bullitt, the U.S. ambassador in Paris, also sent ominous reports about the Nazi danger, but his counterpart in London, Joseph Kennedy, advocated finding some accommodation with Berlin.[3]

The Federal Reserve System, America's central bank, is located in Washington, D.C. at 20th Street N.W. and Constitution Avenue in a four-story classical Georgian marble building featuring a giant eagle on the front. The head of the Fed from 1933 to 1948 was Marriner Eccles, who served as chairman. While the Fed's board of governors made overall American monetary policy, the central bank's gold activity took place at the Federal Reserve Bank of New York, one of twelve regional banks. It ran the day-to-day bullion business, and the nation's gold was stored in the basement of its headquarters at 33 Liberty Street in Manhattan's Wall Street area. The bank president from 1928 to December 1940 was George L. Harrison. Fed Vice President L. Werner Knoke, who had worked for years in private banking, handled daily gold operations.[4]

With Nazi threats becoming ever stronger throughout Europe, Morgenthau, at two meetings in early 1938, told the president bluntly "the world is drifting rapidly towards war." He brought along to one luncheon meeting statistics showing how much the ten leading countries had spent on armaments during the past five years. The numbers were ominous. Germany had quickly built a modern military that had all the latest technology, while other countries were still struggling to get out of the Great Depression and had spent little on national defense. The treasury secretary bluntly warned Roosevelt, "The European countries are gradually going bankrupt through preparing for war. You are the only person who can stop it."[5]

The president was none too happy with that news and jokingly fired back, "I feel like throwing at you either a cup and saucer or the coffeepot."[6] Nonetheless, Morgenthau had gotten the president's attention, and FDR began bringing him into the inner circle on international and defense issues.

Gold began flowing into the U.S following the March 12, 1938 *Anschluss* of Austria, but the pace picked up sharply that September following the Munich agreement that dismantled Czechoslovakia. The reason was not just that European countries were worried that their national treasures might fall into the hands of the Nazis. Countries were suddenly spending heavily to buy war materiel in anticipation of a new European conflict. The U.S. was the world's leading industrial power, and it could quickly turn out the new weapons, especially the airplanes. Countries such as Britain, France and the Low Countries badly needed to catch up militarily with the Germans, and those nations purchased many of the munitions with gold. In addition, they sent it abroad for safekeeping. In the spring of 1938, gold was moving to the U.S. at the rate of $4 million a month, but in the nine months between July 1938 and April 1939 more than $3 billion landed in New York City, with nearly $2 billion of that coming from Britain alone. Even Mussolini's Italy was sending bullion to New York. In 1939 and 1940, the Italians deposited $25 million in gold at the New York Federal Reserve.[7] Gold was arriving either to buy weapons or to get it away from the danger in Europe.

Morgenthau closely monitored the gold that was flooding into the U.S. both to protect it from Nazi confiscation and to pay for weapons, and he kept the president informed of developments. The topic was a frequent subject at the weekly lunches between the two men. The president also put his treasury secretary into a key position to oversee the sales of weapons to the Allies even though that work was far from his portfolio. Morgenthau dealt closely with Harry Hopkins, FDR's top personal aide on foreign affairs, on the issue of getting armaments to Europe. Morgenthau was thus at the heart of the action in dealing with both the Allied defense requirements and the European gold shipments whether they were to buy war goods or to keep bullion out of Nazi hands. The storage location for bullion in the early war years was the New York Federal Reserve, where it was in underground vaults in lower Manhattan. Morgenthau received daily reports from the New York Fed of gold arrivals.

The treasury secretary wished that Roosevelt would have moved faster to bolster the democracies, but he recognized that the president could not get too far ahead of the American public, which was still largely isolationist. At staff meetings, Morgenthau and others voiced concerns that the whole gold system was becoming unstable because the U.S. held so much.

In October 1938, the French government sent businessman Jean Monnet to Washington to investigate the possibility of making large purchases of American aircraft and supporting equipment. He told Morgenthau that the French would be buying about one thousand planes. Paris had one of the largest stores of gold, but they worried nonetheless about how they were going to pay for the huge armament build up. The English-speaking Frenchman had earlier sold cognac in Canada for his family firm J. G. Monnet & Co. He had also worked for the Chinese government. He was well known and respected both in Washington and Wall Street circles.

Britain decided to establish a similar operation, which it called the British Purchasing Commission.[8] The director was Arthur B. Purvis. During World War I, he had been sent to Canada to buy naval supplies and then stayed there and went into business in Montreal. He became president of Canadian Industries, a chemical company that made munitions. When war again loomed, he returned to Great Britain to help with rearmament. Morgenthau held Purvis in high regard, saying that he had "never known a man who was more determined to do this job well.[9] Monnet later suggested to Winston Churchill that the two countries coordinate their work so they wouldn't get into bidding matches. The result was the Anglo-French Purchasing Board.

The political situation in Europe continued to worsen. On March 15, 1939, Germany marched into the remaining part of Czechoslovakia that it had not gotten in the Munich agreement, and a week later absorbed Memel on the German-Lithuanian border. Memel was a spit of land that had been part of the German Reich before World War I. It was given to the new nation of Lithuania at the Versailles Peace Conference. It was only ninety miles long and twelve miles wide and had 145,000 inhabitants that had a slight German majority but also a large Lithuanian minority. The Nazis had their eye on it because the Memel port would be strategically important during a possible invasion of the Soviet Union, something Hitler was already planning, despite the Molotov-Ribbentrop pact. On March 20, 1939, German Foreign Minister Joachim von Ribbentrop himself traveled there and demanded its return to the Reich. After two days of browbeating, the Lithuanian government at 1:00 in the morning of March 23 agreed to turn the area over to Germany. It was another easy Nazi conquest, and Hitler himself triumphantly sailed into the Memel harbor later that very same day.

With war rumors running wild in the last days of August 1939 following the Ribbentrop-Molotov agreement, Britain spent nearly $2.5 million in gold trying to protect the value of the pound. U.S. ambassador Joseph Kennedy sent Washington a message saying, "England is busted now." According to the Bank of England's Montagu Norman, his country's financial situation was "worse than tragic." He predicted that the entire world's gold would soon be in the U.S. and "there will be no hope for the world . . . at least none for Europe."[10]

Two months later and after the fall of Poland in September 1939, FDR asked Henry Morgenthau to take on the job of coordinating weapons sales to all the governments at war with Hitler. Since the failure of the Allies to pay off their World War I debts still loomed in the background, Monnet suggested setting up a dummy corporation in Canada so that the western allies could obtain credit. Morgenthau agreed.

In February 1939, French Premier Paul Reynaud had told Washington that he had enough gold to buy six thousand American airplanes. An armada of European ships was soon heading to New York with central bank gold and returning to Europe with planes and guns. Sometimes the bullion arrived on military vessels, and sometimes it came on merchant ones. Usually it was carried on foreign ships, but it also came on American vessels as well. The New York Federal Reserve staff, which had been handling only a few shipments of gold a month from both Europe and Asia, was suddenly logging in several each week.

Most gold movements came from major countries such as Britain and France, and some days Railway Express trucks went to the New York and New Jersey docks to pick up shipments and bring them to the New York Federal Reserve. By the spring of 1939 gold flowed in at an historic rate. Just in the month of March, eight ships carried to New York City a total of 1,427 crates and cases of British gold valued at $1.2 billion. The SS President Roosevelt arrived from Britain on April 23 with 453 boxes of bullion. The following week, the SS Manhattan brought in another 434 cases from the Bank of England. In the first ten days of May, four ships arrived from British ports with a total of 974 cases. The American ship SS Harding alone made three cross-Atlantic bullion trips, one in late March, one in early April, and one in early May. The cargo totaled another thousand cases. New York Fed officials were nervous because many ships could not get maritime insurance in view of the risks involved.[11]

Smaller countries such as Holland, Belgium, Denmark, Norway, Sweden, Romania, and others also sent their bullion to New York City. Between the end of March and mid-April 1939, the Belgian Central Bank sent four shipments. A fleet of Dutch vessels, all with the names of birds preceded by the word black, arrived between late March and late April. They included the Black Gull, the Black Falcon, the Black Osprey, the Black Heron, the Black Tern, the Black Eagle, and the Black Hawk. The value of gold on board the ships ranged between $150,000 and nearly $2 million.[12]

On September 1, 1939, L. W. Knoke, the New York Fed official who handled the incoming gold, dictated a memo for the record of a conversation he had that day with the Bank of England. He asked officials for instructions on how to handle the flood of gold coming in so quickly. The *Queen Mary* had just arrived with a shipload, and $12 million in bullion was due on the *Samaria*. He wrote: "I explained that the rush of gold over the weekend was on such a scale that we had to make preparations beforehand."[13]

The New York Federal Reserve balance sheet of September 30, 1939 showed that thirty-nine countries had parked some of their national gold in the vault in lower Manhattan.[14] It was arriving so fast by April 1940 that the New York Fed decided to begin charging for services that had up until then been free as a gesture of good will among central banks. The Fed now charged 33.5704 cents for each gold bar received and 22.6007 cents for each bar sent to the Assay Office to test its purity.

Shortly after the Germans took over the Czech rump state of Slovakia in March 1939, President Roosevelt asked Morgenthau to look into what actions the administration could take to help the Allies get more weapons without asking Congress again for new trade legislation. The Secretary assigned Harry Dexter White, his top aide, to come up with a plan for waging economic warfare on Germany. On April 8, 1939, White presented a preliminary report on "the possibility of depriving the aggressor countries of needed strategic war materials." The study zeroed in on nine products that were vital for war, but which Germany had in only short supply. They were: manganese, copper, tin, rubber, petroleum, nickel, manila fiber, tungsten, and cotton. White estimated that Germany had to spend $100 million a month to import the commodities needed to keep its war machine running.[15]

White did not yet realize that the Nazi strategy was to pay for those products with gold stolen from its victims. White proposed purchasing stores of the strategic materials to keep them out of German hands or establishing international agreements to stop the Nazis from getting them. Morgenthau asked the president to support a billion-dollar program to buy up the three most strategic products: oil, tin, and manganese. After consulting with his war, navy, and state departments, though, Roosevelt decided that the price tag was too high, and the administration eventually asked Congress for $10 million, a fraction of what was needed to do the job.[16]

Following the invasion of Poland on September 1, 1939, however, the Roosevelt Administration moved with a new urgency to help the western allies militarily even though the American public still opposed entering another European war. The Neutrality Act of 1935, which had been regularly renewed with only minor changes, imposed an embargo on all war materials and to all parties in the conflict. On September 21, 1939, the president asked Congress to replace that with a new policy that became known as Cash and Carry. It would allow arms sales under stiff conditions. The primary ones were that the buyers had to pay immediately in convertible currencies or gold and had to provide their own transportation for their purchases. Moreover, foreign vessels picking up military hardware could spend only twenty-four hours in a U.S. harbor. Since it often took longer than a day to unload gold and then load heavy equipment such as airplanes, the western allies used Halifax, Canada as a drop-off and pick-up harbor. Vessels brought gold from Europe destined for the New York Federal Reserve and picked up war goods. Cash and Carry was designed primarily to help Britain and France. The new proposal passed Congress relatively quickly and became law in November.

On February 5, 1940, Harry Dexter White informed Morgenthau that France and Britain would soon buy $1 billion worth of airplanes and spend even more on other weapons. He added that they still had $14 to $15 billion in foreign exchange assets, but warned that at the rate they were purchasing they might spend half of that within a year. White speculated that each had left roughly $6.5 billion in gold.[17]

Morgenthau began getting regular reports on world gold shipments from the New York Federal Reserve. The inflow to the U.S. had been only about $100 million per year in the 1920s and early 1930s, but in 1935 had jumped to $1.7 billion, and in 1939 was likely to hit $3 billion. On Tuesday February 6, 1940, the U.S. bought $22.5 million in gold from the Bank of England, $1 million from the Dutch, and $410,000 from Belgians for a total on that one day of $23.9 million. An additional $3.2 million came via

Canada. The Fed received a cable from the Bank for International Settlements to transfer $2.7 million from its account to the Turkish National Bank. The traffic was staggering:

- The Bank of Iceland sent $800,000.
- The Bank of Latvia sent $11 million.
- The State Bank of the U.S.S.R. on September 27, 1939, sent 160 bars of gold via San Francisco.
- The Bank of Romania in late December 23, 1939, sent $845,486 and on March 5, 1940, another 84 more bars worth $1.2 million.
- The Bank for International Settlements in the fall of 1939 made two shipments to New York worth $6.3 million.
- The National Bank of Hungary in late February 1940 sent $3 million.
- The Ministry of Foreign Affairs of Afghanistan even contacted the U.S. embassy in Paris to ask about the New York Fed's gold policy.[18]

By the fall of 1939, it was hard to shock the U.S Treasury policymakers, but in November 1939 the British Exchequer stunned even Treasury Secretary Morgenthau by selling $50 million more in gold. Between the beginning of the war in September 1939 and early 1940, British gold sales amounted to $125 million, and the sales of securities were $112 million.[19]

The Scandinavian countries were particularly nervous about being invaded and losing their gold. Sweden took the lead, and its central bank president Ivar Rooth often spoke for other Nordic central banks. He sent messages to New York City for the Danish Central Bank, asking if Finnish gold could be sold for delivery in Stockholm. The Federal Reserve said no. It did not want to take the added risk of getting it from Stockholm to New York. In February 1938, Rooth sent a letter to New York Fed president George Harrison, saying that he had "long contemplated to distribute gold holdings belonging to the bank." Sweden had significant deposits in London, but he wanted to move them out of harm's way. As war dangers increased, the Swedish banker was soon shipping large amounts of bullion to New York at his own cost. In June and July of 1938, he sent $15 million on four separate sailings. In October 1939, he transferred $25 million and then in December another $5.9 million. A week before Christmas in 1939, Sweden's Rooth sent a year's end message to the New York Fed's Harrison, "We must also think of the possibility that we might become the next victim of the Russian bear. We pray for peace in 1940, but we prepare for the worst."[20]

By the early months of 1940, the influx of gold into the U.S. from Europe was so great that there was a risk that it could destabilize the international monetary system. More than sixty percent of the world's gold was now in the U.S., as compared to twenty-three percent in 1913 or thirty-eight percent in 1929.[21] In the spring of that year and with that trend only growing greater, Morgenthau asked Harry Dexter White to work on a major study on the subject. He called his long report "The Future of Gold." The Treasury Secretary had been invited to give a talk to the Women's Division of the Democratic National Committee, and he hoped that his aide's work might make its way into the speech. The professor came out in White's work, however, and the study turned out to be akin to an academic treatise. At one point, though, he alarmingly wrote: "Suppose the war lasts more than three years? Suppose it lasts five years? At the rate gold is now coming in—$2 billion to $3 billion a year—we would assuredly have most of the world's gold by the end of the war." White also delved into the future of the world monetary system. In many ways, he was exploring issues that would be the basis for the 1944 United Nations Monetary and Financial Conference that was held in Bretton Woods, New Hampshire near the end of the war that was then just beginning.[22]

Morgenthau met with White in Sea Island, Georgia in the spring to go over his work. The secretary reiterated his support for gold, saying that he "felt it did not matter whether the government was a democracy or a totalitarian government or whether its economy was socialism or free enterprise, it would still use gold for international transactions." White agreed. The two concluded, though, that White's work was too dense and theoretical for Morgenthau's upcoming speech and would go over everyone's head including his own. So the secretary's staff produced a more popular talk that stressed the strength of the U.S. economy and the role of gold. The secretary gave his talk in Washington on May 3, and it received good press reviews, which pleased him because he was not a natural public speaker and rarely spoke at public forums. Emil Puhl, the new power at the Reichsbank after the ouster of Hjalmar Schacht, read a copy of the speech and wrote a letter to the U.S. financial attaché in Berlin about his own views on bullion: "I am personally of the opinion that the role of gold in the monetary respect need not by any means have been played out provided all parties concerned can arrive at a reasonable solution of the gold problem."[23]

After his speech to the Democratic women, Morgenthau left for an R-and-R visit to Chicago. At 3:00 on Sunday morning May 5, he woke up and scribbled a note to his secretary on a small pad supplied by the Shoreland Hotel, where he was staying. He noted the date and time and then wrote: "Please tell Dan Bell I want enough money to move all the remaining gold out of N.Y. City to Kentucky. He should speak to me Tuesday." Morgenthau underlined the word "all" three times and put his initials at the bottom. In the morning his son asked why he had gotten up in the middle of the night and written a note.[24]

Two days later, Morgenthau was back in his Washington office. At his regular morning staff meeting he explained his middle-of-the-night note, saying, "I got to worrying about three or four billion dollars worth of gold laying in New York." Undersecretary Dan Bell explained that Fort Knox had the capacity to hold about $15 billion dollars in gold, but was only about one-third full. He figured it could store at least $9.5 billion more. Bell proposed sending about $7.5 billion to Kentucky. An irritated Morgenthau replied that he wanted to ship $10 billion, adding, "I will take it over to the president myself. It is the height of stupidity when it cost a million and a half dollars not to remove ten *billion* dollars to a place of safekeeping."[25] In his memo to the president Morgenthau recommended that "in the current calendar year" the government should ship "approximately $9 billion of refined gold from New York to Fort Knox. He estimated that this would require a supplemental budget appropriation of $1.6 million. Roosevelt approved the proposal.

Morgenthau learned that same day that the treasury had just received $21.8 million in gold from Canada, Britain, Switzerland, and Portugal. In addition the Netherlands had wired that it would be soon sending $3.7 million more. Nazi propaganda claimed that the U.S. was simply trying to grab all of Western Europe's gold, and the British press also angrily reported that the U.S. now had seventy percent of the world's bullion.[26] The Bank of England had previously been the major location where countries parked their bullion for protection, but with London no longer looking like a safe location, it was now going to the U.S. Large shipments from Switzerland, Sweden, and Portugal landed at the New York Federal Reserve for safekeeping, and it was sometimes gold that they had received from Germany. Without realizing it, the U.S. was actually helping finance the Nazi war effort by giving Hitler's partners a secure place to store stolen bullion.[27]

The national press was slow to pick up on the historic influx of gold to the U.S. In June 1940, though, the papers finally paid attention. The *New York Times* and the *Washington Post* carried breathless headlines such as "May Gold Imports Double; Britain Ships Heavily," "Half Billion of European Gold Enters U.S. in 2 Days," and "$225,000,000 in Gold Arrives Over Week-End." The Nazi invasion of the Low Countries and France had precipitated the latest panic. The *New York Times* in a story datelined June 4 reported, "One of the greatest mass movements of gold in history is now under way."[28]

A series of memos the Treasury staff sent to Secretary Morgenthau showed starkly how the U.S. was gathering up nearly all the world's central bank gold. One on July 1, 1940, reported that the U.S. during the previous month had purchased $662.8 million, with $242.7 million of that coming from Britain and $332.9 million from France. Moreover, it stated that in the ten months between September 1939 and June 1940, those two European countries had sold the U.S. $1.7

billion in gold (France $900.7 million, and Britain $766.8 million). At 2014 prices, that would have amounted to $60 billion.[29]

In the first full year of World War II, from September 1, 1939 through August of 1940, the U.S. took in $4.1 billion in bullion from mainly European countries. Harry White noted in a report in late September 1940, "This is by far the largest sum of gold ever received by us or any country in a like period. We now have slightly over 70 percent of the monetary gold held by governments and central banks. We actually hold 80 percent of the world's monetary gold if we include earmarked gold held here."[30]

On October 28, 1940, Henry Morgenthau wrote in a memo that London had just ordered $1.6 billion in war materials and was preparing for an additional one of $3.3 billion. Unless there was a change in American policy, the purchases would all have to be paid for in gold.[31]

Chapter Thirteen

DENMARK AND NORWAY
FALL QUICKLY

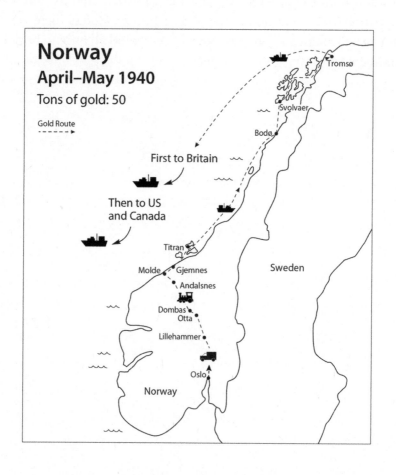

Norway
April–May 1940
Tons of gold: 50

Gold Route

Tromsø

Svolvaer

Bodø

First to Britain

Then to US
and Canada

Titran

Molde

Gjemnes

Andalsnes

Sweden

Dombas

Otta

Lillehammer

Oslo

Norway

On September 27, 1939, the day Warsaw fell, Hitler told the heads of his three military services that he wanted to open his next offensive in the west as soon as possible. The initial objective was to conquer the Low Countries of Holland, Belgium, and Luxembourg, but that objective was soon enlarged to include northern France. This was the same area where German forces in World War I initially had great success, but then got bogged down in trench warfare and eventually lost the war. Hitler remembered those days with both agony and anger. He vowed that this time it would be different.

Hitler issued Führer-Directive Number Six on October 9 for the invasion of the four countries, expecting that it would be launched in only a few weeks. Just ten days later, General Franz Halder, the chief-of-staff of the German army high command, presented the first draft of the operation code-named Case Yellow. Hitler wanted to begin the offensive on November 12, 1939, the day after the signing of the humiliating armistice ending World War I. Hitler stated that his objective was to conquer "as much territory as possible in Holland, Belgium, and northern France to serve as a base for the successful prosecution of the air and sea war against England and as a wide protective area for the economically vital Ruhr."[1]

The invasion date, though, kept slipping, and on the morning of January 10, Army Major Hellmuth Reinberger was carrying Wehrmacht plans for the invasion on a flight from the Loddenheide airport near Munster to Cologne, which then had to make a forced landing in Vucht, Belgium. He had been specifically ordered to take the train to avoid just such an accident, but he flew so that he could spend some extra time with his new wife. In a panic, the major tried to burn the secret documents and nearly set himself on fire in the process. When the Belgians discovered the contents, they quickly distributed them to officials in Holland, France, and Britain. Hitler was livid when he learned what had happened, but he might not have been all that unhappy because he had never thought highly of the original plan.[2]

Upon further reflection and pressure from his naval commander Admiral Erich Raeder, Hitler changed his mind and decided to invade Denmark and Norway first in order to eliminate the possibility that Britain could use those countries in the future as a forward base in a conflict with Germany. When British forces stopped a German vessel in Norwegian waters and searched it, Hitler was more determined than ever to neutralize the two Nordic countries. On February 19, he ordered new plans be drawn up for the invasion of the two Scandinavian countries. The code name was *Fall Weserübung* (Case Weser Exercise) after the Weser River in northwestern Germany.[3]

The area was also important to Nazis war plans because it was the gateway to high-quality Swedish iron ore, which came from the Kiruna area in the far northern part of the country. Germany had to import large amounts of iron ore because of the low quality of its own, which was not weapons grade. Admiral Raeder, the head of the navy, later wrote, "Swedish ore for steel was the heart of our war economy and without which our armament industries would have died overnight."[4] There were only two ways for Germany to transport the Swedish ore to the *Vaterland*. One route was via the Swedish port of Luleå in the Baltic, but that was frozen from December to May. The second was via the Norwegian port of Narvik, which was open all year long. The Nazi war effort, Raeder argued, could not rely on getting iron ore only half the year via Luleå. Germany therefore needed to control the port of Narvik.

Generals Wilhelm Keitel and Alfred Jodl recommended that Hitler appoint General Nicholaus von Falkenhorst, a member of an old military family, to command *Weserübung*. He had served during World War I in Finland as a military advisor helping the Finns fight the Russians, which gave him experience fighting in the Nordic area. He had also been successful in the Nazi invasion of Poland. At the time, he was commanding an army corps stationed in the Rhineland town of Koblenz. Hitler and Falkenhorst met for the first time on February 21, and the Führer talked with him only about his experience in Finland.[5]

After a brief talk, Hitler ordered the general to return at 5:00 that afternoon with a plan to occupy Norway. The Germans lacked proper maps of the country, so Falkenhorst went to a nearby book-store and bought a Baedeker travel guide. As he said later, he had "to find out just what Norway was like. I didn't have any idea." The general quickly saw that his biggest challenge was going to be Nor-way's long 1,500-mile coastline. After working up his plan at the nearby Kaiserhof hotel, Falkenhorst returned to the Führer at the scheduled time. His proposal was similar to one a naval taskforce had already made, and Hitler appointed him to lead the operation.

The occupation of Denmark was not originally part of *Weserübung*. It was included later because German military leaders wanted to gain control of airbases in northern Denmark in order to facilitate airborne attacks on Norway. Air Force Marshal Hermann Göring also insisted on having a larger role for his Luftwaffe. Falkenhorst and his staff easily agreed.

On February 29, Hitler approved Falkenhorst's final battle plan, and the following day put out a four-page war directive. Only nine copies were made. The first sentence said that the objective was to occupy both Norway and Denmark, while the second sentence gave the rationale: "This would anticipate English action against Scandinavia and the Baltic, would secure our supplies of ore from Sweden, and would provide the Navy and Air Forces with expanded bases for operations against England." The attack on Norway was renamed *Weserübung Nord*, while the one against Denmark was *Weserübung Süd*. For the first time in military history, the German attack on Norway would involve army, navy, and air force units. Hitler wrote in the order: "It is of the utmost importance that our operations should come as a surprise to the Northern countries as well as to our enemies in the West. This must be kept in mind in making all preparations."[6]

Attacks on the two countries were to take place simultaneously down to the minute. The paratroop landings at the civilian airport on the outskirts of Oslo were to be made at precisely Weser Hour plus 185 minutes. A top priority was to capture the Danish and Nor-wegian kings, Christian X and his younger brother Håkon VII, their governments, as well as the gold stocks of both countries. Deception was a major part of the planning. All the ships in the German flotilla sailing north were given dummy British names that were to be used in wireless communications with Norwegian officials in order to conceal their true nationality until the last possible moment.

By March 20, Falkenhorst had finished his planning and was ready to go to war. The only thing left was to set a date and time for the invasion. The navy wanted to launch it during the period of long, dark nights, when units would have the maximum natural protection while ships and troops were transported north from German ports. The afternoon of April 2, Hitler and his top military officers conducted a final review of the war plans. Hitler decided that Weser Day would be April 9, a week later, with the invasion beginning at 5:15 A.M. Berlin time.

It was widely known in European central bank circles by this time that capturing gold was an integral part of Nazi invasion strategy. In December 1939, Sweden, Denmark, and Norway held talks about protecting their national treasure, which they called their "golden inheritance." They all agreed to ship large amounts to the U.S. Denmark was in the greatest danger since it shared a border with Germany, so it sent as much as possible and as fast as possible to New York. A first shipment departed in December 1939, and by the end of the month, one-third of the country's bullion was in the U.S. The pace continued in the new year, and on February 13, 1940, two thousand bags of gold arrived in New York City aboard the *SS Randsfjord*. Just six days later, another two thousand bags landed on the *SS Trafalgar*. The Danes had the Federal Reserve melt down 20 million Reichsmark worth of gold coins that they owned into bars. The last Danish shipment arrived in early March, and by then the Bank of Denmark vault was empty. The government gave Henrik Kauffmann, Copenhagen's ambassador to the U.S., full authority over the gold.[7] The Norwegians had also been diligent in protecting their gold. Nicolai Rygg, the director of the country's central bank, devised a detailed plan that included both sending it abroad and protecting what remained at home. After the Nazi invasion of Poland, the bank began shipping bullion out of the country, largely to the

New York Federal Reserve. By January 1940, more than 170 tons, seventy-one percent of the country's entire holdings, were outside the country. The remainder was kept in Oslo because of a government rule requiring it to be legal backing for the country's currency.

Rygg lobbied government leaders to reduce the amount of gold that had to be kept in Oslo during a time of crisis. The law was finally approved on April 8, the day before the invasion. He also ordered the construction of three bombproof vaults in different parts of the country where the metal could be stored. One was near Oslo, one was in Stavanger on the west coast, and the third was in Lillehammer, 112 miles northwest of the capital. Construction on the Lillehammer vault was only completed in January 1940.

In early April, Rygg finalized plans to begin transporting the gold there. The fifty tons of gold was packed in 1,503 wooden crates and thirty-nine small barrels and was ready to be moved. The boxes each weighed between fifty-five pounds and ninety pounds, while the barrels were 175 pounds. Shipments were due to start the following day on April 10.[8]

Britain's Winston Churchill, the new First Lord of the Admiralty, also had his eye on Swedish iron ore. He wanted to stop the flow of it by mining the offshore area near Narvik in Norway's far north. The British cabinet hesitated, but he won support from the new French Prime Minister Paul Reynaud for the plan, and on April 3, the British cabinet authorized the mining and ordered it to begin on April 8. Churchill named the action Wilfred after a cartoon character. A supplementary operation codenamed Plan R4 called for British and French forces to invade four Norwegian ports, Narvik, Trondheim, Bergen, and Stavanger, "the moment the Germans set foot on Norwegian soil, or there is clear evidence that they intend to do so."[9]

The German occupation of Denmark went flawlessly. Military historian Douglas Dildy has called the German invasion the "briefest ground campaign on record." Although anti-Hitler German officers had warned Danish leaders of an invasion, the cabinet refused to mobilize out of fear of precipitating a retaliatory

German action. On April 9, at precisely 5:15 A.M., the first invading troops crossed the Danish border just north of Flensburg. The Falkenhorst plan called for a three-pronged attack aimed at the island of Zeeland, the capital Copenhagen to the east, and directly north to Jutland.[10]

An integral part of the operation was a parachute jump at the military airport at Aalborg. This was to be the first paratroop attack in the history of warfare. Another important objective was to capture quickly both Copenhagen, the capital, and the king, Christian X. The German troopship *Hansestadt Danzig* landed at Langelinie Pier in center city Copenhagen at 6:00 A.M. At nearly the same moment, German planes roared low over the capital and dropped leaflets urging Danes to be calm and cooperate with the Germans. British ambassador Howard Smith wrote in his report on the invasion that the leaflets were "written in a bastard Norwegian-Danish, a curiously un-German disregard of detail."[11]

German troops first marched to Kastellet, an old fortress that housed military barracks, which they captured without firing a shot. The invaders then attacked Amalienborg, the royal castle where the king was meeting with his cabinet and top military leaders. Danish guards resisted, and one was killed. Prime Minister Thorvald Stauning and Foreign Minister Edvard Munch then urged the king to halt the fighting. The king asked General William Prior, the commander in chief of the Royal Danish Army, whether he thought "our soldiers had fought long enough." The general at first replied no. Shortly before 8:00 in the morning, the government broadcast an order over Danish radio not to resist, and at 8:34, the Danish war was over.[12]

The two top German officials in the country, General Kurt Himer and Minister Cecil von Renthe-Fink, met with the king at 2:00 that afternoon to make sure that he would not try to escape. Himer reported back to Berlin that during the conference the king's "whole body trembled." He also indicated that he and his government would do whatever was necessary to avoid further bloodshed. As the meeting was ending, the king said to Himer, "General, may

I, as an old soldier, tell you something? As soldier to soldier? You Germans have done the incredible again. One must admit that it is a magnificent work."[13]

The German invading force perhaps knew that there would be no gold in Denmark. Two months before the invasion, the *Neue Zürcher Zeitung*, the leading newspaper in German-speaking Switzerland, published an article about the Danish economy that said most of the country's gold was now stored in New York City. The following month the German press picked that up, reporting that "international high finance" had "abducted" the Danish gold and taken it to the U.S. The article demanded that in the name of the German people it be returned to Denmark.[14]

Months after he had returned to Copenhagen from the U.S., Carl Valdemar Bramsnæs, the head of the central bank, wrote a long report of this trip that he left in his records. Both its length and detail has surprised historians, who now believe that he wanted to put in writing the decision to ship out the bullion. That way he could explain to German invaders why the vaults were empty. Sure enough, in June 1941, a German diplomat showed up at the Danish central bank office and asked for the Danish gold reserves. He questioned the story that it had been shipped to the U.S. The bank governor was only too happy to show his long 1939 memo.[15]

The plans for *Weserübung Nord*, the invasion of Norway, called for a German diplomat to make a presentation of German demands simultaneously with the beginning of military actions at 4:15 A.M. The invasion was to be spearheaded by German warships attacking cities at the end of fjords on the country's long coastline: Narvik, Trondheim, Kristiansand, Bergen, Oslo, Egersund, and Arendal. Since there was no contiguous land between Germany and Norway, all the Wehrmacht forces had to arrive by ship or plane.

Carl J. Hambro, the president of the Storting, Norway's parliament, was asleep at home just after midnight, when his wife woke him to tell him that air-raid alarms were going off all over the capital. Hambro took a cab to the foreign ministry, where a cabinet meeting was taking place. The invasion left Prime Minister Johan

Nygaardsvold, a long-time supporter of neutrality and minimum national defense, stunned into inaction. Hambro, however, seized the moment and directed his nation's response.

Curt Bräuer, the German minister in Oslo, arrived at the Norwegian foreign ministry at 4:15 A.M. to deliver the German ultimatum. Foreign Minister Halvdan Koht was in the cabinet meeting, but left to meet the German in the ministry's library. There was no electricity in the building because of a blackout, so the men talked by the light of two small candles. Bräuer handed him a fourteen-page typed document, and then gave a verbal synopsis. He warned there would be brutal consequences if there were any "foolish resistance."[16]

After the German diplomat finished his speech, Koht replied that he would have to submit the demands to his government. The minister pressed for a quick reply, saying that the occupation had to be completed before nine o'clock that morning. Koht returned to the cabinet session, but soon returned with the answer: Norway was going to defend its neutrality and resist the German invasion. It was now 5:30, and a grey dawn was breaking across the capital.

"Then there will be fighting," Bräuer replied. "And nothing can save you."

"The fighting is already in progress," said Koht.[17]

When the German left, the cabinet decided that the entire royal family, King Håkon, Crown-Prince Olav, Princess Ingeborg, and their three children, plus the cabinet and Storting members would leave as soon as possible to the town of Hamar eighty miles north. The special train would depart from Oslo's Eastern Central Station at 7:00 A.M.[18]

The Nazis expected little or no military resistance because Norway lacked a substantial army, having traditionally considered neutrality to be their only form of defense. There could be some token mobilization, which would take weeks to carry out. Norwegian military equipment was also antiquated. Nazi plans called for more than 12,500 German forces to be involved on the first day of the invasion, with another 54,500 arriving in the following ten days. Norway had a permanent army of about 7,000 men.

Every ship in the German Nazi navy took part in the attack. The most prized ship was the *Blücher,* the newest heavy cruiser. It had only recently completed sea trials and sailed out of Bremen on April 8 heading north to Norway. Its mission was to capture Oslo. On board were 1,000 Wehrmacht soldiers including General Erwin Engelbrecht and a group of commandos with orders to capture the gold stored at the Bank of Norway.

Shortly before midnight, the first German ship entered the Oslo fjord. At 3:30 A.M., Rear Admiral Oscar Kummetz, the *Blücher*'s commander, ordered his vessel to slow to eight knots and move into the narrowest point of the fjord. The capital was now only twenty miles away. On the shore across from the village of Drøbak stood the Oscarsborg Fortress, a vintage installation built in the 1850s. It housed two 280 mm guns made by Krupp, the famed German arms manufacturer. They were nicknamed Moses and Aaron. A single shell weighed 560 lb. The fort also had an anti-torpedo battery that was also an antique.[19]

Colonel Birger Eriksen, sixty-five, the commander of the Oscarsborg, had only recently been called back to active duty as war tensions mounted. Just before dawn, he looked out into the darkness and saw a small flotilla sailing towards him. Towering above smaller vessels was the heavy cruiser, rising out of the water like some Colossus of Rhodes. Searchlights from the fort briefly lit it up. Eriksen initially was not sure what to do because he hadn't been given any specific orders on how to handle such a situation. Moreover, he could not even tell if the incoming ships were German or British since both navies had been active recently in Norwegian waters. There was little communication between Eriksen and his superiors. He was on his own. As he looked out from a grassy hill between Moses and Aaron, Eriksen knew that he could fire only one round. He would have no chance to reload. At 4:21 A.M., the *Blücher* was only about 1,800 yards away when the colonel barked out the order for the Krupp guns to fire. He knew he would either be decorated or face a court martial.[20]

The first shell hit the German ship in front of the aft mast and set off explosions that started fires in the command tower. Only a few seconds later, the second one slammed into the port side gun turret and caused still more blazes. On-shore batteries then began firing at the flotilla. Eriksen was sure of the nationality of the burning ship when he heard the strains of *Deutschland Über Alles,* the German national anthem, from the stricken cruiser.[21]

German Captain Kurt Zoepffel after the war recounted the scene aboard the *Blücher:* "Suddenly an ear-splitting roar of thunder rends the air. The glare of the guns pierces the darkness. I can see three flashes simultaneously. We are under fire from two sides. The guns seem to be only about five hundred yards away. Soon bright flames can be seen leaping from the ship. The dreaded shout: 'Ship on fire,' was heard. 'Steering gear out of order.' 'Fire apparatus out of order.' One grave report after another reached the bridge."[22]

Two-and-a-half hours later, and after the fire had spread to stored ammunition, Admiral Kummetz ordered the vessel abandoned. At about 6:30 A.M., the *Blücher* rolled over on its port side and began sinking. Norwegians estimated that about 1,000 men went down with the ship, but later studies put the figure at more like 400. Both Kummetz and Engelbrecht jumped into the ocean in full uniform and swam safely to shore. They eventually arrived in Oslo about midnight.[23]

As soon as the Germans arrived in the Oslo Fjord, Norway's military leaders contacted the Bank of Norway's Nicolai Rygg, who told them that he wanted to start moving the country's gold to Lillehammer right away. The central bank headquarters, a three-story granite structure, was located near the harbor where the *Blücher* should have docked. Opposite the bank stood the nation's department of defense. The bullion had already been packed in anticipation that it might have to be moved north at any time. Rygg now directed the loading operation with the help of more than fifty bank employees. Twenty-six trucks were borrowed from Oslo companies to move the cargo north. A maximum of two tons of bullion were put on each truck to avoid overloading.

A driver and two bank employees acting as guards were aboard each vehicle. One of the two guards sat next to the driver, while the other was in back in the cargo area. The guards were armed with pistols. Each truck left for Lillehammer as soon as it was loaded.[24] The last one departed at 1:30 P.M., which was almost exactly the same time as the first airlifted German soldiers arrived in Oslo. Rygg headed for Lillehammer after the last truckload had departed.

On April 11, a member of the German embassy in Oslo and a Wehrmacht major from von Falkenhorst's staff arrived at the Norwegian Central Bank and demanded the gold. Sverre Thorkildsen, a vice director, told them that it had been moved out two days before, and no one there knew where it had gone. The Germans left unhappy, but could do little about it. Later Hitler sent a top official from Berlin to Oslo, who forced reluctant bank officials to tell him that the gold was in Lillehammer, a city the Nazis did not yet control. Furious, the German said that everyone involved would have *"Der Kopf Kaput"* (Their head cut off).[25]

Soon after the fighting started, General Otto Ruge took over as commander-in-chief of all Norwegian forces from Major General Kristian Laake, an elderly leader who was already scheduled to go into retirement. Ruge had his headquarters in Oyer, twelve miles north of Lillehammer. He sent one of his top officers to Lillehammer to work out a way to move the gold as soon as possible further north.

The new plan called for taking it first to Åndalsnes, a small town about 150 miles to the northwest that was a rail center and had a small harbor. There they would put the gold on a ship that would take it to Molde, a nearby town with a harbor large enough for a British warship to dock and take on cargo.

Since trucks were easy targets for Nazi air attacks, the military planners decided to put the gold on a train camouflaged to make it look like simple freight cars and haul it to Åndalsnes. Ruge didn't like the proposal, which seemed highly risky, but he felt he had no choice. With German forces closing in on Lillehammer, Finance Minister Oscar Torp assigned Fredrik Haslund, an official with his Labor Party, to oversee the gold transport. A car as well as a colonel and a major were put at his disposal, and Haslund recruited a team of men for the job, telling them only that they were going to do road work and should bring picks and shovels. The army ordered the city lights blacked out for safety and to conceal what was going on, while Ruge sent two officers and thirty soldiers to guard the train.[26] One of them was Nordahl Grieg, a famous poet and nephew of composer Edvard Grieg. He was a footloose world traveler, who had fought briefly in the Spanish Civil War on the Republican side. He was then living outside of Lillehammer with his girlfriend. As soon as fighting began, he enlisted.

In Lillehammer at 10:00 P.M. on April 18, a small contingent armed with only pick axes and shovels gathered. The local sheriff spread the word that they were going to work on the city's defense fortification. A half hour later, the police blocked all roads surrounding the Bank of Norway building and the local train station. By 3:00 A.M. the next day, everything was in place to move 1,542 cases of gold from the bank vault to trucks that would take them to the train. There were now 818 large cases, 685 small ones, and 19 barrels. In addition, there were two steel cases. One contained Norwegian currency bills, and the other had official documents. There was a temporary snafu, when the director of the Lillehammer branch couldn't remember the combination to the vault, which he hadn't written down out of fear that the Germans might capture him. After some tense moments, he finally recalled it.[27]

Late that evening, the engine chugged its way out of the station. On board, in addition to bank officials, were security forces under the command of Major Bjørn Sunde. The Norwegians heard the news that the first British troops coming to help them had arrived in Åndalsnes. Along the way three German soldiers looking for the king stopped the train and asked for its official documents. They inspected the train, but didn't open any boxes.

The gold train pulled into the port city of Åndalsnes at 5:00 A.M. on April 20. The formerly quiet village was now bustling with British Royal Marines heading south to fight near Lillehammer. German aircraft were attacking the town and the British, and the city had clearly become too dangerous for the gold. Major Sunde had often skied in the area and remembered an area up in the valley that was steep and would provide a good natural bomb shelter. Haslund phoned Finance Minister Torp to tell him the plan: they would move the train about ten miles and park it in a tunnel.

The Norwegian cabinet meanwhile had decided to send all the bullion to Britain in three shipments in order to reduce the risk of it all being captured by the Germans or lost at sea. Four officials, including ministers Oscar Torp and Trygve Lie, went to Åndalsnes to meet with British Captain Philip Vian and work out the details.

At 11:00 that night, the four Norwegians walked into Vian's headquarters. The British officers were very agitated. One of their comrades had barely missed being killed in Åndalsnes, but finally the visitors got a chance to interject and tell them that they wanted to turn over their entire merchant marine fleet of more than eleven hundred ships to the Allies. Now the Norwegians had Captain Vian's attention, and he quickly replied, "That is an impressive number, and I will immediately send a letter to the Admiralty." They then discussed the gold, explaining that it was hidden nearby in a railway tunnel. Vian clapped his hands and shouted with an enthusiasm, "Well done! Gentleman, I think it is the first time in our history that a captain has been woken up in the middle of the night and offered more than one thousand ships and £16 million in gold."[28]

The German offensive north from Oslo through the Gudbrands Valley advanced relentlessly despite deep snow. When Allied forces withdrew from Lillehammer on April 21, the Wehrmacht quickly took over the city. Two Berlin treasury officials accompanied by Gestapo agents soon arrived at the Bank of Norway office to check on the gold. No one in town knew the combination to the vault, but a locksmith eventually opened it. When the Germans turned on the lights and walked into the vault, they found only a few banknotes worth about $30.[29]

During the night of April 23-24, three British cruisers, *Galatea*, *Glasgow*, and *Sheffield*, arrived in Åndalsnes with fresh British troops to throw into the battle. The town by now was little more than a mountain of war rubble. Haslund soon received orders to load the first 200 cases of the country's gold onto the *Galatea*, which would leave immediately for its return trip to Britain as soon as it was unloaded. Grieg and the gold, though, were still two hours away at the Romsdalen station up valley. When he received word to start moving the bullion, workmen separated wagon #8138, which contained two hundred large cases, from the rest of the cars. Then Haslund and sixteen soldiers scrambled into a passenger wagon, and the three-car train headed to the port.[30]

Once there the Norwegians broke the seal on the wagon, removed the cases, and carried them to the *Galathea*, where they placed them in the ship's armored room. The ship's paymaster received the key, and Haslund provided him with a receipt to sign that read, "Received from the Norwegian Government Ministry of Finance, represented by the Norwegian Finance Minister Oscar Torp, the following parcels containing gold bars and/or gold coins: two hundred cases, each weighing approximately 45-50 kilograms (100-110 pounds)." The receipt further stated that the cases were "to be shipped via an English port and safely forwarded to the Bank of England." The commander of the *Galathea* signed it.[31]

Back in the mountains the situation was getting worse. Fredrik Haslund first decided to get rid of the two chests that contained currency and bank documents. He gave them to a Norwegian couple with orders to deliver them to Finance Minister Torp, who was then in Molde with the rest of the cabinet. While waiting for news that another load of gold could be put on a second British vessel, Haslund sought to round up trucks in case the rail link were cut. Five days passed, but still no new messages arrived.

Finally, the group received word that it was no longer safe to remain in Romsdalshorn. They should move the remaining gold out of the railroad area. The Germans would soon be marching down the valley.

An officer in a nearby transportation unit rounded up twenty-five trucks and drivers to make the transfer. It took all night to load the remaining 1,322 boxes and barrels. An armed guard was placed on each truck, and the group departed, traveling in a half-mile-long convoy. Haslund and Grieg rode in the lead car. The two men had almost reached Åndalsnes, when three German planes began dropping bombs and strafing the trucks. Following instructions issued before the caravan had left, the vehicles stopped on the shoulder of the road. The men scurried to get under cars and trucks, hoping that the Germans would run out of ammunition and leave. The attack lasted about an hour, but no one was killed.[32]

The Norwegians got back in the vehicles and continued to the port. More German planes arrived just as the convoy entered Åndalsnes. Their main target was a torpedo boat in the harbor, but bombs were also falling close to the trucks. Miraculously none took a direct hit. Because of the heavy fighting, it was decided to go to the harbor in Molde, which was thirty-five miles away. The cargo would then be loaded on the British cruiser *Glasgow* along with the king and cabinet. The convoy continued the trip over unpaved country roads. Late in the day, it reached Åfannes, where a ferry captain offered to take them across the fjord. Haslund did not want to risk doing that in daylight, so the men waited for nightfall and went on two ferries. The crossing took six hours. The convoy finally reached Molde just before dawn. The trucks stayed just outside the city limits, while the leaders made a phone call to Minister Torp to get new instructions. The drivers and men by now had been traveling forty-eight hours without sleep.

The boxes of gold were put in a temporary holding location in the cellar of the Oscar Hansen clothing factory under a concrete floor topped with heavy planking. The next day German bombs fell constantly, with some even landing on the textile plant. The gold, though, was safe. Four trucks that had been damaged on the trip had to be abandoned, but Hansen was able to get two replacements to carry the load.[33]

Early in the morning of April 28, British General P.G.T. Paget received orders from London to evacuate his troops out of Central Norway in order to concentrate their efforts further north. At 5:00 A.M. he informed General Ruge, the commanding Norwegian officer, of the British decision. The Norwegians were already unhappy with the disappointing support they had received from the British. When he heard the news, Ruge said bitterly, "So Norway is to share the fate of Czechoslovakia and Poland. But why? Why withdraw when your troops are unbeaten?" He then turned around and walked away. After cooling down, Ruge went back, and told Paget, "But these things are not for us to decide, general. We are soldiers, and have to obey."[34]

While the final war drama was being played out, the men with the gold convoy bunked down in Molde at a junior high school, where they stayed from the morning of April 26 to the afternoon of April 29. Guards watched over the gold. At one point a fire broke out and spread to houses nearby. The small unit of men fought the flames and rescued some containers that held gold coins.

Haslund at last received a message to move his cargo to the main Molde pier by 10:00 P.M. The *Glasgow* would be arriving with two destroyers as escorts. One ship was going take the Norwegian cabinet members, top civil servants, and the country's king and crown prince to Tromsø, the country's northern-most city. The captain was insistent that the ship had to leave at 1:00 A.M. so it could be clear of the coast before it was light. Allied and German forces near there were fighting the fiercest battle of the invasion. Tromsø would be the Norwegian government's last stand on national soil. German attacks on the city and harbor continued relentlessly. Finance Minister Torp, who was following the fate of the gold from a villa outside the city along with Ole Colbjørnsen, a director of the Bank of Norway, agreed that the bank official should accompany the gold to London.[35]

Trucks carried the remaining gold to the Apotekderkaien dock in Molde, where it was transported in two small ships to the *Glasgow*. Colbjørnsen tried counting them as they arrived on board, but eventually the system broke down. Just lugging the fifty-pound boxes onto the ship was enough work. King Håkon watched from the bridge as the Norwegians carried boxes up the steep gangplank. A young British sailor suggested that they grease it with soap so that the boxes would move more easily.

The process, though, was taking too long, and the Norwegian gold team decided that they had to drive the remainder through the burning city directly to the ship. Four trucks carrying ten tons of gold each then weaved their way down a small road. Just as they were reaching the dock, a German plane began dropping bombs. British sailors aboard used the cruiser's fire hoses to spray a path for the trucks through the fire. From the deck of the *Glasgow*, Colbjørnsen realized all the gold could not be loaded, so he ran down the gangplank and yelled to Haslund, "Fredrik! You'll have to get the rest up north as best you can!"[36]

Then Colbjørnsen scrambled back up the gangplank, the last man to get on board. Sailors cut the mooring lines holding the ship to the dock, and the *Glasgow* slowly pulled out of the Molde harbor with twenty-eight Norwegians, including the king and crown prince, plus twenty-three tons of gold on board. Anti-aircraft guns blasted away at German aircraft still determined to sink the vessel, and much of the quay was now on fire. The *Glasgow*, though, avoided a direct hit.[37] Back at the dock, Fredrik Haslund made a quick check and discovered that he still had some 18 tons of gold. Someone tried to cheer him up by saying that saving at least half a loaf was better than nothing, but that didn't give him much consolation.

Earlier the Norwegian gold team had learned about the *Driva*, a 330-ton steamship that hauled passengers and freight among the islands on Norway's west coast. It was currently docked at a pier on the other side of the city, and the captain was willing to help the war effort. The trucks again made their way through piles of war debris and the stench of burning human and animal flesh to the dock where the ship was moored. The totally exhausted soldiers immediately loaded the remaining gold onto the *Driva*. German planes continued to drop bombs, but no damage was done. The vessel left the harbor as fast as possible with the remaining gold aboard.

The next day, Haslund set out to round up more fishing vessels and located two similar, but smaller, ships to help with the job.

While on his scouting trip, he learned that a German plane had attacked the *Driva*. It was now beached north of Molde on the island of Visnes. Its bow had gotten stuck in the sand. The quick-thinking captain, though, refloated the ship by moving the heavy gold to the stern and then headed toward the ferry landing in the fishing port of Gimnes for repairs.[38]

Haslund realized that the Germans were now attacking every ship in sight. Local police urged him to use small fishing boats known as puffers to transport the gold further north. They normally carried four to six fishermen and poked along at the rate of just six to eight knots. Their great advantage was that they could travel at night and slip between islands without German airplanes spotting them. Haslund quickly located five puffers, the *Heimdal*, *Bard*, *Leif*, *Gudrun*, and *Svanen*. The two-hundred-and-sixty boxes of gold were then divided equally among four of the vessels and loaded in complete darkness. Guards traveled in the last fishing boat, so they could rescue a gold boat if it got into trouble. A local official gave the little armada's captains a detailed route for how to go from island to island.[39]

At dawn on May 1, the puffers left the harbor. They stopped frequently, but had no contact with local residents to protect the secrecy of their mission. The gold team tried to ignore rumors, which were rife. Haslund decided that if the Germans stopped them, he would hide the gold on an uninhabited island or sink the vessels in shallow water.

The ploy worked, and the puffers attracted little attention. In the uninhabited Lammevågen bay in the town of Inntian, the bullion was transferred to two bigger and more seaworthy fishing boats, the *Alfhild II* and the *Stølvaag*, and they set off for the port of Sauøy.[40] The two skippers were seasoned seamen who knew the coastline as well as they knew the layouts of their own cottages. The local sheriff also arranged for the crews to go overland. Meanwhile, the Germans continued to push the Norwegian and allied troops northward.

Haslund directed the whole expedition from the *Stølvaag*, with Nordahl Grieg acting as his deputy and Hanna Eilertsen as the cook for the crew of four. The *Alfhild II* had six men aboard. By then the nights were getting shorter, so they were sometimes forced to travel in daylight. One day a Germany pontoon plane flew directly over the *Stølvaag* seemingly without noticing it. When they came close to a battle between German planes and British destroyers, the two ships headed for shore, where they hunkered down for several hours. In the middle of the Andfjorden fjord the *Stølvaag* almost ran into a submerging German submarine that was only thirty yards away.

Finally on the morning of May 9, the two vessels anchored in a small bay near Tromsø, and the crews walked into town. After learning that his boss Torp was due there the next day, Haslund wrote out a full report of what had happened. Two days later, the boxes of gold were brought to the Bank of Norway's office in town and the contents were counted. Everything was present and accounted for. Torp inspected the boats and thanked the crews for their bravery. He also decided to send Haslund to Britain with the remaining gold and asked Nordahl Grieg to go with him as his assistant. The British Consul in Tromsø was instructed to contact the Norwegians when the transfer of gold to the British should take place.[41]

While they were killing time waiting for the British to take the gold off their hands, the cook on Haslund's ship became sick. A doctor came aboard the *Stølvaag* and diagnosed her as having scarlet fever. Haslund explained that he had also been suffering from fever and a sore throat for several weeks. The doctor said he undoubtedly had been carrying the illness and had infected the cook. The doctor was stunned that Haslund had undergone his incredible ordeal with a walking case of scarlet fever. By then he was no long contagious, and the voyage continued.

Despite the chaos of war and the struggle to keep the gold away from the Germans, Nordahl Grieg somehow found time to write a patriotic poem entitled simply "May 17, 1940." That is the Norwegian Independence Day, and he read the poem to his fellow countrymen over Norwegian radio from the station in Tromsø. Its most poignant lines:

We fight for the right of breathing
Now, but a day shall be
When Norsemen shall breathe together,
The air of a land set free.[42]

The *Stølvaag* was needed for other naval action, so the gold was transferred to the *Alfhild II* on the night of May 19-20. Now all the remaining gold was in the hands of Haslund and Grieg, and one or the other always stayed on board the ship to watch over it at all times.[43]

Close to midnight on May 21, the British consul came out to the *Alfhild II* and told Haslund and Grieg to deliver their cargo to the British cruiser *Enterprise*, which was just then dropping anchor in the Tromsøysundet strait. Two days earlier, when the ship arrived with the cruiser *Devonshire*, German planes had attacked them. One bomb fell only twenty-five feet away, but miraculously no damage was done. British sailors quickly loaded the last eighteen tons of Norwegian gold onto the *Enterprise*.

The Germans undoubtedly had no idea of the mission of the *Enterprise* and the *Devonshire*, but on the evening of May 23 Nazi aircraft attacked them at anchor and one large bomb fell again only a few yards away. Later while the cruisers were refueling in the harbor, Nazi planes again bombed the *Enterprise*, but again there was no serious damage. The two ships finally left on the morning of May 24 and received an order to head for Great Britain that evening.

They arrived at Scapa Flow in Scotland on May 27 and then traveled down the western coast of Britain, arriving at Plymouth on May 29 at 5:00 in the morning. A representative from the Bank of England met the ship and had the 547 cases, 302 large and 245 small ones, transferred to a train that had a military guard. Haslund again demanded and received a receipt for the gold from the Bank of England official.[44]

On June 1, Sir Cecil Dormer, the British Minister to Oslo, flew to Tromsø and informed the Norwegian government that all Allied forces were being withdrawn from their country in order to strengthen units fighting further south. Germany had invaded

Holland, Belgium, and France on May 10, and the war there was going badly. The Norwegian government held its last meeting on native soil on June 7. That afternoon the cabinet, king, and crown prince boarded the British cruiser *Devonshire* in a light summer rain and set out for Gourrock near Glasgow. They arrived in Scotland the morning of June 10 and traveled by train to London. Britain's King George met his royal counterpart at the railroad station and took the two by car to Buckingham Palace, where they stayed for a few days before beginning nearly four years in exile. The king sent back a radio broadcast to his country explaining that he had left and pleaded: "All we ask of you is: Hold out in loyalty to our dear fatherland!"[45]

The Norwegian cabinet soon decided that it had become too dangerous to keep the nation's gold in London. France was on the brink of falling to the Nazis, and it was believed that Britain would be the next target. Hitler had already given General Keitel orders to plan for *Unternehmen Seelöwe* (Operation Sea Lion), the cross-Channel invasion.

Despite the serious danger from German U-boat attacks in the North Atlantic during the summer of 1940, the Norwegian government voted to ship the country's gold to Canada and the U.S. Canada, as a member of the British Commonwealth, was already in the war, but the United States was still a neutral. The cabinet decided, though, to keep in London one ton of gold, worth approximately $1 million, to pay for the costs of the government-in-exile, the king, and his family.

Major Arne Sunde, who had directed the escape of gold from Åndalsnes on the *Galatea*, was now in London and became part of a taskforce for the shipment across the Atlantic. He decided that the Norwegian merchant ship *Bomma*, a 1,450-ton freighter, would first make a test run to see if it could safely arrive in North America. The vessel had been built in 1938, and its captain Louis Johannesen had been at sea since he was a teenager during the age of sail. Johannesen and his ship had recently escaped from Molde under the nose of the Germans.[46]

The *Bomma* was repainted a dull gray, and its name was removed to make it look like a non-descript cargo ship. In early June, the vessel left Falmouth on Britain's south coast to begin the trip across the Atlantic. Two Norwegians who had been with the gold during most of its odyssey, Ole Colbjørnsen from the Bank of Norway and Fredrik Haslund, were assigned to make the first trip. Haslund was unhappy with the new assignment because he wanted to return to Norway and continue the fight. The plan was to deliver part of the gold to the Bank of Canada in Montreal and part to the U.S. Federal Reserve in Washington, D.C. Lloyd's of London insured the gold against loss at sea for $52,000 per million dollars of value.

Colbjørnsen and Haslund traveled to Falmouth on June 10, and inspected the cargo. The cases had been repacked in London, and the numbers were registered on a new manifest. Ten tons of gold was packed into 120 small boxes and 130 larger ones. They were then put on a towboat and carried out to the *Bomma*, which was anchored in the outer harbor. Colbjørnsen, Haslund, and Captain Johannesen watched over the cargo until it was safely in the hold under lock and key.[47]

The *Bomma* left Falmouth at 2:00 in the morning on June 15. Three hours and forty minutes later, it joined a convoy near Lizard Point, the southern-most spot in Britain. The formation consisted of thirteen vessels, mostly armed. One small destroyer served as escort. The *Bomma* was unarmed, but had anti-magnetic equipment to protect it against mines. After setting out, the convoy poked along on a zigzag course at eight knots to lessen the danger of being attacked.

The weather on the crossing was good, and the trip smooth. After nine days at sea, the convoy was broken up, with each ship going its own way. The *Bomma* increased its speed to thirteen knots and headed toward the Gulf of St. Lawrence with plans to make a first stop in Montreal. Soon, however, heavy fog rolled in, and the temperature fell rapidly. Colbjørnsen was fearful of hitting an iceberg and ordered the captain to change the course to due south. The captain suggested landing in either Boston or New York City, but the banker overruled him in favor of Baltimore. He thought that the arrival of the gold would be less conspicuous there, and he also wanted to be near the Federal Reserve's headquarters.

While the *Bomma* was still in the Atlantic, Wilhelm Morgenstierne, the Norwegian Minister in Washington, hastened to set up a gold account with the Federal Reserve in New York so that the cargo could be deposited upon arrival. He had been in frequent contact with American officials in both Washington and New York for several days about the imminent arrived of the valuable cargo. On June 24, the minister sent a special delivery letter to L. Werner Knoke, a vice president of the Federal Reserve, asking to open a gold account in the name of the Royal Norwegian Government. He explained that he had the power of attorney to "operate all accounts and other assets in the United States belonging to the Norwegian Government."[48]

When the *Bomma* arrived in Baltimore at 5:30 A.M. on June 28, Captain Johannesen and his crew ran into problems because the Norwegians didn't have any document giving them permission to import gold. So the captain declared that the ship had no cargo on board and only had ballast for stability. Armed U.S. Customs officials boarded the *Bomma* and forbid everyone except the captain from leaving the ship.[49]

With the help of Morgenstierne, Colbjørnsen and Haslund were finally allowed to travel to Washington. Not knowing what to expect in the U.S., they took with them two bags that each contained one thousand twenty-kroner gold coins. They figured that would cover any expenses, but left them temporarily at the Federal Reserve's Baltimore office. Once in Washington, they arranged to ship 130 cases of gold to the Federal Reserve Bank in New York and 120 cases to the Bank of Canada in Montreal. The Federal Reserve board finally approved the Norwegian gold account the same day the bullion arrived.

The evening of July 1, the *Bomma* moved to Canton Pier 3 and with a small army of police and customs agents standing guard, the ship's crew moved the gold into three armored trucks. Captain Johannesen wrote in his log that the disembarkation was finished at 10:00 P.M. The gold went to the Camden railroad station, where a special one-car train carried it to New York City. The rest of the shipment left by train for Canada. That same day, Minister Morgenstierne sent the Federal Reserve's Knocke a letter asking that the gold from the *Bomma* be put in the Norwegian account. The minister gave the value of the gold as "approximately" $6 million. Following an agreement with the Federal Reserve, Colbjørnsen stayed in the U.S., while Haslund traveled to Montreal to meet with Norwegian and Canadian officials about the gold that would be arriving there.[50] Following that first successful trip, a Norwegian armada began bringing gold to North America. Later shipments were limited to a maximum of six tons. By the end of July 1940, eleven Norwegian ships had successfully carried the entire Norwegian gold horde, with the exception of the ton kept in London, across the North Atlantic. Thirty-four tons went to the Bank of Canada and were stored in Ottawa, while 14.7 tons eventually went to the New York Federal Reserve Bank.[51]

Only one stray bag of Norwegian gold was lost in the whole transport, when a box was damaged aboard the *HMS Glasgow* on its way to Britain. A sailor on board stole a bag of Hungarian gold coins from the box. He then went on a drinking spree on the Glasgow waterfront, paying for drinks with his new wealth. He was quickly arrested, and given ninety days of detention. The remaining coins were sent to the Norwegian account at the Bank of England.[52]

While still in Washington in early August 1940, Fredrik Haslund wrote an official report on the rescue of the Norwegian gold. At the end of it, he modestly stated that his success "would not have been possible without the energy and the devotion to duty of many persons." He suggested that after the war everyone who helped him should be awarded a gold 20 kroner coin with a picture of the Norwegian king on one side and a "suitable inscription" on the other. No rewards, though, were ever given out to the courageous men who saved Norway's gold.[53]

Chapter Fourteen

ITALY CRUSHES ALBANIA

Albania
April 1939
Tons of gold: 2.6

Gold Route

Holland

Belgium

Luxembourg

East Prussia

Berlin

Germany

Poland

Slovakia

Bohemia and Moravia

Hungary

France

Switzerland

Romania

Yugoslavia

Italy

Albania

Rome

Tirana
Durrës

Greece

A lbania has spent most of its history being kicked around by its bigger neighbors. Greece, Rome, and the Byzantine Empire at various times ruled the poor, rugged land torn between the western and eastern cultures. Ismail Qemali, a veteran leader of the Albanian nationalist movement, declared his country's independence on November 28, 1912, and he became its first head of state. The London Peace Conference of 1912-1913 recognized it as an independent country, but then World War I turned the Balkans into a bloody battlefield. After the war, the Versailles Conference initially split up Albania's territory among Greece, Italy, and Yugoslavia. Woodrow Wilson in the name of national self-determination, however, torpedoed that plan.

In its early years, Albania endured a series of unstable governments. Ahmed Bey Zogu, the son of a prominent landowner, became the country's first president in January 1925 and turned it into a police state. On September 1, 1928, the Albanian parliament declared the country a kingdom, and Zogu named himself King Zog of the Albanians. He aligned his nation with Mussolini as a way to protect it from other neighbors. Italy is only forty miles east across the Adriatic Sea.[1]

Albania remained a poor country with virtually no industry that survived mostly on peasant farming. It was anxious, though, to get on the fast track to the modern world. Italy became an important partner in its financial development. Albania also tried to have close relations with Britain because of its financial center and as a counterbalance to Italy. Neville Chamberlain called Albania a Baltic Belgium, meaning that it was a small country that had to be protected from powerful neighbors. Zog was aware of the danger of getting too close to Mussolini, and once told the British minister, "Never will I fall into the hands of Italy."[2]

For a young country with an undeveloped economy and little financial experience, Albania had a surprisingly sophisticated central bank. The National Bank of Albania (*Banka e Shqipërisë*) was established in the summer of 1925 with capital of 12.5 million gold francs. Italian financiers put up three-quarters of the start-up money, which gave them the dominant role in the country's economy. The other investors were Yugoslav, Swiss, and Belgian banks.[3]

Not surprisingly since foreign bankers ran the financial institutions, the Albanian government and its central bank were very conservative. They kept a tight hand on the economy, and inflation was almost nonexistent. The nation's founders believed strongly in gold. The currency was the lek, and the monetary system was based on the Albanian gold franc. The central bank issued gold coins in denominations of 10, 20, and 100 francs in addition to silver and nickel pieces in smaller denominations. Paper money was backed by forty percent gold. The bank's bullion holdings increased from 1.9 million gold francs in 1927 to 9.2 million in 1938.[4] Looking back at that era, the International Currency Review of 1977 wrote, "Before the Second World War, the Albanian franc was one of the strongest currencies in Europe. The notes of the Albanian National Bank issued from March 1926 onwards were, in effect, bullion certificates."[5]

Once the central bank was established, the government worked hard to build up the gold holdings even more by having private citizens turn in their jewelry and other gold pieces in exchange for the country's new paper currency. That private gold was then put into the central bank reserves. Whenever possible, the bank also bought more gold in London.

Albania had the unfortunate experience to be in the middle of European politics between the wars. Mussolini was both nearby and on the march. His early success in conquering Ethiopia in 1935 had turned him into a new international figure, but Hitler's rapid rise to power around the same time eclipsed Il Duce. Mussolini viewed his Fascist rival with admiration, envy, and suspicion. German intentions in the Balkans, which he considered to be his own sphere of influence, also worried him. By 1938, Albania looked like a close and an easy target for Rome and a way for Italy to reestablish its leadership of Europe's fascist movement.

Count Galeazzo Ciano, Mussolini's son-in-law and foreign minister, took the lead within the Rome government in advocating an invasion of Albania. Ciano also promised Mussolini great mineral resources in the undeveloped country, although he had little research to back that up. The Italian leader, though, was a reluctant warrior, and Italy's Albanian adventure eventually became largely Ciano's war.[6]

The count hoped that the king would be slow to fight because of his concern for the impending arrival of an heir to his throne. Zog in April 1938 married Géraldine Apponyi de Nagy-Appony, a half American and half Hungarian princess, in a lavish wedding. Count Ciano attended the ceremony, and Hitler sent a red Mercedes as a wedding present. Queen Geraldine's main job was to provide the new kingdom with an heir, and she was soon pregnant. Ciano believed the pregnancy would be a distraction and keep the king's mind off politics, writing in his diary, "There is, above all, an act on which I am counting: the coming birth of Zog's child. The king loves his wife very much, as well as his whole family. I believe that he will prefer to insure to his dear ones a quiet future. And frankly I cannot imagine Geraldine running around fighting through the mountains of Unthi or the Mirdizu in her ninth month of pregnancy."[7]

Zog sensed that the Italians might cause trouble and tried to recruit allies, but he had little success. Britain's Neville Chamberlain showed no interest in standing up to the Nazis. The United States was trying to stay out of all foreign commitments despite recent German aggression. Neither Greece nor Yugoslavia was about to offer any help to their former enemy.

In December 1938, Count Ciano presented an invasion plan to Mussolini. The Italian leader tentatively approved it, but did not set a date for its implementation. Zog soon got wind of the danger, and in March of 1939 sent a message pleading, "Albania now is in Italy's hands, for Italy controls every sector of the national activity. The king is devoted. The people are grateful. Why do you want anything more?" Zog also sent a request for help to Hitler, but received no sympathy.[8]

By late March and after the Germans had overrun both Austria and Czechoslovakia, Mussolini drew up an eight-point list of demands that was sent to Zog. It included giving Italy access to all of Albania's ports, airports, and communication facilities. Albania would have become a vassal state totally under Italy's control. Zog might survive, but only as a puppet king. It was clear that failure to implement the demands would be the grounds for an invasion, and likely a brutal one at that for a small nation still recovering from war.[9]

Zog immediately began playing for time and told Ciano that he was willing to go along with the demands, but said that his government was refusing. The Italians at that point concluded that it was going to be impossible to browbeat the king into capitulation, and so Italian troops prepared to invade. Marshal Pietro Badoglio, the country's military leader and the hero of the invasions of Libya and Ethiopia, opposed the move, but other Italian generals were willing to go along. A new demand was then set to King Zog, with the warning that if he did not accept it the Italians would invade on April 7. Mussolini this time sent his own personal ultimatum.[10]

The Italians purposely did not consult Hitler on any of their moves against Albania. Mussolini and Ciano were not really interested in any peaceful solution with Albania. They wanted to show Hitler their country's military might in order to have a more powerful hand in European politics. Ciano wrote in his diary on April 4 that Il Duce "would prefer a solution by force of arms."[11]

On April 5, Her Majesty Queen Geraldine gave birth to a son, who was named Crown Prince Leka. The king ordered a 101-gun salute. The Albanian royal family now had its heir. The king asked the U.S. minister in Tirana, Hugh Grant, whether mother and child could obtain political asylum in America. The U.S. agreed. The birth had been complicated, but the queen still received a doctor's permission to travel, and so she and her two-day old son headed south toward Greece.[12]

Shortly after seeing his heir, Zog received a new ultimatum from Rome. He also learned about the attitude of the British toward the Italian-Albania situation. Prime Minister Chamberlain in response to a question in Parliament on whether Britain had any interest in Albania said, "No direct interest, but a general interest in the peace of the world." He then left for a week of fishing in Scotland. Ciano was pleased.[13]

The Italian invasion began on April 7 at 5:00 A.M. and met virtually no resistance. Zog wanted to retreat into the hills and lead a guerilla fight against the Italians, but the Albanian parliament told him to leave the country. The Italian offensive turned into something of a circus fire drill. The invading force consisted of twenty-two thousand men and four hundred planes, three hundred small tanks, and a dozen warships. The Albanians had about four thousand poorly trained soldiers and a few policemen. Yet in the port city of Durres, locals and a few soldiers drove the first invaders back into the sea. The Italians, though, successfully landed in a second attempt. The capital of Tirana fell at 10:30 A.M. on the day of the invasion without a shot being fired. Historian Bernd Fischer wrote, "The bungled invasion did the fascist leadership a great service; it made clear to them how totally unprepared Italy was to fight a major war."[14] Count Ciano, though, triumphantly flew his own plane to the capital of Tirana, where he found the streets empty.

King Zog went on the radio at 2:00 in the afternoon to make a brave appeal for national unity and resistance, saying, "I invite the whole Albanian people to stand united today, in this moment of danger, to defend the safety of the country and its independence to the last drop of blood." The only trouble was that Albania at the time had less than two thousand radios, and the Italians soon jammed the airways.[15]

Not long after giving the speech, the king left and the following afternoon he arrived in Florina, a small town in northern Greece. Italian radio claimed that he had stolen 550,000 gold francs from the central bank before leaving. The British foreign office later learned that Zog had £50,000 in gold as well as $2 million in a Chase Manhattan Bank account. Whatever he had was enough to pay for a long life in exile. He and his wife and child traveled first to France and then to Britain. After the war he ended up in Egypt as the guest of King Farouk. Rumors were that Zog paid him $20 million for that refuge.[16]

In the years leading up to the war, the Albanian Central Bank, which was largely under the influence of Italian bankers, had been shipping its gold to the Bank of Italy in Rome for safekeeping. By the time Mussolini's forces invaded, the vast majority of it was already in Italy, and the ownership was turned over to the Bank of Italy after the fall of Zog. That amounted to eight million gold francs weighing in at 2.4 tons. The Italians got only 280 gold francs when they took over the Albanian Central Bank in Tirana plus five million more in coins and jewelry from residents.[17]

Following the Allied invasion of Italy in September 1943, the Italians ousted Mussolini, but the soon Nazis put him back in power. On April 16, 1944 Berlin ordered Albanian officials to sign a protocol giving the Germans fifty-five cases of gold that had been stored at the Bank of Italy. They were sealed with steel strips and stored in secret tunnels. Germany military units near the end of that year picked up both the Italian and Albanian central bank gold and sent it to the Reichsbank in Berlin. It remained there until February 1945, when it was evacuated with other seized Nazi gold and art treasures to the salt mine in Merkers, Germany.[18]

Chapter Fifteen

HOLLAND FALLS
IN FOUR DAYS

Holland

May 10, 1940

Tons of gold:
Still in Holland 192.4

Gold Route

To New York

To London

IJmuden

Amsterdam

Schiphol Airport

The Hague

To London and then to New York

The Hook

Rotterdam

Holland

Germany

Belgium

The period between the fall of Poland in October 1939 and the invasion of Western Europe in May 1940 has gone into history with many names. It was a time of peace, but the world was waiting anxiously for more war. Americans called it the Phony War; the French named it the *drôle de guerre* (funny war); Churchill deemed it the Twilight War; and to cynics it was the *Sitzkrieg* (sitting war) or the Bore War. Semantics aside, Hitler, after securing his truce with Russia in the east, used the next few months to prepare a major military offensive in the west.

Originally Nazi generals planned to invade Western Europe in November 1939, with a war strategy similar to that of World War I. Hitler was not too happy with the plan, considering it insufficiently daring. Then on January 10, 1940, that document accidently fell into Allied hands. German regulations forbade officers from taking secret papers on flights near enemy or neutral territory. But as we now know, the newly wed major who was ordered to take the war plans between two locations in Germany, went by plane instead of train so that he could spend an extra night with his bride. And thus the Allies were able to get a hold of the invasion plans via the Belgians who intercepted the major's lost aircraft. Hitler was not all that unhappy because he had never liked the original proposal.[1]

General Erich von Manstein, perhaps the most brilliant strategist of World War II, provided exactly what the Führer wanted. The general came from a long line of officers and at the time was chief-of-staff of General Gerd von Rundstedt, the commander of Army Group I. Manstein supported the new ideas of General Heinz Guderian, who had studied the intra-war work on tank warfare done by Britain's J. F. C. Fuller and B. H. Liddell Hart as well as France's Charles de Gaulle. Army Chief of Staff Franz Halder originally opposed Manstein's proposal, and Hitler first heard about it from his chief adjutant. On February 17, 1940, he had a working breakfast with newly appointed corps commanders, a group that included Manstein. He so impressed Hitler that the Führer kept him until 2:00 P.M. to discuss his ideas in detail.[2]

Manstein's revised plan, which was ready only a week later, was codenamed Case Yellow. It broke the western offensive into northern and southern operations. The two would start simultaneously. The northern one against Holland and northern Belgium had to be a fast and crushing operation because that would be just a setup for the more important southern offensive. This would be a surprise thrust through Luxembourg and southern Belgium before German forces attacked northern France at Sedan on the Meuse River. The genius of the plan, which Hitler modified some and actually improved, was a tank attack through the Ardennes forest, which was then considered to be a natural barrier to an invasion. The boldness and heavy use of armored vehicles greatly appealed to Hitler. The plan now had the name *Operation Sichelschnitt* (Cut of the Sickle). Hitler also called in Guderian to ask him what he would do when he reached Sedan, and the tank enthusiast said he would drive right to the English Channel. That, though, was too bold for Hitler and the top military brass, and a final decision on that part was put off until later.[3]

After officials at *De Nederlandsche Bank* (The Netherlands National Bank) learned how the Nazis had captured the national bank gold when they invaded Austria and Czechoslovakia, they began looking for ways to protect their own holdings, which were among the largest in the world. As an historic financial center and global trader, Holland traditionally had large amounts of bullion in its vaults. Dutch military leaders repeatedly told political leaders that they could protect it over the years, and so they became complacent, figuring that even if there were an invasion they would have time to evacuate the gold via the country's many ports. Nonetheless, central bank officials discussed various ways of protecting it, including the possibility of storing the metal in one of the country's famous polders, the low-lying land behind the dikes.[4]

A new cabinet was more realistic about the Nazi threat, however, especially in light of what was happening to their eastern neighbors, and the central bank began quietly shipping large amounts of bullion out of the country, primarily at first to Britain, the world's traditional storage destination and a nation with which Amsterdam had strong historic ties. At the time, the Dutch Central Bank owned 555.8 tons. Later the Dutch also sent bullion to the Federal Reserve in New York, which now looked to be safer than London. In September 1938, Central Bank President L.J.A. Trip confidentially told the country's prime minister and minister of finance that Holland had ƒ546 million guilders of its gold abroad, with seventy-five percent in Britain and twenty-five percent in the U.S. When the Germans attacked Holland, the Dutch had more than eighty percent of its bullion at the New York Federal Reserve. The central bank, though, still had 192 tons in the country on the day of the invasion.[5]

In November 1939, Dutch officials received news from German opposition sources that Hitler was making plans to invade Holland as part of his plan to conquer Western Europe. The Dutch Central Bank staff at the main office in Amsterdam then hurriedly packed up ƒ125 million in gold bars and ƒ41 million in coins, so they would be ready to move on short notice. It was stored in the basement of its three-story building constructed in 1868 that stood amid gabled mansions in the city center on a street named Oude Turfmarkt. A small circular railroad track provided quick and easy access, and the national treasure could make a quick departure via canal. The plan was that it would go by small boat through the canal to the North Sea, and there would be loaded on bigger ships. While that storage facility was quaint and historic, the Dutch had more of its bullion stored at its more modern branch office in Rotterdam, forty-five miles south. The central bank still had 192.4 tons of gold in the country, with one-third in Amsterdam and two-thirds in Rotterdam. That amounted to thirty-five percent of its total holdings.[6]

Political and bank officials had long agreed that if the country were invaded, the government, not the central bank, would have responsibility for protecting the country's most valuable asset. London and Amsterdam also reached a secret agreement that in case of a crisis, British torpedo boats would escort Dutch ships evacuating gold to safety. When war fears increased again in late April 1940, the Dutch decided to ship an additional ƒ100 million to the United States, while the government continued to move bullion in small amounts to Britain. The last shipload of gold left from Rotterdam aboard the vessel *Delfdijk* with $3.5 million in gold. After landing in Portsmouth, England for repairs, it continued on to New York. The final air shipment before the invasion took place by air on May 7 on a 9:00 A.M. KLM flight to London that carried 1.6 tons. The next departure of 263 bars was scheduled to leave Rotterdam by sea on May 11. The gold was all packed and set to go.[7]

The Rotterdam central bank facility, which opened in 1907, was a mighty fortress located in the center of the city on a street called *Boompjes* or Little Trees. There were three vaults located underground at the back of the building. The concrete roof was 30 centimeters thick and was reinforced with concrete iron beams. At the entrance to the vaults were double steel doors. The main access was at *Boompjes* 72, which was on the backside away from Rotterdam's famous network of inland waterways. The Rotterdam evacuation plan was similar to the Amsterdam one. The gold would leave by canal in front of the bank and go out to the North Sea, where it would be transferred to a larger vessel and taken out of the country.[8]

May in Western Europe is a beautiful time of year. Winter can sometimes drag into late April, but then on May Day nature always seems to flip a switch and turn on spring. Early May 1940 was a perfect example. For the first two weeks, there was no rain and the skies were blue. In Paris on May 1, the traditional lilies of the valley were on sale at every corner, while in Holland tulips were in full bloom. In London on May 9, Sir Alexander Cadogan, the Permanent Under-Secretary at the Foreign Office, wrote in his diary, "Lovely day–tulips almost at their best and everything smiling, except human affairs."[9]

The German army and air force had been ready for months to launch its next invasions, but military leaders kept postponing the date, in part because they were waiting for perfect weather so that Germany's powerful new Luftwaffe would be at its deadly peak efficiency. The second week of May 1940 turned out to be ideal Hermann Göring weather. It was also Whitsun, a popular three-day religious holiday in Western Europe when many people go away for short vacations to enjoy the start of spring. That began on Saturday, May 11, but some people slipped away early.

France, Belgium, and Holland all knew that something was coming because of a steady stream of intelligence tips, mainly from the anti-Hitler group led by an opposition group that included Wilhelm Canaris and Hans Oster, who worked in German military intelligence, and Hans Bernd Gisevius of the Interior Ministry. Even the Vatican received news that a German invasion could be expected on about May 10, and the new pope, Pius XII, passed warnings along to the Dutch.[10] The best information came from Colonel Hans Oster, a top official in Wehrmacht intelligence. On May 9, he had dinner in Berlin with Colonel Jacob Sas, the Dutch military attaché, whom he had been warning of an imminent attack. While they dined, Oster explained that the offensive was likely to start at dawn the next morning. The final decision was to be taken at 9:30 that evening. After the two men finished eating, they walked through quiet Berlin streets to the office of the German High Command. Sas stayed outside on Bendlerstraße, while Oster went in to see if there might have been another delay. A half hour later, the German officer came out and tersely told Sas, "There has been no cancellation. The invasion is to begin." In a veiled reference to Hitler, Oster added, "The swine has gone to the western front."

Sas quickly telephoned the news to military leaders in The Hague, the country's seat of government. Oster also warned the Belgian military attaché in Berlin. At 3:00 A.M., German diplomats in Brussels and The Hague delivered a memorandum to the respective foreign ministries stating that Germany was invading the countries "to forestall a projected Anglo-French action."[11]

Early in the morning of May 10, Hitler and his two closest generals, Wilhelm Keitel and Alfred Jodl, arrived in Münstereifel, a small spa resort in western Germany only twenty-five miles behind the Wehrmacht units that would soon march into Belgium. The Führer claimed he had been so nervous the night before that he hadn't slept. The three encamped in a small field bunker called the *Felsennest*

(Rocky Eyrie) that had just four rooms. At the assigned time, one hundred German divisions began rolling into Luxembourg, Belgium, and Holland. Virtually every plane in Göring's Luftwaffe took off into the air. Winston Churchill would later write: "Four or five millions of men met each other in the first shock of the most merciless of all wars to which record has been kept."[12]

At that crucial moment in European history, neither Britain nor France had a government. London was in the midst of a political crisis. Parliament had lost confidence in Neville Chamberlain because of his accommodating policies toward Hitler going back to the *Anschluss*; but Churchill had not yet been appointed to replace him. The French cabinet had also fallen the afternoon before, a routine occurrence during the country's Third Republic. The government of Paul Reynaud was technically out of office, but President Albert Lebrun the evening before had asked him to continue in power for a few days.[13]

German General Fedor von Bock launched the thirty divisions of the Wehrmacht's Group B into the region stretching from Northern Belgium in the south to above Amsterdam in the north. The primary target was the area the Dutch called *Vesting Holland* (Fortress Holland), the country's stronghold that included the cities of Amsterdam, Utrecht, Rotterdam, Leyden, and The Hague. Water surrounds the region on three sides, and the Dutch were supremely confident that their networks of dikes would stop a German offensive. Three years before, Dutch Prime Minister Hendrik Colijn had explained proudly to Winston Churchill how he could with just the push of a button open the locks on his country's famous dikes. Torrents of water would swamp an invading German army in its tracks.[14]

Many Dutch leaders had been confident that their traditional policy of neutrality, which had kept their country out of World War I, would work again. Only after the Germans sent their armies into the Rhineland in 1936 did politicians slowly become nervous and begin a serious armament program. Ironically, they tried at first to buy some of their weapons from Germany. Berlin, though, wasn't interested in arming potential targets. It was impossible, however, for Holland in a short time and given the country's small military budget to build a force capable of standing up to the mighty Wehrmacht. Holland was totally unprepared for the onslaught that hit it.

At about 1:30 in the morning of May 10, a large formation of German bombers flew high over the country heading west. Alert Dutch defense units surmised that they were going to Britain. When the planes reached the North Sea, however, the pilots turned around and headed back east. Then they bombed two major targets: The Hague and Rotterdam. Amsterdam was not a primary target, and the Dutch believe that was perhaps because Hitler, a student of architecture, liked the city just as he later admired and spared Paris. German paratroop units, Berlin's new attack weapon, which had first been used only a month before in Denmark, began landing in Holland.[15]

Just as in Denmark and Norway, a prime German objective here was to capture the country's royalty and its government. First they had to secure key airports, and after that motorized units would speed to The Hague and take Queen Wilhelmina prisoner. She had been queen since 1898 and was the symbol of the country's unity. She was not a modern monarch who only showed up for ribbon cuttings and stayed out of politics. On the contrary, the strong-willed woman regularly got into the daily affairs of her cabinet and had close relations with the country's military leaders. She had said early and repeatedly that if war came, she wanted to follow the World War I precedent of Albert, the king of the Belgians, who had remained in his country throughout the fighting and occupation.

The German offensive was swift and initially successful. Troops quickly controlled two airfields near The Hague. After temporarily stunned Dutch troops recovered, however, they drove the invaders back and took a large number of prisoners. Just as in Norway, the master race's invasion was not going according to schedule.

In Rotterdam twelve Nazi seaplanes landed on the Nieuwe Maas waterway in the center of the city, which had been opened in 1872 to keep the port of Rotterdam accessible to seafaring vessels. The primary German objective was to capture the city's key bridges that were the gateway to Fortress Holland and to the water defense that Colijn had described to Churchill. If the Germans grabbed them intact, their troops could quickly move into the heart of the country. Nazi commandos, dressed in local police uniforms, pretended to be leading captured German prisoners and then turned and attacked the Dutch troops.

The Nazis took the strategically vital Gennep railway bridge, but a fierce battle was fought over the Willems Bridge. Only about 500 yards from where all the fighting was taking place stood the Rotterdam branch of the Dutch Central Bank. If the Nazi forces were able to capture the bridge quickly, the gold stored there would fall into their hands. Although the Germans captured the southern end of the bridge, Dutch marines managed to control the northern end. They set up military units in the Witte Huis, an eleven-story art nouveau hotel built in 1898 that was Europe's first skyscraper. Because of its height and the soft, damp Rotterdam soil, the building had been constructed of iron, steel, and cement on one thousand pilings. That now made it a mighty defense fortress. From the top floors, Dutch marines fired in all directions. Gradually the Nazi troops had to retreat from all their positions except one in a tall bank and insurance building directly opposite the Witte Huis.

The evening of May 9-10, Queen Wilhelmina had stayed in The Hague with her family at the royal rural residence Huis ten Bosch, one of her three homes. At 4:00 A.M., she woke her daughter Crown Princess Juliana and said simply, "They have come." She didn't need to say anything more. Juliana was sleeping in the palace's air-raid shelter with her daughters Beatrix, aged just over two years, and Irene, who was eight months old. Major Sas had also warned Prince Bernhard, Juliana's husband, of the invasion. The coded Sas message: "My aunt is sick." The prince had passed the news along to Wilhelmina.[16]

Bernhard, a German by birth, had been a member of the Nazi party in his student days and married Juliana in 1937. Three years later, the Dutch people still weren't totally sure where his loyalties lay. The royal family soon heard the sound of anti-aircraft fire from outside the palace, and German airborne troops led by SS General Kurt Student began landing. German planes dropped leaflets with the warning, "The city is surrounded by strong German troops. Any resistance is senseless." The general had orders to capture the queen. If she refused to cooperate, he was to arrest her and send her to Germany.

General Henri Gerard Winkelman, the commander of the Dutch military, urged the royal family to leave Huis ten Bosch, which was located in the middle of a forested area of The Hague and would be easy for the enemy to capture. He proposed they go to their Noordeinde Palace in the heart of the city, which was only two miles away and had a stronger air-raid bunker. It was also nearer the coast in case the royals had to escape by sea. At this point Dutch leaders still thought they could handle the royal family's evacuation without any outside help.

Just before leaving, the queen at 8:00 A.M. issued a statement calling the invasion a "flagrant breach of conduct" among "civilized nations." The family departed in two taxis, rather than their official limousines, so as to attract as little attention as possible. The queen rode in the lead car. The crown princess, the prince, and their two daughters traveled in the second one. As they left, the prince fired a machine gun at a German plane, but did not hit anything.[17]

After an emergency communications link was set up between London and The Hague, Churchill sent a message to the queen asking simply, "What about your evacuation?" The British placed a high priority on keeping royalty on their side. The Dutch military attaché in London was already working with the British to get some of their fastest warships to Holland to rescue both the country's first family and the national gold.

No one knew whether the strong-willed Queen Wilhelmina would leave her country. Her highness was determined to get Princess Juliana, her daughter and royal heir, out of Holland. She represented the future of the House of Orange-Nassau monarchy, and it was imperative that her life be saved. Wilhelmina quickly requisitioned *Torpedo Boat 51* from the Dutch navy and made plans to send the Crown Princess and her family to southern Holland and, if necessary, to France. That plan, though, fell through when the Germans quickly captured the region where the ship was located. The only real option now was to get the heir to London with the help of the British navy.[18]

Central Bank President Trip in the early hours of the invasion worked the telephones to his offices in both Amsterdam and Rotterdam from his home in The Hague. Their first priority was to get their precious metal out of the country. The gold in Amsterdam had fortunately never been unpacked after the November invasion scare. It was still in the basement of the Romanesque bank headquarters at the Oude Turfmarkt. Directly in front of the building was one of the capital's many canals. The gold stored in the basement could be moved easily from the vault in wagons with the help of a small train and put into boats that would take it to bigger ships and evacuated. That escape, though, was not used. During the afternoon twelve trucks arrived in Amsterdam and picked up ƒ125 million guilders worth of gold bars plus ƒ41 million in gold coins. With an armored truck from the Dutch Central Bank acting as escort, the trucks raced to IJmuiden, a port city located at the mouth of the North Sea Canal.

Bank representatives immediately contacted the Royal Dutch Steamboat Company (KNSM) to arrange transportation, but found that it had already sent most of its vessels out to sea in advance of the anticipated invasion. There were only three ships left, the SS *Perseus*, the SS *Titus* and the SS *Iris*. The company was willing to lease them despite the war dangers. The gold was too heavy for just one vessel and the *Perseus* was not ready to leave, so bank officials decided to take the other two. The Dutch are infamous in Europe for bargaining hard over prices, so it was not surprising that the bank and the shipping company quickly got into an argument over the cost of leasing the boats. The company said the price would be ƒ830,000, but Deputy Bank Director A.M. de Jong said that was too much. He counter offered ƒ415,000, but the shipping company responded that was not enough. De Jong quickly pointed out that the company had sent ships empty to Britain. Surely the lower price was better than nothing.[19]

While the haggling was going on, the bank president was on the phone with the Bank of England explaining the Dutch problem getting their gold out of the country. Once off the phone, he impatiently told de Jong that there were a hundred other more important things to do at this time of crisis than haggling over the price of the boats. He told him just to make a deal! The two sides finally agreed on ƒ500,000.[20]

The *Iris* and the *Titus* soon departed for the port of IJmuiden to pick up 70.6 tons of gold bars from the Amsterdam bank office. Klaas de Jong, the captain of the *Iris*, had learned about the German attack early that morning. He was waiting for a favorable tide to start a scheduled trip to Italy and was anxious to leave, but he quickly contacted his office and asked what he should do. With a brusqueness common to ship commanders, he insisted that the crew stay. Policemen eventually came aboard the *Iris* and told the crew that as soon as the country had been invaded, they had become members of the military. So they were now under army orders. The police also had all the seamen sign pledges of loyalty to the country.[21]

With the crew becoming more nervous by the hour, de Jong waited for instructions. Finally at 5:00 in the afternoon, he was told to move his ship into a nearby dock and prepare to leave. As soon as it was dark, he heard the sound of trucks bringing the cargo to the ships. When they arrived, workmen quickly loaded the steel-belted boxes on board. No one had told the captain what they contained, but the workers knew because of the weight. Once the cargo was aboard, an official of the Dutch bank had the captain sign a receipt for eighty-seven million guilders. No one had told de Jong where he was supposed to go, but he figured that he would learn later. With its siren blaring, the vessel slowly pulled away from the dock and immediately ran into the bedlam of boats trying to leave Holland. It was now dark, which gave the *Iris* some cover, but also made it harder to see the mines the Germans had dropped in the canals. The captain finally received a simple order: "Get away and try to reach England." He was also told that a naval escort would pick him up once he was in open ocean and lead him to his final destination.

For the next two hours the *Iris* inched its way through the harbor. De Jong decided to go out into the North Sea and head southeast toward the Belgian coast since it was a route he knew well. He hoped that he could reach there by dawn. Everything was going fine until shortly after the sun came up. A German plane spotted the *Iris* and dove right at the ship with its machine guns firing. Miraculously no serious damage was done. Following the attack, de Jong broke radio silence and sent a radio message asking where the escort was that was supposed to take him to Britain.[22]

Soon a second Nazi plane appeared in the sky, and the captain sent another message, "Attacked again." Operators in Amsterdam replied: "Escort is on the way." Eventually de Jong saw on the horizon lights from the cruiser *HMS Arethusa* and the destroyer *HMS Boreas.* Using a signal light, the *Boreas* flashed the message: "Are you the *Iris.*" De Jong replied: "Yes." The British ships, which had been looking for both the *Titus* and the *Iris,* ordered the vessel to follow them toward the English Channel. For several hours the Dutch ship chased the two larger crafts as they zigged and zagged to throw off enemy vessels. Finally, the three ships pulled into the Thames estuary and headed toward Tilbury. At 5:20 P.M. on May 11, the captain signaled the harbor control officer that he wanted to enter the docks, and the escort ships left. As the *Iris* pulled up to the dock, the British officer on duty shouted, "You must be a very important ship with such an escort!" De Jong barked back, "Mind your own business."

Once he tied up, the captain told British guards that he had to see the commander at once, adding sternly, "No one must leave my ship!" When he got to the main office, the officer on duty asked matter-of-factly what was on board. De Jong replied, "My cargo is only gold." Armed guards then quickly surrounded the vessel. When he returned to the *Iris,* de Jong saw off in the distance the *Titus* at anchor. The British ship *Keith* had met it out at sea and brought it in. The gold from both the *Iris* and the *Titus* was soon loaded onto trucks and taken to the Bank of England.[23]

At The Hague early in the evening of May 10, everything was going badly for the Dutch. The royal family was better protected at the Noordeinde Palace, but the German army, helped by some Dutch traitors, had taken up positions directly in front of the building. Snipers in a nearby house shot at anyone who left the palace. In addition, more German airborne troops were falling from the skies. Prince Bernhard returned sniper fire from the palace with a hunting rifle. He also got into a fistfight with a Dutch army officer, who had gone over to the Nazi side and tried to enter the palace.

The Dutch government was still working to get the royal family and more gold out on a British ship, but was having problems coordinating everything. The queen lamented, "If anything happens to my daughter, I will shoot myself." Prince Bernhard wanted to stay behind and fight for his adopted country against his native nation, but the queen insisted that he leave with his family. Wilhelmina was determined to remain in Holland, saying she would kill herself rather than let the Nazis take her prisoner.[24]

Late in the afternoon, central bank officials in Amsterdam finished packing twelve trucks and one of its steel-plated vans with gold. When the last one was loaded, the caravan took off for IJmuiden, where British ships waited to take the bullion to Britain. The van with a bank director on board made a detour to the palace to pick up Princess Juliana, her family, and some staff. The group quickly scrambled on board. Beside the driver was an armed bodyguard, who carried the royal family's crown jewels in a cardboard box tied with string. Value: $6 million. After the war, Prince Bernhard told the British author Alfred Draper, that in the back of the van were boxes of gold covered with straw. The two royal children were sitting on them. The van had no identification marks except the license plate G44645 on the front bumper. There were only two small windows on the side of the van. Prince Bernhard posted himself next to one window, while E.J. van Olathe, a submarine commander attached to the queen, sat at the other. With tears in her eyes, Juliana cried, "I have a feeling I will not see my mother again." Despite continuous fighting around them, the vehicle had no military escort because that might have attracted attention.[25]

The black van stayed off the main roads, taking three hours to go the thirty miles between The Hague and IJmuiden. Dutch roadblocks stopped the security truck from time to time, but quickly let the group proceed once soldiers recognized the royals inside. Having no idea who was in the vehicle, German soldiers randomly shot at it, although no serious damage was done. Bernhard ordered everyone not to return fire, fearing that would only attract more attention.

At the dock mayhem prevailed. Hundreds of fearful Dutch citizens crowded along the docks desperate to get on British ships or anything that would take them out of the country. German dive-bombers attacked the crowds, and Nazi Stukas staged dogfights against the diminished, but determined, Dutch Army Aviation Brigade. The most frightening moments occurred when German planes fitted with sirens that let out high-pitched screams dove toward the crowds. The aircraft came in from the direction of the sun and were invisible until only seconds before they flew over the tops of ships and then soared back into the sky. Gunners returned fire, but scored few hits.

HMS Codrington, a British destroyer commissioned ten years earlier, left Britain on May 10 with orders to go to IJmuiden and evacuate Princess Juliana and her family. The commander was Captain G. E. Creasy. The previous December the ship had taken King George VI to France to visit troops, and the following month took Prime Minister Chamberlain and Winston Churchill, then the First Lord of British Admiralty, to inspect the French battlefronts. The ship had also been in northern Norway to support that country's battle with the Nazis.[26]

The *Codrington* pulled into the IJmuiden harbor without the benefit of a pilot boat, but accompanied by *HMS Hyperion* and *HMS Windsor*. Captain Creasy made three unsuccessful attempts to dock, but finally landed on the fourth try and tied up at about 9:00 P.M. He was dismayed to learn that his royal passengers and their valuable accompanying baggage had not yet arrived. At a half hour before midnight, the royals finally scrambled aboard. Even though German aircraft couldn't have known who was on the vessel, the planes quickly attacked the *Codrington*. Bernhard asked the crew not to fire back lest it draw more attacks. With the insouciance of a toddler, Princess Beatrix watched the spectacle with her baby sister sitting in her lap.[27]

After the royal family finally reached the *Codrington*, the destroyer immediately departed. Just then, a German plane dropped a magnetic mine setting off an underwater explosion that severely rocked the mighty vessel, but did no serious damage. Captain Creasy ordered full steam ahead, and the ship was soon out into the North Sea heading to Harwich on Britain's southeast coast. The destroyers *HMS Vivacious* and *HMS Venetia* escorted her home. A flotilla of small ships desperate to escape Holland also accompanied the convoy. The *Codrington* arrived that same day at 8:00 A.M., and Captain Creasy wrote in his log: "The Royal party disembarked after giving me the honour of their presence for breakfast at 09.15."[28]

A month later, the crown princess and her two daughters left Britain for Canada to get even further away from Hitler's war. The royal party arrived in Halifax on June 11 aboard the Dutch vessels *Java* and *Tromp*. The following day, two French captains who were picking up American aircraft visited her on the *Java*. The Princess was gracious but cried much of the time and told them of the horrors that had happened to her country. At noon she took a train to Quebec and went into an exile that would last nearly five years.[29]

On May 10, the British Admiralty sent the destroyer *HMS Wild Swan* to the Hook of Holland on the North Sea coast near the entrance to the Nieuwe Waterweg shipping canal. It was under the command of Lt. Commander John Younghusband.[30] Rotterdam is about sixteen miles inland from The Hook. Aboard the ship were Commander J. A. C. Hill and a team of demolition experts. The British were concerned about the large fuel-storage areas located in Holland out of fear that they might fall into Nazis hands. Hill had earlier made a secret trip there to scope out such a plan. Now his orders were to implement it.[31]

At 6:31 P.M. Lt. Commander Younghusband received a message from London that read: "Dutch foreign minister states that there is a large amount of gold at Rotterdam. Estimated weight 36 tons. It is essential to get gold out tonight." Local authorities said it was too dangerous for the *Wild Swan* to go to Rotterdam. Earlier that same day German Stukas had sunk the Dutch destroyer *Van Galen* on the Nieuwe Waterweg. The *Wild Swan* could attract too much enemy attention and suffer the same fate. After Hill and Younghusband huddled, they decided that Hill would go to Rotterdam on a smaller Dutch ship and pick up the gold. Younghusband would stay in the harbor on the *Wild Swan* and let out his mooring lines to twenty feet to make it difficult for any enemy to come aboard. Gunners also manned their stations.

Residents of the village of Maassluis near the Hook of Holland woke the morning of May 10 to the roar of German warplanes flying overhead. This was home to a fleet of small pilot boats whose job was to guide bigger ships into Rotterdam. The crew of *Pilot Boat 19* was called to duty even though it was their day off. The ship was under the command of Sea Lieutenant IJsbrand Smit. While the captain and crew waited for an assignment, they watched German planes landing and disembarking soldiers. Finally at 8:15 P.M., *Pilot Boat 19* departed from Hook of Holland. Destination: Rotterdam. Aboard the ship were Hill and his demolition party plus nineteen Dutch crew members.

It was not the ideal boat for the assignment because it had no degaussing equipment that would protect it from magnetic mines the Nazis had been dropping in the waterways. But this was a war, and Commander Hill had to take what was available. *Pilot Boat 19* moved slowly through the chilly waters. The crew and the soldiers peered out into the dark looking for mines. At about midnight and long after the vessel had passed the area on its way to Rotterdam, a German Henkel 115 airplane dropped new mines in the Nieuwe Waterweg near Rozenburg Island, only about four miles from the Hook of Holland.[32]

Hill and his team arrived at the Lekhaven dock in Rotterdam at 10:30 P.M. It was not the closest one to the central bank office, but it would have been dangerous to try to get any nearer. Nazis now occupied the southern and eastern parts of town and were moving in on the rest. The Rotterdam branch of the Dutch National Bank was located only two hundred yards away from an area the Germans now controlled. Nazi troops had earlier attacked the facility, but Dutch machine gunfire had driven them back.

There were nearly 114 tons of gold still in the Rotterdam bank's vaults, and the Dutch had hope that they would manage to get all of it out of the country. The immediate British task, though, was to get at least some on *Pilot Boat 19*. During the day of May 10, the bank staff had packed the gold into boxes, and they recruited Dutch marines to help move it. Officials requisitioned four trucks, which marines drove across narrow canal bridges to the bank's back door, only a short distance away from the heart of the fighting. With just flashlights to guide them, the men went down into the unlit vaults and carried the heavy boxes through darkened halls to the waiting vehicles. Members of an infantry unit also helped with the loading. There still remained just over 102.8 tons in the bank, but that would have to be removed later. From positions on nearby bridges and in trees, German sharpshooters fired at anything that moved.

Dutch marines then drove the four vehicles toward *Pilot Boat 19* at the Lekhaven dock. Slowly they made their way down dark back streets amid continued shooting. The Dutch had the advantage of knowing their way around Rotterdam's winding streets and narrow bridges. A half hour later, the small caravan arrived at the boat. The marines unloaded the cargo, which took about two hours to complete. Members of the British demolition unit also helped. The work was tough and progressed slowly because each box weighed more than one hundred pounds, and the men worried about slipping on the narrow gangplank. They finally loaded eleven tons. The bullion was stored near the cabin. They could have taken more, but the captain was worried about the boat's stability because the weight was mainly on the deck, rather than in the hold. Hill and the boat's crew set out at 4:45 A.M. for the return trip to the Hook of Holland and the *Wild Swan*, some twenty miles away. There were no other ships on the waterway, so it was a tempting target.[33]

At 5:30 A.M., daylight had broken and *Pilot Boat 19* was getting closer to The Hook. The ship had only about another ten miles to go. Just as it approached the city of Vlaardingen, a powerful explosion rocked the whole area. A Nazi magnetic mine that had been dropped into the water after *Pilot Boat 19* had passed the area on its way to Rotterdam blasted the ship into two pieces. Large hunks of wood catapulted into the air, and just six of the twenty-two men on board survived the blast. Most of the crew had been in the ship's sleeping area below deck. The mine struck the boat two-thirds from the bow, where the gold was stored. One of the survivors was projected across the canal and drowned because he didn't know how to swim. Workers from a nearby factory rushed to help, but could do little. Willem Pottinga, a crewmember and one of the survivors, was below deck when the explosion occurred and swam to safety dragging the body of a sailor he assumed was dead. He wanted the family to have a chance to bury the man. The person was actually alive, and a doctor resuscitated him. But the gold quickly sank to the bottom of the Nieuwe Waterweg.

At 7:45 A.M., Dutch military authorities informed Lt. Commander Younghusband on the *Wild Swan* that a magnetic mine had blown up *Pilot Boat 19*, killing most of those on board and all the British soldiers.[34]

On the evening of May 12, Queen Wilhelmina telephoned Britain's George VI to ask if she could go into exile in his country. As his majesty quipped later, it's not often that a king gets a phone call from a queen in the middle of the night asking for refuge. The destroyer *HMS Hereward* arrived on May 13 to take Wilhelmina to Britain. When she boarded, the always feisty queen said she wanted to go to Flushing in the southwestern part of the country, where fighting continued. The British captain said that was impossible, so her majesty left for Britain escorted by *HMS Vesper*. Churchill would later say that Wilhelmina was "the only real man among the governments-in-exile in London." Her ship arrived that same day in Harwich, and she traveled from there by train to London. When she arrived at Liverpool Station, Wilhelmina walked proudly up to the king with a gas mask slung over her shoulder. King George VI greeted her with a kiss on both cheeks.[35]

At 6:00 P.M. on May 13, six British destroyers began the final evacuation of Hook of Holland. *HMS Windsor* rescued members of the Dutch government as well as British, Belgian, Norwegian legation staffs and 400 refugees. Remaining soldiers and citizens continued to fight heroically, to the consternation of the Germans, who still could not believe the Dutch resistance. On May 14, Hitler decided to end the northern offensive quickly. The more important operation aimed at France was due to reach its crucial point in a few days, and he wanted that to stay on schedule. So he sent out War Directive 11, stating coldly, "Political as well as military considerations require that this resistance be broken immediately." It called for the "rapid reduction of Fortress Holland." Göring ordered an air bombardment of Rotterdam similar to earlier Nazis attacks on civilian targets in Guernica, Spain and Warsaw, Poland. German planes carpet-bombed the city with 1,150 110-lb. and 158 550-lb. explosives. Huge sections of the town were leveled, and there were immediate reports of 30,000 deaths. The figure was later reduced to about 850. One of the few buildings that survived the Nazi air attack was the Witte Huis, which is still standing proudly in the center of the city today.[36]

At dusk that night, General Winkelman, the commander of the Dutch military, ordered his troops to stop fighting. The next morning at 10:00, German and Dutch officers signed a capitulation order.[37]

Under the Dutch-German armistice agreement, the Dutch were charged with cleaning up the country's many waterways, which were now cluttered with the flotsam and jetsam of the invasion. German officials at the time knew nothing about the gold resting at the bottom of the Nieuwe Waterweg. The Netherlands National Bank on June 1, signed a contract with a salvage company to search the area where the pilot boat had sunk. Divers pulled up 75 bars on the first day of the rescue operation and 169 on the second. They were all turned over to the Rotterdam bank. A month later, a German merchant who had a shop nearby told the new Nazi harbor commander in Rotterdam about the golden *Pilot Boat 19* disaster. The Dutch by then had salvaged about 750 bars. A German court ruled that the gold belonged to the Reich. In October 1940, the Dutch Central Bank said in view of that they were not going to continue the salvage operation. By then they had found 816 bars.

After the war, the Nieuwe Waterweg was deepened and expanded; and during that work more gold bars were uncovered and local workmen got some of the treasure. Six bars have never been accounted for and might have been stolen. In any case, they were never found. The channel is today much deeper than it was in 1940, and no one believes that any gold remains at the bottom of the waterway.[38]

After the Nazis consolidated their hold on the country, they began sending the gold left at the Rotterdam branch to Berlin. The first shipment of 536 bars weighed 6.7 tons. Six more shipments were later made, with the last one departing on October 18, 1943. During the next two years, the Dutch shipped 192.7 tons of gold to Berlin.

In the Netherlands, as in other occupied countries, the Nazis captured privately held gold. Dutch citizens were forced to sell their bullion coins and small bars to the Dutch central bank, which paid them in guilders. The bank had to pass them along to Berlin. The Dutch, instinctively law-abiding people, complied with few protests. Citizens sold 35.5 tons of gold to the state bank.

Germany's *Devisenschutzkommandos* were also active in collecting private Dutch gold and other valuables held in private banks. With a bank employee always present, they opened every safety deposit box in the country. The process took a year to complete and resulted in a haul of nearly ten tons of gold bars plus ƒ4.2 million in gold coins and millions more in American, French, Swiss, Belgian, and German currency. All that private wealth was handed over to Göring's Four Year Plan, but was stored at the Reichsbank.[39]

As the war dragged on, the Nazis found new ways to confiscate Holland's remaining gold and foreign currency. On March 24, 1941, Arthur Seyss-Inquart, the Austrian Nazi who became *Reichskommissar* of Holland, demanded that the country pay 500 million Reichsmark for so-called occupation costs. For starters, ƒ75 million had to be paid within two weeks in gold. The Dutch eventually sent ƒ1.2 billion per year to Berlin as occupation payments for the entire war.

Starting in March 1942, Berlin also demanded that the Netherlands help pay for the cost of Germany's invasion of the Soviet Union. This was called their contribution to the "fight against Bolshevism." The allotted Dutch amount was 50 million Reichsmark per month, with 10 million of that paid in gold. Since the invasion of the Soviet Union had started nine months earlier, the initial installment was 90 million Reichsmark in gold.

Central Bank President L.J.A. Trip resigned in protest to Nazi policies in March 1941, but the Germans simply replaced him with a compliant successor, Meinoud Rost van Tonningen, a leader of the Dutch Nazi party and also secretary-general of the finance ministry. In March 1943, he sent a message to Seyss-Inquart that virtually all the treasure that had been left in the vaults or in private accounts was now in Berlin.

Small amounts of gold were found in December 1944 and February 1945 in regional central bank offices in Arnhem and Meppel. In Arnhem the Nazis discovered 32 bags of gold coins that weighed a little less than one ton, and in Meppel they got 1.4 tons. The Arnhem gold went directly to Berlin, but that in Meppel did not because the Germans thought the Soviets would confiscate it when they reached Berlin. It went instead to the regional Reichsbank branch in Würzburg in Bavaria. The last Dutch gold arrived in Germany on February 26, 1945.

The Dutch lost a total of 145.6 tons of gold to the Nazis, the second largest amount of any nation after Belgium. That consisted of 104.9 tons taken from central bank vaults, 28.8 tons robbed from the public, 9.6 tons from *Pilot Boat 19*, and 2.3 tons from Arnhem and Meppel. The valiant Dutch and British efforts under the most dangerous and difficult circumstances possible succeeded in saving 70.6 tons.[40]

Chapter Sixteen

BELGIUM AND LUXEMBOURG TRUST FRANCE

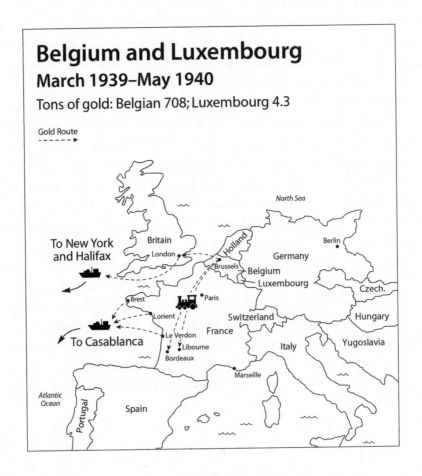

Belgium and Luxembourg
March 1939–May 1940
Tons of gold: Belgian 708; Luxembourg 4.3

Gold Route

To New York and Halifax

To Casablanca

Britain
London
Brussels
Belgium
Luxembourg
Germany
Berlin
Czech.
Hungary
Switzerland
France
Italy
Yugoslavia
Paris
Brest
Lorient
Le Verdon
Libourne
Bordeaux
Marseille
Spain
Portugal
Atlantic Ocean
North Sea
Holland

Throughout history Belgium has been Western Europe's bloody crossroads. During the Middle Ages it was one of the world's richest regions and a major center of the industrial revolution. Unfortunately, it has also been the region where the Germanic and Latin cultures collided and fought brutal wars. Wellington defeated Napoleon at Waterloo just outside of Brussels. Armies of Germany, France, and Britain in World War I, fought to a stalemate there, and as the poem recounts, "In Flanders Fields the poppies blow/Between the crosses, row on row."

Belgium has been a nation state only since 1830, when its often-quarrelsome citizens in the two regions of Wallonia and Flanders united just long enough to throw out their Dutch rulers. In that era Britain was a superpower, and London guaranteed Belgium's independence and neutrality as well as that of Luxembourg, its neighbor to the southeast. The Belgians, though, selected Leopold from the House of Saxe-Coburg and Gotha in Germany to be the first King of the Belgians. The new country was an uneasy mixture of Catholics and Protestants, industrialists and farmers, and Flemish and French speakers. It regularly suffered through recurring political crises, and between June 1936 and September 1939, Belgium had six different governments struggling unsuccessfully to deal with both an economy that had not recovered from World War I and the rise of Nazi power next door. The young Leopold III believed staunchly that the country's neutrality was its only hope for escaping a repetition of World War I, while Belgian politicians mostly looked to London and Paris for protection.

The Grand Duchy of Luxembourg is a small and hilly agrarian country located at the spot where France, Belgium, and Germany meet that had a population in 1940 of about 300,000. Powerful neighbors had often overrun the country. Celts and Romans as well as France, Poland, Spain, Austria, Holland, Belgium and Prussia have at times ruled the tiny nation. During World War I, it tried to be neutral, but German troops occupied it. Nevertheless, Grand Duchess Marie-Adélaïde remained with her people in her country during that entire conflict.

Luxembourg had long sought economic relations with larger and stronger nations. Prior to World War I, it had a customs union with Prussia, but denounced it at the end of the war. Following the war the country tried to unite economically with France, but Paris had no interest. So it turned to Belgium, establishing an economic union in 1921, which included a monetary union.

The Grand Duchy had a central bank, the *Caisse d'Épargne de l'État du Grand Duché de Luxembourg,* although the institution did not have the authority or resources of other national banks. Prior to World War I, the Luxembourg government held no gold, but during the economic crises of the 1930s it began accumulating bullion. By the end of the decade, it had a stockpile of 357 bars of gold weighing 4.3 tons. The Caisse d'Épargne also held 93.5 kg of gold belonging to the J. P. Pescatore Fund. The founder of that organization was a wealthy Luxembourger who had made a fortune in French business and in 1892 established a home for the country's elderly. The gold provided financing for it.[1]

Luxembourg gold was initially stored at home, but when war fears increased the government in 1938 sent it to Holland. Officials, though, ran into transportation problems, and the following year asked the Belgian government to take it over and to protect it the same way that they were handling their own bullion. Brussels agreed.

The *Banque Nationale de Belgique,* as it is known in French, or *Nationale Bank van België,* its name in Flemish, began a program after World War I to modernize and decentralize its gold holdings. Much of the metal stored in its Brussels headquarters was shipped to new facilities in three towns around the country. The new storage facilities were solidly built and had underground vaults made of reinforced concrete. Some gold was also shipped to Antwerp and Ostend, Belgium's two main port cities, from which the national treasure could be moved quickly, most likely to London. Eventually only about fifteen percent of the country's precious metal remained in the capital. Drawing on their experience in World War I, bank officials operated in the belief that in a new conflict they would have enough time to move the gold away from the fighting.

In the late 1930s, Belgium enjoyed a dramatic increase in its gold holdings because of an influx of hot money coming from France. The Popular Front government in Paris launched leftist economic policies that frightened wealthy citizens, who sent much of their private fortunes in gold bars and coins to Belgium and Switzerland. As a result, Belgian gold holdings increased by ten percent, and by the end of the decade the national stockpile totaled more than 600 tons, a large amount for such a small country.[2]

Following the Munich agreement in the fall of 1938, leaders of the Belgian bank became concerned about the safety of their holdings. The board also discussed whether in case of an invasion members should remain in the country or flee to France or Britain for the duration of the conflict. A large number of Belgians had escaped to France during World War I. In order to live there, though, they needed to convert their Belgian francs into French francs. Believing that was likely to happen again in a new conflict and would put a major burden on the country's gold and foreign currency reserves, Belgian bank officials felt they had to keep large stores of bullion to pay for potentially huge sales of Belgian francs for French ones.

At the time, Georges Janssen headed the Belgian Central Bank. Born in 1892 and a lawyer by training, he had successful careers as both a barrister and a law professor before joining the privately held *Société Belge de Banque* in 1932. He was named head of the national bank in 1938. Janssen was not a politician and generally followed the instructions of cabinet members, especially the minister of finance. He suffered recurring bouts of phlebitis, which sometimes hampered his work. Camille Gutt, the finance minister when the war broke out in May 1940 and later the strongman of the cabinet-in-exile, described him as having a "slightly dictatorial temperament."[3]

Following the Nazi seizure of Austria's gold in March 1938, the Belgian bank appointed three top officials, Hubert Nassau, Louis-Jean Mathieu, and Henri Sontag, to draw up a plan to protect the country's treasure. They recommended sending one-third of it to Britain, one-third to either Canada or the U.S., and keeping one-third in the country. The final portion was required by law to remain within the country's borders as backing for the currency. Gutt and Janssen agreed to the proposal. At about that same time, Janssen contacted Montagu Norman about shipping gold to Britain. He agreed and assured Janssen that news of the Belgian gold's move would remain secret and not be included in any public information his bank published. In July 1938, the first shipments left Brussels and Antwerp for London.[4]

The Belgian bank at the same time contacted officials at the New York Federal Reserve and began shipping bullion there. By the end of March 1939, Belgium had 308.6 tons at the Bank of England in London and 117.5 tons at the New York Fed. Some Belgian officials, though, worried about leaving their most valuable property there because their country had not paid back the U.S. for World War I loans. Brussels officials feared that the Americans might seize it as payment for bad debts. The cost of insuring and shipping it across the Atlantic was also increasing all the time, and U-boat attacks made shipping dangerous. As a result, officials finally decided to keep most of their bullion in Europe by moving it to neighboring France.[5]

Over five days in November 1939, the Belgians sent four shipments containing 178 tons of gold in 4,449 sealed cases to the French National Bank offices in Bordeaux and Libourne, both in the southwestern part of the country and thus far from Germany. The transfers were done as earmarked accounts, the same arrangement that Brussels had with the Bank of England. Under French rules, that meant once the gold was turned over to them, the Belgians had no further access to it. They could not even retrieve the banknotes that they had sent to their neighbor. Brussels officials were not given the key or combination to the vaults where their national treasure was located. Those bank reserves were now entirely under French control.[6]

When a new Belgian government took office in early 1940, Finance Minister Gutt decided that all of the gold remaining in the country should be shipped to southwestern France. Belgian bullion began arriving in France so quickly that Pierre Fournier, the governor of the French bank, informed Belgium in February that his staff no longer had time to verify the exact contents of all the containers. He said that in the future his office would only acknowledge the number of crates received with their seals intact. In May 1940, the Belgians sent 730 cases in three separate shipments to three different destinations, Bordeaux, Toulouse, and Mont-de-Marsan. On May 8, just two days before the German invasion, the Brussels central bank had inside the country only 7.5 tons out of its total holdings of 707.8 tons. The Belgian central bank now had 45.6 percent of its gold at the Bank of England, 31.3 percent at the Bank of France, 21.8 percent at the New York Federal Reserve and 1.2 percent at the South Africa Reserve Bank.[7]

The centerpiece of the Belgian strategy against a German invasion was based on its ultramodern Fort Eben-Emael, built between 1931 and 1935. Considered at the time to be the world's best military fortification, even better than France's Maginot Line, it was designed to protect three strategic bridges over the Albert Canal that ran from Antwerp, Belgium to Maastricht, Holland. Belgians believed that the canal provided them with a natural defense line. The fort was built in a jagged mountainous area near the junction of France, Belgium, Holland, and Germany, about twelve miles northeast of Liège, Belgium, and six miles south of Maastricht, Holland. The natural defensive barrier of the mountains, now augmented by the fort, reassured Belgium's leaders that their Maginot Line would hold. Belgian military strategy was built on the premise that Fort Eben-Emael would hold out for five days until French forces could arrive. The fort, though, was still right in the path of a Nazi invasion.

During the spring of 1940, the Wehrmacht's Koch Storm Detachment practiced a daring raid to neutralize the defense structure. At 3:30 A.M. on May 10, the morning the German western offensive began, eleven large gliders tethered to Ju-52 planes left in the dark from Cologne, seventy miles away. Forty-five miles into their mission and over the city of Aachen, nine gliders were released at 8,000 ft. They silently soared into Belgian territory and landed on top of the fort. The German soldiers attacked the fort's turrets with explosives and flamethrowers. The Belgians responded with a heavy defense, but the fortress was now protecting the Nazis on top of it. In only a few minutes the battle ended. More than a thousand Belgian troops were taken prisoner, and the bridges over the Albert Canal were quickly seized. The road to the North Sea through Belgium was now open, and Nazi panzers began rolling toward the Belgian-French coast.[8]

On May 15, the Belgian cabinet left Brussels in a caravan of cars to establish a new base of operations in Ostend on the country's North Sea coast. The city had lovely, wide beaches and also had the advantage of being only a short ferry trip to Britain. The government had previously agreed that if the cabinet relocated, the head of the central bank should remain with the ministers. The scene in the beach resort was sometimes surreal. One night Gutt invited Janssen and others to join him for a gastronomic feast on the grounds that at least the Nazis would not enjoy the food they were having. The menu included a truffle omelet, and they drank Champagne, toasting to the "final victory," even though they knew defeat would come first.[9]

German planes bombed Ostend on the night of May 17-18, and the cabinet reluctantly decided to leave Belgian territory for France, stopping first in Le Havre. Gutt and Janssen early in the morning of May 18 headed to Paris. It took two days to get there because refugees blocked the roads. Janssen went immediately to the French National Bank and established his bank's new headquarters there. In early June, and while both Fournier and Janssen were still in Paris, the French central bank president informed his Belgian counterpart that his country would be moving the Belgian gold out of the country with France's bullion and asked if that was okay with them. Janssen gave his approval, but the details or destination were never discussed. He later tried to get more information, but the French told him little, explaining that the information was a military secret.[10]

King Leopold III, who had taken over formal command of the Belgian Army, had a showdown meeting with his own cabinet on the evening of May 24-25 concerning war strategy at Château de Wynendaele in West Flanders. Present were the four leading members of the government: Prime Minister Herbert Pierlot, Foreign Minister Paul-Henri Spaak, and Ministers Without Portfolio Arthur Vanderpoorten and Henri Denis. The ministers urged the king to leave the country with the government, but he refused. Pierlot bluntly reminded him that only the government, and not he, could surrender. The politicians were escaping to France, but the king wanted to remain in Belgium with his troops, whatever the outcome. His father Albert I had not left during World War I. He would do the same. Leopold added that he would consider a government-in-exile to be an attack "against me." In his memoirs Spaak wrote that the king "gave off the cuff answers to our questions" and "had no clear idea of what being a prisoner would mean." The ministers finally departed realizing that their country's future had become a struggle between their view and the king's.[11]

Belgium had only a small amount of gold physically in the country, but it still had a huge hoard of its national currency in Ostend. It had just arrived in trucks and some in hearses. The central bank had recently printed enough paper money to service the country's economy for three to six months. The 500 million Belgian francs weighed 120 tons and were packed in 241 cases that rested in the cellar of a local bank. It was worth $70 million. By then it was impossible to ship cargo by train or truck to France. Hubert Ansiaux, the bank's thirty-seven year old inspector, was now in charge of it. He rustled up a dozen helpers and a truck that had been left behind to deal with the currency.[12]

While trying to devise a plan to get his valuable property to Britain, the only destination left, Ansiaux on the late afternoon of May 25 was near the harbor in Ostend. All the ships had by then left for safer waters. He was rapidly running out of both hope and ideas. The Germans had been dropping magnetic mines there for days, and no ship would dare to dock. In desperation he and his team put together a last ditch plan to make a giant bonfire of currency bills right there at the dock. That seemed the only way to keep the money out of Nazi hands. Ansiaux was skeptical, though, because he knew that the tight blocks of currency would burn very slowly and might still end up with the enemy.

Then almost miraculously and before the match was lit, a Belgian pilot boat named simply the *A4* suddenly appeared outside the Ostend breakwater. The privately owned vessel normally led ships into harbors along the English Channel. The Belgian military had requisitioned it at the start of hostilities, and it was coming from the besieged French port of Dunkirk. Although the Germans had mined the Ostend waters, the *A4* had been demagnetized, so it was probably safe to land. The vessel, though, was virtually defenseless, having on board only a small canon and a machine gun. Carefully the *A4* eased its way into the dock. As soon as it was dark, Nassau's small team loaded the ship. When it was filled to the gills, the boat slowly pulled out of the harbor with no lights on. As the *A4* sailed past Dunkirk at 10:00 P.M., the crew could see the city in flames. The Belgian ship arrived in the harbor of Dartmouth on the English coast at dawn on May 26. The ship had carried coal before the war, and now everyone aboard had a black face. Ansiaux immediately telephoned the Bank of England and asked what to do with his hoard of cash. The British replied that they would put it in their London vault, where it remained for the duration of the war.[13]

Leaving Paris in front of the German invasion, central bank governor Janssen moved south, trying to stay in touch with French National Bank officials, who were also attempting to remain a few steps ahead of the invasion. Pierre Fournier first went to Poitiers in the west-central part of the country and then further south to Mont-de-Marsan. Communication between the two central banks, however, was terrible. On June 15, the Belgian sent a telegram to Fournier asking him for news about the gold, but the message never arrived. Two days later, though, the two bankers finally met in person.

By then a million Belgian refugees were trying to run away from the war on France's narrow country roads along with millions of fleeing French citizens. As feared, the Belgians were creating a financial crisis by exchanging their own francs for French ones so that they could pay for food and shelter. Janssen was caught in the dilemma of refugees demanding local currency for survival, while at the same time trying to protect his country's gold. Because of the heavy demand for French francs, the value of the Belgian currency was collapsing. On May 10, 100 Belgian francs were equal to 144.4 French francs, but soon the Belgians for the same amount of money could buy only one-third as many goods as they could only a few days earlier. Four days later, French officials unilaterally set the exchange rate at parity. They explained that they had to protect their own currency and introduced strict rules regulating how much money people could exchange. The French bank also unilaterally withdrew 37 tons of gold that the Belgians had deposited to settled the heavy currency sales. Eventually the two countries reached an agreement that half of all Belgian government debt would be settled at the end of each month in gold, dollars, or foreign currency convertible to dollars. Repurchases of Belgian banknotes, though, had to be paid in gold. Between May 28 and June 18, Belgium turned 65 tons of gold over to the French.[14]

Near midnight on May 27, King Leopold capitulated to the Wehrmacht without consulting his cabinet or his allies. The young king thought the French had already lost the war and felt he was doing what was right for his people. The German-Belgian ceasefire began the next morning at 11:00. William C. Bullitt, the American ambassador in Paris, sent a message to President Roosevelt that reflected the opinion not only of the Belgians but also of most Europeans, "Since a king without honor was nothing, the King no longer existed. The prime minister of Belgium denounced the king's action this morning on the radio and announced that it was illegal since the act had to be countersigned by the prime minister. He called on all Belgians to go on fighting."[15] The prime minister, himself, though, was no longer in the country.

The Belgian surrender left a twenty-mile wide hole in the Allied defense lines, which infuriated both Britain and France. French people, who only a few days earlier had befriended the refugees, began attacking them.

The morning after the capitulation, Nazi General Walter von Reichenau, who had led the German 6th Army during the invasion, arrived at the Château de Laeken Palace, three miles north of Brussels. He was stunned to find that Leopold III had not fled to Britain. He called Hitler and asked for instructions. The Führer said his prisoner king should be incarcerated in the Royal Palace of Laeken three miles north of Brussels. Werner Kiewitz, a German colonel, was assigned to be the king's military adjutant. Shortly afterwards, Leopold asked him to send Hitler a telegram requesting that it be "immediately demanded of France that the Belgian State treasure, which was by then in an unknown hiding place in France south of Bordeaux, be restored forthwith to Belgian hands." There is no record that Hitler acted on his puppet king's request.[16]

Hubert Ansiaux, who was now in London, was meeting regularly with Bank of England officials and the Churchill government to find a way to get the Belgian gold out of France and onto a British ship just as London had done with the Dutch gold only weeks before. The nervous Belgians now also talked about transporting their bullion to the U.S., despite the cost and danger of a transatlantic shipment.

On June 10, the Reynaud government left Paris in a panic for destinations south, stopping first in Tours and four days later arriving in Bordeaux. The Belgian central bank team followed them south. Conditions had become so bad that the Belgians could not stop for the night in the same small towns where the French were staying. Communication between them eventually broke down, just as the fate of the Belgian gold was going into an abyss.

The French government of Paul Reynaud grew weaker as an anti-war coalition in his cabinet gathered strength. Reynaud finally resigned on June 16, and Marshal Philippe Pétain, the hero of World War I, replaced him and quickly sued for peace. The Belgians were now more determined than ever to get their gold out of France and ideally out of French hands.

At 6:00 A.M. on June 18, Ansiaux arrived in Bordeaux with a British naval officer aboard a private plane from London. Their plan was to put as much Belgian gold as possible on the British cruiser *HMS Arethusa*, which was then moored in Le Verdon at the mouth of the Gironde estuary north of Bordeaux. The two were in contact with British naval sources and believed that, if necessary, they could get more ships there to pick up additional bullion. Ansiaux met first with Gutt and Janssen, who were also there, and all agreed on the plan to load the Belgian gold onto British vessels.[17]

Ansiaux also met with a French official with whom he had worked earlier while evacuating the Belgian gold to France. The Belgian learned that his country's gold was not located in either Bordeaux or Libourne. It had all been shipped to another port, and the destination was a military secret. The fate of the Belgian gold was now entirely in the hands of the French navy.

The frustrated Belgian finally rushed to find Finance Minister Gutt, whom he discovered sleeping in his car at the Place des Quinconces in the heart of Bordeaux. There were no longer any available hotel rooms in the city. After Ansiaux explained the situation, Gutt decided to confront Yves Bouthillier, who had just taken over as France's finance minister. The Belgian already had contempt for him from earlier encounters, calling him Uriah Heep. Gutt went to Bouthillier's office in Bordeaux full of rage, with the objective of getting back his country's gold. The minister wasn't there, but an elderly doorman whom he knew said that the minister always ate dinner with his aides at 10:00 P.M. at the Ecu d'Argent restaurant. Gutt arrived there an hour early and waited outside. When the minister finally stepped out of his car, Gutt grabbed him by his lapels and shouted, "I'm sorry to have chased you so far, but the matter is urgent. Where is our gold?"

Continuing in the angry tone, Gutt charged that France had not lived up to its promise to protect the Belgian gold. He also shouted that a British ship was ready to evacuate it. He wanted the gold on that vessel. Bouthillier was rattled, and said he would be meeting with Admiral François Darlan, the head of the French navy, the next morning at eight o'clock and would tell him that a British ship was ready to evacuate the Belgian gold. Gutt had no confidence in the French minister and doubted Darlan would help him, but he left.[18]

The indefatigable Ansiaux returned to the French bank and repeated his demand that the gold be transferred to the British ship. The discussion ended abruptly when a French official entered the room and announced that the navy ship carrying the Belgian and Luxembourg gold had just departed and was headed for open ocean. The gold of the two countries was totally in the hands of the French Admiralty, and everything was a military secret.[19] Belgium and Luxembourg had entrusted their gold to the French government on a perilous journey to a destination unknown. The plight of the French, Belgian, Luxembourg, and Polish gold was just beginning.

Chapter Seventeen

THE FALL OF FRANCE

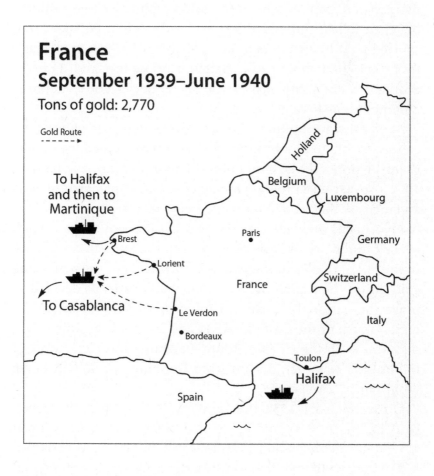

France
September 1939–June 1940
Tons of gold: 2,770

Gold Route

To Halifax
and then to
Martinique

To Casablanca

Brest
Lorient
Le Verdon
Bordeaux

Paris

Holland
Belgium
Luxembourg
Germany
Switzerland
France
Italy
Toulon
Halifax
Spain

A t the apogee of the international gold standard era in the early nineteenth century, France was among the largest holders of that valuable metal, although its reserves fluctuated greatly depending on the country's erratic economy. France suffered repeated bouts of inflation and frequent currency devaluations that wiped out people's savings in paper currencies, which is why citizens were strongly attached to gold. Stories about peasants hiding their savings under mattresses were true, and the French trusted a gold Napoleon coin more than any bank or government. The country's reserves in the early-to-mid 1930s reached a peak of more than $5 billion, when the world's economies were tanking, but then fell in the mid-1930s, when the leftist Popular Front spurred wealthy investors to move their valuables to financially friendlier countries such as Belgium or Switzerland. France's economy went south just as the Nazis began goose-stepping around Europe.[1]

As war threats mounted, French government leaders used the country's gold to buy weapons for a war that seemed inevitable. Clément Moret, the governor of the Banque de France, in January 1932 also started a program to reduce the amount stored in Paris and increase that held in his bank's regional offices. In July 1938, bank officials drew up a six-day evacuation plan for getting all of the bullion out of Paris. Shortly after the Munich conference in the fall of that year, thirty trucks took most of the remaining gold out of the capital. In May 1939, bank officials decided to move the national treasure to the center of the country to a region north of the Garonne River and south of the Loire River on a line with the cities of Tours, Le Mans, and Flers. Most of the bullion was then distant from Germany, while still being within mainland France.

On September 1, 1939, the day World War II began, the French bank had most of its gold in regional offices. In addition, it had 171.1 tons in London and 165.5 tons in New York City. Paris also had some special funds in the U.S., bringing the country's total gold holdings to 2,770.3 tons. With war fears running high, the bank

Franklin D. Roosevelt in 1934 wrote a personal dedication to Henry Morgenthau, Jr., his close friend and partner in power: "For Henry from one of two of a kind." *Courtesy of the Franklin D. Roosevelt Photo Collection, Morgenthau Folder.*

In Munich in the early days of his rise to power, Hitler returns the Nazi *Sieg Heil* salute to members of his paramilitary units. They had a hypnotic dedication to their *Führer. Courtesy of the Bundesarchiv Berlin Photo Collection.*

Adolf Hitler liked to get away with close aides at his mountain retreat outside the village of Berchtesgaden in the Bavarian Alps. From left to right: Hitler, Martin Bormann, who became his secretary, Hermann Göring, the head of the Luftwaffe, and Baldur von Schirach, the leader of the Hitler Youth organization. *Courtesy of the Bundesarchiv Berlin Photo Collection.*

Hjalmar Horace Greeley Schacht considered himself a master of both economics and politics and mistakenly thought he could control Hitler. Schacht, the president of the Reichsbank, alone among the people around the Führer refused to wear the Nazi uniform. *Courtesy of the Bundesarchiv Berlin Photo Collection.*

The Reichsbank headquarters in the heart of Berlin was a showpiece building for the new Nazi regime. Hitler personally presided over its groundbreaking in 1933. *Courtesy of the Bundesarchiv Berlin Photo Collection.*

Hjalmar Schacht with two of his young protégés. In the center is Karl Blessing, and to the right Emil Puhl. Hitler fired Blessing in January 1939, but Puhl stayed on to the very end. *Courtesy of the Bundesarchiv Berlin Photo Collection.*

Belgian Gold

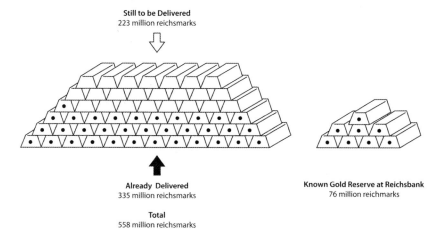

Still to be Delivered
223 million reichsmarks

Already Delivered
335 million reichsmarks

Total
558 million reichsmarks

Known Gold Reserve at Reichsbank
76 million reichmarks

This internal Nazi document explained the capture of the Belgian gold. At the time Germany had almost run out of bullion because of its heavy military spending. *Courtesy of Bundesarchiv.*

Joseph Goebbels, the Reich Minister of Propaganda, enthusiastically gloated over the gold captured in Nazi-occupied countries. Reichsbank President Walther Funk was at the right. *Courtesy of Bundesarchiv Freiburg, Belgium's Contribution to the German War Economy, March 1, 1942.*

Sailors loading gold onto ships in the convoy that took both King George VI and British bullion to Canada in the spring of 1939. *Courtesy of the Imperial War Museum Photo Collection.*

Royal Canadian Mounties protected the British gold that had arrived with the king and took it to the Bank of Canada. *Courtesy of the Imperial War Museum Photo Collection.*

Sailors inspecting a box of French gold that was about to be shipped across the Atlantic Ocean to safety at the New York Federal Reserve in lower Manhattan. *Courtesy of Banque de France, Keystone France.*

Holland's Princess Juliana and her family, plus some of the Dutch gold, traveled in this central bank van from a palace in The Hague to a British ship waiting to evacuate them. *Courtesy of the Dutch National Bank Photo Collection.*

The Nazi cruiser *Blücher* was torpedoed as it arrived at the Oslo fjord, which set back German plans to capture the Norwegian central bank gold on the first day of the invasion. *Courtesy of the Norwegian Maritime Museum.*

The French shipped large amounts of gold to Halifax. Bullion was dropped off, and then those same ships turned around and took American war materiel back to Europe. *Courtesy of Banque de France Photo Collection.*

The French got all of their gold out of the mainland, and much of it ended up in their African colonies, where locals helped them move it inland. *Courtesy of Banque de France Private Photo Collection.*

After the Nazi invasion in June 1941, the Soviets moved their most valuable goods—gold, Lenin's body, and Hermitage artworks—to safety beyond the Urals. *Courtesy of David M. Trachtenberg.*

HOTEL SHORELAND
5454 SOUTH SHORE DRIVE
CHICAGO

3 am
5-5-40

84

Dear Mrs Klotz:

Please tell Dan Bell I want enough money to move _all_ of the remaining gold out of N.Y. City to Kentucky. He should speak to me Tuesday

Best Regards, HM Jr

The note Treasury Secretary Morgenthau wrote in the middle of the night ordering that the gold stored at the New York Federal Reserve be moved immediately to Fort Knox. *Courtesy of Morgenthau Diaries, Franklin D. Roosevelt Presidential Library.*

Harry Dexter White was the key staff person for Treasury Secretary Henry Morgenthau. White's influence grew greatly during the war, but no one in the government realized he was also a secret Soviet agent. *Courtesy of the Library of Congress Photo Collection.*

Harry Hopkins traveled to Moscow in July 1941 to ask Joseph Stalin how the U.S. could help the Soviets militarily following the Nazi invasion. Famous photographer Margaret Bourke-White of *Life* magazine happened to be there on another assignment. She said Stalin had the coldest eyes she had ever seen. *Courtesy of Getty Images.*

Dock workers in both Manhattan and New Jersey first unloaded boxes of bullion that had arrived from European central banks. *Courtesy of the New York Federal Reserve Photo Collection.*

The precious cargo was then put into armored Brinks trucks and taken to the New York Federal Reserve Bank in Manhattan. The boxes were small but heavy. *Courtesy of the New York Federal Reserve Photo Collection.*

So much was arriving, especially in 1939 and 1940, that the underground vault was soon filling up, and the staff had to work overtime just to verify the contents and check it all in. *Courtesy of the New York Federal Reserve Photo Collection.*

Security was heavy at both ends of the shipments to Fort Knox. The gold was moved by escorted trucks to Pennsylvania Railroad train cars and then transferred by trucks to the vault. *Courtesy of the United States Mint.*

Armed guards on watch at the railroad siding before the shipment arrived. *Courtesy of the United States Mint.*

The U.S. Post Office had overall responsibility for moving the precious cargo safely south. *Courtesy of the United States Mint.*

To ensure security, trucks pulled right up to the doors of the train before unloading. *Courtesy of the United States Mint.*

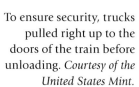

The sight that American G.I.s saw after they blasted open the door. Reichsbank officials had carefully lined up bags of gold, each containing two bars, into long rows. *Courtesy of the Harry S. Truman Presidential Library Photo Collection.*

General Eisenhower and his staff examined both the bags of bullion and the priceless museum art that the Nazis had hastily packed and sent south by train from Berlin. *Courtesy of the Harry S. Truman Presidential Library Photo Collection.*

Colonel Bernard Bernstein examines the contents of a suitcase of valuables taken from inmates of Nazi prison camps. U.S. soldiers at first thought it was simple war booty, but the colonel knew it was from Jewish victims. *Courtesy of the Harry S. Truman Presidential Library Photo Collection.*

A box of gold wedding rings discovered near the Buchenwald concentration camp in southern Germany. *Courtesy of the Holocaust Museum Photo Collection.*

TOP: Refugees trying to flee Berlin in early 1945 after the bombing of the Reichsbank building in February. LEFT: Hjalmar Schacht, in May 1945, at the Dachau concentration camp. The Nazis had arrested him in July 1944 after the attempt on Hitler's life. *Both photos courtesy of Bundesarchiv Berlin Photo Collection.*

then began to concentrate the precious metal that remained in the country at its Atlantic ports.

Only ten days after the invasion of Poland, the French treasury sent a message to the national bank instructing it to work with the French Admiralty to send some gold to the Middle East as soon as possible. The bank dispatched 57 tons on three shipments from Marseilles to Syria and Lebanon, which France ruled under an agreement dating to the end of World War I. On January 6, 1940, Paris shipped an additional 55 tons to Ankara, Turkey as part of a joint operation with Britain, which sent its own separately. The two countries, which had a military alliance with Turkey, gave it gold to buy arms in the hope that it would remain neutral in the new war.[2]

The major French use of its national gold was to buy weapons in anticipation of a war against Germany. Jean Monnet's mission to buy American weapons, primarily airplanes, was successful, but the real question was whether the military goods he was buying would be in place and have skilled military men to run them before the anticipated Nazi offensive. Those fears increased when the western democracies saw how easily the Nazis rolled over Poland. Monnet returned to Paris for consultations, and French leaders urged him to buy even more. He lamented that the American public still strongly opposed getting into Europe's troubles. Roosevelt recognized the danger, but average citizens did not. Monnet later wrote, "Never, perhaps, has the role of the President of the United States been so important, or so lonely."[3]

The French navy set up a special task force of ships in late 1939 called Force Z to handle transportation of the gold. It initially consisted of three vessels. The naval code word for gold in secret internal communications was "macaroni," and one early message asked: "Can you ship your macaroni to Halifax?" Ships carrying gold left from the French west coast port of Brest, dropped the payment off in Canada, and then returned to France with planes. The gold went by train from Halifax to the New York Federal Reserve. Three shipments between November 1939 and March 1940 moved a total of 347 tons of macaroni from France to the U.S. The French initially had a limit of 100 tons of bullion per ship, but over time that increased to more than twice as much. The first shipment started on November 11, when the French National Bank sent a convoy made up of the *Marseillaise*, the *Jean de Vienne*, and the *Lorraine*, to Halifax with 100 tons of gold. The following March three more ships, the *Algérie*, the *Bretagne*, and the *Bérne*, landed in Halifax with 147 tons.[4]

In the first days after the invasion of the Low Countries in May 1940, the world's attention was focused on the rapid fall of Holland and Belgium. The more important part of the German attack, however, was the slowly developing thrust of the Nazi southern flank. At a war-planning meeting in mid-December 1939, General Franz Halder, the chief of the German general staff, had pointed on a map to the densely forested Ardennes area and declared, "Here is the weak point. Here we have to go through!"

General Gerd von Rundstedt, the commander of Army Group A, directed that operation, and under him were two key officers, Heinz Guderian and Erwin Rommel. They were to lead the attack across the Meuse River in the Belgian town of Dinant and then drive deep into France.

The Germans invaded along a forty-mile front, west of the Maginot Line. Guderian's troops easily rolled through Luxembourg, and by 10:00 A.M. they were on the Belgian border. Rommel's two panzer units were also soon into the Ardennes, where they moved more slowly than anticipated but kept pressing forward even at night. The headlights of their vehicles led the way in the dark. The Germans had the advantage of better communications because they had radio contact between tanks and aircraft. German tank commanders could order their air force to bomb specific areas just before an attack, and then go in for the cleanup. The French army had nothing like that. The Nazi operation on the first two days went according to plan; units passed through the Ardennes with only minor difficulty. Twelve hundred German tanks were soon heading toward France. On the evening of May 11, Rommel sent his wife the cheery message: "Everything wonderful so far."[5]

The German objective was Sedan, a city on the Meuse River with historic importance to both the French and the Germans. It was there in 1870 that Prussian units captured emperor Napoleon III and effectively ended the Franco-Prussian War. In 1918, French and American units defeated the Germans in the Battle of the Argonne Forest. Five days later that war ended.

Near midnight on May 12, Rommel's troops reached the Belgian side of the Meuse River. French forces were well entrenched on the other bank in front of the city of Sedan. Both sides brought in their air forces for support, but Nazi planes were much more effective. The intensity of the air battle increased in the afternoon, and dive-bombing Stukas terrified both French soldiers and civilians. At 3:00 P.M. the air attacks abruptly stopped, and German troops began to cross at three points along the river, using new tactics developed during training near the wine town of Bernkastel on the Mosel River. Rommel's goal was to be ten miles past the river by nightfall. He encouraged his men by telling them that the enemy was in full retreat, and at one point jumped into the water to help pull a raft forward. By 4:00 P.M., German troops were largely on the French side of the Meuse.

May 14 was mostly a day of consolidation, with heavy equipment still crossing the river in preparation for the next stage of the attack. The tank units of Guderian and Rommel again led the way. As General Manstein wrote after the war, the goal was "the envelopment of the whole French Army with a powerful right hook." The Germans successfully trapped Allied armies in Belgium and northern France, leaving each group too weak to make a meaningful response to the rapid Nazi offensive.[6]

After dark and with the Germans largely across the river, the local French commander sent a message to headquarters saying that there had been "a rather serious pinprick." That evening Ambassador Bullitt was meeting with French War Minister Édouard Daladier, when General Maurice Gamelin, the army's supreme commander, called to tell him about the collapse of Allied defenses at Sedan. Daladier shouted into the phone, "It cannot be true! Impossible!"

The stunned minister finally told his general to attack immediately, but the general responded that he did not have enough men. Finally after fifteen minutes of pointless exchanges, Daladier hung up. He and Bullitt walked over to a wall map to see how far the Germans had advanced. Gamelin had told them that the French city of Laon had fallen. That meant the Wehrmacht was only seventy-five miles from Paris, and there were no French units in the way to stop them.

Bullitt bluntly asked, "So it means the destruction of the French army?"

Daladier replied, "Yes, it means the destruction of the French army."[7]

Only four days into the war, Lucien Lamoureaux, the minister of finance, telephoned Pierre-Eugène Fournier, the governor of the French central bank, and told him that the government had decided to move all the country's gold out of the country. Paris at that point had just short of two thousand tons located around the country plus the Belgian, Luxembourg, and Polish gold. The first objective was to move the bullion from the central part of the country to three major ports: Brest on the Atlantic coast of Brittany in the north, Le Verdon also on the Atlantic but in the south, and Toulon on the Mediterranean coast. The shipments to Toulon and Le Verdon were to take place mostly by train. The deliveries to Brest, which were the largest, were both by train and truck, which became a nightmare because roads north of Paris were packed with Belgian and French refugees trying to escape the conflict.[8]

At 7:30 on the morning of May 15, French Premier Reynaud woke up the new British Prime Minister Winston Churchill, who had taken office only five days earlier. Speaking in English, the Frenchman said with great agitation, "We have been defeated; we have lost the battle." Churchill attempted to calm him, saying that the situation could not be that bad. Reynaud responded frantically, "The front is broken near Sedan." Churchill again tried to soothe him, but Reynaud repeated, "We are defeated; we have lost the battle." Finally, the prime minister said he would fly to Paris to discuss the situation. He added that he would ask his war cabinet to approve sending to France the British planes intended for his own country's defense.[9]

Churchill left London for the French capital with two top military aides, General John Dill, the vice chief of the Imperial General Staff, and General Pug Ismay, the prime minister's military aide. When they arrived, the group went first to the British embassy and then to the Quai d'Orsay, the foreign ministry, which is located on the left bank of the Seine River in the heart of Paris.

The three visitors were ushered into Reynaud's study at 5:30, where Reynaud, Defense Minister Daladier, and General Gamelin, the supreme commander of French armed forces, were waiting. The entire group remained standing as they discussed the dire situation. The French said the German army had made a fifty- to sixty-mile breakthrough at Sedan. Gamelin explained that German armored units had advanced with a speed that no military man thought possible. Then the room was silent. Using his schoolboy French, Churchill finally asked about the country's strategic reserves, the units every military commander keeps on hand for just such an emergency. Gamelin shook his head and replied simply, *"Aucune."* None. He had none.

Churchill walked over to a window and looked down at the Quai d'Orsay's courtyard, where foreign ministry officials were throwing wheelbarrows of documents onto a bonfire. The smell of burning paper drifted up to the room where the meeting was being held. No one had to explain that the French government was preparing to evacuate the capital. Churchill finally asked Gamelin where he would attack, and the commander simply replied, "Inferior numbers, inferior equipment, inferior method," and shrugged his shoulders. Wrote Churchill in his war memoirs: "There was no argument; there was no need of argument."[10]

After the Allied summit, the French went back to waging a war that many of the country's leaders felt had already been lost, and Churchill returned to London, where some members of his cabinet, including his foreign minister Lord Halifax, seemed open to a settlement with Hitler in order to avoid an invasion.

French military leaders remained convinced that their major problem was the lack of aircraft, and the Reynaud government rushed to buy more planes from the U.S. Paris would pay for them with gold just as it had done during the Phony War that had now morphed into a bona fide conquest. France, though, had problems that something as simple as more planes could not solve. The country's morale was broken, and its army was in chaos and retreat. Many French leaders were already resigned to defeat. Communications, between one part of the country and another, between one government department and another, or even with foreign countries, were difficult, if not impossible. Refugees flooded French roads. The Luftwaffe controlled the skies and strafed the caravans of farm wagons and automobiles. Drivers hopelessly tried to protect themselves by putting mattresses on their roofs. At a time when everything had to work, nothing worked. As the French lamented, their country was *en pagaille*—in a mess.

On May 16, the day after the Anglo-French meeting, an order went out from Paris to the commander of the naval installation in Toulon telling him to contact nearby French Bank offices to pick up gold that was to be shipped to Canada on the aircraft carrier *Béarn*. The following day the navy sent out a series of cables explaining the gold operation in greater detail. The Admiralty had arranged for a convoy that would include three ships. The *Béarn* would leave from Casablanca, the strategically important French port on the Atlantic coast of French Morocco, while two light cruisers, the *Jeanne d'Arc* and the *Émile Bertin*, would depart from Brest. They would all drop off gold in Halifax and pick up war materiel to bring back to France. The vessels were all relatively new, and the maximum amount of bullion allowed was raised from 100 to 200 tons per ship. The *Jeanne d'Arc* had been launched in 1931 as a naval training ship, but had gone into war service in late August 1939. The commanding officer was Rear Admiral Albert Rouyer. The *Émile Bertin* had entered active duty in January 1934, and in the fall of 1939 had carried the Polish gold from Beirut to Toulon. Commodore Robert Battet was still the senior officer on board.[11]

The *Béarn* was assigned to carry 194 tons of gold, while the *Jeanne d'Arc* and the *Émile Bertin* would carry 212 tons between them. After unloading the cargo in Halifax, the *Béarn*, because of its speed, was to return immediately to France with as many airplanes as it could get on board. Its destination would be decided later. While waiting for their departure and out of fear of hitting recently laid German magnetic mines in the harbor, the *Jeanne d'Arc* underwent a demagnetization process. At least one French National Bank staff member would travel with each gold shipment.

On May 18 in the early morning, twenty trucks filled with gold for the *Béarn* began arriving at the Toulon docks. Loading was completed just before midnight, and tugs then pushed the ship out to sea. Two French torpedo boats, the *Chacal* and the *Léopard*, escorted the aircraft carrier into Mediterranean waters. With the two French ships still protecting it, the *Béarn* headed for Casablanca. The following morning, three other escorts took over, and on the morning of May 21 they guided the gold ship into port. Twenty-four hours later and after repairs were made and the fuel tanks topped up, the *Béarn* departed, heading north. Two large ships, the *D'Entrecasteaux* and the *D'Iberville*, escorted it for the first part of the trip.

The departures of the two gold ships from Brest were equally flawless. The *Jeanne d'Arc* and *Émile Bertin* were both docked at the Quai de Laninon on May 20, when trucks carrying bullion began arriving at 7:00 in the morning. In each vehicle a gendarme rode shotgun next to the military driver. Sailors aboard the *Émile Bertin* knew exactly what was in the heavy containers because of their experience a few months before with the Polish gold, and they warned the Jeanne-d'Arc crew about the heavy lifting. The cargo consisted of 4,233 wooden boxes that each contained 110 pounds of gold.[12]

When Rear Admiral Rouyer returned that evening to the *Jeanne d'Arc* after the ship had been loaded, one of his officers told him that during the afternoon the crew had heard a message over the radio from someone calling himself "The Traitor of Stuttgart." In perfect French he had said: "We wish a bon voyage to the two cruisers who are leaving Brest to carry gold from the Banque de France to the U.S." So much for military security.

On the evening of May 21, the *Jeanne d'Arc* and the *Émile Bertin* pulled out of Brest. The French navy that same day sent a message labeled "very secret" to its attachés in London and Washington outlining the mission and instructing them to have everything ready for the arrivals in Halifax. The two messages named the three ships and gave their estimated arrival as "about June 1." They also said that the vessels would be carrying an "important weight of precious metal." The order reiterated that the *Béarn* should load as many airplanes as possible and immediately return to France.

Three days later, Hitler had a triumphant meeting with his generals in northern France. The invasion had been a total success. It had gone so well that he thought his units were racing *too* rapidly across northern France. German tanks were by then only a day from the Atlantic port of Dunkirk. The Führer told General von Rundstedt to regroup his units in preparation for the next phase of the invasion, which was the drive toward Paris. That would begin on May 31. German units stopped twenty miles from the coast. Hitler's order said, "Dunkirk is to be left to the Luftwaffe."[13]

The pause in the Nazi offensive allowed the Allies to evacuate thousands of troops from Dunkirk to Britain. On May 27, the British began the rescue operation that in nine days saved 338,226 men to fight another day. Tons of British and French weapons had to be left behind, but the soldiers survived. According to von Rundstedt, Hitler deliberately let the Allied armies escape because he believed it would facilitate an early settlement with Britain, but that was probably post-war rationalization. The more likely explanation was that the Führer wanted to let Göring's air force share in some of the glory that up until then had gone to the army. General Manstein later called the order, "One of Hitler's most decisive mistakes."[14]

At dawn on May 25, the *Béarn*, *Jeanne d'Arc*, and *Émile Bertin* converged on the Madeira Islands, their agreed meeting point. By 7:30 A.M. they were in sight of each other. With the *Béarn* in the middle, the three ships then left on a course to Halifax at twelve knots. The captains of each wanted to arrive as soon as possible, but had to stay together, which caused complications. The *Émile Bertin* could travel as fast as forty knots, but that would eat up a lot of fuel. The other two ships had slower maximum speeds and had less fuel. The three captains balanced off speed and fuel consumption.

The three commanders maintained radio silence for most of the trip in order to avoid tipping off the Germans about their location. They listened, however, to radio reports of war developments in northern France. The news was terrible. At one point the navy broadcast, "The country has all its eyes fixed on Boulogne, Calais, and Dunkirk."

On May 31, the three ships broke radio silence to inform officials in Halifax that they would arrive the next day at about 4:00 P.M. The French had already alerted the New York Federal Reserve that a shipment was coming, and the French National Bank official aboard the *Béarn*, sent a message to the other ships that all the gold on his vessel should leave by train for New York City as soon as they arrived.

At 8:00 A.M. on June 1, two Canadian military planes began circling the three ships. An hour later, both the British naval station in Bermuda and the Canadians warned the French vessels that an enemy submarine was at the entrance to the port. In response, Admiral Rouyer on the *Jeanne d'Arc* increased his speed to seventeen knots and put his ship on a zigzag course. The French vessels as well as Canadian escort ships soon pulled into the harbor. The *Jeanne d'Arc* was the first ship to land, arriving at Pier B at 11:30 A.M., followed by the *Béarn* a short time later.

The gold on the *Béarn* was unloaded and put directly onto an armored train; as soon as the job was finished it left for the New York Federal Reserve. Between 6:00 A.M. and 2:00 P.M. the next day, the crew of the *Émile Bertin* transferred its gold to another train. The bullion from the *Jeanne d'Arc* was put in railroad wagons between noon and 6:00 P.M.

After some delay, the Admiralty in France finally sent new instructions to the three ships in Halifax: FIRST RETURN AS SOON AS

POSSIBLE THE CRUISER ÉMILE BERTIN TO BREST STOP PROCEED AT A GOOD PACE STOP SECOND JEANNE-D'ARC WILL STAY IN HALIFAX UNTIL NEW ORDERS FROM HERE STOP THIRD LET ME KNOW AS SOON AS POSSIBLE DATE APPROXIMATELY WHEN THE AIRCRAFT LOADING OF BÉARN WILL BE FINISHED STOP.

The vessels responded: ÉMILE BERTIN WILL LEAVE 3 JUNE ARRIVE BREST 9 JUNE STOP LOADING BEARN COMMENCED YESTERDAY BUT LACKING MANY PARTS AND AWAITING HALIFAX STOP TOTAL TIME OF ASSEMBLY AND LOADING MAY LAST EIGHT TO FIFTEEN DAYS DEPENDING ON THE ARRIVAL OF PARTS STOP WILL BE PRECISE AS SOON AS POSSIBLE STOP.[15]

Despite the French navy's bravado, the French Admiralty did not have enough ships to evacuate quickly all the country's gold holdings plus the bullion that France was guarding for foreign countries. More and more of the country's commercial ships had to be pressed into service. Gold was now even traveling on passenger liners. One of those was the SS *Pasteur*, a luxury cruiser that was the pride of the French South-Atlantic Company. It had been designed to carry 751 people across oceans in style. The luxury steamer's owners were so proud of it that they had arranged for the French post office to put it on four million postage stamps that were slated to come out simultaneously with its launch. The war, though, upset that plan. The *Pasteur* had not been commissioned when the French navy took it over and gave orders for it to go to Brest and pick up four hundred tons of "precious metal" that was to be taken to Halifax. The shipment was later cut in half for security reasons.

On June 2 at 9:00 P.M., the *Pasteur*, accompanied by two escort ships that would stay with it for the first twenty-four hours of the voyage, left Brest for Halifax with 213 tons of gold. It was a highly risky trip since the ship had no on-board means of defense, but it did have one great advantage. It could travel at twenty-four knots, twice as fast as the convoy that had included the *Jeanne-d'Arc*. Only six days later, the *Pasteur* entered the Halifax harbor. The gold was immediately transferred to an armored train guarded by Canadian mounted police. Representatives of the Royal Bank of Canada carefully checked the weight of all the containers before they were deposited in vaults in Ottawa. Although this shipment was to buy still more planes, the *Pasteur* couldn't carry them back. Its luxury cabins and ballrooms were not appropriate for large aircraft. The ship's captain eventually received orders to leave Halifax for New York City, where it would have stabilizers installed for the return trip to Europe.[16]

While the commanders and the crews of the *Jeanne d'Arc* and *Béarn* were waiting for their ships to be loaded with war materiel, French sailors in Halifax learned that Italy had declared war on France and Britain. Speaking at the University of Virginia that same day, an angry President Franklin Roosevelt said, "The hand that held the dagger has struck it into the back of its neighbor." Mussolini's war objective was modest. As he told his army chief of staff, "I only need a few thousand dead so that I can sit at the peace conference as a man who has fought."[17]

French commanders in Halifax were realistic enough to know that their country's military situation was now hopeless, but they remained determined to continue fighting. On June 15, Curtiss planes from the U.S. arrived by air in Halifax, and by 10:00 P.M. twenty-three fighter aircraft, forty-eight bombers, and twenty-five transport planes were on the deck of the *Béarn*. The captain left for Casablanca the following morning. Six fighter aircraft and eight liaison planes were loaded that night on the *Jeanne d'Arc*, and that ship was also ready to leave. The next morning the two vessels, escorted by a Canadian torpedo boat, pulled out of Halifax.[18]

That same day in Paris shortly after 7:00 P.M., four German military officers arrived at the French National Bank in Paris. The building was on the rue de La Vrillière near the Louvre Museum. The Nazi Economic Squad wanted to pick up any gold that was still there.

The soldiers were immediately taken to the office of Henry de Bletterie, the bank's controller general, where several other officials were also present. A decidedly cool meeting ensued.

"What's the name of your president?" demanded a German soldier.

"Monsieur Fournier, governor of the Banque de France," replied de Bletterie.

"Where is he?"

"In unoccupied France."

"Who's replacing him?"

"The controller general."

"What's his name?"

"De Bletterie."

"Do you have any gold, currencies, foreign valuables? How much?

"We no longer have anything here such as gold, currency or valuables. There remain about 200,000 to 300,000 francs in bills."

"Where did the valuables go?"

"Far from here in unoccupied France."

"Do you have any safety deposit boxes?"

"Yes, we have safety deposit boxes. About eight hundred."

"And in your branches?"

"We also have them there. We could telephone and find out how many there are in the Seine Department."

"Useless for now. Do you have the keys to the boxes?"

"We have the keys to the underground chambers, but we don't have the keys for each deposit box. Those are in the hands of customers, and we have neither the right nor the possibility to open them."

"As of now, by higher authority, going down to the safety deposit boxes is formally forbidden."

"I protest against that order, and I demand a written order from an authorized, qualified, and superior official. I cannot take under consideration an oral order coming from someone of whose qualifications I know nothing."

"My uniform is not sufficient for you? I act by order of superiors, and that should be enough for you."

"That's not enough for me."[19]

The German entourage then left, but returned a few minutes later accompanied by a Nazi officer who described himself as the head of a *Devisenschutzkommando* unit. At 8:15 P.M., the entire group went down to the basement, where the vault was located. The huge 11,000-square-meter storage area had been built in 1927 and was held up by 658 gray marble columns. The main door, which rotated on a rail, weighed seven tons. Two different keys were needed to enter.

Without a word being said, the Germans looked around. After an hour of searching, they finally had to admit that there was not a bar of gold left in the Paris vault. De Bletterie did not volunteer that at precisely that moment French bank officials and their staff in several locations around the country were doing everything they could to get the last French national treasure out of the country.[20]

Late in the evening of June 16, Prime Minister Paul Reynaud resigned, and Marshal Philippe Pétain formed a new cabinet that included a majority of ministers who wanted to end the war. Just after midnight, Paul Baudouin, the new French foreign minister, called in the Spanish ambassador and asked if his country would act as an intermediary to the Germans "with a view to the cessation of hostilities and the settlement of conditions for peace." At 9:00 A.M. the next morning, General Charles de Gaulle left Bordeaux on a British plane to exile. He already had vague plans to organize a Free French army to continue the war against Hitler. Later that same day, Pétain announced over the radio, "I approached the adversary last night to ask him if he is ready to explore with me, as between soldier and soldier, when the fight is over and in an honorable circumstance, the means of ending hostilities."[21] In a radio appeal made on June 22 to the people of France, de Gaulle called for his countrymen to continue the fight and pointed to the many resources the country still possessed: "There remains a vast empire, an intact naval fleet, and lots of gold."[22]

Admiral François Darlan, the commander of the French navy, sent a message to his entire fleet, signing with his new secret moniker Xavier 337: FIGHT FIERCELY TO THE END AS LONG AS A REGULAR AND INDEPENDENT FRENCH GOVERNMENT HAS NOT GIVEN A CONTRARY ORDER. DISOBEY ORDERS FROM ALL OTHER GOVERNMENTS. NO MATTER WHAT ORDERS ARE RECEIVED, NEVER ABANDON TO THE ENEMY A COMBAT SHIP INTACT.

The captain of the French liner *Pasteur* was still in New York City on June 17, when he learned from American newspapers that his country was pleading for an armistice. He immediately contacted the French naval attaché to ask for instructions. French officials were concerned that the U.S. might seize the ship in New York City in order to keep it out of Nazi hands and ordered him to return immediately to Halifax. While en route, the French Admiralty sent a message telling him that if he had not yet left to remain in New York City or head for Dakar, the capital of Senegal, a French colony in Africa. That port city was located on the Cap-Vert Peninsula, which stuck far out into the Atlantic Ocean 1,500 miles south of Casablanca and nearly 4,000 miles southeast of New York City. The communication, though, did not get through, and the *Pasteur* headed for Halifax. It arrived on June 19 and was ordered to leave immediately for Dakar.

At 1:00 P.M. on June 18, the *Émile Bertin* again pulled into the Halifax harbor, this time tying up at Pier 4. It had left Brest on the evening of June 11 with 254 tons of gold, 3,986 sacks of coins and 796 cases of bars. The previous day while at sea, the crew had heard news of Pétain's peace petition. When the ship landed, Edouard de Katow, the French National Bank representative on board, decided to leave the bullion where it was until he had received new instructions. The Canadian train that was ready to take it to Ottawa would just have to wait.[23]

As soon as the ship was safely tied up, an officer from the French naval mission in the harbor came aboard and gave Commander Battet a message that had arrived a few hours earlier. It read: AS SOON AS ARRIVE IN HALIFAX ÉMILE BERTIN SHOULD MAKE ROUTE AS FAST AS POSSIBLE TO FORT DE FRANCE WITH CARGO ON BOARD STOP. Fort-de-France, the capital of Martinique, had one of the largest harbors in the Caribbean. The ship was almost out of fuel oil, so the first thing Battet did was have the tanks filled, which was done late that night.[24]

The next day just before noon, the French commander met with Vice Admiral Stuart Bonham Carter, the commanding British officer at Halifax; their meeting quickly turned hostile. Carter gruffly told Battet that the French officer's assignment was finished and that he was taking over the French ship. The British admiral explained that he had received orders from London not to let any French vessels leave the harbor.

The French officer responded furiously: "Such an attitude is contrary to all traditions of maritime honor and to all international rules."

Carter replied just as tartly: "I am obliged, also myself, to obey the instructions of my government . . . if necessary by force."

The British admiral warned, "We have our batteries." But the Frenchman barked back, "I also have cannons."[25]

Diplomatic cables soon flew between France, Canada, Britain, and the U.S. While the British did not want the ship to end up in Nazi hands, the Canadians opposed using force to stop the French. Canadian Prime Minister W. L. Mackenzie King got into the fight, saying sternly, "We control our own country and will not be governed by an Admiralty point of view, but by the position of Canada as a whole." Battet received another message from France, repeating the earlier cable to leave port with the gold. It also requested a confirmation that the instructions had been received. Following intense talks but no progress, Battet at 9:00 A.M. on June 21 sent a message to the French Admiralty saying, FOLLOW YOUR ORDERS TO LEAVE BY FORCE STOP CHANCE OF SUCCESS ONE IN THREE STOP.[26]

At noon that same day, Admiral Bonham Carter went aboard the *Émile Bertin* to have lunch with Battet. The French officer had ordered his ship's kitchen to prepare a special meal that would show off his country's culinary achievements. As an extraordinary lunch passed in front of the two officers, the mood improved. There was less confrontation, and the two veteran naval officers talked candidly. Finally and unexpectedly, Bonham Carter told Battet that his ship could leave the port. He added, "Get out fast."[27]

With neither a pilot boat nor a tug to help it depart, the *Émile Bertin* at 6:00 P.M. pulled away from the dock and turned south toward Martinique. Sailors aboard the French ship quickly noticed that the British heavy cruiser *HMS Devonshire* was following. Battet responded by pushing his ship's speed up to thirty-four knots and left the slower vessel in his wake. The British ship was short of fuel, and the next morning it turned around and headed back to Halifax.

The *Pasteur*, which had received orders to follow the *Émile Bertin*, did not leave the harbor. The British seized the luxury cruiser and used it as troop ship for the rest of the war under the British flag.

On June 23, the British war cabinet discussed the French gold that was on its way to Martinique. According to the report of the meeting, "The Prime Minister emphasized the importance of getting possession of these two ships [*Béarn* and *Émile Bertin*] and the gold that was aboard." It also said, "We could announce that we should keep the gold in trust for the French Empire, but that they must not fight for it." The cabinet ordered the *HMS Dunedin* to proceed at full speed to Martinique, where its captain was to make contact with the most senior French official to "get him on our side." The cruiser was also instructed to keep the French ships within sight. If the vessels stayed in Martinique well and good, but if they moved, the *Dunedin* should follow them so that they could be intercepted. The war cabinet feared that they might slip across the Atlantic and land at Dakar.[28]

The *Émile Bertin* docked safely in Martinique on June 25. Waiting for its arrival outside the harbor was the *Dunedin*, which was soon joined by the *HMS Trinidad*. The two ships then set up a blockade. The French vessel would not be going anywhere without the British.

Two hundred fifty Senegalese troops unloaded the 255 tons of gold and moved it two-and-a-half miles to the military installation Fort Desaix. It took four days to complete the transfer. The cargo was placed in three vaults, where 300 soldiers guarded it. Boxes and bags holding the metal had deteriorated during the trip south because of heavy rain and high humidity, so the French commander ordered new wooden containers made.

The situation in Martinique remained tense for several months. The U.S. considered the Caribbean to be its backyard and part of its zone of influence. Washington quickly made its interests known. Admiral John Greenslade, the U.S. Chief of Naval Operations, twice visited Fort-de-France, and on the second trip told French Admiral George Robert, whom Pétain had named the High Commissioner of the French Antilles, that neither French ships nor the gold could leave the island without American permission. U.S. vessels also joined the British in guarding the entrance to the Martinique harbor. The French later decided that if either the Germans or the

Allies attempted to take over the gold at Fort Desaix, they would sink it in 1,000 meters of Caribbean waters.

The French Admiralty sought to get as many ships as possible to Martinique. Just after 8:00 P.M. on June 24, it sent out a message to all its vessels at sea and to naval installations saying that hostilities between France and Germany and Italy would end at thirty-five minutes after midnight French summer time. Less than a hour later, the navy sent a special message to the *Jeanne d'Arc* and the *Béarn*, which were then in the middle of the Atlantic: DO NOT TURN OVER TO ANYONE INDUSTRIAL CARGO WITHOUT FORMAL ORDER STOP. It was too late; their gold was already in Canadian hands.

At 6:07 A.M. the next morning, the French Admiralty sent out another cable: ORDER TO BEARN AND THE JEANNE D'ARC PROCEED TO FORT-DE-FRANCE STOP ACKNOWLEDGE RECEIPT STOP. The two vessels did not reply, so the following day, another message went out: THE FOLLOWING IS A REPEAT AND A CONFIRMATION STOP ORDER TO BEARN AND JEANNE D'ARC TO PROCEED TO FORT-DE-FRANCE ACKNOWLEDGE RECEIPT STOP. This time the message got through. The two ships quickly turned around and checked their fuel levels to make sure they had enough to make it to Martinique. The captains calculated that if they traveled at only twelve knots they could reach their destination with a little fuel oil left.[29]

France soon had a small flotilla docked in the Martinique harbor, and in short order there were also 2,500 French sailors on the island. In addition to the three former gold ships there were nearly thirty smaller French vessels. The *Béarn* was there with about one hundred airplanes that it had picked up in Halifax but never delivered. A short distance away on the French island of Guadeloupe was the cruiser *Jeanne d'Arc*. The war was over for the French sailors and their ships, and the American Navy was now carefully watching the situation in Martinique to make sure that the gold did not move.[30]

Chapter Eighteen

THE VATICAN'S
SECRET GOLD

Vatican
June 1940
Tons of gold: 7.7

Gold Route
- - - - - ▶

Denmark

Baltic Sea

Liverpool

To New York

Britain

Holland

Belgium

Berlin

Germany

Luxembourg

Bohemia and Moravia

Atlantic Ocean

France

Switzerland

Yugoslavia

Italy

Rome

Portugal

Spain

Yugoslavia

Algeria

Tunisia

Mediterranean Sea

As Nazi armies in the dark days of May 1940 marched across Western Europe conquering nations at will and grabbing as much gold as they could to finance their future conquests, even Vatican City, the city-state enclave within Rome that is the international headquarters of the Roman Catholic church, became desperate to safeguard its gold.

American presidents over the decades often had an uneasy relationship with the Vatican. The United States has a strong history of separation between church and state, and that made the men in the White House uncomfortable dealing with an institution that combines them. Anti-Catholicism in the U.S. was strong at times, such as during the Know-Nothing Movement in the mid-nineteenth century, which attempted to stop the flow of Irish and German immigrants. The papacy and the U.S. government, in fact, had not had official contact from the fall of the Papal States to the Kingdom of Italy in 1870 until 1933, when President Franklin D. Roosevelt asked James Farley, his former campaign manager and then postmaster general, to see if he could normalize relations. He visited Rome in 1933, and met with Pope Pius XI.

With Mussolini and Hitler on a brutal mission to dominate Europe, Roosevelt realized that the militarily weak democracies were not equipped to block them. On the evening of December 22, 1939, the president telephoned Myron Taylor, a life-long Episcopalian, and asked him to become his "personal representative" to the Vatican. He would have the rank of ambassador extraordinary. The title was chosen carefully so that the president could avoid any political controversy that might have arisen if he gave Taylor the title ambassador. The White House announced the appointment the next day. At the time, thirty-eight nations had representatives accredited to the pope. In a later letter confirming the Vatican offer, Roosevelt wrote Taylor, "I may from time to time request you to serve as the channel of communications for any views I may wish to exchange with the Pope."[1]

Taylor at the time was one of the most esteemed businessmen in America. After graduating from the Cornell University Law School in 1894, he first practiced law and then went on to a spectacular career as a Wall Street lawyer. He made a fortune by introducing transparent window envelopes. He also bought up poorly run textile companies and created a management process known as the Taylor Formula. In the 1920s, he turned around the then financially troubled U.S. Steel, which at the time was the largest corporation in the world. He won a reputation for corporate enlightenment in 1937, when his company agreed to collective bargaining with the Congress of Industrial Organizations (CIO). That made U.S. Steel the first industrial firm to unionize. Taylor served as its chairman and CEO until 1938.[2]

Taylor began a new diplomatic career that same year, when he represented the U.S. at a conference at Évian-les-Bains. France wanted to find new homes for the thousands of Jews that Hitler had forced out of Germany by his anti-Semitic policies, but didn't want to take them all itself. Representatives from thirty-two countries and thirty-nine private organizations attended the meeting. Before it started, Hitler announced that he would let Jews leave Germany for other countries. The U.S. and Britain quickly made it clear that they would not accept large numbers of Jewish refugees, and the conference was widely considered a failure.

When Roosevelt asked Taylor to go to the Vatican, the pope was Pius XII, who had taken up his job only on March 2, 1938. For many years he had been widely touted as *papabilus*, the Latin term Vatican insiders gave to a cardinal deemed to be a potential pontiff. He had served as papal nuncio to Germany from 1917 to 1929 and later negotiated with Hitler the *Reichskonkordat* agreement that sought to protect the church in Germany at a time when the Nazis were waging war on all religions. It was signed in July 1933, only six months after Hitler came to power. Roosevelt met the future Pope Pius XII in the fall of 1936, when he was still known as Cardinal Eugenio Pacelli. On a visit to the U.S., FDR entertained him at his presidential retreat in Hyde Park, New York, and they discussed the European situation.[3]

When Taylor left the U.S. for his new assignment on February 16, 1940 aboard the Italian ship *SS Rex*, the president, who was vacationing aboard the *USS Tuscaloosa*, sent him a cable saying, "Good luck happy voyage and write me soon." Taylor carried with him Roosevelt's hand-written letter to the pontiff dated February 14, 1940. It stressed their "common ideals of religion and of humanity" and the "reestablishment of a more permanent peace."[4]

Once Taylor was in Rome, the pope quickly received him and accepted his credentials. The two had a private forty-five minute session, discussing European politics with a concentration on the future objectives of both Hitler and Mussolini. The pontiff was pessimistic about Hitler's agenda, while he described Mussolini as "undecided and wavering." Pius XII added that the Italian public was "opposed to war." The pope ended the meeting by telling Taylor that he could have "daily access day or night whenever desired." That same evening a picture of Taylor presenting his credentials to the pope was on the front page of the Vatican daily newspaper *L'Osservatore Romano*. That was quickly followed by a full-page story also on the front page under the headline, "A Program of Liberty, Cooperation and Peace Marks the Constant Relations Between the Holy See and the United States."[5] Italian fascists made a big thing about the non-ambassadorial status of Taylor at the Vatican, calling it an insult to all Italians. So Roosevelt secretly made him a counselor, which had the benefit of giving him both more status and diplomatic immunity.

Taylor met with the pope again less than a week later and also quickly held talks with several other top Vatican officials. In addition, the one-time businessman established a good working relationship with other ambassadors to the Holy See, especially François Charles-Roux, the French representative, and Sir D'Arcy Osborne, the British one. The three soon became close friends. Taylor enjoyed unprecedented access to the Vatican and received a detailed report on the private meeting in March between Pius XII and German Foreign Minister Joachim von Ribbentrop. Taylor also earned a reputation in Rome for being a bit stiff. British author Owen Chadwick, in a history of British relations with the Vatican during the war, called him "a rhadamanthine kind of man; not pompous, but he seemed to survey humanity as from a pedestal."[6]

By late March, Taylor was getting reports from the Vatican about the threat of a German invasion of the Low Countries within a month. Pius XII also personally warned him of the impending Nazi offensive. The Vatican still hoped that it might be able to stop Mussolini from joining Hitler's new offensive.

In a cable to Washington on April 20, Taylor reported that he had learned that Hitler would make a surprise attack on the Low Countries before the end of the month. He said that the Vatican's secretary of state had "earnestly repeated the necessity for speedy action" to stop such a move that "should be taken within two or three days." The U.S. did nothing, but Secretary of State Cordell Hull on April 25 cabled Taylor saying, "although no action taken, this does not mean it is not carefully considered."[7]

At that same time, the Italian government launched a new attack on the papacy. On April 25, Mussolini bellowed, "The Vatican is the chronic appendicitis of Italy." The government centered its attack on L'Osservatore Romano, and the Fascist leader Roberto Farinacci called the paper "the servant of the enemies of Italy and the evident mouthpiece of the Jews."[8] A newspaper he owned called upon readers to beat up anyone found reading the Vatican paper. The paper later wrote, "Judas sold Christ for 30 dinarii. The gentlemen of L'Osservatore Romano are ready to do worse."[9]

The Vatican's source of information during this period were anti-Hitler officers within the German military, who were warning that an attack on Holland, Belgium, and France would take place in early May. The tips were correct. France's Charles Roux wrote Taylor that he had seen the pope about the invasions and that Britain's Sir D'Arcy Osborne was going to see him as well. The Frenchman called the attacks a "shameful action enterprised by Germany in violation of the international law." Roux also told Taylor that it would be "comforting" to him and Osborne to "feel your presence in Rome for a few days to come."[10]

That, however, did not happen. Only two days later the American diplomat had to leave for Florence to get emergency medical treatment. A few weeks before at a diplomatic dinner in Rome, he had eaten bad lobster and become quite ill. Since he had undergone two operations just before Roosevelt named his as his personal representative, Taylor took his health seriously. The Florence doctor had been recommended to him.[11]

Before leaving, Taylor had an hour-long meeting with the pope to discuss the German invasion. He learned that the Vatican had warned Dutch Crown Princess Juliana about an imminent attack during her visit to the Vatican just days before it took place. The pope also passed along to Taylor Mussolini's reply to the pontiff after the invasion. The Italian leader had ominously warned the pontiff, "I cannot, however, give absolute assurance that it will be possible for us to remain non-belligerent until the end."[12]

Taylor was back in Rome on May 17, and four days later sent an emergency message directly to the president, rather than through the State Department. The letter began: "The Vatican Secretary of State has asked of you the following favor." It went on to explain that the Vatican State had a "sizable amount of gold on deposit in a bank in a belligerent country." It turned out that the gold was then stored in Britain. The short cable said that the Vatican wanted to "deposit for safekeeping in trust with New York bankers." Taylor wrote that papal officials wanted to sell gold and to be assured that "as in case of other states with deposits in America that the gold will be intact and in all ways free under our laws." Church leaders had no experience in this type of operation and were terrified that it would become known. The cable ended: "Vatican very anxious to avoid any publicity."[13]

The issue was given to the Federal Reserve since it handled gold matters, but officials were at something of a loss about what to do. Working out the details of the Vatican gold transfer was handled by telephone so as not to leave a written trail. The Federal Reserve officials were used to making such transactions with other central banks or commercial banks, but not with the Vatican, which did not have a central bank. At times Federal Reserve offficials seemed to be all thumbs, not knowing whether the Vatican could be considered a government. There were also concerns in Washington that the Vatican in the past had been too cozy with Hitler and Musso-lini. The Fed at one point attempted to shift the issue to the State Department, but officials responded that it didn't have relations with the papacy because it "had no diplomatic standing." Fed vice president L. Werner Knoke replied in a memo that he understood the department's position because the New York Fed "at the very beginning tried to get away from handling this business."[14] During a telephone conversation between George L. Harrison, the head of the New York Fed, and Marriner Eccles, the chairman of the Federal Reserve Board in Washington, Harrison started the call by saying, "I'll talk, Marriner, as though I were talking with you." He went on to explain that he had received a phone call from the Treasury Department and that someone had dictated over the phone a memo that had arrived from Rome. It said: "The Vatican State would like to ship to New York for deposit and safekeeping with New York bankers a sizeable amount of gold bars which it does not wish to sell." The memo also noted, "The Vatican very much desires to avoid any publicity on the matter." Rome also wanted a reply by the next day.[15]

Harrison explained that he would usually have taken up such a matter with his board, "but the time factor makes it impossible to do that." He said that his bank had never before dealt with anything but another central bank or a government, and he was unsure about where the Vatican fit. He then said he thought his bank could take responsibility for the matter, under its institutional power "to deal in gold."[16] Eccles ended the talk with another appeal for secrecy, saying, "It's terribly important, I can see, that this thing is kept quiet."[17]

The Federal Reserve board in Washington held a special meeting at 2:00 P.M. and agreed to Harrison's suggestion that he handle the issue under the power it had "to deal in gold." A Washington Fed official called New York at 4:00 P.M. to say that it "imposes no objection to Federal Reserve declaring itself willing to open a gold deposit account for the Vatican State."

Treasury Secretary Morgenthau learned of the request on May 21, and the following day Secretary of State Hull sent a cable to Taylor saying, "It has been arranged with the Federal Reserve of New York that the Vatican gold be held on the same basis as the bank holds the gold of other foreign accounts."[18] The State Department passed that news along to Taylor in Rome at the end of the working day on May 22. The dispatch signed by Secretary of State Cordell Hull said that appropriate instructions and signatures would be needed, but "the gold shipment which is desired by the Vatican does not need to be held up in any way by this."[19]

Shortly after the Vatican learned that it could send gold to the U.S., Giovanni Fummi, an international financial wheeler-dealer, traveled to London to arrange for the shipments. The investment house Morgan Grenfell held the gold. Cardinal Luigi Maglioni, the papal Secretary of State, also became involved in the operation. In addition, the Vatican informed Lord Halifax, now the British ambassador in Washington, and Kingsley Wood, the Chancellor of the Exchequer, about the transfer.[20]

The British firm Morgan Grenfell shipped the gold from London in early June. On June 11, Secretary Morgenthau received a memo from the Federal Reserve saying that about ten tons of gold was due to arrive the following day. J. P. Morgan told the Fed that the papacy was anxious that the delivery not be publicized and asked that all communications be conducted with the apostolic delegate in Washington. The Federal Reserve wanted to work through the U.S. embassy in Rome, but Vatican officials said that was too dangerous. It wanted to deal with New York and Washington.

On June 10, a J. P. Morgan official informed the New York Federal Reserve that the Vatican had sent it two shipments. The first, which amounted to 112 gold bars in 28 boxes, arrived from Liverpool aboard the SS Aracataca on June 14 at Manhattan's Pier 56. It was valued at $1.6 million. A second shipment of 432 bars aboard the SS Britannica landed in New York on June 21. The value of that was $6.1 million. A Fed statement two days later showed that the New York Fed had put $7.7 million in gold into a new Vatican account, which had the name Amministrazione Speciale della Santa Sede, Stato della Città del Vaticano (Special Administration of the Holy See, Vatican

City State). A confirming letter on August 5, reported that the first ship carried 45,162.8 ounces of gold and the second 173,844.2 ounces. The New York Fed agreed to charge the Vatican $966.03 per quarter for storage. On February 27, 1942, an additional 104 bars worth $1.5 million arrived at the New York Fed.[21]

The Vatican became an active Fed client. It later purchased $1 million in Swiss francs from Switzerland, and then ten days later it sent 2.1 million escudos to Lisbon. In November 1942, the Vatican paid $1 million for seventy-one bars of gold for its account in a deal arranged by J. P. Morgan.[22] The U.S. government also found it convenient to have a Vatican connection. In December 1942, it sent the equivalent of $3,000 in lira through the Vatican to Howard Tittmann, an American diplomat who had taken political refuge in the Vatican because of fascist threats.

The same day that the cable about the Vatican's gold request went out, Taylor sent a message to Roosevelt saying that he wanted to return to Washington in June "to consult with you." It was unclear whether he was doing that because of war developments or his own medical problems. At the end of the message he added simply, "Leaving tonight for Florence."[23]

Taylor on that same day also wrote a longer memo to Roosevelt about developments in Europe in view of the Nazis attacks in Western Europe. He ended the downbeat report with: "It is considered that the next effort of the Germans will be against Switzerland in order to turn the flank of the French army such as they are trying to do in the case of Holland and Belgium at the Northern end of the line."[24] Two days later, Secretary of State Hull sent Taylor a "confidential message from the president," that stated: "I believe that under existing conditions it is unwise to plan more than twenty-four hours on anything."[25]

On May 23, Taylor had a long farewell audience with the pope, the fifth meeting since the American arrived in Rome at the end of February. In a cable report of the meeting sent to Washington, Taylor wrote that the pope and the secretary of state "were appreciative of your prompt action in regard to the request they had made through me [regarding the gold]." The pope also told Taylor that he thought Italy would enter the war "within the next two or three weeks," but that he could do nothing to stop Mussolini.

By then Rome was becoming an ugly place for the papacy. Crowds in the streets were shouting "Down with the Pope! Down with the French! Down with the British!" When the pope left the safe confines of Vatican City to celebrate a mass in Rome, an angry crowd shouted at him, "Death to the Pope!" Taylor sent a cable to Washington about newspaper attacks on the pope that said, "He needs all the support that can be given him."[26]

On February 27, 1942, the Fed's Knoke reported to his board of governors that an additional $1.5 million in gold had been received from the Vatican State, which brought the amount now held in two accounts to just over nine tons. That bullion remained at the New York Fed for the duration of the war.[27]

In a cable to President Roosevelt on June 14, Taylor finally explained his mysterious urgent trip to Florence, writing, "I regret to advise you that I have been for the last two weeks very ill in Florence. Professor Batianelli, surgeon, and Professor Fugone, medical advisor, urge me as soon as I am able to travel to return home for a time."[28] Taylor spent most of June and all of July in Florence in the hospital, and correspondence between the ambassador and Washington was interrupted for several weeks. On July 29, President Roosevelt sent his envoy a cable saying, "I am delighted you have come through the operation so well, and I need not tell you that you have been in my thoughts." He ended it with the admonition, "Take care of yourself."[29]

In a telegram to Roosevelt on August 2, Taylor said he would be back in Rome on August 19 for a Vatican conference and suggested that he leave Europe after that via Lisbon. He explained the need for the trip by saying, "In view of great European change past and to come, I feel it desirable to return home the week of the 26th to confer with you."[30] The following day, Taylor had an hour-and-a-quarter audience with the pope, but the special envoy sent the president only a vague report, writing, "I hesitate to present them in a telegram and in view of the fact that no immediate or urgent action is suggested. I believe it best to reserve a complete report for the time when I can call on you upon my return to the United States."[31]

Taylor flew to Lisbon on September 22 and then continued on to New York City. His illness had cut short his mission to the Vatican before it had hardly started. Nonetheless, he had been there to handle the church's gold shipment to the New York Federal Reserve. The Vatican and the New York Fed continued to keep up a steady stream of messages concerning the papacy's financial dealings, which were now mostly handled through the church's office in Washington.

Taylor spent most of World War II in the United States, making only a few short trips back to Rome. In the summer of 1942, Roosevelt asked him to return to ask Pope Pius XII to speak out against German atrocities against the Jews. The president was also anxious to explain his support for the Soviet Union. Pius was strongly anti-communist, and continued his outspoken opposition to Stalin despite the war against Hitler. Roosevelt was anxious to stop American bishops from becoming strongly anti-Soviet, which would make it more difficult for him to support Moscow's war efforts. Taylor showed the pontiff concrete proof of the killing of Jews in concentration camps. In his annual Christmas Eve message that year, Pius said, "Humanity owes this vow to those hundreds of thousands who, without any fault on their part, sometimes only because of their nationality or race, have been marked down for death or gradual extinction." Critics, though, said that he should have been tougher and more direct. Later in the war, Taylor also lobbied Roosevelt not to bomb Rome.[32]

The following year, Taylor played a significant role in Mussolini's departure from the war. In 1943 and working with the apostolic delegate in Washington, Taylor encouraged the Vatican to push Il Duce from power. Pius at first was cautious and skeptical, but eventually supported installing a new Italian government. When Roosevelt learned of that he replied, "Myron, this is the first break in the war. It is wonderful."[33]

Chapter Nineteen

ESCAPE TO CASABLANCA

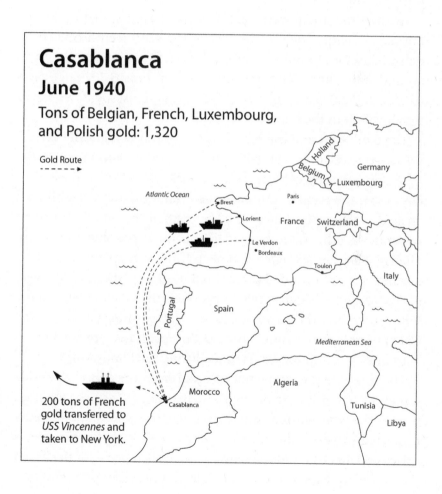

Casablanca

June 1940

Tons of Belgian, French, Luxembourg, and Polish gold: 1,320

Gold Route

Holland

Belgium

Germany

Luxembourg

Atlantic Ocean

Paris

Brest

Lorient

France

Switzerland

Le Verdon

Bordeaux

Toulon

Italy

Portugal

Spain

Mediterranean Sea

Morocco

Algeria

Casablanca

Tunisia

Libya

200 tons of French gold transferred to *USS Vincennes* and taken to New York.

With the war going badly and the collapse of France imminent, the French National Bank's René Gontier on Sunday morning June 9, arrived in Brest with instructions to take another gold shipment to the U.S.[1] He and two other bank officials already in Brest went immediately to the office of Admiral Philip Brohan, the head of the French navy's operation there. This facility, which juts out into the Atlantic from Brittany, was the country's most important military base. It was also an ideal location for more gold shipments. Gontier said that the next convoy might carry as much as 900 tons.[2]

At the time, there were 16,201 cases of gold stored at Fort de Portzic, a facility built at the end of the seventeenth century to defend the city. The bullion had come from fifty-nine branch offices around France and included 4,329 boxes of coins, 9,797 large cases of bars, and 2,075 bags of coins. The navy had just spent two weeks moving it all to the fort.[3]

The bank staff and the French navy were systematically getting the cargo ready to be shipped, when on Friday June 14, 1940, the first alert warning of German air attacks sounded in Brest. Two days later, the French Admiralty sent out a message that all gold located in the ports of Brest and Lorient, another naval port sixty-five miles south, had to be loaded as soon as possible onto ships. The French navy, though, was able to find only six private vessels to carry it. They included three small passenger ships, *El Mansour*, *El Djezaïr*, and *El Kantara*; two larger ones, the *Ville d'Oran*, and the *Ville d'Alger*; and the *Victor Schoelcher*, a cargo ship that before the war carried bananas from Africa to Europe. It had already helped with one gold shipment to Halifax during the Phony War.[4]

The round trip for carrying the gold from the fort to dockside was about ten miles. Finally two days later at 5:00 P.M., the loadings began. The work started systematically with each container being inspected to verify the contents. There were eight trucks, and a driver and an armed navy guard manned each one. Gontier asked the sailors to work as late as possible, but because of the military blackout they had to stop at 9:00 P.M. During the night German planes dropped mines into the harbor, but the diligent crew started work again the next morning at 6:00.[5]

In mid-morning, an agitated Gontier went to the office of Admiral Brohan and bluntly told him that the loading was going too slowly. He demanded more trucks, but the officer replied that he didn't have any. Gontier responded that at the rate they were going it would take a week to finish the job. By that time the Germans would be there. Instead of eight trucks, he wanted twenty bigger vehicles. He insisted that the navy should requisition all the trucks in the area. When he failed to get the answer he wanted, Gontier took his request to the admiral's boss. The higher-ranking officer said he doubted he could locate more than a dozen, and he eventually found ten. That evening everyone at the port heard Marshal Pétain announce that he was asking the Germans for a peace settlement. Someone stuck a handwritten note on a wall saying that the loading had to continue. Gontier also told the navy that work had to continue day and night until the job was finished.[6] A bank official phoned from Bordeaux and told him to get all the ships out of the harbor one by one as soon as they were loaded. The navy countermanded the order, saying that for safety reasons all the ships had to go out together. The *El Djezaïr* was ready to depart at 4:00 A.M. with 203 tons in its hold, but it had to wait.[7]

When Gontier returned to the fort the next day, more trucks had somehow miraculously appeared, and loading was faster. The French navy had discovered eleven six-ton trucks that the British had abandoned in their rush to get to Dunkirk. Enemy air attacks continuously halted the work, and some twenty bombs fell on the road between the fort and the docks.[8]

Three hours later, Admiral Traub, the head of the maritime region, received a phone call telling him that German armored vehicles had captured the city of Rennes, one hundred thirty miles away. There were no military units to stop the invaders before they reached Brest. A new order went out that every ship had to leave the port by 6:00 P.M. Gold was now being moved even during aerial attacks. Officers distributed spiked tea and wine to keep the men working. They explained that they certainly were not going to leave any wine for the conquering Germans. All the ships were now being loading simultaneously and frantically. At one point Gontier urgently yelled to one of the captains, "All gold must be shipped." The captain shouted back, "We're already doing the impossible."[9] At 1:00 in the afternoon, one of the port's tugboats hit a magnetic mine only a few hundred yards from the El Djezaïr.

Realizing that they desperately needed more men to work at the fort, navy officers in the middle of the afternoon decided to enlist inmates from the nearby Pontaniou prison. The men were promised that they would be pardoned as soon as the job was finished. The navy men then quickly put in a new security check. Each prisoner was given a small piece of paper with a number on it that had to be returned after he delivered the gold.

At 5:00 P.M. on June 18, the last truck left the fort. An hour later, the El Kantara sent out an optical signal saying: "Loading finished. We're setting off." Several smaller and slower boats not carrying gold were trying to leave the port at the same time. Every ship's captain and all those on board were living in fear that they would hit a mine and set off an explosion. Slowly, the five gold ships pulled away from the docks one by one. Once outside the harbor, they formed two columns, and their escort ships, the Milan and the Epervier, led them to open ocean. While the flotilla was leaving, the dispatch boat Vauquois hit a mine only a few hundred yards from the convoy. Back on shore, men torched the stocks of fuel, and fire lit up the sky. The two-day and two-night evacuation of the gold from Fort Portzic had been a success. The first five ships carried twenty-tree thousand cases that contained 1,120 tons of bullion.[10]

While the French gold was being rescued in Brest, the Polish and Belgian gold that had been turned over to the French was in equal danger. On June 7, the French navy had sent out an order: BELGIAN AND POLISH GOLD MUST ARRIVE IN LORIENT MONDAY JUNE TEN STOP.[11] The Polish gold that had been in Nevers now had to go north by train.[12] The Belgian gold that had been turned over to the French National Bank was stored near Bordeaux and would also be moved by rail. Admiral Hervé de Penfentanyo, the Navy's harbormaster at Brest, ordered that the Polish and Belgian gold should be stored in a place where it could be "rapidly removed in a very short period of time." The shipment went smoothly despite the war, and on 5:00 in the afternoon of June 13, Admiral Penfentanyo sent out a message: 1208 CASES OF POLAND AND 4944 CASES OF BELGIUM STOCKED AIR-RAID SHELTER STOP SUPPLY FLEET STOP COULD BE PICKED UP IN TWENTY-FOUR HOURS STOP.[13]

Two-and-a-half hours later, the French admiralty sent the cargo ship *Victor Schoelcher* a message that read HEAD TO LORIENT STOP. Captain Moevus was instructed to leave that night and proceed at a speed that would get it there early the next morning. The admiralty's message: YOU HAVE TO PICK UP GOLD STOP MARITIME HARBORMASTER THERE WILL GIVE YOU THE NECESSARY ORDERS STOP ABSOLUTE SECRECY STOP.[14]

The ship arrived the next morning, at 6:35, and Moevus went on shore to get instructions from Admiral de Penfentanyo. He learned that his cargo was Belgian and Polish gold, which was packed and ready for shipment. The cargo consisted of 6,152 cases, with each weighing about 120 pounds. The admiral ordered him to pick up the cargo and leave port as soon as possible. The gold was currently stored in an air-raid shelter, but trucks and the police would get it to the dock. The captain said he had on board two men, a reserve lieutenant and a banana trader, who could handle security. Loading began immediately and continued without interruption, even through air-raid alarms. The torpedo boat *Epée* was assigned to be the escort out of the harbor.

Most of the Polish National Bank's board members had by then left France for Britain, but they had assigned Stefan Michalski, also a board member, to remain with their gold. Michalski, his son, and the director of the French National Bank's Lorient vault, monitored the operation with the care of a mother eagle fluttering around her nest.

Shortly before midnight, the navy harbormaster sent out a message saying that the Germans had dropped mines and until further notice no ships could depart. At 2:00 A.M. an explosions expert arrived to look at the situation. He said that dredgers would have to be brought in before it was safe to depart. Sailors came up with a jerry-rigged solution, but even that would not be ready until afternoon. In the meantime, the gold was to stay on board, but everyone had to get off the ships.

Before leaving the *Victor Schoelcher*, Michalski asked the captain, "Do you know our destination?"

Moevus replied, "No."

"Neither do I, but I think that it should be either Canada or the Caribbean," said the Pole.

Everyone in the harbor soon learned that the Germans expected to be there the next morning. There was no way that the de-mining could be completed by then. At an emergency meeting of top officials, Captain Moevus spelled out his pessimistic options, which were all bad. Even though the Germans would not be there until the following day, the Luftwaffe at any time could sink the *Victor Schoelcher* in shallow waters an easily retrieve the gold. He could also scuttle the ship, but the enemy would probably still pull it out of the water. Then he presented his plan. He proposed sailing out to open ocean following the mouth of the river. He would be passing parallel to the rocks on the coast. "That way, I would have the best chance of being far away from the mines," he said. "Once I'm outside the harbor, I'll sail with the *Epée* on a westerly route and wait to receive instructions for our destination."[15]

Admiral de Penfentanyo was skeptical, but finally approved the captain's risky plan. He didn't have any better solution. The ship would leave at midnight. The staff offered to provide navigation equipment that the captain would need. The meeting was just breaking up, when a Lorient banker pulled up in a truck that was carrying some public and private papers. He asked the captain where he was going and if he could go on the ship as well. Moevus replied that he didn't know his destination, but given how fast the enemy was coming it could only be Africa or America. The banker said that he did not have authority to take the papers outside France.

The captain replied that the only assurance he could give was that he was going abroad. The man reluctantly left.

The *Victor Schoelcher* departed as planned on June 18. Orders to evacuate Lorient had been received two hours prior. All the people on board and in the harbor held their breath as Moevus sailed the route he had described. They expected that at any moment the ship would explode, but *Victor Schoelcher* kept bravely slipping through the water. The captain stayed in touch with officials on shore using marine flags. When it finally passed the ancient Port-Louis citadel, the last dangerous location, he signaled that he was going to proceed on a course west-by-southwest for the next twenty-four hours. The *Epée* replied, "I am on a 248 course."[16]

The happiest man on board was Stefan Michalski, who told the captain, "I sincerely thank you for the perfect execution of this evacuation, and I ask you to please transmit my thanks to the staff whose disciplined ardor and courageous efforts permitted this success."

Moevus received a message shortly before 6:00 P.M. instructing the *Victor Schoelcher* and the *Epée* to stay in the nearby Iroise Sea, where the water more than 100 meters deep. He should wait there for the flotilla from Brest to arrive. Those ships had left at almost the same time and were sailing at eighteen knots, without lights. A little before midnight, all the ships simultaneously saw each other in the dark. An escort ship sent out the message: FOLLOW US STOP COURSE 230 STOP SPEED EIGHTEEN KNOTS STOP. Moevus responded: THAT'S VERY PRETTY STOP. The *El Djezaïr*, though, answered: MY MAXIMUM SPEED 15.5 KNOTS.[17]

After aligning themselves and coordinating their speed, Moevus cabled: IN EVENT OF SEPARATION DON'T KNOW OUR DESTINATION.

The admiral replied: DESTINATION CASABLANCA.

A few hours later, the *Jean-Bart* left the port of Saint-Nazaire and took over escort duties. With everything finally a little calmer, Gontier of the French National Bank, who was aboard the *El Djezaïr*, asked the Admiralty to inquire how many cases he had on board. Moevus replied: LEFT WITH 4944 CASES BELGIAN GOLD AND 1208 CASES POLISH GOLD STOP HEAD OF THE CONVOY IS POLISH BANK DIRECTOR STOP. The five ships from Brest also sent the lists of their cargo. The six ships together were carrying 22,669 cases and bags containing 1,120 tons of bullion. The value of the cargo at the 1940 price of $35 an ounce was $1.3 billion.

At 10:00 in the morning on June 19, the *Victor Schoelcher* received a message from the French Admiralty instructing it to leave the convoy and head for Royan, a port at the mouth of the Gironde River estuary in southwestern France. Captain Moevus and Michalski were stunned, and the captain asked the *El Djezaïr*, the lead ship, to explain. The captain could only say that he had gotten a message two-and-a-half hours earlier telling him that the *Victor Schoelcher* should make the detour. The captain of the *El Djezaïr*, sent a message asking for a clarification, and the order was repeated that the *Victor Schoelcher* should go to Royan. By then, Michalski was furious and shouted: "I demand that you send the Admiralty an official protest from me in the name of the Polish government that I represent to the risks that this order causes the gold of the Polish State Bank."[18]

A message came back saying that navy officials in Royan would be responsible for the gold until further notice. The *Victor Schoelcher* did not hear anything for two hours, and shortly after noon, Captain Moevus again asked for confirmation. This time he got no reply. He later heard reports over his radio from a French ship saying that planes had attacked it and that another vessel that had been torpedoed. At 10:30 P.M., the captain sent out another message: NO RESPONSE TO MY REQUESTS STOP CARRYING 250 TONS GOLD STOP UNLESS ORDERS TO THE CONTRARY ON A ROUTE TO CASABLANCA STOP POSITION 270 SPEED 15 KNOTS STOP.

Finally just before 1:00 in the morning, the French Admiralty sent back a message saying that the earlier one had not come from them. It added: VICTOR-SCHOELCHER PROCEED ON ROUTE TO CASABLANCA AND PLEASE CONFIRM RECEPTION STOP. Moevus by then was certain the first message had not come from the French admiralty but was probably a ploy of German warfare.[19]

With little to do but listen to the radio, the captain and Michalski continued toward North Africa. On June 21 they heard that the unescorted Belgian passenger steamer *Ville-de-Namur* had been hit by two torpedoes and sunk. In the afternoon they heard an SOS from the vessel *Yanarville*, which had been torpedoed. At 11:00 P.M., the *Aragaz* radioed that it had been hit by submarine, and at midnight the *Asheres* reported it had been attacked five miles off Spain's Cap de la Nau.

Finally on Sunday, June 23, Michalski and Moevus saw the Moroccan coastline, and the gold flotilla with its rich cargo soon pulled into Casablanca.[20]

The French National Bank still had many more tons of gold left inside the country. Bank officials decided not to use a Mediterranean location since Italy might soon enter the war on Hitler's side. Le Verdon, a port near Bordeaux on the Atlantic coast, was the alternative departure point.

Charles Moreton, a veteran French National Bank official who only recently had taken over as head of the office at Boulogne-sur-Mer in northern France, had just arrived in Paris on May 24 for a temporary assignment. At 6:30 that evening, he got a phone call instructing him to be in the office of the bank's secretary general in ten minutes. When he arrived, Moreton was told to get on the 10:00 P.M. train to Bordeaux. There he was to organize a shipment, out of France and away from the Nazis, of approximately 200 tons of gold from ten regional bank centers. The gold would then leave Le Verdon for a still undetermined location, and he was to go with it. When he got to Bordeaux, he should have pictures taken for a passport because he might be going abroad. That's all he was told.[21]

Moreton's formal assignment letter said he was to accompany the shipment to Canada, where it was to be deposited at the Bank of Canada's Ottawa office. It did not say exactly how the bullion was supposed to get to Canada, but indicated there might be a temporary stop in Casablanca.[22]

The following morning at 11:00, Moreton's train from Paris pulled into Bordeaux four hours late. The city was overrun with wounded soldiers, refugees, and men on their way to the front. He described it a "total nightmare." Nonetheless, he and a small crew put together a large shipment of gold that had arrived from a variety of locations. Bordeaux had two railroad stations, Saint Jean and Saint Louis, and often he did not know where it would arrive until a couple of hours before the gold actually showed up. He used taxis to move his cargo between stations. At one point a train carrying seventeen tons derailed, and it took five hours to get everything back on the track. Finally at 9:00 P.M. on May 28, a twenty-three-car train was ready to leave the Saint-Louis station for the nearby port of Trompeloup-Pauillac. The cargo would then be taken to a *paquebot*, a small ship that traditionally carried mail and a few passengers. One was docked sixty miles away in Le Verdon. Moreton had to wait another twelve hours for his train to depart because there was only one very busy track.[23]

Following a two-hour trip to the port, the banker's crew was about to move the boxes of gold from the train to the ship, when two customs agents ambled up and asked him what they were shipping out of the country. He explained it was part of France's national gold, adding with irritation that this was a matter of national defense. He also mentioned that he was an official of the Banque de France. That didn't impress the civil servants. They demanded to see a signed document authorizing the shipment. Impatiently, Moreton explained that he was a bank director on special assignment. A soldier accompanying him richly enjoyed the bureaucratic confrontation, but the banker called the whole affair "grotesque."[24]

At last officials at the bank office in Bordeaux sent someone with the proper papers for the obstinate customs officials, and then a small team of men loaded 3,080 heavy sacks and 758 cases that weighed more than 300 tons onto a requisitioned passenger ship. During the transfer, a few sacks broke, and gold coins went rolling in all directions although most were quickly rounded up. A bank official arrived with Moreton's passport and a fistful of French francs, Moroccan francs, U.S. dollars, and British pounds to get him through the unknowable voyage he faced. The immediate destination was Casablanca, but Moreton still thought he would ultimately be going to Canada.[25]

Finally on June 3, the ship received orders to fill the ship's tanks with fuel and then pick up their torpedo escort *Hardi* before heading south toward Casablanca. While waiting for its instructions, Moreton got to know the ship's crew. All but one had been working for maritime companies before being called up for war duty. While still at sea on June 5, they learned that the British were evacuating Dunkirk. The banker wrote in his report of the journey that night, "At the end of this sad day, despite a glassy sea and beautiful weather we sadly and quietly smoked pipes or cigarettes near the captain's bridge until 10 P.M." There was a submarine alert the next day near Cadiz, Spain, and a French ship sank a German sub.

Later that day, Moreton's ship pulled into Casablanca. A group of small but stocky Arab dockworkers quickly moved the heavy boxes and bags of gold from the ship to the vaults of the Moroccan State Bank. Customs agents spent nearly a day verifying the contents. The French navy didn't have a ship that could take the gold to Canada, so it was not clear how it was going to cross the Atlantic.

When Moreton returned to his hotel in Casablanca at noon on June 7, he learned that Julien Koszul, a French National Bank inspector, had arrived by plane that morning with new instructions. The gold was due to depart on the *USS Vincennes*, which would be arriving in two days. The two men were to go on board and monitor the transfer.[26]

After the German invasion of France began, American Ambassador Bullitt met almost daily with Premier Reynaud and knew well the dangers facing the country and its gold. In cables Bullitt pressed President Roosevelt to help the French war effort by supplying them with weapons, despite American neutrality. In a telegram on May 28, the ambassador wrote, "I ask you solemnly and urgently to send immediately a cruiser to Bordeaux for two purposes: First to bring to Bordeaux immediately from 5 to 10,000 Thompson submachine guns caliber .45 model 1928 A-1, and one million rounds of ammunition; and second to carry away from Bordeaux the entire French and Belgian gold reserve. The French reserve is

550 tons. The Belgians 100 tons." He added ominously, "The French have no ships available."[27]

Bullitt temporarily interrupted his telegram, but returned to report, "Reynaud has just told me that if we can send a cruiser to Bordeaux or any other port, he will put the entire gold reserve on it and send it to the U.S." Roosevelt replied that he would send three warships to pick up the bullion at Saint-Jean-de-Luz on the Atlantic coast near where France and Spain meet.[28]

Reynaud was grateful for the American offer, but several of his cabinet members believed that both the British and the Americans had become shameful vultures at France's most dangerous time. They charged that London wanted to grab France's navy, while Washington was after its gold. The Reynaud cabinet eventually decided to send only 200 tons more to the U.S. for safekeeping. The rest, or about eighty percent of the country's remaining gold including what they were holding for Poland and Belgium, would go to France's colonies, and the French navy would handle the shipment.[29] Since transporting the gold on U.S. ships would have violated American neutrality, the transfer had to be done at sea, and the ownership of the bullion had to be transferred for the duration of the trip from the French to the Americans. Saint-Jean-de-Luz was also now too dangerous a location, so it was decided to load the gold in the open ocean off Casablanca.

On May 29, Washington dispatched the USS *Vincennes* and two destroyers to pick up the gold. After a two-day stop in the Azores, it continued to Casablanca. Loading the gold aboard the American ship started at 6:00 A.M. on June 10 and ended at 9:00 P.M. The work was just wrapping up, when everyone heard on the radio that Italy had declared war on France. That cast a dark cloud over Moreton and Koszul, who were going to have dinner on the ship. They were pleased that the vessel had a French name, but were not impressed with the American food, which they thought had been served too rapidly. The next morning the two Frenchmen sent a message to the French navy for relay to the French bank saying, "All well. We're returning as soon as possible." The *Vincennes* left the next morning for the U.S. with $242 million of gold on board that was immediately deposited at the Federal Reserve when it arrived in New York.[30]

Moreton and Koszul found their way back to mainland France on an Argentinian ship, arriving at Le Verdon at 9:00 in the evening of June 18. German mines by then were all over the harbor, and they watched in horror as a ship hit one and exploded. Their vessel rescued some of those on board, but fifty minutes later they watched the ship sink. When they finally arrived at the central bank's Bordeaux office at 9:00 P.M., they had to sleep on the floor. Most Bank of France executives had moved there after the fall of Paris. Shortly after Moreton fell asleep, a German bombing raid woke him with a shock, and five blockbusters fell near the bank.[31]

The next afternoon, he received a new assignment. Bank of France Governor Fournier said he was calling on him because he had "experience and his first trip had gone very well." Another official protested that Moreton had just returned from a dangerous mission, but Fournier replied, "Exactly. He's been vaccinated and fears nothing. He'll handle our business very well."[32]

Moreton was happy to leave Bordeaux because a suffocating defeatism prevailed at the bank. At the same time, though, he was worried about his wife whom he hadn't heard from since he left home more than a month earlier. He feared that she was on France's crowded roads along with thousands of other refugees.

The banker had only fifteen hours to pull together a whole host of things and get them to the ship that would take him back to Casablanca. His cargo included two hundred cases of Swiss gold as well as bags of foreign currency in large denominations that had been left at a Bordeaux train station. There was also gold from regional offices that had arrived after he left on his first trip. Finally there was a large, heavy container of valuables that the Banque de l'Indochine had given the French. It belonged to Bao-Dai, the emperor of Vietnam. Moreton's assignment was to get all that to the *Primauguet*, a navy light cruiser that was docked at Le Verdon. The ship was already carrying a number of bags and boxes of gold. At 6:00 that night, Moreton left Bordeaux for the port. When he arrived two hours later, war was exploding around the harbor, and the area was almost totally dark because of an enforced blackout. It was also raining hard.[33]

The banker quickly learned that German planes had attacked the *Primauguet*, and that it was damaged and located about fifteen miles away. He grabbed a nearby drunk fisherman, and told him they had to find the ship. A gang of inebriated fishermen plus a few sober bank employees loaded his cargo onto the fishing boat. Work began at 11:00 P.M. and finished three hours later. Moreton then jumped into a dripping cargo net with two suitcases and was lowered onto the twelve-foot trawler.

Despite the darkness and rain, they had to find the *Primauguet* downstream somewhere in the Gironde estuary. The fishing boat luckily made radio contact with the larger ship, and two hours later they reached it. The captain failed in his first five attempts to pull his boat close enough for the gold and passengers to be transferred, but he finally succeeded on the sixth try. Since it was dangerous to use the wet gangplank to transfer the cargo, the crew loaded it into nets that dropped it onto the deck. The net broke on the last transfer, but the two containers fell on the ship's deck. The job was finally finished early the next morning, and Moreton went on board. He immediately took several showers hoping to get rid of the smell and feel of oil that permeated everything. The smell, though, lingered for days.[34]

The *Primauguet* departed quickly, and once out to sea, the voyage went smoothly in contrast to the chaos it had just left behind. While traveling they learned over the ship's radio that the armistice agreement with Germany had been signed. They also received notices that the British fleet might soon attack French ships. The ship's captain received an instruction that if there were British officers on board, he should watch them closely and disembark them in the first French port.[35]

The trip was uneventful, and the *Primauguet* pulled into the Casablanca harbor two days later at 10:00 in the morning. The armistice with Germany had gone into effect at 1:30. The ship had made the trip at a rapid speed of twenty-five knots. There was not a single place, though, for the ship to dock. The captain and Moreton went ashore in a dingy to see Admiral Emmanuel Ollive, who briefed them on conditions there and told them that he was now urging all French gold ships to go immediately to Dakar, where their cargo would be far from the Germans. At 11:30 A.M. a message went out from the French Admiralty: ALL SHIPS CARRYING PRECIOUS METAL SHOULD BE DIRECTED TO DAKAR STOP. Moreton, though, wanted new instructions from his Bank of France superiors. Since it was too risky to leave the gold on board, he decided to transport it to the vault of the Bank of Morocco. The process took twenty-three hours, and the cargo was finally officially weighed in at fifteen tons.[36]

The next day, Moreton sent a coded message to his bosses in Bordeaux: POSTAL PACKAGES ARRIVED AND HOUSED WELL STOP FATHER AND SON LEFT THE DAY BEFORE YESTERDAY DIRECTION DAKAR WITH MANY FAMILY MEMBERS STOP HARD TO LODGE HERE STOP AWAIT YOUR INSTRUCTIONS FOR GRANDSONS STOP.[37]

Chapter Twenty

BRITAIN ON THE BRINK

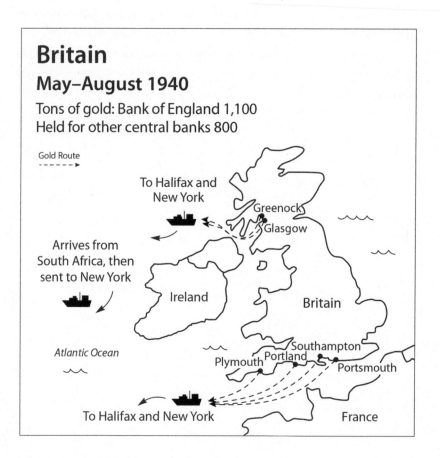

Britain
May–August 1940
Tons of gold: Bank of England 1,100
Held for other central banks 800

Gold Route
- - - - - ->

To Halifax and
New York

Greenock
Glasgow

Arrives from
South Africa, then
sent to New York

Ireland

Britain

Atlantic Ocean

Southampton
Plymouth Portland
Portsmouth

To Halifax and New York

France

It was called the miracle of Dunkirk, but others in the United Kingdom viewed it as something other than a miracle with regard to Churchill's handling of the war. During nine days in May and June 1940, a ragtag armada of ships evacuated 338,226 Allied forces from under the noses and guns of Nazi armies to Britain to fight another day. The new Prime Minister Winston Churchill had no illusions that his country had suffered a horrific setback. In a speech to the House of Commons on June 4, 1940, he called the events in France "a colossal military disaster," and added "wars are not won by evacuations."[1]

Many members of the British establishment at the time did not think Churchill was up to the job of leading the country in wartime. He had just botched the Allied effort to help the Norwegians in their struggle against Hitler. The day after the new prime minister's appointment, John Colville, his private secretary, wrote in his diary: "There seems to be some inclination at Whitehall to believe that Winston will be a complete failure and that Neville [Chamberlain] will return."[2]

The failure on the continent, though, led some nervous Britons to reach for their gold. Mrs. Edith Parr, a housewife from the Isle of Wight, wrote in a letter to the *Times of London*, "Let us beat our enemies by learning from them. The Italian women, in the Abyssinian War, gave up their wedding rings, receiving in exchange rings of baser metal." Kingsley Wood, the Chancellor of the Exchequer, picked up the idea, and argued that it might raise £20 million for the war effort. Churchill rejected that extreme measure unless it became necessary to shame the Americans into coming to his country's aid, but he still liked to quote Lord Macaulay's poem "Horatio at the Bridge":

Romans in Rome's quarrel
Spared neither land nor gold.[3]

The British were already aware of the Nazi gold strategy and the importance of getting the Bank of England's reserves out of the country and to safety abroad. In addition, Britain was custodian of hundreds of tons of bullion for other nations, much of which had just been sent over for safekeeping in the past three years. Always lurking in the back of the minds of British leaders, however, was the fate of the White Star Line's *SS Laurentic* during World War I. Launched in 1908, the ship at first carried passengers from Liverpool to Canada, but in the Great War it became an armed merchant cruiser. On January 25, 1917, the vessel hit two mines north of Ireland and sank within an hour. It was carrying 43 tons of gold stowed in the second-class baggage room. After the war, Royal Navy divers recovered most, but not all, of the bullion. That tragedy was never far from the minds of the men making decisions about what to do with Britain's gold now that the German threat had finally reached their shores.[4]

While the United States was the destination of choice for the British bullion, America's strict neutrality stance caused complications. The obvious alternative was Canada, a member of the British Commonwealth and, just like the U.S., an ocean away from the war. It was also close to the U.S., the world's major supplier of war materiel, which was demanding payment upon delivery in gold or hard currency for its weapons.

The Bank of Canada had only recently become a member of the club of world central banks, opening its doors on March 11, 1935. Graham Towers, thirty-eight, was the first governor. He naturally looked to London for guidance, and Britain's legendary Montagu Norman became his tutor. Early in 1936, British officials first voiced interest in shipping gold abroad for national security reasons and began sending £2 million a month.[5] Canada was also an important gold producer, and Norman indicated he wanted to buy some at auction. By the end of 1936, the Bank of England had deposited 3,304 bars in Ottawa, and a year later that number was up to 4,748 bars.[6] The Bank of Canada, in effect, became the shadow Bank of England for the duration of the war.

Immediately after the *Anschluss* in March 1938, the Bank of England's Harry Siepmann asked the Bank of Canada if his country might purchase, transfer, and ship "up to an amount of $250,000,000 or more" of gold to them. Towers informed Canadian Finance Minister Charles Dunning about the request, who answered that his country was "most willing to be of assistance in any way we can."[7] The pace quickly picked up. One shipment arrived on May 9, 1938, just in time to go into the bank's new vault located under Wellington Street in Ottawa. Trains took bullion from the docks in Halifax directly to the capital, with Royal Canadian Mounted Police guarding the operations. When a journalist noticed the train pulling into the station, the event became big news. After that, the bank was more discrete.

By the end of 1938, Britain had parked 10,219 bars in Ottawa, and Belgium, France, and Switzerland were inquiring about shipping their own bullion. In December 1939, the Swedish National Bank also asked about sending some.[8] The Bank of Canada at the beginning of 1940 had just three foreign gold accounts, but by the end of the year, it had eleven.

Sir Frederick Phillips, undersecretary of the British Treasury, proposed in an early 1939 memo that the government take private gold holdings, foreign currencies, and internationally marketable securities to Canada in order to "prevent the export of domestic capital." All British residents would be "required to offer gold coin or bullion in their possession for sale to the Treasury." Securities would also have to be sold to the state "at a prescribed sterling price."[9] The measure passed Parliament with little public notice. John Colville, a cabinet insider, wrote in his diary the next day, "Yesterday the Government obtained permission from the House to take over fuller power than any British Government has ever possessed. The purpose is largely that if we are invaded, or otherwise in extremis, the rights of individuals and institutions must not be allowed to stand in the way of the country's safety."[10]

At the time, Prime Minister Neville Chamberlain was anxious to solidify ties to both Ottawa and Washington. While Canada was a member of the British Commonwealth, he wanted to make sure the country would participate if there were a new war with Germany. He was also wanted to strengthen relations with President

Franklin D. Roosevelt. So at Chamberlain's urging, King George VI and Queen Elizabeth in the spring of 1939 traveled across the Atlantic to visit both countries. It would be the new, and nervous, monarch's first venture onto the international stage. He had only recently been thrust on the throne after his older brother abdicated, and British leaders were concerned about how well the royal couple would perform in its new roll. He had a stammer and was socially ill at ease.

Britain used the George VI trip as an opportunity to move some gold to North America. On March 29, Undersecretary Phillips sent a letter to the Admiralty proposing the "dispatch of vessels to Canada in connection with His Majesty's visit." The original plan was to send fifty tons of bullion on two escort ships accompanying the Royal Mail ship *Empress of Australia*, which would be carrying the king and queen. His Majesty, though, considered that too risky and scaled back the project. The accompanying *HMS Southampton* carried 1,207 boxes of bullion, while *HMS Glasgow* had 1,000. That still amounted to £30 million of bullion. Bank of England trucks carried the treasure to the departure harbor for the royal party, but no one noticed the special cargo.[11]

The king and queen were big hits in both countries. Large crowds greeted them as they visited every province in Canada, and Roosevelt, who believed strongly in personal diplomacy, laid everything on thick for the first visit of a sitting British monarch to its former colony. The king and queen visited the World's Fair in New York City and also spent four days at FDR's home in Hyde Park, New York. During a picnic fit for a king, the president enthusiastically pushed his majesty to try his first hotdog.

The royal trip, though, was only a brief, happy hiatus from war. The Nazi invasion of Poland on September 1, 1939, increased the urgency for getting more British gold out of Europe. Later that month, Sir John Simon, the Chancellor of the Exchequer, sent a letter to Winston Churchill, the new First Lord of the Admiralty, alerting him to the need for moving more bullion across the Atlantic. He wrote urgently, "It is essential for us to ship gold to the value of £40 million . . . from South Africa via England to North America as early as possible." South Africa was the world's largest bullion producer in addition to being a member of the Commonwealth. Simon went on to explain that the country had "a great hoard at Ottawa, but as you know the demands on it in recent months were enormous."[12]

War Cabinet Secretary E. E. Bridges on October 6, 1939, urged stepping up shipments to the new world. He wrote: "It will be for the Treasury in collaboration with the Bank of England, and the Foreign Office, to examine the possible means of getting the bullion and negotiable securities into the same place of safety. The transport of many hundreds of tons of bullion presents a difficult problem and the loading would take a long time." The plan was Britain would also evacuate the gold of Belgium, Holland, and other countries that had sent their own bullion to London for safety. Bridges wrote that the total weight would amount to about 1,800 tons, and said that the evacuation was a matter of the "utmost importance" and "would present a considerable problem if it had to be undertaken in a hurry when transport facilities were disorganized."[13]

The Chamberlain government agreed with the Bridges suggestion, and the British navy turned over the job of shipping it to Captain Augustus (Gus) Agar, a holder of the Victoria Cross, the country's highest military honor. He received it for almost single-handedly sinking a Soviet cruiser in World War I. Tall, lean, and courtly, Agar credited his naval success to growing up the last of thirteen children. At the time, he commanded the HMS Emerald, which was on blockade duty in the North Atlantic, which was infested with U-boats. His ship and the HMS Enterprise, commanded by his friend Captain Jack Egerton Broome, were ordered to head for Plymouth "with all dispatch."[14]

Once there, the two captains were told to stock up on supplies and get ready for the new assignment. Only Agar knew what it was. Just before sailing, a small railway truck pulled up to the dock alongside the two ships and began offloading cases of what was described as "special secret explosives." At 3:00 A.M., sailors started carrying packages weighing about 130 pounds each onto the vessel, while policemen carefully counted the cargo both at the delivery truck and then again at the ship. The speculation among crew members was that they were headed to Freetown, Sierra Leone or the East Indies. Only Agar knew the cargo was bullion and that they were really going to Canada. Once out at sea, the two vessels rendezvoused with a cruiser and a battleship. The convoy arrived in Canada a week later. During the trip the crew faced heavy seas and dense fog. The *Emerald* lost overboard many pieces of equipment, including a lifeboat. The four ships, though, proudly steamed into the Halifax harbor, which was already packed with nearly one hundred British vessels carrying war goods or food back home. Royal Canadian Mounted Police and a special train were waiting at the dock and quickly spirited the gold away.

After the Canadians left, the four commanders chatted about Britain's historic Order in Council rule dating back to the Napoleonic Wars, which gave ship captains carrying bullion one-eighth percent of the cargo's value when it was safely discharged. In May 1936, Agar's friend Captain Charles Morgan had rescued Emperor Haile Selassie, and his gold, when he escaped from Ethiopia. At the end of the voyage the emperor offered to pay the captain the traditional fee. Morgan, though, politely declined to take it. The officers in Halifax jokingly lamented that the British Treasury a few years before had cancelled the Order in Council regulation. Agar later wrote in his autobiography, "Otherwise Jack Egerton Broome and myself might have collected quite a nice little sum for our retirement."[15]

Thirty British gold shipments took place in the year between King George VI's visit to Canada and the May 1940 Nazi invasion of the Low Countries. All of them went to Canada, and most were valued at only £2 million or £3 million. But more—much, much more—was soon heading that way.[16]

Only two weeks after the Nazi invasion of Western Europe, the situation for Britain looked ominous. Dutch, Belgian, and French defenses had quickly crumbled, and the Germans were marching toward Paris. A British cabinet meeting on May 21 was realistic and pessimistic. On May 21, Sir Alex Cadogan, the Permanent

Undersecretary for Foreign Affairs, wrote in his diary, "A miracle may save us: otherwise we're done."[17]

That same day, Undersecretary Phillips sent Sir RVN (Hoppy) Hopkins, the second treasury secretary, a terse, hand-written, one-page memo outlining the country's gold situation. The report, which was soon in Churchill's hands, stated that the country had £80 million in Ottawa, £25 million in South Africa, £6 million in India, and £40 million in transit. In addition, Britain had £280 million more in London and was holding another £200 million in bullion for a variety of central banks. Total British gold holdings: 1,600 tons, and it had to be evacuated as soon as possible. The report noted that the best temporary storage facility outside London was in Southampton on Britain's south coast, but Hopkins wrote that was "unsuitable" in view of the threat of an attack from German-controlled coastal areas of France and Belgium. The Nazis were already assembling a fleet to invade Britain.[18]

The following day, Cadogan wrote in his diary in an almost throwaway line, "Cabinet this morning discussed legislation for this afternoon giving Government full powers over property and persons. This ought to have been done twelve months ago."[19] The war measure was certainly late, but it was the most sweeping grant of authority ever given to an elected government in British history. It passed Parliament without any discussion. The press did not understand the implications of the legislation, which basically changed the rules of Britain's private economy. According to an old British saw, Parliament can do anything except turn a man into a woman. The Churchill cabinet was doing something almost as historic. In addition to shipping all of the nation's gold out of the country, the government was going to send stocks and bonds to Canada. During meetings in the director's parlour at the Bank of England, a small team of officials from the British Treasury, the Bank of England, and the Admiralty began drawing up a plan to evacuate the country's wealth.[20]

On May 25, Basil Catterns, the deputy governor of the Bank of England, sent Sir Frederick Phillips a two-page memo on "the steps that could be taken to protect the assets of this country." Based on talks with the Admiralty, officials knew the navy could ship £300 million in gold to Canada by the end of the month and perhaps £350 million later. Catterns added that the government had to deal not only with privately held gold in Britain but also that of its "customers," referring to foreign governments such as Holland or Belgium. He recommended that all the country's stock certificates be collected and "shipped to Canada by a vessel specifically chartered for the purpose." Catterns thought that could be done "within a couple of weeks." Phillips further suggested that £300 million in British currency notes be "put on board a boat under military guard and kept either in dry dock or, say, somewhere in the Mersey so that, if necessary, the boat could be taken out to sea and sunk." The objective of all the proposed measures was to make sure that if Hitler did successfully invade Britain, the Nazis would not find any gold, currencies, or securities to further finance their war.[21]

That same day, top Treasury and Bank of England officials met to work out details for shipments to Canada that were to take place in June. The size of the gold movements now increased dramatically. In a convoy of three vessels due to leave on May 30, two merchant ships would each carry £10 million and a battleship would take £30 to £40 million. Going forward, battleships were to haul a maximum of £50 million. The British navy in June 1940 moved £200 million in gold, while commercial vessels transferred £100 million.

Government officials also drew up a plan for putting any securities that the Nazis could market abroad "out of reach of the Germans if they were to gain a foothold in this country." Since London was the world's financial capital, many foreign investors kept large sums of stocks and currency there. All those stock certificates and bearer bonds had to get out of Britain. Shares held by foreign residents from countries ranging from Argentina to the United States, would also be shipped to Canada without their knowledge.

Finally, the government set out a plan to collect British paper currency from around the country that could be destroyed quickly in case of an emergency. New bills for distribution in London alone weighed about 115 tons, and it would take an estimated twenty-three five-ton trucks fifteen hours to remove the money from vaults and load it onto vehicles. Officials hoped that they would not have to take this step, but they had to be prepared for every eventuality.[22]

On May 26, Phillips gave Sir Kingsley Wood, the Chancellor of the Exchequer, a status report on the evacuation of the country's wealth. At the top of the first page of the three-page, hand-written memo were the words "Highly Secret." It stated that there was £630 million in British gold to be shipped out. In addition, London was holding bullion worth £70 million for France, £85 million for Belgium, £10 million for Norway, £25 for Holland, £8 million for Czechoslovakia, plus a few smaller accounts. Foreign deposits, wrote Phillips: "Say £203 million." He added, "All the gold in the Bank of England is being packed and this process will be completed in a week." The goal was to "break the back of the whole job by end-July."[23]

Sir Fredrick also pointed out that unexpected problems were developing with the financial security plan. One example: "Newly printed bank notes tightly packed are unfortunately terribly hard to destroy in a hurry." Ominously he concluded, "This involves taking fearful risk which we would not contemplate for a moment in normal times: we shall for instance be sending £50 million on one battleship. . . . We must assume also I think that the risks will increase as time goes on."

He concluded his report with the simple question, "Shall we go ahead?"[24]

Chancellor Wood scribbled at the bottom: "Let us do nothing at the moment about [telling] the other countries as we do not wish to give them the impression that we have got the wind up. Let us renew that side of the question from day to day." The British government did not inform foreign gold holders that their shipments might be at risk. On May 30, Jacques Rueff, the deputy governor of the French National Bank, replied to his counterpart B. C. Catterns, "I know the difficulties of these transfers and the responsibility they impose on those who undertake them. Permit me, in thanking you for your proposals, merely to say that any increase in the percentage which might seem possible to you in the near future would be welcomed here."[25]

The three days of May 26, 27, and 28, 1940 were perhaps the most crucial period of World War II. The British war cabinet met several times a day, as the situation on the battlefield continued to deteriorate. Churchill asked the king to declare Sunday the 26th a day of national prayer, and Britons across the country turned out at churches as if the king had given a royal command.

A growing split over war strategy between Churchill and his foreign secretary Lord Halifax was becoming more obvious at every cabinet session. Halifax wanted to send out diplomatic feelers to see if Mussolini might act as an intermediary for some kind of an agreement between London and Berlin. Churchill considered that a dangerous step on the slippery slope toward surrender. Halifax wrote in his diary that the prime minister "talked the most frightful rot."[26]

On Monday May 27, the British put out the order for *Operation Dynamo*, the evacuation of Allied forces from Dunkirk. That evening King Leopold III of Belgium asked Berlin for an armistice, leaving a giant hole in the Allied lines. At a cabinet meeting Halifax confronted Churchill, pressing him to declare whether he would consider any peace terms at any time. Most of the members thought the answer was no. Halifax had already told Cadogan that he could no longer work with the prime minister. In perhaps the most dramatic moment in British history, Halifax interrupted the second of three cabinet meetings that day to ask Churchill to join him for a walk in the garden. Neither man ever revealed what was said during their stroll. The two men returned, and the meeting continued. Britain, though, did not ask for peace conditions.[27]

It was without a doubt the worst possible moment to be moving billions of dollars of valuables across the Atlantic. From July to October 1940, German U-boats were at their most deadly. Admiral Karl Dönitz told Allied interrogators after the war that at the time, "Conditions were made particularly favorable for the U-boat war against shipping in the Atlantic." The German navy was at peak capacity, and it could use the Spanish Bay of Biscay ports for repairs and refueling instead of having to make long sea trips back to Germany. Submarines went out into the waters near Britain, fired at will, and then quickly returned to be refitted in northern Spain. "The sea routes were now, so to speak, at the front door," Dönitz later explained. "The U-boat losses were exceptionally small," and it led the Germans, according to Dönitz "to entertain the idea of deciding the war in our favor by a rapid invasion of England."[28]

On May 30, the battleship *HMS Revenge* undertook the first major gold shipment across the Atlantic. Vessels would now carry bullion worth more than $150 million (£40 million). Two speedy steamships, the *SS Antonia*, a Cunard vessel that previously brought emigrants across the Atlantic, and the *SS Duchess of Liverpool*, another passenger boat that was evacuating children to Canada, accompanied the *Revenge*. Each of them carried $40 million (£10 million) in gold. It was a risky undertaking even with the best of planning. In June, fifty-seven Allied ships went to the bottom of the Atlantic Ocean.[29]

An even bigger convoy was ready to depart near the end of that month. One afternoon in the middle of June, five Bank of England executives were called to the director's parlour and asked if they would undertake a totally secret mission abroad. That was all they were told. Everyone said yes and then rushed to pick up their passports and tell their wives to get ready to leave the country. The men knew only that they would be departing on a ship from Greenock, Scotland, while their wives would be on a separate ship sailing from Liverpool. Each staffer was allowed to take just one suitcase. Alexander Craig of the bank's Foreign Exchange Control department was the group's senior official.

The *SS Emerald*, which had earlier escorted King George VI to North America, was to be the lead ship in the convoy. Captain Agar was no longer its commander because he had been reassigned to Operation Lucid to create the plan for a last ditch effort to protect the country if the Germans invaded. Berlin was already assembling landing craft. Agar was going to set the English Channel on fire by directing a fleet of burning ships at the invaders. The plan was modeled after Drake's never-used strategy to stop the Spanish Armada in the sixteenth century, which appealed to Churchill's love of history. Fortunately, the plan never had to be implemented this time, either.

Captain Francis Cyril Flynn was now captain of the *Emerald*. Four destroyers were assigned as escorts. Philip Vian aboard *HMS Cossack* led the group. Only two months earlier, the Norwegian government had turned over to him that country's gold as well as its entire merchant fleet.

The *Emerald* carried 2,229 boxes of gold worth £30 billion plus nearly five hundred boxes of securities with a nominal value of at least £200 billion. The gold was stored in the ammunition lockers, while the stocks and bonds were tucked into every nook and cranny on the ship. The crew learned what the ship was carrying during the loading, when a few containers of ingots crashed to the floor and broke open. Because of the wartime dangers, this shipment, and all those to follow, could not be insured.[30]

The weather forecast for the voyage was as bad as it could be: heavy rain and fog were predicted for the first several days. Sailors loaded the *Emerald* on June 22 and 23. Then an hour before midnight on June 24, the ship pulled away in deep fog. Visibility was still poor when the ship passed Northern Ireland and entered the Atlantic. Shortly after the departure, the Bank of England's Alexander Craig chatted with one of the officers, who told him that Flynn had just received a message from the Admiralty that "a couple of German U-boats" were waiting for them. The British vessels were among the Royal Navy's best and could travel at high speeds, but gale winds forced them to slow down. Vial's destroyer led the convoy, and he stayed in a zigzag course for safety reasons. Eventually the officer sent a message that it would be safer for the *Emerald* to travel alone so that it could travel at a higher speed. The escorts then turned around and returned to base. As they pulled away, the *Cossack* flashed a signal-lamp message: Godspeed.[31]

The five Bank of England officials, who were unaccustomed to foul ocean travel, were dreadfully seasick for the first three days out. Finally on the fourth day, the storm subsided, and they played darts and bridge or read. Once he was free of the escorts, Captain Flynn increased his speed to a brisk twenty-eight knots, and early in the morning of July 1 the crew and bank officials saw Canadian destroyers off in the distance coming out to bring them to shore. The *Emerald* docked at 7:30 A.M. A Canadian National train as well as officials from the Bank of Canada greeted them. It took twelve hours to unload the vessel, but at 7:00 P.M. the train left on an overnight trip to Montreal.

Upon arrival at the Bonaventure Station, guards jumped off coaches to set up a protection perimeter. David Mansur, acting secretary of the Bank of Canada, and Sidney Perkins of the country's Foreign Exchange Board were the official greeters and immediately approached Alexander Craig. The Brit said casually, "Hope you won't mind our dropping in unexpectedly like this, but we've brought along quite a large shipment of fish." The British code name for the Canadian shipments was Operation Fish, although the Admiralty called the cargo "margarine." He quickly added, "Actually, the fish are a very large portion of the liquid assets of Great Britain. We're cleaning out our vaults. In case of invasion, you know. The rest will be coming over shortly." The cargo was then split up, with the gold going on by train to the Bank of Canada vault in Ottawa, while the securities went to the Sun Life Assurance Company in Montreal.[32]

Only a few days after the *Emerald's* cargo was safely stored in Canada, five more ships left Britain in the biggest British convoy of the war. It was also the largest treasure shipment in history on either land or sea. Two British navy vessels, the battleship *HMS Revenge* and the cruiser *HMS Bonaventure*, departed from the River Clyde in Scotland. In the North Channel between Ireland and Scotland, they met up with three former cruise liners: the *Monarch of Bermuda*, *Sobieski*, and *Batory*. The last two ships belonged to the Free Poland navy. Four destroyers also joined as escorts. The commander of the entire operation was Admiral Ernest Archer, who had taken command of *Revenge* the year before. This would be his fourth bullion voyage. Between them the ships carried a cargo of

£450 million. Also on board was a team of British officials on their way to a crucial financial meeting in Washington.

The ship was so full that the captain sent back a message saying, "We are now in a stage where the ship's chaplain is sleeping on his altar." The ship carried twelve-inch and fifteen-inch guns as well as an anti-aircraft battery. Sailors slept near the weapons in case of emergency. *Revenge* joined the other vessels in the convoy at 7:00 P.M. The following day, it dropped a depth charge in hopes of hitting a German submarine. Sure enough, the ship's crew soon saw a huge splash off the port bow.[33]

Two-thirds of the way to Halifax, the *Sobieski* reported mechanical problems and had to slow down. Admiral Archer ordered Captain Jack Egerton Broome, who was now the commander of the *Bonaventure*, to leave the convoy and help the Polish ship. The vessels detoured to the closer landfall at St. John's, Newfoundland. The three remaining ships stayed on course for Halifax, and tied up there at 1:45 P.M. on July 12. The gold and securities were offloaded to secure vehicles, and it took until 10:00 the next morning to finish the job. At one point, a box broke, and a heavy ingot dropped through a hatchway to the fourth deck. A sailor looked down and shouted, "Is that gold okay?" A middy barked back, "What about our bloody heads!"

With the *Bonaventure* leading the way, the two laggard ships sailed through heavy fog and floating ice for more than two days toward St. John's. The worried captains knew they would not see an iceberg until they were almost on top of it. The two vessels finally stopped dead for twelve hours and waited for better weather. Finally at 5:15 A.M. on July 12, they separated at the entrance to the St. John's harbor. The *Bonaventure* headed for Halifax, arriving there the next morning, while the *Sobieski* landed in St. John's. All five vessels—and their cargo—were now on the safe side of the Atlantic. When his ship docked, Commander Humphrey Jenkins, the executive officer on *Revenge*, told the Bank of Canada's Sidney Perkins, "I'll be glad to get rid of this margarine."

British officers were always watchful to make sure that nothing was lost to sticky fingers during the transport. When the *Revenge* arrived, it appeared that three cases of gold were missing. A bank official thought something might have happened during the loading. A mess steward, who was preparing a drink, overheard the bankers talking about it and said, "Perhaps I've got what you're looking for. I've been tripping over something since we left." He went into the kitchen area and found three boxes stored amid cases of Scotch whiskey. Nothing was missing!

It took five special trains to transfer this mega shipment of bullion from Halifax to Ottawa. Each consisted of ten to fourteen wagons, and 150 cases were loaded on the floor of each coach. Two guards were locked in the cars and watched the valuables during four-hour shifts.[34]

The securities were again sent to the three-story basement of the Sun Life building in Montreal. One hundred twenty retired bankers, brokers, and investment secretaries recorded the information about what they nicknamed "our bundles from Britain." The Buttress Room on the third basement was quickly filled, and bank officials immediately started construction of a new vault that would be sixty feet square and eleven feet high. Officials used 870 old railway tracks to reinforce its three-foot cement walls. Two different keys were required to enter the vault, which trainloads of securities soon filled. It took 900 filing cabinets to store all the stock certificates.

The size of the gold and securities transfers declined after the first two trips. The war in the Atlantic continued, but the bulk of the London gold was now safely in Canada. The final transfer of a British navy ship took place in April 1941 aboard the *HMS Resolution* and carried only £3 million in bullion. The last one, on the merchant ship *Ida Bakke*, brought just £1.25 million.

While most of the gold went from London to Halifax, the British also sent significant amounts across the Pacific Ocean to the U.S. and Canada. Between November 1939 and April 1940, forty-eight shipments traveled from Cape Town to Sydney and then on to Canada. There were also deliveries from Bombay and Hong Kong to Honolulu and San Francisco. Those totaled more than £100 million.[35]

On June 30, 1940, Sir Frederick Phillips was able to report to his bosses that outside of gold held by individuals only £280 million remained in Britain, and there was a decline of £125 million in just the two previous weeks. Of that, the Bank of England owned only £20 million. The rest was the property of the central banks of Argentina, Belgium, Czechoslovakia, France, Holland, Norway, Poland, Switzerland, and Yugoslavia. Phillips added that the next week two convoys involving battleships and ocean liners would carry £132 million. The rest should be leaving in July, so the great British evacuation was just about over.[36]

Only a week after the Nazis invaded Poland in 1939, President Franklin Roosevelt sent a letter to Winston Churchill, who was then First Lord of the Admiralty. The two men had met during World War I, or at least the president thought they did. He said they met in London during World War I, when Churchill was First Lord of the Admiralty and Roosevelt was Assistant Secretary of the Navy. Roosevelt remembered the occasion, but Churchill did not. The First Lord quickly responded to the White House message, signing his answer with the code name: "Naval Person." Their exchanges continued throughout the war, totaling more than two thousand messages. After Churchill moved to 10 Downing Street to be prime minister, he sent the president a special message, asking if the cable traffic could continue. Churchill that night signed off as "Former Naval Person."[37]

A year into the war, the prime minister was anxious to stop paying for American military equipment with cash on the barrelhead because he knew his country would soon run through all the gold that was now on the western side of the Atlantic. At the end of 1940, Roosevelt suggested that the U.S. send navy ships to South Africa to pick up British gold as payment for some destroyers. Churchill politely, but firmly, rejected the idea. He wrote that loading gold in Cape Town "will disturb public opinion here and throughout the Dominions and encourage the enemy, who will proclaim that you are sending for our last reserves." Later, though, Britain did ship gold from South Africa to Washington.[38]

Despite Britain's success in getting its gold to North America, the country still faced a desperate financial situation. On August 21, Chancellor of the Exchequer Sir Kingsley Wood sent the war cabinet a brutally candid report entitled "Gold and Exchange Resources." It was marked "TO BE KEPT UNDER LOCK AND KEY." It opened with the blunt statement, "I am seriously perturbed by the rate at which our gold and exchange resources are now disappearing."[39]

Wood discussed the issue the following day at a noon cabinet meeting. He showed that between January 1, 1940 and mid-August 1940, the country's total assets had fallen from £775 million to £490 million, with gold and dollar holdings dropping from £525 million to £290 million. Looking forward to the period from July 1940 to June 1941, he predicted, "We could lose some £800 million of gold and foreign exchange as compared with the previous estimate of £410 million." He then glumly concluded, "If we continue to lose gold at the rate we have experienced in the last six weeks, we should have none left by the end of December." Wood once again brought up the possibility of requisitioning British wedding rings and other gold jewelry, but dismissed the idea himself saying that it "would not produce more than £20 million."[40]

Germany's London blitz commenced on September 7, 1940, and the American public began to realize fully what was happening to beleaguered Britain. Edward R. Murrow, a radio reporter for the CBS network, brought the horror of the attacks into America's living rooms. The America First Committee, whose most prominent member was Charles Lindberg, still opposed getting into the war, but a counter-organization called The Committee to Defend America by Aiding the Allies was beginning to build a following.

Churchill on the afternoon of May 15 sent Roosevelt his first message in his capacity as prime minister. He bluntly wrote, "We shall go on paying dollars for as long as we can, but I should like to feel reasonably sure that when we can no more, you will give us the stuff all the same." Both leaders knew that nothing could happen until the U.S. got through the quadrennial national circus known as the presidential election. Roosevelt was running for an unprecedented third term.[41]

Behind the scenes in Washington, administration policy makers were busy looking for new ways to help Britain, even though they could not talk about it in public because of the upcoming election. Treasury Secretary Henry Morgenthau took the lead. In June, he asked the British to send a team of top officials to discuss both the country's financial needs and its finances. London sent Sir Frederick Phillips. During the candid talks, he admitted that at the current rate of war spending, Britain by June 1941 would need "massive assistance."

Lord Lothian, the British ambassador to Washington, tipped off the American public to a change in British policy shortly after Roosevelt's election victory in November. It came in the form of a well-planned quip to reporters. The diplomat had been in London working on a strategy for how to deal with the Americans after the election. Nazi bombings were raining down on the British capital day and night. During a long flight back to the U.S. aboard a Pan Am Clipper, Lothian pondered what he would say to the reporters he knew would greet him when he landed at New York's LaGuardia Airport. He finally decided to let it all hang out. After disembarking on November 25, he flippantly told them: "Well, boys, Britain's broke. It's your money we want."[42]

Roosevelt was furious and let the British embassy know it. The ambassador's aides admonished him for the undiplomatic comment, but he replied, "I know I shall get my head washed in London and in Washington, but it's the truth, and they might as well know it." One of his deputies later wrote, "Never was an indiscretion more calculated."[43]

At that time, Britain had already spent nearly $5 billion to buy U.S. weapons. The country didn't have much left in the kitty, and that could not be disposed of quickly or easily. As Churchill explained in his memoirs, "Up to November we had paid for everything we had received. We had already sold $335 million worth of American shares requisitioned for sterling from private owners in

Britain. We have paid out over 4,500 million dollars in cash. We had only 2,000 million left, the greater part in investment, many of which were not readily marketable. It was plain that we could not go on any longer in this way. Even if we divested ourselves of all our gold and foreign assets, we could not pay for half we had ordered, and the extension of the war made it necessary for us to have ten times as much."[44]

After his long and tiring presidential campaign, Roosevelt on December 3, left on a long trip to the Caribbean aboard the *USS Tuscaloosa* with Harry Hopkins, his global troubleshooter. Hopkins was so close to the president that he actually lived in the White House. Before joining the New Deal, he was a social welfare worker in New York City. His first job for Roosevelt was fighting unemployment, but gradually he drifted to foreign affairs. FDR ran the big foreign policy issues out of the White House, calling on his special aide Harry Hopkins and to a lesser degree Sumner Welles, Undersecretary of State to handle the crucial problems. Hopkins was very sickly, having had an operation for cancer of the stomach in 1937, and also suffered from malnutrition. He spent a lot of time in and out of the hospital.

While relaxing on the cruise, the two men discussed the European war. The president on December 9 received by navy seaplane a four-thousand-word memo from Winston Churchill that was perhaps their most momentous correspondence of the whole war. As a consummate political tactician, the prime minister had timed it to arrive shortly after the election.

No British document during the war was more carefully crafted than Churchill's four-thousand-word plea for financial help. The prime minister had supreme confidence in his own eloquence, but this time he was open to editing. The first draft, for example, raised the possibility that Britain might invade the Irish Republic to occupy its ports in order to wage the Atlantic war. Ambassador Lothian warned him that even such a suggestion would outrage the large Irish-American community and hurt Britain's cause. That paragraph was dropped. Another sentence said, "I should not myself be willing even in the height of this struggle to divest Great Britain of every conceivable saleable asset." Upon second thought, Churchill realized that Britain had to be willing to put everything on the line. That also fell by the wayside.

In the final draft, Churchill confidently wrote: "The danger of Great Britain being destroyed by a swift overwhelming blow has for the time being very greatly receded." He did not ask for the U.S. to send troops to Europe, writing, "Shipping, not men, is the limiting factor." Accompanying the memo was a statistical supplement that spelled out in detail the British naval losses from June 2, 1940 to November 24, 1940. It was a bleak picture: Britain had lost 372 ships.

In point seventeen of the nineteen-point document, Churchill wrote, "Last of all I come to the question of finance. The moment approaches when we shall no longer be able to pay cash for shipping and other supplies." The key words were underlined.

Churchill then made his pitch: "If, as I believe, you are convinced, Mr. President, that the defeat of the Nazi and Fascist tyranny is a matter of high consequence to the people of the United States and to the Western Hemisphere, you will regard this letter not as an appeal for aid, but as a statement of the minimum action necessary to the achievement of our common purpose."[45]

Roosevelt and Hopkins discussed Churchill's cable for hours aboard the *Tuscaloosa*, and the day after they returned to Washington, the president at a press conference took the first step toward a new American foreign policy. Reaching for a homey metaphor, he told reporters: "Suppose my neighbor's home catches fire, and I have a length of garden hose four or five hundred feet away. If he can take my garden hose and connect it up with his hydrant, I may help him to put out his fire. I don't say to him before that operation, 'Neighbor, my garden hose cost me $15; you have to pay me $15 for it.' I don't want $15. I want my garden hose back after the fire is over."[46]

On January 10, 1941, the administration introduced legislation in Congress officially named "An Act Further to Promote the Defense of the United States." It became known as Lend-Lease. Instead of buying weapons, the Allies going forward would get them for free. Theoretically the foreign countries were going to return them later, but that never happened. The bill was patriotically listed as H.R. 1776. The next month, Churchill helped the political process along when he said, "Give us the tools, and we will finish the job." Roosevelt signed Lend-Lease into law on May 11, 1941. The primary recipient was Britain. Churchill later called Lend-Lease "the most unsordid act in the whole of recorded history."[47]

In his year's end fireside chat on December 29, 1940, Roosevelt urged American industry to join in a mammoth national program to build weapons for the world's democracies to fight the evil posed by the Axis powers of Germany, Italy, and Japan. He warned, "Never before since Jamestown and Plymouth Rock has our American civilization been in such danger as now." Then he made his pitch: "We must have more ships, more guns, more planes—more of everything. And this can be accomplished only if we discard the notion of business as usual. We must be the great arsenal of democracy."[48]

After the legislation was enacted, the Reichsbank's Emil Puhl was in Basel for a monthly meeting of the Bank for International Settlements. He stopped in at Thomas McKittrick's office and asked, "What does this Lend-Lease mean? We don't understand it."

McKittrick explained how the new policy worked and added, "We're getting our industrial organization in shape for our entry into the war."

Puhl's face dropped so dramatically that McKittrick thought he was going to faint. Finally the German muttered, "My God. If you're right, we've lost the war."[49]

Chapter Twenty-One

DESTINATION DAKAR

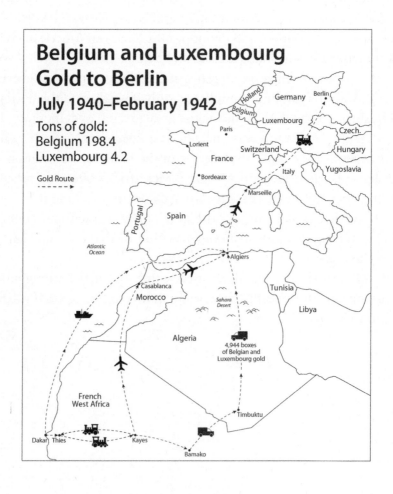

Belgium and Luxembourg Gold to Berlin

July 1940–February 1942

Tons of gold:
Belgium 198.4
Luxembourg 4.2

Gold Route
- - - - - ▶

Holland

Belgium

Germany

Berlin

Luxembourg

Czech.

Paris

Lorient

Switzerland

Hungary

France

Italy

Yugoslavia

Bordeaux

Marseille

Portugal

Spain

Atlantic Ocean

Algiers

Casablanca

Morocco

Tunisia

Sahara Desert

Libya

Algeria

4,944 boxes of Belgian and Luxembourg gold

French West Africa

Timbuktu

Dakar Thies

Kayes

Bamako

Philippe Pétain's new French government ruled only forty percent of the country, while the Germans occupied the rest, including Paris. The capital of the rump French state was the small provincial town of Vichy, while the French central bank's headquarters was located forty-five miles away in Clermont-Ferrand. Initially, it was uncertain who had authority over France's institutions. The Nazi part of the country was clearly under the Wehrmacht's boot, but Pétain's authority in Vichy was questionable because it was not known whether the French public or civil servants would answer to his new regime.

It was also not clear to whom France's far-flung empire answered. Pétain appointed Admiral George Robert High Commissioner of the French Antilles, and he technically had authority over the French gold in Martinique. The American and British navies, though, had battleships just off shore to make sure it didn't go anywhere. An important part of the French central bank's staff now worked outside the country, and no one knew their future. French bank officials working abroad eventually set up an informal group that dealt with the institution's international issues independent of mainland France. General Charles de Gaulle, who was operating out of London, put together an army that called itself the Free French, which continued the fight against Germany. Thanks to British help, it began gathering strength.

The Bank of France's staff was proud of their heroic efforts under difficult circumstances, but they learned a few horror stories about things that had gone badly wrong during the evacuation. Bags of gold had been left on railroad platforms. Two officials from the bank's office in Bayonne simply showed up with six bags of gold, eighty-eight sacks of paper currency, and 130 containers of coins. How many more cases were there like that? The ship *Clairvoyant* had arrived with just one ton of gold. Fortunately and almost miraculously, all the gold ships from Brest and Lorient made it safely to Casablanca and under orders had gone on to Dakar.

Bank officials now also had time to investigate how much gold had been lost or stolen along the way. They learned to their dismay that a case of gold weighing a total of 110 pounds had fallen into the harbor in Brest during the loading. Six bags of coins had also seemingly been lost. A few sacks had broken open during transport, and 166 gold pieces were stolen on the *El Kantara*, although the perpetrators were later caught. The *Ville d'Alger* lost at least 10 sacks, and a case was missing from the *Ville d'Oran*. In June 1941, the bank finally admitted that nearly a half-ton had been lost during the evacuation. Given the massive amount that was handled in chaotic circumstances, the whole operation was a remarkable achievement. On June 28, Moreton received a message from the French Admiralty telling him that officials had finished an inventory of the gold that had arrived in Dakar. It weighed in at 1,097 tons.[1]

On July 3, Charles Moreton met with Admiral Ollive, who said that the French Admiralty had warned him about the danger of a British attack on the ships in Dakar. The French navy had decided to move all the gold as soon as possible to a safer inland location. The bank's René Gontier, who had arrived from Brest on the *El Djezaïr*, had already left for Dakar to monitor the transfer, but he needed some help. Ollive asked Moreton to assist him, offering to get him there overland by car and plane.[2]

French naval intelligence was correct, and at almost the same time as the two Frenchmen were discussing their next moves, a British naval task force bombed the French fleet anchored at Mers-el-Kébir on the Mediterranean coast of French Algeria. At the time, much of the surviving French fleet had been docked there. The attack resulted in the deaths of 1,297 French servicemen. A battleship was sunk and five other vessels were badly damaged. Churchill had told the French that he was worried about their fleet ending up in the hands of the Germans, although Admiral François Darlan had given his personal assurance that would never happen. He said that if necessary, he would send it to Canada. Churchill, though, didn't trust the admiral or perhaps wanted to make a political point by showing that the British lion could still roar. Cordell Hull, the American Secretary of State, later had a long discussion with the prime minister about the event and wrote in his memoirs, "Since many people throughout the world believed that Britain was about to surrender, he (Churchill) wanted by this action to show that she still meant to fight."[3] The attack was not Britain's finest hour.

At 3:00 in the morning of July 5, a military car picked up Moreton at his hotel and took him seventy miles to Port Lyautey near Rabat in Morocco. The following morning, the banker had a five-hour car ride to a small military outpost, where he picked up another vehicle that took him to a second military camp. He reached there at 7:00 the next morning. Then he boarded a seaplane already carrying fourteen men. It had just reached cruising speed, when a British aircraft attacked it, but then departed. After that close call, Moreton's pilot told his passengers that he was not sure he had enough fuel to make the trip. The plane eventually landed after eleven hours in the air at Port Etienne in Mauritania, where everyone spent the night. The brave travelers left the next morning on a treetop flight that rarely rose above 1,000 feet and finally landed in Dakar at 4:30 in the afternoon.[4]

After Moreton arrived, he went immediately to the ships and helped Gontier and the others finish that day's work moving the gold. The French military was taking it off the ships in the port and moving it by train to a garrison in the town of Thiès forty miles inland. The bullion had started arriving on July 4. The navy had wanted to unload the five ships at the same time, but Gontier insisted that for security reasons they handle only one vessel at a time. Troops started with the *El Kantara* and then unloaded the *Victor Schoelcher*. The *Ville d'Alger* was handled last. Moving heavy cases in the middle of summer in tropical Africa was difficult, and the men could not work more than eight hours on a shift. While having dinner aboard the ship, an officer gave Moreton five 20 franc gold coins that had fallen out of a ripped sack somewhere along the way.[5]

The French central bank gold was now spread far and wide around the world. The largest amount, 735.7 tons, was in Dakar. In addition there were 476.5 tons at the New York Federal Reserve,

345.5 tons at the Canadian National Bank in Ottawa, 258.1 tons at the Bank of England in London, 254.2 in Martinique, and 10.4 tons in Casablanca. The French had rescued a total of 2,080.4 tons from the Germans.[6]

On the morning of July 8, Moreton and Gontier left in a military vehicle for Thiès to check out the final destination for the African gold. The heat was stifling, but they amused themselves watching monkeys run alongside their car. The mosquitoes and ants were not as much fun. Never far from their thoughts was the possibility of another British attack. When they arrived at the outpost, the two men saw that French soldiers had strung barbed wire around a large brick bunker where the gold was stored. Workers were still moving crates into the building. Moreton was intrigued by what he saw, and later wrote in a report on his trip: "Negroes of the most beautiful black that I had ever seen carried the boxes. They were completely nude except for a very small string between their buttocks."[7]

Security was tight. It took two keys and two people to open the bunker's main door. The last gold train arrived just after the bank officials. When everything was unpacked and counted, there were 20,576 cases from four countries: 14,424 French, 1,208 Polish, and 4,944 Belgian and Luxembourg.[8]

That same night, Moreton received a message telling him to return the next morning to Casablanca and report to Admiral Ollive. Twelve hours later, he took off on the long flight back to Casablanca. There was only one stop along the way, and the trip soon became monotonous. There was nothing but sand and then more sand to see below until the plane reached the Atlas Mountains. When he landed, Moreton had another confrontation with a French customs agent because he was still carrying the money he had been given weeks earlier, when he thought he might be going to Canada. He had no proof he was legally bringing it into the country. Finally, though, the official let him go.

During his next two months in Morocco, Moreton handled routine central bank business and handled non-gold shipments to the French National Bank headquarters in Clermont-Ferrand. He also sent five tons of gold to Lisbon to settle a debt of the French Foreign Ministry. Finally on September 30, Moreton left Casablanca by train on a four-day trip to Algiers, where he picked up the passenger ship *Lamoricière*, which took him to Marseilles. A week later, he arrived in Clermont-Ferrand. After four-and-a-half months of adventures unknown to the average bank civil servant, Charles Moreton's war had ended. It was the kind of adventure that few bankers ever had, and he later wrote a long account of it for his grandchildren.[9]

Three articles in the Compiègne armistice agreement signed in June 1940 dealt with economic issues. The most important set out the procedure of French payments to Germany for the occupying forces. That amounted to 20 million Reichsmark ($4.8 million) per day. The Germans ruled that it was perfectly legal under Article 52 of the 1907 Hague Conventions Governing War.

The armistice also set up the Wiesbaden Commission to handle occupation issues. General Otto von Stülpnagel, a German officer, and General Charles Huntziger, from France, initially headed it. There were eventually two groups, one dealing with military issues and the other for economic questions. Hans Richard Hemmen, a career German diplomat who specialized in economic affairs and the newly appointed German Plenipotentiary Minister in France, headed the economic section. The French joked that he meant trouble since his name in their language means "to impede." His counterpart on the French side was Yves Bréart de Boisanger, the new head of the French Central Bank. The economic commission initially met in Wiesbaden, Germany, but later also had sessions in Paris.[10]

The Germans at first were unaware that the French had moved large stocks of gold to the Caribbean and Africa. Paris officials led them to believe that in the last days of the invasion they had sent it all to North America. Slowly, though, they began to learn about what had happened from Paris civil servants in a strategy that was later labeled collaboration. Five weeks after the fighting stopped, on July 19, 1940, an irritated Hemmen handed over a six-point questionnaire to Bréart de Boisanger, demanding information about the whereabouts of all French gold on June 22, the day of the armistice. The Nazis specifically demanded to know what had happened to the gold of Poland, Belgium, Luxembourg, Holland, Norway, and what they called the "former Czechoslovakia." The French dragged out the process as long as they could, but finally supplied the information, admitting that some of the gold had been sent to Dakar.[11]

French civil servants have a well-earned reputation for being brilliant negotiators, and they now masterfully obfuscated in order to avoid turning over any gold that was still under their control. The Vichy French also sought to win German understanding by saying that they did not want it to fall into British hands. Hemmen, though, kept pressing for the return of the bullion to mainland France. Bank officials then argued that it was much too dangerous to send it anywhere by ship, but the Germans said they would send Luftwaffe planes to pick it up. The Vichy French rejected that offer on the grounds that the risk would be even greater if it were shipped by air.

Both the French and the Germans were by then concerned that General de Gaulle and his small military force might set up a base in Africa and capture the gold in Thiès, only forty miles by train from Dakar, and only eighteen miles as a plane flies. It was also less than twenty miles from sandy beaches, where Allies troops could land.[12]

At a meeting of the Wiesbaden group on September 12, Hemmen ordered the French to give him "as soon as possible" a detailed report about the location of all French, Belgian, and Polish gold. The German also demanded that all the bullion be transferred further inland to a more secure location.

Bréart de Boisanger responded eight days later. He informed the Germans that he was so concerned about the gold's security that France was already moving it to Kayes, a town known as the "pressure cooker" because of its extreme heat. It was about 300 miles from the coast, so a naval rescue operation was impossible. The city was then in Senegal, although today it is part of Mali. It was an important transportation center at the point where the Dakar-Niger railroad line met the Senegal River, and shipments could thus be made by boat, road, or rail. The city's real appeal to the French, though, was its isolation. A train from Dakar ran only three times a week and took eighteen hours. River travel was difficult in the dry season, and virtually impossible in the wet months.

The French banker still strongly objected to the German proposal to send the gold to Europe, insisting that it was safer to leave it where it was. He pointed out that the British were now stopping and inspecting Vichy warships at sea. Hemmen again replied that he could send German planes to pick up the valuable cargo. The Frenchman answered just as passionately that it wasn't feasible to ship 100 tons of gold by air. Hemmen said he had at his disposal twenty or thirty planes, and later even suggested sending a convoy of trucks overland from Kayes to Algiers and then flying the bullion to Marseilles. The French answered every German suggestion with a counter-argument, and the standoff dragged on.[13]

German and Vichy concerns about the British and de Gaulle were correct. In late September 1940 they attacked Dakar. The two groups had different goals. The British were worried that the Nazis would take over the port of Dakar, which juts out into the Atlantic Ocean from the hump of West Africa. That would have been an ideal location from which to launch submarine warfare against the Allies. De Gaulle, on the other hand, was looking for a place to establish a base in Africa to rally French forces to his cause.

They also both shared an interest in the tons of gold the French had sent to Africa. Polish and Belgian officials in London had already told the British about it. Churchill in a letter to General Jan Smuts, the South African Prime Minister, wrote, "Besides the strategic importance of Dakar and political effects of its capture by de Gaulle, there are £60 or £70 million Polish gold wrongfully held in the interior."[14]

A squabble soon broke out in London among French, British, Belgian, and Polish refugees about what to do with the gold once it was captured. Everyone had his own idea about how to spend it. They finally decided that the British would use it to purchase American war materiel for the Free French forces.

Using all of his famous eloquence, Churchill, in a talk with de Gaulle, painted a glorious scenario: "Dakar wakes up one morning, sad and uncertain. But behold, by the light of the rising sun, its inhabitants perceive the sea, at a great distance, covered with ships. An immense fleet! A hundred war or transport vessels." Free French envoys land and go directly to the resident governor-general, while overhead French and British planes drop leaflets saying that they had come in peace. Only a few shots would be fired before surrender. Then de Gaulle and the governor-general would dine together and toast to the final victory.[15]

Reality turned out totally different. The invasion was a debacle. The British provided few ships; the French offered few soldiers. De Gaulle had to arrive in Dakar on a Dutch vessel. The Allies did not realize that the Vichy French had quietly sent a squadron of its own ships through the Mediterranean to reinforce Dakar. The ensuing confrontation turned into a battle between Vichy French and Gaullist French forces.

The weather also turned against the invaders. Africa is supposed to be nothing but sunshine, but the Franco-British forces arrived in a thick fog on September 23. Following Churchill's script, de Gaulle's representative landed with a letter for the local governor-general. But instead of welcoming him, the port commander arrested him. Then a fierce French vs. French battle broke out. Vichy loyalists in a Dakar fort bombarded Allied ships in the harbor. The *Richelieu*, a French battleship sent there to keep it out of Nazi hands, joined in the fight against the British and Free French. De Gaulle attempted to land, but scrubbed the operation when the British could not guarantee him air cover. As the general wrote in the his memoir, "Decidedly the affair was a failure." There were reports afterwards that the proud general was so depressed that he considered suicide.[16]

The Germans at the Wiesbaden talks were also interested in the 254 tons of French gold that had been sent to Martinique. Both sides had learned through the press that Americans and French representatives had reached an agreement not to ship it back to France. The Germans demanded that be done, and the French initially replied that they knew nothing of such an arrangement. Later they had to admit that there was such an understanding, but insisted that it had nothing to do with the armistice between France and Germany since the decision was taken before the cease-fire.[17]

At a meeting of the Wiesbaden group on October 10, 1940, Hemmen demanded once again that steps be taken to get the Belgian gold out of Africa. Although he and the Vichy French constantly referred to it as the Belgian gold, it also included the ninety cases of Luxembourg bullion. Hemmen announced that the Germans would initially make five planes available for the operation, and each flight would carry two or three tons. He presented the French with a schedule that would finish the project in two months. The Vichy representatives immediately protested the use of German planes in a French colony. The Nazis were by then exasperated at all the foot dragging.[18]

While Bréart de Boisanger continued to stall, Hemmen went around him to Pierre Laval, who ran the Vichy government on a day-to-day basis under Marshal Pétain. Laval was the most conciliatory top French official, and he had Pétain sign the agreement to move the Belgian and Luxembourg gold to Europe. No one from those two countries signed the accord. Georges Janssen, the head of the Belgian bank, was ill, which may have been true or it may have been a diplomatic illness since he didn't want to acquiesce under duress. Two Nazis who ran the Belgian central bank's daily operations approved the agreement in the name of Belgium and Luxembourg. The final accord specified that the French National Bank "accepted" responsibility to restore to Belgium the gold "in the state in which was received." The plan was to send it from Kayes to Marseilles, where it would be taken to the local French bank office. Germans would then take control of it and send it by train to Berlin. The first shipment of 2.4 tons left Kayes by air on November 4, 1940, on a flight that took it to Agadir, Morocco, and Oran, Algeria before landing in Algiers. It finally arrived by air in Marseilles on November 6 and was then quickly shipped to the Reichsbank in Berlin. Belgian gold was later sold to a variety of Germany's gold partners: a total of

109 tons went to Switzerland, thirty tons to Romania, three tons to Turkey, and one-third of a ton to the German embassy in Bucharest.[19]

On January 26, 1941, a Belgian official in occupied France sent a coded cable to the top Belgian diplomat in the U.S. telling him what was transpiring. It read: "Janssen health good. Situation bad. Yellow family traveling from Kayes via Algiers and Oran and Marseilles to the German family on Air France. You should retain the French family Yellow in New York. Hope is in you." The next-to-the-last sentence was a suggestion that Belgium sue the Bank of France in a New York City court to get back their gold. The case was filed in the U.S. because the French had large gold holdings on deposit at the Federal Reserve, which the Belgians hoped would be used to pay them for their losses. The case was eventually halted because it was impossible to get key European officials to New York to testify because of the war conditions. Eventually in 1944, the French government gave the Belgians 198 tons of bullion, the amount that Paris turned over to the Nazis.[20]

A variety of ways were later used to get the Belgian and Luxembourg gold from Kayes to Marseilles. Transportation took place by truck, ship, air, and railroad. The project eventually took eighteen months to complete. Much of the delay was based on the difficulties of getting the cargo to Algiers. A French official wrote in August 1940, that it was impossible to make shipments over land during the wet season. American diplomats in Africa kept close track of the deliveries and sent reports back to Treasury Secretary Morgenthau in Washington. There was little that the U.S. could do, however, except watch it happen.[21]

Many of the later shipments went inland nearly four hundred miles by train from Kayes to Bamako, then by large trucks six hundred miles to Gao, and finally in smaller trucks 1,400 miles through the historic town of Timbuktu and the Sahara Desert to Colomb-Béchear in Algeria. Sometimes the bullion was carried on the backs of camels. The last leg of the trip was by train to Algiers. Other shipments went upstream on the Niger River and sometimes ran into drought conditions that had lowered the water level. Local

Africans then had to push the boats upstream. As a result of all the complications, trips that were supposed to take days ended up taking weeks. The average shipment to Marseilles at one point lasted three-and-a-half months. French officials told American diplomats about the German demand, and the U.S. officials abroad kept a careful eye on the traffic. There was some discussion about shooting down an Air France plane carrying gold, but that never happened.[22]

Whether the shipments went by boat to Algiers via Dakar or across the Sahara, they all landed in the Algerian capital, where Air France planes took them to Marseilles. During a flight on February 8, 1941, a British plane attacked four French aircraft carrying gold. Three of them returned safely to base, and the last landed at the Marseilles airport. After that, flights were temporarily grounded, but they eventually resumed, mostly at night. The gold shuttles across the Mediterranean also faced constant fuel shortages since the first priority remained the Nazi war effort and all Nazi planes, ships, and tanks had fuel priority.[23]

A year after the French-held gold repatriation started, only 2,013 out of the 4,944 boxes of gold had arrived in Berlin, and Hemmen demanded that the job be finished quickly. He demanded that everything should be done by airplane, in order to prevent any more bureaucratic foot-dragging. Finally on June 5, 1942, French officials sent a message to the Armistice Commission announcing, "The transport of Belgian gold is completed." It had taken 231 flights to transport the cases from Algiers to Marseilles.[24]

The Germans in February 1941 forced Luxembourg to ask formally for both the French and the Belgians to send their gold to Berlin. By that time, a Nazi *Gauleiter*, a paramilitary officer, was running the Grand Duchy. The Germans paid a nominal price in Reichsmark for the bullion. After the war, German officials claimed that they didn't owe the country anything because the Nazi government had technically paid for it.

After all the Belgian and Luxembourg bullion arrived in Berlin, it was transferred on September 9, 1942, to fund Göring's Four Year Plan, although the metal was stored in Reichsbank vaults. The

Germans also offered to pay Belgium for its gold with Reichsmark, but the proceeds could only be used to buy German goods. The Belgians would also have to pay all the transportation costs, including getting it out of Africa. Brussels officials refused the offer, sending a reply to Berlin on December 22, 1942, that maintained that the Bank of France's delivery of it "had been done without the consent or participation of the National Bank of Belgium." The Reichsbank in July 1943 set a value at 552,378,318.20 RM ($221 million) for the gold. Berlin also stated that if Belgium again refused to accept payment, the issue would be handed over to a German court. Belgium never responded.[25]

The relentless Nazi pressure on the French and finally the willingness of the Vichy government to accommodate Berlin cost the Belgians heavily. The gold arrived just at the time the Nazis were running out of resources to finance their war machine. The Belgians lost 198.4 tons of gold to the Germans once France fell, the largest amount of any country during the war.[26]

The Germans also had their eyes on the Polish gold, claiming that it too should be sent to mainland France and then to Berlin. The French again used a strategy of delay to hold off the Nazis, claiming first that the Polish government-in-exile had run up a huge debt with them that was greater in value than the gold they held. The French thus argued that the bullion actually belonged to them and was the property of neither the Germans nor the Poles. Without citing any specific amounts, Bréart de Boisanger in the Wiesbaden talks maintained there was only "a relatively small amount" of Polish gold. At one point in the negotiations he got his courage up enough to say, "The French government is not going to give the Polish gold to anyone."[27]

The fate of the Polish gold eventually turned into a debate that only lawyers could love. The Vichy French argued that since the Germans had decreed that Poland no longer existed as a country, there was no longer a Polish central bank. The Germans, on the other hand, changed their argument and now argued that the French government should return 1,200 cases of gold not to them but to the Polish government in Warsaw, which of course they controlled.

In March 1941, Hemmen suggested that the Polish gold be sent to the French National Bank offices in Clermont-Ferrand, but that never took place. The following September, the Germans demanded that the Polish gold in Kayes be sent to Algiers and transported to mainland France "in the same way as the Belgian gold." That, however, also never happened.[28]

The German ability to get gold out of Africa was greatly reduced after the Anglo-American invasion of North Africa in 1942 that eventually drove German and Italian armies out of the area. The Nazis were by then more concerned about defending the military gains they had made in Europe than getting their hands on the remaining Polish and French bullion sitting in the heat of Senegal.

∾

With the Germans out of Africa, the Polish government in London and the Polish National Bank sent Stefan Michalski to meet with representatives of the Free French forces in North Africa about taking over custody of the Polish gold. The two sides easily worked out a plan for the French to turn it over to the Polish government in exile.

In the spring of 1944, a convoy of six American naval vessels including the escort cruiser *USS Block Island* was on anti-submarine patrol near the Cape Verde Islands just off the coast of Africa. They were called hunter-killer groups, and their main job was to sink U-Boats; their weapon of choice was depth charges dropped to destroy or disable the submarines underwater. Occasionally they hit a whale. On March 23, Lt. Commander Edward N. W. Hunter on the *USS Breeman* and Lt. Commander S. H. Kinney on the *USS Bronstein* received orders to leave that group and proceed to Dakar. The two captains assumed they were going to check out signals from a German submarine. Soon they received a secret message ordering them to pick up a cargo of gold and take it immediately to New York City on the safest and most direct route possible.

The two ships pulled into dock at Dakar in the early afternoon of March 25, and the two captains checked in with the Vice Admiral William Glassford, the chief of the American naval mission there. The French had already brought the Polish gold from Kayes to Dakar and were ready to load it. After the workday at the French naval base was finished and only a few officers were still there, a caravan of French army trucks rolled up to the dock with loads of gold. Soldiers with bayonets guarded the transfer, while Senegalese sailors carried the heavy containers that each held four bars packed in sawdust. All the boxes had an iron band with a seal and the initials BP (*Bank Polski*). The Senegalese workers deposited them on the deck, and then American sailors gave Michalski a receipt for the crates. The American sailors, as so many people before them, were stunned at the weight of a box of gold. So they rigged up a block-and-tackle to lower them below deck.

The *Breeman* and the *Bronstein* left Dakar just before midnight the same day and headed directly for New York City at the speed of eighteen knots. They arrived at the Brooklyn Navy Yard in the late afternoon of April 3. The following day, Brinks armored trucks picked up the $60 million in Polish gold and moved it to the Federal Reserve vault in Manhattan. It had been quite an odyssey since leaving Warsaw on September 6, 1939.[29]

BALKAN DISTRACTIONS

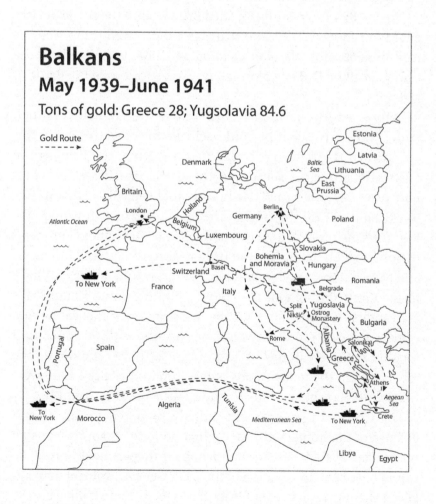

Balkans

May 1939–June 1941

Tons of gold: Greece 28; Yugsolavia 84.6

Afterwrapping up his rapid victory over the Low Countries and France in late June 1940, Hitler turned his attention to his next target: Great Britain. Churchill knew what was coming and on June 18 warned the British parliament and public in perhaps the greatest speech ever made in the English language. He said: "The Battle of France is over. I expect the Battle of Britain is about to begin. Upon this battle depends the survival of Christian civilization . . . Let us therefore brace ourselves to our duties and so bear ourselves that, if the British Empire and its Commonwealth last for a thousand years, men will still say, 'This was their finest hour.'"[1]

No one had successfully invaded Britain since the Battle of Fishguard in February 1797, and that was a short-lived thing. The last real invasion took place on October 14, 1066, when William the Conqueror, the Duke of Normandy, was victorious at the Battle of Hastings.

Before sending ground troops across the English Channel, Hitler wanted to see if he could achieve his objective in the air, and turned that job over to Hermann Göring, the head of the Luftwaffe. After his success in the Battle of France, he had a new title: *Reichsmarschall*. He brashly told the Führer that in five weeks he could rid the skies of the Royal Air Force. It would take four days, he promised, to defeat the Royal Air Fighter Command in Southern England. He would then start a four-week offensive, and Nazi bombers and long-range fighters would destroy military installations throughout the country and obliterate Britain's aircraft industry. Code name for the invasion: *Unternehmen Seelöwe*. (Operation Sea Lion). It would be the first military operation fought exclusively in the air. Just in case air power did not do the job, however, the many canals of Belgium in the fall of 1940 were filled with Nazi boats ready to undertake a naval invasion.[2]

The Churchill government quickly prepared for an all-out defense of the homeland. The cabinet on June 30 approved using poison gas to fight off German troops if they came ashore. That would have been in violation of the 1925 Geneva Protocol that outlawed chemical warfare, but Britain was ready to do it if it were the only way to defeat a Nazi invasion. The government also organized 1.5 million volunteers into the Home Guard, a secondary line of defense behind the military. Beaches were mined, and anti-landing barricades were built. Britain took over the contracts to buy aircraft the French had ordered in the U.S., which meant there would be no shortage of planes. Perhaps most importantly, the Royal Air Force had a new and powerful secret weapon: RADAR, an acronym for RAdio Detecting And Ranging. For years scientists in several countries had been working on a way to establish an early-warning system that would alert defenders to incoming airplanes. British scientists perfected the technology in early 1940.

Hitler on August 1 issued War Directive No. 17, which ordered the Luftwaffe "to overpower the English Air Force with all the forces at its command and in the shortest possible time."[3] A few British planes made a token attack on Berlin in August, and Hitler retaliated by ordering a massive bombing of London. Young RAF pilots who took to the air were both brave and successful. Despite heavy losses, they held their own. Late that month, Churchill told Parliament in another of his stirring speeches, "Never in the field of human conflict was so much owed by so many to so few."[4]

Göring missed his deadline by a long shot; and when the air war dragged on into the fall Hitler contemplated alternative military moves. He once again thought time was not on his side. The United States might soon come into the conflict on the British side, even though he figured it would take its military two years to gear up. Still heady after his rapid successes in the spring, the Führer also began to consider doing what he had vowed never to do: wage war on two fronts. He rationalized that he could temporarily put aside the invasion of Britain and quickly defeat the Soviet Union, which he considered to be militarily a house of cards that would collapse easily. Then he could turn back to Britain and finish it off.

In October 1940, Hitler toured his newly conquered Western Europe realm to meet with his allies. He never liked to fly, although he had been forced to do so during his early days in politics. Now he ruled much of Western Europe, and he could travel by train. His private rail car made its first stop on October 23, in the French-Spanish border town of Hendaye in France. In a meeting at the train station, Hitler pressed General Francisco Franco to join the war against Britain, promising that Spain could take over Gibraltar. A key Hitler objective was to get Britain out of the Mediterranean. Franco dodged, insisting that he was more interested in obtaining territory in French Africa. The Nazi leader was also anxious to get a naval base on Spain's Canary Islands to wage the Atlantic war, but the Spaniard stalled him on that as well. The meeting ended in deadlock with forced smiles. Hitler later complained to Mussolini, "Rather than go through that again, I would prefer to have three or four teeth taken out."[5]

Hitler's train next took him to the village of Montoire-sur-le-Loir in central France, for a meeting with Marshal Philippe Pétain, the country's new head of state. The location was selected because of its proximity to the Paris-Hendaye rail line. The two men shook hands on the railroad platform, and that picture would haunt the French war hero to his grave. During their confab in Hitler's private car, Pétain tried to get German help in putting down de Gaulle's rebellion in French Africa, but he gave no support for the Führer's agenda. So no success there, either.

The next train stop was Florence for a session with Mussolini. The two men had met at the Brenner Pass only three weeks earlier, and two conferences in such a short period reflected their growing estrangement. Each leader had been playing coy, providing little information about his future plans. Hitler had not let on at the earlier meeting that he would be going into Romania only a few days later to protect his oil supplies. Mussolini was furious when he learned that. He bellowed to Count Galeazzo Ciano, his son-in-law and foreign minister, "Hitler always faces me with a fait accompli. This time I am going to pay him back in his own coin. He will find out from the newspapers that I have occupied Greece."[6]

Mussolini planned to invade Greece on October 28. Six days before, he sent Hitler a letter informing him of his plans without specifying a date. In order to be not too offensive, he backdated his message to October 19. The Führer learned about the contents by phone on October 24, while he was in France. He then demanded an immediate conference. Mussolini casually suggested October 28. When Hitler got off the train that morning in Florence, Il Duce greeted him with the happy announcement, "Führer, we are on the march! Victorious Italian troops crossed the Greco-Albanian frontier at dawn today." Their meeting was tense and unproductive, and Mussolini's invasion quickly turned into a fiasco.[7]

With the Soviet Union at the top of Hitler's agenda, Germany faced a messy situation on his southern flank in the Balkans, which stretches from Yugoslavia and Romania in the north to Greece and Turkey on the Mediterranean. The Balkans were a relatively small place where trouble seemed to just happen. Squabbling powers there had drawn Europe's big powers into World War I. Hitler believed he had to protect his southern flank before turning his armies on Moscow.

The Balkans had been a key part of the German economic strategy after Hjalmar Schacht unveiled his New Plan of 1934, which reoriented the Nazi economy toward that region. It was economically poor but rich in the raw materials that the German war machine desperately needed. The Balkan states were geographically close to the Reich and accepted payment in gold. The region produced the crucial raw materials, especially copper, that Harry Dexter White had identified for Morgenthau as crucial for Germany's war machine. Emil Wiehl, a German Foreign Office economic specialist, in 1939 had said, "Copper is a life and death matter." A shortage of it in early 1940 hurt both the Luftwaffe and the army, and forced the German navy to curtail U-boat production. Yugoslavia also produced aluminum. Hungary was an important source of bauxite, an aluminum ore. Turkey had large deposits of chromium, exporting 40,000 tons annually to Germany, as well as tungsten, both of which are vital ingredients for making high-quality weapons out of Germany's low-grade iron ore. But the most important war materiel of all was Romanian oil. The country was Europe's second biggest producer after the Soviet Union, and

Germany's largest supplier. Despite the success of German chemical companies in making synthetic fuel from coal, petroleum was still essential to keep Nazi tanks rolling, and vastly cheaper than the synthetic option. Between February 9, and March 10, 1943, the Germans sent Romania a total of 30 tons of gold to pay largely for petroleum. In February, Berlin transferred an additional 10.4 tons to Switzerland for Romania, using stolen Belgian gold. Nazi Germany paid a total of $53.8 million for Romanian oil. Some of that bullion also found its way to the U.S. In January 1941, Romania sold 13.8 tons of gold to the New York Fed.[8]

The Soviet Union, though, was also increasingly active in the Balkans. German Foreign Minister Ribbentrop invited his Soviet counterpart Molotov to a November meeting in Berlin, where he proposed that Germany, Italy, Japan, and the Soviet Union divide the world into large spheres of influence. The talks deadlocked largely because the foreign ministers both had their eye on the Balkans. Molotov insisted the fate of Romania and Hungary was important to Moscow, and wanted to know "what the Axis contemplated with regard to Yugoslavia and Greece."[9] Once back in Moscow, Molotov sent Ribbentrop a formal reply saying that the Soviet Union would join the other three nations only if it could sign a mutual defense pact with Bulgaria and establish a base for land and sea operations near the Dardanelles, which connects the Black Sea and the Mediterranean Sea. Talk of four spheres of influence died a quiet death.

In September of 1940 Hitler postponed plans for the invasion of Britain. On December 18, 1940, Hitler signed off on Operation Barbarossa, the invasion of the Soviet Union. The opening line of the war directive: "The German Armed Forces must be prepared, even before the conclusion of the war against England, to crush Soviet Russia in a rapid campaign."[10]

Before the Nazis could turn to Barbarossa, however, they had to clean up the situation in Greece and Yugoslavia. Both countries were worrisome not only because the Soviet Union considered that area to be its backyard but also because the British had an active presence and close relations with both nations. The Germans feared that either London or Moscow could cause trouble in the south at a time when they wanted to be launching a powerful invasion of the Soviet Union through central Europe.

Greece in October 1940 easily halted the Italian invasion and pushed Mussolini's troops back into Albania. Greece, however, was both politically unstable and diplomatically fickle. King George and many Greeks favored an alliance with Britain, but General Ioannis Metaxas, the country's dictator, leaned toward the Axis powers. The question was whether the king or the general would stage a coup first.

Yugoslavia was equally in turmoil. Hitler put heavy pressure on Prince Paul, the regent for seventeen-year-old King Peter II, which included a visit to Berchtesgaden. Nazi threats worked, and the country became a member of the Tripartite Pact on March 25. The following day, however, Yugoslav Royal Air Force officers with British inspiration staged a coup in the name of King Peter. After the rebellion, Churchill said the country "had found its soul."[11]

On March 27, 1941, Hitler signed War Directive No. 25 ordering a massive attack on Yugoslavia. It stated: "Yugoslavia must be "regarded as an enemy and beaten down as quickly as possible." The invasion, which included troops from Germany, Italy, Hungary, Romania, and Bulgaria, began on April 6 with the carpet-bombing of Belgrade. The offensive ended on April 17 in Yugoslavia and on April 27 in Greece.[12]

The Germans were still worried about the British presence on the island of Crete, and on May 20, 1941, they launched *Unternehmen Merkur* (Operation Mercury), an airborne invasion, the first in military history. Both British and German military leaders valued the island because of its proximity to Egypt, the Suez Canal, and the route to India. German paratroopers suffered heavy casualties, but the main airfield on the western side of the island soon fell into Nazi hands, and the whole island was subdued in ten days. Because of the heavy casualties, however, Hitler nixed future airborne invasions.

A memo of the New York Federal Reserve reported on April 19, 1941, that Greece's gold reserves had been generally estimated to be about 28 tons.[13] By the time the Axis armies invaded, the National Bank of Greece had shipped twenty-five tons of gold out of the country to the safety of other central banks, with most of it going to the Bank of England via Egypt. The British sent a navy ship to undertake the operation. Greece had seven tons safely in New York. Some, though, still remained in the hands of private banks and individuals. The national bank as a precaution packed ten cases of valuables that could be readily moved on short notice. They contained both gold and silver coins. The boxes were bound with a steel strapping and marked with the bank's seal in wax and the letters ETE for the name in Greek of the national bank. There was nearly a ton of gold, and ton-and-a-half of silver.

On April 12 and with Axis units consolidating their hold over the country, the Greek National Bank assigned two officials, Nicolas Lavas and Panayotis Tsimicalis, to take over authority of the ten cases and move them to Crete. They soon left the mainland for the Bank branch in Heraklion, the largest city on the island.

In early June 1941, German authorities took over the town and demanded the keys to the vaults in the Bank of Greece's office. The Nazis then searched the storage area in the presence of the branch manager. On June 17, Major Eberhard von Künsberg also arrived at the bank. He was the head of a special SS unit charged with confiscating local artworks and other valuables in invaded countries. The Nazis had great hopes of a rich haul in Greece. Künsberg picked up the ten cases, which in a document were identified as "three cases containing gold and seven cases containing silver."[14]

Citizens holding gold coins in Greece were required to deposit them in a semi-state banking institution known by the French name *Caisse des Dépot et Consignations* (Cashier of Deposits and Consignments). They were then given drachmas, the local currency, in exchange for the gold. The Caisse retained the coins in its vaults, and the Germans confiscated them. They included mainly British, Turkish, French, and Italian coins. The Germans later learned of other holdings and picked up small amounts on the Greek mainland in August 1941 and on Crete on April 1944. Another 116 kilograms of gold was found in the Salonika branch of the Bank of Greece, and a total of 12.5 tons was taken from private individuals. Later 6.5 tons of gold was taken from Greek Jews who were deported to Germany and died in concentration camps.[15]

The Yugoslav government had substantially more gold than Greece, and much of it had left the country before the Axis powers invaded. In early May 1939, and shortly after the Germans had taken control of Czechoslovakia and Memel, the National Defense Council of Yugoslavia decided to move most of the nation's bullion abroad to London and New York. On May 20, 1939, the Yugoslav destroyer *Beograd* docked in Plymouth Harbor in Britain with 7,344 bars of gold. The Yugoslav attaché in London was there to greet it. The Yugoslavs eventually stored nineteen tons in Britain.[16]

The United States, though, was the major destination for Belgrade's gold. The Yugoslavs in June 1940 first sent four shipments to the New York Fed and then later five more. By the end of November 1940, the New York Federal Reserve was holding 17 tons of Yugoslav gold. With the Axis threat rising rapidly, a New York Federal Reserve report in February 1941 estimated that the Yugoslavs still had inside the country "not less than" 131 tons that it wanted to move to a safer location. A month later, Belgrade was so desperate to get bullion out that they sent 22 tons to Argentina and Brazil and also shipped some to the Bank for International Settlements in Switzerland. On March 18, 1941, a Yugoslav shipment arrived at Pier 34 in New York City with seventeen tons of bullion for the Federal Reserve.[17]

On April 5, the day before the invasion, the National Bank of Yugoslavia told the Bank for International Settlements in Basel to convert all its accounts, including its gold, into dollars and deposit that in the New York Federal Reserve. Two days later, the BIS sent $2.7 million to the Yugoslav account at the New York Federal Reserve.[18]

The last minute frantic shipments were successful, and by the time the Axis powers controlled Yugoslavia in mid-April, the country had just twelve tons of gold left in the country, which was mostly in coins. Bank officials decided to move nearly ten tons of that to the bank's Uzice Branch in western Serbia, where it was stored in vaults. The location was close to the Adriatic coast, a potential route for shipping it abroad. Immediately after the Nazi invasion began, several of the National Bank's managers and the Yugoslav minister of finance traveled to Uzice to check on the bullion.[19]

With the Germans on the march, the bullion was next shipped nearly 120 miles further west to the town of Mostar. General Miojko Jankovic called the manager of the local branch on April 13 and relayed a wireless order he had just received to send the bullion to Nikšić, a city sixty miles north in Montenegro. During that evening, 204 cases of gold left in trucks headed for the new location. In the town of Bileca, the cargo was transferred to a train. It finally arrived at its destination on April 15.

Bank officials decided to move it by truck to the nearby Trebjesa Grotto, where it would stay until the Yugoslav Air Force could carry it out of the country from an airport in Nikšić. The seven remaining Do-17K bombers in the Yugoslav Air Force flew there to evacuate King Peter II, members of the Yugoslav government, and the gold.[20] During that operation, however, only twenty of the 204 cases of the country's gold reserves were airlifted out. Five Do-17Ks planes were destroyed, and the remaining boxes of bullion remained on the tarmac. The Italians seized them and sent them to the Bank of Italy. After the fall of Mussolini and German occupation of Italy in 1944, they went sent to the Reichsbank.[21]

Ten boxes of gold had been dispatched by truck to the Ostrog Monastery, a massive structure built into the hillside where Gavrilo V, the Orthodox Patriarch of Yugoslavia, had recently taken refuge. The German First Panzer Group, commanded by Paul von Kleist and known as *Panzergruppe von Kleist*, reached the monastery at 5:00 in the morning on April 25. Accompanying the unit was Wilfred Oven, a war reporter who wrote the following news story:

"The Gestapo in collaboration with the Wehrmacht has discovered an important part of the Serbian State treasure concealed in the inaccessible mountains of Montenegro. The coterie of traitors that surrounded the young King Peter had previously, like so many governments in allegiance to England, endeavored to send their state treasures to the British Isles. That attempt failed in Serbia.

"The town of Nikšić was still asleep when we left by a narrow winding path that led up the mountains. The mountain scenery here is wildly romantic, filled with ravines and steep rocks. There was a mountain torrent a hundred meters below. There we caught sight of the monastery that lies within an opening made in the almost perpendicular mountainside. This had been the goal of the king when he fled. It is also our goal. The monastery seemed still asleep when we arrived, except for the monotonous chanting of monks in the chapel. The place was soon awoken by our arrival. The doorman, who had a bad conscience, appeared and seemed at once to understand what we were after. He told us that the prior was still in bed. We told him we wanted to see him. We also told him that everyone in the monastery was to assemble in one of the rooms before we began our search. When the leader of our expedition asked whether everyone was present, he told us that everyone was there except for two monks who were in a building still higher on the mountain that was the real monastery.

"We believed him and began our search. One locked door interested us. From the outside it appeared to be the entrance to a storage room. Although the servant of the prior assured us that it contained nothing of interest, we were anxious to investigate. Finally, after the prior saw that we had hammers and crowbars, he produced the key. When we opened the door, we found ourselves in a comfortably furnished clubroom with chairs around a table. There was a door opening to another room, and who should we find there but the Patriarch of Yugoslavia Gavrilo!

"He had just finished putting on his richly ornate vestment, when we showed him two pistols that he had hidden away in his cupboard. Apparently the Patriarch was ready to fight Germany with more than just spiritual weapons. Later we found other weapons: rifles, numerous pistols, and large stores of ammunition. There is no doubt that it was only our sudden appearance that had prevented these weapons from being used against German soldiers.

"Although the Gestapo had quite reliable clues that led to this monastery, the Patriarch maintained that he knew nothing of any treasure. It was only after we made him understand that he might be shot for having concealed weapons that he asked us to follow him. He then led us down to a mountain cellar that had an iron door. By the light of four torches, we saw piles of boxes, equipment, and state documents. Then we proceeded through a narrow and damp passage where there was the smell of smoked hams and meat. We found ourselves in a larder filled with a countless number of sausages, hams, sacks of flour, sugar, coffee, and other foodstuffs. But there we also found canvas sacks that we couldn't open. They were sealed with chains and locks. There could be no doubt about the contents. We dragged them into the sunlight.

"For the first time in my life, I carried 25 million on my back because each of these sacks had a neat little label on which was written: Contents 25,000,000. . . . Gradually 375 million were brought out and put on a truck. But still more important were the chests, each of which was so heavy that two men had difficulty carrying one. This was mint gold. We had a splendid haul."[22]

The Gestapo later sent a jeep to the upper monastery building and seized nearly a ton there. The Germans got a total of 9.6 tons of gold in Yugoslavia. Italian troops captured a total of 124 boxes of gold, including forty-two cases that had been left on the road between Cetinje and Hercegnovi and eighty-two in the town of Nikšić. They were all sent to Rome. The rest was temporarily left in the hands of Yugoslav authorities, but eventually it too was dispatched to Italy. There still remained 32 cases of gold stored in the Franciscan Monastery in Kaptol, Zagreb, which stayed there until the end of the war.[23]

On April 29, 1940, Yugoslav Finance Minister Juraj Šutej told a meeting of the Yugoslav government-in-exile in Jerusalem that only 9.2 tons of gold remained in the country.[24] Almost twice as much was by that time stored in the New York Federal Reserve.[25]

Chapter Twenty-Three

THE SOVIET UNION
STARES INTO AN ABYSS

Soviet Union

1941

Tons of gold: 3,000

Gold Route

To New York
and London

O n December 18, 1940, Adolf Hitler issued War Directive No. 21. Only nine copies were made. The military operation was named Operation Barbarossa, and the target was the Soviet Union. Barbarossa was a charismatic twelfth century Holy Roman Emperor, who was constantly at war. The Führer was going to do what he had said he would always avoid: wage war on both the eastern and western fronts simultaneously. Confident that the fall of Britain was only a matter of time and could be finished easily, he now turned his attention to an attack on the communist country. Hitler had an almost irrational hatred toward communism and wrote in *Mein Kampf*, "The problem of how the future of the German nation can be secured is the problem of how Marxism can be exterminated."[1]

The minerals-rich area of the Ural Mountains was also an essential part of Hitler's vision of his future Reich. The Soviet Union was to provide the raw materials and agricultural products needed for his massive land empire that would dominate Europe for a thousand years. The inferior ethnic groups living there would be killed, and Germans would move in and harvest the area's riches.[2]

War Directive No. 21 set the invasion date at "May 15 or soon after." Hitler expected another lightning victory just as he had enjoyed in Western Europe during May and June 1940. "We have only to kick in the door, and the whole rotten structure will come crashing down," he confidently declared. In the instructions on the conduct of the war for the army's Economic Operations Staff East, there was a section called "Raw Materials, Management of Goods." Item two stated: "Gold reserves and foreign currency are to be secured. Further action will be taken by the Economy Command upon notification."[3]

Russia enjoys a great wealth of natural resources, especially minerals, and has historically been a major gold producer. At the beginning of the reign of Czar Alexander III in 1881, Russia had just 195 tons of bullion holdings, which rose to nearly 700 tons at the end of his reign in 1894. Under the ill-fated Nicholas II, they soared again to reach 1,250 tons at the beginning of World War I.

The czarist government, though, sold off much of its bullion during the war to buy weapons and used it as collateral for loans. At the beginning of the Russian revolution in 1917, the country's holdings were down to 1,102 tons, with two-thirds of that stored in Britain, France, the U.S., and Japan. Most of the country's remaining bullion had been moved for safekeeping from Petrograd, the capital located at the foot of the Bay of Finland on the Baltic Sea, inland to the Volga region, mostly to the city of Kazan.[4]

During the civil war, which lasted until 1921, both the Red Army and the anti-Bolshevik White Army fought to capture the national treasury. The Red army managed to evacuate only 4.5 tons early in 1918. Admiral Alexander Kolchak, the head of the Imperial Russian Navy, became the leader of the forces fighting the Reds, and their bullion was called Kolchak's Gold. He set up his government in Siberia, with the center in Omsk. Kolchak enjoyed some early success, but his military units were eventually pushed back into Eastern Siberia, and he sent some of his gold abroad. Some of Kolchak's gold was sold off during the civil war to buy weapons and thus ended up in the U.S. and Britain. He was killed in February 1920. Some went to royalists living abroad and some fell into Bolshevik hands.[5]

The new communist government in 1918 sent 98 tons of gold to Germany as part of the Brest-Litovsk Treaty that took the Soviet Union out of World War I. Some of the new country's gold also had to be given to the victors of World War I, including France and Britain. In June 1921, the People's Commissariat of Finance announced that the Communist government had returned 323 tons of gold to the new capital of Moscow, where it was stored in the Gosbank, the new Soviet central bank.[6]

In a 1921 article in *Pravda* entitled "The Importance of Gold Now and After the Complete Victory of Socialism," the country's new leader Vladimir Lenin famously said, "When we are victorious on a world-wide scale, we will make public toilets out of gold on the streets of the world's largest cities."[7] He had a more immediate and practical purpose for it during the period of state capitalism, when the nation was recovering from the ravages of the civil war and building a new industrial country. The national railroad, for example, used gold to buy 1,000 locomotives from Sweden. The government also made use of it to support national communist parties and world revolution through the new Comintern. Stalin succeeded Lenin in 1922, and he initially showed little interest in gold. Production remained low, and the reserves dropped to 141.3 tons in 1925.[8]

In the late 1920s, Stalin changed the national gold policy and sought to expand mining. He brought in a team of experts to rebuild the industry as part of his first Five Year Plan. Alexander Serbrovsky, a famed Soviet scientist, led the program and hired the American mining engineer John Littlepage, who became the deputy Gold Commissar. Production increased almost five-fold between 1929 and 1936. By 1933, output was back to pre-World War I levels and the Soviet Union was once again among the world's largest producers. By 1935 the central bank holdings had risen to 626 tons. The country was selling much of it abroad to finance industrialization.[9]

The U.S. broke diplomatic relations with Moscow in December 1917, after the fall of Czar Nicolas II, and did not recognize the country even after it became clear that the communists were in power to stay. That policy changed, however, early in the administration of Franklin D. Roosevelt. The Soviets at the time were interested in purchasing American equipment for its industrialization program, which was difficult without diplomatic ties. At the time, the United States had few Soviet experts. The top one at the State Department was William C. Bullitt, who had married the widow of John Reed, an American Communist whose first-hand account of the Russian Revolution was entitled *Ten Days That Shook the World*. Reed died in 1920 and was buried in the Kremlin Wall.

In late September 1933, Roosevelt surprised Treasury Secretary Henry Morgenthau at one of their weekly luncheons by asking him, "What would you think of bringing this whole Russian question into our front parlor?" The next day Morgenthau had lunch with Bullitt, who proposed a new U.S. policy toward the communist nation.[10] The secretary suggested that the U.S. offer the Soviets diplomatic recognition and also sell them $100 million worth of agricultural and industrial goods. He worked with Bullitt in early planning, but eventually turned the entire project over to the diplomat. Stalin later sent the urbane Maxim Litvinov, the People's Commissar for Foreign Affairs and a veteran of the Russian Revolution, to Washington as ambassador. Roosevelt had a lighter touch. He sent comedian Harpo Marx to Moscow as a good-will ambassador. The two countries established diplomatic relations in November 1933.

The United States and the Soviet Union were natural partners. The Americans could provide industrial equipment for Moscow, and the Soviets had gold to pay for it. So it was not surprising that trade flourished, with Roosevelt and Morgenthau watching developments closely. American exports to Moscow went from $8.9 million in 1933 to $33.4 million in 1936, while U.S. imports jumped from $12.1 million to $21.4 million in the same period.[11]

Morgenthau in April 1937 suggested to the Soviets that the central bank of the Russian Federation open an account with the Federal Reserve Bank of New York to handle earmarked gold transactions, which they did in June. Moscow made an initial deposit of $100,000. As part of the new relationship, the New York Fed staff produced a detailed study of the Soviet gold industry since the Russian Revolution. Given Soviet secrecy in such matters, it was more guesstimates than hard facts. It showed that the Soviet bank's official balance sheet on January 1, 1937, reported assets of $120 million, with twenty-four percent of that in gold. It estimated that the country's bullion stocks were worth $1.2 billion, with the central bank holding $300 million. The study estimated that in the fifteen years since 1923, the Soviet Union had exported $730 million of the $1.2 billion in gold that it mined. The Soviet Union was the world's second largest producer after South Africa. Moscow now probably had twenty-one percent of the global gold market. The study predicted that the Soviet Union in 1937 would buy $30 million in goods from the U.S., with most of that going toward products such as aircraft engines.[12]

In August 1939, the Soviet central bank sent the New York Fed a cable saying that they would soon be sending a first shipment of gold from Leningrad to New York. On September 27, the State Bank delivered 160 bars of gold to San Francisco. The following month a second shipment worth $11 million arrived.[13] While most of the bullion arrived in New York City and was taken immediately to the Federal Reserve vault, some also landed in San Francisco after crossing the Pacific Ocean. The gold departed from the port of Vladivostok on the Pacific Coast. There were two routes out of the harbor. In the winter, when the northern way was frozen, it left by the southern one. The bullion was stored at the U.S. Mint in San Francisco, which had been built originally to handle the California gold rush. The funds were immediately booked in the Secretary of the Treasury's special account.[14]

Soviet gold shipments to the U.S. continued at a good pace, especially after the European war began in September 1939. Some of the shipments went to Chase Manhattan Bank and Guarantee Trust in addition to the Federal Reserve. In the middle of July, the Treasury Department received a message that ten tons would soon arrive in either San Francisco or New York. It came in mid-August. In mid-September $5.6 million worth landed in San Francisco. On October 11, Morgenthau gave the Soviet Union government a $50 million advance to buy weapons in expectation of new gold shipments for the next six months. Later that month the *SS Dneprostroy* arrived in New York with $5.5 million in bullion. On November 6, the *SS Azerbaidjan* pulled into San Francisco with $6 million in bullion, and on December 10, the *SS Transbalt* landed in the same harbor with $6.8 million. The *SS Donbass* also docked in New York with a bullion cargo of $6.6 million. Also that month, Morgenthau told the press that the U.S. had purchased an addition $30 million in gold from Russia.[15]

Moscow sold plenty of bullion to other western countries during this period. Between December 8 and 26, 1939, the Soviets exported nearly 90 tons. Britain bought 23.2 tons, the U.S. 18.9 tons, Germany 12.5 tons, Holland 27.5 tons, and Switzerland 7.9 tons. In the first three months of 1940, the Swiss acquired an additional 20 tons of Soviet gold. Shipments continued to the U.S. in 1940, with several going via Vladivostok to San Francisco. In the first half of 1941, the bulk of the 60 tons that the Soviets exported went to the U.S. and Switzerland, with only a small amount going to Germany.[16]

On June 22, 1941, Hitler launched history's mightiest invasion against the Soviet Union. Armies of the Axis nations attacked on a front 1,800 miles wide. The 150 divisions were made up of three million men, of which two-and-a-half million were Germans. The nineteen panzer divisions had three thousand tanks. There were also 7,000 artillery pieces, 2,500 aircraft, and even 600,000 horses.[17]

Armchair historians immediately compared the date with Napoleon's invasion of Russia in 1812. He crossed the Neman River into that country on June 24 with a half million men and reached Moscow on September 14. The Russians, though, refused to surrender, and the French leader left Moscow on October 19 with about 100,000 men and 40,000 wagons filled with war spoils. The retreat turned into a disaster, as Russian soldiers attacked the retreating *Grande Armée*. The French claimed that *Général Hiver* (General Winter) defeated them. Historians estimate that only about 20,000 soldiers made it back to France.[18] Would Hitler succeed where Napoleon had failed? The Germans certainly thought so. Göring's air force expected to be back fighting Britain in the air after two months of duty on the eastern front. Hitler, however, attacked six weeks later than his original plan because of his detour into Yugoslavia and Greece to protect his southern flank.

Stalin had plenty of warning that an attack was coming. His own military had been telling him for months. In late April, Churchill informed him through the British ambassador in Moscow that the Germans would soon attack. Roosevelt sent a similar message. Stalin, though, could not bring himself to believe them, as while he trusted no one else, he trusted Hitler.

The Soviet leader at the time was also receiving secret notes from Hitler. The Nazi leader wrote him at least two known letters, one on December 31, 1940, and another on May 14, 1941. In the second one Hitler admitted that there was a Nazi military build-up on the

Soviet border, but said it was being done to prepare for an invasion of Britain "away from the eyes of the English opponent and in connection with the recent operations in the Balkans." He added that "on my honor as a head of state" there would be no attack on the Soviet Union. As Alexander Solzhenitsyn later wrote, Stalin, the man who trusted no one, trusted Adolf Hitler.[19]

At 8:00 P.M. on June 21, Stalin was in a meeting at the Kremlin, when he received a phone call from General Georgy Zhukov, the chief of the general staff, telling him that a German noncommissioned officer had just surrendered to Soviet troops and told them that an invasion would start the next morning at 4:00. Zhukov asked for permission to mobilize, but Stalin barked back, "Permission not granted. This is a German provocation." The Soviet leader then soon departed for his dacha just outside Moscow and went to bed. Semen Timoshenko, the People's Commissar of Defense, and Zhukov slept that night in their offices.[20]

At 3:45 A.M., Zhukov again telephoned Stalin, but the duty officer at the dacha said he was sleeping. The general replied, "Wake him immediately. The Germans are bombing our cities." Three minutes later, Stalin was on the phone, and Zhukov repeated the news. There was a long silence on the phone, and the general asked, "Did you understand what I said?" More empty air and finally the Soviet leader said, "Tell Poskrëbyshev [his executive assistant] to summon the whole Politburo."[21]

The first day of the war was a monumental disaster for the Soviet Union, whose air force lost 1,200 aircraft that day alone. The Politburo met and agreed that a speech to the nation had to be made, but Stalin was too shattered to do it. For most of the day, he was also still in denial, believing the invasion might be Hitler's plot to get him to attack first. So the task fell to V. M. Molotov, the People's Commissar for Foreign Affairs and Stalin's closest toady. The announcement was more propaganda than news, claiming that only two hundred people were dead. It concluded with a stirring call, "Our cause is just. The enemy will be crushed. Victory will be ours." Many believe that Stalin wrote the final three sentences.[22]

Historians have hotly debated Stalin's role in his country's defense during the first week of the war. Nikita Khrushchev in his memoirs indicated that the Soviet leader went into shock and became dysfunctional. Khrushchev, though, was not in Moscow and based that opinion on hearsay. At the time, he was in Ukraine with Zhukov attempting to stop the Nazi invasion. The Kremlin kept logbooks of Stalin's meetings during that period, and those show he was active most of the time. He always had strange working habits, so his schedule was not unusual. On June 26, for example, he was at the Kremlin from 12:10 P.M. until just before midnight, meeting with twenty-eight different people. He normally arrived at the Kremlin at about 2:00 in the afternoon, pulling up in a small caravan. For security reasons, no one ever knew out of which one he would emerge. Then he worked late into the night.[23]

On June 27, Stalin arrived for work at 4:30 in the afternoon. He immediately summoned the Politburo and met with them until 9:30. Some military leaders also attended. On the agenda was what to do with the country's most valuable properties to protect them from the invasion rolling from the west. The four most precious items were the country's gold stocks, the Romanoff crown jewels, diamond holdings, and artworks of the famed Hermitage Museum in Leningrad. The group also discussed safeguarding industrial valuables and important raw materials, but decided that those four most important items had to be shipped far inland, safely away from the invaders.[24]

The Ural Mountains run through Russia from north to south, from the Arctic Ocean to the Ural River. This chain of mountains is generally considered the natural boundary between Europe and Asia. The highest peak at 6,217 feet is Mount Narodnaya. The Politburo plan was to evacuate the country's most precious properties to the foothills of the eastern side of the mountains, so they would be behind the Urals. The title of the Council of People's Commissars document No. 144: "On the Evacuation from Moscow of the State Deposits of Precious Metals, Precious Stones, the Diamond Fund of the U.S.S.R., and the Treasures of the Kremlin Armory."[25]

Item one in the order dictated that all the listed goods be sent to the cities of Sverdlovsk and Chelyabinsk. The directive did not state how, but they went by train. The first city was the administrative center of the Urals. It was then called Sverdlovsk, but today is known as Yekaterinburg. It was just shy of 900 miles due east of Moscow. The second destination was 120 miles south and slightly east. It was named Chelyabinsk. Both locations are on the eastern side of the Urals. The seven-point document also gave general instructions to several state agencies. The People's Commissariat of Forestry, for example, was to supply the wooden boxes to carry the valuables. The People's Commissariat of Communications Lines had to obtain the necessary trucks and trains. The People's Commissariat for Internal Affairs, the feared secret police, was assigned to get "the necessary number of employees and military guards for escorting and guarding the evacuated treasures." The final instruction to both the secret police and the Ministry of Finance was that the whole operation had to be completed "within three days." Nikolai Bulganin, the deputy prime minister and head of the State Bank of the Soviet Union, signed the document.

Since the Russian Revolution, the Soviet State Bank's holdings had been a closely guarded secret, and starting in the 1930s, the Soviet State Bank had been under the thumb of the country's secret service. The official gold holdings remained stable at 375 tons, which was the amount the country held to back its paper currency. The nation's total gold holdings, though, had recently reached nearly 3,000 tons. Most of that was to be sold to the west.

The Politburo gave overall responsibility for executing its directive concerning the nation's most precious items to Gokhran, the State Precious Metals and Gems Repository, which dated back to Peter the Great in the early eighteenth century. Its most important job before the Russian Revolution was to safeguard the czar's crown jewels, but it was also responsible for the safety of all the country's gold. Traditionally, valuables were stored in safety boxes that had three locks to which three different people held the keys. The head of the organization after the revolution was Yakov Jurovsky, who had also carried out the royal family's execution in July 1918. Following some charges of missing gold, the agency was put under the state secret service, which still had that job in June 1941. Gokhran's headquarters were immediately transferred to Sverdlovsk, and gold as well as diamonds were stored in facilities in the cities of Novsibirsk and Chelyabinsk.[26]

The first of three trains carrying 2,800 tons of gold left Moscow on June 30, and the last one departed on July 2. It took some 100 Pullman carriages to do the job. It left from the Northern railroad station and traveled along the Trans-Siberian railroad line. Soldiers from the Kremlin garrison took care of loading the gold into wooden crates. They were all numbered and recorded. Military guards traveled on each train. The first shipment proceeded without any stops until it reached the Kirov region about halfway to its destination. The commanding officer then halted the train after noticing cracks in the floor of one of the carriages, which undoubtedly was due to the weight of the gold. After the floor was repaired, the trip continued. It took four days to reach the final destination, where cadets from a military school helped with the unloading. Youngsters were selected because officials thought they were less likely than their parents to steal any gold. The last train arrived in Sverdlovsk the night of July 5.[27]

The Politburo was also determined to protect the Soviet Union's most revered relic: the embalmed body of the nation's founding father, Vladimir Lenin. General Nikolai K. Spiridonov, the commandant of the Kremlin, proposed to Lavrentiy Beria, a candidate member of the Politburo and head of the secret service, that it be sent "deep inside the country." Lenin's waxen figure had been on display for a decade in a darkened mausoleum in the center of Moscow's Red Square. Soviet citizens often waited for hours to file past the open casket and pay homage to the body. It was the communist version of making a pilgrimage to Mecca or Lourdes. Lenin had to be protected as much as the country's gold, diamonds, and paintings by being safely on the other side of the Urals. The Politburo discussed the issue on June 26 and decided to send it to a remote location where there were no military installations, which might be a target for Nazi bombers. The following day the Politburo took the decision to move the body. General Spiridonov suggested that several professors travel on the train "to take care of the body."[28]

On July 2, the Council of People's Commissars approved the evacuation of Lenin's body. Senior Major Dmitry Shadrin of the secret police was given the job of handling the details. Stalin signed the resolution. Another order, signed by General Spiridonov, specified that Lenin was going to Tyumen, a town 1,100 miles east of Moscow. The document also stated that the shipment included the leader's heart as well as the bullet lodged in his body in an assassination attempt. Lenin traveled aboard a super luxury Pullman-style train, pulled by Joseph Stalin Locomotives that had Stalin's name emblazed across the front. There were only three wagons, one for the body and the other two for scientists assigned to protect it and security guards. According to legend, Stalin came to see the body the night before it left and said solemnly, "Under Lenin's banner, we won the civil war. Under the Lenin banner, we will defeat this wily enemy."

The body left Moscow the next day aboard the climate-controlled train that was also equipped with special springs to avoid any damage to the corpse. No one except the operation commander knew the final destination. The honor contingent maintained its same mausoleum ritual of changing guards every two hours. The train arrived after a flawless voyage on the morning of July 7. The body was transferred that evening to an old school building in the center of town that had been turned into an agricultural college. The honor guards continued their duties.[29]

Soon after Lenin's body went east, Plant No. 171, the country's only facility for making chemically pure gold by turning imperfect metal into pure gold to be used in ingots, was also moved. Beria took personal charge of that operation. The plant was moved using several trains to the city of Novosibirsk, which is known as the capital of Siberia. Along with it traveled 600 engineers and workers to operate the facility. The first rail cars arrived on July 21. Eventually 118 railroad cars were needed to complete the job. Within months it was back in operation, producing 300 tons of gold annually.[30]

While the evacuations of the most valuable properties went smoothly, things were not going nearly as well on the battlefield. On June 27, the same day that the Politburo decided to ship the national treasure east and a week after the invasion had begun, an angry Stalin and his four closest aides, Beria, Molotov, Georgy Malenkov, who handled Communist Party personnel matters, and Anastas Mikoyan, the People's Commissar for External and Internal Trade, went to see generals Timoshenko and Zhukov. Minsk, a city of 300,000 and capital of Belarus, was on the brink of falling, which happened the following day. The strain of the last few days by then had gotten to Stalin, and he lashed out at Zhukov, "What kind of chief of staff panics as soon as the fighting starts, loses contact with his forces, represents nothing and commands nobody?" The general was so crushed that he left the room in tears. Stalin seemed only more disgusted and told Mikoyan, "Lenin left us a great state, and we've shitted it away,"[31] although Stalin himself was largely to blame for the lack of military preparedness. His massive purge of the military only three years before had left the army both weakened and dispirited. No one, though, dared mention that.

There are no records of Stalin making phone calls on June 29 or 30. He holed up at the Kuntsevo Dacha just outside Moscow. Kremlin aides telephoned and left messages to call back, but he never did. The dictator led a hermit's existence at the facility in the middle of a forest. He worked out of one room and slept on the sofa surrounded by telephones and books.

On June 30, Molotov called the other Politburo members to a meeting in his Kremlin office and proposed that a new state body be established to run the war effort. The group easily approved the measure. It would later be called the State Committee of Defense. The Presidium of Supreme Soviet of the U.S.S.R., the Council of People's Commissars of the U.S.S.R., and the Central Committee of the Communist Party of the Soviet Union all quickly approved it.[32]

The inner circle of communist leaders then left for Stalin's dacha, arriving there at 4:00 P.M. When they walked in, Stalin was slumped down in an armchair. Bulganin later said that his pockmarked face was haggard, and he appeared gloomy.[33] Mikoyan confirmed that in his memoirs. Stalin looked at his guests and almost in a mumble said, "Why have you come?" He may well have thought they were there to arrest him.

Speaking for the group, Molotov said they had decided that the government needed a new structure to concentrate power and run the war.

"Who should head it?" Stalin asked.

Molotov quickly responded, "You, of course."[34]

Stalin may have been testing them to see if a coup was in the works, or he may have been suffering from a deep depression. His hero Ivan the Terrible did that by pretending he was dying to see how his associates reacted. Then he had a miraculous recovery and punished the ones whose actions he didn't like. Stalin called his aides "blind kittens" and could have been handling them in the same way as the czar. In any case, he got the answer he wanted to hear.

The next day he was back at work in the Kremlin, and on July 3, he finally made his first radio address to his country since the invasion. He dropped some of his normal communist rhetoric in favor of a patriotic appeal to all of his country's citizens. The new approach was evident from the opening line when he called out to, "Comrades, citizens, brothers and sisters, men of our Army and Navy! I am addressing you, my friends!"[35] Russians called the historic battle against Napoleon the Patriotic War. Stalin named this one the Great Patriotic War.

The battle, though, continued to go badly. On July 11, 1941, the Wehrmacht crushed the Soviet Union's 19th Army near Vitebsk in Belarus and not far from Smolensk, where there was a branch of the Soviet central bank that had a small quantity of gold bars and coins as well as silver. Eight trucks of the treasure were sent along the Old Smolensk road toward the city of Vyazma, but it came under fire and only five of the trucks reached the village of Otnosovo. When a bomb hit one of the vehicles, it exploded and coins and currency flew through the air. It was clear that no one could go any further, so Soviet soldiers burned the currency and buried the coins. Two trucks, which contained four tons of bullion and a half-ton of jewelry, continued until they too were surrounded by Nazi troops.[36]

Stalin soon gained an unexpected ally in his battle against Hitler. Harry Hopkins, Roosevelt's international troubleshooter, had just finished a trip to London, where he had met with Churchill to work out details for funneling military aid to Britain. On July 25, Hopkins sent the president a cable saying, "I am wondering whether you would think it important and useful for me to go to Moscow . . . I think the stakes are so great that it should be done. Stalin would then know in an unmistakable way that we mean business on a long-term supply job."[37]

The president jumped at the suggestion and instructed Sumner Wells, the acting Secretary of State, to send a message to Stalin saying that the president was sending Hopkins to Moscow in order to talk "with you personally" about how the United States could help "the Soviet Union in its magnificent resistance against the treacherous aggression of Hitlerite Germany."[38]

After receiving the go-ahead from Washington, Hopkins asked Churchill to provide a Royal Air Force plane to take him to Stalin. In order to avoid the fighting on the continent, he left on a twenty-four hour flight to Archangel in the far north part of the Soviet Union. From there Hopkins took a four-hour flight to Moscow. A large delegation of Soviet officials greeted him there, but quickly ran into trouble with his name. They called him Garry Gopkins because the Russian letter "h" is pronounced like the English letter "g."[39]

Hopkins had two long meetings with Stalin that lasted more than five hours. Following Stalin's work habits, they began late in the afternoon. The American quickly picked up that he terrified everyone around him. They called him simply the *Vozhd*—the Boss. When Hopkins in the first session quickly asked what his country needed, Stalin rattled off a long list that included aircraft guns, one million rifles, machines guns, aviation fuel, aluminum for airplanes, and more. Stalin added that he was confident that his tanks were better than the best German ones. "Give us anti-aircraft guns and aluminum, and we can fight for three or four years." He scribbled on a piece of paper his top four priorities and gave it to Hopkins:

1. light anti-aircraft guns
2. aluminum for airplanes
3. 50-calibre machine guns
4. 30-caliber rifles

The aluminum impressed Hopkins, who thought that anyone asking for that was thinking long term and wouldn't be surrendering anytime soon. In a long report to Roosevelt, Hopkins wrote, "Mr. Stalin expressed repeatedly his confidence that the Russian lines would hold."[40]

At a second meeting the two men went over the details of shipping goods via ports such as Murmansk and Archangel in the far north rather than through either the Persian Gulf-Iran route or the Pacific Ocean-Vladivostok one. Stalin was particularly concerned about the latter, fearing that the Japanese would attack his ships. Murmansk, on the other hand, was ice-free all year long, and Archangel could be kept open with the help of icebreakers. At the end of the session the famed *Life* magazine photographer Margaret Bourke-White, who was on assignment in Moscow, popped in and took pictures of the two men. She moved around the office trying to capture the drama of the war moment and became intrigued by the Soviet dictator's eyes. She said they were the coldest she had ever seen.

Stalin's translator in the talks said after the war that Stalin always had a high regard for Hopkins because "he was the first who came after the terrible blow we got from the Germans."[41] At the suggestion of Hopkins, Roosevelt sent Averill Harriman to handle the follow-up work on getting military equipment to the Soviet Union. Even though the U.S. was still not yet formally at war, the Allied Big Three Powers to fight Hitler were in place.

Following the Hopkins visit to Moscow, Morgenthau's Treasury Department established its own contacts with the Soviet Union with the help of Harry Dexter White, the Treasury Secretary's top aide and a secret Soviet agent since the 1930s.[42] At his initiative on December 24, 1941, White met with Andrei Gromyko, who was the counsel of the Soviet embassy in Washington and would go on to be his country's longtime foreign minister. It is not certain, but likely, that Gromyko knew of White's ties to Moscow, although he did not mention that in the report of the meeting. The two had many more meetings during the war, and White was an open champion of the Soviets within the Roosevelt administration.[43]

Hitler and German military leaders were delighted with the initial success of their invasion. On July 3, 1941, General Franz Halder, chief of staff of the army, wrote in his diary, "On the whole, then, it may be said even now that the objective to shatter the bulk of the Russian army this side of the Dvina and Dnieper has been accomplished. It is thus probably no overstatement to say that the Russian Campaign has been won in the space of two weeks."[44]

Only two months later, however, the situation looked very different. On September 5, another German officer glumly wrote, "No victorious Blitzkrieg, no destruction of the Russian army, no disintegration of the Soviet Union." Later that month, Göring issued orders to German troops to "live off the land." In early November, General Guderian, the hero of the Nazi invasion of France, wrote his wife, "We have seriously underestimated the Russians, the extent of their country and the treachery of their climate. This is the revenge of reality."[45]

Never in warfare, though, had so many prisoners been taken so quickly. In the three battles in Smolensk, Uman, and Gomel between August and October 1941, the Wehrmacht captured two million Soviet soldiers. Following Göring's economic directive known as the Green Folder, the Germans instituted a policy of starving the local population. The three-pronged strategy was to kill 30 million people and eliminate the country's Jews with the Final Solution. Germans would then populate an empty, but fertile land.[46]

Total victory remained elusive for the Nazis, even though their troops by November 1941 had advanced 600 miles into Soviet territory. The Wehrmacht now controlled most of the industrialized part of the country and nearly half of the population in a region as large as Britain, France, Italy, and Spain combined. Hitler made another fatal mistake on August 21, when he told his commanders that the primary objective was not to capture Moscow, the heart of the nation's government as well as a major industrial complex, but to seize Crimea and the coal-mining region of the Ukraine, and then circle back to the capitol. By the end of September, the German military had devastated five more Soviet armies and taken 665,000 prisoners, but its forces had lost vital time in getting to Moscow. Field Marshal Fedor von Bock, the commander of Army Group Center, on October 2 resumed the drive toward Moscow. That was more than a month later than originally planned. The code name of the new offensive: Operation Typhoon. He had early success, but still lost some 35,000 men, 250 tanks and artillery pieces, and several hundred trucks. Fuel and ammunition supplies soon ran dangerously low. German forces traveled along the Mozhaisk Highway and were within 40 miles of the capital. The French had traveled that same road in 1812. Panic struck the capital, and people began evacuating the city. Most of the Soviet bureaucracy left for Kuibyshev 500 miles to the southeast. Martial law was declared. Stalin, though, remained in the capital after Zhukov assured him that it would not fall.[47]

On November 20, Bock moved his headquarters near the front lines. On December 2, German advance troops reached the Moscow suburb of Khimki, fourteen miles from the Kremlin. From there, German officers were able to see the spires of the Soviet capital through field glasses. That, however, marked the closest the army ever got to Moscow. The German High Command two days later decided that Army Group Center was "at present incapable of mounting a counterattack without bringing forward substantial reserves."[48]

Bock's staff began planning an orderly withdrawal. He angrily wrote in his diary, "We could have finished the enemy last summer.

We could have destroyed him completely. Last August, the road to Moscow was open. We could have entered the Bolshevik capital in triumph and in summery weather. The high military leadership of the Fatherland made a terrible mistake when it forced my army group to adopt a position of defense last August. Now all of us are paying for that mistake." If Hitler had stayed with his original date to launch Barbarossa, Bock would have arrived at the door of Moscow in mid-October rather than at the beginning of December, when General Winter was primed to launch his own attack.[49]

On 6 December and with the temperature -50 degrees Celsius, Zhukov's troops launched a huge counterattack. German troops retreated all along the Moscow front, destroying whatever equipment they could not salvage. The attack was slow but relentless. Several days later, the German High Command ordered a halt to all offensive operations. The Wehrmacht was losing twice as many men from frostbite as from enemy attacks.[50]

By mid-December, German forces had retreated more than 50 miles from the capital, and Hitler relieved Bock of his command. *Général Hiver* had once again defeated an invasion of Russia.

On December 7, 1941, the Japanese attacked Pearl Harbor, and the following day the American Congress declared war on the Empire of Japan. Four days after that, Hitler supported his Axis partner by declaring war on America. The European conflict was now a global conflict, and with America in the war, the balance of military might was now on the side of the Allies. In January, the Red Army launched a surprise counter offensive that ultimately broke the German front. The relentlessly fierce battles lasted until spring and have gone into history as the Rzhev Meat-Grinder. Nazi forces were pushed westward, with the army lines moving as fast as 25 miles a day. The tide of war had changed.

The traffic of arms going east and gold going west picked up sharply at the end of 1941 and during early 1942. In mid-November 1941 the Federal Reserve Bank in San Francisco sent to the New York Fed a message that it had just received $5.6 million in gold aboard the SS *Azerbaidjan*. On January 6, 1942, Morgenthau's

Treasury Department put out a press release announcing that it had purchased $20 million more gold from the Soviet Union.

Bullion continued to be necessary in getting weapons to the Soviets because there was a strong group in Congress that did not want Moscow included in the Lend-Lease program. They lobbied at first to restrict it only to Britain and Ireland. In the end Congress passed an extension to the law to include the Soviet Union. Although Lend-Lease had been signed into law in March 1941, countries still had to pay for weapons in gold or other assets until September of that year. The program was not fully in operation until the following July. The Soviet Union eventually received $11.3 billion in goods through Lend-Lease, second only to Britain.

The most vital Allied supply route to the Soviet Union during World War II was the 1,500-mile long Murmansk Run that Stalin had outlined to Hopkins. Located nearly one thousand miles north of Moscow on the Barents Sea, Murmansk was the Soviet Union's safest entry point. Convoys of thirty or more ships carried war hardware from ports in Scotland and Iceland to the beleaguered country that was now bearing the brunt of the Nazi offensive. The route had been busy before the Hopkins trip to Moscow, but shipments picked up sharply afterwards.

In October 1941, Morgenthau told his staff that the U.S. would be soon buying $30 million in Soviet gold as an advance payment for more military hardware. That later went up to $40 million. Moscow wanted to make sure that payment issues did not hold up the delivery of war goods. Allied ships, unfortunately, were floating targets for Nazi planes, ships, and submarines working out of military installations in Norway. Dozens of Allied vessels went to the bottom of the Arctic Sea. Enough got through, however, to keep a military pipeline to the Soviet Union open, and ultimately that turned the tide against the Nazis.[51]

Immediately after the Hopkins visit to Moscow, the Soviet tanker *Batumi* arrived in San Francisco with gold. In early 1942, the pace of Soviet shipments picked up sharply. Most of the gold arrived in the U.S., but some also went to Britain. The SS *Cairo* in February took twelve tons to London, which was then sent on to New York. The *HMS Kenya* took ten tons to the U.S.

On April 28, 1942, the convoy named PQ 11 was ready to depart from the Soviet harbor to return to Britain. Among the escorts was *HMS Edinburgh*, a 10,000-ton cruiser that was 613 feet long and had a maximum speed of 32.5 knots. It had two-dozen large guns and carried four aircraft on board. It was the largest and most powerful vessel in the group and had a crew of 850 men. Rear Admiral Stuart Bonham Carter was the convoy's commander. He had fought World War I at sea, and early in the new conflict had commanded the Third Battle Squadron that protected Atlantic convoys landing in Halifax.

The day before the *Edinburgh* was due to leave, nearly one hundred small wooden boxes arrived at dockside and were stored in a bomb room on the starboard side deep inside the vessel. The cargo was supposed to be top secret, but one of the containers fell on the deck during the loading and smashed open. Everyone now knew the secret. The ship was carrying 93 boxes containing 465 bars of gold. Total weight: five-and-a-half tons worth just over $6 million. The Soviets were sending it to the U.S. to buy weapons.[52]

The second day at sea, the *Edinburgh* was steaming along fifteen miles in front of the other convoy ships. At about noon, the Nazi sub *U-456* began following it. Captain Max-Martin Teichert, the commander of the German submarine, stalked the British ship for five hours and then gave the order to fire a torpedo. The shot hit the starboard side near the bomb room and the gold. The badly damaged *Edinburgh* headed back to Murmansk, which was now 250 miles away. The *HMS Foresight* gave it a tow, but the two vessels had to limp along at only four knots.

Captain Teichert called in three German destroyers to help him finish off the *Edinburgh*, and the group finally caught up with the British ship on May 2. In an ensuing battle the crippled vessel quickly sank a German ship, but then a Nazi destroyer scored a direct hit on the side of the *Edinburgh*, which miraculously continued limping along through the night. Rather than let the Germans capture the cruiser and its gold, Bonham Carter took the decision every commander dreads. He instructed the *Foresight* to fire a torpedo at the *Edinburgh* at a range of 1,500 yards. The ship and its bullion quickly sank, with the stern going down first. Some of the men aboard were lost, but others were picked up by other vessels. As the *Edinburgh* slipped into the freezing dark waters, British sailors on nearby vessels saluted. Treasure hunters in the 1980s found much of the gold from the sunken ship and brought it up.[53]

That catastrophic loss of gold, however, did not stop the Soviets from sending more. On April 10, 1942, the Convoy QP 10 was returning nearly empty after dropping off weapons. It was headed for Reykjavik, Iceland. The group included sixteen merchant ships and five destroyers. The British cruiser *Liverpool*, one of the escorts, carried twenty-six tons of gold. Shortly after the convoy departed, German U-boats and aircraft began attacking the Allied ships. The fierce encounter lasted three days. Four merchant vessels were sunk, and another had to return to the Soviet Union. The convoy's escorts, though, shot down six Nazi planes and damaged others. The *Liverpool* and its gold survived, and the treasure was soon on its way to the New York Federal Reserve. The Murmansk convoys continued to send a steady flow of gold to the U.S. On July 30, 1942, the Soviet vessel *SS Smolny* arrived in Nome, Alaska from Vladivostok with $3.7 million in gold. That was one of the last gold shipments, as finally Lend-Lease kicked in.[54]

As a result of their courageous efforts in moving the central bank gold and the Hermitage treasures to the far side of the Urals and because Soviet citizens held little personal gold, the Nazis captured only a small amount of gold in the Soviet Union. According to postwar studies done for the Nuremberg Trial, the country lost only a ton-and-a-half of gold bars and twenty-three tons of gold fragments and jewelry despite having suffered the lion's share of human casualties in World War II.[55]

Chapter Twenty-Four

MELMER GOLD

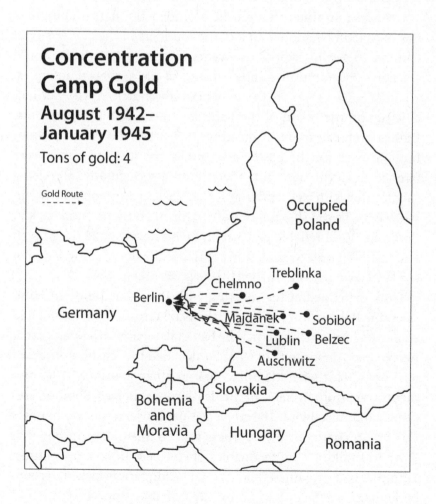

Concentration Camp Gold

**August 1942–
January 1945**

Tons of gold: 4

Gold Route

Occupied
Poland

Treblinka

Chelmno

Berlin

Germany

Majdanek

Sobibór

Lublin

Belzec

Auschwitz

Slovakia

Bohemia
and
Moravia

Hungary

Romania

GEORGE M. TABER

W alther Funk, the president of the Reichsbank in the summer of 1942 called Emil Puhl and asked him to come to his plush office at the Reichsbank building in Berlin. Puhl was the managing vice president and the person who ran the bank's day-to-day operations since Funk lacked the finance background for the job. He was more interested in the trappings of power than actually doing the work. Puhl was a bank careerist and a complex figure. A member of the Nazi party since 1934 and one of only two board members who had survived the purge when Hitler fired Schacht, Puhl climbed to a high level in Hitler's Reich.

At the same time, though, he attended the Berlin church of Pastor Martin Niemöller, one of the founders of the Confessional Church in Berlin, who spent years in the Sachsenhausen and Dachau concentration camps because of his anti-Nazi activities. Hjalmar Schacht was also a member of the church. As the German delegate on the board of the Bank for International Settlements, Puhl attended its monthly meetings in Switzerland. He sometimes brought back for the pastor new books about religion that were banned in Germany. While there, Puhl also regularly attended a cabaret that satirized Hitler and the Nazis. Few people in Berlin knew what he did in Basel outside of his BIS business, and back in Berlin he was a reliable civil servant who never spoke out of turn and followed orders. He left his ethics at the door and was one of the key Germans who made Hitler's government work.[1]

Funk explained at the meeting with Puhl that Heinrich Himmler, the Reichsführer of the SS, the Nazi terror organization, had contacted him and asked that the bank take charge of valuables that people had "deposited" in what Funk called the "eastern occupied territories." He then told Puhl to "ask no other questions." The shipments were from inmates in the death camps Bełżec, Sobibór, Treblinka and Auschwitz. The conversation between the two bankers was full of euphemisms, but there was no misunderstanding that Funk was talking about valuables of concentration camp victims. Himmler had explained that his own headquarters lacked a secure enough storage facility to house the valuable property. Funk told

Puhl that the material had to be handled with utmost secrecy. Nothing they were discussing was to be put on paper. Funk told him to work out the details with Oswald Pohl, the head of the economics department of the SS and also a concentration camp inspector. Funk said that Himmler and Finance Minister Lutz Schwerin von Krosigk had already reached an agreement on the matter.[2]

Funk and Himmler were now leaving the job of handling the concentration camp valuables to their deputies, and Puhl could expect to receive a phone call from his counterpart in the SS before long. The vice president immediately tried to get out of taking the war booty, calling it "inconvenient" and adding that he didn't know the consequences of such action. Funk assured him that there would be only a few shipments. In the end, the two men agreed that the Reichsbank would make its services available to the SS. They also decided that SS members would deliver and unpack the material delivered to the bank. The final admonition was that no one was to be told the origin of the goods. Only a dozen or so Reichsbank officials ever knew about the operation.

Puhl later met with SS Brigade-Führer Karl Hermann Frank and Obergruppenführer Karl Wolff, both high ranking SS officers, to work out the details of the shipments, and all agreed to handle everything verbally and to put nothing in writing. Puhl informed Bank Director Frommknecht, the member of the board in charge of the vault, who called in Albert Thoms, the manager of the Precious Metals Department and the person who would be running the day-to-day operations. Frommknecht explained that the SS would soon be bringing him deliveries, again emphasizing that they came from the "eastern occupied territories."

The two men then went to see Puhl, who said that the matter was to be kept "absolutely secret" and that the delivery would include several different types of valuables including jewelry. Puhl warned Thoms that if anyone ever asked him about it, he should not discuss the subject. Thoms was given the names of two SS officers whom he should contact if he had any questions about the upcoming deliveries.

Thoms protested that he would need to use outside experts to evaluate the material they were talking about, but Puhl said that should be handled some other way. The deputy suggested that the jewelry be dealt with exactly as the bank had treated earlier confiscated Jewish property in the aftermath of *Kristallnacht* in 1938 by sending it to the Municipal Pawn Shop in Berlin, which would then later forward a payment to the bank. Puhl accepted the proposal.[3]

After going back to his office, Thoms called one of the names he had been given and learned that in two weeks SS Hauptsstrumführer Bruno Melmer would deliver the first shipment. The SS had already decided that it would be better if he arrived in civilian clothes, although other soldiers in uniform would accompany him to help move the valuables expeditiously. Bank officials gave the name Melmer to all the deliveries, and a tag with that word was put on each container the SS delivered. Thoms and his staff followed orders and did not put the letters "SS" anywhere in the bank's books.

The first shipment arrived on August 26, and the contents were immediately distributed to various bank departments. The currency and stock certificates went to the currency group, while the jewelry and gold coins stayed in the Precious Metals Department. The items generally arrived in battered suitcases, although some were also in canvas bags. Melmer provided his own list of the contents at each delivery, and received a receipt for the goods when he left. Unloading the first shipment took four days, but the second one only two.

It had been agreed between the bank and the SS that the proceeds of shipments would be deposited in a new SS account at the German Finance Ministry. The code name for the account was Max Heiliger. There was no such person, and it is an example of SS humor since in German the surname means "Holy One." Max is a common German first name.

The deliveries were erratic. There was one in August 1942, then three in September and back to one in November. In March 1944, there were four shipments.[4] The concentration camp suitcases contained a wide variety of items. One listed simply as Case 71, for example, held 1,536 bracelets made out of gold, silver, and lacquer. In another there were 2,656 gold watchcases. In a third was Polish currency totaling 850,300 zloty. Some contained hundreds of pieces of silverware. Teeth fillings were separated into gold and silver containers, and in one of the early suitcases there was twenty-two pounds of dental silver. The first gold teeth appeared in the November 1942 delivery. Eighteen bags contained bars of silver and gold. There were also gold cufflinks, tiaras, silk stockings, and Passover cups, as well as pearl necklaces. In short, the cases contained anything people who had been told they were being relocated to a new place would have wanted to take with them.

Thoms passed along as much of the Melmer deliveries as he could to other organizations, without telling them the origin of the goods. Jewelry went to the Municipal Pawn Shop in Berlin, as he had suggested. Items in good condition, such as gold bars, were sent directly to the Prussian Mint, where they were melted and given predated identification numbers to hide their original identity. Boxes of gold wedding rings also went to the Prussian Mint. Lower quality gold from other jewelry went to Degussa, a German precious metal company, which smelted it into higher-quality bars. Several Reichsbank officials were charged with handling other specific goods.[5]

After the first shipment arrived at the Reichsbank, Oswald Pohl of the SS called Emil Puhl and asked him if he knew about the deliveries. The banker said yes, but then added that he did not want to talk with him about it on the phone. He asked the SS officer to come to his office so they could discuss the matter in person. Pohl arrived with an assistant and said that he already had a large quantity of jewelry in Berlin and wondered if he could bring it to the bank. Puhl replied that he would try to arrange it. After the war, the bank managing vice president told interrogators that he informed the board of directors about the first shipment at its next meeting. No one raised any objections to this new work with the SS.[6] Bruno Melmer personally delivered all of them until late in the war, when Sturmführer Furch took over the job.

In early 1943, some of the packages began carrying stamps identifying them as Lublin or Auschwitz. The Reichsbank staff knew that those were the names of death camps. Puhl rarely visited Thoms and his operation, but on one occasion Funk had a dinner for Oswald Pohl, the Himmler aide. Before they ate, Emil Puhl took the concentration camp inspector down to the cellar vaults so that he could see the suitcases of looted valuables that his men were bringing to the bank.[7] After a few months of deliveries, Puhl telephoned Thoms and asked him how the operation was going. The vice president said that he thought they would soon be over. Thoms replied that it looked to him like they were increasing.

When the Allied bombing of Berlin became devastating and targeted, it was more and more difficult to handle the shipments of prison camp gold and other valuables. Piles of unopened suitcases began to stack up in the Reichsbank basement. Degussa's main facilities were destroyed by Allied attacks in late 1944, and it could no longer smelt gold.

Thoms told American interrogators that the total value of all of the deliveries was about ten million marks, but he was likely underestimating it. At the official 1940 dollar-mark exchange rate of 2.5, that would have been the equivalent of $4 million. Bernstein calculated the Melmer proceeds from the deliveries at $10 million. While most of the bullion was in small amounts, 125 pounds came in the form of bars. Later post-war estimates ranged between $2.5 million and $5.0 million, but no one knows for certain. In addition, there were 6,427 gold coins. Those two categories alone amount to nearly eleven tons. The theft of valuables from people on their way to death camps ranks among the most despicable of the many Nazi atrocities. The seventy-sixth and last Melmer delivery arrived at the Reichsbank on January 27, 1945.[8]

Eisenhower was not comfortable with money and gold issues, but he had someone to handle them for him. In the summer of 1942, General Eisenhower sent Secretary of War Henry L. Stimson a message saying that he would need an expert to handle financial and monetary issues when American armies began invading Nazi-held parts of North Africa and Europe. Stimson picked up the phone and asked Morgenthau if he had someone for Eisenhower.

The Secretary of the Treasury replied that Bernie Bernstein, his assistant general counsel, was just the man. Morgenthau thought he had both the youth and the experience needed for the obviously demanding job. Bernstein immediately received the rank of Lt. Colonel and was soon working for Eisenhower in London. When allied forces soon invaded North Africa and Italy, Bernstein handled delicate occupation issues such as local currency values and military script.

In a May 8, 1945 report entitled "SS Loot and the Reichsbank," Bernstein estimated the value of the Melmer deposits to be $14.5 million.[9] In his conclusion he wrote: "The sums estimated by Thoms appear to be an understatement for the loot handled by the Reichsbank since 1942. Certainly they cannot begin to represent the total extent of the operations of the SS economic department, which for 12 years has disposed of the personal and household valuables of millions of racial and political victims of the calculated Nazi policy of extermination."[10]

In Bernstein's May 1945 monthly report to General Clay, he updated his estimate on the amount of Melmer gold deposited at the Reichsbank. This was based on further interrogations of Albert Thoms and other bank officials. A 1998 study by William Z. Slany, a U.S. State Department historian who did extensive work on the topic for the 1997 London Gold Conference, estimated the amount of looted SS bullion at $4.6 million.[11]

There is no doubt that some gold taken from concentration-camp victims has found its way into bars and today sits in the world's central banks vaults, probably including those of the New York Federal Reserve. Several ingots of Melmer gold were sold to Switzerland and then moved into the traffic of central bank bullion.[12] It is impossible, though, to determine how much. When gold is melted down and resmelted, it loses all identification. It would be like trying to identify a grain of wheat in a loaf of bread.

Chapter Twenty-Five

DRAGGING EVERYTHING OUT ITALIAN STYLE

A merican and British troops scrambled ashore on the island of Sicily on July 10, 1943 to begin the British and American attempt to recapture the European mainland. Churchill, who desperately wanted to go on the offensive, called the area the continent's "soft underbelly." Stalin had also been pressing the Americans to launch an offensive to relieve his troops on the eastern front. Only nine days later, the American air force bombed Rome, targeting a steel factory, a freight yard, and the main airport. Those blows ended Benito Mussolini's final hold on the Italian people. The country's Grand Council of Fascism, the party's ruling body, on July 25 voted no confidence in him and asked King Victor Emmanuel to resume his full constitutional powers as leader of the country. Later that day, the king ordered Il Duce arrested. Following the fall of the Italian leader, the Nazis quickly moved ten divisions into Italy to shore up the country in anticipation of an Allied invasion of the mainland.[1]

Italian military units moved Il Duce around the country after his arrest and eventually imprisoned him in the Campo Imperatore Hotel at Gran Sasso d'Italia in the Apennine Mountains about eighty miles north of Rome. He did not stay there long. On September 12, SS Lt. Colonel Otto Skorzeny led a Nazi commando unit in gliders that landed near the resort and without firing a single shot overwhelmed 200 *carabinieri* guards. Skorzeny told Mussolini, "The Führer has sent me to set you free!" Mussolini replied: "I knew that my friend would not forsake me!"[2]

The Germans immediately took Mussolini to Berlin, where Hitler was appalled by his one-time mentor's physical and emotional deterioration. Nonetheless, the Führer made him the leader of a new puppet state called the Italian Social Republic. Its nominal capital was Rome, but that was too close to the invading forces so it operated out of the town of Salò on Lake Garda in northern Italy. Mussolini was now the total tool of Hitler.

Early in the war, the Italian fascist government had undertaken a study to find a central location in the country where its bullion could be easily protected. At the time it was located at the *Banca d'Italia* (Bank of Italy) headquarters in Rome at the Palazzo Koch, a palace on Via Nazionale. Mussolini selected the small town of L'Aquila, which was in a narrow valley about sixty miles northeast of Rome. The government began printing paper currency there, but the gold was never moved. With the war going badly for the Italian fascists, officials decided to look for another location. The country's finance minister argued that it should go to the mountainous Trentino-Alto Adige region north of Venice. Before that could be accomplished, however, Mussolini was ousted. Bank governor Vincenzo Azzolini suggested distributing the bullion among several cities around the country to reduce the risk that the Allies would capture it intact. Marshal Pietro Badoglio, the head of the military, wanted it sent to an Italian bank near the Swiss border, but that too was nixed.[3]

At a meeting of the Bank of Italy's board on July 28, Azzolini pushed through a plan to move the bullion out of Rome, although the destination was still not clear. Less than two weeks later on August 10, 1943, the banker met with General Badoglio to work out the details. The actual creation of the plan went slowly. At one point in September, there was even a proposal to ship the bullion to Sardinia, which the British and Americans had already liberated. Finally the general told Azzolini that he and other bank officials should work out a plan to move it north by train.

Four days later, the Italian government declared Rome to be an open city in hopes of avoiding Allied air attacks. The country was still nominally in the hands of Italian Fascists, but the Germans in early September took over both the capital and the central part of the nation. Hitler named Rudolf Rahn, a career foreign service officer who had just been appointed ambassador, to take up the new post of plenipotentiary in Italy. The Germans were now effectively running the country, and Rahn was the new boss.

Four German organizations were soon anxiously looking to get their hands on the Italian gold: Himmler's SS, Hermann Göring's Four Year Plan, Joachim von Ribbentrop's Foreign Office, and Walther Funk's Reichsbank. Ribbentrop had not previously been a major player in confiscating central bank gold, but this time he demanded to be part of the action because he was desperately looking for ways to finance his spying operations abroad. His people operated all over Europe and the Middle East under the cloak of diplomacy, and bullion was the coin of the realm for their operations.

Ribbentrop became the strongest of the four because his man Rahn was the top official on the ground in Italy. The Reichsbank's Funk had little clout in Berlin; his role by then was largely technical and dealt with gold shipments. Göring, whose influence had slipped badly after his failure to defeat Britain in the summer of 1940, wanted to ship the bullion immediately to Berlin, where it would reside at the Reichsbank but be under his control. Himmler also tried to get into the action, but was excluded. Rahn successfully argued that the Germans could not risk the total collapse of the Italian economy and the chaos that might ensue if the bullion were moved to Germany. He also recognized that he would be more powerful if the treasure remained under his control in Italy.

The leaders of the Italian Social Republic and the Germans easily agreed that their immediate priority was to get the bullion out of Rome and up to northern Italy, where it would be far from invading Allied forces. An exception was made, though, for 2.3 tons of Albanian gold, which the Italians had captured during their invasion of that country in April 1939. It had simply been sitting in the Italian central bank vaults since then. That was immediately packed up into fifty cases and sent to Berlin on September 17, 1943.[4]

The Nazis were not the only ones with their eyes on the Italian gold. The Bank for International Settlements also closely monitored the situation. Officials there were nervous about the bullion because that was a guarantee for their investments in Italian financial markets. Shortly after the BIS began operations in 1930, it made investments in member countries including Italy. Those were backed by Swiss gold francs, and at the beginning of World War II were valued at 54.5 million Swiss gold francs or $18 million. The bank was now anxious to protect its investment in Italy.[5]

BIS boss Thomas McKittrick on September 9, sent Azzolini, who was an ex-officio BIS board member as well as head of the Italian central bank, a message about his organization's concerns. McKittrick followed that up the next month with a formal demand that the Bank of Italy immediately ship three tons of gold to the BIS. He wrote that this was being done because of Italy's "uncertain future." The Basel institution actually just wanted to make sure the bullion didn't fall into either Allied or Axis hands. Raffaele Pilotti, a top BIS official and also an Italian, traveled to Rome to discuss the issue with Azzolini, who was outraged at the request. He protested that it was an insult and had never been asked of any other BIS member. Gradually, though, the Italian banker began to realize that if he did not agree to the offer, all of Italy's bullion would end up in Berlin. It was better to keep at least some in a different secure place.[6]

Anticipating that the Nazis would soon be coming for the Italian gold, Niccolò Introno, the Italian bank's deputy director general, came up with an ingenious plan to protect at least some of it. He proposed to Azzolini in the middle of September 1943 that they hide the bullion by constructing a false wall in the bank's underground vault. They could build it in such a way that there would be a new entry into the vault that would camouflage the change. In another ruse, bank officials would backdate documents to show that they had sent bullion to Potenza, a town in southern Italy that was under heavy bombing and would probably soon be in Allied hands.

Azzolini approved the plan, but ruled that only half of the gold should be placed behind the false wall. Bullion was then moved into the hidden area, and masons started building the dummy wall, which was completed during the night of September 19. Only a few hours after work was completed, Ambassador Rahn sent Azzolini the official document ordering that the country's gold be moved immediately to northern Italy. The Nazis dictated that it had to be turned over to their representatives, who would have control of it.[7]

At about the same time, Azzolini learned that the Germans had captured a hoard of Italian government records, and he feared that they had probably learned the size and location of the country's gold holdings. Potenza still remained under fascist control, and it would be easy to check whether gold was stored there, as they were planning to claim. On the morning of September 20, Azzolini met with Finance Minister Etorre Combi, who told him the Nazis had said that some of the gold had be sent to Berlin immediately, and he had only until 3:00 P.M. to reply. If the bank did not agree, the Germans would simply seize it. Stalling was no longer an option, and Azzolini decided the ploy of the hidden wall was perhaps too clever by half. He ordered the just-finished wall torn down.

The Bank of Italy's never-executed trick may have been the inspiration for Robert Crichton's post-war novel *The Secret of Santa Vittoria*, in which Italian peasants hide millions of bottles of wine in a communal village cellar in order to keep it out of Nazi hands. The book was made into a movie with the same name that starred Anthony Quinn.

In the hectic days after the fall of Mussolini, the Italian Central Bank sent small amounts of gold to its branch offices around Italy and to the country's colonial outposts in Benghazi, Rhodes, and Addis Ababa. Those faced a variety of fates. The Bologna branch received just over one hundred pounds, but there are no records of what happened to it after it arrived. It simply vanished. The Milan office attempted to protect more than a half-ton of bullion by producing documents showing it now belonged to various groups or institutions. During the night of September 7-8, 1943, two lots were hidden in a well, and records were forged to show that it had been shipped to Turin. That gold also simply disappeared.[8]

A German military unit finally arrived at the Bank of Italy office early in the afternoon of September 20, with orders to move the gold north by air the next day. A representative of the Reichsbank was to accompany it. Leading the group was Lt. Colonel Herbert Kappler, the SS officer who had rescued Mussolini. The Italians again stalled, and Azzolini insisted that it was much safer to send it by train and that Italians should guard it. His unspoken fear was that if it left by air, the plane could well end up landing in Berlin. The Germans eventually agreed, but insisted that they provide security. Then seemingly just to show who was boss, the Germans the next day sent five tons by air. Between September 22 and 28, 119 tons of gold left Rome on two trains, and were immediately deposited in the vault of the Bank of Italy office in Milan. The shipment included twenty-three tons from countries Mussolini had invaded: eight tons from the National Bank of Yugoslavia, fourteen tons from Vichy France, and one-third of a ton from Greece.[9]

Italians still legally had custody of all the treasure in Milan, but Germans effectively controlled it and would determine its fate. Azzolini and the other Italian officials continued to drag their heels as much as they could about further shipments. Once all the gold had arrived safely, the Germans posted guards outside the vaults where it was stored. After Italian officials protested, the soldiers left but the Nazis received three keys to the storage room.

Always anxious to demonstrate his power, Göring again got back into the action. He demanded that the gold be sent from Milan to a location closer to Germany, arguing that Milan was too vulnerable to Allied bombing. Ribbentrop eventually agreed that it move again on the condition that it remain under the authority of his man Rahn. The Reichsbank at one point got into the debate on the side of Azzolini, who continued his bureaucratic battles to keep it from being moved. He now argued that the Allies could still bomb it even if they moved it into the Alps, and proposed just leaving it in Milan. The Germans by now, though, paid no attention to the Italian central banker.[10]

On October 18, less than three weeks after the bullion arrived in Milan, Göring proposed shipping it to the village of Franzensfeste. It was in the Italian Alps area of Trentino-Alto Adige, or as the Germans called it Südtirol, near the Brenner Pass that led to German-occupied Austria. One of Europe's mightiest fortresses was located there.

Napoleon in 1805 invaded Austria, and Prince Klemens von Metternich, that country's long-time foreign minister, always feared a repeat of the humiliation. The Brenner Pass is the lowest mountain route across the Austrian Alps, and thus the most natural invasion road. So shortly after the Napoleonic wars ended in 1815, Metternich proposed building a fortress that could stop a future attack. The Hapsburg Empire began construction on the Franzensfeste Fortress on June 17, 1833, and Emperor Ferdinand I of Austria inaugurated it on August 18, 1838. A railroad link was built in 1867. The area became part of Italy after World War I, and it became known by its Italian name Fortezza.

The structure consisted of massive bunkers and extensive tunnels, where weapons, ammunition, or anything precious could be safely stored. At the entrance were three twelve-foot-tall pillars carved out of granite. Each weighed eighteen tons. Behind the first entrance was a second door built just as solidly. A Hapsburg double-headed eagle looked down menacingly on the courtyard below. One hundred yards from the tunnel entrance stood a small chapel with a steeple. Visitors could reach the fort only via a winding mile-long road that was easily defended. Riflemen had a 360° view of anyone daring to climb the mountainsides. In short, it was the perfect place to store a country's gold.[11]

Berlin went through the formality of asking Mussolini for permission to ship the gold there, and he quickly agreed. A contingent of Germans officials then went from Berlin to Fortezza to examine the facility. They recommended a few minor changes to make it even safer, such as more lighting and a new reinforced wall inside with an iron trellis.[12]

On December 13, Finance Minister Domenico Pellegrini Giampietro sent Azzolini a terse order: "According to the agreement reached by the German government and the Italian government, the gold transferred to Milan and deposited there will now be transported to another location in northern Italy in the province of Bolzano, using the same methods that were used in the transfer from Rome to Milan." Pretending not to understand the direct command, Azzolini responded that there were no facilities in the city of Bolzano where the gold could be stored. When the minister received that message, he picked up the phone and ordered him to ship the bullion, saying sternly, "You must know that if you do not do this, they will seize the gold and take it to Germany." Fortezza was not an ideal location from the point of view of the Italians, but it was still better than having it in Berlin. On the morning of December 16, the gold left Milan by train. Both SS guards and Italian central bank officials accompanied it.[13]

The bullion arrived at its destination that night. According to documents that arrived with it, there were 175 barrels and 20 bags. A group of German soldiers were enlisted to move it into the fortress, but that became too much heavy lifting for them. Fifty Russian prisoners-of-war then took over the job. The gold was stored in rough-hewn caves at the bottom of the towering cliffs. Due to high humidity in the caves, some of the bags were soon damaged.

The Berlin contingent that had overseen the transfer departed at the end of the following day, but twenty-six German soldiers remained at the fortress to guard the treasure. Two Bank of Italy officials also took up residence.

The Germans originally demanded that no Italians have anything to do with the Fortezza gold, but they later allowed bank people to monitor the comings and goings into the vault. That did not change the reality that the bullion, which had been on Italian territory while in Rome or Milan, was now officially in Germany, where the Italians had no authority. The Alpenvorland unit of the Wehrmacht controlled that part of the Austrian Alps now and now had ultimate control of Italy's gold.

The bullion had hardly arrived in Fortezza before Göring, Ribbentrop and Funk were again fighting over it. The first to act this time was the Reichsbank's Funk, whose deputy, Puhl, wanted to help out his old BIS colleague Azzolini. In January 1944, the two central bankers met in Moltrasio on Lake Como, where the Bank of Italy now had its headquarters. Paul Hechler, the top German official at the BIS, put together the plan to ship some of the Italian bullion to Switzerland. Azzolini's attitude was now totally different than it had been to the first BIS proposal just after the fall of Mussolini. He realized that if the gold did not go to the bank, it would find its way to Berlin. The two men thus quickly worked out details for a shipment to Basel.[14]

On April 20, four train cars carrying 23.4 tons of gold left Fortezza. It consisted of 10.8 tons for the Swiss National Bank in Bern, and 12.6 tons that would be dropped off in Basel at the BIS. Five days later, the Italian Central Bank transferred three more tons to the BIS, bringing the total there to 15.8 tons. Azzolini would later claim that he arranged the payments to protect his country's reputation for fulfilling its legitimate obligations and to guard its international reputation. The deal, though, would not have been done if it had not satisfied the interests of the Nazis, the Italian Fascists, and the BIS. It also showed that the first priority of any central banker is to his institution.[15]

Plenty of Italian gold still remained in Fortezza, and Göring, as head of the Four Year Plan, insisted he needed money for "common war operations with Italy," while the foreign minister said he needed it for "particularly secret operations of the ministry of foreign affairs." In early January 1944, Göring proposed giving the Italian Social Republic 50 million Reichsmark ($20 million) in exchange for part of the gold. Negotiations soon began, with Mussolini and his Finance Minister Domenico Pellegrini Giampietro representing the Italian side. The Bank of Italy had no role in the talks and was not even informed that they were taking place.

An agreement was reached on February 5. Rahn signed it for the German side, while Stefiono Mussolini, the secretary general of foreign affairs, and Pelligrini Giampetro, the finance minister, endorsed it for the Italian Social Republic. The accord made "the entire amount of gold owned by the Bank of Italy available to the Ambassador and Plenipotentiary of Greater Germany in Italy." The seventy-one tons of Italian gold was now officially in the hands of Rahn. Under a new diplomatic agreement, gold worth 141 million Reichsmark ($31.3 million), just under half the total amount, was immediately handed over to Berlin as a "contribution to the joint war effort." In addition, gold valued at 250 million lira ($12.5 million) was given in "restitution" for the Yugoslav gold, 100 million lira ($3.3 million) went to the German foreign ministry to pay for its undercover operations abroad, and 50 million lira ($2.5 million) was used to settle a Nazi claim against the Italian state. Azzolini did not even learn of the agreement until three weeks after it was signed. The 50.5 tons of gold in 175 sealed boxes and 435 sealed bags left Fortezza on February 29 and arrived in Berlin three days later.[16]

When German officials inspected the Fortezza gold, their calculations turned out to be significantly lower than the Italy's because various boxes or bags did not contain as much metal as was listed. The total shipment was nearly a ton short. The bulk of the gold was nonetheless sent immediately to the Reichsbank since it still had the safest vaults in Berlin. One hundred thirty-five sacks with a combined weight of just over eight metric tons, though, were given directly to the foreign ministry. Ribbentrop was so anxious to get his gold that he sent one of his own officials to meet the train at the Berlin station. He also wanted to make sure he got coins denominated in dollars, francs, and other currencies, which would be easy for foreign ministry agents to use in their secret operations. Ribbentrop also took a few bars.

Shipping the last Italian gold to Berlin dragged on for many months. Some Italian officials such as Finance Minister Pellegrini Giampietro were willing to hand over the remaining bullion. Others, including Azzolini, were now trying to separate themselves from the gold deliveries to Berlin and from Mussolini's republic, which seemed to be on the losing side of the war. In May 1944, the Nazis were back demanding that 21.5 metric tons still stored in Fortezza be shipped to Berlin. This time the Reichsbank's Maximilian Bernhuber handled the negotiations for the Germans, while Azzolini opened them for the Italians. Both he and his successor in the gold talks, Giovanni Orgera, procrastinated, but finally the irate Finance Minister Pellegrini Giampietro ordered the central bank to hand over the bullion.

On October 21, 1944, the Italians shipped to Berlin 153 barrels and 53 bags of gold coins, weighing in at 21.5 tons. It arrived four days later. That brought the total amount sent in two consignments to 71 tons, but that was still a ton less than the amount recorded by the Bank of Italy. The Germans were beginning to notice that Italian deliveries were always a little lighter than the declared weight, which they passed off as simply Latin inefficiency. From the second shipment, 1,607 bars were delivered to the Prussian Mint and resmelted into bars that were given German identification marks. Another 141 were sent to the Degussa company for refining and made into bars. In total, the Bank of Italy sent 69.3 tons of its own gold to Berlin, in addition to 8.3 tons of Yugoslav bullion and 6.6 that belonged to the Bank of France.[17]

Following the latest shipments to Germany, there still remained in Fortezza 153 boxes and 55 sacks totaling 25 tons of gold. When American army forces liberated the area in the spring of 1945, they discovered it and turned it over to the Bank of Italy.[18]

While the shipments were being made, Azzolini had been looking out for himself. He was able to persuade officials of both Germany and the Italian Social Republic to let him go to Rome, but then he never returned north. Rome fell to the Allies on June 5, 1944, and only two days later Italian newspapers began a campaign against him because of his role during the war. On July 10, the British interrogated him and removed him from his position at the Bank of Italy. He was also placed under house arrest. The new Italian government later charged him with collaborating with the enemy and turning the country's gold reserves over to the Nazis. While in jail for his trial, he worked as the prison librarian. During all that time, the Reichsbank's Puhl and the staff of the Bank for International Settlements exchanged messages lamenting his treatment and trying to figure out how to help their old friend.[19]

Azzolini's trial took place in three sessions between October 9 and 14, 1944. The state demanded the death penalty, but judges instead gave him thirty years in jail and required him to pay back the Bank of Italy for the losses it had suffered in its branches, which was totally unrealistic. The sentence accused him of being "significantly docile and servile toward the Nazi-fascist regime and not doing anything to save the gold when it was still possible to do so." He remained in jail until September 1946, when the court considered a plea for amnesty. Judges that time annulled the conviction, saying that he should "cease to be condemned and penalized further." The judges even praised him, writing, "All the behavior of Azzolini revealed not a willingness to favor the gold plundering by the Germans, but actually an opposing willingness to resist them, using all the shrewdness that the time and the circumstances allowed him to use."[20]

While the Nazi regime was concentrating on capturing the Bank of Italy's gold, the Nazi SS went after smaller amounts held by Rome's 12,000 Jews. SS Lt. Colonel Herbert Kappler on September 26, 1944 ordered two of the community's elders to collect 50 kilos of gold within thirty-six hours. He warned them that if they failed, he would arrest two hundred Jews and send them to the Russian front. Roman Jews reached into their family treasures and also turned in gold from synagogues. When Pope Pius XII heard about the demand, he authorized Catholic churches to make loans of gold to the Jews to help them reach their absurdly high quota. The bullion was quickly collected, although the elders said they were having difficulty raising the amount out of fear that if they said they had it, the Germans would simply ask for more. They ultimately assembled 80 kilos but delivered only 50.3, holding back the rest for later use. An SS Captain at first incorrectly weighed the metal and then lashed at the Jews for not turning over enough. A second weighing showed that they had slightly more than demanded.[21]

The gold was shipped to SS headquarters in Berlin addressed to SS General Ernst Kaltenbrunner, Himmler's deputy. Kappler included with it a letter reminding the general of the plan to use Jews in Rome as laborers. He received back a strong rebuke saying that the Nazi objective was "the immediate and thorough eradication of the Jews in Italy." A roundup soon followed. At the end of the war, Allied soldiers found the crate of Jewish gold from Rome still unopened in Kaltenbrunner's office.[22]

Chapter Twenty-Six

PARTNERS IN GOLD

Nazi Partners
1938–1945
Value of Nazi gold shipped: $779 million

Gold Route
-------->

Finland

Norway

Stockholm

Sweden
$59.7 million

Estonia

Latvia

Denmark

Lithuania

East Prussia

Soviet Union

Holland

Germany

Berlin

Poland

Atlantic Ocean

Belgium

Luxembourg

France

Bohemia and Moravia

Slovakia

Hungary

Romania
$52.2 million

Basel
Bern

Switzerland
Swiss National Bank
$389.2 million
Swiss Commercial Banks
$61.1 million
BIS: $21.5 million

Yugoslavia

Bucharest

Black Sea

Portugal
$43-49 million

Italy

Bulgaria

Albania

Madrid

Spain
$140 million

Lisbon

Greece

Ankara

Turkey
$10-15 million

Algeria

Tunisia

Mediterranean Sea

Aegean Sea

Morocco

Chapter Twenty-Six

PARTNERS IN GOLD

W ithout the help of a few key co-conspirators, the gold the Nazi regime seized from invaded countries would have simply sat untouched and gathering dust in the Reichsbank vaults. It would not have played a major role in helping Hitler achieve his war objectives. Because of those partners, however, Germany was able to turn the stolen bullion into an important tool for waging World War II. A few nominally neutral countries were willing to turn stolen bullion into currencies that could be used to buy crucial war materiel. Without Romanian oil, Portuguese and Spanish tungsten, Turkish chromium, Swedish iron ore, and a few other items, along with key countries such as Switzerland that were willing to facilitate the sales, the German war machine would have ground to a halt long before May 1945. German leaders at the apogee of their power in 1941 were confident that they would continue conquering countries and eventually hold most of the world's gold. The Reichsbank's Walther Funk in a speech in Rome on October 20, 1940, said categorically, "By the end of the war, the gold which we need will be ours."[1]

The most important Nazi partner was Switzerland, which accepted a large amount of stolen gold. American officials with access to Reichsbank documents, calculated after the conflict was over that at least $398 million of the $579 million the Nazis stole ended up in Switzerland. Documents uncovered in a Swiss bank investigation of wartime activities confirmed that as early as June 1942, the Swiss Central Bank assumed the gold they had `received from Germany had come from occupied countries. For a while the Swiss even considered melting down bullion they had and turning it into new bars to hide its provenance.[2]

Germany had long enjoyed strong economic and ethnic ties with its neighbor to the south. At the time of World War II, nearly three-quarters of Switzerland's population were native German speakers, providing a strong bond between the two countries. When the Nazis in the spring of 1940 invaded Western Europe, however, Swiss leaders were terrified that their country might be the next victim. Hitler had just shown that he did not respect the neutrality of Holland or Belgium, so why would he treat Switzerland any differently? That put the small nation in a dangerous and no-win situation. If it were cozy with Berlin, London and Washington would be furious and perhaps retaliate. If it followed orders from the Allies, the Nazis would have been equally outraged and could easily occupy the country.

Switzerland was totally pro-Swiss and amoral when it came to financial transactions with the Nazis. Every nation looks out for its own self-interest. That is nothing new. What was different in World War II was that Switzerland turned a blind eye to the well-known German atrocities in order to continue its profitable financial transactions with the Nazi regime, particularly when it came to dealing in gold. For much of the war, the Swiss pedaled the idea to the Allies that it was just a poor little neutral nation being pushed around by the big, bad Nazis. In reality, it voluntarily leaned toward Germany and its golden coffers. Swiss political leaders for most of the war were only too happy to work with Berlin. The Allies made their first warning against dealing in stolen property in July 1941, but it was not until April 11, 1945, that the Swiss halted its purchases of Reichsbank gold. By then, the German defeat was obvious.

The harshest critics in recent times of Switzerland's war record in gold transactions have been the Swiss themselves. Jean Ziegler, a professor of sociology and former member of the Swiss Confederation's National Council, the country's federal parliament, in 1997 published a highly critical account of his nation's wartime activities entitled *The Swiss, the Gold, and the Dead*. In it he wrote: "Switzerland escaped World War II by virtue of shrewd, active, organized complicity with the Third Reich. From 1940 to 1945 the Swiss economy was largely integrated with the Greater German economic area. The gnomes of Zurich, Basel, and Bern were Hitler's fences and creditors."[3]

The Swiss Independent Commission of Experts, which began an investigation of the country's activities during the war in December 1996, finally and officially recognized the country's complicity in Hitler's atrocities. Nine Swiss and foreign historians plus a support staff of one hundred archivists had freedom to roam through Switzerland's wartime records. Their final report was published in March 2002. The report was twenty-seven volumes long. Some Swiss nationalists said it did not take into account wartime conditions, but it was generally accepted as an honest and accurate study.

At the beginning of the war most of the gold transactions between Germany and Switzerland were done by private banks. The National Swiss Bank, though, took over the business in October 1941. Switzerland's importance in the Nazi gold traffic was staggering. Three-quarters of the German bullion that was shipped abroad went through Switzerland. Between 1940 and 1945, the Nazis sold 101.2 million Swiss francs of bullion to private Swiss banks and 1,231 million through the Swiss National Bank. That was all stolen gold. The bank also dealt with Turkey, Spain, Romania, Sweden, and Portugal, which all had products the Nazis needed and would accept payment in Swiss francs.[4]

The peak period of the Nazi gold traffic was between the fourth quarter of 1941 and the first quarter of 1944. That was when they got their hands on the Belgian and Dutch gold. The Swiss franc and gold were the oil that made the machine work. The Germans bought Swiss francs from Switzerland in exchange for gold. The Nazis paid countries supplying them with vital war products in either gold or Swiss francs. The neutrals were happy to take either.[5]

The gold-for-raw-materials business was no secret. As early as October 1940, American newspapers carried stories about how it worked. In the summer of 1943, the head of the French National Bank, Yves Bréart de Boisanger, presented the Swiss with solid information that stolen Belgian gold, which the French had turned over to the Nazis, was being used in international transactions. The same was true of stolen Dutch gold. Some of the metal now owned by neutrals found its way to the New York Federal Reserve since the American government during the war made no attempt to ascertain its origin.

The system worked for central bank and concentration camp gold. Dutch and Belgian bank gold was smelted and new numbers and dates were added so they looked like old Reichsbank bars. The Nazis smelted private gold in the same way. Three gold bars of the third Melmer delivery, which took place on November 27, 1942, were sold to Switzerland on January 5, 1943. The trade was so advantageous for the Nazis that it soon became unthinkable that they would invade Switzerland. As the Bergier Final Report said, "Switzerland had–in effect–bought its freedom from German attack."[6]

After the war, the Swiss government claimed it had not realized that it was dealing in gold stolen from central banks or robbed from concentration camp inmates. That is totally specious. Switzerland during the war was the world's main gold market, and anyone watching gold transactions would have realized that Berlin's official pre-war holdings were by then exhausted. The Bergier Report again noted, "Evidence that German gold had been stolen was presented in Swiss newspapers, in particular the *Neue Zürcher Zeitung*, in August 1942."[7] Bergier concluded that by the summer of 1943, there was "irrefutable evidence that the German gold had been looted."[8] In a post-war interrogation, the Reichsbank's Emil Puhl, who had made gold deals with Swiss officials as late as April 1945, confirmed that the directors of the Swiss National Bank knew that they were accepting stolen Belgian gold.[9]

In a minor, but still distasteful, example of Swiss complicity with the Nazi regime, Adolf Hitler had his personal bank account at the Union Bank of Switzerland in Bern, where he stored royalties from the sale of *Mein Kampf*. SS Lieutenant Max Amann administered the account.[10]

The Bank for International Settlements was another important partner in the Nazi gold effort, and its role became the subject of major controversy during the war. Since Hjalmar Schacht had played a key role in its birth, he knew exactly how it worked and how Germany could use it. The staff in Basel included dedicated Nazis who promoted Nazi policies up to the very end of the war. It was another convenient channel for the Nazis to launder stolen gold, and during the war the Reichsbank deposited 13.5 tons of bullion with the BIS.[11]

Although the still young banking institution had been widely criticized for the role it played in delivering a large share of the Czech gold to Berlin in 1939, it continued to do business with Germany. BIS President Thomas H. McKittrick traveled to Berlin after taking over the organization in January 1940 to meet Walther Funk. They had both only recently taken up their jobs. McKittrick throughout the war had cozy relations with Nazi leaders, in particular with Puhl. The American defended his actions by saying that he was protecting an organization that would have a major role in rebuilding Europe after the war. He also had regular contact with Allen Dulles, who was running out of Bern, Switzerland the Office of Strategic Services, the forerunner of the Central Intelligence Agency. McKittrick kept Dulles informed about Puhl's travels.[12]

In May 1940 after the invasion of the Low Countries had begun, a large concentration of German military units was spotted just over the border from Basel, where the Bank for International Settlements was located. McKittrick also heard reports that Switzerland was about to be invaded. The bank hastily moved its headquarters and staff eighty miles south to the Grand Hôtel in the village of Château d'Oex. Paul Hechler, the top Nazi at the BIS, told McKittrick, "I think you are the most important man for us to get out of Basel." The staff remained there until October and then returned to Basel.

McKittrick's first term as BIS president was coming to an end, and it was unclear whether he would be reappointed. Because of wartime conditions, the BIS could no longer hold regular board meetings. German Foreign Minister Ribbentrop felt strongly that McKittrick should be replaced. When Puhl asked Paul Hechler, the top German official in Basel, for his opinion, he responded that it was best to keep the American because he was only an easily managed figurehead. A new person, the two Germans said, might cause the Nazis problems. McKittrick made a dangerous trip back to the U.S. in late 1942 to meet with Washington officials so he could make sure that they approved his reappointment. The Roosevelt administration was still unhappy with the BIS, but no one stopped the move. He stayed at the BIS until 1946, and later went to work with W. Averell Harriman in the startup days of the Marshall Plan.[13]

Some of the stolen central bank gold that neutral countries and the Bank for International Settlements obtained from Nazi Germany ended up in U.S. and Canada during the war. Countries did not trust leaving it in Europe for fear that it might fall into German hands. During the war, both Washington and Ottawa had a difficult time determining which bullion was legitimate and which was pilfered.

At the Bretton Woods conference in the summer of 1944, which drew up a new global monetary system, the Norwegian delegation introduced a resolution calling for the "liquidation of the Bank for International Settlements in Basel at the earliest possible date." It also proposed naming a commission to investigate "the management and the transactions of the Bank during the present war." Harry Dexter White, the American co-chairman of the meeting, approved the initiative, saying, "I think it would be a salutary thing for the world." Resolution VI of the Bretton Woods final document stated bluntly that "accepting looted gold and concealing enemy assets would not go unpunished."[14]

Sweden was another important German partner. At the same time that Ivar Rooth, the head of the Swedish Central Bank, was writing letters to his counterpart at the New York Federal Reserve Bank lamenting his country's dire economic prospects, he was also doing good business with Berlin.[15] Early in the war, Stockholm, for safety's sake, moved a substantial amount of bullion to southern and western Sweden. It still had seventy-nine percent of its gold reserves in the country in 1939. But then it began shipments to London and New York City. The country's gold and foreign exchange holdings increased substantially during the conflict. It bought 77 million Swiss francs worth of gold.[16]

Sweden sold the Nazis large amounts of war material, primarily ball bearings and high-grade iron ore used for munitions. The country at the time had eighty percent of the European market for ball bearings, which were needed for tanks, ships, and guns. The

Swedish company SKF (Svenska Kullagerfabriken or Swedish Ball Bearing Factory) sold so many ball bearings to Germany during the war that Europeans jokingly said the initials really stood for Süddeutsche Kugelfabrik (South German Ball Bearing Factory). The Nazis paid for the war goods with gold or Swiss francs. Stockholm also allowed the Nazis to send troops through its country during the invasion of the Soviet Union in 1941.

The Swedish Central Bank did a lively business in bullion with the Nazis. In May 1940, it bought two tons of gold from the Reichsbank. Then a month later, the German bank deposited three more tons in Stockholm. In the fall of that year, it got an additional eight tons. More gold exchanges were made in 1941 and 1942. In some cases, the Swedes were buying the gold with their currency, which the Germans undoubtedly used to finance war. The Reichsbank's Puhl visited Stockholm in the spring of 1942, and the Swedes soon set up an account in Berlin to hold their gold so that it would not have to be physically moved. Between November 1942 and December 1943, the Swedes acquired 15.5 tons of Nazi gold, and also bought a ton of German gold coins in the summer of 1944. In addition, they also bought large amounts of gold from Switzerland that was probably originally German. A study after World War II showed that in 1943 and 1944 Sweden received stolen Belgian and Dutch gold from Germany. Between 1949 and 1955, Sweden gave back $15 million of looted gold to Holland and Belgium. It also turned over to the Allies $66 million in liquidated assets.[17]

Foreigners living in Sweden were allowed to hold bank accounts in the country until February 1941, and some refugees left their money there when they departed for a safer location. A study by Swedish banks in the 1960s showed that there had been 9,032 such accounts with balances totaling 3.4 million Swedish crowns. In 1972, the banks donated 1.2 million Swedish crowns to the Swedish Red Cross to start a special fund for the victims of Nazism. As with Switzerland, when the war turned against the Nazis after 1943, the Swedes tried to improve relations with the Allies.[18]

Portugal and Spain both received substantial amounts of gold from Germany in payment for their shipments of raw material to Berlin. According to Swiss records, Portugal bought 536.6 million Swiss francs worth of bullion, while Spain purchased 185.1 million. The two Iberian Peninsula countries were primarily suppliers of tungsten, a crucial mineral for making weapons-grade armaments. Portugal sent mainly sardines and tungsten to Germany, but Spain shipped a host of minerals in addition to tungsten, including pyrite, zinc, and lead. Lisbon's trade with Berlin grew substantially during the war, going from only 1.8 percent of the country's exports in 1940 to 24.3 percent in 1942. Records show that 20.4 tons of Belgian gold ended up in Portuguese hands. A 1940 handwritten note of Antonio Salazar explained how it all worked. He wrote: "The Banco de Portugal has obtained gold seized in the occupied countries. It has paid for this in escudos that can be converted into dollars."[19]

Portuguese gold started arriving at the New York Federal Reserve in January 1940, and later the traffic picked up sharply. From January to October the amount of earmarked bullion jumped from eight tons to seventy-four tons. Almost all of that came in the second half of the year. Gold was transported first by train from Berlin to Lisbon and then by ship to New York.

In November 1947, the Allies demanded that 38.3 tons of stolen gold that Portugal had obtained from Nazi Germany be returned to its original owners. The Portuguese contested the ownership of all but 3.9 tons.[20]

At the end of the war, a U.S. diplomat in Madrid estimated that Spain had received 85 tons of looted gold from Nazi Germany. The Clinton Administration's Gold Team, which prepared the London Gold Conference of 1997, estimated that Spain received 94 tons of gold between 1942 and 1944.[21] In June 1942, ten steel cases of gold that had an estimated weight of a half ton were sent from the French border town of Hendaye to the Bank of Spain in Madrid. From February 1942 and May 1944, sixty tons moved from Switzerland to Spain. Franco in 1945 still received 187 million Swiss francs of laundered German gold in payment for tungsten.[22]

Romania lived dangerously in the shadow of both Nazi Germany and the Soviet Union, and it was not in a position to stand up to either of them. Berlin wanted Romanian oil to power the Nazi army, air force, and navy. Germany's big chemical companies had succeeded in manufacturing synthetic oil from coal, but the Wehrmacht needed more than they could produce. Romania in March 1939 signed an agreement with Berlin that allowed the Nazis to take over the development of Romanian natural resources. On December 21, 1939, a further accord obliged the country to furnish Germany with 1.8 million tons of oil in 1940. That was a jump from the 1.2 million the previous year. During the war, Romania increased its gold holdings at the Bank for International Settlements by 96 tons. In February 1943, the Reichsbank transferred thirty tons of gold to Romania. A year later, it sent 10.4 tons to Switzerland that was destined for Bucharest.[23] Between July of 1940 and May of 1943, the Reichsbank sent 47.8 tons of gold to the Romanian National Bank. Virtually all of that was to pay for oil, and two-thirds of the gold was stolen Belgian bullion. The Germans in addition deposited 10.4 tons in a Romanian account at a Swiss bank.[24]

Turkey's chromium was another crucial raw material for the Nazi war machine. Chromium, the raw material for chrome, has been compared to yeast in bread. You don't need a lot, but a little is essential. Chrome was used in the production of tanks, cannon barrels, aircraft engines, submarines, and many other war goods. Germany has very little chromium. Turkey, though, had nineteen percent of global output in 1939, which made it the world's second largest producer after the Soviet Union. Nazi Germany imported 11.7 tons of chromium in 1933; but from January to August 1939, just before the invasion of Poland, it bought 96.2 tons. In 1944, one-third of German chromium imports went into tank production. That kept the Nazi war machine working. Turkey's central bank gold holdings rose from 27.4 tons in 1939 to 216 tons in 1945. All the new bullion directly or indirectly came from Germany. In July 1942, the Reichsbank sent Albert Thoms and Kurt Graupner, two of its top gold officials, to Turkey to accompany a shipment of two tons of bullion.[25]

Two private German banks also played roles in laundering stolen Nazi gold, including that taken from concentration camp inmates. Deutsche Bank, which had its headquarters in Berlin, was the country's largest financial institution. It was founded in 1879 and had long operated internationally. During the Nazi era, it played a major role in the so-called aryanization of the German economy, which meant removing Jews from any positions of authority. One of the bank's rising stars was Hermann Abs, who became a member of the board at age thirty-seven in 1938. He remained a power in German finance until the 1970s. Deutsche Bank was in the middle of several gold deals during the war. Between October 1941 and August 1944, it moved nearly five tons from the vaults of Creditanstalt-Bankverein in Vienna to the Istanbul office of Deutsche Bank, which was known there as Doyçe Bank. It made a profit of 629 million Reichsmark on that deal. At the end of the war, Deutsche Bank still owned 3.6 tons of gold.[26]

Dresdner Bank, another major German financial institution, bought a total of 5.8 tons of gold from the Nazis. It made money buying gold at international prices and then selling it for a much higher level especially in Turkey. Some of that was concentration camp gold. Dresdner was the favorite bank of the SS's Heinrich Himmler. During the war it gobbled up Bohemian Discount Bank in Prague, Societa Bancara Romana in Bucharest, Handels- und Kreditbank in Riga, Kontinentale Bank in Brussels, and Banque d'Athenes in Greece. In addition, it gained majority control of Croatian Landerbank and Kommerzialbank in Kraków and Deutsche Handels- und Kreditbank in Bratislava. It likewise took over French interests in the Hungarian General Bank and the Greek Credit Bank, and it founded the Handelstrust West in Amsterdam. Dresdner also controlled the Banque Bulgare de Commerce in Sofia and Deutsche Orient-Bank in Turkey. Dresdner still had in its vaults 4.2 tons of gold on the day the Reich surrendered.[27]

Another crucial partner for the Nazi gold program was Degussa, the precious metals company, which played a major role in German economic history. When Bismarck founded the empire in

1871 following the Franco-Prussian War, the new nation needed a central bank since the national government had eliminated the currencies of the country's principalities. At that time, Degussa was a small privately-owned firm known as Friedrich Roessler Söhne that purified gold and silver. It was located close to the Frankfurt mint. The family firm quickly expanded its operations and become a public company that could handle all of the government's metal purification. The name Degussa was the acronym of its German initials.[28]

The company was a perfect fit for Schacht's autarky policy, and it received generous government subsidies. Degussa handled most of the government's smelting operations, which consisted mainly of purifying gold by removing other alloys until it was nearly one hundred percent pure. The process goes back three thousand years. The metal was then turned over to the Prussian Mint, which produced standard-sized gold bars and put on a Reichsbank stamp and serial number. Much of the Dutch and Belgian gold as well as the Melmer jewelry and coins went through Degussa before being sold as German bullion. In order to hide the origin, the date on the bars was backdated. An Allied air attack in March 1944 badly damaged the Degussa facility, putting it out of operation for the remainder of the war. A postwar study of the company's records showed that it had melted down 2,260 bars of gold. Most of those were originally from Italy, Holland, and Belgium.[29]

Chapter Twenty-Seven

THE ALLIES FINALLY CRACK DOWN

After the Nazis successfully captured the Italian gold in the fall of 1944, they did not steal a substantial amount more before the end of the war. Berlin officially had been fairly successful in keeping their gold theft out of the general public eye and their laundering operations secret. German financial reserves, both hidden and published, reached a peak in the middle of 1943, when gold holdings stood at about 300 tons, double what they were at their nadir in 1936. Ninety percent of the gold was hidden, and Swiss banks remained a friendly partner, buying and selling Nazi gold and making generous profits.[1]

On February 22, 1944, the U.S. government issued the Allied Gold Declaration stating, "The United States would not recognize the transference of title to looted gold which the Axis at any time held or had disposed of in world markets."[2] Britain and the Soviet Union made similar declarations the same day. It was a political document aimed at convincing neutral countries to stop accepting Nazi gold and also getting their cooperation with returning it to the rightful owners. That now cast a long shadow on future bullion transactions.[3]

Henry Morgenthau's treasury department had already been considering for several years how to handle Germany's economy after the battles were over. He worked closely with Harry Dexter White, who had just come off his great success at the Bretton Woods conference, and Bernard Bernstein, who had previously been on the treasury staff but since October 1941 had been on loan to General Eisenhower. White was now a far different man than the junior professor from a small college who joined the treasury department a decade earlier. While Morgenthau was tired after eleven years at the highest levels of the Roosevelt administration, White was at the peak of his intellectual power and ready to push his policy agenda. In the past he carefully kept his political opinions to himself, but now that Moscow was an ally he no longer held back his views. "The United States had not been doing enough for the Soviet Union," he said at a morning staff meeting with irritation. He also secretly turned over to the Soviets the American printing plates for the U.S. occupation currency in Germany.[4]

Morgenthau and White collaborated so closely on post-war policy toward Germany that it is impossible to know what was Morgenthau's work, what was White's, or indeed even what was the Soviet Union's. There is no doubt that they all shared the belief that Germany should never again dominate Europe. The Soviet Union wanted a weak Germany, so that it could control the continent and expand communism. It could be that White, its undercover agent, was simply following orders. Only four days before Morgenthau and his top aide made a trip to Europe to sell their tough German program, White had a meeting with a Soviet agent who had the code name Kostov.[5] White may have honestly believed that turning Germany into a weak, rural nation was the only way to avoid a new war. No one knows for sure, but the similarity of the Soviet view and the Morgenthau-White position was clear. White said at one meeting with British officials devoted to post-war Germany, "Our objective was to see that Germany was never again in a position to wage war. Everything else was incidental to that objective. If, to obtain that objective, it was necessary to reduce Germany to the status of a fifth-rate power, that should be done."[6]

President Roosevelt initially supported that approach, saying, "We have to either castrate the German people, or you have got to treat them in such a manner so they can't just go on reproducing people who want to continue the way they have in the past."[7] By this time, however, FDR had started to fail physically. When Morgenthau presented him with his plan on Germany, the treasury secretary was shocked by the president's decline, writing in his diary, "He is a very sick man, and seems to have wasted away."[8]

The State Department, on the other hand, was much more conciliatory toward Germany, arguing that it would be impossible to keep the country down permanently. The strongest cabinet opponent to Morgenthau's policy was Secretary of War Henry L. Stimson, who said that the plan "would lead to the starvation of thirty million Germans." He said that Morgenthau assumed that the Germans would live "happily and peacefully" on soup kitchens.[9]

By the summer of 1944, however, Allied governments and their intelligence services had learned the broad outlines of the skullduggery. The Foreign Economic Administration, a new cabinet-level operation President Roosevelt launched in 1943 to reduce conflict and confusion among U.S. agencies, first proposed the program. Washington then went seriously into economic warfare by attempting to block Nazi assets located in safe havens abroad. The great impetus was to make sure that there would be no repetition of the sorry tale after World War I. The Allies were determined to prevent another Hitler and another world conflict.

The shape of post-war Europe was a key issue on the table in September 1944, when Roosevelt met with Churchill in Quebec. Morgenthau gave the president a four-page memo before he left. The title said it all: Program to Prevent Germany from Starting a World War. His plan for breaking up the country was to give a large section of eastern Germany to Poland and a western part to France. There would be an independent South Germany nation, and the Rhineland and Ruhr would be under international control. The plan also had minor humiliating ideas such as that no German would be able wear a military uniform or be in a military parade.[10]

The British prime minister at a dinner the first night of the conference tore into Morgenthau's proposal, calling it "unnatural, unchristian, and unnecessary." Morgenthau was not used to anyone treating him that way. The treasury secretary later wrote that Churchill slumped down in his chair and viciously attacked him. "I have never seen him more irascible and vitriolic than he was that night. He used me, so to speak, to draw the venom." Meanwhile, Roosevelt said little.[11]

Churchill, though, was in a weak position because he was once again begging for American help. This time he needed it for his postwar economy. Great Britain had paid a heavy price for fighting the war alone for so long. His nation's top economist, John Maynard Keynes, warned him ominously that its economic future looked grim because of its heavy debt. Churchill was reduced to asking Roosevelt, in a reference to the White House dog, "What do you want me to do? Get up and beg like Fala?"[12]

The prime minister swallowed Morgenthau's Germany program in order to obtain the financial aid his country desperately needed. The two leaders signed their Top Secret Directive on Germany that stated: "The program for eliminating the war-making industries in the Ruhr and the Saar is looking forward to converting Germany into a country primarily agricultural and pastoral in its character." Anthony Eden, the British Foreign Secretary, angrily objected.[13]

Morgenthau had temporarily won the battle, but when the details of the accord reached American newspapers, the public outspokenly opposed the rural Germany solution and criticized Roosevelt. Such a mean and vindictive program was not the way Americans did things, even after this terrible war. Some people wondered what had happened to a nation whose president after an even more bitter conflict had advocated a policy of "malice toward none and charity for all." War Secretary Stimpson, Secretary of State Cordell Hull, and Churchill all opposed the Morgenthau plan. Roosevelt, who always knew which way the political winds were blowing, began putting some distance between himself and his close friend.[14]

Bernard Bernstein in December 1944 returned to Washington from Europe to lobby for Treasury's tough approach toward Germany. He had several meetings at the White House and succeeded in tightening up the language in a paper on gold and currency policy toward the Nazis. The new administration text called for "long-term foreign exchange control . . . to eliminate Germany's war potential, to prevent her re-nazification and to supervise her economic policies." That policy was put into the U.S. Army's Financial and Property Control Technical Manual.[15]

In early February, the western allies met with Joseph Stalin in Yalta in Crimea. Germany had clearly been defeated, even though the conflict dragged on, and war reparations were the major issue for the Allies. Stalin wanted to take huge amounts of money and machinery out of Germany and to set up a large border buffer zone between the Soviet Union and Germany. Eugen Varga, a leading Soviet economist, proposed that the Allied financial reparations amount to between 800 and 1,000 billion gold rubles. That would have been about eight times the amount demanded of Germany at the end of World War I. Stalin proposed somewhat less, with a disproportionate amount going to Soviet Union because it had lost the most men in the conflict.[16]

The Big Three finally papered over their disagreement on reparations, and in the communiqué agreed to disagree until their next meeting after the war had ended. The Soviets thought reparations should be $22 billion, with fifty percent going to them. The final secret protocol stated that all reparations should be paid within two years.[17]

Nazi Propaganda Minister Joseph Goebbels seized on the Morgenthau Plan as proof of how the Allies were simply going to "get rid of thirty to forty million Germans." Hitler railed that it would mean "the uprooting of 15 to 20 million Germans and transport abroad, the enslavement of the rest of our people, the ruination of our German youth, but above all, the starvation of all Germans." Albert Speer said later that, "the Morgenthau Plan was made to order for Hitler and the Party, insofar as they could point to it for proof that defeat would finally seal the fate of all Germans."[18]

General Eisenhower reported that after the proposal became known, German soldiers waged war with "a noticeable and fanatical zeal. The Germans are convinced they are fighting for their very existence." American intelligence experts thought that the German response to the Morgenthau plan was the German attack in the Ardennes in December 1944 that became known as the Battle of the Bulge attack.[19]

Morgenthau had White write a quick book that would appear under Morgenthau's name entitled *Germany is Our Problem*. It contained such hyperventilating prose as, "Fanatical young corporals will be dreaming of another chance at world conquest and reminding each other in beer halls. . . . They will get the chance for the industrial leaders of Germany already are laying their plans to mobilize for World War III."[20]

Morgenthau informed Roosevelt that he was working on a book about the German threat that he wanted to show him. The president's reaction, which he relayed through Eleanor Roosevelt was, "Why a book now?" He later also asked the treasury secretary to delay publication.[21]

The president in early April 1945 left for an extended stay in Warm Springs, Georgia to recuperate from his travels. Morgenthau was anxious to make his case for a tough German policy directly to the president, so he traveled there to see his old friend in person. In his diary he wrote, "I was terribly shocked when I saw him, and I found that he had aged terrifically and looked haggard." The treasury secretary made his pitch, and the president had a jovial talk. Roosevelt told some stories about Germans. He reminded the treasury secretary about a time when Germany's Hjalmar Schacht cried about his poor country in the Oval Office. Morgenthau wasn't interested in anecdotes, and said, "Look, Mr. President, I am going to fight hard, and this is what I am fighting for. A weak economy for Germany means that she will be weak politically, and she won't be able to make another war." FDR replied that he agreed with him "one hundred percent."[22]

Franklin D. Roosevelt died the next afternoon.

Chapter Twenty-Eight

RICH DISCOVERY
IN A SALT MINE

Destination Merkers
February–April 1945
Tons of gold: 219

Gold Route
- - - - ->

Denmark

Britain

Holland

Belgium

Germany

Berlin

Remagen   Merkers

Patton's Third Army

Luxembourg

Slovakia

Bohemia
and Moravia

Hungary

Switzerland

France

Italy

Yugoslavia

By the beginning of 1945, the end of the Third Reich was near. The once famed Luftwaffe was history, and Hitler's promised wonder weapons, the V-1 and V-2 guided missiles, or "flying bombs" as they were called, were too few in number and inaccurate to stop the British and American offensives on the western front or the Soviet one in the east. American, Soviet, and British planes relentlessly pounded Berlin. Even Joseph Goebbels, the German Minister for Propaganda and Enlightenment and the last true believer, recognized the war was over.[1] On the morning of January 12, Soviet Marshal Georgi Zhukov, the hero of his country's defense of Leningrad, launched the final offensive against the Third Reich from the east. His goal: Berlin. The Soviets had 6.7 million men under arms on the eastern front, twice as many as the beleaguered Germans.[2] Fierce German resistance initially slowed Zhukov's attack, but by early February the Soviets were at the Oder River, Germany's eastern border and fifty miles from the capital.

A tempting target for Allied bombers was the Reichsbank building in the center of Berlin, where the Germans kept their gold. One of the city's tallest structures, it stood out on the bank of the Spree River across from the Romanesque Berlin cathedral. Hitler had commissioned the structure in 1933 as an early edifice for his new Berlin. Famed Bauhaus architects such as Walter Gropius and Ludwig Mies van der Rohe entered the design competition, but Heinrich Wolff won. The massive structure of reinforced concrete covered with stone slabs had narrow windows and looked like a bunker. Hitler attended the groundbreaking in 1934, and the building went into service in 1940. It was considered virtually indestructible and a fitting home for Germany's Fort Knox.

The Reichsbank headquarters was also an important target for Soviet forces attacking from the east. Lavrentiy Beria, the head of the secret police and Stalin's closest aide, had assigned General Ivan Serov, his number-two man, to get to the gold at the Reichsbank. He was equal in rank to commanding military officers.[3]

In January 1945, Reichsbank President Walther Funk went to Hans Lammers, the head of the Reich Chancellery and Hitler's gatekeeper, and asked to see the Führer to discuss moving Germany's gold and the bank's operations out of Berlin. A few days later, Funk received the reply that Hitler was opposed to that and also turned down a suggestion to move the central bank's headquarters out of Berlin. Lammers said Hitler would tell him when it was time to do that.[4]

A massive attack on Berlin took place before noon on February 3, devastating the capital and the Reichsbank. Nearly a thousand U.S. B-17 bombers dropped thousands of bombs on the city, killing nearly three thousand Berliners and leaving 120,000 homeless.[5] Large sections of the Reichsbank were now rubble, and the staff was forced to work in the cellar. The currency printer was destroyed, but the printing plates survived. Nonetheless, a severe currency shortage soon developed, causing the country's already weak economy to slow down even more. The bank had to scramble to get paper money into circulation at its branch offices.

The bombing gave new urgency to protecting the Reichsbank's gold. Funk returned to the Reich Chancellery that same day and this time insisted on seeing the Führer. Lammers let him. Funk explained the situation and said that his prime objective now was to continue to operate the country's economy, which might be impossible if there were another bombing like that one. Hitler insisted that the bank headquarters remain in Berlin, but agreed that some of the staff could leave the capital.

Two days later, Funk wrote a memo to his staff telling them what was being done as a result of the "terror raid." He said Hitler had told him, "No matter what the conditions, the Reichsbank must maintain for the whole of Germany a properly regularized banking system. That is essential for the prosecution of the war, the rationing of the population, and for the financing of the armed forces, state, and party."[6]

Funk believed that the gold was essential not only to the continued financing of the war but also to provide the money for an eventual Fourth Reich that SS Boss Heinrich Himmler had proposed at the end of 1943. That was to be an *Alpenfestung* (Alpine

Fortress) in the area that stretched from Bavaria to northern Italy. The plan was that Germany's leaders would retreat to that mountainous area and wait for better times. Allied generals learned about the plan and took it very seriously.

After the war began going downhill in 1943, gold started to spill out into a variety of Nazi organizations. Each agency handled its bullion in its own way and to achieve its own goals. Foreign Minister Ribbentrop, who had obtained a major part of the stolen Italian bullion, used it to pay for diplomatic operations abroad and for foreign informants.[7] Göring's Four Year Plan and the SS also had their own stashes.

The vast majority of the gold, though, remained in the hands of the central bank. In July and August 1943, the Reichsbank had taken a minor step to decentralize it by shipping twenty tons to eighteen regional bank offices for safekeeping. Some of those, such as Stettin and Frankfur (Oder), were in the eastern part of Germany and were now in the path of the Soviet offensive.

Following the February 3 attack, the Reichsbank officials decided to send most of the remaining gold to Thuringia, a heavily forested area known as the green heart of Germany. It was in the center of the country just north of Bavaria. The central bank quickly delivered a shipment of gold to its office in Erfurt, the capital of Thuringia. Funk advocated moving the bank's new headquarters there.[8]

The German economics ministry had already requisitioned the country's salt mines so that they could be used for underground storage of valuable goods. The first shipment of state documents was sent to Thuringia in May 1944, and the following month, the state library in Berlin dispatched its most precious books, some dating back to the 1500s, to a mine there. By the spring of 1945, nearly two million books were stored and the library of the Prussian State Opera and the Library of Fine Arts were located in twenty-five depositories. The cities of Bremen, Lübeck, and Rostock stored public and private records in the village of Merkers, as did Henschel and Krupp, two major corporations that had strong ties to the Nazi war machine. At one point the Luftwaffe sent 40,000 bottles of liquor there to be used as a stimulant in case of military emergencies. After several incidents of workers getting drunk, however, the liquor was removed.[9]

Wintershall, Germany's second largest chemical company after I.G. Farben, had several mines in Thuringia, including one named Kaiseroda in Merkers. Reichsbank officials selected that as the place to store both gold and currency because it was not only one of the largest mines but also had a stable humidity level, which would be important for safeguarding paper currency. Kaiseroda was located 2,000 feet underground and had 30 miles of tunnels, providing excellent protection from Allied bombs. Sitting in the middle of a green valley with hills in the distance, the plant looked like a small village, with a complex of red-brick buildings, bridges, and cobblestone streets. Its billowing smokestacks and giant elevator dominated the rural skyline.

The original plan was to evacuate only Reichsbank valuables, but officials from the Prussian state museums asked to safeguard some of its paintings and other artworks in the complex since it provided more protection than their own facilities. Eventually about one-quarter of the most important works of art from state museums, including engravings by Albrecht Dürer and paintings by Renoir, traveled along with the first shipment of gold. The paintings, often still in their frames, were put in wooden crates that sometimes held several priceless pieces. Eventually about a thousand items were shipped south.[10]

The Reichsbank staff packed up the gold and other valuables with as much care as possible under the wartime circumstances. Two gold bars were put into individual cloth bags, while gold coins went into their own containers. Bundles of German and foreign currency were put into small gunnysacks. Items were sent to various locations for handling, including gold and silver jewelry that SS guards had taken from concentration camp inmates, which had arrived too late to be sent to the Prussian state mint for smelting into bars.

On February 11, only eight days after the massive bombing that had devastated the Reichsbank building, a special gold train with twenty-two cars left Berlin. Dr. Witte, a member of the bank's board of directors, and Albert Thoms, the head of its Precious Metals Department, accompanied the shipment. The train arrived in Merkers without any delay, but it took four days to unload and store it in the Kaiseroda mine. The valuables were put into a large storage room with a steel door that could be locked. The room was named simply "number eight."[11]

Near the end of February, the Reichsbank closed its gold books in anticipation of the evacuation of the national treasury from Berlin. The closing balance for gold was $256 million.[12] The end was near. A second Reichsbank train left Berlin on March 11, this time with only four cars. It carried about $2.5 million Reichsmark of bullion plus large amounts of foreign currency, including Norwegian kroners, Dutch guilders, French francs, and American dollars. Thoms again accompanied the shipment, and Reichsbank Director Frommknicht joined him. This time it took only two days at the mine to unload the smaller shipment.[13]

Thoms again returned to Berlin to pick up another shipment, but decided to return to Merkers with a truck, which would be more versatile than railroad cars. He left Berlin on March 23 and stopped briefly at Erfurt, but because the city was running out of food pushed on to Merkers. Also joining the Reichsbank group leaving Erfurt were Dr. Werner Veick, the head cashier of the Reichsbank's Foreign Notes Department, Dr. Otto Reimer, the chief cashier of the Reichsmark Department in Berlin, and a bank employee whose job was to arrange transportation between Berlin and Merkers. The national shortage of currency was growing ever more acute, and the government could not even pay some soldiers in cash. The main job now was to move Reichsmark currency that had already been sent to Merkers back to the capital, so it could be distributed to regional offices. The bank's previously efficient operation, along with the whole country, was sliding into chaos.[14]

Easter holiday is one of Germany's most important holidays, lasting from Good Friday through Easter Monday. In 1945, it ran from March 30 to April 2. Even in wartime, Germans stopped for

Easter, and only a few trains ran. The last gold shipment reached Merkers on April 3 at 4:00 in the morning.[15]

After spending only a few hours in Merkers, the transportation specialist from Berlin drove away from the Kaiseroda mine in a two-and-a-half-ton truck with 200 million Reichsmark in packages of hundred-mark bills plus an additional fifty or so packages of foreign currency. Before leaving, he explained that on his trip back to the capital he would stop at the regional Reichsbank offices in Erfurt, Halle, and Magdeburg to distribute currency.[16]

With the help of Polish POWs, German bank officials hauled out of the salt mine one thousand bags of currency that each contained one million Reichsmark. The plan was to load it all onto a railroad car in nearby Bad Salzungen and take it to Berlin. The Germans later learned that Allied bombers had destroyed a bridge the train was supposed to go over, closing another escape route. After working all day underground moving bags of paper money, Veick and Frommknicht were dead tired and decided to return to a casino where they were staying for the night. "We'll have to see what tomorrow brings."[17]

The next morning, the two men were back working in the mine, when they learned that American forces would be moving into city shortly. Frommknicht told Thoms, "Let's go to the entrance and see if we can slip away." Frommknicht had a driver, and their plan was to leave immediately for Berlin. When the driver arrived, he locked the door to room #8 and gave the key to a guard. He then told Veick to go get his suitcase and return immediately to join him on the trip to Berlin. Veick left quickly, but by the time he returned to the mine, American soldiers had entered Merkers. Frommknicht and Thoms had also disappeared. A mine director said he'd seen them leave on foot, but added, "I don't believe they will get far."[18]

U.S. troops marching through the village just before noon on April 4 saw German civilians unloading bags out of a truck. The G.I.s stopped and asked what was in them, and the locals replied, "currency." The Americans, though, just kept marching. In the mayhem of war, military units, displaced persons, prisoners-of-war, and civilians were all blending together.

At about 9:00 on Friday morning, April 6, U.S. soldiers Pfc Clyde Harmon and Pfc Anthony Cline were guarding a road about six miles from Merkers, when two women approached them walking through the village of Bad Salzungen about six miles from Merkers. A military curfew was in place, so they should not have been on the road, and that is when the soldiers met with the two women, one pregnant, who revealed the various activities that had been going on at the Kaiseroda mine. It was this mine where the women had seen Germans offloading gold and other valuable things. The next day, the G.I.s went to the mines, blasted the door blocking entrance to a storage room, and found hundreds of bags of gold as well as containers filled with jewelry taken from concentration camp inmates.[19]

Just before 8:00 P.M. that night, Reichsbank President Funk and his wife Luisa were at their rural home south of Munich in the village of Bad Tölz. Hitler had given the house to him in 1940 for his fiftieth birthday. They were listening to the BBC on the radio, even though that was illegal. BBC correspondent Robert Reed came on the air. The first thing he said was this was his 143rd radio report and that it had been censored. Then he announced: "This morning American soldiers working in a twenty-one-hundred-foot-square salt mine broke through a red brick wall and found one-hundred tons of German gold."[20]

Luisa Funk said later that her husband was "heart broken" by the news and told her that everything was now "finished." A general was supposed to have blown up the mine if enemy forces ever got close to it. The Nazi plan, Funk explained, was that it would have taken two to three years to excavate the gold, and that during that time Germany would be able to stabilize itself politically under Hitler's leadership. The gold was going to be used to rebuild the country after the war.[21]

In Berlin that same night, Propaganda Minister Joseph Goebbels learned about the Merkers discovery from United Press, the American news service. He was furious and dictated to a secretary for his diary, "Sad news from Mülhausen in Thuringia. Our entire gold reserves amounting to hundreds of tons and vast art treasures, including Nefertiti, have fallen into American hands in the salt mines there." He went on to rant against Reichsbank President Walther Funk, saying that the gold and art should never have been moved out of Berlin and that he had "always opposed" the transfer. Goebbels also complained that this had only happened because German trains had not run over Easter, the weekend before.[22]

Outside Paris the next day, Col. Bernard Bernstein, a member of General Eisenhower's staff, was enjoying a late Sunday breakfast. He and Ike's other aides had moved there from London after the liberation of the city the previous August. They were now working out of Louis XIV's spectacular Versailles Palace in the *Grande Écurie* (Big Stable). As he walked away from his breakfast in the mess, Bernstein had under his arm a copy of *Stars and Stripes*, the GI's daily newspaper. When he arrived at his office, he looked at the front page. The lead story was about the war in the Pacific and carried the headline "Carrier Planes Sink Japs' Greatest Warship." Just below that was a report about the European war with the headline "15 Mi. From Bremen." It was a two-paragraph story in bold type, though, that captured Bernstein's attention. The headline: "Reich Gold Hoard Captured." The Associated Press reported that Third Army forces had found 100 tons of gold bullion plus large amounts of French francs and other currencies.[23]

Only a few minutes later, Bernstein received a phone call from General Frank McSherry, the deputy assistant chief of staff at Eisenhower's headquarters, which was then located in Rheims, France. The general told Bernstein that General Patton had asked Eisenhower to take over responsibility for the gold. McSherry added that Eisenhower wanted his financial officer to assume charge of it and move the valuable cargo to a more secure location. McSherry then ordered Bernstein to get to Merkers as soon as possible. The original plan was for him to fly to Frankfurt/Main and then proceed by car to Merkers, only eighty miles away. But by then, it was too late in the day to fly that far, so Bernstein flew instead to Rheims to meet with both McSherry and General Lucius Clay, who was due to head the military government in Germany after the war was over.

Bernstein met the generals the next morning, and at the end of their talk, Clay asked him if he had any questions. The colonel replied, "Only one, General. May I act as it seems to me to be wisest to do?" Clay replied, "Yes." Bernstein then left for Frankfurt.[24]

Even before he got to Merkers, Bernstein had to decide whether to move the gold and artwork to the Ehrenbreitstein Fortress across the Rhine River from Koblenz or to the Reichsbank's branch in Frankfurt. The fortification had been overlooking the Rhine since 1000 BC, and the current version dated back to the seventeenth century. After visiting both locations, Bernstein picked Frankfurt. Ehrenbreitstein was already full of documents, and it was also considered an inappropriate site for the art. Frankfurt, on the other hand, was a good place for storing both gold and art. An added plus was that the bank was only a mile from the I.G. Farben building, which had already been selected to be the U.S. army headquarters after the war.[25]

Bernstein then continued on to Merkers, where he visited the gold vault and interrogated two captured Reichsbank officials, Werner Veick, the head cashier of the Reichsbank's Foreign Notes Department, and Otto Reimer, the chief cashier. Veick claimed that he didn't know much about the gold, but said that Albert Thoms, who had been captured while trying to escape from Merkers, "knows all." Reimer admitted that he and other bank employees had loaded one thousand bags of currency with the intent of taking them back to Berlin or to local Reichsbank offices. A bank official also revealed that they now had only about four tons of gold left in Berlin.[26]

Later that evening, Bernstein left for Patton's headquarters. After the colonel explained the lay of the land in Merkers to the general, he said he thought the gold should be moved to Frankfurt. Patton confidently told the young subordinate that the Germans were not going to "push me" out of the area and that the gold could simply remain in the mine. Bernstein agreed that the Germans were unlikely to recapture Merkers, but added that under the recent Big Three agreements at Yalta, that area of Germany would be in the

Soviet sector of occupation. Bernstein then added, "We certainly want to get all of this out of here before the Russians get here." Patton was astounded with that information and immediately approved moving the gold to Frankfurt, where it would be safely inside the American zone. The Soviets later demanded that the gold be shipped to them, but Washington ignored the request.[27]

The following day, Bernstein returned to Merkers and interrogated Dr. Paul Rave, the assistant to the director of the Prussian state museums, who had accompanied the Berlin artworks to the mine. The Germans were cooperating, and everything was starting to fall in place.[28]

An advance team of the Allied monuments, fine arts, and archives unit had already arrived in Merkers on April 8. They were museum directors, curators, and art historians who were following just behind the conquering armies rescuing artworks that the Nazis had stolen from museums and private collections all over Europe. George Stout, who before the war had been an art conservationist at Harvard's Fogg Museum, was the leader of the cultural operation. Although only a lieutenant in rank, he was the best American art man in uniform. He had landed at Normandy and traveled with troops rescuing priceless pieces of culture.

A minor turf battle quickly developed between Bernstein's men and those of Stout. Was this primarily an operation to rescue gold or to protect art? Stout wanted his boss, Britain's Geoffrey Webb, to come to Merkers to direct the art operation. When Patton learned of that, he sent an order telling Bernstein that this was to be an American-only project. "No damn limeys," exclaimed the general. The arts men felt they were being treated as second-class citizens, while the gold guys were running the show. The art team, however, were professionals and went to work checking on the conditions in which the art had been stored and preparing to move their part of what had been found in the salt mines. In some cases, they found priceless pieces sitting in pools of water. Many paintings were wrapped only in brown paper, and a few had been ripped during transport.[29]

Bernstein and Stout together inspected nearby mines where they had been told more art had been stored. Berlin museum experts initially sent pieces to the Ransbach mine one hundred miles west, but the Americans decided it wasn't an appropriate place and moved them to Merkers. Stout found forty-five cases that contained works by Dürer and Holbein as well as an estimated two million rare books. In the nearby Philippstal mine the Americans discovered countless more old books and maps. They also interrogated Dr. Shawe, a Berlin librarian who was responsible for manuscripts.[30]

When Bernstein returned to his housing on April 11 after a hard day in the salt mine, a message from Patton was waiting for him. It said that he should be at the entrance of Kaiseroda mine the next morning at 9:00. Bernstein dutifully followed orders, but no one showed up at the assigned time. Finally at about 10:30, a jeep pulled up. On the front was a plaque with five stars. That could be only one person: Five-Star General Dwight Eisenhower. Eisenhower and Generals Patton and Omar Bradley also hopped out of the vehicle. They were all there to inspect the Merkers mine. Bernstein led the group to an old wooden elevator shaft, an ancient contraption that carried them down to the bottom of the mine twenty-one hundred feet below. As the generals descended in the open elevator, Bernstein had a terrible thought: the guy operating it was a German! Bernstein, though, didn't say anything. Patton quipped that if the cable snapped, "Promotions in the United States Army would be considerably stimulated." Eisenhower shot back at the irrepressible Patton, "OK, George, that's enough. No more cracks until we are above ground again."[31]

With Bernstein as their guide, the generals toured room number eight. The original press report of 100 tons of gold had vastly underestimated the cache. There was probably double that and more, but no one knew for sure because they could only count the number of bags and suitcases. Perhaps to relieve their tension, the generals returned to joking. Bradley told Patton that if they were still in the "old freebooting days, when a soldier kept his loot, you'd be the richest man in the world." Patton didn't say a word, and just grinned. The artworks didn't impress Patton much. He wrote in his memoirs, "The ones I saw were worth, in my opinion, about $2.50, and were of the type normally seen in bars in America."[32]

Bernstein explained that the suitcases were filled with gold and silver items perhaps taken from concentration camp inmates. The generals already knew about the camps since U.S. forces four days before had liberated a slave labor camp in the nearby village of Ohrdruf. At one point during their tour, Eisenhower saw some writing in German on a wall and asked if Bernstein could translate it. The colonel, who knew Yiddish, replied that it said, "The State is Everything and the Individual is Nothing." Eisenhower muttered to himself that he found that an appalling doctrine. The generals stayed underground for an hour. There had still been some talk of shipping all the gold and artworks to the U.S., but Bernstein told them that he favored moving everything simply and quickly to nearby Frankfurt. The brass agreed.[33]

Following the visit to the Kaiseroda mine, the three generals and officers accompanying them went to Ohrdruf to tour the death camp. "It was the most appalling sight imaginable," Patton later wrote. The group saw a table where inmates had been whipped; forty naked bodies were now stacked on it. Nearby there was a pyre made of railroad ties. Patton later wrote with disgust, "In the pit itself were arms and legs and portions of bodies sticking out of the green water which partially filled it." The war-hardened Eisenhower wrote in a letter to General George Marshall, "The visual evidence and the verbal testimony of starvation, cruelty and bestiality were so overpowering as to leave me a bit sick."[34]

The group ended the day at Patton's headquarters, where the generals stayed up late talking about the horrific scene they had just witnessed. The need to loosen up after the visit to the concentration camp got them back to joking. Eisenhower asked Patton what he'd do with all the gold. Never at a loss for words, Patton replied there were two schools of thought among his men: one group thought that it should be made into medallions with one going to "every sonuvabitch in Third Army." The other wanted to hide it and use it to buy weapons the next time Congress cut the army's appropriation. Eisenhower looked over to Bradley and said, "He's always got an answer."[35]

About midnight the group finally headed for bed. Patton went to a nearby van, where he slept. He had forgotten to wind his watch, so he turned on the BBC to get the time. The broadcaster was just announcing that President Roosevelt had died. Patton returned to the others and told them. The three generals talked until 2:00 A.M. about what this might mean for the conduct of the war.[36]

Back at Merkers, Bernstein was still interrogating Reichsbank officials and others who might know something about the shipments of gold and art. He finally had his first opportunity to question Albert Thoms, who had left the mine with Frommknicht on foot the day the Americans marched into the village. The two Germans had hoped to get back to Erfurt. They had been walking along a road when G.I.s in jeeps drove up to them. The two ran into the forest and separated, but Thoms was eventually captured. In his questioning, the Reichsbank employee was evasive and provided some false information. He denied, for example, that the gold was stolen. The German also initially said that deliveries of concentration camp gold had started only recently. They actually had begun in August 1942. When presented with conflicting evidence, Thoms began changing his story and eventually became a valuable source of information, although he often still stretched the truth. He admitted leaving Berlin with records of the gold shipments, but claimed he had shipped the documents back to Berlin or that Frommknicht had destroyed them, adding that he was with him when the records were burned. The records later turned up in Merkers. Thoms remained vague and evasive during numerous interrogations and for years to come about his role with the captured gold.[37]

Bernstein spent most of his time preparing for the shipment of all the treasure, both gold and art, to Frankfurt. Before starting the operation, he had a preliminary inventory made of the gold, other metals, and currency. It indicated that in addition to the Reichsbank bullion there were 62 bags of Italian gold, 2.8 billion Reichsmark, and 711 bags of American $20 gold coins.[38]

At 7:30 in the morning of April 14, thirty-two ten-ton trucks arrived from nearby Mainz to transfer the gold and art to Frankfurt. Soldiers began taking bags out of room #8 at 9:00. Jeeps had already been moved down to the bottom of the mine, so that G.I.s only had to get the goods onto trailers that jeeps pulled to the surface. Then the contents were loaded onto trucks. Four crews consisting of both enlisted men and officers did the work. Bernstein set up a system of checks to make sure no one pocketed a brick of gold, although that would have been difficult given a bar's weight. An officer and a soldier stood at the door of the vault, and the senior person called out the contents as they were taken out the door and put on a jeep. The enlisted man wrote the number on his sheet, which became the shipping ticket. It then went up a shaft, and an officer accompanied the gold as it moved from the vault door to the top of the shaft. When it reached ground level, the jeep was checked again before one of two crews of fifty soldiers working in shifts loaded the cargo onto a truck. The names of the driver, the assistant driver, and the guard plus their army serial numbers were all listed on the sheet.

Bernstein hovered over the whole operation like the bride's mother at a wedding. During the night and until the trucks had left Merkers, air patrols flew over the site. Bernstein later bragged that it took his group less than a day to load all the gold, while the Germans had spent four days to handle just the first shipment. The trucks were loaded to the max, and one had broken down shortly after being filled but was quickly replaced. Before departing, the colonel made another inventory of the eleven thousand bags, boxes, and cases, in particular the 8,037 gold bars. The loading was finally finished at 7:45 A.M. on April 15. Fifteen minutes later, the trucks departed with a five-platoon escort for Frankfurt.[39]

Bernstein accompanied the cargo in an armored vehicle and sent some of his staff ahead to Frankfurt to make sure everything would be waiting for them upon arrival. The trucks took a direct route to Frankfurt, traveling only a few miles before getting on one of the Reich's prized *Autobahnen*. The convoy exited the highway just before entering the bombed-out city and then turned into the bank property from Adolf Hitler Straße, arriving in Frankfurt at 2:00 P.M. The cargo then went through the same inventory control as it had in Merkers, and unloading was only finished the next day at 3:30 P.M.

It took forty hours to load the artworks onto twenty-six ten-ton trucks, and one hundred POWs helped with the work. Three loads of paintings left with the gold, and the rest departed later in a separate convoy. The second shipment, which was dubbed Task Force Whitney, left Merkers at 8:50 A.M. on April 17. It arrived at the Reichsbank building the same day at 1:00 P.M. and unloading started at 3:30. Bernstein used the same control system for the art at both ends of the trip as he had for the gold. After everything was in place, the U.S. army installed an anti-aircraft emplacement on the roof of the bank building, the entire block was surrounded by barbed wire and a Sherman tank was stationed in front. After all, the gold there was now the richest hoard in the world outside of Fort Knox.[40]

The gold was also unpacked and weighed again. There were a total of 4,100 bags of bars each weighing 55 pounds, and 3,000 bags of coins topping the scales at 81 pounds each. A note from Bernstein to General Clay on August 19 set the value of the gold at $262,213,000. In the report he said that an additional $32 million had been discovered in Austria that belonged to Hungary.

After the bullion had been moved to Frankfurt, General McSherry called Bernstein and told him that General Bedell Smith, Eisenhower's Chief of Staff, wanted five gold coins to make into medals for President Roosevelt, even though he was now dead, Prime Minister Churchill, British Field Marshal Bernard Montgomery, General Eisenhower, and Army Chief of Staff General George Marshall. Bernstein said that was a rather unusual request since Eisenhower's headquarters had issued strict regulations against looting.

The order, though, was then cancelled. McSherry later explained to Bernstein what had happened after the phone call. He said the two generals were on their way to the Frankfurt bank to pick up the five gold pieces, when McSherry explained what tough security

Bernstein had put in place to prevent looting. After driving a little further, Smith told the driver to turn around and go back to headquarters. When Eisenhower and Clay heard about it, they also nixed the idea.[41]

While directing the movement of the gold and art, Bernstein also put into place an operation to pick up some of the gold the Reichsbank had moved to its regional offices around Germany. Bank and mine officials had told him that large amounts of bullion and foreign currencies were located there, so Bernstein and a small task force at first went to seven nearby locations. From bank records, he knew that 241 boxes had originally been sent from Merkers to regional Reichsbank offices. In Weimar, the first stop, the Americans interrogated the bank staff until 3:00 in the morning and learned that 25 bags of gold had been shipped there on April 2, but had then been moved again. The bank in Apolda had initially received 40 bags of gold, but those were returned to Berlin on April 7. Nuremberg got 15 bags of bars on April 1, but officials said it had been moved to Halle for safer keeping.

Bernstein asked to have an infantry regiment help him track down the riches. He knew it was going to be a difficult job, going from location to location over badly damaged roads. The army brass, however, said it could not afford to that many men away from their primary job of fighting the war. He and his group were able to commandeer only a couple of jeeps. Thoms, who had originally been hostile to the Americans, was now cooperative and went along on the search.

They had some success:

- Forty bags of gold had gone from Weissenfels to Halle, where another sixteen boxes were found. Two contained both gold and $2 million in American currency.
- They found eighty-two bars of bullion in each of the Zwickau, Eschwege, and Coburg branch offices.
- Officials in Erfurt said they had received eighty bags of gold, but it had been moved on April 4 to an unknown location.

- At the Reichsbank office in Plauen, American soldiers blew off the door of a vault where they found thirty-five bags of gold that had been deposited in April 1944 for Heinrich Himmler, the head of the SS. His coin collection was also there, and some for the bags contained $20 gold coins.

The search for additional gold lasted until June. Fourteen tons were eventually recovered and sent to Frankfurt in seventy-eight shipments.[42] The picture that emerged from the long search of Reichsbank offices and interrogations shows how the once mighty German central bank in the last days of Hitler had collapsed. On April 30, Director Rudolf Himpe at the Coburg bank, for example, admitted to Bernstein's men that just before American troops occupied the area, he had buried forty-one bags of gold, weighing just over a ton, under a chicken coop and a pile of manure in a friend's garden a mile from the bank. High-ranking officials such as Reichsbank President Funk and Foreign Minister Ribbentrop in the last days of the war traveled around the country with bags of gold and currency. Officials placed their last best hope in gold, and as late as the 1960s, NATO troops on patrol found Nazi gold in the Bavarian forest.[43]

During the late spring and summer of 1945, officials from several countries arrived in Frankfurt and tried to identify property that had been stolen. French and Belgian officials were particularly anxious to determine whether the gold the Belgians had given the French for safekeeping in 1940 could be found. Unfortunately, the Nazis had smelted down much of it along with Dutch and Italian gold and then restamped it with predated markings. Much had been sold to Switzerland, and it was now very difficult to determine the original owner.

In May 1945, Eisenhower's office asked the U.S. Treasury and the Bank of England to send experts to conduct an official audit of all the gold in Frankfurt. Five experts, three Americans and two British, spent four months assessing the treasure. Their work took several months and examined the Merkers haul closely. Eight bags of rare gold coins had been set aside because it was believed that their numismatic value was probably higher than their gold content.[44]

Bernstein on September 6 sent his military bosses a thirty-page summary of his work recovering gold entitled "Report on Recovery of Reichsbank Precious Metals." It is the most comprehensive study of the American gold findings in Germany up to that date. It showed that they had captured $238.5 million in gold at Merkers and an additional $14 million at other locations, mainly Reichsbank offices. In addition, there was $270,469 worth of silver, 35,000 ounces of platinum, and small amounts of the platinum group such as palladium, whose value still had to be determined. The value of the concentration camp gold, though, had not yet been appraised. Bernstein proudly stated that the Americans had recovered 98.6 percent of the Nazi gold.[45] The final estimated value of all the gold caches made that same day set the value at $256 million.[46]

Bernstein's statement was a bit chest beating. He had no way of knowing how much gold remained undiscovered. The Germans had certainly moved it all around the area they occupied, and there was no way to know whether a few gold coins or a random bar was not stuffed under someone's bed. Charges were later made that some American soldiers had taken gold from Merkers as war trophies. One bag of Dutch gold guilders that arrived at Frankfurt, for example, had been ripped open, and 340 coins were missing. Art expert Robert Posey, one of the Monument Men, wrote his wife on April 20, 1945 that he had seen American soldiers filling a helmet with $20 gold pieces. He wrote that it was so heavy that he couldn't lift the helmet. He claimed that he had refused to take any, and those went back into a sack. Posey claimed the gold was worth $35,000. The U.S. Army later made an investigation into missing gold coins, and Bernstein was questioned about it on April 24, 1945. But no one was ever charged.[47]

When the Soviet army captured Berlin, General Serov from Zhukov's staff liberated the ruins of the Reichsbank. Major Fedor Novikov ordered the vaults to be opened, where Soviet troops found just 2.4 tons gold, twelve tons of silver coins, but millions in banknotes from countries the Germans had occupied. The Soviets may have also picked up gold in Reichsbank branch offices in eastern Germany on their way to Berlin, but they never told their Allied partners. In the end, Moscow captured an estimated $4.3 million in Nazi gold.[48]

The gold that Albert Thoms and other Reichsbank officials evacuated to Merkers in the dying days of World War II constituted the largest amount still in Nazi hands. It represented, though, only one-fifth of the bullion that the Nazis looted from European central banks over the course of the entire war.

Chapter Twenty-Nine

THE *GÖTTERDÄMMERUNG* OF GOLD

By the spring of 1945, the Third Reich was all but finished. The German people, though, still had to suffer through Hitler's operatic self-conflagration of their country. Following the failure of the Ardennes offensive of December 1944, the Nazi military was a burnt-out case, and the regime's leaders sleepwalked their way into history. Soviet armies moved slowly but relentlessly from the east, destroying everything in their way and raping women with abandon, while the Americans and British attacked from the west with less brutality. A useless fire bombing in February leveled the historic cultural city of Dresden, the Florence on the Elbe, and left 25,000 dead. On Sunday, April 1, Goebbels wrote in his diary, "This is the saddest Easter Day I have ever had in my life. From all corners of the Reich news causing fresh anxiety floods in through the day. A prolonged series of air raids has wrought fearful devastation in the Reich during the last 24 hours."[1]

On April 12, the Berlin Philharmonic gave its last performance of the war in the capital. Albert Speer, the closest person Hitler had as a friend, had organized an event for the Nazi hierarchy. Speer told the orchestra to leave Berlin immediately after the concert, which ended appropriately with the finale to Wagner's *Götterdämmerung*. Even at that catastrophic moment, however, Berliners, who are famous for their humor, were saying that the optimists were learning English and the pessimists were learning Russian.[2]

Just over a week later, Hitler on April 20 celebrated his fifty-sixth birthday at his Berlin bunker with his ministers and cronies, but after the maudlin celebration many of them headed out of the capital with their own plans. *Sauve qui peut*. Speer went to Hamburg, Göring to Bavaria, and Himmler headed north in hopes of starting talks with Swedes about a brokered peace. After the birthday celebration, Göring told Hitler he was leaving for Obersalzberg in Bavaria. The Führer replied simply, "Do what you want."[3]

A latecomer to the war was Hungary, which the Germans had invaded in March 1944 after Hitler received news that his long-time ally was seeking a deal with the Allies. Nazi control on the ground, though, did not change much. With the Wehrmacht in retreat, the Nazi SS had set up a major program to collect Jewish valuables, including gold, currency, paintings and rugs. The Hungarian government estimated they were worth $350 million at the time, although others said it was less than half that. All the goods were packed onto the forty-two-car train that started moving north into Austria on the night of March 29-30.[4] It was called the Hungarian Gold Train. First French and then American troops captured the train, and the property was eventually put under U.S. army control. Much of the valuables disappeared, and Americans were charged with stealing it. High-ranking officers reportedly took plenty of things for their private collections. The case dragged on for years, even in American courts, and ended with no one totally satisfied.

A second Hungarian gold case involved the country's central bank bullion. The Hungarian National Bank decided to move its personnel and the country's thirty-two tons of gold out of Budapest and sent it west by train toward the advancing Americans. The destination for the bank officials was the town of Spital am Pyhrn in Austria. Two hundred Hungarian policemen and 500 bank employees were there to guard the stash, but most of all to make sure that they surrendered to the Americans and not the Soviets. Bank officials sent messages to the American forces telling them that they were holding it in the cellar of an old monastery that was guarded by a Hungarian Royal Police unit. When Patton's Third Army arrived in Spital am Pyhrn, it took over the national treasure without a fight. A Hungarian colonel also handed over the historic Holy Crown of Hungary or Crown of Saint Stephen, the country's most precious object, to an American colonel. It was later decided not to put the Hungarian gold into the general pot of Nazi gold to be dealt with after the war. Instead American military officials with great fanfare returned it to the Hungarians in August. It consisted of 2,669 gold bars on a train that Allied forces claimed had been Eva Braun's private car that carried it to Budapest. It was widely believed that the delivery was really made to better relations with the Soviets, since Hungary was going to be in Moscow's zone of influence, and so they were really turning the gold over to the future communist rulers of Hungary. St. Stephen's Crown, though, was not included in the transfer.[5]

Perhaps the most bizarre episode in the chaotic days at the end of the war involved some Yugoslav gold. Nazi occupiers in April 1941 had installed the Ustaša, a revolutionary movement with German support, to head the Independent State of Croatia. Post-war intelligence reports said that the Ustaša had anywhere from $600,000 to $35 million in Nazi gold. The organization had its own army that terrified the countryside with a brutality that shocked even Heinrich Himmler. The Croatian State Bank had just under one ton of gold in Switzerland, which was handed over to Marshal Tito, the new ruler of Yugoslavia, in July 1945. It had an additional ton in a Swiss bank, and that was also turned over to the new government. On the night of May 7-8, 1945, and with the end in sight, the Ustašas reportedly grabbed a quarter ton of gold from the Croatian State Bank and then set off in two directions. Some of them left in a truck headed for Austria. The vehicle broke down near the small town of Wolfsberg, where Ustaša officers broke open a case and handed it to comrades trying to escape. Then they reportedly turned over the rest to a Franciscan monastery run by a fanatical Catholic group that had strong ties with the Vatican. The Croatian Roman Catholic priest Krunoslav Dragonović allegedly took it to Rome in July and turned it over to the pope. The Croatian delegation at the 1997 London Gold Conference insisted, "These facts exclude any possibility that the NDH (Ustaša) gold was stored in the Vatican."[6]

The cache of Yugoslav bullion has since been lost in claims and counter claims. Emerson Bigelow, a U.S. Treasury official with connections to American intelligence groups, on October 21, 1946 sent a message to the U.S. Treasury Department saying that "approximately 200 million Swiss Francs was originally held in the Vatican for safekeeping. According to rumor, a considerable portion was sent to Spain and Argentina through the Vatican's 'pipeline,' but it is quite possible this is merely a smokescreen to cover the fact that the treasure remains in its original repository." That has been called the "Bigelow Report," but is actually only a three-paragraph note that reads more like gossip than solid intelligence. The following year, William Gowen, an agent of the Office of Strategic Services, sent a message to Washington saying that the gold had been sent to the College of San Sirolamo Degli Illirici, which is located within the walls of the Vatican. Swiss banks supposedly helped with the transfer. That again was never verified. There is no doubt, though, that the Vatican and the U.S. Army Intelligence Corps helped some Ustaša leaders escape to Argentina.

The Vatican has kept its silence about the Yugoslav gold story, and no one outside the church knows where it went and how much was involved. The Eizenstat Commission in the late 1990s used all the weight of Washington to break the Vatican's silence as part of its study of the World War II gold, but church officials steadfastly refused to participate. A lawsuit was also filed in the U.S., but that too could not break Vatican secrecy.[7]

In the early months of 1945, gold was spilling out all over Germany, with top Nazis grabbing some in the hope that it might help them and their families survive. Many top officials had their private stashes. Joachim von Ribbentrop, who had grabbed tons of Italian gold, sent part of it out of Berlin. Eighty-one sacks were placed in the cellar of Schloss Fuschl, a castle near Salzburg, Austria. More went to the Liebenau monastery just outside Worms and to a castle in Mühlhausen in Thüringen. Some also went to a factory in the village of Gaissau Hintersee in the Salzkammergut area near Salzberg, Austria. Ribbentrop finally sent several tons to Schleswig-Holstein in the north, where he planned to make his last stand. Later, 1.8 tons of coins belonging to the Foreign Ministry turned up near the town of Itzehoe thirty miles north of Hamburg.[8]

Gestapo leaders had their own stores of gold and foreign currency. Ernst Kaltenbrunner, the number-two man in the SS and one of the authors of the Final Solution, in mid-April was named the commander of the German forces on the southern front. He quickly set up his headquarters in the village of Altaussee in the central part of his native country, where he used to ski. He shipped his hoard out of Berlin on a special train in the final days of the war. When American soldiers captured Kaltenbrunner in a mountain lodge, he was carrying papers that identified him as Dr. Unterwegen. He had thrown away his Nazi identification into a nearby lake shortly before American soldiers arrested him.[9] His young mistress Countess Gisele von Westrap told the Americans that he had two chests of gold, but she did not know where they were located. Later 130 pounds of gold were discovered near the mansion where Kaltenbrunner had lived. American G.I.s discovered abandoned gold in the strangest places. They found nearly two thousand Austrian gold coins plus bars of gold in an abandoned hay wagon next to a railroad station in a small town in Austria.[10]

Other SS units took some of the Reichsbank's Melmer gold for their own use. In October 1944, the SS moved gold coins worth an estimated $25 million to Bad Sulza near Weimar, and another truckload of gold and foreign currency to Salzburg in late April 1945. Both shipments were to be used for food and bribery by Nazis going to ground. Otto Skorzeny, an SS Lt. Colonel sent a staffer to

Salzburg to get more money, and he returned to the SS headquarters in the town of Radstadt with 50,000 gold francs.[11]

Germany quickly descended into economic chaos. Since the Reichsbank had a difficult time sending new currency to its regional offices around the country, the wheels of commerce slowed down. Factories ran short on raw materials, and companies could not pay employees. Soldiers were not paid either. Bartering became widespread, as farmers traded milk or eggs for whatever they could get in exchange. With roads and bridges bombed out, traffic moved slowly. The unit known as Organisation Todt, which was building facilities in France for the new V-1 and V-2 rockets that Hitler still hoped would bring victory, had to use gold to keep its operation functioning.

In March 1945, Reichsbank Vice President Emil Puhl was shuffling between the Southern Germany city of Konstanz, where the bank had a branch office, and Switzerland. He was desperately trying to sell Nazi gold to either the Swiss or the Bank for International Settlements. He wrote letters to Walther Funk in Berlin about how it was becoming more and more frustrating to get anything done. He complained about his loneliness and not knowing what was happening to his family, and the pressure the "Anglo-Saxons" were putting on the Swiss to stop gold sales. On March 19, he wrote in a four-page letter, "In general it is much worse that I even imagined in my most pessimistic expectations." He had stopped at the Bank for International Settlements in Basel before going to the Swiss capital in Bern and wrote that he was "very disappointed" by the situation he found there. President McKittrick, after extensive consultations with the American embassy in Bern, told Puhl he would no longer accept gold from the Reichsbank. That killed agreements to send two shipments to the BIS, one for six tons and one for a ton and a half. The Swiss National Bank, though, was still willing to take bullion despite Allied pressure, but it was not delivered from Konstanz before the the war ended.[12]

On April 6, Puhl wrote a more upbeat ten-page letter after the Swiss agreed to sign the agreement to buy Nazi gold. He wrote: "It is pleasing to note again and again in all these events how strong the cultural ties are that connect our two countries, even if the political opinion of the broad mass is not in our favor today." He lamented, though, that he had lost contact with this wife and youngest son who are now in "enemy-occupied territory."[13]

Although the Reichsbank had gotten the bulk of the country's gold out of Berlin in early 1945, there was still a lot floating around the capital at a variety of organizations. Lt. Colonel Friedrich Josef Rauch, who was known by the name Fritz, was the adjutant of Hans Lammers, the head of Hitler's Reich Chancellery, the center of the Nazi state machinery. A veteran Nazi who had participated in the Munich beer hall putsch and fought in the Balkans, Rauch was relatively new to his powerful position in Berlin. Nonetheless, he convinced Lammers that the government had to get all the remaining valuables out of Berlin before either the Americans or Soviets got there. He proposed sending it to the area of Southern Germany and Northern Austria, a region he knew well since he was born in Munich. Diehard Nazis such as he still hoped to establish there the National Redoubt that Heinrich Himmler had proposed.

The Reichsbank had in Berlin some gold plus plenty of currency and the material for printing new money to keep the economy functioning. Other organizations also had their private war chests. The *Devisenschutzkommandos* of Hermann Göring had plenty of jewelry and foreign currency taken from people in invaded countries. Himmler's SS, which ran the concentration camps, also had its riches. Rauch wanted to move all that south.

Lammers quickly approved the proposal and took the plan to Walther Funk, who was already trying to get the last Reichsbank bullion and currency out of Berlin. Lammers and Funk together took their plan to Hitler, who was now in dark depression in his bunker. He had already decided to die in Berlin, but agreed to let them take the remaining treasure out of the city.

Reichsbank officials led the operation to get as much as possible of the nation's remaining riches to Bavaria. Officials found two freight trains, the *Adler* (Eagle) and the *Dohle* (Jack Daw), and assigned eighty employees to accompany the valuables to Munich. When the two trains were hooked together at the Lichterfelde-West train station, only half of them were on board. The rest were taking their chances and staying in the capital. The trains carried 25 boxes and 365 bags of gold, millions of dollars of foreign currencies including British pounds and American dollars, plus 500 million Reichsmark, 200 packets of blank paper, and 34 boxes of printing plates to make even more German currency. The foreign money came largely from Göring's *Devisenschutzkommandos*. Hans Alfred von Rosenberg-Lipinsky, a bank board member, directed the whole operation. There now remained in the bombed-out Reichsbank headquarters only 2.5 tons of gold.[14]

The next day, Walther Funk also left Berlin along with August Schwedler, an SS officer and also a Reichsbank board member. They departed in a car driven by Funk's chauffeur, Bernard Miesen, who brought along his wife and three children. The group pulled out of Berlin at five o'clock in the afternoon on April 14 and joined a caravan that ultimately included six trucks carrying gold and other goods. In total there were fifteen people. They traveled through the night, arriving in Munich at 11:00 the next morning. Funk did not stop there, though, going instead to his country home near the village of Bad Tölz.[15]

During the next few days, the driver took Funk and Schwedler on several trips around the area so that they could get the lay of the land and decide where to hide the gold. They first went to the Reichsbank office in Munich, which was located on Briennerstraße, one of the four royal boulevards in the heart of the city. There they discussed plans to protect the gold that would be arriving soon. They also went to Berchtesgaden to meet with Hans Lammer, who had escaped from Berlin by claiming poor health.

The Reichsbank gold train from Berlin to Munich quickly turned into a nightmare. Because of both mechanical problems and the war conditions, it crept through Dresden and the spa town of Marienbad. The wagons were a tempting target for Allied bombers, and the leaders of the convoy feared they might lose the whole shipment. When the gold train pulled into Freising, a town just north of Munich, the entire city and the railroad station were on fire. One wagon broke down and had to be replaced. The train eventually split into two units, with the *Dohle* remaining behind for repairs. Some of its cargo was off-loaded into trucks that headed for Munich. Traveling was slow because the roads were filled with dead cattle and horses as well as fleeing refugees. Trucks also had difficulty finding gasoline. One of the shipments that arrived finally by truck included twenty vehicles that carried four thousand gold bars.[16]

The early choice for a place to store the gold was a coal mine in Peißenberg, a small town about sixty miles southwest of Munich. It had an extensive network of caves dating back to the seventeenth century. Schwedler decided to check it out while waiting for the trains to arrive. Their driver took him and three Reichsbank staffers to Peißenberg, where they met with mine officials and inspected the facilities. They found water in several of the tunnels and realized that this was not the site to store their bullion, much less the paper currency, which would quickly become waterlogged. Schwedler took three mysterious bags with him into the mine, but then returned with them to the car. He went back to Funk's mountain hideaway to discuss the situation with the bank president, who by then was drinking heavily. They agreed that Peißenberg was not the place to store the gold.[17]

Lt. Colonel Rauch, who had already been in Bavaria for a while, had decided that the best temporary location for the gold was the barracks of the *Gebirgsjägerschule* (Mountain Infantry School) in Mittenwald. This was a village located at the foot of the North Tirol Alps sixty miles south of Munich and near Garmisch-Partenkirchen, the mountain resort that had been host to the 1936 winter Olympics. The poet Johann Wolfgang von Göthe once described Mittenwald as a "living picture book." The *Gebirgsjäger* was an elite light infantry unit and part of the *Waffen–SS*. Members wore a distinctive Edelweiss insignia on their sleeves and caps. The commander of the

Mittenwald troops was Colonel Franz Pfeiffer, a war hero and recipient of the coveted Iron Cross.

The two colonels decided to store the gold at first in a bowling alley in the basement of the officer's club. The first shipment of bullion arrived in Munich on the *Adler* and was quickly sent there. Once it had arrived, bank officials who had traveled with it from Berlin immediately did an inventory. There had been 365 bags of bullion when it left Berlin, with two bars in each container. One of the bankers said it was an easy number to remember because it was the same as the days in a year. When officials finished their inventory, however, they were missing one bag. The Reichsbank staff searched the whole area and recounted, but they were still one short. No one could figure out how it could be missing. The controls since they left Berlin had been very strict. Bank officers questioned everyone, including the staff at the school and all who had been on the train. Nothing showed up. A few days later, someone lit a fire in the bowling alley's stove, and it began to belch smoke. Two bars of gold were wedged in the chimney. Most likely a member of the Berlin staff had planned to come back later to recover the two bars.[18]

The gold from the *Adler* was still waiting for a long-term hiding place, when the *Dohle* train finally pulled into the Munich-West train station on April 25 with the remaining load. It was too late to move it in trucks to Mittenwald, so it remained there for the night. The next day twenty-five more crates of bullion were moved south by truck.[19] All the Berlin gold was now at the *Gebirgsjägerschule*.

A final hiding place, though, still had to be found. Funk met again with Lammers in Berchtesgaden near midnight at the end of April to discuss what was going on with the gold and also what they were both personally going to do in view of the impending arrival of the Americans. This time the central bank president arrived with the three bags that Schwedler had been carrying before. Currency was in two of them and two bars of gold were in the third. Before leaving, Funk turned the sacks over to a local Bavarian official.

Funk, Lammers, and Schwedler finally met at the Berghof and discussed what to do with the gold, which was clearly not safe in the long run at the *Gebirgsjägerschule*. With everything closing in on them, they decided to give Rauch responsibility for taking all the valuables into the mountains and burying them.

Lammers and Funk after that basically waited for Allied forces to arrive, and they were soon arrested. Funk had been drunk much of the time. German soldiers drifted away from their units, as men tried to make private deals by surrendering to the Americans. Skirmishing broke out between SS loyalists committed to fighting to the very end and the Freedom Action Bavaria movement, an anti-Hitler group that wanted to get rid of the Nazis before the Americans arrived. The battle for Munich, which had already been badly damaged by bombing, began early in the morning of April 30 and was over by the end of the day. Wehrmacht soldiers received papers stating that they had been legally relieved of duty.

Schwedler, though, stayed on the job. Nearly a week later, he and the driver went back to Mittenwald for more meetings with Pfeiffer and Rauch. Bavaria now was in total chaos, and to make matters worse winter had returned. Temperatures dropped rapidly, and there were six inches of snow on the ground.[20]

Although the two officers knew that the end was at hand, they decided to move the remaining Reichsbank gold and foreign currency one more time to a safer place than the *Gebirgsjägerschule*. The destination was an area near the Walchensee (Lake Walchen), Germany's largest and deepest lake. Some fifteen miles due north of Mittenwald, it was a remote location that the Americans would only find later. The two colonels were now in charge of the gold operation. Funk simply waited to be arrested, and Schwedler only rarely checked in on what had happened.

The remaining valuables were worth at least $15 million and consisted of more than 700 gold bars, 34 boxes of printing plates, and 200 containers of blank currency paper. The gold weighed about ten tons, and all the items to be hidden totaled some seventeen tons. No one was any longer conducting detailed inventories.[21]

One of the officers at the *Gebirgsjägerschule* was the son of Hans Neuhauser, the chief forester of the Walchensee area, who owned a two-story house in the woods a short distance southwest of the lake. He agreed to keep the Reichsbank goods in the family storage room, previously a stable, for a short time before they would be moved to a long-term location nearby. It took three days to transfer all the valuables to the Neuhauser house.[22]

From there, and with the help of pack mules, the soldiers began re-locating everything up the steep Steinriegel mountain nearby. They moved 364 bags of gold, 25 boxes of it, 96 bags of currency, and 34 packets of blank currency paper. Fearing that the currency and blank paper would not survive being buried in the damp soil, they camouflaged it well above-ground behind logs, timbers, and bushes in a shelter resembling a bunker.

The gold was next moved to a still higher location on the mountain near the hamlet of Einsiedel. Deep in the woods, the soldiers dug large holes three- to four-yards long, wide and deep, and added wooden planks along the walls to reinforce the hiding places.[23] Since gold does not deteriorate even in moist conditions, no one worried about putting it in the damp earth. They carefully hid the location, putting a tree stump and other pieces of natural debris around the spot where they had dug. A few makeshift booby traps were also put in place. The whole process was not completed until April 30. The printing plates for Reichsmark currency now seemed worthless, so the soldiers took them out in a boat and dumped them into the Walchensee.[24]

Schwedler wanted to see the gold hiding place and pressed the two colonels to take him there. After walking two hours up the mountain near the lake, they found the hiding spot.

Only a few days later, American forces marched into the Walchensee area, but they had no idea what riches were stored on the mountains near the lake.[25] The *Amis*, as the locals called them, immediately started arresting males who looked as if they had just discarded their Nazi uniforms. The G.I.s soon heard vague reports about gold transfers between Munich and the *Gebirgsjägerschule* in

Mittenwald. The people who knew what had happened, though, were not talking. When it became known that gold was involved, Allied officers called in help from Colonel Bernstein's operation. The British also sent a general to assist with the investigation. They worked for weeks piecing together a bit of information here and a piece there. An American officer interrogated Funk about the gold, but he provided nothing because he knew nothing. The Allies were sure that something had taken place near the Walchensee, but they were not sure exactly what or how big was the stash. They also learned that forester Neuhauser had been involved and that Josef Veit, a sanitation worker at the school, and Heinz Rüger, who was on the Mittenwald staff, had helped in moving the gold and currency to the mountains.[26]

It took a month for the Americans and British to amass enough details about the hidden gold to start a serious search. Finally on June 6, the American and British soldiers accompanied by Veit and some sawmill workers went by truck to the Walchensee. They walked into the forest near the Neuhauser house and then climbed further up to Einsiedl. Eventually they reached near the summit in the crags above the Obernach power plant. The Americans carried metal detectors. The G.I.s knew that the Germans who had hidden the gold had done their work with the help of pack mules, so they followed stool droppings through the woods. They also found hoof marks. For a long time, the men heard nothing but the sound of their boots clomping on the forest floor. Finally the metal detectors let off loud whistles. The group stopped and looked around. Nearby they saw empty wine bottles and discarded food cans.

The group immediately began digging, and they pulled from a hole some heavy bags. The booby traps did not explode. Stenciled on the sack were the words *Reichsbank Hauptkasse Berlin* (Reichsbank Main Cash Desk Berlin) They opened them, and found two gold bars. It was obviously the *Gebirgsjägerschule* gold, so they continued digging until they had searched the whole area. They ultimately found a rich hoard of bags of gold and sacks of currency. They also uncovered blank currency paper and boxes of jewelry.[27]

The prize, though, was the 364 bags that contained 728 gold bars that the Reichsbank staff had brought from Berlin. American Major William R. Girler and Captain Walter R. Dee signed papers acknowledging that they had received them. The two officers estimated that they contained a total of 9.1 tons of gold. Perhaps as many as one hundred gold bars and all the Swiss francs, though, were missing. The contents of the shipment from Berlin had not been counted in weeks, and there is no doubt that much of it was gone. The Americans believed the locals had taken it, while the locals thought the Americans had. Plenty of the Reichsbank gold had obviously slipped away in the mayhem of war and would never be found. It was later estimated that at least a half-ton of bullion and an unknown amount of currency, which might have included more than $120,000 in American dollars, had disappeared.[28]

The Bavarian Criminal Investigation Department in the early 1950s did a thorough study of the Walchensee gold and presented its findings on January 8, 1953. By that time, Colonel Pfeiffer and Lt. Colonel Rauch had both immigrated to Argentina, where they lived for many years as successful businessmen working for a metallurgy company. It was always suspected that they had put away enough Reichsbank gold to finance their new life. There were also reports of two American colonels seen just after the war with large rucksacks filled with gold and British pounds. People also claimed to have seen Pfeiffer and Rauch with American officers, who had plenty of valuables. When the owner of a nearby hotel was murdered, there were stories that she had taken part in the plot to steal valuables. One of the Reichsbank officials, who had traveled on the gold train from Berlin committed suicide in 1946, and other bank employees believed that he was the one who took the two bars that ended up in the stovepipe. No one, however, was ever charged in the case.

After living many years in Argentina, Rauch returned to Bavaria where he spent his last years; Pfeiffer returned to Austria, where he lived until his death. The two men took the complete story of what happened at the Walchensee with them to the grave.

Over the years since 1945, many stories have surfaced about tons of gold being lost at the *Gebirgsjägerschule* and the Walchensee. The favorite one among Germans is that the *Amis* (Americans) had stolen the gold. It also seems that unnamed Bavarians got some. Large amounts of currency, both dollars and pounds, were later dug up, for example, in gardens. No one was ever charged, even after the long and thorough investigation by Bavarian authorities in the early 1950s. Several writers have attempted to unravel the story of the Bavarian gold, without success. Henriette von Schirach, whose husband was the Nazi youth leader and *Gauleiter* of Vienna, lived in the area after the war and wrote the book *The Price of Glory*. She called the gold story a "tragicomedy." The British writer W. Stanley Moss in *Gold Is Where You Hide It* told a similar tale. Two British writers, Ian Sayer and Douglas Botting, in the 1984 book *Nazi Gold* did the most exhaustive work, but failed to solve the mystery. They too charged an American cover up. Sayer told the London Gold Conference that more than $3 million had been stolen in Mittenwald and Einseidl. The Gold Team's final report in 2000 stated, "The Gold Team developed many leads regarding small and large misappropriations of gold bullion by elements of the U.S. Third Army in Germany and by U.S. intelligence agents in Austria and Germany," but admitted that more research had to be done on "this politically sensitive issue." That has never done, and there is no doubt that American G.I.s stationed in Bavaria at the end of the war pilfered small amounts of bullion that were later uncovered.[29]

In the late 1980s, researchers discovered two gold bars in Bavaria that originally belonged to the Belgian Central Bank, but had been melted down by Degussa and given a date prior to 1938. They were perhaps part of the Mittenwald gold. The German government in September 1996 gave them to the Tripartite Commission for the Restitution of Monetary Gold, which sent them to the Bank of England. The proceeds were later distributed to Tripartite claimants.[30]

Chapter Thirty

THE END OF
A SORDID TALE

Götterdämmerung
April–May 1945

Tons of gold: 50

Gold Route
- - - - - ▸

Denmark

Itzehoe

Holland

Germany

Berlin

Belgium

Mühlhausen
Weimar

Bohemia
and Moravia

Worms

Luxembourg

Slovakia

Munich

Salzburg

France

Mittenwald Walchensee
Switzerland

Altaussee

Hungary

Italy

Yugoslavia

The final Big Three meeting of World War II took place in the summer of 1945 in Potsdam just outside bombed-out Berlin. The cast sitting around the table this time was dramatically different from the previous one held only five months earlier. Harry Truman was now the U.S. president. Churchill and Labor party leader Clement Attlee initially both participated, but then Churchill left after he lost his country's parliamentary election. With two novices at the table, Stalin bargained tougher than ever. He was also in a strong position because the Red Army now controlled the Baltic states, Poland, Czechoslovakia, Hungary, Bulgaria, and Romania. The Soviets demanded an enormous amount of reparations from their occupation zone in the now divided country as well as thirty percent of all German external investments and gold. That almost ended the meeting in its tracks.

The three leaders signed a final agreement on August 2 that basically let each of the three have power over its occupation zone. The Soviet Union renounced "all claims in respect of reparations to shares of German enterprises which are located in the Western Zones of Germany." Early in the conference Stalin made a formal claim to some of the gold found at Merkers, saying that he would be satisfied with thirty percent of it. But later he surprised his colleagues by announcing he would make "no claims to gold captured by the Allied troops in Germany." One can only speculate why Stalin took that unexpected step. Perhaps Soviet troops had already collected substantial amounts of gold on their way to Berlin, and he did not want to share it. Whatever the reason, Moscow was not part of further gold discussions. France was not invited to Potsdam, but Britain and the U.S. created a French zone out of their territory. World War II was over; the Cold War had begun.[1]

As a follow-up to the Potsdam summit, the Paris Conference on Reparations took place in November and December 1945. Part III of the conference's final statement set out the immediate post-war gold policy. The Tripartite Gold Commission was set up to judge the various claims and divide the captured bullion among the victims. James Angell, the leader of the U.S. delegation, argued successfully that the only moral and logical solution was to allot Nazi gold captured by the Allies to countries on the basis of how much they had lost. Allied armies had not collected nearly enough to satisfy all the demands. The participants finally agreed that recovered bullion would be distributed to countries "in proportion to their respective losses of gold through looting or by wrongful removal to Germany."[2] The agreement covered all gold moved after March 12, 1938, the date of the *Anschluss*. Moreover, any monetary gold recovered from a third country and taken to Germany, such as the Yugoslav or Albanian holdings that wound up in Rome, would also become part of the pool.

Ten countries submitted claims, which totaled more than twice the amount that had been turned into the Allied gold pool. The ten countries demanding restitution were Albania, Austria, Belgium, Czechoslovakia, Greece, Italy, Luxembourg, Netherlands, Poland, and Yugoslavia. They collectively asked for the return of 735 tons, but the Allies validated only 514 tons. The Trilateral Commission eventually obtained only 336.4 tons of captured gold for distribution to the claimants.[3]

There was no attempt to deal with personal gold that the Nazis had seized because it was impossible to track that gold back to its original owners. That, however, became a nagging problem that hung around World War II reparations for years.

The commission's first job was to determine the merit of the claims, and it disallowed a large portion of them. In the end, though, there were still fifty percent more claims than the commission had gold. Most of the cases were settled quickly and relatively easily, with more than eighty percent of them resolved between 1947 and 1950. Despite the initial success in quickly distributing most of the bullion to the rightful owners, the organization operated out of Brussels until September 1998. It was an international organization that refused to go out of business.

By the late 1950s, the only item of importance still on its agenda was the Albanian claim to the gold that Italy had taken in April 1941, when it invaded the country. The Trilateral Commission quickly recognized the Albanian case for the gold, which at first had gone into the Italian Central Bank but then was taken by the

Germans when they occupied the country in 1944. Enver Hoxha ruled the People's Socialist Republic of Albania from 1944 until his death in 1985. The country isolated itself from the rest of Europe and leaned toward communist China.

A naval incident took place in October 1947 involving two British destroyers, which were seriously damaged by Albanian mines planted in the Channel of Corfu. Gunfire was also exchanged between the two countries. Britain demanded reparations for the damages, but the Hoxha government refused. Britain then blocked the delivery of a ton of Tripartite gold to Albania. The case eventually went to the International Court of Justice, which ruled in favor of the British. The Albanians, though, still refused to pay. The standoff was only settled in 1996 with the end of the cold war and the death of Hoxha. Britain settled the case. At that point the Tripartite Commission had no outstanding gold claims.

Also high on the post-war agenda of the Allies was punishment of the countries that had profited from collaborating with the Nazis. There was widespread anger toward several nations that had been nominally neutral, but had either openly or clandestinely helped the German war machine. The most important of those was Switzerland, but the list of alleged offenders also included Sweden, Spain, Portugal, Turkey, and Argentina. Romania had also been a major supporter of the Wehrmacht as a key supplier of petroleum, but it was now in the Soviet sphere, and the west did not seek to punish it economically.

In early 1946, the U.S., Britain, and France invited Switzerland to send a delegation to Washington to open a discussion about its wartime economic activities. London and Paris did much more business with the Swiss and were less enthusiastic than the Americans about prosecuting them. U.S. officials, by then, had calculated that "at a minimum" the Nazi regime had transferred at least $200 million of looted gold to Switzerland.[4] Statistics later released by the Swiss National Bank showed that it was a major buyer of German gold from the last quarter of 1941 through the first quarter of 1944.[5] Swiss diplomats blustered and stonewalled for months until the U.S. negotiators were worn down and accepted a settlement for the payment of just $58.1 million. That went into the gold pool. Former Swiss parliamentarian Jean Ziegler wrote in his book *The Swiss, the Gold and the Dead* that his compatriots "lied their heads off at Washington in 1946." In 1951, the amount was negotiated down to $28 million.[6]

Later negotiations with Sweden, Spain, Portugal, and Turkey took place against the backdrop of the new Cold War. Sweden signed its deal with the Allies in July 1946. William Slany, the chief historian of the Department of State, wrote later that the agreements were "clearly a foreign policy aimed at ensuring normalcy in the gold trade, good relations with the neutral in the pos-war era, and the neutrals in the post-war era and reassuring the New York Federal Reserve that it could continue to buy gold unfettered by considerations of origin."[7]

Spain, Portugal, and Turkey were members of NATO, and the U.S. was putting together military plans for the defense of Western Europe and the Middle East. Sweden remained neutral, but leaned west. The U.S. negotiated a treaty with Spain that permitted it to build a major air force re-supply facility in that country, which was important for the Pentagon. Spain had received $90 million in Nazi gold, but eventually gave the Tripartite Commission a token $114,329. Portugal and the U.S. signed a treaty giving landing rights to the American military in the Azores. Turkey allowed the U.S. to build military bases in its country, which were used for spying on the Soviets during the Cold War. Sweden's compensation took the form of donations to refugee groups as well as payment for stationing American and British forces in Europe.

As a result of these deals, several countries were able to keep their ill-gotten gains from World War II. In the late 1990s, the Clinton Administration put together a group headed by Under Secretary of State Stuart Eizenstat that was called the Presidential Advisory Commission on Holocaust Assets. Unofficially it was known as the Gold Team. It did extensive research on stolen Nazi assets, and was critical of the agreements the neutrals made with Hitler. Switzerland received the most criticism, and it also protested that the deal with Portugal, "effectively washed all looted bars." Lisbon acknowledged receiving less than four tons of gold. Spain was suspected of getting 94 tons of looted gold between 1942 and 1944, but was held responsible for obtaining only eight bars. The Gold Team report further complained that the Turkish government had been willing to surrender $3.4 million in gold to the Allies, but had never signed the accord. In high dudgeon it said: "To this day the Turkish government has not surrendered a single coin or bar of restitution for the looted gold that it received during the war in payment for chromite and other strategic commodities."[8]

The Eizenstat work was the first serious attempt to examine the fate of private gold during World War II. Worldwide research into that dark corner of World War II was brought together at the London Conference on Nazi Gold in December 1997. Eizenstat also detailed his long work on the subject in his book *Imperfect Justice*. The meeting made a major contribution to the understanding of an historic tragedy that had previously been almost ignored. The final report pulled back the curtain on the evil of Adolf Hitler, a man of hate. He and his fellow Nazis had attempted to build a Reich that would endure for a thousand years by stealing gold from Europe's central banks and from millions of concentration camp prisoners.[9]

EPILOGUE

O n the last day of February 1946, almost a year after the war ended, the French navy sent out the message: ORDER TO THE MONTCALM TO MAKE DIRECT ROUTE TO CHERBOURG STOP. The 350 tons of gold that had arrived in Martinique in June 1940 finally set out from the Caribbean on its way home. There were 9,766 wooden boxes aboard, each weighing just over one hundred pounds. When the cargo arrived in France, most of the bullion, which consisted largely of coins, was smelted and turned into bars. Once again the country's gold, one of the world's largest holdings of the precious metal, was home. It was the biggest return of World War II gold.[1]

Humankind never seems to lose its fascination for gold. Some people love it; some hate it. Few are indifferent. Perhaps that has something to do with the price, which has had lots of volatility in recent times but has risen sharply in value. In the last eighty years, the price of the metal has gone from $35 an ounce to nearly $2,000. The world's two most populous countries, China and India, have millions of gold bugs, which means the metal is likely to remain popular. Many academics, though, still mutter about it being a barbaric relic.

World War II did not end gold's role in the international economy. Bullion remained paramount for the world's political and financial leaders, and it would play an important role in rebuilding the world economy. The international monetary system that Harry Dexter White pushed through at the Bretton Woods Conference of 1944 reaffirmed the primacy of gold as an instrument of international debt payments between nations. It also raised the U.S. dollar to the honored position of being on a parity with gold. It was the only currency with that status. During the initial years after the war, Bretton Woods worked fairly well. Countries wanted dollars to buy American cars, steel, machinery, and more for their economic recovery. In November 1961, eight major countries attempted to maintain the gold standard by setting up the London Gold Pool. They defended the price at $35 per troy ounce by interventions in London, the largest bullion market. In March 1968, though, that collapsed. America's predominance in gold holdings continued slipping, and foreigners soon held more than the U.S.[2]

Starting in the 1960s, the U.S. was spending heavily on both the Great Society social programs and the Vietnam War without any appropriate tax increases, which caused serious balance of payments problems. The results were large deficits and a weakening American currency. The dollar eventually became overvalued, and the global monetary system ran into trouble. The post-war financial system was really only operational from 1959 to 1968.

Critics complained that Bretton Woods gave the U.S. an unfair advantage in global business. Charles de Gaulle, the president of France, became the leader of the anti-Bretton Woods offensive. At a press conference in 1965, he launched the first attack. He also strongly endorsed bullion, saying, "In truth, one does not see how one could really have any standard criterion other than gold." Starting three years earlier, France had begun converting its surplus dollars into gold, buying as much as $150 million a month and having it shipped to Paris. U.S. gold holdings were soon only about half what they had been at the end of the war. Jacques Rueff, a long-time Banque de France official, provided the intellectual firepower for the French attack.[3]

The U.S. successfully fought off the French assault, but the American currency continued to be weak, especially against the post-war economic powers, Germany and Japan. Washington continued to lose more and more gold to countries such as Portugal and

Spain who began following the French lead. Finally on August 15, 1971, President Nixon closed the gold window and refused to sell the metal, thus essentially ending Bretton Woods, although it limped along for a while. It was a traumatic episode for the world economy and became known as the Nixon Shock. The price of bullion on the world market began rising, and by the end of the 1970s was more than $800 an ounce. It then fell to less than $300 for several years before roaring back in the late 1980s to $500. It took another long slide in the 1990s, but has come back strong in the new millennium.[4]

Many economists, central bankers, and finance ministers would be happy for gold to just go away as a global system of value and be no different than other metals such as copper or iron. At the turn of the new century, gold was down to about $270 an ounce and falling. Gordon Brown, the British Chancellor of the Exchequer, thought he saw the handwriting on the wall and announced that he would sell fifty-eight percent of his country's gold reserves. Between 1999 and 2001, he sold off four hundred tons at about $275 an ounce. That turned out to be one of history's greatest financial blunders. The price was soon once again rising. The chancellor had sold at the bottom of the market, and that period became known as Brown's Bottom.[5]

In more recent times, the price of gold has fluctuated widely on international markets, but has been generally rising. There have been several spikes, which were usually concurrent with inflation or political unrest. Gold continues to retain its allure as a safe haven in times of trouble. The historic high closing London fixed price was on September 5, 2011, when it reached $1,896.50 an ounce.[6]

According to experts, less than 200,000 tons of bullion have been mined in history. Current world production is about 2,500 tons per year, and the four largest producers are China, Australia, the United States, and Russia. Together they mine nearly half of new global output.

Central banks still hold about twenty percent of the world's gold. Since 1999, some two-dozen nations, including the U.S., have had an agreement not to sell more than four hundred tons per year. They have also stated as their policy was that "gold will remain an important element of global monetary reserves." A few countries such as Holland and Belgium have nonetheless quietly sold off bullion. Switzerland was the last major country in the world to go off the gold standard, which it did only in 2000.

Gold remains a product that many people trust because they lack confidence in politicians, who seem all too ready to debase the currency so that they can operate irresponsible economic policies, steal the national treasury, or run it as a Ponzi scheme. The words of Herbert Hoover to Franklin Roosevelt in 1933 still ring true: "We have gold because we cannot trust governments."[7]

As for my personal view of gold, dear reader, I follow the recommendation of my investment consultant Paul Koether, who has been a friend and watched over my money for many years. He advised me to put some of my retirement nest egg into gold. So I own gold coins. They might be useful in the next apocalypse.

Appendix I

STATISTICS OF NAZI GOLD

Germany was historically a major holder of central bank gold, but just prior to the war the country had only a small amount because of its ongoing economic problems. Following orders from Reichsbank President Hjalmar Schacht, the holdings as early as 1933 were divided between published accounts and hidden ones, so that the world would not know how much the country actually had. Nazi leaders needed gold to buy critical war material on the international market. Before the world conflict began, Germany captured a large amount of bullion in Austria and a smaller cache in Czechoslovakia. Most of that, though, was soon spent on armaments, and the bullion holdings were again low when World War II began with the invasion of Poland. The Nazis captured much more after their invasion of Western Europe in 1940. Almost all of the gold seized during the war had been confiscated by the end of 1940. Although the world's public was outraged by the theft of bullion as well as other valuables from private individuals, in particular concentration camp inmates, that was a relatively small amount when compared with what was stolen from central banks.

Reichsbank Holdings in 1938 Prior to Nazi Aggression[1]
Published	$28.6 million
Hidden	$120.5 million
Total	$149.1 million

Stolen Central Bank Gold[2]

Austria	March 1938	$91 million
Czechoslovakia	March 1939	$45 million
Danzig	September 1939	$4.3 million
Netherlands	May 1940	$137.2 million
Belgium	May 1940	$204.9 million
Luxembourg	May 1940	$4.8 million
Yugoslavia	April 1941	$3.8 million
Greece	April 1941	$7.4 million
Italy	December 1943	$64.8 million
Albania	September 1943	$2.6 million
Hungary	March 1944	$32.2 million
	Total	$598 million

Appendix II

PARTNERS IN GOLD

Switzerland was by far the most important way for Germany to unload its stolen gold and buy war goods. Nearly eighty percent of all the bullion shipments between the Reichsbank and other countries went through Switzerland. In the first two years of the war, Berlin dealt mainly with private Swiss banks, but the Berne government in October 1941 stopped that and demanded that business be done with the Swiss National Bank. That small country that was home to a major international central bank remained a good Nazi partner until late in the war, when the Allies announced the Gold Declaration of January 1944. The U.S., Britain, and the Soviet Union declared that they would not recognize the transfer of looted gold and would not buy it from any country that had not broken relations with Axis countries. Nonetheless, the Reichsbank's Emil Puhl was still selling bullion to the Swiss in the spring of 1945. The Swiss government's Bergier Report in 2002 confirmed that the Swiss knew by 1943 that the Nazi gold it was accepting was taken both from central banks and citizens of occupied countries.

Bank Recipients of Nazi Gold During World War II[3]

Swiss National Bank	$389.2 million
Swiss Commercial Banks	$61.1 million
Spain	$140 million

Sweden	$59.7 million
Romania	$54.2 million
Portugal	$43-$49 million
Turkey	$10-15 million
Bank for International Settlements	$ 12 million

Sales to Private Swiss Private Banks in 1940-1941[4]

Swiss Bank Corporation	$36.3 million
Bank Leu	$12 million
Union Bank of Switzerland	$7.6 million
Basler Handelsbank	$1.8 million
Eidgenössische Bank	$0.1 million

Sales to the Swiss National Bank (1940-1945)[5]

1940	222 million Swiss francs
1941	349.9 million
1942	493.2 million
1943	609.3 million
1944	257.4 million
1945	15.7 million
Total	1,947.8 million Swiss francs

Other Nazi Gold Sales[6]

Soviet Union	$23 million
Japan	$4.2 million
Bank for International Settlements	$21.5 million

Appendix III

POST WAR

Despite all the gold the Allies seized from defeated Germany, the Reichsbank ended the conflict with nearly twice as much as it had prior to the war. Ten countries made claims to the Tripartite Commission for the Restitution of Monetary Gold. Most of the cases were settled within two years after the commission started its deliberations in 1945. The organization, which had its headquarters in Brussels, existed for much longer largely because of the lack of a settlement for the Albanian claim. Britain blocked it because of three incidents involving British ships in Albanian waters just after World War II. After that dispute was finally settled, the Commission was dissolved on September 9, 1998. It was recognized from the beginning that no country would get total restitution since so much more gold was stolen than had been recovered. The victim countries received about two-thirds the amount that the commission recognized they had lost.

Reichsbank Gold Holdings at the End of World War II[7]
$256 million

Total Nazi Gold Trade 1938-1945[8]

Reichsbank gold transactions	$909.2 million
Looted from central banks	$475 million

Seized from individuals, both
    German and others $146 million
Nazi spent during the war
    and lost gold $645 million

Gold Recovered in Germany in 1945[9]

U.S. Army recoveries from
    April-December 1945 $262.2 million
Merkers $238.5 million
Reichsbank branches $14 million
Other locations $9.7 million
Bullion Soviet army seized
    at the Reichsbank in Berlin $4 million

Tripartite Commission Restitution of Monetary Gold[10]

	Claimed	Recognized
Netherlands	145.7 tons	110.2 tons
Italy	73.4	69.3 tons
Albania	2.6	2.3 tons
Austria	91.3	78.3 tons
Czechoslovakia	45	13.3 tons
Yugoslavia	12.3	2.7 tons
Belgium	204.9	198.4 tons
Greece	12.6	none
Luxembourg	4.3	4.2 tons
Poland	138.7	(Danzig only) 4.1 tons

ENDNOTES

PROLOGUE

1. Greater glory to come: Charles M. Province, *Patton's Third Army*, p. 223.
2. Your just reward: "Absolute War" in *The Poems of George Patton*.
3. Down the road: NACP RG 331 Bernstein Report to Brig. Gen. F.J. McSherry G-4. /390/46/9/2. Function in ETOUSA Operations: Merkers-Harringen-Frankfurt Areas in Germany 9 April to 22 April 1945. Dated 26 April 26, 1945.
4. Back to Merkers: *Ibid.*
5. Arrested all the mine executives: *Ibid.*
6. Cardboard or wooden containers: NACP RG 260 Monthly Report of Financial Aspects of the Allied Occupation of Germany, April 1945.
7. Property in world history: NACP RG 331 Report of Developments in Removal of Treasure from Kaiseroda Mine at Merkers, Germany sent to Brig. Gen. McSherry April 8, 1945. Arthur Smith, *Hitler's Gold*, p.163.

CHAPTER ONE: THE GLITTER OF GOLD

1. The human race: Gerard Loeb, *Battle for Investment Survival*, p. 102.
2. Period of time: Peter L. Bernstein, *The Power of Gold*, p. 367.
3. A barbaric relic: John Maynard Keynes, *Monetary Reform*, p. 172.
4. On each side: Peter L. Bernstein, *The Power of Gold*, p. 3, and World Gold Council.
5. Second Millennium B.C.: Fernand Braudel, *Memory and the Mediterranean*, p. 61.
6. Things go smoothly: Thucydides, *The History of the Peloponnesian War*, VI, 34, 2, the Jowett Translation.
7. In great quantities: Fordham University, Internet Medieval Sourcebook. www.fordham.edu. *Christopher Columbus: Extracts from Journal*.
8. Most productive eras: *Ibid. Columbus Letter to the King and Queen of Spain, 1494*.
9. An ounce: World Gold Council paper by Timothy Green, Central Bank Reserves, www.gold.org.
10. Pre-war level: The Churchill Centre, www.winstonchurchill.org, speech May 4, 1925, House of Commons.
11. In the bourgeois sense: Joseph Schumpeter, *History of Economic Analysis*, p. 406.
12. The twenty-first century: Peter L. Bernstein, *The Power of Gold*, p. 372.
13. Vote for Gold: *Ibid.* p. 369.
14. In his mattress: Benjamin P. Thomas and Harold M. Hyman, *Stanton*, p. 319.
15. Limit the power of government: Liaquat Ahamed, *Lords of Finance*, p. 169.
16. The toothpaste tubes: Felix Rohatyn, *Dealings*, p. 3.
17. Worth of gold: Noel Barber, *The Week France Fell*, p. 298.

18. Before a higher god: Adolf Hitler, *Mein Kampf*, Vol. 2, Chapter 2.
19. Europe's national depositories: Arthur L. Smith, Jr., *Hitler's Gold*, p. 163. Hjalmar Schacht, *Gold for Europe*, p. 13.
20. All hazards get gold: Peter L. Bernstein, *The Power of Gold*, p. 15.

CHAPTER TWO: SPANISH PRELUDE

1. Half a million dead: Hugh Thomas, *Spanish Civil War*, p. 900.
2. In its vaults: Angel Viñas, *The Financing of the Civil War* in the book *Revolution and War in Spain 1931-1939*, p. 267.
3. National parliament: Gerald Howson, *Arms for Spain*, p. 2.
4. Sisters were killed: Paul Preston, *The Church's Crusade Against the Republic*, p. 53.
5. Religion and the church: Papal Encyclicals Online, Pius XI, *Dilectissima Nobis*. www.papalencyclicals.net.
6. Nationalists and Catholicism: Hugh Thomas, *Spanish Civil War*, pp. 938-939.
7. Plotted a coup d'etat: Gerald Howson, *Arms for Spain*, pp. 5-15.
8. Funeral of democracy: Hugh Thomas, *Spanish Civil War*, p. 5.
9. Republican-controlled Madrid: Oliver Todd, *Malraux*, p. 181.
10. Planes to Franco: Hugh Thomas, *Spanish Civil War*, 331-334. Angel Viñas, *The Financing of the Civil War*, p. 253.
11. Until March 1937: *Ibid.* Angel Viñas, p. 268.
12. From your country: Hugh Thomas, *Spanish Civil War*, p. 338.
13. Spanish Republic: Oliver Todd, *Malraux*, p. 183.
14. Bullion to France: Angel Viñas, *The Financing of the Civil War*, p. 268
15. Pessimistic reports: Daniel Kowalsky. *Stalin and The Spanish Civil War.* Chapter 1.
16. And code breakers: *Ibid.*, chapter 9.
17. The artillery fire: W.G. Krivitsky, *In Stalin's Secret Service*, p. 71.
18. Agency's economic department: Edward Gazur, *Alexander Orlov*, p. 14.
19. On September 16: Alexander Orlov, *Reader's Digest*, December 1966, pp. 31–43.
20. Gave to Franco: RGASPI, Fond 17, op. 166.
21. The good life: Bolloten, p. 143.
22. Million gold dollars: Louis Fischer, *Men and Politics*, p. 356.
23. All with aviation: Kowalsky, Daniel. *Stalin and The Spanish Civil War*, chapter 3.
24. The best security: Edward Gazur, *Alexander Orlov*, p. 85.
25. For the government: Angel Viñas, *The Financing of the Civil War*, p. 228.
26. The Spanish gold: W.G. Krivitsky, *In Stalin's Secret Service*, p. 87.
27. In Soviet Russia: Alexander Orlov, *March of Time*, p. 384.
28. Time of delivery: Gerald Howson, *Arms for Spain*, p. 122.
29. By Schwed personally: Alexander Orlov, *March of Time* pp. 381-382.

30. To that country: *Ibid.* p. 385.
31. To store munitions: *Ibid.* pp. 385-387.
32. Bank of America: *Ibid.* p. 387.
33. Arriving Soviet vessel: Alexander Orlov, *Readers Digest.*
34. Carry each box: Alexander Orlov, *March of Time* p. 91
35. When he could: Alexander Orlov, *Reader's Digest.*
36. Soon be over: Alexander Orlov, *March of Time* p. 391.
37. Settle the problem: Edward Gazur, *Alexander Orlov,* p. 93.
38. Checked and weighed: *Ibid.*
39. Be legally meaningless: RGVA RF, Fond 05, Litvinov Files, op. 16, P.114, file 1.
40. Sure of your figure: John Costello and Oleg Tsarev, *Deadly Illusions,* p. 262.
41. Your figure to anybody: *Ibid.*
42. End to end: W.G. Krivitsky, *In Stalin's Secret Service,* p. 98.
43. On November 7: RGASPI, Yurii Rybalkin, Operatsija "Iks".
44. Most of them Portuguese: Burnett Boilloten, *The Spanish Civil War,* pp. 149-152.
45. Their own ears: Orlov papers. NACP RG 46, Box 77.

CHAPTER THREE: ADOLF HITLER'S ARGONAUT

1. Always called Hjalmar: Hjalmar Schacht, *My First Seventy-Six Years,* pp. 10-22.
2. His stiff formality: Jacobsson, Erin, *A Life for Sound Money,* p. 119.
3. His complex character: Harold Deutsch, *Hitler and His Generals.* BA PRO, C/23/83/18.
4. Quantity of other goods: Hjalmar Schacht, *Gold for Europe,* p. vii. David Ricardo, *On the Principles of Political Economy and Taxation,* Part 1.2.
5. Edge of a volcano: Hjalmar Schacht, *My First Seventy-Six Years,* p. 177. Frederick Taylor, *The Downfall of Money,* pp. 202-205.
6. Travelling third class: Hjalmar Schacht, *My First Seventy-Six Years,* p. 187.
7. With a lifetime tenure: Frederick Taylor, *The Downfall of Money,* pp. 329-336.
8. Before Roosevelt's election: Hjalmar Schacht, *The Stabilization of the Mark,* p. 129.
9. Standard for the world: Hjalmar Schacht. *My First Seventy-Six Years,* pp. 194-200.
10. For its replacement: *Ibid.,* p. 264.
11. Two billion per year: Margaret Macmillan, *Paris 1919,* pp. 102 and 192.
12. Never to have signed: Hjalmar Schacht, *My First Seventy-Six Years,* p. 247.
13. Wearing that night: IMT 3936-PS.
14. Into practical action: *Ibid.,* p. 279.
15. Dangerous power play: IMT, XVI, 224. Paul Enzig, *Germany's Default,* p. 41.
16. As their predecessors: IMT, Vol. 13, May 3, 1946 morning and IMT 456-D.
17. Rule through them: Liaquat Ahamed, *Lords of Finance,* p. 480.

18. With a forceful Heil: IMT 457-EC.

19. Can save Germany: IMT Vol. 13, May 2, 1946, p. 567.

20. Führer's position entirely: IMT 2409(a)-PS.

21. Means of the state: *The Goebbels Diaries*. February 3, 1933, p. 240. Alan Bullock, *Hitler a Study in Tyranny*, p. 258.

22. With an iron fist: IMT D-203.

23. Such a clear picture: IMT EC-439.

24. Then also denied it: Shirer, p. 194, IMT 3740-PS.

25. Unemployed off the street: Hjalmar Schacht, *My First Seventy-Six Years*, pp. 302-303.

26. Descending on Germany: Richard Evans, *The Coming of the Third Reich*, p. 354.

27. Never happen again: William Carr, *Arms, Autarky and Aggression*, pp. 21-36.

28. Get its payoff: Joseph Borkin, *The Crime and Punishment of I.G. Farben*, pp. 44-60.

29. Shall swim in it: Trevor-Roper, Hugh, *Hitler's Table Talk*, pp. 623-624. Hartmut Berghoff, *Business in the Age of Extremes*, p. 139.

30. Army before economics: Hitler, Adolf, *Hitler's Second Book*, p. 99.

31. The Nazis needed: Albert Speer, *Inside the Third Reich*, pp. 316-317.

32. Needed with gold: Jacob Weixelbaum Publications and Research, *The Contradiction of Neutrality and International Finance*, www.jasonweixelbaum. wordpress.com.

33. Clandestine operations abroad: Hans Fredrik Dahl, *Quisling*, pp. 145-152.

34. All the attention: Hjalmar Schacht, *My First Seventy-Six Years*, pp. 307-313.

35. Been complete flops: IHT November 23, 1945. John Weitz, *Hitler's Banker*, pp. 168-169.

36. Service of warfare: Hjalmar Schacht, *My First Seventy-Six Years*, p. 320.

37. Our political opponents: IMT 1168-PS. IMT January 11, 1946.

38. Spent on dinners: IMT Vol. 13, Friday, May 3, 1946.

39. Via Mefo financing: IMT Document Schacht-7.

40. Half billion Reichsmark: IMT 493-USA and EC 497.

41. And other purposes: IMT 014-EC and 835-USA.

42. Have taken place: IMT document 835-USA. Ralf Banken, *Edelmetallmangel und Großraubwirtschaft*, p. 241.

43. And even dangerous: William Edward Dodd, *Ambassador Dodd's Diary, 1933-1938*, p. 254.

44. The Protestant Reformation: Schacht, *My First Seventy-Six Years*, p. 349.

45. But steadily deteriorated: *Time* magazine, January 30, 1938, *My First Seventy-Six Years*, p. 386.

CHAPTER FOUR: FRANKLIN D. ROOSEVELT'S ARGONAUT

1. Soon dropped out: Henry Morgenthau III, *Mostly Morgenthau*, pp. 213-214.

2. Without a degree: Herbert Levy, *Henry Morgenthau, Jr.*, pp. 215-217.

3. And deep friendship: *Ibid.*, p. 246.
4. New York State weekly: *Ibid.*, p. 239.
5. Incumbent Herbert Hoover: John Morton Blum, *From the Morgenthau Diaries* Vol. 1, pp. 31-34.
6. And other businesses: *Ibid.*, pp. 35-50.
7. No one's here: Bernard F. Stanton. *George F. Warren Farm Economist*, pp. 404-414. *Time* magazine cover story November 27, 1933.
8. Before Roosevelt's election: Bernard F. Stanton, *George F. Warren Farm Economist*, p. 410.
9. Standard for the world: Peter L. Bernstein, *The Power of Gold*, p. 318.
10. For paper currency: *Ibid.*, pp. 319-322.
11. Off the gold standard: Liaquat Ahamed, *Lords of Finance*, p. 461.
12. Prop up world currencies: *Ibid.*, pp. 466-471.
13. So-called international bankers: University of California Santa Barbara, The American Presidency Project. www.presidency.ucsb.edu, Franklin D. Roosevelt, 96. Wireless to London Conference July 3, 1933.
14. End of western civilization: Liaquat Ahamed, *Lords of Finance*, p. 460.
15. Fist into a pillow: Arthur Schlesinger, Jr. *Coming of the New Deal 1933-1935*, p. 239.
16. The world market: The American Presidency Project, University of California Santa Barbara. www.presidency.ucsb.edu, Franklin D. Roosevelt fourth fireside chat, October 22, 1933.
17. Secretary of the navy: John Morton Blum, *Roosevelt and Morgenthau*, pp. 45-53.
18. Put into bankruptcy: Liaquat Ahamed, *Lords of Finance*, p. 473.
19. Old pink whiskers: *Ibid.*
20. Standard on the booze: Keynes Open Letter to the President, published in the *New York Times* on December 31, 1933.
21. Doing it together: Blum, *From the Morgenthau Diaries*, Vol. 1, p. 73.
22. Foreign exchange rates: The American Presidency Project: Message to Congress, Recommending Legislation on the Currency System, January 15, 1934.
23. Going to $12 billion: Liaquat Ahamed, *Lords of Finance*, p. 474.
24. Between 1923 and 1934: CIA study of October 17, 1955. CIA/SV/RR 121 titled "Soviet Gold Production, Reserves and Exports Through 1954."
25. Access to the powerful: Henry Morgenthau III, *Mostly Morgenthaus*, pp. 309-314.
26. All the time: HM 3:327.
27. To economic revival: Bernard F. Stanton, p. 431. Liaquat Ahamed, *Lords of Finance*, p. 477.

CHAPTER FIVE: HERMANN GÖRING GRABS CONTROL

1. Horace Greeley Hjalmar Schacht: William L. Shirer, *The Rise and Fall of the Third Reich*, pp. 259-262.

2. Carin von Kantzow: Roger Manvell and Heinrich Fraenkel, *Goering*, pp. 55-62.

3. Swedish drug clinic: Irving, David. *Göring*, pp. 83-89.

4. With brutal efficiency: William L. Shirer, *The Rise and Fall of the Third Reich*, pp. 213-226.

5. Called Göring amoral: IMT 3936-PS.

6. Will protect you: Stephen H. Roberts, *The House that Hitler Built*, p. 63.

7. The hall roared: Roger Manvell and Heinrich Fraenkel. p. 148.

8. Fight major conflicts: German History in Documents and Images, Vol. 7, www.germanhistorydocs.ghi-dc.org.

9. The same deadline: *Ibid*.

10. Steadfastly carried out: *Ibid*.

11. Country for imports: IMT EC-416 and EC-244.

12. Faith is justified: Hjalmar Schacht, *Confessions of The Old Wizard*, p. 338.

13. Produce at home: *Völkisher Beobachter*, September 10, 1939.

14. Had the chance: William Carr, *Arms, Autarky and Aggression*, pp. 51-52. Schacht Interrogation September 26, 1945, TD, University of Connecticut, 7971-2.

15. Rest of the world: *Foreign Affairs*, January 1937.

16. Saw the Führer: Schacht interrogation, September 26, 1945. TD, 7971-2.

17. Approved it in July 1938: IMT EC-243. Bernice Carroll, *Design for Total War*, pp. 135-137.

18. Bombing the factories: Joseph Berkin, *The Crime and Punishment of I.G. Farben*, pp. 128-134.

19. Throughout the war: Berenice Carroll, *Design for Total War*, pp. 145-146.

20. In northern France: Hartmut Berghoff, Jürgen Kocka, and Dieter Ziegler: *Wirtschaft im Zeitalter der Extreme*. Ralf Banken article *"Hiergegen kann nur mit freier Fahndung eingeschritten werden–Die Arbeit der deutschen Devisenschutzkommandos 1938 bis 1944."* Katrin Isabel Krähling, *Das Devisenschutzkommando Belgien, 1940-1944*. GFAB MA RW 36/217.

21. Orders only from him: IMT EC-376.

22. In the least: Hjalmar Schacht, *My First Seventy-Six Years*, pp. 369-370. IMT EC-248.

23. Go to war: IMT 244-EC.

24. His former activity: IMT EC-248, PS-3730, EC-252.

25. The Nazi government: Schacht Interrogation on October 12, 1945, TD 7972, EC-248 and PS-3730.

26. Further Mefo spending: Schacht Interrogation, October 12, 1945. TD, 7972.

27. Reichsmark of Mefo bills: TD, 7975-1.

28. I'm fond of you: Hjalmar Schacht *My First Seventy-Six Years*, p. 375.

29. Because he'll faint: Albert Speer, *Inside the Third Reich*, pp. 97-98.

30. To my successor: Hjalmar Schacht, *My First Seventy-Six Years*, p. 377.

31. Pick up on it: Harold James, *Schacht's Attempted Defection from Hitler's Germany*.

32.   Untiring working strength: IMT 3021-PS, 97-EC.
33.   Sitting in your chair: Hjalmar Schacht. *Account Settled*. p. 104.
34.   Dismissed the threat: Martha Dodd, *Through Embassy Eyes*, pp. 236-240.
35.   Enlightenment and propaganda: IMT 35-5-PS and 2828-PS.
36.   Within their ranks: Albert Speer, *Infiltration*, p. 66.
37.   Hands of Hermann Göring: John Weitz, *Hitler's Banker*, pp. 209-221. Ralf Banken, *Edelmetallmangel und Großraubwritschaft*, p. 241.

CHAPTER SIX: THE CLUB FOR CENTRAL BANKERS
1.   Reichsbank's Hjalmar Schacht: Liaquat Ahamed, *Lords of Finance*, pp. 23-72.
2.   After World War I: Barry Eichengreen, *Golden Fetters*, pp. 224-245.
3.   The hotel room: Hjalmar Schacht, *My First Seventy-Six Years*, pp. 250-251.
4.   Coordinate national policies: Gianni Toniolo, *Central Bank Cooperation at the Bank for International Settlements*, pp. 35 and 46-58.
5.   Largely of economists: *Ibid.*, p. 62.
6.   Flowing behind him: Erin E. Jacobsson, *A Life for Sound Money*, p. 102.
7.   His Jewish counterpart: Hugh Trevor-Roper, *Hitler's Table Talk*, pp. 432-433.
8.   Do not understand: John Maynard Keynes, *The Great Slump of 1930*, p. 1.
9.   Stable as possible: Liquat Ahamed, *Lords of Finance*, pp. 375-379.
10. DNA of the BIS: Gianni Toniolo, *Central Bank Cooperation at the Bank for International Settlements*, p. 131.
11. The basis of gold: Bank for International Settlements website Fifth Annual Report. BIS website: bis.org/publ/arpdf/archive/ar1935_en.pdf.
12. Signed his letters Heil Hitler: Gianni Toniolo, p. 225. William Slany, *U.S. and Allied Efforts to Recover and Restore Gold and Other Assets Stolen or Hidden by Germany During World War II*, p. 189-193.

CHAPTER SEVEN: AUSTRIA BECOMES THE FIRST EASY PIECE
1.   And note taker: *Hossbach Memorandum*, 1937. *Documents on German Foreign Policy*, Series D, Vol. 1. pp. 29-39.
2.   Bores his guests: Galeazzo Ciano, *Diary 1937-1943*, p. 233.
3.   Period of Nazi aggression: Yale University. Avalon.law.yale.edu/imt/hossbach.asp.
4.   Discussion of armaments: *Ibid.*
5.   The armed forces: William Shirer, *The Rise and Fall of the Third Reich*, p. 318.
6.   Demands one Reich: Adolf Hitler, *Mein Kampf*, p. 3.
7.   March into Austria: Kurt von Schuschnigg, *Austrian Requiem*, pp. 3-27.
8.   Residing in Czechoslovakia: William Shirer, *The Rise and Fall of the Third Reich*, pp. 332-333.
9.   People and Fatherland: Kurt von Schuschnigg, *Austrian Requiem*, p. 39.
10. Was a mistake: Dieter Warner and Gerhard Tomkowitz, *Anschluss*, p. 97-99.
11. Treated as friends: William Shirer, *The Rise and Fall of the Third Reich*, pp. 337-342.

12. Regard to Austria: Dieter Warner and Gerhard Tomkowitz, *Anschluss*, p. 48-50.
13. The scheduled referendum: IMT C-102.
14. By phone at 2:45: Kurt von Schuschnigg, *Austrian Requiem*, pp. 45-48.
15. Nazi government popular: Götz Aly. *Hitler's Beneficiaries*, pp. 81-83.
16. As soon as possible: IMT 182-C. Dieter Warner and Gerhard Tomkowitz, *Anschluss*, p. 140.
17. Homeland to the German Reich: *Ibid.*, p. 194.
18. Return to the building: Norbert Schausberg, *Der Griff nach Osterreich*, pp. 35-50.
19. Account of the Reich: IMT 2313-PS.
20. Value of 1:1: IMT EC-421.
21. At a rapid rate: HM 115:198.
22. The Vienna bank: IMT E-297-A.
23. New York City: TCA Austria, November 4, 1947. NACP RG59/62D115 Box 14.
24. The takeover simple: *Ibid.*
25. From Austrian Jews: Ralf Banken, *Edelmetallmangel und Großraubwritschaft* p. 291.
26. Escape from persecution: *Ibid.*, pp. 292-302.
27. Million Reichsmark: Adam Tooze, *The Wages of Destruction*, pp. 245-246.
28. Countries they invaded: GFA, R2501/6446.
29. Balance of payments constraint: Adam Tooze, *The Wages of Destruction*, p. 246

CHAPTER EIGHT: AN INSIDE JOB AGAINST CZECHOSLOVAKIA
1. Tons of gold: Eduard Kubu, *Czechoslovak Gold Reserves and Their Surrender to Nazi Germany*, The London Conference, pp. 245-248.
2. Earlier October: *Documents on German Foreign Policy*, Series D, Vol. II, no. 221, pp. 357-62.
3. Way to German authorities: William L. Shirer, *The Rise and Fall of the Third Reich*, p. 376.
4. And flames up: *Jodl Diaries*, IMT EC-405 and PS-178.
5. The Sudeten Germans: Richard Evans, *The Coming of the Third Reich*, p. 674.
6. Fallen from heaven: John Toland, *Adolf Hitler*, pp. 650-651.
7. Cabinet and parliament: *Ibid.* p. 655.
8. Relationship of confidence: William L. Shirer, *The Rise and Fall of the Third Reich*, pp. 391-401.
9. On September 29: Harold C. Deutsch, *Hitler and His Generals*, pp. 401-410. William L. Shirer, *The Rise and Fall of the Third Reich*, pp. 404-412.
10. We know nothing: BBC Online Archives: "Chamberlain Addresses the Nation on His Negotiations for Peace."
11. Peace in our time: *BBC On This Day.*
12. Generals urged restraint: TD, 7971-2.
13. The Slovak economy: *Documents on German Foreign Policy*, Series D, Vol. VI, pp. 947-48.

14. Orders of the Führer: IMT, XXVIII, p. 373. Jodl Diary, p.167.
15. From that angle: *The British War Bluebook*, Speech by the Prime Minister at Birmingham on March 17, 1939.
16. Deliver 12.5 tons: Eduard Kubu, *Czechoslovak Gold Reserves and Their Surrender to Nazi Germany*, p. 246. Gianni Toniolo, *Central Bank Cooperation at the Bank for International Settlements*, p. 204.
17. Had 74 tons left: Gianni Toniolo, *Central Bank Cooperation at the Bank for International Settlements*, p. 546.
18. Under German control: IMT, Morning session, May 3, 1946.
19. Remaining Czech gold: Eduard Kubu, *Czechoslovak Gold Reserves and Their Surrender to Nazi Germany*. pp. 246-247. Gianni Toniolo, *Central Bank Cooperation at the Bank for International Settlement*, pp. 205-206.
20. In the telegram: J.S. Beyen. *Money in a Maelstrom*. pp. 137-140.
21. Unilaterally to block it: BA, Treasury Papers, T160/1417.
22. To the Germans: Eduard Kubu, *Czechoslovak Gold Reserves and Their Surrender to Nazi Germany*, p. 246. Thomas McKittrick Papers, Harvard Business School Library, carton 9, f.2. Gianni Toniolo, *Central Bank Cooperation at the Bank for International Settlement*, p. 546.
23. Anticipation of war: Gianni Toniolo, *Central Bank Cooperation at the Bank for International Settlements*, p. 205-213.
24. That was a lie: Paul Einzig, *In the Centre of Things*, pp. 186-194.
25. Out of Hitler's hands: *Ibid.*
26. Governments of those days: J.S. Beyen, *Money in a Maelstrom*, pp. 137-140.
27. I'll say you are: HM 170:124-129.
28. At that point: *Ibid.*
29. You look at it: *Ibid.*
30. Half to Switzerland: Eduard Kubu, *Czechoslovak Gold Reserves and Their Surrender to Nazi Germany*, pp. 245-248.
31. The former Czechoslovakia: *Ibid.*, pp. 245-249. Colonel Bernard Bernstein report to Lt. General Lucius Clay, November 1, 1945. NACP RG 260 File 940.607.

CHAPTER NINE: MUTINY AT THE REICHSBANK
1. Results of our policy: IMT 611-EC.
2. England target 1942: Georg Thomas, *Geschichte der Deutchen Wehr—und Ruestungswirtschaft*, p. 509.
3. The new demand: Adam Tooze, *The Wages of Destruction*, pp. 223-239.
4. Hands of criminals: IMT, May 1, 1946 morning session. Exhibit Schacht-34.
5. Hitler by the throat: IMT, April 25, 1946 morning session.
6. Demanded of me: Ulrich von Hassell, *Von Anderen Deutschland*, pp. 3-31.
7. Then hang me: Edward Peterson, *Hjalmar Schacht*, p. 320.
8. Attack on *Kristallnacht*: John Toland, *Adolf Hitler*, pp. 696-698.
9. Reich was bankrupt: IMT PS-3731.

10. Brink of financial collapse: Adam Tooze, *The Wages of Destruction*, pp. 252-253.
11. After the holidays: Adam Tooze, *The Wages of Destruction*, pp. 297.
12. Likely lead to inflation: Hjalmar Schacht, *Account Settled*, pp. 134-135.
13. Hitler and his methods: IMT, May 3, 1946, p. 72. EC-348.
14. Country's financial situation: IMT 369-EC. Hjalmar Schacht, *Account Settled*, pp. 133-134.
15. Hitler was coming: Hjalmar Schacht, *My First Seventy-Six Years*, pp. 199-200. IMT EC-348.
16. Reichsbank and currency: IMT 369-EC.
17. Dumb and useless: IMT 369-EC.
18. Put off to 9:15: Hjalmar Schacht, *My First Seventy-Six Years*, p. 392.
19. Not sufficiently Nazi: John Toland, *Adolf Hitler*, pp. 695-696.
20. Have kept silent: Hjalmar Schacht, *My First Seventy-Six Years*, p. 392.
21. Any more now: *Ibid.*, p. 393.
22. Good thing Mein Führer: *Ibid.*
23. The Nazi regime: *Ibid.*
24. As Reich Minister: IMT EC-397.
25. Reorganization of Reichsbank: U.S. Berlin Embassy cable to Washington, January 20, 1939. NACP RG 59.
26. Shoot me yet: *Time* magazine, January 30, 1939.
27. Message with Heil Hitler: GFA, Reichsbank folder. Bestand R 25.01.
28. Out of all this: Ulrich von Hassell, *The Ulrich von Hassell Diaries*, p. 33.
29. In the east: Hugh Trevor-Roper, *Hitler's War Directives*, pp. 37-40.

CHAPTER TEN: POLAND'S LONG ODYSSEY

1. First suitable opportunity: IMT L-79.
2. Military might at Poland: IMT EC-28. *The German Campaign in Poland*, U.S. Chief of Staff Report, March 21, 1942, pp. 1-10.
3. Long-delayed economic treaty: William Shirer, *The Rise and Fall of the Third Reich*, pp. 513-530.
4. Lay our hands: IMT PC-699.
5. The latter date: Shirer, *The Rise and Fall of the Third Reich*, pp. 536-542.
6. Poland to September 1: *Ibid.* pp. 540-544.
7. With a red pencil: Hugh Trevor-Roper, *Hitler's War Directives*, pp. 38-40.
8. The alleged victims: David G. Williamson, *Poland Betrayed*, pp. 63-75.
9. War with Germany: BBC Archives. *The Transcript of Neville Chamberlain's Declaration of War*. Shirer, *Berlin Diary*, p. 201.
10. Société de Banque Suisse. Wojciech Rojek, *Odyseja skarbu Rzeczypospolitej*, p. 28.
11. The Reichsbank's holdings: Col. William Brey *Report on Captured Gold*, NACP RG 260, Box 397, NND 775057. Zygmunt Karpiński. *Histoire de l'Or Polonais Pendant la Deuxieme Guerre Mondiale*.

12. Comfortable 256.7 tons: *Bergier Commission Final Report*, p. 39, table 1.
13. Waited for instructions: Eugeniusz Romiszewski, *An Epic Tale of Polish Argonauts*. Zygmunt Karpiński, *Histoire de l'Or Polonais Pendant la Deuxieme Guerre Mondiale*, pp. 2-5.
14. Bar is left inside: Janusz Mierzwa, *Pułkownik Adam Koc*. pp. 15-45.
15. Warsaw's Handlowy Bank: *Ibid.*, Eugeniusz Romiszewski, *An Epic Tale of Polish Argonauts*, pp. 2-10.
16. Ready to be shipped: Wojciech Rojek, *Odyseja skarbu Rzeczypospolitej*, p. 32.
17. And small toddlers: David G. Williamson, *Poland Betrayed*, p. 61.
18. Bank office there: *Report of the Management Board of the Bank of Poland on Deployment of the Gold reserves of the Bank of Poland Before the War and on the Bank's Evacuative Transports Made in September 1939*. Hoover Institution Archives, Polish Collection, 2272/VI.
19. Getting it to France: Wojciech Rojek, *Odyseja skarbu Rzeczypospolitej*, pp. 40-41.
20. Leadership of Floyar-Rajchman: Matuszewski papers, Piłsudski Institute, New York, N.Y.
21. The Romanian side: Wojciech Rojek, *Odyseja skarbu Rzeczypospolitej*, p. 43.
22. Had recently passed: *Ibid.* p. 44.
23. Leave Romanian borders: *Encrypted correspondence between Reichs Ministry of Foreign Affairs and German Embassies in Bucharest and Istanbul*. Hoover Institution Archives, Polish Collection, 2272/VI.
24. On short notice: *Report of the Management Board of the Bank of Poland on Deployment of the Gold reserves of the Bank of Poland Before the War and on the Bank's Evacuative Transports Made in September 193*. Stanford University, Hoover Institution Archives, Polish Collection Letter from K.H.M. Duke, British Eastern European Section, Joint Research Department to J. Weinstein in Hoover Collection.
25. Would be attacked: Eugeniusz Romiszweski, *An Epic Tale of Polish Argonauts*.
26. Confiscated and secured: Hoover Institution Archives, Polish Collection, 2000C71, Eugeniusz Romiszewski, *An Epic Tale of Polish Argonauts*.
27. Him out a receipt: Zygmunt Karpiński, *O Wielkopolsce, złocie i dalekich podró ach*, p. 204.
28. Take the gold: *Ibid.*
29. Took three hours: Adolphe Leportier, *La Bataille de l'Or*, pp. 32-42.
30. Toulon on October 6: *Ibid.*
31. Run its operations: Gérard Cornu, *L'Or Polonais*, Cahiers anecdotiques de la Banque de France, #13. TCA Poland, p. 3. NACP RG59/62D115 Box 22.

CHAPTER ELEVEN: NORTHERN LIGHTS GO OUT
1. Bank for International Settlements: RGAE, Fond 5, op. 1, file 2761, Cit in Elena Osokina, Zolotodlya Industrializatsii: Torgsin, Moskva: Rosspan, 2009, Tablitsa 2, s. 524. Elena Osokina, Gold for Industrialization: Torgsin, Moscow: Rosspan, 2009, Table 2, p. 524.

2. Spheres of influence: Fordham University, fordham.edu, Modern History Sourcebook. The Molotov-Ribbentrop Pact, 1939.
3. More of Poland: Gerhard L. Weinberg, *A World at Arms*, pp. 60-64.
4. Troops in each country: *Ibid.*
5, Accepted their applications: *Ibid.*
6. Soviet state bank: RGAE, Fond 7733. The People's Commissariat of Finance (Narcomfin-NKF) of the URSS, 1918-1946. The Ministry of Finance of the URSS, 1946-1991, RGAE op. 26 (1941), file 1455.
7. Our account subsequently: New York Federal Reserve Latvia folder 261.
8. Gold to Moscow: U.S. Federal Register, Franklin D. Roosevelt, Executive Order 8484.
9. Of that action: RGAE, 2324-26-2685, p. 50.
10. And Polish bullion: Pierre Arnoult, *Les Finances de la France* (1940-44), p. 225.
11. His board members: *Thomas H. McKittrick Papers 1889-1970*, Harvard Business School, Carton 5, f.24.
12. The Baltic States: RGAE, 2324-26-2690.
13. Countries held abroad: RGAE, 2324-26-2779.
14. Protect their independence: Thomas H. McKittrick Interview, Seeley G. Mudd Manuscript Library, Princeton University.
15. All their debts: RGAE, 2324-26-2776, p. 149.
16. Was well underway: GARF, Fond R-6822.
17. Bank for International Settlements: Antti Kuusterä and Juha Tarkka, *Bank of Finland 200 Years*, pp. 62-64.
18. Finns would obey: Nikita Khrushchev and Strobe Talbott, *Khrushchev Remembers*, p.154.
19. On the table: Nikita Khrushchev and Strobe Talbott, *Khrushchev Remembers*, p. 154.
20. Washington's wartime regulations: NYFED, Folder 261 Finland.

CHAPTER TWELVE: THE WORLD'S FORT KNOX
1. Even more harm: Henry Morgenthau III, *Mostly Morgenthaus*, pp. 152-172.
2. But Congress refused: Douglas Brinkley, *World War II: The Axis Assault, 1939-1942*, pp. 99-106. Gianni Toniolo, *Central Bank Cooperation at the Bank for International Settlements 1930-1973*, p. 671.
3. Accommodation with Berlin: HM 219: 23-26.
4. Daily gold operations: Liaquat Ahamed, *Lords of Finance*, pp. 298-320.
5. Can stop.it: HM 55:330-331.
6. Or the coffeepot: HM 54:125-127 and 303-304.
7. Federal Reserve: NYFED Shipping Records 1938-1939, SZ1-SZ32. *Gold Team Report*, p. 9.
8. British Purchasing Commission: Warren F. Kimball, *The Most Sordid Act*, p. 20.

9.   This job well: HM 385:204.
10.   None for Europe: HM 219:23-35.
11.   The risks involved: NYFED, 1939 shipping, SZ1-SZ32.
12.   Nearly $2 million: *Ibid.*
13.   Make preparations beforehand: NYFED England File 261.
14.   In lower Manhattan: NYFED, 1939 financial register.
15.   War machine running: HM 176:269-284.
16.   Do the job: HM 206:223-477.
17.   Bullion in gold: HM 239:207-211.
18.   Fed's gold policy: HM 276:295.
19.   Securities were $112 million: Blum II pp. 106-107.
20.   For the worst: NYFED, Folder 261 Sweden Correspondence.
21.   Percent in 1929: Peter L. Bernstein, *The Power of Gold*, p. 323.
22.   Bretton Woods New Hampshire: Benn Steil, *The Battle of Bretton Woods*, pp. 10-25.
23.   The Gold Problem: HM 275:76-77.
24.   Written a note: HM 206:84 and 114.
25.   Place of safekeeping: HM 260:114.
26.   The world's bullion: Kimball, p. 37. HM 259:401-409.
27.   Nazi war effort: HM 501:271.
28.   Now under way: *New York Times,* June 5, 1940.
29.   Britain $766.8 million: HM July 1, 1940, 278:6.
30.   Gold held here: HM September 23, 1940, 308:359.
31.   Paid for in gold: HM October 28, 1940 325:703.

CHAPTER THIRTEEN: DENMARK AND NORWAY FALL QUICKLY

1.   Economically vital Ruhr: Hugh Trevor-Roper, *Hitler's War Directives,* p. 50.
2.   The original plan: Gerhard L. Weinberg, *A World at Arms,* pp. 109-111.
3.   In northwestern Germany: Erich Raeder, *My Life,* pp. 300-310.
4.   Have died overnight: *Ibid.,* p. 300.
5.   Experience in Finland: Geirr H Haarr, *The German Invasion of Norway,* pp. 8-12.
6.   Making all preparations: Adam Claasen, *Hitler's Northern War,* p. 36. Henrik Lunde, *Hitler's Preemptive War,* p. 64. Earl Ziemke *The German Northern Theater,* p. 17.
7.   Over the gold: C.V. Bramsnaes, *The National Bank During the German Occupation of Denmark,* p. 11.
8.   On April 10: Per Arnt Harnes, *Gulltransporten,* pp. 10-15.
9.   Intend to do so: Winston Churchill, *The Gathering Storm,* pp. 575-585.
10.   North to Jutland: Douglas C. Dildy, *Denmark and Norway 1940,* p. 34.
11.   Disregard of detail: IMT C-66.
12.   War was over: IHT D-627.

13. A magnificent work: William L. Shirer, *The Rise and Fall of the Third Reich*, p. 700.
14. Returned to Denmark: Bo Lidegaard, *Kampen om Danmark*, pp. 25-45.
15. Long 1939 memo: *Ibid.*
16. Any foolish resistance: Halvdan Koht, *Norway Neutral and Invaded*, pp. 69-75.
17. Progress said Koht: *Ibid.*
18. Central Station at 7:00: Carl Hambro, *I Saw it Happen in Norway*, pp. 8-28.
19. Also an antique: Halvdan Koht, *Norway Neutral and Invaded*, p. 30.
20. Face a court martial: Geirr H Haarr, *The German Invasion of Norway*, pp. 126-135.
21. The stricken cruiser: Frank Binder, Hans Schlünz, Hermann Schlünz, *Schwerer Kreuzer Blücher*, pp. 35-45. Geirr H Haarr, *The German Invasion of Norway*, pp. 130-135.
22. Reached the bridge: Frank Binder; Hans Schlünz, Hermann Schlünz, *Schwerer Kreuzer Blücher*, pp. 45-47.
23. Oslo about midnight: Geirr H Haarr, *The German Invasion of Norway*, pp. 138-143.
24. Soon as it was loaded: Per Arnt Harnes, *Gulltransporten*, pp. 13-19.
25. Their head cut off: Bo Lidegaard, *Kampen om Danmark*, p. 47.
26. Guard the train: Hans Christian Adamson and Per Klem, *Blood in the Midnight*, p. 62.
27. Finally recalled it: *Ibid.*, p. 64.
28. Million in gold: Tryve Lie, *Leve eller dø*, pp. 179-180.
29. Worth about $30: Hans Christian Adamson and Per Klem, *Blood at Midnight*, p. 72.
30. To the port: Fredrik Haslund Report. NAN, Oscar Torp (Pa 640), Box 8, File 4.
31. *Galathea* signed it: *Ibid.*
32. No one was killed: *Ibid.*
33. Carry the load: Michael Brady, *Nordic Gold*, p. 4.
34. Have to obey: J.L. Moulton, *The Norwegian Campaign of 1940*, p. 210.
35. Gold to London: Fredrik Haslund Report. NAN, Oscar Torp (Pa 640), Box 8, File 4.
36. Best you can: Hans Christian Adamson and Per Klem, *Blood in the Midnight*, p. 80.
37. A direct hit: *The Day of Destiny in Molde, April 1940*, p. 23.
38. Gimnes for repairs: Fredrik Haslund Report. NAN, Oscar Torp. (Pa 640), Box 8, File 4.
39. Island to island: *Ibid.*
40. Port of Sauøy: *Ibid.*
41. Should take place: *Ibid.*
42. Land set free: G.M. Gathorne-Hardy, *War Poems of Nordahl Grieg*, p. 23.
43. At all times: Hans Christian Adamson and Per Klem, *Blood in the Midnight*, p. 89.

44. Bank of England official: *Ibid.*, p. 94.

45. Our dear fatherland: *All for Norway*, p. 98.

46. Nose of the Germans: Hans Christian Adamson and Per Klem, *Blood in the Midnight*, p. 100.

47. Lock and key: *Fredrik Haslund Report*. NAN, Oscar Torp (Pa 640), Box 8, File 4.

48. The Norwegian Government: NYFED, Correspondent File C261 Norway.

49. Leaving the ship: Fredrik Haslund Report. NAN, Oscar Torp (Pa 640), Box 8, File 4.

50. Would be arriving there: NYFED, C261 Norwegian Correspondence Account.

51. Federal Reserve Bank: Fredrik Haslund Report. NAN, Oscar Torp.(Pa 640), Box 8, File 4.

52. Bank of England: Per Arnt Harnes, *Gulltransporten*, p. 108.

53. Saved Norway's gold: Fredrik Haslund Report. NAN, Oscar Torp.(Pa 640), Box 8, File 4.

CHAPTER FOURTEEN: ITALY CRUSHES ALBANIA

1.   The Adriatic Sea: Miranda Vickers, *The Albanians: A Modern History.*

2.   Hands of Italy: Alessandro Roselli, *Italy and Albania*, pp. xii-xiii.

3.   And Belgian banks: *Ibid.* p. 36.

4.   9.2 million in 1938: *Ibid.*, pp. 48-89.

5.   Effect bullion certificates: *International Currency Review*, July 1977, p. 48.

6.   Largely Ciano's war: Bernd J. Fischer, *Albania at War 1939-1945*, p. 11.

7.   Month of pregnancy: Galeazzo Ciano, *Diary*, p. 208.

8.   Received no sympathy: Bernd J. Fischer, *Albania at War 1939-1945*, pp. 14-15.

9.   For an invasion: Ciano *Diary*, pp. 207-216.

10. Own personal ultimatum: Bernd J. Fischer, *Albania at War 1939-1945*, pp. 19-21.

11. Force of arms: Galeazzo Ciano *Diary*, p. 213.

12. South toward Greece: Bernd J. Fischer, *Albania at War 1939-1945*, p. 25.

13. Ciano was pleased: Jason Tomes, *King Zog of Albania*, p. 230.

14. Fight a major war: Bernd J. Fischer, *Albania at War 1939-1945*, pp. 22-24 and Jason Tomes, *King Zog of Albania*, pp. 215-232.

15. Soon jammed them: Jason Tomes, *King Zog of Albania*, p. 230.

16. For that refuge: *Life* magazine, June 25, 1957. TCA: Albania. NACP RG59/62D115.

17. Jewelry from residents: Arben Puto and Qirjako Qirko, *On the Plundered Albanian Gold by the Nazis*, London Gold Conference, pp. 17-19.

18. In Merkers Germany: *Ibid.*, p. 18.

CHAPTER FIFTEEN: HOLLAND FALLS IN FOUR DAYS

1.   Was insufficiently daring: Alister Horne, *To Lose a Battle*, pp. 172-175.

2.   Ideas in detail: Erich von Manstein, *Lost Victories*, pp. 120-126.

3. Off until later: Alister Horne, *To Lose a Battle*, pp. 158-168.
4. Behind the dikes: Geschiedenis van de Nederlandsche Bank—Vijfde deel De Nederlandsche Bank van 1919 tot 1948. Trips tijdvak 1931-1948 onderbroken door de Tweede Wereldoorlog–Dr. Joh. de Vries. p. 352. Gerard Aalders, *Eksters*, p. 20. TCA Holland, p. 2.
5. In the U.S.: *Ibid.*, p. 21. Corry van Renselaar, *Partij in de marge: oorlog, goud en De Nederlandsche Bank*, p. 48.
6. Its total holdings: *Ibid.* TCA Holland, pp. 2-3. NACP RG59/62D115 Box 23.
7. Set to leave: Alfred Draper, *Operation Fish*, pp. 121-126. Corry van Renselaar, *Partij in de marge : oorlog, goud en De Nederlandsche Bank*, p. 48.
8. Out of the country: Gerard Aalders, *Eksters*, p. 24.
9. Except human affairs: *The Diaries of Sir Alexander Cadogan 1938-1945*, pp. 277-280.
10. To the Dutch: Owen Chadwick, *Britain and the Vatican During the Second World War*, pp. 109-110.
11. Anglo-French action: William L. Shirer, *The Rise and Fall of the Third Reich*, p. 716.
12. Has been kept: Winston Churchill, *The Second World War, Their Finest Hour*, pp. 3-4. Hugh Trevor-Roper, *Hitler's Table Talk*, p. 70.
13. For a few days: Jacques Benoist-Méchin, *Sixty Days that Shook the West*, p. 66.
14. Army in its tracks: Ernest R. May, *Strange Victory*, pp. 229-235. Winston Churchill, *The Second World War, Their Finest Hour*, p. 34.
15. Landing in Holland: Alister Horne, *To Lose a Battle*, p. 259.
16. Along to Wilhelmina: Alfred Draper, *Operation Fish*, pp. 107-112.
17. Not hit anything: *Ibid.*, 109.
18. The British Navy: Gerard Aalders, *Eksters*, pp. 25-28.
19. Better than nothing: *Ibid.*, p. 26.
20. Finally agreed on ƒ500, 000: *Ibid.* p. 27.
21. Loyalty to the country: Alfred Draper, *Operation Fish*, pp. 121-122.
22. Take him to Britain: *Ibid.*, pp. 123-126.
23. Bank of England: *Ibid.*, pp. 125-126.
24. Take her prisoner: *Ibid.*, pp. 116-117.
25. Have attracted attention: Alfred Draper, *Operation Fish*, pp. 116-119.
26. With the Nazis. *Ibid.*; Donald A. Bertke and Don Kindell, *World War II Sea War*, Vol. 2, Ships messages May 10-May 20, 1940.
27. Sitting in her lap: Alfred Draper, *Operation Fish*, p. 121.
28. Breakfast at 09.15: Donald A. Bertke and Don Kindell, *World War II Sea War*, Vol. 2, Listings May 10-May 20, 1940.
29. Nearly five years: Adolphe Lepotier, *La Battaille de l'Or*, p. 133.
30. Commander John Younghusband: Donald A. Bertke and Don Kindell, *World War II Sea War Vol. 2*, Listings May 10-May 20, 1940.
31. Ordered to blow up: Gerard Aalders, *Eksters*, pp. 24-25.
32. Hook of Holland: TCA Holland, p. 2. NACP RG59/62D115 Box 23.

33. A tempting target: Alfred Draper, *Operation Fish*, pp. 131-134.

34. The British soldiers: *Ibid.*, p. 130.

35. On both cheeks: Jacques Benoist-Méchin, *Sixty Days that Shook the West*, p. 89.

36. Center of the city: Hugh Trevor-Rober, *Hitler's Directives*, pp. 64-65.

37. A capitulation order: TCA Holland. NACP RG59/62D115 Box 23.

38. Bottom of the waterway: Interview with Ronald Dijkstra, author of the forthcoming book on the rescue of the Dutch gold, *Failed Gold Transport*.

39. At the Reichsbank: IMT EC-3724.

40. Saving 70.6 tons: TCA Holland, p. 2, NACP RG59/62D115 Box 23. London Gold Conference, pp. 355-358.

CHAPTER SIXTEEN: BELGIUM AND LUXEMBOURG TRUST FRANCE

1. Financing for it: Ernest Mühlen: *Monnaie et circuits financiers au Grand-Duché de Luxembourg*. TCA, Luxembourg. NACP RG59/62D115 Box 21.

2. A small country: Walter and Jan Pluym, *Or à la Dérive*, pp. 8-10.

3. Slightly dictatorial temperament: *Ibid.*, p. 21.

4. Antwerp for London: Herman Van der Wee and Monqui Vrbreyt, *A Small Nation in the Turmoil of the Second World War*, p. 25.

5. Moving it to France: Pierre Kauch, *Le Vol de l'Or de la Banque National par les Nazis 1940-1943*, pp. 6-7.

6. Under French control: BNB, Boekhouding, I, dossier 601.I.

7. South Africa Reserve Bank: BNB, Boekhouding, 2, file 88.02.02.00.

8. Belgian-French coast: Alister Horne, *To Lose a Battle*, pp. 124-125 and 220-223.

9. Would come first: Camille Gutt, *La Belgique au Carrefour*, 1940-1944, p. 125.

10. Was a military secret: Walter and Jan Pluym, *Or à la Dérive*, pp. 6-9.

11. And the king's: Paul-Henri Spaak, *Continuing Battle*, pp. 46-47.

12. With the currency: Herman Van der Wee and Monique Verbreyt, *A Small Nation*, p. 41.

13. Duration of the war: *Revue Générale*, February 1985. *L'Or et les valuers de la Banque Nationale dans la tourmente de 1940*.

14. To the French: Jean Crombois, *Camille Gutt and Postwar Internaitonal Finance*, p. 34. Herman Van der Wee and Monique Verbreyt, *A Small Nation*, pp. 45-67.

15. Go on fighting: Orville H. Bullitt, *For the President Personal & Secret*, p. 433 Bullitt telegram 912.

16. Puppet king's request: Pierre d'Ydewalle, *De Memoires 1912-1940*, pp. 397-398. Roger Keyes, *Outrageous Fortune*, pp. 357-359.

17. Onto British vessels: Revue Générale, Hubert Ansiaux, *L'Or et les valuers de la Banque Nationale dans la tourmente de 1940*.

18. But he left: Camille Gutt, pp. 60-62. His testimony in the case of Daniel De Gorter and Henri Wild v. Banque de France, Supreme Court, County of New York, 1940.

19.   A military secret: Revue Générale, Hubert Ansiaux, *L'Or et les valuers de la Banque Nationale dans la tourmente de 1940*.

CHAPTER SEVENTEEN: THE FALL OF FRANCE

1.   Stepping around Europe: *Federal Reserve Bulletin, January 1941*, Gold, Capital Flow and Trade During War. Liaquat Ahamed, *Lords of Finance*, pp. 376-377.
2.   The new war: Adolphe Leportier, *La Bataille de l'Or*, pp. 80-93. William Slany, *U.S. Allied Wartime and Postwar Relations and Negotiations with Argentina et. al.*, p. xlv. FNB, Box 372. 1280200801.
3.   Or so lonely: Jean Monnet, *Memoirs*, p. 124.
4.   Halifax with 147 tons: HM January 4, 1940, 233:227
5.   Wonderful so far: Alistair Horne, *To Lose a Battle*, p. 283.
6.   Rapid Nazi offensive: Erich von Manstein, *Lost Victories*, p. 121.
7.   The French army: Orville H. Bullitt, *For the President Personal & Secret*, p. 426.
8.   Escape the conflict: Lucient Lamoureux, *La sauvetage de l'Or en 1940*, *Revue des Deux Mondes*, June 1, 1962, pp. 348-360.
9.   Own country's defense: Winston Churchill, *The Second World War, Their Finest Hour*, p. 42.
10.   Need of argument: *Ibid.*, pp. 45-49.
11.   Officer on board: Adolphe Leportier *La Bataille de l'Or*, pp. 107-120.
12.   Pounds of gold: *Ibid.* pp. 121-128.
13.   To the Luftwaffe: *Ibid.*
14.   Most decisive mistakes: Erich von Manstein, *Lost Victories*, p. 124.
15.   As possible stop: Adolphe Leportier, *La Bataille de l'Or*, pp. 129-130.
16.   Trip to Europe: *Ibid.* pp. 148-164.
17.   Man who has fought: Frans de Waal, *Peacemaking Among Primates*. Cambridge, MA: Harvard University Press, 1990.
18.   Out of Halifax: IMT EC-1618.
19.   Enough for me: Tristan Gaston-Breton, *Sauvez l'Or de la France!*, pp. 15-16.
20.   Out of the country: *Ibid.*, pp. 15-25.
21.   Ending hostilities: Jacques Benoist-Mechin, *Sixty Days that Shook the West*, p. 382.
22.   Lots of gold: Internet, ambafrance-us.org/IMG/pdf/General_de_Gaulles_Address_-_June_22_1940.pdf.
23.   Have to wait: René Auque and Paul Carré, *Le Croiseur Émile Bertain*, pp. 68-75.
24.   Late that night: *Ibid. Inspecter General Report by Martial. Banque de France report by Millain on February 2, 1948*.
25.   Also have cannons: Banque de France report on the incidents from June 18-21, 1940. FNB 1060200101-27, 1280199901/91.
26.   In three stop: *Ibid.*
27.   Get out fast: *Ibid.*
28.   Land at Dakar: Martin Gilbert, *The Churchill War Papers*, Vol. II, p. 400.
29.   Fuel oil left: Adolphe Leportier, *La Bataille de l'Or*, p. 139. Martial report to the Banque de France. 1280199901/91.

30. Did not move: HM, 256:156, February 11, 1942.

CHAPTER EIGHTEEN: THE VATICAN'S SECRET GOLD

1. With the Pope: *New York Times*, December 24, 1939. "Envoy to Vatican Ends 72-Year Gap." p. 12. *Wartime Correspondence Between President Roosevelt and Pope Pius XII*. pp. 17-19.
2. CEO until 1938: *Time* magazine, April 22, 1929. W. David Curtiss, *Cornell Benefactor, Industrial Czar, and FDR's Ambassador Extraordinary*, www.lawschool.cornell.edu/library.
3. The European situation: *New York Times*. November 6, 2936, "Pacelli Lunches With Roosevelt." p. 1.
4. More permanent peace: Myron Taylor, *Wartime Correspondence*, p. 11.
5. The United States: FDR, Papers of Myron Taylor, February 28, 1940.
6. From a pedestal: Owen Chadwick, *Britain and the Vatican During World War II*, p. 101.
7. Not carefully considered: FDR, Papers of Myron Taylor, Folder "*Documentation of the Mission of President Roosevelt to his Holiness Pope Pius XII by His Personal Representative Myron C. Taylor 1940-1945.*" April 20, 1940.
8. Mouthpiece of the Jews: Owen Chadwick, *Britain and the Vatican During World War II*, p. 109.
9. To do worse: *Ibid.*, p. 111.
10. Days to come: FDR, Papers of Myron Taylor, May 10, 1940.
11. Recommended to him: W. David Curtiss, *Cornell Benefactor*.
12. Until the end: Taylor fourth audience, FDR, Papers of Myron Taylor, May 11, 1940.
13. Avoid any publicity: FDR, Papers of Myron Taylor, May 17, 1940.
14. Handling this business: NYFED C261 Italy-Vatican State folder, June 12, 1940.
15. The next day: *Ibid.*
16. Deal in gold: *Ibid.* May 22, 1940 memo.
17. Keep quiet: NYFED C261 Italy-Vatican State, June 12, 1940.
18. Other foreign accounts: FDR, Papers of Myron Taylor, May 20, 1940.
19. Way by this: NYFED C261 Vatican State.
20. About the transfer: BA FO 371/25194 and 371/24935/98.
21. New York Fed: NYFED C 261 Vatican State. June 23 report and June 10 memo.
22. Arranged by J. P. Morgan: NYFED C261 Italy State, June 12, 1940.
23. Tonight for Florence: FDR, Papers of Myron Taylor, May 17, 1940.
24. End of the line: FDR, Papers of Myron Taylor, May 17, 1940.
25. Hours on anything: FDR, Papers of Myron Taylor, May 19, 1940.
26. Be given him: FDR, Papers of Myron Taylor, May 17, 1940.
27. Duration of the war: NYFED C261 Italy-Vatican State.
28. For a time: FDR, Papers of Myron Taylor, June 14, 1940.
29. Care of yourself: FDR, Papers of Myron Taylor, July 29, 1940.
30. Confer with you: FDR, Papers of Myron Taylor, August 2, 1940.

31. The United States: FDR, Papers of Myron Taylor, August 20, 1940.
32. To bomb Rome: Robert A. Graham, *The Vatican and Communism During World War II*, pp. 35-40.
33. It is wonderful: W. David Curtiss, *Cornell Benefactor, Part II.*

CHAPTER NINETEEN: ESCAPE TO CASABLANCA

1. Shipment to the U.S.: Tristan Gaston-Breton, *Sauvez l'Or de la Banque de France*, p. 91.
2. As much as 900 tons: Adolphe Leportier, *La Bataille de l'Or*, p. 182.
3. Moving it to the fort: *Ibid.*, appendix and pp. 180-183.
4. The Phony War: *Ibid.*
5. Next morning at 6:00: Tristan Gaston-Breton, *Sauvez l'Or de la Banque de France*, p.91.
6. Job was finished: Adolphe Leportier, *La Bataille de l'Or*, pp. 184-185.
7. Had to wait: *Ibid.*
8. And the docks: Tristan Gaston-Breton, *Sauvez l'Or de la Banque de France*, p. 96.
9. Doing the impossible: Adolphe Leportier, *La Bataille de l'Or*, pp. 187-189.
10. Tons of bullion: *Ibid.*, p. 202.
11. June ten stop: Adolphe Leportier, *La Bataille de l'Or*, p. 178.
12. North by train: *Ibid.*
13. Twenty-four hours stop: *Ibid.*, p. 179.
14. Absolute secrecy stop: *Ibid.*, p. 195. Zygmunt Karpiński sworn deposition in Supreme Court of the State of New York, 1941 in the case Sigismond J. Stojowski et al against Banque de France. Court Index N. 34164-1941.
15. For our destination: Adolphe Leportier, *La Bataille de l'Or*, p. 199.
16. On a 248 course: *Ibid.*, p. 200.
17. Speed 15.5 knots: *Ibid.*, p. 201.
18. Polish State Bank: *Ibid.*, p. 203.
19. Ploy of German warfare: *Ibid.*, p. 205.
20. Pulled into Casablanca: *Ibid.*, 208.
21. He was told: Charles Moreton, *Lettre d'Un Grand-Père*, Cahiers Anecdotiques de la Banque de France.
22. Stop in Casablanca: Charles *Ibid*, Annex II, Cahiers Anecdotiques de la Banque de France. Report d'Oran du Verdon à Casablanca, convoi M. Moreton, June 9, 1940, FNB 1060200101-27.
23. Very busy track: *Ibid.*
24. Whole affair grotesque: *Ibid.*
25. Going to Canada: Charles Moreton, *Lettre d'Un Grand-Père*. Adolphe Leportier, *La Bataille de l'Or* p. 169.
26. Monitor the transfer: *Ibid.*
27. No ships available: Tristan Gaston-Breton, *Sauvez l'Or de la Banque de France*, p. 84. Orville H. Bullitt, *For the President Personal & Secret*, p.434.

28. France and Spain meet: Orville H. Bullitt, *For the President Personal & Secret*, pp. 434-435.
29. Handle the shipment: Pierre Arnoult, *Les Finances de la France (1940-44)*, p. 200.
30. Arrived in New York: Charles Moreton, *Lettre d'Un Grand-Père*. Adolphe Leportier, *La Bataille de l'Or* pp. 164-194. Villard report of February 18, 1948, Banque de France, Villard report of February 2, 1948, FNB 1060200101-27.
31. Near the bank: Charles Moreton report on the voyage of the *Primauguet* from *Le Verdon* to Casablanca June 21, 1940. Banque de France, 1280199901/07.
32. Business very well: *Ibid.*
33. Also raining hard: *Ibid.*
34. Lingered for days: Adolphe Leportier, *La Bataille de l'Or*, p. 224 and Charles Moreton, *Lettre d'Un Grand-Père*.
35. First French port: Charles Moreton, *Lettre d'Un Grand-Père*.
36. At fifteen tons: Adolphe Leportier, *La Bataille de l'Or*, p. 228.
37. For grandsons stop: Charles Moreton, *Lettre d'Un Grand-Père*.

CHAPTER TWENTY: BRITAIN ON THE BRINK
1. Won by evacuations: Martin Gilbert, *The Churchill War Papers*, Vol. II, pp. 240-247.
2. Chamberlain will return: John Colville, *The Fringes of Power*, May 11, 1940, p. 123.
3. Land nor gold: Max Hastings, *Winston's War*, p. 79. *Horatio*: ancienthistory. about.com/library/bl/bl_horatiuspoem.htm.
4. With Britain's gold: www.laurentic.com.
5. Million a month: Duncan McDowell, Bank of Canada, *Due Diligence*, p. 125
6. Up to 4,748 bars: *Ibid.*, summary p. 4.
7. Way we can: BA BOC File A 18-17.
8. About sending some: BA BOC file A 16-2.
9. Prescribed sterling price: BA T177/45.
10. The country's safety: John Colville, *The Fringes of Power*, p. 139.
11. The special cargo. Alfred Draper, *Operation Fish*, pp. 15-17.
12. Months were enormous: *Ibid.*, p. 22.
13. Facilities were disorganized: BA T177/56, Memorandum by War Cabinet Secretary E. E. Bridges from October 6, 1939.
14. With all dispatch: Augustus Agar, *Footprints in the Sea*, pp. 233-240.
15. For our retirement. *Ibid.*
16. Heading that way: Alfred Draper, *Operation Fish*, Appendix.
17. Otherwise we're done: David Dilks, *The Diaries of Sir Alexander Cadogan 1938-1945*, p. 288.
18. To invade Britain: BA, T160.1054.
19. Twelve months ago: David Dilks, *The Diaries of Sir Alexander Cadogan*, p. 288.
20. The country's wealth: Alfred Draper, *Operation Fish*, pp. 150-155.

21. Finance their war: BA T/177/56.
22. For every eventuality: *Ibid.*
23. By end-July: BA T/177/56.
24. Shall we go ahead: BA T160/1054.
25. Be welcomed here: BA 77/177-56.
26. Most frightful rot: BA NC 2/24A and John Lukacs, *Five Days in London*, p. 17.
27. For peace conditions: *Ibid.*, pp. 151-155.
28. Invasion of England: Karl Dönitz, *The Conduct of the War at Sea*, p. 12.
29. The Atlantic Ocean: Alfred Draper, *Operation Fish*, pp. 152-169.
30. Not be insured: *Ibid.*, pp. 209-215.
31. Signal-lamp.message godspeed: *Ibid.*, pp. 206-211.
32. Company in Montreal: Leland Stowe, *How Britain's Wealth Went West*.
33. The port bow: Alfred Draper, *Operation Fish*, p. 215.
34. Four-hour shifts: *Operation Fish*, pp. 213-230.
35. More than £100 million: *Ibid.*, Appendix I and IV.
36. Just about over: BA T160/1054.
37. Former Naval Person: Warren F. Kimball. *Churchill & Roosevelt: The Complete Correspondence. Vol. 1*, p. 24.
38. Our last reserves: Jon Meacham, *Franklin and Winston*, p.81. HM 389:60, April 15, 1940.
39. Are now disappearing: BA W.P. (40) 334.
40. More than £20 million: *Ibid.*40
41. Unprecedented third term: Winston Churchill, *The Second World War, Their Finest Hour*, pp. 24-25.
42. Money we want: Victoria Schofield, *Witness to History*, pp. 112-113.
43. Indiscretion more calculated: *Ibid.*
44. Times as much: Churchill, *Finest Hour*, pp. 369-370.
45. Our common purpose: Warren F. Kimball, *Churchill & Roosevelt: The Complete Correspondence*, Vol. 1, pp. 102-109. BA MR PREM 3/486/1/299-313.A.
46. Fire is over: University of Santa Barbara, The American Presidency Project. www.presidency.ucsb.edu. December 17, 1940 press conference.
47. Whole of recorded history: Churchill speech on November 10 1941 speech at the Mansion House in London. Richard Langworth, *Churchill by Himself*, p. 131.
48. Arsenal of democracy: www.presidency.ucsb.edu/ws/?pid=15917.
49. Interview of Thomas McKittrick, Princeton University Seeley G. Mudd Manuscript Library.

CHAPTER TWENTY-ONE: DESTINATION DAKAR

1. Weighed in at 1,097 tons: Charles Moreton, *Lettre d'Un Grand-Père*, Cahiers Anecdotiques de la Banque de France.
2. Car and plane: Didier Bruneel, *Les Secrets de l'Or*, p. 135. Adolphe Leportier, *La Bataille de l'Or*, p. 251. Pierre Arnoult, *Les Finances de la France 1940-1944*, p. 202.

3. Still meant to fight: Cordell Hull, *Memoirs*, p. 345.
4. In the afternoon: Adolphe Lepotier, *La Bataille de l'Or*, pp. 235-242. Charles Moreton, *Lettre d'Un Grand-Père*.
5. Along the way: Charles Moreton, *Lettre d'Un Grand-Père*.
6. From the Germans: FNB AVdF-1280199901-box 24.
7. Between their buttocks: *Lettre d'Un Grand-Père*.
8. Belgian and Luxembourg: FNB AVdF-1280199901-box 24.
9. For his grandchildren: Charles Moreton, *Lettre d'Un Grand-Père*.
10. Sessions in Paris: Pierre Arnoult, *Les Finances de la France 1940-1944*, pp. 10-15.
11. Sent to Dakar: Adolphe Lepotier, *La Bataille l'Or*, p. 324, Annexe IV.
12. Troops could land: Didier Bruneel, *Les Secrets de l'Or*, p. 134, Pierre Arnoult, *Les Finances de la France 1940-1944* pp. 202-204 and p. 230.
13. Standoff dragged on: Pierre Arnoult, *Les Finances de la France 1940-1944*, pp. 227-236.
14. Held in the interior: Winston Churchill, *Their Finest Hour*, p. 487.
15. The final victory: Henry Adams, *Years of Deadly Peril 1938-1941*, pp. 299-336.
16. He considered suicide: Charles de Gaulle, *Memoirs*, p. 125. Michael E. Haskew, *De Gaulle*, p. 135.
17. Before the cease-fire: Adolphe Lepotier, *La Bataille de l'Or*, p. 318.
18. All the foot dragging: Pierre Arnoult, *Les Finances de la France 1940-1944*, pp. 232-234.
19. Embassy in Bucharest: *Ibid.*, pp. 235-238 and 249-250. Didier Bruneel, p. 138.
20. It eventually did: Herman van der Wee and Monique Verbreyt, *A Small Nation in the Turmoil of the Second World War*, p.187. Ansiaux, Hubert. *L'Or et les valeurs de la Banque National dans la tourmente de 1940*, *Revue Générale*, Brussels, part III.
21. Watch it happen: HM, Book 345.
22. That never happened: Yves Bréart de Boisanger to Hemmen, March 22, 1941, FNB No. 15,733/DE. Pierre Arnoult, *Les Finances de la France 1940-1944*, pp. 255-258. Herman van der Wee and Monique Verbreyt, *A Small Nation in the Turmoil of the Second World War*, p. 184.
23. Nazi war effort: Pierre Arnoult, *Les Finances de la France 1940-1944*, pp. 209-226.
24. Algiers to Marseilles: FNB No. 993 CM/15, Didier Bruneel, *Les Secrets de l'Or*, pp. 137-141.
25. Belgium never responded: Pierre Arnoult, *Les Finances de la France 1940-1944*, p.261.
26. During the war: London Gold Conference of 1997, pp. 67-70 and 538.
27. Gold to anyone: Pierre Arnoult, *Les Finances de la France 1940-1944*, p. 210.
28. Also never happened: *Ibid.*, pp. 218-222.
29. On September 6, 1939: war diary DE104/A4-3 Serial 001-45 and ships logs. NACP RG 24 NND 927605 AND 803052.

CHAPTER TWENTY-TWO: BALKAN DISTRACTIONS

1. Their finest hour: The Churchill Centre, www.winstonchurchill.org.
2. Undertake a naval invasion: Gerhard L. Weinberg, *A World at Arms*, pp. 148-149.
3. Shortest possible time: Hugh Trevor-Roper, *Hitler's War Directives*, pp. 79-80.
4. Many to so few: The Churchill Centre, www.winstonchurchill.org.
5. Teeth taken out: Ciano Diplomatic Papers, p. 402.
6. Have occupied Greece: Chester Wilmot, *The Struggle for Europe*, p. 63.
7. Turned into a fiasco: John Stoessinger, *Why Nations Go to War*, p. 39.
8. New York Fed: Paul Hehn, *A Low Dishonest Decade*, p. 111. Fold3.com #269909657. Jack Bennett report June 11, 1946. Arthur L. Smith, Jr., *Hitler's Gold*, p. 164. New York Fed gold purchase, January 6, 1941, SZ-167.
9. Yugoslavia and Greece: Chester Wilmot, *The Struggle for Europe*, p. 70.
10. A rapid campaign: Hugh Trevor-Roper, *Hitler's War Directives*, p. 93.
11. Found its soul: Winston Churchill War Papers, 1941 p. xxxix.
12. April 27 in Greece: Hugh Trevor-Roper, *Hitler's War Directives*, p. 108.
13. About 28 tons: NYFED, File C261 Greece.
14. Cases containing silver: TCA Greece. NACP RG59/62D115 Box 19.
15. In concentration camps: *Ibid.* pp. 5-15.
16. Tons in Britain: NYFED, File C261 Yugoslavia. London Nazi Gold Conference, Dusan Biber, pp. 411-415. Jacob Hoptner and Henry Roberts, *Yugoslavia in Crisis 1934-1941*, p. 156.
17. Federal Reserve: NYFED, File 261 Yugoslavia.
18. New York Federal Reserve: Gianni Toniolo, *Central Bank Cooperation at the Bank for International Settlements*, p. 219.
19. On the bullion: TCA Yugoslavia. NACP RG59/62D115 Box 22.
20. And the gold: *London Gold Conference*, Dusan Biber, p. 411.
21. To the Reichsbank: *Ibid.*
22. A splendid haul: Wilfried von Oven and Jürgen Hahn-Butry. *Panzer am Balkan–Erlebnisbuch der Panzergruppe von Kleist*. Berlin: Lipert, 1941.
23. End of the war: TPA Yugoslavia.
24. Remained in the country: *London Gold Conference*, Dusan Biber, p. 411.
25. New York Federal Reserve: NYFED, file 261 Yugoslavia.

CHAPTER TWENTY-THREE: THE SOVIET UNION STARES INTO AN ABYSS

1. Can be exterminated: Hugh Trevor-Roper, *Hitler's War Directives*, p. 3. Hitler, Adolf, *Mein Kampf*, ch. IV, p. 155.
2. The area's riches: Hugh Trevor-Roper, *Hitler's Table Talk*, pp. 623-624.
3. Command upon notification: IMT 1743-PS. Albert Speer, *Inside the Third Reich*, p. 238.
4. City of Kazan: Timothy Green, *Central Bank Gold Reserves since 1845*, World Gold Council. RGASPI Fond 5, op.1, file 2761.
5. Into Bolshevik hands: Oleg Budnitskii, Kolchak's Gold: The End of a Legend, russiasgreatwar.org. RGASPI Fond 5, op.1, file 2761.

6. Soviet Central Bank: RGASPI Fond 5, op.1, file 2761.

7. World's largest cities: *Lenin's Collected Works*, 2nd English Edition, Progress Publishers, Moscow, 1965, Vol. 33, pp. 109-116.

8. Tons in 1925: CIA study of October 17, 1955. CIA/SV/RR 121 entitled *Soviet Gold Production, Reserves and Exports through 1954*.

9. To finance industrialization: *Ibid*. GARF, Fond 4433, op. 12a, file 698, Osokina, Torgsin, p. 527.

10. The communist nation: John Morton Blum, *From the Morgenthau Diaries 1928-1938*, pp. 55-57.

11. The same period: NYFED Report June 11, 1937, C261 Soviet Union folder.

12. Such as aircraft engines: *Ibid*.

13. Worth $11 million arrived: *Ibid*.

14. Treasury's special account: *Ibid*.

15. Gold from Russia: NYFED, C261 Soviet Union folder. John Morton Blum, *From the Morgenthau Diaries 1938-1941*, p. 269. HM, 455:313, October 20, 1941.

16. Going to Germany: RGAE 2324-20-4462. HM 259:270, April 30, 1940.

17. Even 600,000 horses: Gerard L. Weinberg, *A World at Arms*, p. 264.

18. Back to France: Adam Zamoyski, *Moscow 1812*, p. 547.

19. Trusted Adolf Hitler: Constantine Pleshakov, *Stalin's Folly*, p. 70. Winston Churchill, *The Second World War, The Grand Alliance*, pp. 303-305. David Murphy, *What Stalin Knew*, p. 189 and Appendix Two.

20. Night in their offices: *Ibid*., p. 6.

21. The whole Politburo: Rodric Braithwaite, *Moscow 1941*, p. 65.

22. Final three sentences: Constantine Pleshakov, *Stalin's Folly*, p. 115. David Murphy, *What Stalin Knew*, p. 218.

23. Into the night: RGASPI FOND 17 OP.164, FILE 659, pp. 67,69.

24. From the invaders. Politburo Protocol 34/34—OP.21-29 June 1941, point 144, 27 June 1941.—Fond 17, op. 166, file 659, pp. 189-190, RGASPI; typed original.

25. The Kremlin Armory: RGASPI No 34/34, point 115, Fond 17, op. 164, pp. 67, 69.

26. Novsibirsk and Chelyabinsk: GARF Fond R6822. Politburo meetings Protocol No 34/34, point 115—Fond 17, op. 164, file 659, pp. 67, 69, RGASPI.

27. Night of July 5: GARF, Fond R-6822.

28. Care of the body: TsAFSB RF, A. 17, op. 25, file 9 pp. 172-173. TsA FSB RF, Fond 17, op. 25, file 9, p. 184.

29. Continued their duties: TsA FSB RF, Fond 17, op. 25, file 10, p. 86, GARF, R-6822-1-377.

30. Tons of gold annually: GARF, R-6822-1-410, p.1. R-6822-1-377, p.4. R-6822-1-409, p. 155, R-6822-1-409, p. 8.

31. We've shitted it away: Simon Sebag Montefiore, *Stalin*, p. 374.

32. Quickly approved it: Rodric Braithwaite, *Moscow 1941*, pp. 82-83.

33. He appeared gloomy: Edvard Radzinsky, *Stalin*, p. 471. David Glantz, *When Titans Clashed*, pp. 62-63.

34. You, of course: Rodric Braithwaite, *Moscow 1941*, pp. 83-84. Edvard Radzinksy, *Stalin*, pp. 468-472.
35. You my friends: www.ess.uwe.ac.uk/documents/stalin1.htm.
36. Surrounded by Nazi troops: Ukrainian Business News enews.com.ua/show/283964.html.
37. Long-term supply job: FDR, Henry Hopkins Papers, Container 306, Book 4. Welles-Hopkins on July 21, 1941, 740.001 EW 19390. PSF: Safe File.
38. Aggression of Hitlerite Germany: *Ibid.*
39. The English letter: Michael Fullilove, *Rendezvous with Destiny*, p. 292.
40. Lines would hold: FDR, Henry Hopkins Papers.
41. From the Germans: Michael Fullilove, *Rendezvous with Destiny*, p. 308.
42. Since the 1930s: Allen Weinstein and Alexander Vassiliev, *The Haunted Wood*, p. 44.
43. The Roosevelt administration: Fond 06, op.3, P. 21, folder 280, AVP.RF.
44. Space of two weeks: Charles Burdick and Hans-Adolf Jacosen, *The Halder War Diary 1939-1942*, p. 446.
45. Revenge of reality: Nikolas Cornish, *Images of Kursk*, p. 7.
46. But fertile land: Rodric Braithwaite, *Moscow 1941*, p. 85. Timothy Snyder, *Bloodlands*, p. 180.
47. Would not fall: Rodric Braithwaite, *Moscow 1941*, p. 85, and David E. Murphy, *What Stalin Knew*, pp. 232-233.
48. Forward substantial reserves: Janusz Piekalkiewicz, *Die Schlacht um Moskau*, p. 205.
49. Beginning of December: Fedor von Bock, *The War Diary 1939-1945*, p. 345.
50. From enemy attacks: Allen E. Crew, *Fighting the Russians in Winter*, p. 12.
51. Against the Nazis: John Morton Blum, *From the Morgenthau Diaries*, Vol.2., pp. 255-272.
52. To buy weapons: GRAE Fond 2324-20-4697.
53. Nearby vessels saluted: Nigel Pickford, *Lost Treasure Ships of the Twentieth Century*, p. 129. RGAE Fond 2324.
54. Lend-Lease kicked in: RGAE Fond 2324-20-4697.
55. Fragments and jewelry: IMT EC 320-2.

CHAPTER TWENTY-FOUR: MELMER GOLD

1. Hitler's government work: IMT 3944-PS. Nuremberg Trial, May 15, 1946 session. Report to Colonel Bernard Bernstein, May 8, 1945 outlining history of the Melmer deliveries. NACP RG 260, Box 423, 940.304.
2. On the matter: IMT, May 7, 1946 session of trial. IMT 3944-PS.
3. Accepted the proposal: NACP RG 260, Box 423, 940.304. Nuremberg Trial May 15, 1945 session.
4. There were four shipments: NACP RG 260, Box 423, 940.304. December 4, 1945 report by A.I. Edelman to Donald W Curtis.

5.   Currency to jewelry: *Ibid.* Colonel Bernard Bernstein reports to Lt. General Lucius Clay for April 1945 and May 1945. IMT 3951-PS.

6.   Work with the SS: Three interrogation statements made by Albert Thoms. NACP RG 260, Box 423, 940.304.

7.   To the bank: IMT PS-445. Statement of Albert Thoms, September 19, 1945.

8.   Reichsbank on January 27, 1945: NACP RG 260, Box 423, 940.304, July 18, 1947 Colonel Bernard Bernstein monthly May 1945 report, OMGUS AG, 1945-46.ort to Lt. General Lucius Clay, part II. TD, Box 330, Folder 7645.

9.   Deposits to be $14.5 million: NACP RG 260 AG 1945-1946.

10. Policy of extermination: NACP RG 260 AG 1945-1946.

11. The same level: William Slany, *U.S. and Allied Efforts to Recover and Restore Gold and Other Assets Stolen or Hidden by Germany During World War II*, pp. 157-163.

12. Central bank bullion: *Bergier Independent Commission*, final report, p. 249.

CHAPTER TWENTY-FIVE: PROCRASTINATION ITALIAN STYLE

1.   Invasion of the mainland: Gerhard L. Weinberg, *A World at Arms*, pp. 593-601.

2.   Not forsake me: Robert Forczyk, *Rescuing Mussolini—Gran Sasso 1943*, pp. 5-15.

3.   That too was nixed: Sergio Cardarelli and Renata Martano, *I Nazisti e L'Oro della Banca d'Italia*, p. 3.

4.   Berlin on September 17, 1943: TCA Italian Report. NACP RG59/62D115 Box 20. Albert Thoms Interrogation, April 12, 1945. NACP RG 2650/390/46/9/2 Box 424.

5.   Investment in Italy: Gianni Toniolo, *Central Bank Cooperation at the Bank for International Settlements 1930-1973*, p. 252.

6.   Different secure place: *Thomas McKittrick Papers*, Harvard Business School Library, Series 2. Business Papers, Letters and memos, October 1942-August 1945.

7.   Have control of it: Sergio Cardarelli and Renata Martano, *I Nazisti e L'Oro della Banca d'Italia* p. 15.

8.   Also simply disappeared: London Gold Conference, pp. 324-325.

9.   Ton from Greece: Sergio Cardarelli and Renata Martano, *I Nazisti e L'Oro della Banca d'Italia* p. 150.

10. Italy central banker: London Gold Conference, p. 324.

11. Store a country's gold: *German Bundesbank, Dokumentation das im Kriege Nach Deutschland Verbrachet Münzgold Italiens, Hergoz Report.*

12. An iron trellis: *German Bundesbank, Dokumentation das im Kriege Nach Deutschland Verbrachet Münzgold Italiens, Hergoz Report.*

13. Officials accompanied it: Sergio Cardarelli and Renata Martano, *I Nazisti e L'Oro della Banca d'Italia*, pp. 22-23.

14. Shipment to Basel: London Conference, pp. 325-326. ICB Asbi.Segretariato Generale, pratt, n 995, fasc.2

15. To his institution: London Gold Conference, pp. 325-326.
16. Three days later: Sergio Cardarelli and Renata Martano, *I Nazisti e L'Oro della Banca d'Italia*, pp. 28-34.
17. Bank of France: London Gold Report, p. 337 and TCA Italian case. NACP RG59/62D115 Box 20.
18. Bank of Italy: *Ibid.*
19. Their old friend: Thomas McKittrick Papers, Harvard Business School Library, Series 2.
    Business Papers, Letters and memos, October 1942-August 1945.
20. Allowed him to use: Biographical Dictionary of Italians, www.treccani.it/enciclopedia.
21. More than demanded: NACP Record Group.226, CIA, doc. 7185. Robert Katz, *The Battle for Rome*, pp. 74-75.
22. In Kaltenbrunner's office: NACP Record Group.226, Entry 112, Misc. X-2 Files, Box 1, Folder 5, Italian Decodes.

CHAPTER TWENTY-SIX: PARTNERS IN GOLD

1. Will be ours: Bergier Commission Report Final Report. *International Commission of Experts Switzerland: National Socialism and the Second World War*, pp. 223-238. Funk speech in Rome GFAB 25.01/70/18/1 p. 549.
2. Hide its provenance: Interview transcript of Thomas McKittrick, Princeton University Seeley G. Mudd Manuscript Library. NACP RC 59 800.515/5-646. Bergier Commission Final Report, p. 12.
3. Fences and creditors: Jean Ziegler, *The Swiss, the Gold, and the Dead*, p. 18.
4. In Swiss francs: Bergier Commission Final Report, p. 239.
5. To take either: *Ibid.*, p. 241-254.
6. From German attack: *Ibid.*
7. In August 1942: *Ibid.*, p. 250.
8. Had been looted: *Ibid*, p. 239.
9. Stolen Belgian gold: *Ibid.*, p. 252.
10. Administered the account: Jean Ziegler, *The Swiss, the Gold, and the Dead*, p. 6.
11. With the BIS: Thomas McKittrick Interview, Princeton University Seeley G. Mudd Manuscript Library. Gianni Toniolo, *Central Bank Cooperation at the Bank for International Settlements*, g. 246.
12. About Puhl's travels: Donald P. Steury, *The OSS and Project SAFEHAVEN*.
13. The Marshall Plan: Gianni Toniolo, *Central Bank Cooperation at the Bank for International Settlements*, p. 224. Thomas McKittrick Interview, Princeton University Seeley G. Mudd Manuscript Library.
14. Not go unpunished: Gianni Toniolo, *Central Bank Cooperation at the Bank for International Settlements*, p. 246. Armand Van Dormael, *Bretton Woods*, p. 205.
15. Business with Berlin: NYFED, Letter from Rooth to Harrison received November 14, 1939, Folder C 261 Sweden.

16. Worth of gold: Bergier Commision Final Report, p. 241-254.
17. Million in liquidated assets: London Gold Conference, Swedish papers, pp. 456-466. London Gold Conference, p. 712.
18. With the Allies: Nazi Gold: The London Conference, pp. 427-479.
19. Converted into dollars: Antonio Louça and Ansgar Schäfer, *Portugal and the Nazi Gold*, p. 24.
20. All but 3.9 tons: William Slany study *U.S. and Allied Wartime and Postwar Relations and Negotiations with Argentina, Portugal, Spain, Sweden, and Turkey*, p. xxxix. Interim Swiss Gold Transaction Report, appendix 1.
21. Between 1942 and 1944: Clinton Administration's Gold Team *Final Report*, p. 42.
22. Payment for tungsten: Jean Ziegler, *The Swiss, the Gold, and the Dead*, p. 72. May 21, 1946 U.S. diplomatic cable from Madrid to Washington.
23. Destined for Bucharest: Thomas McKittrick Papers, Harvard Business School Library, Business Papers, Letters and memos, October 1942-August 1945.
24. At a Swiss bank: NACP RG 260/390/46/9/2 Box 424, 940.603. RG 43.
25. Tons of bullion: Murat Önsoy, *The World War Two Allied Economic Warfare: The Case of Turkish Chrome Sales*, pp. 1-20.
26. Tons of gold: Jonathan Steinberg, *The Deutsche Bank and Its Gold Transactions during the Second World War*, 13-38.
27. The Reich surrendered: Johanes Bähr, *Der Goldhandle der Dresdner Bank im Zweiten Weltkrieg*, pp. 149-160.
28. Its German initials: Peter Hayes, *From Cooperation to Complicity*, pp. 9-15.
29. Holland and Belgium: NACP RG 260, 910.304.

CHAPTER TWENTY-SEVEN: THE ALLIES FINALLY CRACK DOWN
1. Making generous profits: November 14, 1945 monthly report to General Clay, *Fold 3*, #286968215.
2. In world markets: William J. Clinton Presidential Library, Clinton Administration, Gold Team Report, pp. 262-27. HM Diary 698:159.
3. With the allies: Martin Lorenz-Meyer, *Safehaven*, p. 39.
4. Currency in Germany: David Rees, *Harry Dexter White*, p. 177.
5. Code name Kostov: Michael Beschloss, *The Conquerors*, p. 152.
6. Should be done: David Rees, *Harry Dexter White*, p. 248.
7. In the past: John Morton Blum, *Roosevelt and Morgenthau*, p. 572.
8. Have wasted away: HM 766:35-38. HM 770:17-33.
9. On soup kitchens: David Rees, *Harry Dexter White*, p. 262.
10. A military parade: Henry Morgenthau Jr., *Germany Is Our Problem*, pp. 1-4.
11. Roosevelt said little: John Morton Blum, *Roosevelt and Morgenthau*, p. 594.
12. Beg like Fala: Michael Besschloss, *The Conquerors*, p. 130.
13. Foreign Secretary angrily objected: John Morton Blum, *Roosevelt and Morgenthau*, pp. 595-596.
14. His close friend: Martin Lorenz-Meyer, *Safehaven*, pp. 82-84.
15. Control Technical Manual: *Ibid.*, pp. 92-93.

16. In the conflict: *Ibid.*, pp. 71-72.
17. Within two years: Yale University, Avalon Project. Yalta Conference final communiqué, http://avalon.law.yale.edu/wwii/yalta.asp.
18. Fate of all Germans: Albert Speer, *Inside the Third Reich*, p. 433.
19. The Bulge attack: John Dietrich, *Morgenthau Plan*, pp. 70-72, 82.
20. World War III: Henry Morgenthau, Jr., *Germany is Our Problem*, p. 10.
21. To delay publication: John Morton Blum, *Roosevelt and Morgenthau*, p. 627.
22. One hundred percent: John Morton Blum, *Years of War*, pp. 415-420.

CHAPTER TWENTY-EIGHT: RICH DISCOVERY IN A SALT MINE

1. War was over: Hugh Trevor-Roper, *The Goebbels Diary*, pp. xxix-xxxi.
2. The beleaguered Germans: Antony Beevor, *Berlin the Downfall 1945*, p. 11.
3. Commanding military officers: *Ibid.*, pp. 307-309 and 406.
4. Time to do that: Veick Interrogation. BHM, 335. BLI, Netzeband Statement. BA 327D FO1046/24.
5. Leaving 120,000 homeless: Erik Smit, *3 Februar 1945: Die Zerstorung Kreuzbers.*
6. State and party: BA A-327D FO 1046/24. Bernstein papers, Box 2, Harry S. Truman Presidential Library.
7. For foreign informants: Karl Bernd Esser, *Hitlers Gold*, p. 75.
8. New headquarters there: Dr. Werner Veick Interrogation, April 10, 1945. NACP Record Group.331, G-4 Functions in ESTOUSA Operations.
9. Liquor was removed: Maxmillian Rathke Interrogation, Dr. Werner Veick Interrogation, NACP Record Group.331, G-4 Functions in ESTOUSA Operations.
10. Were shipped south: Joseph Abrams, History of the 90th Division 6 June 1944 to 9 May 1945. Bernard Bernstein Report to Brig. Gen. F.J. McSherry, April 18, 1945. SHAEF/G-5/1/13, RG 331, G-4 Functon in Operational and Occupation Headquarters.
11. Named simply #8: U.S. Army interrogations of Albert Thoms and Ernst Funtmann.
    NACP Record Group.331, File 940.401, G-4 Functions in ESTOUSA Operations.
12. Gold was $256 million: Arthur L. Smith, Jr., *Nazi Gold*, p. p. 164.
13. The smaller shipment: *Ibid.* Second and third Albert Thoms interrogations. NACP RG 260, Box 423, 940.304.
14. Sliding into chaos: Veick interrogation. NACP Record Group.331, File 940.401, G-4 Functions in ESTOUSA Operations.
15. In the morning: *Ibid.*
16. To distribute currency: *Ibid.*
17. What tomorrow brings: *Ibid.* Frommknicht and Veick Interrogations. RG 260, 910.304.
18. Will get far: *Ibid.*
19. Concentration camp inmates: RG 331, Report G-4 Functions in ESTOUSA Operations 9 April to 22 April 1945.

20. Tons of German gold: BHM, 335. BLI, Luisa Funk Statement.
21. Rebuild the country: *Ibid.* Karl Bernd Esser, *Hitlers Gold,* p. 286.
22. The weekend before: *The Goebbels Diaries,* pp. 320-321.
23. And other currencies: Bernard Bernstein Oral History July 23, 1975, Harry S. Truman Presidential Library.
24. Left for Frankfurt: *Ibid.*
25. After the war. NACP Record Group.331, File 940.401, G-4 Functions in ESTOUSA Operations.
26. Left in Berlin: Veick Interrogation. April 12, 1945. NACP Record Group.331, G-4 Functions in ESTOUSA Operations. Karl Friedrich interrogation, NACP RG 331 Folder 940.4601.
27. Ignored the request: Bernard Bernstein Oral History July 23, 1975, Harry S. Truman Presidential Library.
28. Fall in place: Oral History Interview with Bernard Bernstein, Harry S. Truman Presidential Library.
29. Ripped during transport: Robert S. Edsel, *The Monuments Men,* pp. 290-295.
30. Responsible for manuscripts: *Ibid.,* pp. 295-297.
31. Above ground again: Greg Bradsher, *Nazi Gold: The Merkers Mine Treasure,* p. 15.
32. Bars in America: George S. Patton, Jr., *War As I Knew It,* p. 292.
33. The brass agreed: *Ibid.*
34. A bit sick: Dwight D. Eisenhower, *Dear General,* p. 223.
35. Got an answer: Omar N. Bradley, *A Soldier's Story,* p.540-541.
36. Conduct of the war: George S. Patton, Jr. *War as I Knew It,* pp. 288-295. Omar N. Bradley, *A Soldier's Story,* pp. 537-541.
37. The captured gold: Albert Thoms first interrogation. NACP RG 260, Box 423, 940.304.
38. $20 gold coins: Bernstein Report to Brig. Gen. F.J. McSherry, April 18, 1945. G-4. /390/46/9/2. Function in ETOUSA Operations.
39. Escort for Frankfurt: Bernstein Report 18 April 1945. *Ibid.*
40. Outside of Fort Knox: James Stewart Martin, *All Honorable Men,* pp.73-74.
41. Nixed the idea: Jean Edward Smith, *Eisenhower in War and Peace,* p. 738.
42. Seventy-eight shipments: Bernstein Monthly Report on Financial Aspects of the Allied Occupation of Germany, April 1945. NACP Record Group.331, G-4 Functions in ESTOUSA Operations. NACP RG 331, SHAEF, 1/13. April 14, 1945. Bernstein Report to C/S Third Army.
43. The Bavarian forest: GFA #20486, pp. 180-183. #20546, 007-105.
44. Their gold content: Bernstein letter to General Lucius Clay, August 19, 1945. NACP Record Group.331, G-4 Functions in ESTOUSA Operations.
45. The Nazi gold: NACP RG, 332. ETO. SGS 123/2 Nixon to Bernstein.
46. Value at $256 million. NACP REG 260, Entry Finance, Box 440, file 940.60.43.
47. Was ever charged: Robert M. Edsel, *The Monuments Men,* p. 300.

48. In Nazi gold: Antony Beevor, *Berlin the Downfall 1945*, p. 406. Arthur L. Smith, Jr., *Hitler's Gold*, p. 164.

CHAPTER TWENTY-NINE: THE *GÖTTERDÄMMERUNG* OF GOLD

1. The last 24 hours: Hugh Trevor-Roper, *The Goebbels Diaries*, p. 296
2. Were learning Russian: Antony Beevor, *Berlin The Downfall 1945*, pp.188-191.
3. Do what you want: David Irving, *Göring*, p. 460.
4. Night of March 29-30: Ronald W. Zweig, *The Gold Train*, p. 91.
5. In the transfer: NACP RG 260, File "History of the Hungarian Gold." Letter Bernard Bernstein to Lucius Clay August 19, 1945. NACP RG 260/390/46/9/2, box 424.
6. Stored in the Vatican: Report of Croatian Delegation, London Gold Conference, p. 242. *U.S. and Allied Wartime and Postwar Relations and Negotiations with Argentina et. al.*, p. xlvii.
7. Break Vatican secrecy: Dusan Biber, Yugoslav Monetary Gold 1939-51. London Gold Conference. Supplement to Report of the Croatian Delegation pp. 238-242. William Slany, *U.S. and Allied Wartime and Postwar Relations and Negotiations with Argentina et. al.*, p. xlvii-xlviii.
8. North of Hamburg: Franz Stonnleithner and Hans Schröder interrogation. Report by Herbert Sorter to Samuel Rose. NND 775057 Fold3 Image #291842964.
9. Soldiers arrested him: Kenneth Alford and Theodore Savas, *Nazi Millionaires*, p. 96.
10. Town in Austria: NACP RG 260 940.304 Melmer file.
11. 50,000 gold francs: Kenneth Alford and Theodore Svas, *Nazi Millionaires*, p. 96.
12. Despite Allied pressure: Thomas H. McKittrick Papers, Harvard University Business School Library: Series 2. Carton 6/25.
13. Enemy-occupied territory: *Ibid.*
14. Tons of gold: Munich Justice investigation, August Strobl statement.
15. Village of Bad Tölz: BHM, 335, Käthe Miesen statement.
16. Thousand gold bars: BHM, 335 BLI Netzeband report. BHM Luisa Funk testimony.
17. Store the gold: BHM, 335. BLI Bernhard Miesen statement.
18. The two bars: BHM, 335 BLI Reichsbank Secretary X statement.
19. South by truck: Karl Bernd Esser, *Hitlers Gold*, p. 312.
20. On the ground: BHM, 335. Bernhard Miesen statement. conducting detailed inventories.
21. Conducting detailed inventories: Karl Bernd Esser, *Hitlers Gold*, pp. 313 and 323.
22. The Neuhauser house: BHM, 335 BLI Gottlieb Berger statement.
23. Reinforce the hiding places: *Ibid.*
24. Into the *Walchensee*: BHM, 335, Alois Ziller statement.

25. Near the lake: Ian Sayer and Douglas Botting, *Nazi Gold*, pp. 46-48.

26. To the mountains: BHM, 335, Heinz Rüger testimony.

27. Boxes of jewelry: BHM, 335, Georg Forstreicher and Anton Bräu testimony.

28. Dollars had disappeared: BHM, 335, BA 20486/000069-77. *Bayerischen Landpolizei* Report.

29. Charged an American coverup: Henriette von Schirach, *The Price of Glory*. W. Stanley Moss, *Gold Is Where You Hide It*. Ian Sayer and Douglas Botting, *Nazi Gold*. Gold Team Final Report, William J. Clinton Presidential Library.

30. To Tripartite claimants: Final Report, Trilateral Commission for the Restitution of Monetary Gold. www.state.gov/s/l/65668.htm. London Gold Conference, p. 811. Gold Team Final Report, p. 9.

CHAPTER THIRTY: THE END OF A SORDID TALE

1. Cold War had begun: wikipedia.org/wiki/Potsdam_Agreement. London Gold Conference, presentation by Gill Bennett, British delegation, p. 689.

2. Removal to Germany: Paris Conference on Reparations, November and December 1945, Final Report, Part III. NACP RG 84.

3. To the claimants: William Slany, *U.S. and Allied Wartime ad Postwar Relations and Negotiations with Argentina, et al.* p. lvi.

4. Gold to Switzerland: April 4, 1946 letter from William E. Rappard, head of the Swiss delegation, to U.S. delegation. NACP RG 84.

5. First quarter of 1944: *Bergier Commission Final Report*, p. 241.

6. Down to $28 million: Jean Ziegler, *The Swiss, the Gold and the Dead*, p. 200. *U.S. and Allied Wartime ad Postwar Relations and Negotiations with Argentina, et al.* p. 172.

7. Considerations of origin: *Final Gold Report*, Presidential Advisory Commission on Holocaust Assets, p. 40, William J. Clinton Presidential Library.

8. Other strategic commodities: *Ibid.*, pp. 43-46.

9. Were mostly Jews: Nazi Gold London Conference, pp. 790-794.

EPILOGUE

1. World War II gold: http:www.anac-fr.com/2gm/2gm_19.htm.

2. More than the U.S: Peter L. Bernstein, *The Power of Gold*, pp. 339-345.

3. For the French attack: *Ibid.* pp. 339-345, *Time* magazine, February 1965.

4. The new millennium: London Gold Fixing.

5. Called Brown's Bottom: Wikipedia, Sale of U.K. gold reserves, 1999–2002.

6. Reached $1,896.50 an ounce: London Gold Fixing.

7. Cannot trust governments: Herbert Hoover, *The Memoirs of Herbert Hoover*, p. 390-391.

APPENDICES I, II, AND III

1. Reichsbank Holdings in 1938: Ralf Banken, *Edelmetallmangel und Großraubwritschaft*, p. 241.

2. Seizure of Central Bank Gold: Tripartite Claims; *Final Report of the Tripartite Commission for the Restitution of Monetary Gold Commission* (NACP RG 59, Entry 5382 [201538-546]; country Tripartite claims and adjudication, William Slany, *U.S. and Allied Wartime and Postwar Relations and Negotiations with Argentina, Portugal, Spain, Sweden, and Turkey on Looted Gold and German External Assets and U.S. Concerns About the Fate of the Wartime Ustasha Treasury*; Eduard Kubu, *Czechoslovak Gold Reserves and Their Surrender to Nazi Germany*, London Gold Conference.

3. Bank Recipients of Nazi Gold During World War II: *Bergier Commission, Interim Report on Gold*.

4. Sales to Private Suisse Private Banks in 1940-1941: *Ibid.*

5. Sales to the Swiss National Bank (1940-1945): *Ibid.*

6. Other Nazi Gold Sales: *Ibid*, London Gold Conference, p. 514.

7. Reichsbank Gold Holdings at the End of World War II: Howard Report, September 6, 1945, NACP RG 59 Files 940.92 and 940.60.

8. Total Nazi Gold Trade 1938-1945: Howard Report, September 6, 1945, NACP RG 59 Files 940.92 and 940.60.

9. Gold Recovered in Germany in 1945: William Slany, *U.S. and Allied Wartime and Postwar Relations and Negotiations with Argentina, etc.* Interrogation of Karl Friedrich Wilhelm, NACP RG 59 Files 940.92 and 940.60.

10. Tripartite Commission for the Restitution of Monetary Gold: Tripartite Commission national case adjudications.

BIBLIOGRAPHY

Aalders, Gerard. *Eksters*. Amsterdam: Boom, 2002.

———. *Nazi Looting*. Oxford: Berg, 2004.

Abrams, Joseph. *A History of the 90th Division in World War II, 6 June 1944 to 9 May 1945*. Nashville: Battery Press, 1999.

Adams, Henry H. *Years of Deadly Peril*. New York: David McKay, 1969.

Adamson, Hans Christian and Klem, Per. *Blood on the Midnight Sun*. New York: W.W. Norton, 1964.

Anderson, James. *The Spanish Civil War*. Westport: Greenwood Press, 2003.

Agar, Augustus. *Footprints in the Sea*. London: Evans Brothers, 1959.

Ahamed, Liaquat. *Lords of Finance*. New York: Penguin Press, 2009.

Alford, Kenneth D. *Nazi Plunder*. Cambridge, MA: Da Capo Press, 2000.

Alford, Kenneth and Savas, Theodore. *Nazi Millionaires*. Havertown, PA: Casemate, 2002.

Aly, Götz. *Hitler's Beneficiaries*. New York: Metropolitan Books, 2005.

Ambrose, Stephen E. *Eisenhower and Berlin 1945*. New York: W.W. Norton, 1967.

Amouroux, Henri. *Le Peuple du Désastre*. Paris: Éditions Robert Laffont, 1976.

Andenaes, Johs. *Norway and the Second World War*. Oslo: Johan Grundt Tanum Forlag, 1974.

Anderson, James A. *The Spanish Civil War*. London: Greenwood Press, 2003.

Andrews, Lewis. *Tempest, Fire and Foe*. Victoria, B.C.: Trafford, 1999.

Arad, Yitzhak. *Belzec, Sobibor, Treblinka*. Bloomington, IN: Indiana University Press, 1987.
Arnoult, Pierre. *Les Finances de la France et l'Occupation Allemande*. Paris: Presses Universitaires de France, 1951.

Auboin, Roger. *The Bank for International Settlements, 1930-1955*. Princeton, NJ: Princeton University Press, 1955.

Auphan, Paul. *The French Navy in World War II*. Annapolis, MD: U.S. Naval Institute, 1959.

Auque, René and Carré, Paul. *Le Croiseur Émile Bertin*. Paris: Éditions de l'Officine, 2002.

Bähr, Johannes. *Der Goldhandel der Dresdner Bank im Zweiten Weltkrieg*. Berlin: Gustave Kiepenheuer Verlag, 1999.

Banken, Ralf. *Edelmetallmangel und Großraubwirtschaft*. Berlin: Akademie Verlag, 2009.

Barber, Noel. *The Week France Fell*. New York: Stein and Day, 1979.

Barkai, Avraham. *Nazi Economics*. New Haven: Yale University Press, 1990.

Beevor, Antony. *The Spanish Civil War*. New York: Peter Bedrick Books, 1983.

———. *Berlin the Downfall 1945*. London: Penguin, 2007.

Bell, P.M.H. *A Certain Eventuality*. Scotland: Robert MacLehose, 1974.

Benoist-Méchin, Jacques. *Sixty Days that Shook the West*. New York: Putnum, 1963.

Bernstein, Peter L. *The Power of Gold*. New York: Wiley, 2000.

Berghoff, Hartmut, Kocka, Jügen, and Ziegler, Dieter. *Business in the Age of Extremes*. Cambridge: Cambridge University Press, 2013.

Bertke, Donald A. and Kindell, Don. *World War II Sea War Vol. 2*. Dayton, OH: Bertke Publications, 2011.

Beschloss, Michael. *The Conquerors*. New York: Simon & Schuster, 2002.

Best, Nicholas. *Five Days that Shocked the World*. New York: St. Martin's Press, 2011.

Bethell, Nicholas. *The War Hitler Won*. New York: Holt, Rinehart and Winston, 1972.

Beyen, J. W. *Money in the Maelstrom*. New York: Macmillan, 1949.

Biggs, Barton. *Wealth, War, and Wisdom*. Hoboken, NJ: John Wiley & Sons, 2008.

Binder, Frank and Schlünz, Hans H. *Schwerer Kreuzer Blücher*. Frankfurt/Main: Ullstein, 1996.

Bingham, Colin. *Men and Affairs*. New York: Funk & Wagnalls, 1967.

Blinkhorn, Martin. *Spain in Conflict 1931-1939*. London: Sage, 1986.

Blum, John Morton. *From the Morgenthau Diaries Vol. 1-3*. Boston: Houghton Mifflin, 1959, 1965, 1967.

———. *Roosevelt and Morgenthau*. Boston: Houghton Mifflin, 1959.

Bock, Fedor von. *The War Diary 1939-1945*. Atglen, PA: Schiffer Publishing, 1996.

Bolloten, Burnett. *The Spanish Civil War*. Chapel Hill: University of North Carolina Press, 1991.

Borio, Claudio. *Past and Future of Central Bank Cooperation*. Cambridge: Cambridge University Press, 2008.

Borkin, Joseph. *The Crime and Punishment of I.G. Farben*. New York: The Free Press, 1978.

Bourgeois, Daniel. *Le Troisième Reich et la Suisse*. Neuchatel: Éditions de la Baconni, 1974.

Bower, Tom. *Nazi Gold*. New York: HarperCollins, 1997.

Bradley, Omar N. *A Soldier's Story*. New York: Henry Holt, 1951.

Bradford, Sarah. *George VI*. London: George Weidenfeld & Nicolson, 1989.

Brady, Michael. *Nordic Gold*. Oslo: Norsk Numismatisk Forlag, 1989.

Bramsnaes, C.V. *The National Bank During the German Occupation of Denmark*. Copenhagen: Nationalbanken, 1948.

Braithwaite, Rodric. *Moscow 1941*. New York: Random House, 2006.

Braudel. Fernand. *Memory and the Mediterranean*. New York: Vintage, 2002.

Breitman, Richard. *U.S. Intelligence and the Nazis*. New York: Cambridge University Press, 2005.

Brinkley, Douglas. *World War II, 1939-1942: The Axis Assault*. New York: New York Times Books, 2003.

Brook-Shepperd, Gordon. *The Storm Petrels*. New York: Ballantine Books, 1977.

Brownell, Will and Billings, Richard. *So Close to Greatness*. New York: Macmillan, 1987.

Bruneel, Didier. *Les Secrets de l'Or*. Paris: Le Cherche Midi, 2011.

Bullitt, Orville. *For the President Personal & Secret*. New York: Houghton Mifflin, 1972.

Bullock, Alan. *Hitler*. New York: Harper & Row, 1952.

Burdick, Charles and Jacobsen, Hans-Adolf. *The Halder War Diary 1939-1942*. Novato, CA: Presidio Press, 1988.

Buruma, Ian. *Year Zero*. New York: Penguin Press, 2013.

Buttar, Prit. *Between Giants*. Oxford: Osprey, 2013.

Cardarelli, Sergio and Martano, Renata. *I Nazisti e L'Oro della Banca d'Italia*. Rome: Editori Laterza, 2000.

Carell, Paul. *Invasion They're Coming*. New York: Dutton, 1963.

Carpozi, George. *Nazi Gold*. Far Hills, NJ: New Horizon Press, 1999.

Carr, John. *The Defense and Fall of Greece: 1940-1941*. Barnsley: Pen & Sword Military, 2013.

Carr, William. *Arms, Autarky and Aggression*. London: Camelot Press, 1972.

Carroll, Berenice A. *Design for Total War*. The Hague: Mouton, 1968.

Casey, Steven. *Cautious Crusade*. Oxford: Oxford University Press, 2001.

Chadwick, Owen. *Britain and the Vatican During the Second World War*. Cambridge: Cambridge University Press. 1988.

Churchill, Winston. *The Gathering Storm*. Boston: Houghton Mifflin, 1948.

———. *Their Finest Hour*. Boston: Houghton Mifflin, 1949.

———. *The Grand Alliance*. Boston: Houghton Mifflin, 1950.

Chuikov, Vasilia. *The Fall of Berlin*. New York: Holt, Rinehart and Winston, 1968.

Ciano, Galeazzo. *Diary 1937-1943*. New York: Enigma Books, 2002.

Clarke, Comer. *England Under Hitler*. New York: Ballantine Books, 1961.

Classon, Adam R.A. *Hitler's Northern War*. Lawrence, KS: University Press of Kansas, 2001.

Clingan, C. Edmund. *The Lives of Hans Luther, 1879-1962*. New York: Lexington Books, 2010.

Dodevilla, Angelo. *Between the Alps and a Hard Place*. Washington: Regnery Publishing, 2000.

Cohan, William D. *The Last Tycoons*. New York: Doubleday, 2008.

Colville, John. *The Fringes of Power*. New York: Norton, 1985.

Cornish, Nik. *Images of Kursk*. Lincoln, NE: Potomac Books, 2002.

Costello, John and Tsarev, Oleg. *Deadly Illusions*. New York: Crown Publishers, 1993.

Craig, R. Bruce. *Treasonable Doubt*. Lawrence, KS. University Press of Kansas, 2004.

Crombois, Jean F. *Camille Gutt and Postwar International Finance*. London: Pickering & Chatto, 2011.

———. *Camille Gutt*. Bruxelles: CEGES Gerpinnes, 1999.

Dahl, Hans Fredrik. *Quisling: A Study in Treachery*. Cambridge: Cambridge University Press, 1999.

Davis, Forrest and Lindley, Ernest. *How War Came*. New York: Simon and Schuster, 1942.

DeGaulle, Charles. *The Complete War Memoirs of Charles de Gaulle*. New York: Carroll and Graf, 1998.

Deutsch, Harold. C. *Hitler and His Generals January-June 1938*. Minneapolis: University of Minnesota Press, 1974.

———. *The Conspiracy Against Hitler in the Twilight War*. Minneapolis: University of Minnesota Press, 1968.

Deutsch, Oswald. *Hitler's 12 Apostles*. Freeport, NY: Books for Libraries Press, 1940.

DeJong, A.M. *Geschiedenis van de Nederlandsche Bank*. Haarlem: J. Enschedé, 1967.

Delarue, Jacques. *The Gestapo*. New York: Macdonald. 1964.

Dietrich, John. *The Morgenthau Plan*. New York: Algora Publishing, 2003.

Dildy, Douglas. *Denmark and Norway 1940*. London: Osprey, 2007.

Dilks, David. *The Diaries of Sir Alexander Cadogan 1938-1945*. New York: G.P. Putnam's Sons, 1972.

Dodd, Martha. *Through Embassy Eyes*. New York: Harcourt Brace, 1939.

Dodd, William E. *Ambassador Dodd's Diary 1933-1938*. New York: Harcourt Brace, 1941.

Dönitz, Karl. *The Conduct of the War at Sea*. Washington: The Navy Department Library, 1946.

Draper, Alfred. *Operation Fish*. London: Cassell, 1979.

D'Ydewalle, Pierre. *De Memoires*. Tielt : Lannoo, 1994.

Eden, Anthony. *The Reckoning*. Boston: Houghton Mifflin, 1965.

Edsel, Robert M. *The Monuments Men*. New York: Center Street, 2009.

Edwards, Bernard. *The Road to Russia*. Barnsley, Britain: Pen & Sword Books, 2002.

Ehrenburg, Ilya. *Fall of Paris*. New York: Alfred Knopf, 1943.

———. *Memoirs: 1921-1941*. New York: Grosset & Dunlap, 1963.

Eichengreen, Barry. *Golden Fetters*. Oxford: Oxford University Press, 1992.

Einzig, Paul. *International Gold Movements*. London: Macmillan, 1931.

————. *Germany's Default*. London: Macmillan, 1934.

————. *Economic Warfare*. London: Macmillan, 1940.

————. *In the Centre of Things*. London: Hutchinson, 1960.

————. *The Destiny of Gold*. London: Macmillan, 1972.

Eisenhower, Dwight. *Crusade in Europe*. New York: Doubleday, 1952.

Eizenstat, Stuart E. *Imperfect Justice*. New York: Public Affairs, 2003.

Esser, Karl Bernd. *Hitlers Gold*. Munich: Books on Demand, 2004.

Evans, Richard J. *The Coming of the Third Reich*. New York: Penguin, 2005.

————. *The Third Reich in Power*. New York: Penguin, 2005.

————. *The Third Reich at War*. New York: Penguin, 2009.

Farago, Laislas. *Burn After Reading*. Los Angeles: Pinnacle Books, 1961.

Feiertag, Oliva and Margairaz, Michel. *Les Banques Centrales à l'Échelle du Monde*. Paris: Science Po, 2012.

Fergusson, Adam. *When Money Dies*. New York: Public Affairs, 2010.

Fischer, Bernd J. *Albania at War 1939-1945*. West Lafayette, IN: Purdue University Press, 1999.

Fischer, Louis. *Men and Politics*. New York: Harper & Row, 1941.

Forczyk, Robert. *Rescuing Mussolini*. Oxford: Osprey, 2010.

Fowler, Will. *France, Holland and Belgium 1940*. Surrey, Britain: Allan Publishing, 2002.
Fullilove, Michael. *Rendezvous with Destiny*. New York: Penguin Press, 2013.

Funk, Walther. *Ein Leben für Deutschland*. München: Zentralverlag der NSDAP, 1940.

Gaston-Breton, Tristan. *Sauve l'Or de la Banque de France*. Paris: Le Cherche Midi. 2002.

Gathorne-Hardy, G.M. *War Poems of Nordahl Grieg*. London: Hodder & Stoughton, 1944.

Gazur, Edward P. *Secret Assignment Spain*. London: St. Ermin's Press, 2001.

Gilbert, Martin. *The Churchill War Papers*. New York: Norton, 1995.

————. *Winston Churchill*, vol. VI. Boston: Houghton Mifflin, 1983.

————. *History of the Twentieth Century*, vol. 1. New York: Avon Books, 1998.

Gisevius, Hans Bernd. *To the Bitter End*. Boston: Houghton Mifflin, 1947.

Glantz, David M. and House, Jonathan M. *When Titans Clashed*. Lawrence, KS: University Press of Kansas, 1995.

Goda, Norman. *Tales from Spandau*. Cambridge: Cambridge University Press, 2006.

Goldstein, Ivo. *Croatia: A History*. London: C. Hurst, 1999.

Goodwin, Doris Kearns. *Team of Rivals*. New York: Simon & Schuster, 2005.

————. *No Ordinary Time*. New York: Simon & Schuster, 1994.

Gordon, David Dangerfield. *The Hidden Weapon*. New York: Harper & Brothers, 1947.

Graham, Helen. *The Spanish Republic at War 1936-1939*. Cambridge: Cambridge University Press, 2002.

Graham, Robert A. *The Vatican and Communism During World War II*. San Francisco: Ignatius Press, 1996.

Green, Timothy. *The New World of Gold*. New York: Walker, 1981.

Greene, Graham. *Ways of Escape*. New York: Simon & Schuster, 1980.

Gritzbach, Erich. *Hermann Göring*. London: Hurst & Blackett, 1939.

Gutt, Camille. *La Belgique au Carrefour 1940-1944*. Paris: Fayard, 1971.

Haarr, Geirr H. *The German Invasion of Norway*. Annapolis, MD: Naval Institute Press, 2009.

Haffner, Sebastian. *Germany Jekyll & Hyde*. London: Secker & Warburg, 1940.

Haining, Peter. *Mystery of Rommel's Gold*. London: Robson, 2003.

Hall, H. Duncan. *North American Supply*. London: Longmans, Green and Co., 1955.

Hambro, Carl J. *I Saw It Happen in Norway*. New York: William Morrow, 1940.

Harriman, Florence Jaffray. *Mission to the North*. Philadelphia: Lippincott, 1941.

Harnes, Per Arnt. *Gulltransporten*. Romsdal: Utgitt av, 2006.

Harris, Whitney. *Tyranny on Trial*. Dallas: Southern Methodist University Press, 1954.

Hart, Matthew. *Gold*. New York: Simon & Schuster, 2013.

Haskew. Michael E. *De Gaulle*. New York: Palgrave Macmillan, 2011.

Hassell, Ulrich von. *The von Hassell Diaries*. Oxford: Westview Press, 1994.

Hasting, Max. *Winston's War*. New York: Vintage Books, 2011.

Hayes, Paul M. *Quisling*. Bloomington: Indiana University Press, 1972.

Hayes, Peter. *From Cooperation to Complicity*. Cambridge: Cambridge University Press, 2004.

Hehn. Paul N. *A Low Dishonest Decade*. New York: Continuum, 2002.

Hewins, Ralph. *Quisling, a Prophet Without Honor*. New York: John Day, 1965.

Hitler, Adolf. *Mein Kampf*. Boston: Houghton Mifflin, 1998.

——. *Hitler's Second Book*. New York: Enigma Books, 2006.

Hobbs, Joseph. *Dear General*. Baltimore: Johns Hopkins Press, 1971.

Holland, James. *Italy's Sorrow*. New York: St. Martin's Press, 2008.

Hoover, Herbert. *Public Papers 1932-1933*. Washington: Government Printing Office, 1977.

Hoptner, Jocob and Roberts, Henry. *Yugoslavia in Crisis 1934-1941*. New York: Columbia University Press, 1962.

Horne, Alistair. *To Lose a Battle*. Boston: Little, Brown, 1969.

Howson, Gerald. *Arms for Spain*. New York: St. Martin's Press, 1998.

Hubatsch, Walther. *Weserübung*. Berlin: Munsterschmidt-Verlag, 1960.

Hull, Cordell. *The Memoirs of Cordell Hull*. New York: Macmillan, 1948.

Ibarruri, Dolores. *They Shall Not Pass*. New York: International Publishers, 1976.

Irving, David. *Göring*. New York: William Morrow, 1989.

Jackson, Julian. *The Fall of France*. Oxford: Oxford University Press, 2003.

Jacobsson, Erin E. *A Life for Sound Money*. Oxford: Clarendon Press, 1979.

James, Harold. *The Deutsche Bank and the Nazi Economic War Against the Jews*. Cambridge: Cambridge University Press, 2001.

Jedrzejewicz, Waclaw. *Diplomat in Paris 1936-1939*. New York: Columbia University Press, 1970.

Jessop, Keith and Hanson, Neil. *Goldfinder*. New York: John Wiley, 1998.

Johnson, Juliet. *A Fistful of Rubles*. Ithaca: Cornell University Press, 2000.

Johnson, Paul. *The Birth of the Modern*. New York: HarperCollins, 1991.

———. *Modern Times*. New York: HarperCollins, 1983.

Karski, Jan. *Story of a Secret State*. Boston: Houghton Mifflin, 1944.

Katz, Robert. *The Battle for Rome*. New York: Simon & Schuster, 2003.

Kauch, Pierre. *Le Vol de l'Or de la Banque Nationale par les Nazis (1940-1943)*. Bruxelles: Institute Belge des Finances Publique, 1956.

Kelly, C. Brian. *Best Little Stories from WW II*. Nashville: Cumberland House, 2010.

Kersaudy, François. *Norway 1940*. Lincoln: University of Nebraska Press, 1990.

Kershaw, Ian. *Fateful Choices*. New York: Penguin Press, 2007.

———. *Hitler 1889-1936*. New York: Norton, 1999.

Keyes, Roger. *Outrageous Fortune*. London: Secker & Warburg, 1985.

Keynes, John Maynard. *The Economic Consequences of the Peace*. New York: Harcourt, Brace and Howe, 1920.

———. *The Great Slump of 1930*. Project Gutenberg Canada Ebook. www.gutenberg.ca.

Khrushchev, Nikita and Talbott, Strobe. *Khrushchev Remembers*. Boston: Little, Brown, 1970.

Kimball, Warren. *Churchill & Roosevelt: The Complete Correspondence*. Princeton, NJ: Princeton University Press, 1984.

———. *The Most Unsordid Act*. Baltimore: John Hopkins Press, 1969.

Kitchen, Martin. *The History of Modern Germany*. Hoboken, NJ: Wiley-Blackwell, 2006.

Klein, Burton H. *Germany's Economic Preparations for War*. Cambridge: Harvard University Press, 1959.

Knudsen, H. Franklin. *I Was Quisling's Secretary*. London: Britons, 1942.

Koht, Halvdan. *Norway Neutral and Invaded*. New York: Macmillan, 1941.

Kowalsky, Daniel. *Stalin and the Spanish Civil War*. New York: ACLS Humanities E-Book, Columbia University Press, 2008.

Kuusterä, Antti and Tarkka, Juha. *Bank of Finland 200 Years*. Helsinki: Otava Publishing, 2012.

Lampe, David. *The Last Ditch*. London: Greenhill Books, 1968.

Larson, Erik. *In the Garden of Beasts*. New York: Crown, 2011.

Lash, Joseph P. *Roosevelt and Churchill 1939-1941*. New York: W.W. Norton, 1976.

Lassaque, Jean. *Le Croiseur Émile Bertin 1931-1961*. Bourg-en-Bresse, France: Marines Éditions, 1995.

Lauryssens, Stan. *The Man Who Invented the Third Reich*. Charleston, SC: History Press, 1999.

Lebor, Adam. *Hitler's Secret Bankers*. Secaucus, NJ: Carol Publishing Group, 1997

———. *Tower of Basel*. New York: Public Affairs, 2013.

Leitz, Christian. *Economic Relations Between Nazi Germany and Franco's Spain 1936-1945*. Oxford: Clarendon Press, 1996.

Lenin Vladimir. *Lenin's Collected Works*. Moscow: Progress Publishers, 1965.

Lepotier, Adolphe. *La Battaille de l'Or*. Paris: Editions France-Empire, 1960.

Levy, Herbert. *Henry Morgenthau, Jr*. New York: Skyhorse Publishing, 2010.

Lidegaard, Bo. *Kampen om Danmark 1933-1945*. Copenhagen: Gyldendal, 2005.

Lie, Trygve. *Leve eller dø*. Oslo: TidenNorsk Forlag, 1955.

Lochery, Neill. *Lisbon*. New York: Public Affairs, 2011.

Loewenheim, Francis, Langley, Harold, Jonas, Manfred. *Roosevelt and Churchill*. New York: E.P. Dutton, 1975.

Longworth, Richard. *Churchill by Himself*. New York: Public Affairs, 2011.

Lorenz-Meyer, Martin. *Safehaven*. Columbia, MO: University of Missouri Press, 2007.

Louçã, António and Dick, Ilse. *Nazigold für Portugal*. Vienna: Holzhausen Verlag, 2002.

Lukacs, John. *The Last European War*. Garden City: Anchor Press, 1976.

———. *The Duel*. New York: Ticknor & Fields, 1991.

———. *Five Days in London*. New Haven: Yale University Press, 1999.

Lunde, Henrik O. *Hitler's Pre-Emptive War*. Philadelphia: Casemate, 2009.

———. *Finland's War of Choice*. Philadelphia: Casemate, 2011.

Mackenzie King, W. L. *The Mackenzie King Record* Vol 1. Toronto: University of Toronto Press, 1960.

MacMillan, Barbara. *Peacemakers*. London: John Murray Publishers, 2003.

———. *Paris 1919*. New York: Random House, 2003.

Malkin, Lawrence. *Krueger's Men*. New York: Little, Brown, 2006.

Malraux, Andre. *Man's Hope*. New York: Random House, 1939.

Mann, Golo. *The History of Germany Since 1789*. New York: Frederick K. Praeger, 1968.

Manstein, Erich von. *Lost Victories*. Novato, CA: Presidio Press, 1982.

Manvell, Roger and Fraenkel, Heinrich. *Goering*. New York: Skyhorse Publishing, 2011.

Martin, James Stewart. *All Honorable Men*. Boston: Little, Brown, 1950.

Marx, Jenifer. *The Magic of Gold*. Garden City, NY: Doubleday, 1978.

Massimo, Dario. *Die Franzensfeste*. Brixen: Eigenverlag, 2007.

Maugeri, Leonardo. *The Age of Oil*. Westport, CT: Praeger, 2006.

May, Ernest R. *Strange Victory*. New York: Hill and Wang, 2000.

Meacham, Jon. *Franklin and Winston*. New York: Random House, 2003.

McCullough, David. *Truman*. New York: Simon & Schuster, 1992.

McDowall, Duncan. *Due Diligence*. Ottawa: Bank of Canada Website, 1997.

Mierzwa, Janusz. *Pułkownik Adam Koc*. Krakow: Historia Iagellonica, 2006.

Milward, Alan S. *The German Economy at War*. London: Athlone Press, 1965.

Monnet, Jean. *Memoirs*. New York: Doubleday, 1978.

Montefiore, Simon Sebag. *Stalin*. New York: Knopf, 2004.

Morgenthau, Henry, Jr. *Germany Is Our Problem*. New York: Harper & Brothers, 1945.

Morgenthau, Henry, III. *Mostly Morgenthaus*. New York: Ticknor & Fields, 1991.

Morrison, Samuel Eliot. *The Battle of the Atlantic*. Boston: Little Brown, 1947

Moss, W. Stanley. *Gold Is Where You Hide It*. London: Andre Deutsch, 1956.

Moulton, J.L. *A Study of Warfare in Three Dimensions*. Athens, OH: Ohio State University Press, 1967.

Moynihan, Daniel Patrick. *Secrecy*. New Haven: Yale University Press, 1998.

Muggeridge, Malcolm. *Ciano Diplomatic Papers*. London: Odhams Press, 1948.

Mühlen, Norbert. *Hitler's Magician*. London: George Routledge & Sons, 1938

Mühlen, Ernest. *Monnaie et Circuits Financiers au Grand-Duché de Luxembourg*. Luxembourg: Université Internationale de Sciences Comparées, 1968.

Müller, Rolf-Dieter and Ueberschär, Gerd. *Hitler's War in the East*. New York: Berghahn Books, 2009.

Murphy, David E. *What Stalin Knew*. New Haven: Yale University Press, 2005.

Nafftel, William. *Halifax at War*. Halifax: Formac, 2008.

Nicolson, Harold. *Diaries and Letters* Vol. II. New York: Atheneum, 1967.

Oestreich, Paul. *Walter Funk, Ein Leben für die Wirtschaft*. Munich: Zentralverlag der NSDAP, 1941.

Önsoy, Murat. *The World War Two Allied Economic Warfare*. Saarbrücken: VDM Verlag, 2009.

Orlov, Alexander. *The March Of Time*. London: St. Ermins Press, 2004.

Orwell, George. *Homage to Catalonia*. New York: Houghton Mifflin Harcourt, 2010.

Oven, Wilfred von and Hahn-Butry, Jürgen. *Panzer Am Balken*. Berlin: Limpert, 1941.

Overy, R.J. *The Nazi Economic Recovery 1932-1938*. Cambridge: Cambridge University Press, 1982.

——. *War and Economy in the Third Reich*. Oxford: Clarendon Press, 2002.

——. *Interrogations*. New York: Penguin, 2002.

Patton, George S., Jr. *War as I Knew It*. Boston: Houghton Mifflin, 1947.

——. *Lines of Fire*. Lewiston, NY: Edwin Mellen Press, 1991.

Paxton, Robert. *Vichy France.* New York: Columbia University Press, 2001.

Pearson, Owen. *Albania in Occupation and War.* London: I.B. Tauris, 2005.

Penrose, Barrie. *Stalin's Gold.* Boston: Little, Brown, 1982.

Peterson, Edward. *Hjalmar Schacht.* Boston: Christopher Publishing House, 1954.

Petrow, Richard. *The Bitter Years.* New York: William Morrow, 1974.

Petzina, Dieter. *Autarkiepolitik im Dritten Reich.* Stuttgart: Deutsche Verlags-Anstalt, 1968.

Phayer, Michael. *The Catholic Church and the Holocaust.* Bloomington, IN: University Press, 2000.

Picaper, Jean-Paul. *Sur la Trace des Trésors Nazi.* Paris: Tallandier, 1998.

Pickford, Nigel. *Lost Treasure Ships of the Twentieth Century.* Washington: National Geographic, 1999.

Piekalkiewicz, Janusz. *Die Schlacht um Moskau.* Berlin: G. Lubbe, 1981.

Pleshakov, Constantine. *Stalin's Folly.* Boston: Houghton Mifflin, 2006.

Pluym, Walter and Pluym, Jan. *Goud Op.Drift.* Leuven: Davidsfonds Uitgeverij, 2011. (Also published in French with the title *L'or à la dérive*).

Pool, James. *Hitler and His Secret Partners.* New York: Pocket Books, 1997.

Preston, Paul. *Revolution and War in Spain 1931-1939.* London: Methuen, 1984.

——. *The Spanish Civil War.* London: Harper Perennial, 1986.

Province, Charles M. *Patton's Third Army.* CreateSpace Independent Publishing Platform, 2008.

Pryce-Jones, David. *Paris in the Third Reich.* New York: Holt, Rinehart and Winston, 1981.

Radosh, Ronald; Habeck, Mary B.; Sevostianov, Grigory. *Spain Betrayed.* New Haven: Yale University Press, 2001.

Raczynski, Edward. *In Allied London.* London: Weidenfeld and Nicolson, 1962.

Radzinsky, Edvard. *Stalin.* New York: Doubleday, 1996.

Rauschning, Hermann. *Hitler Speaks.* London: Thornton Butterworth, 1939.

Raeder, Erich. *My Life.* Annapolis: U.S. Naval Institute, 1960.

Rees, David. *Harry Dexter White.* New York: Coward, McCann & Geoghegan, 1973.

Remarque, Erich Maria. *The Black Obelisk.* New York: Harcourt, Brace and Co., 1957.

Reveille, Thomas. *The Spoil of Europe.* New York: Norton, 1941.

Reynaud, Paul. *In the Thick of the Fight.* New York: Simon and Schuster, 1955.

Ribeiro de Menesies, Filipe. *Salazar.* New York: Enigma Books, 2009.

Rings, Werner. *Raubgold aus Deutschland.* Zürich: Artemis, 1985.

Roberts, Stephen H. *The House that Hitler Built.* New York: Harper & Brothers, 1938.

Rohatyn, Felix. *Dealings.* New York: Simon & Schuster, 2010.

Rojek, Wojciech. *Odyseja skarbu Rzeczypospolitej.* Kraków: Wydawnictwo Literackie, 2000.

Roll, David L. *The Hopkins Touch.* Oxford: Oxford University Press, 2013.

Romerstein, Herbet and Breindel, Eric. *The Venona Secrets.* Washington: Regnery Publishing, 2000.

Roselli, Alessandro. *Italy and Albania.* London: I.B. Tauris, 2006.

Rossino, Alexander. *Hitler Strikes Poland.* Lawrence, KS: University Press of Kansas, 2003.

Russell, William. *Berlin Embassy.* London: Elliott & Thompson, 2006.

Ryan, Cornelius. *The Last Battle.* New York: Simon and Schuster, 1966.

Sayer, Ian and Botting, Douglas. *Nazi Gold.* London: Congdon & Weed, 1984.

Schacht, Hjalmar. *The Stabilization of the Mark.* London: G. Allen & Unwin, 1927.

———. *Account Settled.* London. Weidenfeld & Nicolson, 1948.

———. *Gold for Europe.* London: Duckworth, 1950.

———. *My First Seventy-Six Years.* London: Allan Wingate, 1955.

———. *Confessions of 'The Old Wizard'.* Boston: Houghton Mifflin, 1956.

———. *The Magic of Money.* London: Oldbourne, 1967.

Schausberger, Norbert. *Der Griff Nach Österreich.* Vienna: Jugend und Volk, 1978.

Schecter, Jerrold and Leona. *Sacred Secrets.* Washington: Brassey's, 2002.

Schlesinger, Arthur M., Jr. *The Coming of the New Deal 1933-1935.* Boston: Houghton Mifflin, 1959.

Schmidt, Paul. *Hitler's Interpreter.* New York: Macmillan, 1951.

Schofield, Victoria. *Witness to History.* New Haven: Yale University Press, 2012.

Schumpeter, Joseph. *History of Economic Analysis.* New York: Oxford University Press, 1954.

Schuschnigg, Kurt von. *Austrian Requiem.* New York: Putnam's, 1946.

Sherwood, Robert. *Roosevelt and Hopkins.* New York: Harper & Brothers, 1948.

Schirach, Henriette von. *The Price of Glory.* London: Frederick Muller, 1960.

Shirer, William L. *Berlin Diary.* New York: Galahad Books, 1940.

———. *The Rise and Fall of the Third Reich.* New York: Simon and Schuster, 1960.

———. *The Challenge of Scandinavia.* Boston: Little, Brown, 1955.

———. *The Nightmare Years 1930-1940.* Boston: Little, Brown, 1984.

———. *The Collapse of the Third Republic.* London: Pan Books, 1972.

Shales, Amity. *The Forgotten Man.* New York: Harper Collins, 2008.

Simpson, Amos. *Hjalmar Schacht in Perspective.* The Hague: Mouton, 1969.

Simpson, Christopher. *War Crimes of the Deutsche and the Dresdner Bank.* New York: Holmes & Meier. 2001.

Smit, Erik. *3 Februar 1945: Die Zerstorung Kreuzbers.* Berlin: Bezirksamt Kreuzberg, 1995.

Smith, Arthur. *Hitler's Gold.* Oxford: Berg, 1989.

Smith, Jean Edward. *Eisenhower in War and Peace*. New York: Random House, 2012.

Snyder, Louis. *Encyclopedia of the Third Reich*. New York: McGraw-Hill, 1976.

Snyder, Timothy. *Bloodlands*. New York: Basic Books, 2010.

Spaak, Paul-Henri. *Continuing Battle*. West Sussex: Littlehampton, 1971.

Speer, Albert. *Inside the Third Reich*. New York: Macmillan, 1970.

——. *Spandau*. New York: Macmillan, 1976.

——. *Infiltration*. New York: Macmillan, 1981.

Stafford, David. *Roosevelt and Churchill*. New York: Overlook Press, 2011.

Steil, Ben. *The Battle of Bretton Woods*. Princeton: Princeton University Press, 2013.

Spielvogel, Jackson J. *Hitler and Nazi Germany*. Upper Saddle River, NJ: Prentice Hall, 1992.

Stahel, David. *Operation Typhoon*. Cambridge: Cambridge University Press, 2013.

Stanton. Bernard F. *George F. Warren*. Ithaca: Cornell University Press, 2007.

Steinberg, Jonathan. *The Deutsche Bank and its Gold Transactions during the Second World War*. München: Verlag C.H. Beck, 1999.

Stevens, E.H. *Trial of Nikolaus von Falkenhorst*. London: William Hodge, 1949.

Stoddard, Brooke C. *World in the Balance*. Washington: Potomac Book, 2011.

Stoessinger, John. *Why Nations Go to War*. Stamford, CT: Cengage Learning, 2010.

Stourzh, Gerald and Zaar, Brigitta. *Österreich, Deutschland und die Machte*. Vienna: Verlag der Österreichen Akademie der Wissenschafter, 1990.

Stowe, Leland. *They Shall Not Sleep*. New York: Alfred A. Knopf, 1945.

Surmann, Rolf and Schröder, Dieter. *Der lange Schatten der NS-Diktatur*. Hamburg: UNRAST Verlag, 1999.

Taylor, Frederick. *The Downfall of Money*. New York: Bloomsbury Press, 2013.

Taylor, Myron. *Wartime Correspondence Between President Roosevelt and Pope Pius XII*. New York: Macmillan, 1947.

Táborsky, Eduard. *The Czechoslovak Cause*. London: Witherby, 1944.

Taylor, Robert. *Battle of Britain*. Philadelphia: Casemate, 2010.

Thomas, Benjamin P. and Hyman, Harold M. *Stanton*. New York: Alfred A. Knopf, 1962.

Thomas, George. *Geschichte der deutschen Wehr—und Rüstungswirtschaft (1918-45)*. Boppard am Rhein: Harald Boldt Verlag, 1966.

Thomas, Hugh. *The Spanish Civil War*. New York: The Modern Library, 2001.

Toland, John. *Adolf Hitler*. New York: Ballantine Books. 1976.

Tomasevich, Jozo. *War and Revolution in Yugoslavia 1941-1945*. Stanford: Stanford University Press, 2001.

Tomes, Jason. *King Zog*. New York: New York University Press, 2003.

Thompson, Laurence. *1940*. New York: William Morrow, 1966.

Todd, Olivier. *Malraux*. New York: Knopf/Borsai, 2005.

Toniolo, Gianni. *Central Bank Cooperation at the Bank for International Settlements, 1930-1973.* Cambridge: Cambridge University Press, 2007.

Tooze, Adam. *The Wages of Destruction.* London: Allan Lane, 2006.

Trevor-Roper, Hugh. *Hitler's War Directives 1939-1945.* Edinburgh: Berlin, 2004.

———. *Hitler's Table Talk 1941-44.* London: Weidenfeld & Nicolson, 1953.

———. *The Goebbels Diaries.* London, Book Club Associates, 1978.

———. *The Last Days of Hitler.* Chicago: University of Chicago Press, 1971.

Truffaut, France. *Sauver l'or belge.* Tubize, Belgium: Gamma Press, 1997.

Truman, Harry. *Memoirs 1945: Year of Decision.* New York: New York: Smithmark, 1955.

Turney, Alfred W. *Disaster at Moscow.* Albuquerque: University of New Mexico Press, 1970.

Van der Wee, Herman and Verbreyt, Monique. *A Small Nation.* Leuven: Leuven University Press, 2009.

Van Dormael, Armand. *Bretton Woods.* London: Macmillan, 1978.

Vian, Philip. *Action This Day.* London: Frederick Muller, 1960.

Vickers, Miranda. *The Albanians: A Modern History.* London: I. B. Tauris, 2001.

Waal, Frans de. *Peacemaking Among Primates.* Cambridge, MA: Harvard University Press, 1990.

Wagner, Dieter and Tomkowitz, Gerhard. *Anschluss.* New York: St. Martin's Press, 1968.

Watt, Richard. *Bitter Glory.* New York: Hippocrene Books, 1979.

Weinberg, Gerhard. *A World at Arms.* Cambridge: Cambridge University Press, 2005.

Weinstein, Allen and Vassiliev, Alexander. *The Haunted Wood.* New York: The Modern Library, 2000.

Williamson, David G. *Poland Betrayed.* Mechanicsberg, PA: Stackpole Books, 2009.

Weitz, John. *Hitler's Banker.* Boston: Little, Brown, 1997.

Wheeler-Bennett, John. *Special Relationships.* London: Macmillan, 1975.

Wilmot, Chester. *The Struggle for Europe.* Old Saybrook, CT: Konecky & Konecky, 1952.

Wood, E. Thomas and Jankoski, Stanislaw. *Karski.* New York: John Wiley & Sons, 1994.

Yeadon, Glen. *Nazi Hydra in America.* San Diego: Progressive Press, 2008.

Young, Peter. *World Almanac of World War II.* Englewoods Cliff, NJ: Prentice-Hall, 1981.

Zabludoff, Sidney. *Movements of Nazi Gold.* Jerusalem: Institute of the World Jewish Congress, 1997.

Zamoyski, Adam. *Moscow 1812.* New York: Harper, 2004.

Ziegler, Jean. *The Swiss, the Gold, and the Dead.* New York: Harcourt Brace, 1997.

Ziemke, Earl F. *The German Northern Theater of Operations 1940-1945.* Washington: U.S. Printing Office, 1959.

Zweig, Ronald. *The Gold Train.* New York: HarperCollins, 2002.

———. *World War II Day by Day.* London: DK, 2004.

OFFICIAL PUBLICATIONS

Nazi Gold: The London Conference. London: The Stationery Office, 1998.

The Legacy of Alexander Orlov. U.S. Senate. Ann Arbor, MI: University of Michigan Library, 1973.

The Gold Report of the Presidential Advisory Commission on Holocaust Assets. Washington, D.C.: 2000.

Trial of the Major War Criminals before the International Military Tribunal Nuremberg 1945-1946, Nuremberg, 1949. Washington, D.C.

International Commission of Experts Switzerland: National Socialism and the Second World War. Bergier Report. Zürich: Pendo Verlag, 2002.

Switzerland and Gold Transactions in the Second World War. Independent Commission of Experts Switzerland-Second World War.

The Luxembourg Grey Book. London: The Stationery Office, 1998. New York: Hutchinson, 1942.

Documents on German Foreign Policy. Lansing, MI22: University of Michigan Library, 1949.

Hitler Attacks Norway. Herman K. Lehmkuhl, London: Royal Norwegian Government Information Office, 1943.

The German Campaign in Poland. Robert M. Major, Department of the Army, US Government Printing Office, 1956.

Gold, Capital Flow and Trade During War. Federal Reserve Bulletin, January 1941.

Fighting the Russians in Winter. Allen E Crew, Levenworth Papers, 1981.

U.S. and Allied Efforts to Recover and Restore Gold and other Assets Stolen or Hidden by Germany During World War II. William Z. Slany, 1997, Washington.

The Eizenstat Report and Related Issues Concerning United States and Allied Efforts to Restore Gold and Other Assets Looted by Nazis During World War II. Congressional Hearings, June 25, 1997, Washington.

U.S. and Allied Wartime and Postwar Relations and Negotiations With Argentina, Portugal, Spain, Sweden, and Turkey on Looted Gold and German External Assets and U.S. Concern About the Fate of the Wartime Ustasha Treasury. William Z. Slany, 1998, Washington.

All For Norway. London: Royal Norwegian Government's Information Office, 1942.

ARTICLES, RESEARCH PAPERS, AND BOOK CHAPTERS

Ansiaux, Hubert. *L'or et les valeurs de la Banque National dans la tourmente de 1940. Revue General,* Brussels, February 1985.

Banken, Ralf. *Hiergegen kann nur mit freier Fahndung eingeschritten werden–Die Arbeit der deutschen Devisenschutzkommandos 1938 bis 1944.* Article in the book *Wirtschaft im Zeitalter der Extreme* published by Hartmut Berghoff, Jürgen Kocka, and Dieter Ziegler.

Beaudoux, Henri. *Visite Allemande à la Souterraine,* Cahiers Anecdotiques de la Banque de France, #6.

Blazer, David. *Finance and the End of Appeasement.* Journal of Contemporary History, vol. 40(1), London, 2005.

Bordogna, Muriel. *Transfert d'or de la Banque de France en 1940*. Cahiers Anecdotiques de la Banque de France, # 9.

Bradsher, Greg. *Nazi Gold: The Merkers Mine Treasure*. Prologue magazine, Spring 1999.

Brundeel, Didier. *La Restitution de l'or par les puissances de l'Axe*. Cahiers Anecdotiques de la Banque de France, #32.

Cornu, Gérard. *L'or polonais*. Cahiers Anecdotiques de la Banque de France, #13.

Curtiss, W. David and Stewart, C. Evan. *Cornell Benefactor, Industrial Czar, and FDR's Ambassador Extraordinary*. Ithaca: Cornell Law School.

Dostert, Paul. *L'or luxembourgeois spolié par l'Allemagne pendant la Seconde Guerre Mondiale ainsi que Sa Récupération à la Fin des Hostilités*. Revue d'Histoire Luxembourgeoise, 1 (1998), pp. 1-34.

Einzig, Paul. *Hitler's New Order in Theory and Practice*. The Economic Journal, Vol. 51, No. 201, pp. 1-18.

Golson, Eric B. *Did Swedish Ball Bearings Keep.the Second World War Going?* Scandinavian Economic History Review, vol. 60, No. 2, pg 165-182.

Irwin, Douglas A., *Gold Sterilization and the Recession of 1937-38*. National Bureau of Economic Research, Working Paper 17595.

James, Harold. *Schacht's Attempted Defection from Hitler's Germany*. The Historical Journal, vol. 30, No. 3. (September 1987).

Kubu, Eduard. *Czechoslovak Gold Reserves and Their Surrender to Nazi Germany*. Nazi Gold London Conference.

Louça, Antonio and Schäfer, Ansgar. *Portugal and the Nazi Gold*. Yad Vashem Studies, vol. 27 (1999).

Moreton, Charles. *Lettre d'Un Grand-Père*. Cahiers Anecdotiques de la Banque de France.

Morgenthau, Henry, Jr. *The Morgenthau Diaries*. Springfield, Ohio: Collier's magazine, October and November 1947.

Müller, Rolf-Dieter. *The Mobilization of the German Economy for Hitler's War Aims*. Research Institute for German History, Potsdam, 2005.

Orlov, Alexander. *How Stalin Relieved Spain of $600,000,000*. Pleasantville, NY, Reader's Digest, November 1966.

Plisnier, Oscar. *L'or Belge livré aux Allemands en 1940*. Revue Générale Belge, #52, February 1950.

Porter, Sylvia. *The Great Nazi Gold Rush*. Springfield, Ohio: Collier's, September 15, 1942.

Preston, Paul. *The Church's Crusade Against the Republic*. Published in *Revolution and War in Spain 1931-1939*.

Ritschl, A.O. *Nazi Economic Imperialism and the Exploitation of the Small: Evidence from Germany's Secret Foreign Exchange Balances, 1938-1940*. Economic History Review, LIV, 2 , 2001.

Romiszewsi, Eugeniusz. *An Epic Tale of Polish Argonauts: From Istanbul Towards the West*. Radio Free Europe Collection. Hoover Library, Stanford University.

Gold Team Report, July 2000. William J. Clinton Presidential Library.

Steury, Donald P. *The OSS and Project Safehaven*. CIA Historic Document. June 27, 2008. Amazon Digital Services.

Stowe, Leland. *The Secret Voyage of Britain's Treasure*. Reader's Digest, November 1955.

Viñas, Angel. *The Financing of the Civil War, Revolution and War in Spain 1931-1939*. Published in *Revolution and War in Spain 1931-1939*.

Wolfe, Martin. *The Development of Nazi Monetary Policy*. The Journal of Economic History. Vol. 15. No. 4, December 1955.

Sivertsen, Svien Carl. *The Day of Destiny in Molde, April 1940*. Norsk Tidsskrift for Skøvesen, 2000.

Ziegler, Dieter. *A Regulated Market Economy: New Perspectives on the Nature of the Economic Order of the Third Reich 1933-1939*, Hartmunt Berghoff, Business in the Age of Extremes, pp. 139-152.

INTERNET SITES

Weixelbaum, Jason. *The Contradiction of Neutrality and International Finance:* jasonweixelbaum. wordpress.com

Proceedings and Documents of the United Nations Monetary and Financial Conference. Bretton Woods, New Hampshire, July 10-22, 1944: fraser.stlouisfed.org

Bank for International Settlements, Annual Reports 1935-1945: bis.org/publ/arpdf/archive/index.htm

Vogier, Robert. *The Swiss National Bank's Gold Transactions with the German Reichsbank from 1939 to 1945*: snb.com

U.S. Army, Third U.S. Army. After Action Report, Third U.S. Army: paperlessarchives.com/wwii_third_army_after_action_r.htmlwww.anac-fr.com/2gm/ 2gm_19.htm

Christopher Columbus Reports on Voyages. Fordham University, Internet Medieval Sourcebook: fordham.edu/halsall/sbook.asp.

Timothy Green study Central Bank Gold Reserves Since 1945: scribd.com/doc/119942259/CentralBankGoldReserves-Since-1845

Papal Encyclicals Online, Pius XI, Dilectissima Nobis: papalencyclicals.net

The American Presidency Project, University of California Santa Barbara: www.presidency.ucsb.edu

German History Documents: germanhistorydocs.ghi-dc.org

SS Laurentic: laurentic.com and naval-history.net/OWShips-WW1-08Laurentic.htm

wikipedia.org/wiki/SS_Laurentic_(1908)

Winston Churchill Speeches: winstonchurchill.org

Biographical Dictionary of Italians: treccani.itencyclopedia

Trilateral Commission for the Restitution of Monetary Gold, Final Report: state.gov/s/l/65668.htm

Paris Conference on Reparations, November and December 1945, Final Report: cvce.eu/education/unit-content/-/unit/en/55c09dcc-a9f245e9-b240- eaef64452cae/cf8a7bab-3e2b-4406-a7fb-2a5757198da3/Resources# 5c0dfcd9-2af2-431b-8cbf-e8e288aef30e_en&overlay

Krähling, Katrin Isabel. *Das Devisenschutzkommando Belgien, 1940-1944*: kops.ub.uni-konstanz.de/bitstream/handle/urn:nbn:de:bsz:352-opus-18753/Das_Devisenschutz-kommando_Belgien_1940_1944.pdf?sequence=1

ARCHIVES

Banque de France, Paris (Bank of France)

Banque nationale de Belgique/Nationale Bank van België (National Bank of Belgium)

Bundesarchiv, Berlin and Freiburg (German Federal Archives)

William J. Clinton Presidential Library, Little Rock, AK

Institut für Zeitgeschichte (Institute of Contemporary History), Munich

New York Federal Reserve, New York, NY

Józef Piłsudski Institute of America, New York, NY

Franklin D. Roosevelt Presidential Library, Hyde Park, NY

Harry S. Truman Presidential Library, Independence, MO

ACKNOWLEDGMENTS

I have been for years interested in the story of central bank gold in World War II, and this book has been a longtime work of love. It was also a massive undertaking because it involved so many countries and different foreign languages. One dispirited day I did a quick calculation and figured that I had to research more than two dozen countries with nearly that many languages. I can work in English, French, and German, but not in Norwegian, Albanian, Portuguese, Dutch, Russian, and many others.

The first thank-you goes to Curt Prendergast, my first boss at *Time* magazine, who as the dedication explains, tipped me off to the topic nearly fifty years ago.

Fortunately, I was able to put together a team of people from all around Europe who helped me in a variety of ways. Some tracked down documents; others helped me with translations. Others did translations of reports and even whole books. They all helped me understand their country's wartime history. They also read the chapter about their nation and made helpful suggestions and corrections. The book could not have been done without them. The list starts with two Germans, Dirk Lau in Hamburg and Elisabeth Kaiser in Brussels. They were both patient with many questions and guided me around the shoals of German history. Elisabeth found some crucial books and offered wise counsel. Dirk and I had Skype phone calls to discuss things, and he also did research at the Berlin archives. Both sometimes double-checked my German translations.

They, though, were only the beginning. The list begins with winter neighbors in Vero Beach, such as Jurich Dorawa in Vero Beach, FL, who helped with Polish documents. Hermann Schnabl and Evelyn Kopke-Gripenberg did the same with German, and Boyd Fellows improved the quality of the photographs. Jacek Szafran helped with both Polish translations and his knowledge of his country's history. Jan Emsbro found Norwegian material, and Keith Lewis guided me through maritime terms. Mary Ann Sorrentino translated a crucial Italian book. Tihmir Lerner helped from Croatia. Mari H. Rowland translated the long report written in 1940 by the leader of the Norwegian gold evacuation. Per Arnt Harnes, author of *Gulltransporten*, read the Norwegian chapter. Bo Lidegaard in Denmark translated a crucial section of his book *Kampen om Danmark 1933-1945*. Anders Bergnas, a graduate school friend, helped me in Sweden. When I was in Belgium, Hermann Van der Wee and Walter Pluym, who have both written books about their country's gold saga, were very generous with their time and pointed me to key documents. Van der Wee's book, which was done with his wife Monique Verbreyt, is *A Small Nation*. Pluym's work, written with his brother Jan, is *Goud op Drift* in the Dutch edition and *Or à la Dérive* in the French one.

Officials at the Banque de France were extremely helpful both before and after the week I did research in Paris. Didier Bruneel, the director of the excellent publication *Cahiers anecdotiques de la Banque de France* and the special counselor to the bank's president, helped in many ways. He provided the first solid information about how the Soviet Union saved its gold, and also allowed me to use photographs he had collected for his own book *Les Secrets de l'Or*. When I arrived in Paris, Arnaud Manas, the head of the archives at the French National Bank, had just finished the defense of his doctoral thesis on the Vichy government's gold policy. He gave me a copy of it and also helped me find my way through his archives.

Paul Dostert in Luxembourg has done work on his own country's gold during the war, and he gave him time both to explain what happened and point me to the archives. We also had a pleasant lunch at an outdoor café.

A small team helped in Holland. Alexander Nieuwenhuis put together an excellent program that got me to the right people. Ronald Dijkstra, who was just finishing his own book on the Dutch story, spent a day walking around Rotterdam, retracing the steps of the soldiers who carried gold to a boat that hit a mine and sank and then visiting the site. We also visited the ship museum near the Hook of Holland, where officials told us more about the ship. Gerard Aalders, who has written an excellent book in Dutch about his country's gold, answered all my questions over glasses of Dutch beer. Daphne Dupont-Nivet translated his book for me.

Svetlana Chervonnaya in Moscow deserves all the credit for finding the right Russian documents and then translating them. It would have been impossible to do the Soviet chapter without her. She was also very helpful in unraveling the story of the shipment of Spanish gold to Moscow in 1936.

In Britain, Robert Hart, who was a fellow journalist many years ago in Bonn, worked with me for a week combing the British National Archives outside London for cabinet records and ship logs.

Central bankers have a reputation for being stuffy, but officials at banks from Portugal to Turkey, with many more in between, were generous in providing help in uncovering their stories. Most of the communication was done over the Internet. I would like to thank in particular Jenni Hellström at the Bank of Finland, who sent me the chapter from a history of her bank that dealt in detail with the Finnish story.

Officials in national and central bank archives are the unsung people in the background. They helped find the right documents or photographs. Joseph M. Komljenovich, Julie Sanger, and Marja Vitti at the New York Federal Reserve opened up their collections during two long visits. Officials at the Franklin D. Roosevelt Library and the Harry S. Truman Library were helpful when I visited their archives. The William J. Clinton Library provided documents over the Internet. The staffs of the U.S. National Archives in College

Park Maryland, the Banque de France, the Bundesarchiv in Berlin and Freiburg, the Bayerische Hauptstaatsarchiv in Munich, and at the British National Archives were particularly valuable. I made four long visits to the U.S. National Archives in College Park, MD, and Margaret Shannon and Candace Clifford also did work for me there. Peter Voskamp tracked down some crucial material at the newspaper collection of the Library of Congress in Washington. The staff at the Thomas J. Dodd Research Center at the University of Connecticut opened its wonderful collection of Nuremberg Trial documents. Andy Hollinger of the United States Holocaust Memorial Museum in Washington provided many useful photos from its collection.

Librarians also were essential aides. I thank those at Brown University, University of Rhode Island, Stanford University, the New York Public Library, Princeton University, University of Connecticut, Harvard Business School, Vero Beach, and the Block Island Free Library.

The most important assistance of all came from my wife Jean, who over several years read and edited many early versions of chapters, and from our daughter Lara, who diagnosed computer problems and also created the maps that accompany most chapters and designed the book's photo pages. Both Jean and Lara were always there for me.

Special thanks to Jennifer McCartney for very carefully proofreading the manuscript.

I would also like to give special thanks to Harvey Klinger, my agent now for five books, and to Jessica Case and all the people at Pegasus Books.

INDEX

INDEX

INDEX

INDEX

INDEX

INDEX

INDEX

Lubeck, storage of records in Merkers, 396
Lublin, 138–139, 359
  regional bank office in, 136
Ludwigshafen, Allied seizure of, xiii
Lufthansa, 61–62
Luleå, 174
Luther, Hans
  as German ambassador to Washington, 36
  offering of Schacht the job of ending
    German inflation, 28
  as Reichsbank President, 35
Lutsk, 140
  Polish gold in, 141, 142
Luxembourg
  central bank of, 228
  demands for restitution, 430
  early history of, 228
  German attack on, 206
  gold of, 228, 312
  monetary union with Belgium, 228
  Nazi objective of conquering, 173
  stolen gold of, 440
Luxembourg gold, 312

M

Maassluis, 220
Maastricht, 231
Macaulay, Lord, 285
Madagascar, Jews and Nazi opponent immigration to, 120
Madeira Islands, 248
Magdeburg, Reichsbank offices in, 399
Maginot Line, 110, 231, 242
Maglioni, Luigi, 265
Mainz, Allied seizure of, xiii
Malenkov, Georgy, 345
Malraux, Andre, 12
Manganese
  German need for, 165
  U.S. buy up of, 165
Manila fiber, German need for, 165
Mannerheim, Carl, 156
Manstein, Erich von, 205–206, 243
Mansur, David, 297
Marie-Adélaïde, Grand Duchess, 227
Marienbad, 420
Marseillaise, 242
Marseilles, 317
  Belgian and Luxembourg gold in, 316
  shipment of gold from, 241
Marshall, George, 405
Marshall, James W., discovery of gold in California, 4
Marshall Plan, 381
Martinique, gold in, 254, 256, 307, 310, 435
Marx, Harpo, 337
Marxism, danger of, to Germany, 64
Mathieu, Jean, protection of Belgian assets, 229–230

Matuszewski, Ignacy, x, 139–140, 142, 145, 146–147
Matuszewski Poles, 139
Mauritania, 309
McGarrah, Gates W., 81
McKittrick, Thomas H.
  as president of Bank for International Settlement, x, 305, 366, 380, 418
  relationships with Nazi leaders, 380
McSherry, Frank, 401, 408–409
Mechelen, 205
Mefo bills, 43, 72, 121, 123
Mein Kampf (Hitler), 5–6, 31, 63, 91, 334, 379
Melmer, Bruno, 358, 359
Melmer gold, 355–361
  SS units claim of, 417–418
Memel, 163
  German control of, 319
Menjou, Adolphe, 15
Meppel, 225
Mercantile system, 3
Mercer, Lucy, affair with FDR, 54–55
Merkers
  Allied discovery of, xiv, 401
  audit of gold found in, 410–411
  gold and art treasurers in salt mine in, 203, 410–411
  gold evacuated to, 397, 412
  stealing of gold from, 411
  storage of records in, 396
  turf war between Bernstein and Stout at, 403
Mers-el-Kébir, 308
Metallurgische Forschungsgesellschaft (Metal Research Company) (Mefo), 42–43
Metaxas, Joannis, 327
Metternich, 368
Michalski, Stefan, x, 273, 275, 276–277, 319
Miesen, Bernard, 420
Mies van der Rohe, Ludwig, 394
Miklas, Wilhelm, 96, 97
Mikoyan, Anastas, 345, 346
Milan, 272
Mill, John Stuart, 26
Minsk, 345
Mittenwald, 421–422, 425, 427
Młynów, 142
Moevus, Captain, 273, 274, 276–277
Molde, 183, 188, 190, 193
Molotov, V. M., 340, 345
Molotov, Vyacheslav, 22, 131–133, 316
Molotov-Ribbentrop Treaty, 151–152, 163
Monarch of Bermuda, 297
Monnet, J. G., & Co., 162
Monnet, Jean, 162, 163
  purchase of American weapons and, 241
Mont-de-Marsan, 231, 234
Montoire-sur-le-Loir, 324
Monument Men, 411

INDEX

INDEX

INDEX